Using C/C++
Special Edition

LEE ATKINSON
MARK ATKINSON

PROGRAMMING
SERIES

D0817200

Using C/C++, Special Edition

Library of Congress Catalog No.: 92-63329

ISBN: 1-56529-141-7

96 95 94 93   8 7 6 5 4 3 2 1

Interpretation of the printing code: the rightmost double-digit number is the year of the book's printing; the rightmost single-digit number, the number of the book's printing. For example, a printing code of 93-1 shows that the first printing of the book occurred in 1993.

Trademarks

To our families, without whose patience and support there would have been no book.

From Mark to Paige; your understanding and love made it all worthwhile.

CREDITS

Publisher
Lloyd J. Short

Associate Publisher
Rick Ranucci

Publishing Manager
Joseph B. Wikert

Acquisitions Editor
Sarah Browning

Production Editor
Kezia Endsley

Copy Editors
Ginny Noble
Chuck Hutchinson
Judy Brunetti

Technical Editor
Greg Guntle

Editorial Assistants
Elizabeth D. Brown
Stacey Beheler

Production Manager
Corinne Walls

Proofreading/Indexing Coordinator
Joelynn Gifford

Production Analyst
Mary Beth Wakefield

Book Designer
Scott Cook

Cover Designer
Jean Bisesi

Graphic Image Specialists
Dennis Sheehan
Jerry Ellis
Susan VandeWalle

Production
Jodie Cantwell, Brad Chinn, Michelle Cleary,
Brook Farling, Tim Groeling, Bob LaRoche,
Tom Loveman, Roger Morgan, Angela Pozdol,
Joe Ramon, Caroline Roop, Linda Seifert,
Michelle Self, Susan M. Shepard, Greg Simsic,
Phil Worthington

Indexers
Loren Malloy

Composed in Cheltenham and MCPdigital by Prentice Hall Computer Publishing

ABOUT THE AUTHORS

Mark Atkinson

Mark Atkinson was introduced to computer programming in 1969 with a FORTRAN ballistics program that tracked the Saturn-V rocket and astronauts to the moon. He has been involved with computing continuously since that time, including networking, programming, and writing. He was coauthor for Que's *Using Microsoft C/C++ 7* and *Using Borland C++ 3*. He is currently a systems analyst for the United States Courts.

Lee Atkinson

Lee Atkinson is a 20-year veteran of the data processing industry. He has written code professionally in C, Pascal, COBOL, FORTRAN, PL/I, APL, and a number of assembly languages for machines ranging from the smallest microprocessors to IBM's top-of-the-line mainframes. He is currently an MVS systems programmer for a Mississippi-based regional retail company. He was coauthor for Que's *Using Microsoft C/C++ 7* and *Using Borland C++ 3*.

ACKNOWLEDGMENTS

Grateful acknowledgements are made to the following persons and organizations:

The Que Corporation editorial and production staff—especially Joe Wikert, Kezia Endsley, Ginny Noble, Chuck Hutchinson, and Judy Brunetti—for their patience and guidance.

The American National Standards Institute for permission to quote parts of X3.159

OVERVIEW

Introduction 1

I Introduction to C 7

1 Getting Started with C 9
2 Basic I/O Programming 49
3 Building C Programs 101
4 A Closer Look at C Programs 147
5 Objects, Expressions, Operators, and Conversions 185
6 More About C Functions 237
7 Controlling Program Logic Flow 277
8 Programming with Pointers, Arrays, and Strings 321
9 More About Using Pointers 373
10 File I/O Programming 411
11 Deriving New Complex Data Types 453
12 Portability and Conversion Issues 503
13 Moving to C 529

II C++ Programming Basics 569

14 Objects and Object-Oriented Programming 571
15 Defining Classes and Objects 595
16 Controlling Classes and Objects 665
17 More on C++ Methods and Objects 709

A   ASCII Character Set 753

B   ANSI C Predefined Macros 761

C   ANSI C Function Library 769

D   The FINANCE.C Program 781

E   IBM PC Communications Program 803

F   B-Spline Derivation 825

G   Performance-Measurement Software 827

    Index 839

TABLE OF CONTENTS

Introduction 1

  Purpose of This Book 2

  Who Should Use This Book? 2

  Getting Prepared To Use This Book 3

  The Book's Format 3

  Notation and Conventions 4

  How To Use This Book 5

I Introduction to C 7

1 Getting Started with C 9

  Approaching the C Language 9

    A Brief History of C 10

      In the Beginning: Kernighan and Ritchie 10

      The Move from UNIX to DOS 10

      ANSI Gets Interested 11

      Looking Toward the Future: C++ 12

    Comparing C to Other Languages 13

      Comparing C to Assembly Language 14

      Comparing C to Pascal 14

      Comparing C to COBOL 14

      Comparing C to FORTRAN 15

    A First Look at C Form and Punctuation 15

      How To Look at a C Program 15

      Noticing the C Punctuators 16

  Understanding the Parts of a C Program 18

    Including the Header Files 20

      Including Source Files in General 20

      Header Files and Built-In Functions 21

      Placing the Include Directives 23

      Two Ways to Include 23

Defining Data in C 25
   Setting Aside Memory for Data 25
   Where Do You Put It? 26
What the *main( )* Function Does 27
   Setting Up the Environment 27
   Normal Program Termination 28
Providing User-Defined Functions 28
   Functions Act Like Data 29
   Where Do They Go? 29
Writing a C Program 31
Start with the Right Design 31
A Top-Down Approach to Coding 31
Making Programs Readable 32
   Using Indentation and White Space 32
   Using Comments 33
   Aligning Braces and Parentheses 34
Writing Programs in the C Environment 35
Evaluating the Text Editor 35
What's in a Good C Compiler? 37
   Compiler Features 37
   The Linkage Editor and Compatibility 40
   Project-Management Facilities 41
   Compatibility with Other Languages 43
Command-Line and Integrated Environments 43
   What's the Difference? 44
   Why You Need Both 44
Do You Need a Visual Debugger? 44
   What Is a Visual Debugger? 45
   Features of a Good Debugger 46
   Legitimate Uses of a Debugger 47
Summary 47

2 Basic I/O Programming **49**

The Problem with Input and Output 50
Understanding Stream I/O 53
Comparing Streams, Files, and Devices 54
   Interactive Devices 56
   Data Files 57
   Introducing C Streams 57
The Standard Streams 58
   stdin, *stdout*, and *stderr* 58
   Relating Streams to DOS Handles 61
The Simple I/O Functions 62
Connecting Files to Streams: *fopen( )* 62

Declaring the Stream Data Object 63
Opening the File 65
Closing the File: *fclose( )* 67
Character I/O Functions 68
String I/O Functions 76
Handling I/O Errors and End-of-File Conditions 79
Converting Data Formats 80
The Formatted I/O Functions 83
Displaying Data with *printf( )* 84
Getting Input with *scanf( )* 88
Putting It All Together 90
Coping with Hardware and System Dependencies 91
Using Extensions to Standard C 91
Supporting Extended DOS Streams 92
Programming IBM PC I/O Ports 94
The IBM PC Video-Display Controversy 94
"Glass Teletype" I/O and Standard Streams 95
Getting Around the Problem 95
Summary 98

3 Building C Programs 101

Managing Data in a C Program 102
The Standard C Data Types 102
Working with Constant Values (Literals) 110
Declaring Variable Data 113
Naming Variables 113
Declarators and Declarator Lists 114
Initializing Variables 118
Local and Global Variables 119
Declaring Functions and Passing Parameters 128
Using Full Function Prototypes 130
The Prototype Declaration Format 131
Effects on the Order of Appearance 134
Coding the Function Definition 135
Building the Function Body 136
Writing C Statements 137
Returning Values from a Function 142
Calling the Function 145
Summary 145

4 A Closer Look at C Programs 147

More Detail on Language Conventions 147
The C Character Set 148
Bits, Bytes, and Characters 148

The C Minimal Character Set 150
Handling Special Characters 151
Source and Target Character Sets 161
How C Looks at Your Source Program 161
The Phases of Program Translation 161
Tokens and Translation Units 164
Identifiers in General 165
Using C Reserved Words 166
The Standard Macros and Functions 167
Using Compiler Directives and Macros 168
Revisiting the C Preprocessor 168
The Source File Inclusion Directive 169
Macro Substitution Directives 171
Conditional Compilation Directives 177
Line-Control, Error, Pragma, and Null Directives 180
Predefined Macro Names 182
Summary 182

5 Objects, Expressions, Operators, and Conversions 185

Another Look at Scope and Duration 186
Taking Advantage of Storage Class 186
Determining the Scope of an Object 188
Determining the Linkage of an Object 189
Controlling Initializers for Objects 192
Accessing External Data and Functions 193
Compiling Modules Separately 195
Setting Up the Header Files 200
Coding References to Other Modules 202
Linking the Modules 203
Understanding C Expressions 206
Rules Governing C Expressions 206
Primary Expressions 209
The *rvalue* and *lvalue* Expressions 210
Function Designator Expressions 212
void Expressions 212
Controlling the C Operators 212
Classifying the C Operators 213
Postfix Operators 213
Cast Operators 221
Binary Operators 222
The Conditional (Ternary) Operator *?:* 227
Simple and Compound Assignment Operators 227
The Comma Operator 229
The Key to C: Operator Precedence 229

Converting Data Types to Other Types 231
   Automatic Type Conversions 231
      Type Promotion in Expressions 231
      Implicit Conversion by Assignment 233
   Explicit Conversions with Type Casts 233
   Summary 235

6 More About C Functions 237

Details About Passing Parameters 237
   Pass by Value and Pass by Reference 238
      Parameters Are Passed on the Stack 238
      Passing Parameters by Value 238
      Passing Parameters by Reference 239
   Function Argument Promotions 240
   Function Prototypes with Incomplete Types 242
   Variable-Length Argument Lists 243
Passing Parameters to *main( )* 249
   Accessing Command-Line Parameters 250
   argc and *argv[ ]* 250
   Designing Command-Line Formats 252
Functions That Call Themselves 254
   Understanding Recursion 254
   Avoiding Open-Ended Recursion 256
   Eliminating Recursion 258
Other Ways to Invoke Functions 260
   Using Pointers to Functions 261
   The *signal( )* and *raise( )* Functions 265
   The *setjmp( )* and *longjmp( )* Functions 269
Summary 275

7 Controlling Program Logic Flow 277

Designing Program Loops 278
   Properties of Program Loops 278
   Doing It the Hard Way—Not Recommended 279
   Front-End Condition Checking: *while( )* 284
   Back-End Condition Checking: *do-while( )* 288
   Getting It All: The *for( )* Loop 293
   Altering Logic Flow in a Loop 298
      goto Versus *break* 300
      Using *continue* to Loop Early 302
Programming Conditional Logic 304
   If-Then-Else Statements 305
   More Complex Conditions: *switch( )* 308

The *switch( )* Statement 308
case Labels 309
Using *break;* and *default:* 313
Terminating the Program Early 314
Invoking the System Command Processor 317
Common Extensions to the
    ANSI Standard 318
Summary 319

8 Programming with Pointers, Arrays, and Strings 321

Pointers and Composite Data Types 322
    Reviewing Indirect Addressing 322
    Referring to Pointers and Their Objects 323
    Pointer Comparisons and Arithmetic 327
    When Do You Need a Pointer? 333
Defining Arrays of Variables 334
    Defining One-Dimensional Arrays 335
        Declaring the Array 335
        Referencing Array Elements 337
    Defining Multidimensional Arrays 338
        Declaring the Array 338
        Referencing Array Elements 339
    Pointer and Subscript Equivalence 340
Using Arrays for Smoothing Geometric Curves 342
    Using Arrays to Represent Shapes 342
    Curve-Smoothing Methods: SPLINE.C 343
Using Arrays to Solve Systems of Equations 349
    Using Arrays to Represent Equations 349
    Solving the Equations: GAUSS.C 349
Strings Are Arrays of Characters 352
    The Internal Representation of Strings 353
    Declaring String Variables 353
    Initializing String Variables 354
    Manipulating Strings 354
    Using Strings to Edit Text 356
        Inserting and Deleting Characters 358
        Screen I/O Considerations 360
        General-Purpose String Edit: STREDIT.C 361
Arrays and Strings as Function Parameters 369
    Strings as Function Parameters 370
    Arrays as Function Parameters 370
Summary 371

9 More About Using Pointers 373

Using Pointers with Pointers 373
    Using Multiple Indirection 373
    Referencing and Dereferencing Multiple Pointers 374
Using Pointers to Scan and Parse Text 375
    Creating a Lexical Scanner 376
        What a Scanner Does 376
        Why *strtok( )* Does Not Work Here 376
        How the Scanner Uses Pointers 378
    Creating a Parsing Routine 388
        What "Recursive Descent" Means 388
        Building the Parser 389
    Evaluating Formulas: FORMULA.C 390
Mixing Arrays and Pointers 398
    Defining Arrays of Pointers 398
    Defining a Pointer to an Array 399
Improving Program Performance with Pointers 401
    Using Pointers to Increase Flexibility 401
    Speeding Up Sorting with Pointers 401
Summary 409

10 File I/O Programming 411

Using C's File-Management Functions 412
    Deleting a File with *remove ( )* 412
    Changing the Filename with *rename ( )* 413
    Back to the Beginning with *rewind( )* 414
    Creating and Using Temporary Files 416
Buffered I/O Concepts 416
    What Difference Does It Make? 417
    Buffering and *stdin*, *stdout*, and *stderr* 419
Selecting an I/O Mode for File Streams 421
    Selecting the Access Mode 421
        Open Options for Input Mode 422
        Open Options for Output Mode 423
        Open Options for Update Mode 423
        Summary of Modes 425
    Mixing Reads and Writes in Update Modes 425
    Using Text and Binary File Modes 427
Direct-Access File Programming 430
    Direct-Access Concepts 430
    Using *ftell( )* and *fgetpos( )* 434
    Using *fseek( )* and *fsetpos( )* 435
Direct Access with Hashed Keys 436
Writing High-Performance File Routines 445

Choosing the File Mode 445
Minimizing I/O Overhead 445
  Using *setbuf( )* and *setvbuf( )* 446
  Loading Directly to RAM 449
Common Extensions to the ANSI Standard 449
Low-Level I/O Practices 450
Files in a Networking Environment 450
Summary 450

11 Deriving New Complex Data Types **453**

Defining Structures of Items 454
  Basic Structure Declarations 454
    Defining Structured Data Objects 454
    Using Structure Tags 458
  Accessing Structure Members 460
  Using Bit-Fields in Structures 463
  Combining Structures and Arrays 465
Defining Unions of Structures 469
  The Overlay Concept of Unions 469
  Declaring a Union 470
  Accessing Members of a Union 470
Deriving Types with *typedef* 472
Managing Data in Dynamic Memory 473
  Allocating Memory at Runtime 474
  Keeping Track of Allocations 477
Structures and Unions as Function Parameters 478
Building Linked Lists with Structures 479
Using Enumeration Constants 499
Summary 501

12 Portability and Conversion Issues **503**

Keeping the Spirit of C 504
  The Programmer Is Ruler 504
  Keep It Simple 504
  Make It Unique 505
  Performance Is the Rule 505
A Treaty Between Vendor and Programmer 505
  A Meeting of the Minds 505
  When It Backfires 506
Unspecified Behavior 506
Undefined Behavior 508
Implementation-Defined Behavior 514
  What to Look For 514

Environment 515
Identifiers 515
Characters 515
Integers 516
Floating-Point 516
Arrays and Pointers 516
Registers 516
Structures, Unions, Enumerations, and Bit-Fields 516
Qualifiers 517
Declarators 517
Statements 517
Preprocessing Directives 517
Library Functions 518
Locale-Specific Behavior 519
Quiet Changes to K&R C 520
What Is a Quiet Change? 520
Converting K&R C Programs 521
Environmental Considerations 524
Translation Limitations 524
Common Extensions to ANSI Standard C 525
Environment Arguments 525
Specialized Identifiers 526
Length and Case of Identifiers 526
Scope of Identifiers 526
Writable String Literals 526
Other Arithmetic Types 526
Function Pointer Casts 526
Non-*int* Bit-Field Types 527
The *fortran* Keyword 527
The *asm* Keyword 527
Multiple External Definitions 527
Empty Macro Arguments 527
Predefined Macro Names 528
Extra Arguments for Signal Handlers 528
Additional Stream Types and File Modes 528
Defined File-Position Indicator 528
Summary 528

13 Moving to C 529

Moving to C from BASIC 530
Interpreters Versus Compilers 530
Comparing Data Types 532
Integers 532
Floating-Point Variables 534

Comparing String Types 536
Arrays 539
Operators in BASIC and C 540
Mathematical Operators 540
Relational Operators 541
Logical Operators 542
Conditional Flow Control in BASIC and C 543
Flow Control with *if-then-else* 543
Flow Control with *SELECT CASE* and *switch* 544
Flow Control with *for-next* Loops 545
Flow Control with *do* and *while* Loops 546
Modular Programming 548
Moving to C from Pascal 549
Comparing Data Types in C and Pascal 550
Integers 550
Real Numbers 552
Characters and Strings 554
Boolean 555
Pointers 555
Arrays 559
Using Operators in Pascal and C 560
Mathematical Operators 560
Relational Operators 561
Logical Operators 562
Controlling Logic Flow in Pascal and C 562
Flow Control with *if-then-else* 562
Flow Control Using *case* and *switch* 563
Flow Control with *for* Loops 564
Flow Control with Prechecked and Postchecked Loops 565
Summary 567

II C++ Programming Basics 569

14 Objects and Object-Oriented Programming 571

Objects Are Working Models 572
Data Abstraction Is Data Hiding 573
C Functions as Object Methods 574
Classes Are Abstract Data Types 579
Going Beyond *typedef* 586
What Encapsulation Means 586
Class Inheritance Is Type Derivation 586
Definitions of Object-Oriented Systems 587

Wegner's Definition 587
Zortech's Definition 589
Stroustrup's Comments 590
Other Issues in Object-Oriented Systems 590
Multiple Inheritance 591
Object Implementations: Functional, Server, Autonomous,
and Slot-Based 591
Summary 592

15 Defining Classes and Objects 595

Defining Classes to C++ 596
Setting Up the Class Definition 597
Member Elements: *private:*, *public:*, and *protected:* 604
What Is *this*? 605
Initializing and Destroying Class Objects 608
Constructors and Destructors 608
Copy Initializers 615
Using Class Objects 616
Calling Member Functions 616
Building a Virtual Screen Class 617
Summary 663

16 Controlling Classes and Objects 665

Understanding C++'s Free Store 666
Using the Global *new* and *delete* Operators 666
Defining Your Own *new* and *delete* 672
What About *this* and *::operator new( )*? 678
Defining Objects to C++ 680
What Are Static and Dynamic Objects? 680
Dynamic Objects on the Stack 681
Global Static Objects 683
Static Objects on the Free Store 685
Derived Classes and Inheritance 686
Understanding Code Reusability 686
Reusing Code by Composition 687
Reusing Code by Inheritance 693
Extending Class Capability with Virtual Functions 698
C++ Stream I/O 703
Reading and Writing with *cin* and *cout* 703
Mixing Input and Output Streams 706
I/O Redirection and Streams 707
Summary 707

17 More on C++ Methods and Objects **709**

  Pointers and References in C++ 709
    The Reference Operator 710
    Defining Pointers to Objects 713
    Passing Objects as Parameters 715
    Referencing Other Objects 717
  Overloading Functions 720
    Overloading Member Functions 722
    Overloading Friend Functions 723
  Overloading Operators 723
    What Can Be Overloaded? 723
    User-Defined Type Conversions 745
  Recent Changes to C++ 745
    Multiple Inheritance and Virtual Base Classes 746
    Overloaded Functions and Type-Safe Linkage 747
    Using *const*, *volatile*, and *static* Member Functions 747
    AT&T C++ 3.0 Changes 749
  Summary 752

A ASCII Character Set **753**

B ANSI C Predefined Macros **761**

  #include <assert.h> 761
  #include <float.h> 761
  #include <limits.h> 763
  #include <locale.h> 764
  #include <math.h> 764
  #include <setjmp.h> 764
  #include <signal.h> 765
  #include <stdarg.h> 765
  #include <stddef.h> 765
  #include <stdio.h> 766
  #include <stdlib.h> 766
  #include <time.h> 767

C ANSI C Function Library **769**

  #include <ctype.h> 769
  #include <locale.h> 770
  #include <math.h> 770
  #include <setjmp.h> 772
  #include <signal.h> 772
  #include <stdio.h> 772

#include <stdlib.h> 775
#include <string.h> 778
#include <time.h> 780

D The FINANCE.C Program **781**

Program Structure and Operation 796
Using FINANCE.C Computations 798
   General Business Functions 798
   Interest-Rate Conversion 799
   Time Value of Money 799
   Mortgage Analysis and Amortization 800

E IBM PC Communications Programming **803**

F B-Spline Derivation **825**

G Performance-Measurement Software **827**

Data Areas Used in TIMER.C 831
Reprogramming the Timer Chip 832
Handling the Timer-Tick Interrupts 833
Cleaning Up After High-Resolution Timing 834
Separate Compilation of TIMER.C 835
Converting TIMER.C to Borland C 836
Using the TIMER.C Functions 837

Index **839**

Introduction

The world of C and C++ programming is endlessly fascinating, a world in which you can always find something new and profitable. Computer programming, especially in C and C++, is a world in which you go beyond mastering your environment: You re-create it with each new program.

In this book, you begin (or perhaps continue) the process of learning a language well-suited to creating and manipulating computer environments. C has been characterized as a high-level assembly language, easily capable of controlling your computer's hardware. It is also a particularly powerful high-level language suitable for rapid development of rich, complex programs. In fact, C is both of these things.

C is not *all* things to all people—nothing ever is. It is, however, about as close as you can get to being so, which explains its booming popularity. You can write just about any kind of program in C, from business and scientific applications to operating systems.

This book contains the material you need in order to comprehend all the fundamentals of the C *and* the C++ programming language. We designed it to accomplish this goal in one volume—a rather ambitious task. This book has no pretensions of being encyclopedic, however. The following tradeoffs were therefore necessary in controlling the size of the book:

- The size had to be controlled, but depth of coverage is important. The table of contents shows the range of topics that constitute the fundamentals of modern C and C++. We have tried to cover them in sufficient depth to enable you to write programs with confidence and enjoyment, and to prepare you to move on to advanced skill levels.

- The sample programs teach the language, not specific applications. Large, complex projects belong in other books, and would only consume space and confuse the issues here. We have tried to avoid boring examples, however. The powerful techniques in this book are basic building blocks for the larger projects.

- C is not just C anymore. Beyond K & R C are ANSI C (the basic language) and C++ (ANSI C plus object-oriented extensions). We necessarily place the emphasis on ANSI C, with which you get the basic concepts necessary for an understanding of *all* C programming. Only when you have mastered these concepts are you ready for C++, and we have provided a solid primer for that as well.

Purpose of This Book

The most important purpose of this book is to introduce you to C/C++ programming, and to help you raise your skills from the beginning to the intermediate level. We also hope that this book will be a useful tool that you won't outgrow as you become a more sophisticated C/C++ programmer. Three specific purposes are aimed at achieving these goals. They are as follows:

- Present all the fundamentals of modern C/C++ programming. This includes ANSI C and C++ programming. You do not have to buy several books; this one covers what you need to know to get a sound start in C/C++ programming.

- Teach the C/C++ languages effectively. Learning C/C++, when approached incorrectly, can be confusing and difficult. This need not be so. The process can be a fruitful and enjoyable one. We have made every effort to arrange the material in such a way to hasten your proficiency in C/C++, without leaving you to sink or swim.

- Be a handy reference source. This book is intended to be a single-volume sourcebook about C/C++ programming. To serve that purpose, we have included reference and summary information in both tabular and graphic formats. After you have used this book to learn C/C++, you can use it again to quickly refresh your memory, or to look up an obscure point.

Who Should Use This Book?

Using C/C++, Special Edition is aimed specifically at beginning and intermediate-level C/C++ programmers. You can use this book to learn C/C++ from the beginning and to increase your knowledge and skills.

Those who already have experience with C/C++ will find it useful as well. If you are a longtime C/C++ user accustomed to the old-style programming methods, you can use this book to update yourself on the latest developments in C/C++ programming. All C/C++ programmers can profit from the summary and reference information.

This book is *not* intended to promote the product of any particular compiler vendor. It is about *standard* C/C++—those things that make C/C++ what they are. This does not mean that specific compilers are never mentioned. Doing so would eliminate the possibility of writing sample programs that actually work. The compiler used is noted with each example. The following compilers were used:

Borland C++ 3.1　　　　(Borland)

Microsoft C/C++ 7.0　　　(Microsoft)

There are also occasional notes on features that the different compilers provide as extensions to ANSI C, and on how they differ in implementing some things.

Getting Prepared To Use This Book

To learn C/C++ programming, you need some experience with computers in general, as well as with programming in particular. It *is* possible to learn C as a first language, and this book can help you do that, but it may be a jarring experience. C is a sophisticated language, and seems to embody everything programmers traditionally use to confuse the layperson. You should be familiar with the way computers do things, at the very least, before learning C.

If you are a complete beginner and want to learn C right now anyway, the antidote is simply to read some basic computer books as you go along.

The Book's Format

The material in this book is arranged in two major parts, covering ANSI C fundamentals and then C++ fundamentals. The first part presents and explains the mechanics of the language. Then, the second part shows you how to get started using C++.

Notation and Conventions

To get the most out of this book, you should know how it is designed. New terms and emphasized words are presented in *italicized text* and are defined on first reference. Pay close attention to italicized text. Functions, commands, parameters, and the like are set in `monospace` text; for example, the `main()` function. User responses that must be typed at the prompt appear in **`monospace bold`**; for example:

```
Please Enter Your Name: Erin
```

Placeholders (words that you replace with actual values) in code lines appear in `monospace italic;` for example:

```
long double variable1, variable2;
```

In this example, you would replace `variable1` and `variable2` with the appropriate numbers, depending, of course, on the program you were writing.

Full C and C++ programs appear as listings with listing heads, whereas code fragments appear alone within the text. Tables and figures also help organize material within the chapters.

Two special features have to be mentioned as well. In listings of entire programs, every line is numbered. This makes referring to specific lines easy. Very short code fragments do not have line numbers or listing heads.

Other visual pointers found in this book include:

> Caution boxes that warn you of problem areas, including possible cases in which you might introduce bugs into your program or crash your system.

and

 Note boxes that provide you with extraneous information. Many times, this information will help speed your learning process and provide you with shortcuts in C. Other times, it simply reminds you of information important enough to be mentioned twice!

and

C-Notes Are Boxes of Summary and Reference

Throughout the book are shaded boxes of summary and reference information called *C-Notes*. The title line of the C-Note tells you in which of the following four categories it fits and what kind of information it contains. There are four kinds of C-Notes, as follows.

- *ANSI C Rationale.* These C-Notes contain comments about why the ANSI standard was implemented in certain ways rather than others. This helps in your overall understanding of the language.

- *Old-Style Coding.* Tremendous numbers of C programs were written before the ANSI standard was published. These notes help you read old-style code and convert it to modern style.

- *Compiler Dependency.* Because of the large variety of machines and operating systems with which C/C++ can run, the precise behavior of a surprisingly large number of features was left up to each compiler manufacturer. You should be aware of them if you deal with more than one compiler.

- *Quick-Reference.* Wherever a summary of C/C++ rules or technical information is appropriate, you will find one of these notes. They are handy for quick review or for a bird's-eye perspective of the topic being discussed and are the most common type of C-Note.

How To Use This Book

You can use this book as either a learning resource for C/C++ or as a reference to the language.

The order in which material is presented is designed for C/C++ students. It is not the order you would find in a formal definition of the language. This means that you can read through Parts I and II in sequence and cover the whole language. Do not hurry the reading. Follow the explanations of sample programs in detail—doing so takes you a long way toward understanding how C rules work in practice. Most of all, do not try to memorize the rules. Because you can learn C/C++ best by *writing* C/C++, begin by duplicating the examples, and then branch out to programs of your own. And keep at it.

You can use this book also as a reference. The table of contents is fairly detailed; you can use it to navigate quickly to a particular topic. If the table of contents does not help you locate what you need, try the index. After you have found the discussion of interest, look for tables of information and Quick-Reference C-Notes.

Introduction to C

PART

I

OUTLINE

1 Getting Started with C

2 Basic I/O Programming

3 Building C Programs

4 A Closer Look at C Programs

5 Objects, Expressions, Operators, and Conversions

6 More About C Functions

7 Controlling Program Logic Flow

8 Programming with Pointers, Arrays, and Strings

9 More About Using Pointers

10 File I/O Programming

11 Deriving New Complex Data Types

12 Portability and Conversion Issues

13 Moving to C

Getting Started with C

If you want to learn the fundamentals of the C programming language, you will find everything you need in this book. If you are new to C programming, this chapter is the place to start. If you already have some experience with C, you might want to skim this chapter for a review.

Approaching the C Language

To learn a new language, you need a good overview of the subject as well as the right type of information. Getting the big picture gives you a context that makes the subject meaningful. This chapter gives you an overview of C. You learn about the following:

- The history of C, from K&R to C++

- How C compares to other languages

- How to read and make sense of a C program

- The basic ingredients of a C program

- The process of writing C programs

- What tools you need to write C programs

A Brief History of C

Where did C come from? Why was it developed? What is it good for? Knowing the answers to these questions does not affect whether you can learn C but gives you a sense of context and continuity, a sense of knowing with what you are dealing.

In the Beginning: Kernighan and Ritchie

In 1978, Prentice Hall published *The C Programming Language,* written by Brian W. Kernighan and Dennis M. Ritchie. Thus began the C explosion.

At first, it wasn't really an explosion. C was developed by Dennis Ritchie for use with the UNIX operating system, running on DEC PDP-11 computers at the Bell Laboratories in Murray Hill, New Jersey. In addition to the actual compiler, the UNIX operating system and most of its utility programs were written in C.

Several players other than Kernighan and Ritchie were involved. The software that resulted in UNIX and its companion C began with Martin Richards, who developed a language called BCPL. This language, in turn, strongly influenced the development of the next language, B—yes, really!—by Ken Thompson in 1970 for use with the original UNIX on the DEC PDP-7. By 1972, Dennis Ritchie (working with Ken Thompson) had expanded B into C. The new C added something that B did not have: *data types.*

BCPL and B were designed as *typeless* languages. C, however, was designed with three fundamental types. These fundamental types are *integers, characters,* and *floating-point numbers.* Using these fundamental types makes it easier to control the data your program manipulates.

For some time, C was considered an esoteric language, difficult to learn and confined to DEC machines and UNIX. By the time K&R published their historic book, C was implemented on IBM, Honeywell, and Interdata computers, among others. C was now on the road to notoriety.

The Move from UNIX to DOS

C did not travel directly from UNIX to DOS in one easy step. It first passed through a phase of implementation on 8-bit microcomputers running the CP/M operating system. Although CP/M—a scaled-down derivation of UNIX developed by Digital Research—was quite popular, the C explosion had not truly begun in this phase. A principal reason for this is that 8-bit systems were typically constrained to 64K RAM sizes—C doesn't hit its stride until more memory is available.

The microcomputer memory barrier was broken, and the C explosion began, with the introduction of the 8088 and 8086 family of 16-bit microprocessors in 1980. Continuity was the rule here, too. The DOS operating system was first designed and marketed (also in 1980) by Seattle Computer Products as 86-DOS. Its author, Tim Paterson, deliberately positioned it to make conversion from CP/M easy.

The entry of Microsoft and IBM into the picture virtually guaranteed that software companies would develop products, including compilers, for the new machine and operating system. The success of the IBM PC and its software exceeded all expectations; part of that success was the blooming popularity of C compilers for that environment. C had successfully made the transition from ivory tower programmers to the masses of programmers who code because they like it.

ANSI Gets Interested

Some early writers on C said that C retained so much purity because it was largely the work of only two men—Ken Thompson and Dennis Ritchie. These writers scorned the committee approach to compiler standardization, noting that a camel is "a horse designed by a committee."

There is some truth to this. *ANSI* (American *N*ational *S*tandards *I*nstitute) has been involved in defining criteria for other languages, notably COBOL. A much touted benefit of such standardization is "portability." Our experience with porting COBOL applications from one ANSI standard compiler to another indicates that *complete* portability is a pipe dream. This is true even when dealing with two compilers from the same vendor.

ANSI interest in C, then, does not automatically guarantee a programmer's utopia in which C is just C, no matter what. Yet, a cynical attitude toward ANSI standardization is unfair. Adhering to ANSI standard C definitions has several benefits, and ANSI has done a better job with C than with COBOL.

Codifying Practice

ANSI created a committee, X3J11, with a task to propose what constitutes "standard C." A major concern of the charter given to the committee was that it should *codify existing practice*. This means, whenever possible, that the new standard recognized the common practice of the programmers of that time. The committee did so, with good results. C is still largely what K&R defined it to be, with fewer loopholes and inconsistencies.

The application of this principle to the standard has one extremely important consequence: *most existing code still ran* when handled by a compiler conforming to the new standard. C code was abundant at this time, and its total commercial value was immense; to render the code unusable would have guaranteed that the standard would never have been accepted in the marketplace.

Conforming to ANSI C

No law says that compiler manufacturers *have* to make their product conform to the ANSI C standard. They are free to produce anything they want. Marketing a product that claims to be "ANSI compatible" when it is not, however, is not being wise. Such a violation of programmers' expectations would quickly ruin the product's sales. On the other hand, a compiler that is *only* ANSI-conforming has no practical use. Real-world programs frequently must control their host hardware and operating system not only to achieve adequate performance levels, but sometimes even to supply certain functions.

Both ANSI and the compiler vendors realize that *implementation-dependent extensions* to the standard have to be allowed. The trick is not to advertise them as part of the standard. Thus, you will find that C compilers commonly provide routines for interfacing with DOS, accessing I/O ports, controlling the display, and so on. In fact, you need a compiler that is rich in extensions if you want your programs to amount to much.

Portability Issues

Portability is the capability to use a program's source code, without modification, on more than one vendor's compiler. This is where the tire meets the road, as far as a standard is concerned. A standard that does not promote portability is useless.

This is also where the conflicts arise for a powerful language like C. One of the great benefits of C is that it can control much of its environment directly without having to resort to assembler, even though every environment is different. A 100-percent portable compiler unfortunately does not exist.

The ANSI C committee partly solved this problem by deciding that the standard should give the programmer a fighting chance to write portable code, but not force her or him to do so. What this means to you, the programmer, is a little complex. For a complete discussion of conversion and portability issues, read Chapter 12.

Looking Toward the Future: C++

ANSI standardization did not make the C language popular; rather, C is standardized because it is so popular. Beginning in December of 1989, the ANSI X3J11 committee convened to standardize C++ as well. Work is still being done on the C++ standards, yet C++ is no longer an esoteric tool used by research labs and hackers, as was C. C++ is everyone's route to powerful and portable programming.

NOTE The new C/C++ packages from vendors such as Borland and Microsoft make the road to powerful programming especially easy. When you buy these vendor's C++ package, you are also getting a full-powered C compiler. Even if you don't want to move to C++ for some time, getting Borland C++ or Microsoft C/C++ provides you with a full-featured C compiler for now and a powerful C++ compiler for later.

Object-Oriented Programming

Object-oriented programming systems, or *OOPS* (pronounced as it is spelled) have been around for quite some time. Characterized by their flexibility and power, they are somewhat notorious for poor performance. C++ comes to the rescue—it is both object-oriented and a hot performer.

C++ buys you more than execution speed; it also buys you programming speed. It enables faster development of larger projects by helping you prevent errors and by supplying some tools that C does not have.

Bell Labs Again

Somehow, it seems only fitting that this latest marvel of C efficiency should come from Bell Labs. C++ was developed by one man, Bjarne Stroustrup. Aficionados of C++ fondly refer to his book, *The C++ Programming Language,* published originally by Addison-Wesley in 1986, as "The Book." (*The C++ Programming Language* is now in its second edition.)

C++ is not a complete departure from ANSI C. In fact, ANSI C may be regarded as a subset of C++, because the two borrowed heavily of each other for ideas and methods. In fact C++ is C, *plus* more, hence the name. C++ definitely goes far beyond standard C. It supplies a storehouse of extra tools: encapsulation, data hiding, classes and derived classes, function and operator overloading, and much more.

Comparing C to Other Languages

Like all languages, C has both advantages and disadvantages. Because C's philosophy is to provide straightforward implementation, to commit to fast runtime code, and to furnish a mature function library and a rich operator set, C compares well to other languages.

Comparing C to Assembly Language

No high-level language can beat assembly language at producing fast runtime code or code that's highly compact and tuned. Of all high-level languages, however, C probably comes closest to keeping up with assembly language. Originally a language for system programmers, C remains in touch with low-level components of the system and can be used as a high-level assembler.

In areas in which C is slower than assembly language, C's flexibility and power often more than make up for its lack of speed. The same can be said of code size. C runtime code is always larger than that of a comparable assembly language program, mainly because of the presence of the generalized library functions that make the language so rich and powerful.

Comparing C to Pascal

Originally, Pascal was intended to be a tool used for teaching the fundamentals of programming while masking the more detailed aspects of the hardware and operating system environments. It is therefore more generalized than C and less capable of attaining C's performance levels. Pascal has matured but (unlike C and assembler) is less often used for large development projects such as operating systems and canned packages.

On the flip side, Pascal programmers probably will have less trouble acclimatizing themselves to C syntax than will other programmers. There are many similarities between C and Pascal; the punctuation, the general style of block statements, the way arrays are handled, and the packaging of complex data objects are some of the ways the languages resemble one another. Still, there are enough differences to make the process of converting from one to the other a laborious, tedious job.

Comparing C to COBOL

There are almost no similarities of syntax and construction between C and COBOL. C is a much more free and flowing language than COBOL. It holds nothing of the rigid separation of components found in COBOL's Identification, Environment, Data, and Procedure divisions. C programs always result in significantly faster and more compact runtime code than COBOL programs (at least using the compilers with which the authors are familiar).

Not long ago, COBOL obtained a significant advantage when it adapted to business programming. COBOL has the built-in availability of decimal data and arithmetic. This advantage is proving short-lived, however; the newer C++ compilers have built-in classes that support decimal data and arithmetic, too.

Comparing C to FORTRAN

Justly famous for its number-crunching capability, *FORTRAN* (*FOR*mula *TRAN*slation) was the first language of both of the authors—it has been around for a long time.

FORTRAN is still the undisputed master of number-crunching applications. It is used, for example, in the ballistics programs that run the IBM Federal Systems computers guiding NASA space vehicles. (These systems are based on the 360 mainframe technology—old, but tried and true.)

Could C ever displace applications like this? Conceivably, it could. C programs running on 80386 processors with a math coprocessor, or on the newest 80486 processors, would *significantly* outperform the older technology. C's formula-translating capability is every bit as good as FORTRAN's, and the advanced math functions could easily be added to the function library. What C can't do is overcome the weight of tradition in this case.

A First Look at C Form and Punctuation

Reading the sample C programs is one of the most important parts of mastering the material in this book. If you can't read a program, you certainly can't write one. The first step in learning to read C programs is to learn something about how they are created.

How To Look at a C Program

Suppose that you are sitting at your computer, and that your favorite text editor is running with the source file for a C program on the screen. What do you see? If you are new to C programming, the display may look like the result of an explosion at the local dictionary factory. Don't worry. It really does make sense once you get the hang of it.

You very accurately can define a C source program to be a series of declarations. A *declaration* tells the compiler of which elements it should be informed. You can write a declaration to instruct the compiler how to do the following:

- Recognize a name you created.
- Set aside storage (RAM) for data objects such as variables and constants and (optionally) initialize their values.
- Define the behavior of a function.
- Interpret a particular type of data.

Strictly speaking, *statements* (instructions that do something) are only parts of a function declaration; they never appear outside a function and are not declarations. At this level, *functions* are just collections of statements. From the compiler's viewpoint, looking at the whole program, the entire program is just a collection of declarations that tell the compiler how to generate object code, not how to perform the ultimate task you want the program to perform. For those of you who are not computer scientists, that is a strange way of looking at programming—but it makes sense. Compilers don't know what you are thinking—they know only what you tell them.

You can begin reading C programs before you finish this book because C declarations often make intuitive sense. The very terms used actually tell you something about what is going on. Furthermore, declarations are found mostly in groups of a single type, and those groups are separated by blank lines (*white space,* in C lingo). By putting these clues together, you get an overview of the program's structure and function.

Noticing the C Punctuators

Punctuation in C is extremely important. (If you are not accustomed to it, it is strange, also!) You can use punctuation as a clue to what a program is doing, however. You might want to look ahead now to Listing 1.1, FIRST.C, to see the punctuators in action as they are discussed.

Quick Reference: The C Punctuators

All the C punctuators are predefined. Only the following punctuators are valid:

```
[ ] ( ) { } * , : = ; ...  # ##
```

You cannot use these characters for anything but punctuation in the manner defined by C. The only exception is if these characters are used as data inside a string or character literal.

Both # and ## are actually *preprocessing operators;* they are not included in the ANSI X3J11 document's list of punctuators. But, because they are used only during preprocessing and behave more like punctuators than true operators, they are included here.

Notice first that most the lines in Listing 1.1 end with a semicolon (;). The semicolon is used to terminate all simple statements and declarations in C. For example, in the following statement:

```
i = i * 2;
```

the value of i is doubled and placed back in the variable's location in storage (RAM).

You can identify a *block statement* by noting that it is composed of one or more simple statements enclosed in curly braces ({}). The body of the calc() function is an example of a block statement:

```
int calc( int i )
{
  i = i * 2;
  i++;
  return i;
}
```

Look carefully at the preceding lines. Although each simple statement is terminated with a semicolon, the block statement *does not* end in a semicolon after the curly brace (}). All this means is that the entire group of simple statements inside the braces is to be considered as a single, undivided entity. Either the whole block is executed, or none of it is.

Next, you can easily pick out compiler directives; notice that they all begin with the pound sign (#) in the extreme left column, as in the following example:

```
#include <stdlib.h>
```

Compiler directives are not part of the source code you want translated into object code; they are instructions to the compiler on how to go about the translation process. Because these instructions must be found and interpreted before any real compilation takes place, they are also called *preprocessing directives*. Directives do not need the semicolon to be terminated. If the statement includes a semicolon, it is there for another reason, covered in detail in Chapter 4.

Finally, *comments* play an important role in making a C program readable. Comments are delimited by special sequences of characters that are neither punctuation nor C operators. A comment begins with the sequence /* (a slash and an asterisk) and ends with the sequence */ (an asterisk and a slash). See the first two lines of Listing 1.1. Comments also can appear on the same line with legitimate C statements.

Comments in C++ are slightly different. C++ uses the sequence // to indicate a comment.

The only purpose of a comment is to provide to human eyes some clarification of the program. The compiler replaces the whole comment with a single blank before proceeding with translation.

Sneak Preview: Characters, Arrays, and Strings

It is nearly impossible to discuss the C language without some mention of *strings*. In order to understand strings, you must also have some acquaintance with characters and arrays. These three types of data have the following characteristics:

- A *character* is a data variable that can be printed or displayed, or that can control a display device. Letters, numbers, and punctuation are *display characters*. *Control characters* have the same internal structure as display characters, but are generally invisible and control the way other characters appear on a display device (such as a screen or printer). Chapter 4 gives much more detail on characters.

- An *array* is a group of data variables (all of the same type) that are stored together in the computer's memory. Arrays can be formed from any other type of variables, including characters. An array of integers, for example, is defined by writing:

```
int counts[10];   /* An array of 10 integers. */
```

- A *string* is a special type of array composed of characters. You define a string just like any other array. For example, you might define a name string:

```
char name[40];   /* A name string with up to 39 chars. */
```

This string can contain only up to 39 display characters, because the last array element (position) must be reserved for a *null character*. A null character is a special character that has a numeric value of zero. The null character signals the end of the string, and is not displayable. When you initialize a string with a literal value, you do not have to code the null character, as follows:

```
char name[40] = "John Aloysius Doe";
```

Understanding the Parts of a C Program

Now that you have an idea of how C programs are composed, it is time to look at their ingredients. Listing 1.1 shows the source code for FIRST.C, a short program that has all the basic program components.

Listing 1.1. FIRST.C—A basic program (in Borland C++).

```
1   /* ----        FIRST.C        ---- */
2   /* ---- A short C program. ---- */
3
4   #include <stdio.h>
5   #include <stdlib.h>
6
7   int calc( int i );
8
9   main()
10  {
11    char number_in[4], number_out[5];
12    int i,j;
13
14    puts( "Enter up to a two digit integer." );
15    gets( number_in );
16    i = atoi( number_in );
17    j = calc( i );
18    itoa( j, number_out, 10 );
19    puts( "The calculations on the integer yield:" );
20    puts( number_out );
21  }
22
23  int calc( int i )
24  {
25    i = i * 2;
26    i++;
27    return i;
28  }
```

If you are new to C programming, take a little time to look over Listing 1.1 and get acquainted with a C program's composition. FIRST.C gets a string of characters from the keyboard and converts the string to a number. Then the program calls a function that doubles the number and returns the result. Finally, the new value is converted back to a character string and displayed on the console. Here's how it breaks out by line numbers:

■ Lines 1-2 are comments that give some basic information about the program—its name and ingredients.

■ Line 3 illustrates that you can leave blank lines anywhere in the program to improve its readability.

■ Lines 4-5 are *compiler directives.* In this example, they tell the compiler that some very important information (about the built-in library functions to be used in this program) is contained in the named files. These files are called *header files* because they normally appear at the head of the program.

■ Line 7 contains a *function prototype,* which tells the compiler that the program contains a definition for a function called calc. This function receives an integer *parameter* (something to work with or on), and returns an integer value to the place in the program where the function was called. Once defined, a function can be called again and again from many places in the program (but, as you will later see, not from *every* place). In this book, a function is called simply by its name, followed by a pair of parentheses. The function in line 7 is referred to as calc(), for example. You are expected to understand that the function might have parameters and return some data type, hence the empty parentheses. You can refer to the code listing or fragment for the particular details.

■ Lines 9-21 contain the program's main() function. Every program has a main() function; it is the first function that executes when you run the program. In Listing 1.1, main() gets some input data, converts the data to a number, passes that number to calc() for processing, receives a result, and displays the result on-screen.

■ Lines 23-28 contain the *function definition* for calc(), the function referred to in the function prototype in line 7. calc() performs the task of doubling the number that main() passed to it as a parameter, and returning that result to main().

Including the Header Files

Lines 4 and 5 of Listing 1.1 provide an example of the #include preprocessing directive. It is doubtful that you will ever find a useful C program that didn't have at least one #include directive. What is it and why is it so necessary?

Including Source Files in General

The #include directive causes the compiler to do what you might reasonably expect—to pull in another source file. At preprocessing time, before translation to object code begins, the compiler locates the named source file on-disk (the file in angle brackets), reads it in, and inserts it into the current source at the position of the #include—see Figure 1.1.

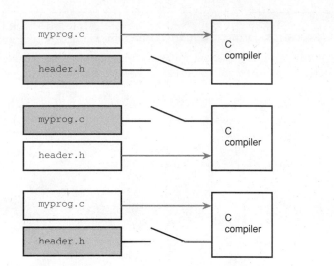

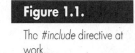

Figure 1.1.

The *#include* directive at work.

Figure 1.1 implies something else about including other source files: The included file can be anything you want it to be, if it is something the compiler can accept when program translation begins. You could break a long source program into multiple text files and reference the files with #include statements for compilation. (Note, however, that this is not a very efficient way to handle complex projects.) Building complex projects is mentioned later in this chapter and discussed in some detail in Chapter 5.

If you have to rekey directives, constants, and similar material every time you want to use them, eventually you will make a typographical error or some other mistake. C programs normally use #include directives to make constants and the like consistent. Ordinarily, you should not place in a header file statements that initialize variables, function definitions (as opposed to declarations, see Chapter 3), or other such animals that belong in the running code.

Header Files and Built-In Functions

The two #include directives in Listing 1.1 are good examples of the way a compiler product makes its library functions and other facilities available to you. These resources are vitally important for writing robust, useful programs.

When you bought your compiler, you got much more than just one compiler program. You got, among other gifts, a whole library of powerful functions that are not part of the C language. These functions are built into the *package,* but not the *compiler;* they don't change the essence of what constitutes C.

Quick Reference: Typical Uses for Header Files

Bjarne Stroustrup, the developer of C++, suggests several uses for header files. Here is a slightly modified list of what a header file should contain:

Type definitions	`struct parts { int stocknum, loc };`
Function declarations	`int area( int length, int width);`
Data declarations	`extern unsigned master_switch;`
Constant definitions	`const int maxsize = 32767;`
Enumerations	`enum toys { top, jacks, slinky };`
Include directives	`#include <graphics.h>`
Macro definitions	`#define TRUE 1`
Comments	`/* This is a header file. */`

Now that you have them, what can you do with them? The compiler manual tells you all about the functions—what they are, how they work, and how to set up a call to them. The important point to understand is that, in some ways, functions behave like variables; they return a value that has a certain type. That is why you can use functions on the right side of an assignment statement, as follows:

```
/* What will happen here? */

double x;               /* Define a variable to use. */
...
x = sqrt( 3.1415926 ); /* Take the square root of PI. */
```

The square root function `sqrt()` is defined to return a double-length floating-point value, but how does the compiler know that? If you have not declared the function somewhere, but use it anyway, the compiler assumes that the function returns an integer. (The integer is the default type in C. Beginning in Chapter 3—and throughout this book—you will see what the acceptable data types are. C can do a great deal with data.) Depending on the brand of compiler you use, this error may or may not get by the compiler or linker. If the error does get by and you try to run the program, your computer probably will go haywire at this point.

How, if you didn't write the function, are you going to declare it to the compiler? That is what the supplied header files are for. The compiler manual tells you not only how to call the function but also which header file to include in the program so the function will work correctly. The ANSI standard header file for the square root function is MATH.H; you should correct the code shown in the preceding fragment by adding the `#include` directive for it, as follows:

```
#include <math.h>
...
double x;                /* Define a variable to use. */
...
x = sqrt( 3.1415926 ); /* Take the square root of PI. */
```

Placing the Include Directives

Where do you place the `#include` directives in the program? C syntax provides for placement just about anywhere. C grammar, however, expects you to declare something before you can use it. (This is as true for supplied library functions as for anything else.)

In Listing 1.1, the `#include` directives are preceded only by a few comments indicating the program's name and purpose. Placing the directives at or near the top of the source file in every case, so you don't accidentally wait too long, is a good idea.

If you do not use any of the functions (or macros or global variables) that a particular header file declares, you don't have to include them—but it normally doesn't hurt to do so. It's a good habit, for example, to always including STDLIB.H and STDIO.H (just in case). They are used so often that they are easy to forget. If the header files are not needed, it does *not* hurt your program in any way to include them.

CAUTION

What happens if you forget to include a necessary header file? You are likely to get some strange error messages at either compile time or link-edit time. Often, the compiler assumes that the reference is to something in another source file and ignores it. The linker then sends the function a message about having encountered an unresolved external reference. Because this can be confusing, double check the header files for the library functions you use and make sure you've included them all.

Two Ways to Include

Listing 1.1 illustrates only one way to write an `#include` directive. The file to be included was written inside angle brackets (< >)—the same characters you use as greater-than and less-than operators. Be extremely careful not to put any extra blanks inside the brackets; if you do, the compiler cannot find the file. For example:

```
#include <stddef.h>        /* The correct method */
```

is not the same as

```
#include < stddef.h >      /* Wrong! */
```

The ANSI standard says that using angle brackets to write an include causes the compiler to search for the named file in "a sequence of implementation-defined places." Thus, the search takes place *only* in specifically designated directories, which are assumed to contain only header files. This is the type of `#include` you should write to include *supplied* header files.

Implementation-defined means that the manner of specifying these directories varies from one compiler and operating system to the next. On MS-DOS systems, for example, a typical way to identify directories is to include a SET `INCLUDE=d:\dirname` string in the AUTOEXEC.BAT file so the directory name string becomes part of the environment that the compiler can check. (For details on how to do this, check the manual for your compiler.) Figure 1.2 shows a setup similar to those used by many popular compilers.

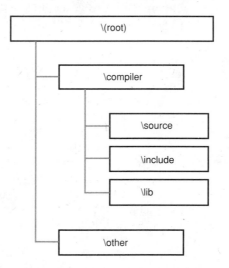

Figure 1.2.

Directories for headers
and libraries.

As you look at Figure 1.2, remember that normally, the \source directory is the current one. You can use the DOS SET command to define PATH, INCLUDE, and LIB specifications for the directories to use for those libraries and files.

The second way to write an `#include` is to enclose the filename in double quotation marks, as follows:

```
#include "myhdr.h"
```

Here, as in the first method, the warning about including extra blanks applies. The ANSI standard says, "The named source file is searched for in an implementation-defined manner." If that fails, the search proceeds as if the first method had been coded. That doesn't say much at all. Every compiler you have used assumes that this syntax means to search first in the current directory and then, if the file is not there, to go back and search as in the first type of #include (that is, as if angle bracket notation was used).

This is the style you should use for including header files you have written. These header files usually are placed in the same directory as the program's source file, not in the directory with the compiler's headers.

NOTE When you begin to write complex programs, you have to learn how to package parts of the program in files that are compiled separately and linked together later. When you compile a group of functions separately, you have to create for them a header file that can be included in other source files, so other functions can access your functions and the variables you want to make *public* (visible to other source files). In Chapter 5's discussion of "Accessing External Data Items: Setting Up the Header Files," you learn more about building complex programs.

Defining Data in C

All programs (whether written in C or in another language) exist to carry out one action: manipulation of data. Some of this data exists only in the program; some of it is moved into RAM from different places by the input and output functions. In either case, the compiler has to know how to set up your program's memory to hold that data. A data item is often called an *object* in C documentation.

Setting Aside Memory for Data

Whenever you *declare a variable* or *use a constant,* you cause the compiler to set aside (*allocate*) memory. This type of memory becomes part of the program—when the compiler writes the runtime code to disk, this type of data (all constants and variables written outside functions) takes up some space in the file.

By using malloc(), calloc(), realloc(), and related functions, you can allocate memory for data dynamically when you run your program. This group of functions acquires blocks of memory from the operating system, outside of the program, at runtime, not compile time. Dynamically allocated data does not take up space in the program file on disk.

For all types of data, however, the compiler must construct your program so the runtime program code can keep track of everything. Therefore, certain types of data are placed in particular parts of memory. On the 80x86 family of processors, data is placed in the code segment, data segment, or stack segment, according to how the data is used.

Figure 1.3 shows how C compilers assign storage for data on 80X86 processors. In the segment layout for the SMALL memory model on an IBM or compatible PC shown in Figure 1.3, data is stored in the _DATA, CONST, _BSS, STACK, and Heap segments, all addressed by the DS register. (The *heap* is where C dynamically allocates memory.)

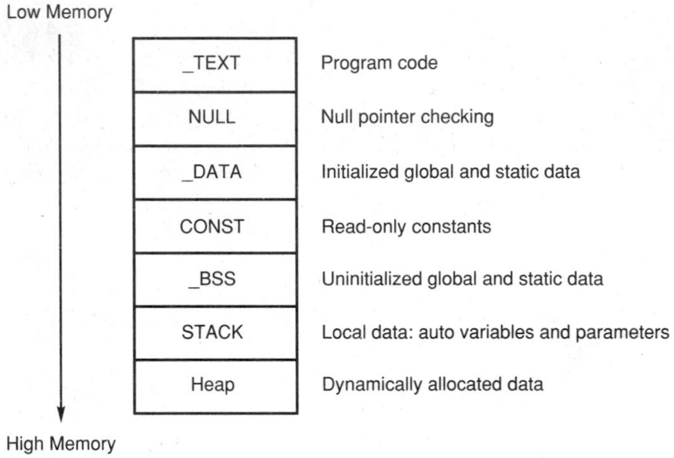

Low Memory

_TEXT	Program code
NULL	Null pointer checking
_DATA	Initialized global and static data
CONST	Read-only constants
_BSS	Uninitialized global and static data
STACK	Local data: auto variables and parameters
Heap	Dynamically allocated data

High Memory

Figure 1.3.

How data-object allocation is handled.

Where Do You Put It?

Look at lines 11 and 12 in FIRST.C (Listing 1.1). These two lines declare data objects the program will use. Line 11 declares two strings (these are *character arrays*—sequences of displayable characters); line 12 declares two integers.

Now notice the location of these declarations—they are inside the body of the main() function. Only the main() function can access these variables directly, either to examine them (*fetch* access) or to modify them (*update* access). The main() function is not prevented from passing the values or locations of these variables as parameters to other functions, but only main() can access them directly.

You can also declare variables outside a function. Such variables can be accessed by all functions in the source file—they are jointly owned by all (presuming that the variables were declared first, before the functions). This distinction gives rise to an important concept in C: *local variables* and *global variables*.

- Local variables are "visible" only in the block (the function or block statement) in which they are defined. These variables have *dynamic duration*—they exist only while the block is active (actually running)—unless you override the duration. As you may recall, a block statement is anything surrounded by curly braces; thus, a function body is a block.

- Global variables are "globally visible" in the source file, and can be made visible to other source files as well. By default, global variables have static duration—they remain valid no matter what part of the program is active.

Even though you don't enclose the entire source file in curly braces, the whole file is considered a block. This point of view may help you understand the general rule: variables are visible only in the block in which they are defined.

T I P

What the *main()* Function Does

You can write any functions you like and call them anything you like—except `main()`. `main()` is the only C function that is *required* in every program. (Lines 9 through 21 in Listing 1.1 contain the `main()` function for the FIRST.C program.) A `main()` function is required for several reasons, as explained.

Assume that you have compiled your program, that no errors occurred, and that you are ready to run it. Now ask this question—how does the computer know which of the many executable instructions in your program to start with?

One of the primary purposes of the `main()` function is that it is the primary entry point for the program. The compiler *always* sets up the executable program file so `main()` runs first.

Setting Up the Environment

Actually, quite a bit of preparation goes on behind the scenes. The compiler creates a program *stub* (short routine) that executes before the code you placed in `main()`. This stub has different purposes, depending on the machine and operating system being used. Generally, the stub sets up access to the command-line parameters you typed at the system command to execute the program. It also sets up the system environment for the program (determining how interrupt keys are handled, what to do if the program aborts, and so on).

Just because the main() function is required, you do not have to put any particular arguments in it. What you supply depends entirely on what you want the program to do. In fact, you don't have to do anything at all. For example, the following is a perfectly legitimate program that compiles correctly and runs without error:

```
main()  /* empty.c */
{
}
```

It just doesn't do anything!

Normally, main() should perform any setup tasks that depend on your application—initializing global variables, opening files, calling the first functions to get started, and whatever else may be called for. In a short program, you may even want to put the majority of the statements in main(), as in Listing 1.1.

Normal Program Termination

The final major function of main() is to provide a mechanism for ending program execution normally. As you might have noticed in the preceding program fragment (EMPTY.C), no statements are necessary to accomplish this. The effect of allowing the program to "fall through" the bottom of main() is exactly the same as the effect of the following code:

```
main()  /* ending.c */
{
  ... /* Some statements go here */
  exit(0);
}
```

ENDING.C terminates the program deliberately but normally. The function call exit(0) invokes a library function that cleans up after the program, returns control to the system, and passes a return code of 0 (or whatever you want) to the system.

Providing User-Defined Functions

Lines 23 through 28 of Listing 1.1 contain a user-defined function: calc(). Such functions are not mandatory, but a C program that had none would be rather strange.

Functions Act Like Data

After you have declared and defined a function, you can invoke it by simply referencing it in an expression, as in line 17 of Listing 1.1:

```
j = calc( i );
```

The reference to `calc()` occupies a position in this statement in the same way a variable or constant does. That is, the compiler presumes that a function has a value. In `calc()`, the `return` statement caused the calculated value of `i` to be passed back to the calling routine. Functions behave like data objects in this way.

You can also invoke a function that stands alone, like this:

```
calc( i );
```

Calling a function without using its result is perfectly legitimate. Any value the function returns is simply thrown away.

Where Do They Go?

Where you place a function in the program depends on where it is declared and on what other parts of the program call the function.

You can, but should not, reference a function before it has been declared. As you might recall, doing so causes certain (not always desirable) default actions to take place. The following methods are all acceptable; some are better than others:

■ You can declare a function by defining it, providing the function body as well as the function parameters. You can now refer to the function anywhere after the definition. If you choose this method, you may find yourself positioning functions as if they were Pascal procedures: with the lowest (most detailed) level near the beginning of the program, followed by higher levels, and finishing with `main()` at the bottom of the program. This is not recommended because it makes reading the program difficult.

■ You can forward declare the function by writing a function prototype early in the program and defining it later. A function prototype is just the header line with no body, as in

```
double do_something( double a_parm );
```

Notice that in the prototype only, a semicolon follows the parentheses. In a definition, you would delete this semicolon and open the function body with a curly brace.

Full-function prototyping, the preferred method, has the following distinct advantages:

■ You can place `main()` at the top of the program, followed by the next highest-level functions, and so on, in a fashion that resembles the program's logical structure. This makes the program much easier to read, and therefore easier to debug.

■ You reduce the risk of referencing a library function before it has been declared. This prevents the accidental return of a data type other than the one you expected (the type of error that can make your program go crazy!).

■ You can now reference functions in any order, from anywhere in the source file.

This last point is important to sophisticated programs. If you use the first method, the current function can be invoked correctly only by functions that follow it. For example, consider this arrangement:

```
void function_a( void ) /* wrong.c */
{
  double n;
  n = function_b();
}


double function_b( void )
{
  ... /* Something goes on here */
}
```

At first glance, this code fragment looks fine. Everything is there, and this is not quite the same as forgetting a header file for a library function. The intended return value is a double floating point, and the function that supplies it has that type. So what happens?

Most likely, you won't even get this one through the compile phase. When a program like this is submitted to the Microsoft C/C++ 7.0 compiler, for example, it stops when the `function_b()` definition is encountered. The resulting error message says that this is a redefinition of the function. This means that, as far as the compiler is concerned, the presumed function type changed suddenly from integer to double float.

In more sophisticated programs, you might even encounter a situation in which `function_a()` may sometimes have to call `function_b()`, whereas at other times `function_b()` calls `function_a()`. For this type of situation, the modern method of full-function prototyping is absolutely necessary.

Writing a C Program

Besides requiring a knowledge of syntax and coding rules, writing a C program requires a good deal of skill and mental preparation. What would happen, for example, if you sat down to write a murder mystery without having considered who did the deed or how? The book would be a haphazard mess. The same is true when you write a C program. You must be prepared first.

Start with the Right Design

For a C program (as for a murder mystery) you have to know the ending before you write the beginning. How else do you know where to start, and how to get there? Thus, decide exactly what you want the program to do before you start coding. The structure of most programs can be represented as a *top-down tree structure*. Well-structured programs tend to call functions in layered groups, or levels. The functions become more detailed or "atomic" as you move down the tree structure—see Figure 1.4.

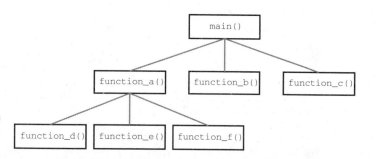

Figure 1.4.

A typical top-down program structure.

A Top-Down Approach to Coding

You don't have to have every line of code in your mind before you approach the keyboard, but you should know how you want the program to behave. You can certainly overlap the program-design and program-coding phases.

An excellent way to do this is to use a top-down approach to both design and coding. Begin with the broadest statement of what the program is to do, and break the logic down one level into a series of major tasks. Now you have the first level of function calls to write into the `main()` function. Repeat the process for each function in that second tier to arrive at a third, more detailed level. At each level, just add to the source code the functions, prototypes, and variables needed (be sure not to put this off—you will forget something).

Program design is a matter of personal style; it can become quite complex if carried out scientifically. A full discussion of it is out of place here. For more information about the process, you may want to read *C By Example* or *C++ By Example,* published by Que Corporation.

Making Programs Readable

Just as you learned to use breaks in the code and punctuation to read C programs, you can take several steps to make your programs readable. They are not difficult to do, and this is the time to start doing them. Later, after you have formed the habit, performing these steps is automatic and painless.

Using Indentation and White Space

C requires only enough blanks so it can recognize keywords and names. Other than that, you can run a program together almost at will. Take another look at WRONG.C, written here with no attention paid to coding style:

```
void function_a(void)/* wrong.c */{double
n;n=function_b();}double function_b(void){/*Something
goes on here*/}
```

It looks like garbage, doesn't it? Writing it this way, however, has not introduced any new errors in the code. Perhaps this example is a little dramatic, but it does prove a point. The way you lay out the text in the program makes all the difference in the world to the human eye.

All you have to do to change the first version of WRONG.C to this second version is to remove unnecessary blanks and line indentations. Although these blanks and indentations are unnecessary to the compiler, but people need them desperately. Both the eye and the brain tend to work in units, rather than a continuous, unbroken spectrum. To sum it up:

- Use blanks to separate individual items, wherever suitable and possible.

- Indent (to the same level) program statements that belong together. Some programmers prefer to indent in two-space increments from one level to the next, some prefer to use four spaces, and some prefer other values. The point is that you should pick a style and stick with it. Consistency is the key to readable code.

You should be aware also that most visual debugger products are able to resolve the current position in a program only to the *closest line of code,* not to a single statement or expression. You may therefore want to confine yourself to writing only one statement per line of source code (or perhaps two, if they are very closely related). If you observe this restriction, you do not have to determine which of several statements on a line has the bug.

Using Comments

Using comments liberally in your programs, especially in those parts where something tricky or difficult is being done, is a good idea. You can clarify your code by using block comments and line comments effectively.

A *block comment* should introduce a major section of code or a function, and can look something like this:

```
/*

   +-------------------------------------------+
   + Function XYZ.
   +  Input Parameters:  int a     A number
   +                     char q    A character
   +  Returns:           char *    A string "a"
   +                               bytes long filled
   +                               with "q"
   +  Purpose:           To illustrate block comments.
   +-------------------------------------------+
*/
```

This is just a suggestion. The style, layout, and contents of such comments are completely up to you, and should suit your own taste. The point is to provide visual separation of useful information.

Line comments also can be quite useful. They can help clarify complicated bits of code, so you or someone else does not have to puzzle over the algorithm whenever you look at it. Here is a trivial sample of line comments:

```
int calc( int i )
{
  i = i * 2;    /* First double the value */
  i++;          /* Now increment it by one */
  return i;     /* And send it back */
}
```

Now the function is not so cryptic, is it? Line comments are extremely useful in complicated sections of code. Use them freely where they are needed, but don't clutter the code unnecessarily with them. The need for white space also applies here.

Aligning Braces and Parentheses

You can use the physical alignment of curly braces and parentheses in combination with white space and indentation to make your programs more readable. The compiler is not affected by comment alignment—use a style that reflects your own taste.

The authors, for example, habitually align braces and parentheses *with each other* when surrounding function bodies (as in the preceding code) or long lists of values (as follows):

```c
static char *month_tab[] =
    { "January",
      "February",
      "March",
      "April",
      "May",
      "June",
      "July",
      "August",
      "September",
      "October",
      "November",
      "December",
      "INVALID"
    };
```

Because this requirement would sometimes consume too many lines and distract the eye, try to align braces and parentheses with their indentation level (rather than with each other) when coding conditional and selection statements, like this:

```c
if ( a == b ) {
  puts( "Serious error!\n" );
  abort();
}
else {
  puts( "Results OK.\n" );
  a = get_next_thing();
}
```

Notice also the use of white space and indentation, and the location of semicolons. Whether you choose an alignment scheme like this is up to you. Again, just pick one and stay with it. Uniformity is important.

Writing Programs in the C Environment

The *C environment* refers to the tools you need to do productive work in C. The minimum set of tools you need includes the following:

■ The particular compiler you choose and its features. The choice of compilers and features varies widely.

■ A good text editor. You need a text editor that at least provides for easy insertion and deletion of characters, cutting and pasting, and scrolling the text. Most modern C compilers for the IBM PC provide a built-in editor.

■ Whether the linker produces code that is compatible with the output of other products.

■ Project-management utilities.

■ A visual debugging tool.

Evaluating the Text Editor

When you buy a compiler, you may receive a text editor with it. Most compilers' packages do include one, so you can write programs even if you have no other editor. Many programmers prefer to purchase a separate editor, even if the compiler package has one. An editor called BRIEF has developed a large following, as has one called SPF/PC. (IBM mainframe programmers like SPF/PC because they are already accustomed to its "feel.")

In either case, you spend the most time with, and become most intimately acquainted with, the text editor. If your text editor is worthless, you do not get much done. Most text editors have only a subset of the important features. A few of these features are listed here:

■ *Large edit buffers.* The best editors enable you to use all the machine's remaining memory. This is important because C programs, at least the sophisticated, useful ones, tend to run long.

■ *A convenient keyboard layout.* Remembering which key does what shouldn't be difficult. Keystrokes should not be awkward. (This can slow you down more than you realize—not to mention the aggravation.) The most popular text editors either support or mimic WordStar's keyboard usage, which although rather awkward, is so universal that most programmers make the keystrokes subconsciously.

■ *Automatic file backup.* When you begin editing a file, the editor should make a backup copy automatically, for obvious reasons.

■ *File-merge capability.* Frequently, as you edit a program, you will find it convenient to copy a file, or part of a file, into your current edit session. If, as often happens, you find that you have already coded something similar to the project you are working on, get a copy of your existing work. There is no need to write your code a second time.

■ *Multiple editing sessions.* Editing your program in one window while looking at some sample code in another window is just one of the advantages of this feature. Unfortunately, not many editors that come with the popular compilers support this feature.

■ *An appealing visual interface.* The editor's screens should look good. It is surprising how quickly you can tire of looking at a poorly designed screen—it can actually disrupt your concentration. The Microsoft C/C++ 7.0 editor shown in Figure 1.5 is an example of an appealing editor.

Figure 1.5.

The Microsoft C/C++ 7.0 editor screen.

Most of the more recent compiler products feature an *integrated development environment* (IDE). When you use an IDE, you don't run the compiler, you run the environment. In that environment, the *built-in* text editor is usually the first screen you see. (Microsoft's C/C++ 7.0 editor is a built-in editor, for example.) In a built-in editor, the other functions (compiling, linking, setting options) are just a menu selection or a hot key away. By contrast, *stand-alone* editors are not part of an IDE. If you choose a stand-alone editor, it should have the same features as an IDE editor (except, obviously, interfaces to the compiler and the linker).

Editors built into an IDE have two extremely helpful features: *error location* and *advanced project make facilities*. These two features can do more to reduce development time than almost any of the others in the package.

In an IDE, compile-time errors are displayed (in the editor) with the cursor positioned on the first error, ready to correct. The screen typically is divided into two windows, with the edit session in the upper portion of the screen, and a list of error messages in the lower portion. These windows stay synchronized. As you select the next error message in the error window, the cursor is automatically repositioned in the edit window.

In an IDE, project make facilities (controlling multiple source files is discussed in Chapter 5) can be considerably automated. The Borland C++ product provides an integrated project make facility as well as a stand-alone make utility. Both integrated project make and stand-alone make facilities require a text file containing make instructions as input. Project files have an extension of .PRJ rather than the usual .MAK (for make files). Project and make files are essentially the same; they differ only in syntax and point of use, not in purpose. The syntax of project files is simpler than that of make files.

The Microsoft integrated environment reaches these same goals by using a *program list*. Here, too, the syntax is simplified. The list of source files is created in a dialog box and stored in a file with the .MAK extension. When the program list is stored to disk (at your request), that list is converted to make-file format and syntax.

Using either vendor's product, you are saved a great deal of effort.

What's in a Good C Compiler?

Assuming that your compiler product provides the minimum set of tools in one form or another, how can you tell whether you have a good product? Again, the answer reflects the authors' opinions—at least, up to a point. Simply keep in mind that an editor's popularity does not always guarantee it will be satisfactory for you. Selecting your C compiler product involves both elements of personal taste and of need.

Compiler Features

There is no point in buying a less than robust C compiler, just because you have yet to learn the language. A full-featured package may seem intimidating at first, because there are so many options to control. You probably will find, however, that you will grow quickly into the more sophisticated product.

Choosing among the leading contenders in the C compiler market is difficult, primarily because the best packages are quite similar in what they offer. Yet there are significant differences. When you start thinking about buying a C compiler, you should investigate at least seven types of features:

- Full ANSI C conformity
- Compile-only options
- Environment support
- Floating-point math support
- Support of low-level features
- Optimization features
- C++ support

Full ANSI C conformity is crucial, and becomes more so. A compiler that does not conform to the standard, or conforms to only part of it, creates unnecessary problems in manufacturing portable programs. The issue of ANSI conformity, however, applies to your programs as well as to the compiler you use.

The ANSI X3J11 committee wisely provided for the distinction between strictly conforming (maximally portable) and conforming programs. This distinction was made to enable the presence and legitimate use of extensions to the standard language. Many of these are necessary to produce practical code for a particular machine or system.

ANSI C Rationale

ANSI C provides for extensions to the language in a conforming implementation (compiler), to provide enhanced *functionality* and *performance*. Don't be afraid to use the extensions. They can be the keys to slick, high-performance programs. Low-level I/O and video I/O functions are two areas in which a compiler vendor is likely to provide extensions (in the form of library functions).

You can reduce the impact of using extensions on portability by encapsulating the nonstandard code in a group of user-defined functions and referring to the nonstandard function calls only in those functions. When porting the program to another machine or operating system, you have to convert only those nonstandard functions, leaving the rest of the program as is.

Compile-only options are needed to provide separate compilation and linkage editing when you construct large, complex projects. This type of option is so universally available that you are unlikely to find a C compiler that does not support it in some fashion.

Options supporting the host environment make much of the difference between professional-quality compiler tools and lesser products. The compiler should provide options for at least the following:

- Generating object-module maps

- Choosing memory models or instruction sets (for IBM 80x86-based machines)

- Selecting the function-calling conventions (to support mixing with other languages, and for performance boost)

- Stack checking at runtime

- Controlling the stack and heap size

- Enabling debugging-support features

For systems programming with C, you might want a compiler that can produce *ROMable* code (such as the code in a PC extension card). And anyone might want to control the names of files output from the compiler (by using a file extension other than .OBJ, for example).

Floating-point math support obviously is important. There are many calculations that require the use of floating-point numbers. The floating-point package should include both floating-point emulation and the capability to use math coprocessor chips directly, without first having to change the source code you write. Control of this feature with a compile-time switch is acceptable, but it is much better if the compiler can detect the coprocessor dynamically and build your program accordingly. Dynamic detection of the coprocessor allows your program to run on any machine, with or without the coprocessor, and without having to be recompiled.

Support of low-level features is mandatory for systems or commercial-grade work. The compiler should enable access to system I/O ports, low-level I/O functions, system interrupt services, direct DOS calls, and ROM BIOS calls. Why? There are two reasons: *speed* and *power*. DOS simply isn't very fast and it doesn't have the capability to perform many functions. Nor does the ANSI standard mandate interfaces to such high-performance services. Later in this book, you are introduced to coping with hardware and system dependencies like these. You should be aware that you will mature rapidly as a C programmer and that you will not only want, but also *need* these features.

Optimization features also are key to large, complex projects. Basically, you can optimize code in only two ways. You can optimize for *speed* or for *size*. Sometimes optimizing for one factor contributes to better efficiency for the other, as well. For many of your projects, you do not have to optimize the code. Later, however, you begin to develop polished, high-performance programs that may require wringing the last bit of performance from the machine, or stuffing the greatest possible amount of code into memory.

Finally, *C++ support* is rapidly becoming a hallmark of the acceptable compiler. C++ is for neither the beginner nor the faint-hearted. It can be an important tool in the future, however, as more and more software products take advantage of object-oriented features. Usually, the newest C packages feature both a C and a C++ compiler.

The Linkage Editor and Compatibility

Most compilers do not produce *load modules* (executable runtime files) directly. Rather, they produce *object modules* (machine code, not yet ready to run). A linkage editor then combines the object modules into load modules, performing such tasks as resolving references to data items and function names in separately compiled modules (it links object modules together). The linkage editor is therefore an important part of the compiler product. The catch is that linkage editors are not always interchangeable. The linkage editor is completely dependent on the specific format of the object file produced by the compiler, and some vendors' compilers produce object formats compatible only with their own linkage editors.

In the IBM-compatible and MS-DOS arena, Microsoft naturally sets the standard with object formats acceptable to MS LINK. All MS language products use this linker, and many other products more or less base their formats on this standard. Even if the level of conformity to the MS object format is less rather than more, however, selecting a compiler product with a companion linkage editor is still important, because Microsoft no longer provides MS LINK with the DOS system, but only with their own language products.

Borland supplies TLINK with the Borland C++ system. This linker is presented as a high-performance subset of MS LINK, with the caveat that code compiled with Microsoft C often cannot be handled because that code has undocumented (proprietary) format object records. The manual does not comment on whether MS LINK can be used with Borland C++ object modules.

No vendor's product is either superior or inferior to any other. You only have to understand the linkage editor you have and what its limitations are.

T I P Remember one caveat when choosing a linkage editor: the compiler package you choose must have a linkage editor and should at least allow the inclusion of Microsoft assembler modules (or modules produced by the vendor's own assembler). Any package that does not is not suitable for advanced work.

Project-Management Facilities

To continue with the idea that you need a compiler product that enables you to grow in sophistication without having to buy a new compiler, you can see that the package should have some facilities that support *complex projects*. These facilities can be more or less sophisticated, but you really need at least two utilities: MAKE and TOUCH. These utilities, which originated in UNIX systems, made the transition with C to the PC and are indispensable to serious programmers.

MAKE automates and controls the compilation and linkage editing of programs made up of several source files. A single *make file* (a text file describing the compile and link-edit steps) can control generation of one or several complex programs. MAKE differs from the integrated project-management facilities mentioned earlier, in that it is a separately run utility program. Living without such a utility is possible, but there are some important advantages to having MAKE:

- You don't have to remember which object modules go together to make up a load module. You record this information once in the make file, thus completely eliminating the risk of forgetting anything when regenerating the programs.

- You can record dependencies of one source file on another in the make file. MAKE notes when changes are made to a module (by comparing dates and times), and automatically recompiles or relinks any modules dependent on the first.

- MAKE saves a great deal of time, because it recompiles or relinks only modules that actually need it. A DOS batch (.BAT) file, by comparison, can only recompile and relink everything.

- Although you generally can handle much more complex projects with MAKE than you can with IDE facilities (as described earlier), this is not always true. MAKE can be used also in those rare cases when you must use the stand-alone compiler rather than the integrated environment.

TOUCH is a companion utility to MAKE. There are times when you have to force the recompilation or relinking of a module, although the date or time stamps on the files involved have not changed. TOUCH updates the date and time stamps of source or object files, making them more recent than dependent files. Then when MAKE runs again, it rebuilds from the TOUCHed files.

TOUCH can be either a separate utility, as in the Borland products, or it can be integrated into the MAKE utility, as in Microsoft's C/C++ 7.0 (called NMAKE). If you find that you are using a package that does not supply any form of TOUCH, you can supply one yourself! Listing 1.2 shows UCTOUCH.C, which is an example of how to write such a program in Borland C++ (plain C style).

Listing 1.2. UCTOUCH.C—A user-written *TOUCH* utility (for Borland C++).

```
1   #include <dos.h>
2   #include <io.h>
3   #include <string.h>
4   #include <stdio.h>
5   #include <stdlib.h>
6   void main( int argc, char *argv[] )
7   {
8     struct time t;
9     struct date d;
10    struct ftime f;
11    FILE *tfile;
12
13    if ( argc < 2 ) {
14      puts( "Specify a filename." );
15      abort();
16    }
17    if ( NULL == ( tfile = fopen( argv[1], "r" ) ) ) {
18      puts( "File open error." );
19      abort();
20    }
21    gettime( &t );
22    f.ft_tsec = t.ti_sec;
23    f.ft_min  = t.ti_min;
24    f.ft_hour = t.ti_hour;
25    getdate( &d );
26    f.ft_day   = d.da_day;
27    f.ft_month = d.da_mon;
28    f.ft_year  = d.da_year - 1980;
29
30    setftime( fileno( tfile ), &f );
31    fclose( tfile );
32  }
```

The program in Listing 1.2 uses library functions (`gettime()`, `getdate()`, and `setftime()`) that are unique to Borland C++. They are not part of the ANSI standard library, nor are they necessarily found in the same form in other vendor's compilers. You will have to convert those functions to the forms used by your own compiler.

Compatibility with Other Languages

Earlier in this chapter, you saw a brief comparison of C to other languages. Clearly, some languages are better suited than others for certain tasks. In some cases, building a single program from modules compiled in more than one language is desirable. When that is true, the compilers involved must be able to do several tasks in compatible ways. One of the most important of these tasks is using the system stack to pass parameters to subroutines.

Suppose, for example, that you have written a fancy new C program, the performance of which could be improved considerably by recoding one of its functions in assembly language. Suppose also that you know the stack is used to pass parameters to the function, and that the part of the stack used to do this is called a *stack frame*. Which parameters are placed at the top of the stack frame and which at the bottom? How do you code the assembler routine to access the individual parameters correctly?

Doing this requires a knowledge of how the C compiler generates code internally, as well as a knowledge of assembler. To make the problem worse, suppose that the other language is not assembler, but some other high-level language—FORTRAN, for instance. Now you have no control over handling the passing of parameters. Both compilers do it in a specific way. Do they match in their parameter-passing methods?

Matching dissimilar compilers for use is a matter of some research. You have to know, not guess, their characteristics before you start. The authors have never seen a C compiler (although there may be one somewhere) that could not somehow interface to an assembler routine. Beyond assembler interfacing, however, the rule is *do your homework*.

The search for compatible compilers can be a deceptive one. You might think, for example, that the Borland C++ and Turbo Pascal compilers can be used together, especially because Borland C++ enables you to declare functions that use a Pascal calling convention. Can you use them together? No! The Pascal calling convention is a Borland C++ feature used to enhance performance, but output from the two compilers is not everywhere compatible and you cannot mix object modules from them.

Command-Line and Integrated Environments

As important as an integrated development environment is to rapid construction of programs, it cannot be used at times. When the integrated development environment can't be used, you must resort to the command-line compiler.

What's the Difference?

The command-line environment is a manual environment. You must edit the program with a stand-alone editor (you can use an IDE editor, but only for editing), execute the compiler, then execute the linkage editor. Each command must be typed at the system prompt (the DOS c> prompt, for example), and each utility must be run to completion before the next can be run.

Obviously, you lose all the advantages of automation when you use a command-line environment. You also lose a corresponding increment of speed in the development process. Why would you ever want to work in the command-line environment? There are some good, but infrequent, reasons for having it available.

Why You Need Both

You should have a command-line version of your compiler because the compiler's full range of functions is usually available there. Most of the compiler's options are available in the integrated environment, but a few may not be. To use these extra options, you have to specify (in the command that invokes the compiler) the options you want. Suppose, for example, that you want to use Borland C++ to compile a C program, generating only assembly language output, not an object module. The command-line parameters would look like this:

```
bc -S first
```

This command compiles the FIRST.C program, with assembler output. You could then fine-tune the resulting assembler source for very high performance and assemble it separately, or simply study it to see how the compiler handles different C source statements.

Sometimes, the command-line compiler is the only way you can compile a sophisticated program. (Just what type of program this is depends on the compiler.) The Microsoft C/C++ and Borland C++ compilers can handle in-line assembly statements directly, whereas other compilers require you to compile from the command line and have a separate assembler available.

Do You Need a Visual Debugger?

You *do* need a visual debugger. Testing the program is an inescapable part of program development. Almost invariably, the result of testing is *debugging*—finding and fixing problems with the code. Fixing code without a debugger can be difficult, to say the least.

If the compiler you select does not have an integrated development environment with debugging built in, at least verify that a visual debugger is available as a separate package. If none is available, you are strongly suggested to stay away from that particular package.

> Make sure the compiler you buy either has a built-in debugger or that a visual debugger is available as a separate package.

CAUTION

What Is a Visual Debugger?

The great advantage of a visual debugger is its interactive nature. It shows you what is going on in the program and enables you to control execution of the program.

As the program is being executed (by you, as slowly as you like), a visual debugger displays the source code on-screen, indicating with a current-position pointer the next statement to be executed. At every step, you can see what is about to happen. Figure 1.6 shows the screen displayed by the Borland's Turbo Debugger as FIRST.C is being debugged.

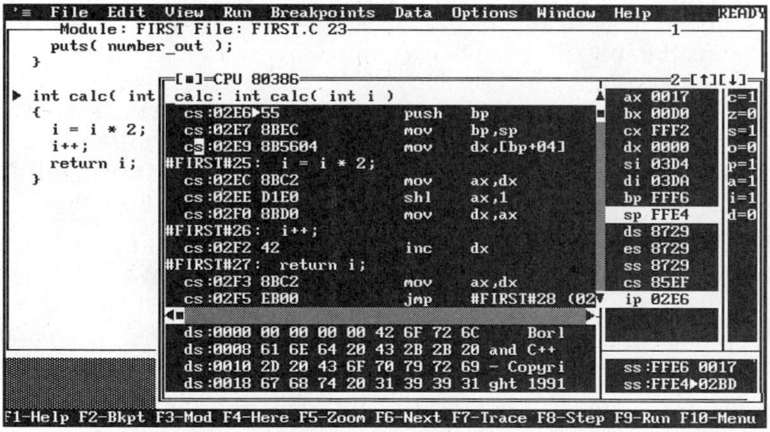

Figure 1.6.

Borland's stand-alone Turbo Debugger.

The solid triangular pointer to the left of the source code statements indicates the current position. As you can see, execution of the program has been traced to the calc() function.

Features of a Good Debugger

Figure 1.6 also shows several other items the debugger can track and display. This is just a sampling of the features a good debugger provides. Some of the features to look for in a debugger are described in this section.

■ *Integrated environment and stand-alone versions of the debugger.* Debugging in an IDE can be convenient for short programs, whereas a stand-alone debugger is essential for large or extremely complex programs. Although having both types of debugger is not absolutely essential, it certainly is helpful.

■ *Step-over and trace-into execution. Stepping over* enables you to execute a program one line at a time. If a line contains a function call, the call is treated like a *black box* (the function is executed, but the display continues to show the calling line of code). *Tracing into* also executes one line at a time, but when a function call is encountered, the visual display follows execution down into the called function. Both methods of debugging are appropriate at different times.

■ *Multiple display windows.* Being able to track several different types of program information on-screen and to switch easily and rapidly to another type of display is important to quick, efficient debugging.

■ *Breakpoint and variable watch support.* You can execute the program one line or statement at a time. Sometimes this is necessary, but it can be extremely time consuming. By setting breakpoints, you can speed debugging considerably. You can flag as a breakpoint the last statement or line you know to be working correctly, then let the program execute at full speed until the breakpoint is reached. Setting up a variable *watch window* by telling the debugger which variables to "watch" (continuously) is also very helpful. Again, you can allow the program to execute at full speed while you observe how the selected variables are being changed.

■ *System and environment displays.* To find errors in complex programs, debugging occasionally must get extremely detailed. When this need arises, you may want to look, for example, into the system hardware registers or the condition of the program stack. A good debugger enables you to do so.

■ *Interactive modification of the program. Interactive modification* does not mean rewriting the source code on the fly. However, you may want to observe the effects of changing the value of a variable that has been corrupted by some part of the program. If, by correcting such a value, you cause the program to run correctly, you have isolated the problem to a narrow range of possible causes.

■ *Support of multiple source files.* Many programs (of any complexity and consequent usefulness) are composed of several independent source files. A good visual debugger loads and displays the different source files at the correct times. Debugging large programs would be nearly impossible without this feature.

The features listed here, although by no means an exhaustive list, cover the more important features of a visual debugger.

Legitimate Uses of a Debugger

The purpose of a debugger is to locate the cause of problems in a program, or to verify that a *specific* section of code is working correctly. Surprisingly, debugging tools, especially the more sophisticated ones, are easy to abuse. That is, you can easily confuse *debugging* with *testing,* and use the debugger as a testing tool.

This type of mistake is subtle and can lead to problems. The temptation is to assume that because you have "gotten inside" the program while it executes, you have also verified every aspect of its execution. That is not automatically true.

Using a debugger does not guarantee that you have successfully predicted every situation that might arise while running the program. There is no substitute for adequately designing a program, nor for taking the time to thoroughly design the test cases for it. After you have done these two safeguards, you can use a debugger to verify correct operation of the program under all the circumstances it might encounter.

Summary

This chapter introduced you to the world of C programming, with only a broad overview of what goes into building a C program. The purpose of the chapter is to give you a sense of context, a foundation of the concepts that guide and control writing C programs. This chapter discussed the following:

■ Where C came from, and the context in which it was developed. You learned something about the flavor of the language.

■ A comparison of C to several other languages, painted in broad strokes. C compares well to other languages but does not replace all other languages. (They wouldn't exist if there were no need for them.)

■ An introductory to C form and punctuation. You must understand its form to read—and later write—C programs. They are also the concepts that initially confuse new students of C programming.

■ The basic parts of a C program: header-file inclusion directives, data definitions, the `main()` function, and user-defined functions. All but the most simple C programs contain all these parts.

■ The first steps in writing a C program. Here, you not only learned the basics of how to design a C program, but also how to make it readable for later correction or modification.

■ What tools a C programmer needs. The text editor is important, because you interface with it more often than with any other part of a C compiler package. The compiler, to be useful to you, must have the right features. You also saw the difference between integrated development environments and command-line environments—and why both must be available. Finally, you learned that a visual debugger is a crucial item in the C programmer's tool bag.

Now you have a platform from which to work. In the next chapter, "Basic I/O Programming," you launch into the nuts and bolts of C programming, examining the basics of C input and output functions.

Basic I/O Programming

Because a computer program that does no input or output probably is a program that doesn't do much of anything, this chapter is placed early in the book so that you can begin to write meaningful programs as soon as possible. The purpose of this chapter is twofold: to introduce you to the basics of I/O programming in C and to introduce you to the philosophy behind I/O programming in general. In this chapter, you do the following:

■ See some of the reasons why new programmers often have trouble with I/O programming. Understanding what you are trying to do is the best way to begin understanding how to do it.

■ Learn about the C I/O environment. This environment includes C data streams, the types of I/O devices, and file handling.

■ See how to deal with C's predefined, or standard, data streams.

■ Learn how to write programs using both the simple and the formatted I/O library functions, as well as how to convert data formats after inputting items.

■ See what it costs to do I/O programming without using the library functions. Doing this gives you the following: (1) an appreciation for the library I/O functions; (2) knowledge of how I/O is implemented on an IBM PC and compatibles; and (3) two useful utilities—a working communications program to build on later, and a high-performance version of the DOS MORE utility.

The Problem with Input and Output

I/O programming often presents the programmer-in-training with unexpected difficulties. The answers to the following three questions unravel much of the mystery of I/O operations and prepare the way for a discussion of C's stream I/O functions:

- What precisely is I/O?

- How far do the operating system and other components go in masking the complexity of I/O?

- What built-in facilities does your C compiler provide for interfacing with the I/O system?

I/O is nothing more than moving data from secondary storage into main storage (*input*, or *read* operations) and out of main storage into secondary storage (*output*, or *write* operations). In the process, one or more types of cache (high-speed buffer) memory may be used.

Each type of memory is characterized by its *speed* (how fast the CPU can access it) and *persistence* (how long it retains data). The block diagram in Figure 2.1 shows how the components of a digital computer system relate to one another.

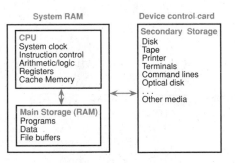

System RAM   Device control card

CPU
System clock
Instruction control
Arithmetic/logic
Registers
Cache Memory

Main Storage (RAM)
Programs
Data
File buffers

Secondary Storage
Disk
Tape
Printer
Terminals
Command lines
Optical disk
. . .
Other media

Figure 2.1.

Memory in relation to system components.

Main storage is the memory inside your PC's system unit. This is where your programs reside while they are run, and where they manipulate data. Main storage is often called RAM, or *random-access memory*. RAM has fast access time (typically around 100 nanoseconds, or billionths of a second) and short-term persistence (only as long as the computer is powered on).

Secondary storage is a collective term signifying a group of objects called simply *I/O devices*, or *peripheral devices* (meaning *outside the computer*). In this book, the term *I/O device* is used because it implies the read-write operations the devices perform.

I/O devices differ drastically from main memory in both speed and memory persistence. A fast hard disk drive may have an access time of 28 milliseconds (about 280,000 times slower than main memory). Comparisons to instruction execution speed are similarly disproportionate. The original IBM PC, running at 4.77 MHz, could execute its fastest instructions in 210 nanoseconds, or about 133,333 times faster than the previously mentioned hard disk can set up for an I/O operation (without actually performing it).

This is why I/O is the single greatest roadblock to high-performance programs. However, some I/O devices (like disks and tapes) have long-term persistence. They can retain recorded data for many years, even when the computer is switched off.

There are only two basic ways to perform an I/O operation (read or write): *memory-mapped I/O*, and channel or *port I/O*. Although the exact manner of implementation of these methods may vary from one computer to another, all I/O operations fall into one of these categories. Later in this chapter, you see examples of both methods of handling I/O on the IBM PC.

A program performs memory-mapped I/O by moving data bytes into and out of an area of RAM designated for a particular device. The area of RAM is the same as, and is part of, the system's normal RAM used by programs and data. The instructions used are those for moving data bytes around elsewhere in RAM. Figure 2.2 shows how memory-mapped I/O is used for controlling a PC display terminal.

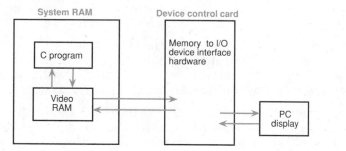

Figure 2.2.

Memory-mapped I/O implemented for a PC display.

High-performance disk drives (both floppy and fixed disks) use an even more sophisticated method of memory-mapped I/O called *direct memory access* (DMA) in which a peripheral device can read and write directly to RAM. DMA involves complicated programming as well as special support circuitry.

Port I/O is more complex for several reasons. A program maintains data in RAM, but only for its own use. The data must be fetched from the RAM areas (buffers) and sent to the I/O device through a special machine instruction that writes to the port. Similarly, input operations read data from the port, leaving it to the program to dispose of the data in some way. When doing direct port I/O, the software must be concerned with the input and output of control information as well as data. Figure 2.3 illustrates these operations.

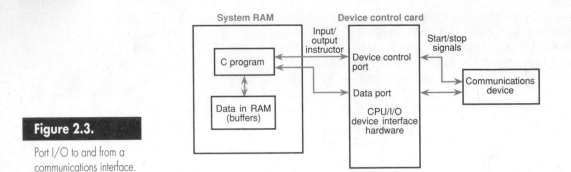

Figure 2.3.

Port I/O to and from a
communications interface.

The complexity of port I/O doesn't stop with data transfer. As you can see from Figure 2.3, there is a *device control port* as well as a data I/O port. Control ports are used to inform the device whether the next operation is input or output, how to set up for it, whether to clear and reset, and so on. Disks also use control ports as well as DMA—an extremely complicated but necessary arrangement.

Fortunately for programmers, this kind of overhead programming does not have to be written directly into every program. Responsibility for such control functions is divided among several pieces of code:

■ The device controller circuitry handles the most time-sensitive and delicate activities, such as timing disk rotation and stepping the read/write head into position. These functions are built into the controller card at the factory; you do not have to worry about them.

■ The system BIOS (an acronym for Basic I/O System) sends requests to and receives status information from the device controller circuitry by reading and writing the control ports assigned to a particular device. The BIOS also reads and writes data through the assigned data ports.

■ The operating system (such as DOS, OS/2, or UNIX) converts your program's logical I/O requests into physical I/O requests and passes them to the BIOS. A logical request might involve requesting a particular record number from a file. Converting it to a physical request would involve calculating the sector number on disk where the data resides. The operating system also receives status information about the operation from the BIOS and passes the information back to your program.

■ The compiler's built-in I/O functions do a variety of tasks covered in this discussion of I/O. Typical functions do such tasks as keeping track of the next available record number, noting whether I/O operations are successful, and converting I/O requests into the operating system's format. Standard C I/O functions make all I/O appear to the program as if the data flows in and out of the program as a continuous stream of characters (bytes).

■ It remains for your code to use the built-in I/O functions. You request that the next character or block of characters be read or written. You will begin to see how to do that in the following sections of this chapter.

A lot goes on behind the scenes. From the programmer's point of view, most of the complexity is hidden behind the services provided by the compiler's built-in functions and the operating system services. Figure 2.4 summarizes the division of responsibility for I/O among the different components.

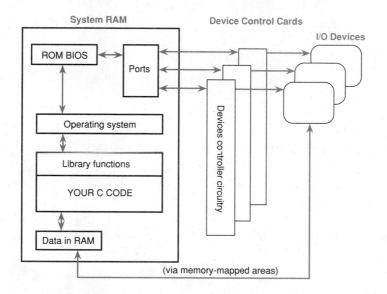

Figure 2.4.

Division of I/O responsibilities.

Understanding Stream I/O

In ANSI standard C, all I/O appears to the program as a continuous stream of characters or perhaps groups of characters. Stream I/O was adopted as the standard method for several reasons, of which the following are prominent:

■ Stream I/O provides device independence; the C programmer does not have to write I/O functions for each specific type of device. With stream I/O, a C program sees a file as a continuous stream of text characters, even if they are stored in widely separated chunks (blocks) scattered over a disk.

■ Stream I/O permits a C program to access files in a standard way, independent of its physical format on an external storage medium. An important side effect of device independence is that file access is the same from one compiler to another.

■ Stream I/O not only provides for buffering of input and output data, whenever the devices used permit that, in a uniform way, but also enables the programmer to tune I/O performance by controlling buffer size.

Comparing Streams, Files, and Devices

Streams, files, and devices are all related; they make up a hierarchy of concepts. This simple hierarchy can be explained briefly by the next two statements.

■ Streams are always associated with an external file.

■ A file may be a collection of related data that resides on a storage device, or a file may be an interactive device.

Although you, the programmer, may not be directly aware of it, the way files are buffered differs from one device type to another. The specific differences are described in the upcoming discussions of device types.

Buffering is an important part of I/O, and streams are buffered whenever possible (depending on the I/O device being used). What is a buffer, and why is it important?

A *buffer* is a block of RAM into or from which the I/O functions read or write a large chunk of data. This activity may be going on behind the scenes even if your program is requesting only one character at a time.

Standard C provides three types of buffering for streams:

■ *Unbuffered I/O* starts a new I/O operation for every character of data transferred.

■ *Line-buffered I/O* collects characters into lines of text, with a newline character at the end of each line, before making them available to the program.

■ *Fully buffered I/O* reads or writes an arbitrary but usually fairly large number of characters at a time.

Controlling buffers may seem like a lot of trouble. You are probably wondering, Why do it?

Buffers perform a *speed-matching function*. If your program read or wrote only one character, there would be no problem; but a typical program reads and writes many thousands of bytes. Without a speed-matching mechanism, the program would spend most of its time waiting for I/O and would take an intolerable amount of time to run.

Remember that I/O devices are several orders of magnitude slower than the computer itself, largely due to *setup overhead time*. This is particularly true for devices like disks, which maintain relatively large amounts of data. Several factors contribute to overhead time for disk I/O operations:

■ The library functions must translate your request into a form acceptable to the operating system. They must also update control information about the stream kept within the C program.

■ The operating system must translate the request into a form acceptable to the BIOS. Control information kept in the operating system is updated also.

■ The BIOS then outputs the request to the disk controller. Provisions must be made for handling the physical transfer of data to or from RAM and for recognizing when I/O activity is complete.

■ The disk controller activates the particular drive, steps the read/write head to the correct track (seek time), notes the head's position on the track, and waits for the correct sector to rotate under the head (rotational delay, or latency).

Whenever this overhead can be avoided (or at least worked around), program performance increases. On single-user systems, such as PCs running DOS, your program must come to a complete halt while it waits for I/O. The only way to reduce that overhead is to reduce the number of I/O "starts" by providing efficient buffering of data.

To illustrate this point, we set up a test file and program. The program read the file (18,738 bytes of text) repetitively, significantly increasing the buffer size on each pass. The unrealistically small initial buffer size of 16 bytes was multiplied by eight for each repetition, resulting in a final buffer size of 8K bytes (not nearly as large as it might be). Read time for the file decreases rapidly as buffer size increases. The point of diminishing returns will be reached eventually, however, when no increase helps. Figure 2.5 graphically shows the results of this test.

Read time

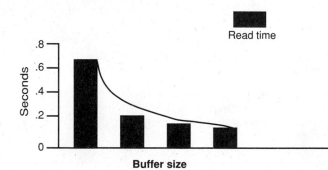

Buffer size

Figure 2.5.

The effects of buffer size on read time.

Even though the test system was already running an intelligent disk-buffering package, read time dropped from 0.6913 to 0.1479 seconds, nearly a fivefold improvement. (See Appendix G for a description of the timing software used.)

Interactive Devices

Interactive devices differ from other I/O devices in that they don't provide long-term storage of data and are designed to interact directly with a user of the system. Common examples of interactive devices are video displays, keyboards, and communications ports. Figure 2.6 shows how interactive devices relate to the computer system.

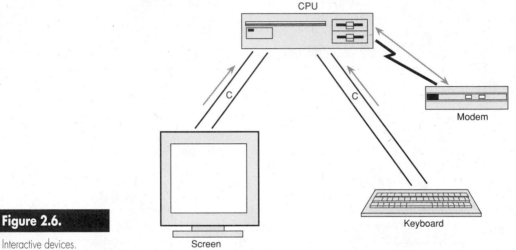

Figure 2.6.

Interactive devices.

Interactive devices may be either completely unbuffered or only line buffered. In *unbuffered files,* as the term implies, each byte or character is read or written immediately. The library functions do not place the byte in an intermediate RAM area. Some of the simple keyboard input library functions, for example, use unbuffered I/O.

The keyboard may also be *line buffered.* Characters are received and stored in RAM until you press the Enter (Return) key. Then the newline character is added to the buffer, and the whole line of text is sent to your program.

Data Files

Data files are not themselves devices, as are interactive "files." Instead, data files are collections of data that reside on storage devices. Files on a storage device share the space available. The most common storage devices are diskettes and hard disk drives. A volume directory keeps track of where everything is. Tracks on disk are closer together than the eye can see. Each track is divided into sectors, each of which contains a fixed amount of data (see Figure 2.7).

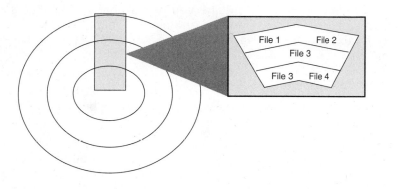

Figure 2.7.

Files on storage devices.

Data files are, in the nature of the case, fully buffered. This means that the buffer is made large enough to be efficient but that it does not necessarily correspond to logical lines of text. You can still read lines of text from data files, but doing so involves having the library routines retrieve data from the buffers and building the line of text.

Even when you seem to be reading a fully buffered file, one character at a time, the buffers are in action behind the scenes. This was the case, for example, in the test run illustrated in Figure 2.5.

Introducing C Streams

Is it buffered? Is it not buffered? If it is buffered, how large is the buffer? Is that efficient? With C streams as implemented by the standard C library functions, you can write reasonably efficient file-handling programs and never worry about the details of buffering. In Chapter 10, "File I/O Programming," you learn how to plan for and implement procedures for high-performance I/O code—but you don't have to do that for many of the tasks for which you write C programs.

Streams may be classified as *text* or *binary*. Although the file associated with the stream is the same in either case, there is an important distinction in the way the library functions handle I/O for text and binary streams.

Text streams (files) can be understood in an intuitive way—they are files that contain text data which people can read immediately. The stream of characters in text files is organized into lines, which also are understood in the ordinary way. Each line is terminated by an end-of-line character (or characters). According to the standard, the lines in a text file must be capable of containing at least 254 characters. A text file can be read and written also as a binary file.

The library functions perform some translation of some special characters when reading or writing text files. The characters that physically indicate end-of-line (usually a carriage return and line-feed pair of characters) are transformed into a single newline character. Certain other characters also are recognized. A tab character, for instance, causes the display position on-screen to be changed when it is written to the video display.

Binary streams (files) are so named because they are read and written bit for bit exactly as found in the physical file, with no translation of characters. Characters (unsigned characters) are still being handled, but now the program must determine what to do with special characters.

Facilities for handling binary files are provided so that you can work with any data that does not fall into the category of text. There are quite a few of these files—the .EXE and .COM files that compilers and linkers must produce, data files that contain numeric information in internal formats (to save disk space, for example), and many others.

The Standard Streams

Standard C provides three streams that always are associated with input or output files. These are the *standard input* (stdin), *standard output* (stdout), and *standard error* (stderr) streams.

The standard streams are text streams; you normally do not have the option of treating them as binary files. The standard streams always are available for immediate use and require no preparatory action on your part. In fact, some of the library functions assume the presence of standard streams, so that you do not have to name them explicitly.

stdin, stdout, and *stderr*

The standard I/O files are prepared for use by the C initialization code in a process normally hidden from the programmer. The associated files are *opened* at program start-up and *closed* at program termination (unless the program is aborted). Shortly, you will learn how to open and close files to associate them with streams.

One feature of standard I/O is that *I/O redirection* can be used to vary the actual places the input and output go. stdin usually gets its input from the system console, and stdout usually sends output to the system console. This can be changed with redirection. Incidentally, I/O redirection is supported almost identically in DOS, UNIX, and OS/2. The manuals for these systems document how to use redirection at the command-line level. All you have to do in your program is use the standard streams.

In standard C, the list of library functions for I/O is reasonably rich. Any of the stream functions can refer to the standard streams (except purely control functions), and eight functions assume that a standard stream is meant so that you do not have to specify a stream name in the function call. Table 2.1 summarizes these eight functions and shows their more general counterparts, which can refer to any stream.

Table 2.1. I/O functions that assume standard I/O.

Implies stdxxx	Requires Stream Name	Action of Function
printf()	fprintf()	Formatted output
scanf()	fscanf()	Formatted input
vprintf()	vfprintf()	Formatted output, variable argument list
getchar()	getc(), fgetc()	Character input
gets()	fgets()	String input
putchar()	putc(), fputc()	Character output
puts()	fputs()	String output
perror()	None	Send error message to stderr only

With these eight I/O functions, you can do just about any file I/O you want without having to name a stream explicitly. With I/O redirection available, it can also be disk file text I/O.

Listing 2.1 is a short program named STREAM.C. It illustrates the equivalence of getc() and getchar(), and of putc() and putchar(). STREAM.C also shows a couple of interesting points about standard stream I/O that you need to see in action before they are explained. Take the time now to type Listing 2.1 into your C editor and then compile and run it. After that, read the discussion that follows the listing.

Listing 2.1. STREAM.C shows character I/O (for Borland C++).

```
1   /*+------------------------------------------------------------
2    +                        STREAM.C
3    + This short demo shows how getchar() and putchar()
4    + relate to getc() and putc().
5    +------------------------------------------------------------
6   */
7
8   #include <stdlib.h>
9   #include <stdio.h>
10
11  main()
12  {
13    char char_buffer;
14
15    /* do it the easy way first */
16
17    printf( "\nType in a line, up to 80 characters, and " );
18    printf( "the computer will repeat\n" );
19    printf( "it using getchar() and putchar().\n" );
20    while ( ( char_buffer = getchar() ) != '\n' )
21      putchar( char_buffer );
22
23    /* now do it the hard way */
24
25    printf( "\n\nPlease type another line. This time the " );
26    printf( "computer will use the\n" );
27    printf( "functions getc() and putc().\n" );
28    while ( ( char_buffer = getc( stdin ) ) != '\n' )
29      putc( char_buffer, stdout );
30  }
```

Even though the listing header indicates that this is a Borland C++ program, it contains only code that conforms to standard C. Because this program contains only standard C code, it runs equally well using the Microsoft compiler.

The presence of the printf() function calls is only incidental to the program. (That function is covered a little later in this chapter.) Right now, the calls to getchar() and putchar() in lines 20 and 21 and the calls to getc() and putc() in lines 28 and 29 are of interest.

Did you notice that they are used without preamble of any kind? These function calls either imply or explicitly name only stdin and stdout streams. No preparation is needed—they were already open (see the section "Connecting Files to Streams: fopen()" a little later in this chapter) and ready when the main() function began to execute.

Now reflect on how the program behaved when run, compared to the function calls in the while loops. Think about those loops for just a moment. The way the program is written, a character is read, and the same character is immediately written to stdout.

That is not the way the screen looked, however, when the program was run. You were able to type the entire string and press Enter before the string as a whole was echoed on the screen. For example, suppose that you typed the letters *abc*. They would have appeared on the screen like this:

```
abc
abc
```

But if each character is output immediately after it is read, why did it not appear like this instead?

```
aabbcc
```

The reason is *line buffering*. The ANSI C standard requires only that the stderr not be fully buffered, and that the stdin and stdout streams be fully buffered but not if they are associated with interactive devices.

On an IBM PC or compatible, the system console is actually two interactive devices: the keyboard and the video display. Therefore, the stdin and stdout streams are not fully buffered—they are *line buffered* in most C compilers (this is not a guarantee, by the way).

This explains the program's behavior. Characters are read and immediately output—to the stdout *buffer*. They are not sent physically to the display until the whole line has arrived, signaled by the end-of-line character (the Enter keystroke). Hence, the input and output characters remain unmingled.

Relating Streams to DOS Handles

DOS relates files (either interactive or data files) with integer numbers called *file handles*. DOS also has standard input and output handles (as well as error, auxiliary, and print handles) to which C relates its standard streams. Table 2.2 relates the standard C streams to the DOS handles for standard I/O.

Table 2.2.   C streams and DOS handles.

C Stream	DOS Handle	I/O Type
stdin	0	Standard input
stdout	1	Standard output
stderr	2	Standard error message
stdaux	3	Standard asynchronous communications
stdprn	4	Standard printer output

There are five standard streams in DOS, and most C compilers for this environment extend the support for standard streams to support them all. The last two streams shown in Table 2.2 are not part of ANSI standard C, however.

The Simple I/O Functions

In the following sections, you learn the specific I/O functions and ways to implement I/O in your programs. The simple I/O functions are presented first because, being relatively uncluttered in both syntax and operation, they are easiest to learn.

The simple stream I/O functions are those that do not separate and interpret data content, except to supply newline characters at the ends of strings in text mode I/O. A character is just a character, and a string is just a string to the simple I/O functions. They are not concerned with which character or with what is in the string. One important exception to this rule is the class of characters called *control characters*, which make the I/O behave in certain ways. They are pointed out in this chapter and are discussed in detail in Chapter 4, "A Closer Look at C Programs."

A small, easy-to-remember group of four simple I/O functions—getchar(), putchar(), gets(), and puts()—helps you remember their more explicit counterparts listed in Table 2.1. The remaining simple I/O functions are getc(), fgetc(), putc(), fputc(), fgets(), and fputs().

Connecting Files to Streams: *fopen()*

The names you assign to streams in your program are different from the filenames stored on disk. *Stream names* are C identifiers, whereas *filenames* are string data values. Thus, in normal I/O function calls, you can use a short but meaningful name that does not have to be a long, quoted string.

The `fopen()` function brings the stream name and filename together. It associates the string value (the filename on disk) with the stream name you choose. It asks DOS (or another operating system) to open the file identified by the string value and to return the numeric file handle.

When the file handle is successfully received, it is stored (with other information about the state of the stream, such as where in the file the next I/O takes place, buffer location, error and end-of-file conditions, and so on) in a control block, usually called the `_iob`. Figure 2.8 illustrates the relations of your program, the operating system, and the `_iob`.

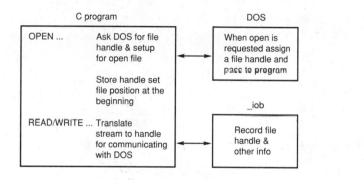

Figure 2.8.

The relation of streams to handles.

Declaring the Stream Data Object

Before opening the stream, you must declare it to be a data object. It is not a simple data object, such as `int`, but its complexity is hidden in the `#include` file. You declare the stream like this:

```
#include <stdio.h>

...


main()
{
  FILE *input_file;

  ... open and use input_file,
  ... then close it when done.


}
```

Here the stream `input_file` is declared to be a *pointer*—a variable that contains the address of another variable—to a data object of type `FILE`. (See the next C-Note for a quick introduction to pointers.) The definition of the `FILE` is in the STDIO.H header file; don't forget to include it. You must type the word `FILE` in *uppercase letters*.

Sneak Preview: C Pointers

A *pointer* is a variable whose contents are the *memory address of another variable* rather than a data value directly. Use an asterisk (*, the *indirection operator*) to define a pointer:

```
int a;   /* a plain integer */
int *b;  /* a pointer to int */
```

To get an address value into the pointer, use an ampersand (&, the *address-of operator*) to extract the address of another variable:

```
b = &a; /* address of a placed in pointer b */
```

To get to the data in a variable being pointed to, use the indirection operator in an expression or statement (as opposed to the original pointer definition):

```
int c;
c = a;   /* assign a data value to c */
c = *b;  /* assign the same data value to c */
```

Using the indirection operator to extract a data value being pointed to is called *dereferencing the pointer*. If you refer to a pointer *without* the asterisk, you are dealing with an address value:

```
int a;   /* an integer */
int *b;  /* a pointer to an int */
int *c;  /* another pointer to int */
...
b = &a;  /* get an address into the first pointer */
c = b;   /* the value of b is an address ! */
```

A pointer has an *indeterminate* value before it is initialized: it cannot yet be used. A pointer may also have a *zero value* even when initialized, in which case it should be understood to point to nothing at all. Such a pointer is called a *null pointer*. Most compilers supply a predefined macro name—NULL—that defines a zero pointer value. The main idea, however, is that *the value of a pointer is the address of another variable* or another area of memory.

This stream object is declared inside the main() function, which means that the stream can be used directly only with this function. In order for another function to use it to do I/O, a pointer to the stream object would have to be passed to that other function as a parameter. You will do that anyway, when you call the open function.

Opening the File

Once you have defined a stream object—which is also called a stream variable or file variable, but is always a pointer type variable—you must open the stream (file) before you can use it for reading and writing data. The STDIO.H header file declares the `fopen()` function like this:

```
FILE *fopen( const char *filename, const char *mode );
```

It is more instructive, though, to illustrate how you use `fopen()` in this way:

```
FILE *input_file;
...
char filename[40]; /* 40-byte string holds name */
...
input_file = fopen( filename, "r" );
```

This means, first, that the function returns a pointer to an object of type FILE. You assign that pointer to the stream variable name. The value of this pointer is also the means of determining whether the open function was successful. If it was not successful, `fopen()` returns a null (empty) pointer. Most C compilers have already defined a macro with the name NULL (in uppercase letters) that you can use to check this result.

The first parameter inside the parentheses of a call to `fopen()` is a pointer to a string containing the name of the file (as it exists on the disk) that you want opened. The const type modifier means that the `fopen()` function does not intend to change this name string. The filename can be either a string variable or a string constant, as in the following example:

```
fname[40] = "c:\usr\check.dat";
/* define 40-byte string */
...
input_file = fopen( fname, "r" );
```

This is equivalent to

```
input_file = fopen( "c:\usr\check.dat", "r" );
```

because either method opens the file in exactly the same way. Now the general procedure to open a file looks like this, including error checking to see whether the `fopen()` call worked:

```
#include <stdio.h>
...

main()
{
  FILE *input_file;
```

```
input_file = fopen( "c:\usr\check.dat", "r" );
if ( NULL == input_file ) abort();
... use input_file,
... then close it when done.
}
```

Now the stream has been opened, and the result of the operation verified. If the pointer returned to the program was NULL, an error occurred, and the program was *aborted* (abnormally terminated using the standard library function abort()).

The second parameter inside the parentheses of the function call is the *file mode parameter*. The mode determines exactly how reads and writes to the file take place. The file mode in the preceding code fragment is "r", or *read* mode. There are three basic modes:

- ■ "r" indicates that the stream is to be opened in *read-only mode*. You cannot write to a read-mode file. If the file does not exist, or if any other problem occurs, the open fails and returns a null pointer.

- ■ "w" indicates that the file is to be opened in *write-only mode*. You cannot read from a write-mode file. If the file does not exist, an attempt is made to create it; if the file does exist, its length is truncated to zero, and it is written over (old contents are destroyed) from the beginning. If either action cannot be carried out, the open fails, and a null pointer is returned.

- ■ "a" indicates that the file is to be opened in *append mode*. Append mode means that you can only write in the file—and only at the end of the data already present. New information is appended at the end, even if you use the fseek() function to reset the current position elsewhere, such as at the beginning of the file. If the file does not exist, it is created. If the file cannot be created or otherwise accessed, the open fails, and a null pointer is returned.

Using any one of these modes opens a file as a *text file*. You can add a b to the end of the mode strings to open a file in binary mode: "rb", "wb", and "ab" are all valid modes. These and other advanced file modes are covered in detail in Chapter 10, "File I/O Programming."

The ANSI standard for C has one loophole that can affect append processing in binary mode. When a binary file is created, the standard allows an implementation of C to append any number of null characters to the end of that file (to fill out a sector or block). If the binary file is then opened for append-mode processing, the current position may be *beyond* the actual end-of-file because of the padding characters. Because DOS takes care of such padding, this normally is not a problem for DOS-based compilers. You should, however, know whether your particular compiler can be so affected.

The preceding file-open facilities are all you need in order to read, write, and append data to files. Figure 2.9 summarizes the effects of the modes of opening files, including the direction of data flow and positioning within the file.

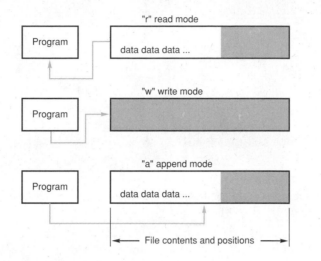

Figure 2.9.

fopen() access-mode actions.

Closing the File: *fclose()*

After you have opened and used the file, you should close it. Closing the file performs two important tasks. First, it releases the stream from the file so that the stream can be reused. Second, and even more important, it ensures the accuracy of write-mode files. It does this by physically writing to the storage device any tag-end data in output buffers.

The ANSI standard for C specifies that you can count on having the buffers *flushed* (cleared with a write, if needed) like this only if you actually perform the close. Many compilers have a feature that closes all open files properly when a program terminates *normally*. If, however, you forgot to close a file and your program crashes, you lose the data.

The function prototype for `fclose()` is also in STDIO.H and has the following syntax:

```
int fclose(FILE *stream);
```

The `fclose()` function returns an integer to the program, indicating the outcome of the operation. This integer is zero if the close was successful; a negative integer (usually –1) is returned if the close was not successful. This negative integer is represented by an ANSI-required macro name, EOF (for "End Of File").

The entire sequence of events, as developed so far, results in a program that looks like this:

```
#include <stdio.h>
...

main()
{
  FILE *input_file;

  input_file = fopen( "c:\usr\check.dat", "r" );
  if ( NULL == input_file ) abort();
  ... use input_file,
  fclose( input_file );
}
```

Even though `fclose()` returns an integer result, it was not checked in this code fragment—it was simply thrown away.

For an output (write-mode) file, ignoring the results of `fclose()` would not be a good idea. Instead, you should take some action, such as that shown in the following example:

```
if ( fclose( output_file ) == EOF ) {
  printf( "Error closing %s.\n", filename );
  abort();
}
```

This would at least give the person running the program a chance to know there was a problem and to do something about it.

Character I/O Functions

In C, characters frequently are handled as if they were integers. This is especially true when characters are passed to functions as parameters. As you can see from the Quick Reference C-Note "Character I/O Function Prototypes," they are passed as integers.

Quick Reference: Character I/O Function Prototypes

```
#include <stdio.h>

...
```

```
int getchar(void);
int getc(FILE *stream);
int fgetc(FILE *stream);
int putchar(int c);
int putc(int c, FILE *stream);
int fputc(int c, FILE *stream);
```

You can pass an unsigned character (one byte) to the library functions. It is converted (*cast*) to an integer before use by the function. (C has the capability to change the data type of a variable under certain circumstances. This capability to change data types is called *typecasting* and is covered in more detail in Chapter 5.)

Now it's time to put all this knowledge to work. You can begin by using the simple character I/O functions to write a program you can use—one that protects the data in your private files. The program, called CIPHER.C, encrypts your text files according to a key that only you know.

Because this program is significantly longer (131 lines) than any of those earlier in this book, consider for a moment what you want the program to do and how it will work.

CIPHER.C should be able both to encrypt a file for security and to decrypt it again so that you can use it. Therefore, it needs to accept a command-line parameter that indicates which action is to be taken. If you use the lowercase letter *n* to mean "encrypt the file" and use the lowercase letter *d* to mean "decrypt the file," the command to execute the program (so far) looks like one of the following:

```
cipher n ...
```

```
cipher d ...
```

Next, you should be able to tell the program which file to use. Because you don't want to use redirection or piping in this case, another command-line parameter is in order.

For simplicity's sake, so that the user of the program does not have to type a file extension when running the program, assume that the extension of the *plaintext file* (the unencoded file) is always .TXT, and that the extension of the encrypted file is always .ENC. Now the command-line information looks like one of the following:

```
cipher n filename ...
```

```
cipher d filename ...
```

An encryption key, definable by the user, also must be available. This key is the third and last command-line parameter. The complete command looks like one of these:

```
cipher n filename string

cipher d filename string
```

This string is used internally to generate an unsigned character (byte field) which, in turn, is used to encrypt (or decrypt) every character in the text file. If this string contains no blanks, it can appear without punctuation. However, because this is C, the string can also be quoted if you want to use something difficult to guess. For example, you could encrypt a file named ACCTDATA.TXT with this command:

```
cipher n acctdata "phone plug 123"
```

Note that the *exact* same key string must be used to decrypt the file; otherwise, the result will be garbage.

If the user types the command cipher, without using any command-line arguments, the program should respond by displaying basic instructions for use and then terminate normally.

Now that you know the requirements for the program, take a few minutes to examine its structure, as shown in Listing 2.2.

Listing 2.2. CIPHER.C supports data encryption (for Borland C++).

```
 1   /*+---------------------------------------------------------
 2    +                      CIPHER.C
 3    + This program uses basic character I/O to support a
 4    + binary transformation data encryption scheme.
 5    +---------------------------------------------------------
 6   */
 7
 8   #include <stdlib.h>
 9   #include <stdio.h>
10   #include <string.h>
11   #include <conio.h>
12
13   FILE *normal_file, *cipher_file;
14
15   static char *help[] =
16     {
17       "- - - - - CIPHER.C - - - - -",
```

```
18          " ",
19          "CIPHER.C requires that you enter"
20          "three arguments on the",
21          "command line when you start the program:",
22          " ",
23          "        encrypt:        cipher n name string",
24          "        decrypt:        cipher d name string",
25          " ",
26          "You enter the file name without an extension. CIPHER",
27          "appends an extension of \".txt\" to the normal text",
28          "file and \".enc\" to the encrypted file.",
29          " ",
30          "The third argument generates an encryption key. This",
31          "argument can be any string. If it contains blanks,",
32          "enclose it in double quotes.",
33          ""
34        };
35
36   int open_file( char *process_type, char *file_name );
37   unsigned char generate_key( char *key_string );
38   void encode_file( unsigned char key_value );
39   void decode_file( unsigned char key_value );
40
41   main( int argc, char *argv[] )
42   {
43
44     int hold_char;
45     int i;
46     unsigned char key_value;
47
48     if ( argc < 4 )
49     {
50       clrscr();
51       for ( i=0; *help[i]; i++ ) puts( help[i] );
52     }
53     else
54       switch ( *argv[1] ) {
55         case 'n':
56                   printf( "File encoding started\n" );
57                   if ( ! open_file( argv[1],argv[2] ) ) {
58                     printf( "\n\nCan't open file.\n" );
```

continues

Listing 2.2. Continued

```
59                        exit( 8 );
60                    }
61                    key_value = generate_key( argv[3] );
62                    encode_file( key_value );
63                    fcloseall();
64                    break;
65          case 'd':
66                    printf( "File decoding started\n" );
67                    if ( ! open_file( argv[1], argv[2] ) ) {
68                       printf( "\n\nCan't open file.\n" );
69                       exit( 8 );
70                    }
71                    key_value = generate_key( argv[3] );
72                    decode_file( key_value );
73                    fcloseall();
74                    break;
75          default:
76                    printf( "Invalid option, try again.\n" );
77      }
78    return( 0 );
79 }
80
81 int open_file( char *process_type, char *file_name )
82 {
83    char name1[25], name2[25];
84
85    printf("Opening files.\n");
86    strcpy( name1, file_name );
87    strcpy( name2, file_name );
88    strcat( name1, ".txt" );
89    strcat( name2, ".enc" );
90
91    if ( process_type[0] == 'n' ) {
92      normal_file = fopen( name1, "rb" );
93      cipher_file = fopen( name2, "wb" );
94    }
95    else {
96      cipher_file = fopen(name2, "rb" );
97      normal_file = fopen(name1, "wb" );
98    }
99
```

```
100    if ( ( normal_file == NULL ) || ( cipher_file == NULL ) )
101      return 0;
102    else
103      return 1;
104  }
105
106  unsigned char generate_key( char *key_string )
107  {
108    int i = 0, j = 0;
109    unsigned char key_value = 0;
110
111    while ( ( j = key_string[i++] ) != '\0' ) key_value += j;
112    return key_value;
113  }
114
115  void encode_file( unsigned char key_value )
116  {
117    int temp_char;
118
119    while ( ( temp_char = fgetc( normal_file ) ) != EOF ) {
120        fputc( temp_char ^ key_value, cipher_file );
121    }
122  }
123
124  void decode_file( unsigned char key_value )
125  {
126    int temp_char;
127
128    while ( ( temp_char = fgetc( cipher_file ) ) != EOF ) {
129        fputc( temp_char ^ key_value, normal_file );
130    }
131  }
```

The first item of interest in Listing 2.2 is line 13. Two streams (normal_file and cipher_file) are declared. Notice again that they are actually declared as pointers to objects of type FILE.

Lines 15 through 34 contain the definitions of the help text. The declaration

```
static char *help[] = { ... };
```

indicates that help is an *array of pointers* to strings. From the overview in Chapter 1, you already know that a string is an array of characters. The square brackets [] indicate an array of some kind. In this case, it is an array of char *, or pointer to character, which is how you point to (not define) a string. Finally, the token static is a storage class modifier. (Chapter 5, "Objects, Expressions, Operators, and Conversions," has details on storage class.) Its purpose here is to supply a syntax that allows the array of pointers to strings to be initialized directly in the declaration. This is done by the series of string literals inside the {} braces. Notice that the strings in the list are separated by commas.

Because this is an *initializer list,* not a block statement of the kind described in Chapter 1, the whole thing is followed by a semicolon, even though curly braces ({}) are used. The very last string in the help text is a *null string* (one with nothing in it). This string acts as a "fence," so that the program can detect the end of the array of strings (see line 31).

Lines 36–39 contain function prototypes for the user-defined functions defined later in the program. You could define the user functions before main(), and before they were referenced anywhere, but the method used here is preferred. If nothing else, it prevents inadvertently calling a function that has not been defined.

The main() function is contained in lines 41–79. This time—instead of just empty parentheses—some parameters are declared for main():

```
main( int argc, char *argv[] ) ...
```

This method of declaring main() is how C programs can access the command-line parameters typed by the user to execute the program. The first, argc, is an integer that has the count of parameters present in the command line. This count includes the program name. For instance, because cipher requires the program name plus three parameters in order to run correctly, argc has a value of four.

char *argv[] is another array of pointers to string (as was help). Because arrays are indexed from zero, the program name from the command line is pointed to by argv[0], the action parameter (n or d) is pointed to by argv[1], and so on.

On entry to main(), the number of command-line arguments is checked in line 48. If it is less than 4, something was left out, and the help text must be displayed. This is one of those places where the marvelous compactness of C code can be seen. The entire logic for doing this is found in one line (51), in the following single for loop:

```
for ( i=0; *help[i]; i++ ) puts( help[i] );
```

The integer i is used to step through the array of pointers. Look at the parts of the for loop control structure in the following three paragraphs.

i=0 sets the index variable to its initial value.

The cryptic *help[i] notation checks to see whether the end of the array has been reached. *help[i] refers to the *value* of the first character in the ith string in the list. Because the last string is null, this expression evaluates to zero (false), ending the loop.

The i++ expression uses the *postfix* increment operator (named for obvious reasons) to update the value of the index variable. This is done *after* the logic for each pass of the loop is performed.

The main part of the work is done in the switch statement (lines 54–77). This is just a fancy if-then-else arrangement. Look at the switch statement—you can see its intent. If the value of *argv[1] is an n, encoding is requested; if a d, decoding is requested. The default keyword is a special case that indicates what to do if none of the indicated values were matched in one of the case statements.

In both case statements, there is a function call to fcloseall(). This is not an ANSI standard function. It is an extension that the compiler (in this instance, Borland C++) provides for convenience.

The user-defined function open_file() is found in lines 81–104. It returns an integer, as does the fopen() function it calls. The purpose of this function is to associate the file with the .TXT extension with the stream named normal_file, and to associate the file with the extension .ENC with the stream named cipher_file. (The arrangement of if statements does this.)

A word also should be said about the generate_key() function. It converts the cipher key *string* into the cipher *key,* a single unsigned character—one byte. The method, known as a *checksum,* is simply to step down the string, adding the value of each character to the cipher key. When you develop a checksum, any carries or overflows from the addition are thrown away. The one-byte checksum is used to encode the plain text file by exclusive-ORing its value with each character of the input file. This is why you need to use exactly the same key string for encryption and decryption.

The meat of the program is in the two simple functions encode_file() and decode_file(), found in lines 115–131 of Listing 2.2. The process is the same in both cases. Only the direction of translation differs.

The fgetc() library function is used for inputting characters, and fputc() is used for outputting characters. The entire encryption/decryption process can be accomplished in a single short while loop, as in the following example:

```
while ( ( temp_char = fgetc( normal_file ) ) != EOF ) {
    fputc( temp_char ^ key_value, cipher_file );
}
```

The while statement contains a conditional expression within the parentheses—positioned almost like parameters in a function call—that determines when the loop is finished. Here, the conditional expression is being used not only to read characters, but also to check for the end-of-file condition. First, the character is read, using fgetc(), and placed in the variable temp_char. The next level of parentheses means that the result of that read is to be compared to EOF. If EOF is not true (! *>>=), the while continues.

In a manner similar to the open and close functions, `fgetc()` returns an integer/character, while the character is passed to `fputc()` as a parameter. The character actually passed is the exclusive-OR of the input character and the cipher key.

Suppose that the bit pattern of the input byte is 11001010 and that of the cipher key is 01110111. Encoding the input byte yields the following:

```
    11001010
XOR 01110111
    ════════
    10111101
```

To decode, just take the ciphertext (encoded) character and XOR it again, with exactly the same key:

```
    10111101
XOR 01110111
    ════════
    11001010
```

String I/O Functions

Frequently, dealing with text files as collections of lines of text (as opposed to collections of simple characters) is convenient or necessary. The string I/O functions provide for this need. Strictly speaking, the ANSI standard classifies the string I/O functions as character functions, because they also do no particular data formatting. The string I/O functions are summarized in the Quick Reference C-Note "String I/O Function Prototypes."

Quick Reference: String I/O Function Prototypes

```
#include <stdio.h>

...

char *gets(char *s);

char *fgets(char *s, int n, FILE *stream);
int puts(char *s);
int fputs(const char *s, FILE *stream);
```

`gets()` and `puts()`, of course, assume that a standard stream is being used. `fgets()` and `fputs()` streams must be opened and associated with a file before use. All four of the functions require a pointer to a string as a parameter, to or from which the I/O takes place.

In contrast to what you have seen so far, both string input functions return a pointer to a string. If the input function was successful, this will be a pointer to the same string that was passed as a parameter. If the function was not successful, it will be a null pointer. You can test for this condition with a statement like the following:

```
char line_in[81];
...
if ( NULL == gets( line_in ) ... /* do something */
```

The puts() and fputs() functions return integers to the caller. These integers have the same meaning as before—zero means successful I/O, and EOF means either that the end-of-file was reached or that there was an error.

fgets() introduces something new. Its second parameter is an integer that specifies the maximum number of characters which can be input so that the I/O operation does not overrun the area allotted for it. In the example

```
char in_stuff[80];
...
fgets( in_stuff, 80, in_file );
```

the integer is 80. Actually, this integer is one more than the number of allowed characters, because C strings are terminated by a null (binary zero) character, which takes up one of the array positions. In this fragment, then, only 79 characters could be input. If the end of the text line has not been reached by that time, the library function clips the string short, reserving the rest of the line for the next input request.

If the end of the line is reached, the physical end-of-line indicator(s) is converted to a newline character, and this character is placed in the receiving string. In most cases, this is what you want. If it is not, you have to write the code to remove the newline character from the string (see FMORE.C in Listing 2.9 later in this chapter).

Listing 2.3 puts this new knowledge to work. The purpose of program NUMBER.C is to read a text file; prefix each line with its corresponding line number; and write a new, numbered, text file.

Listing 2.3. NUMBER.C shows number text files (for Microsoft C/C++ 7).

```
1   #include <stdlib.h>
2   #include <stdio.h>
3
4   main( int argc, char *argv[] )
5   {
6     FILE *source_in;
```

continues

Listing 2.3. Continued

```
7    FILE *source_out;
8    char name_in[41] = "";
9    char name_out[41] = "";
10   int line_num = 0;
11   char line_buf[255];
12
13   /* ----- Check command-line parameters ----- */
14
15   if ( argc < 2 ) {
16     printf( "\nSupply a program name to number.\n" );
17     exit( 8 );
18   }
19
20   /* ----- Set up filenames ----- */
21
22   strcpy( name_in, argv[1] );
23   strcpy( name_out, name_in );
24   if ( !strchr( name_in, '.' ) ) {
25     strcat( name_in, ".C" );
26     strcat( name_out, ".NUM" );
27   }
28   else {
29     char *p = name_out;
30     while( *p != '.' ) p++;
31     *p = '\0';
32     strcat( name_out, ".NUM" );
33   }
34
35   /* ----- Open input and output files ----- */
36
37   if ( NULL == ( source_in = fopen( name_in, "r" ) ) ) {
38     printf( "\nCan't locate %s, exiting.\n", name_in );
39     exit( 8 );
40   }
41   if ( NULL == ( source_out = fopen( name_out, "w" ) ) ) {
42     printf( "\nCan't locate %s, exiting.\n", name_out );
43     exit( 8 );
44   }
45
46   /* ----- NUMBER THE FILE ----- */
```

```
47
48    while ( fgets( line_buf, 255, source_in ) )
49      fprintf( source_out, "%3d  %s", ++line_num, line_buf );
50
51    /* ----- Close input and output file ----- */
52
53    fclose( source_in );
54    fclose( source_out );
55  }
```

Like CIPHER.C in Listing 2.2, NUMBER.C expects a command-line parameter—
the name of the file to be numbered. The code is designed to accept a
filename, with or without an extension. If you supply the file extension, it can
be anything you want it to be. If you do not supply one, it is assumed to be .C.
(There is a good reason for this—this is the program we used to number the
sample programs for this book.) In either case, the output file is forced to have
the extension .NUM.

The logic to handle the file extensions is in lines 22–33. The code uses the
strcpy() (string copy) function to move the strings around, the strcat()
(string concatenate) function to splice the pieces together, and the strchr()
(string character search) function to look for a period and thus determine
whether the name has an extension.

If there is an extension and the output filename must be forced to .NUM, lines
29–32 handle the situation. The code uses a temporary pointer variable p to
step through the string to the period and then overlay it with a null character,
effectively truncating the string there. Then the proper extension can be
concatenated to it. You might want to adapt this logic for CIPHER.C in Listing 2.2 to generalize its filename-handling logic.

The while loop in lines 48 and 49 is the workhorse of the program. This loop
provides another example of the compactness possible with C syntax. The
conditional expression for the while is nothing more than the call to fgets().
Because a nonnull pointer is returned for each successful read, the loop
continues (nonzero = true). When end-of-file is reached, fgets() returns a null
pointer, and the loop ends (null = 0 = false).

Handling I/O Errors and End-of-File Conditions

Clearly, some means is needed to separate end-of-file conditions from error
conditions. These conditions are not at all the same, and you frequently must
know which is which (instead of just assuming something). There are four
standard functions for handling these conditions:

- `void clearerr(FILE *stream);`

  `clearerr()` clears the end-of-file condition, an error condition, or both for the named stream. It returns nothing.

- `int feof(FILE *stream);`

  `feof()` tests the named stream for the end-of-file condition. If end-of-file has been reached, the function returns 1, or true. If not, it returns 0, or false.

- `int ferror(FILE *stream);`

  `ferror()` tests for an error indicator for the named stream. If an error has occurred, the function returns 1, or true. If not, it returns 0, or false.

- `void perror(const char *s);`

  `perror()` prints a text error message. If an error has occurred, the library function detecting it will have set an internal variable `errno`. `perror()` uses `errno` to index into an array of strings (like the `help` text array in Listing 2.2) to locate a message describing the problem. `perror()` first prints the string `s` (which was passed to it as a parameter), followed by a colon and a blank, and then followed by the system error text. You provide the string `s`, which can be anything informative you want to use.

Here is an example of the use of `ferror()` and `perror()`:

```
if ( ferror( some_stream ) )
  perror( "C detected file error" );
```

Converting Data Formats

Later in this chapter, you will learn how to use formatted I/O functions to extract specific fields from input text. Later in the book you will learn how to use library functions to break a string into tokens, and even how to construct your own text-scanning and parsing routines. Sometimes, even then, simply converting a string to a numeric internal format is useful. The six standard functions converting data formats are these:

`atof()`	`atoi()`
`atol()`	`strtod()`
`strol()`	`stroul()`

The header file to include for these functions is STDLIB.H. The following paragraphs, with examples, summarize how these data format conversion functions are used.

```
double atof(const char *nptr);
int atoi(const char *nptr);
long int atol(const char *nptr);
```

The ato...() functions convert ASCII text strings, pointed to by nptr, to double-float, integer, and long-integer numbers, respectively. These functions, which have been around since K&R introduced C, are still so useful that they have been incorporated into the ANSI standard. These three functions do not have any error-recognition mechanism; what happens if an error occurs is strictly up to the specific implementation.

```
double strtod(const char *nptr, char **endptr);
```

strtod() converts a string pointed to by nptr to a double-precision float. White space in front of the number is skipped, the number is converted, and conversion is stopped at the first character that cannot be converted. endptr points to the first character that was not converted. Calling this function is a little different. Here is how it works:

```
char *where;
char numstring[20] = "   3.1415926*";
double numval;
...
numval = strtod( numstring, &where );
```

When this statement is executed, the value of pi is converted from the string and placed in numval. Because the asterisk cannot be converted to a number, conversion stops, and where is made to point to the asterisk. Notice especially that the parameter endptr is a pointer to a pointer, and the address-of operator (&) is used in the function call to make sure that the argument passed to the function matches the formal parameter requirement (pointer to pointer). Don't forget this little point when you use the strto...() functions.

The strto...() group of functions does detect and report errors. If no conversion can be performed, 0 is returned. If successful conversion would cause overflow, either the plus or minus HUGE_VAL macro value is returned, and the system variable errno is set to the predefined value ERANGE.

```
long int strol(const char *nptr, char **endptr,
    int base);
unsigned long int stroul(const char *nptr,
    char **endptr, int base);
```

These two functions perform the conversion for long and unsigned long integers, respectively. Error detection works the same way. Overflow in strol() returns LONG_MAX or LONG_MIN; overflow in stroul() returns ULONG_MAX. In both cases, errno is set to ERANGE.

These functions have the added option of providing a way to specify the base number system in which the input string number is written. If the base is given as 0, an ordinary decimal constant for these data types is expected. Otherwise, the base can be from 2 to 36.

The program STRTOX.C in Listing 2.4 illustrates the use of these functions. Look at the code, and then get right to the subject of formatted I/O.

Listing 2.4. STRTOX.C (for Borland C++).

```
1   #include <stdlib.h>
2   #include <stdio.h>
3   #include <ctype.h>
4   #include <limits.h>
5   #include <conio.h>
6   #define long_const(x) #x " is an unsigned long integer."
7
8   main()
9   {
10    char double_string[] =
11      "+2.9979250e8 is the speed of light.";
12    char long_string[] =
13      "2341, 2347, 2351, and 2357"
14      " are consecutive prime numbers.";
15    char ulong_string[] = long_const( ULONG_MAX );
16    char *pointer;
17    long i = 0;
18    int count;
19
20    clrscr();
21    printf( "%s\n", double_string );
22    pointer = double_string;
23    printf( "Half the speed of light is: %f\n\n",
24        strtod( pointer, &pointer ) / 2 );
25
26    printf( "%s\n", long_string );
27    pointer = long_string;
28    for ( count = 1; count <=4; count ++ ) {
29      i += strtol( pointer, &pointer, 0 );
30      while ( !isdigit( *pointer ) ) pointer++;
31    }
```

```
32    printf( "The sum of the prime numbers is: %ld\n\n", i );
33
34    printf( "%s\n", ulong_string );
35    pointer = ulong_string;
36    printf( "%lu is the decimal value"
37            " of this unsigned long int.\n",
38            strtoul( pointer, &pointer, 0 ) );
39  }
```

The Formatted I/O Functions

The formatted I/O library functions are perhaps the most commonly used functions in ordinary C programming. They are without a doubt handy routines to have around.

The purpose of the formatted I/O routines is to format text data found in continuous strings into discrete data objects (fields), and vice versa. Each formatted I/O function accepts as one of its parameters a *format string* that controls the conversion process. The format string can contain both text and *conversion specifiers,* which state the precise manner of conversion of one of the data parameters being processed. The format string and conversion specifiers differ slightly for input and output function types. Refer to the next C-Note for examples of the formatted I/O function prototypes.

Quick Reference: Formatted I/O Function Prototypes

```
int printf(const char *format, arg1, ..., argn);
int fprintf(FILE *stream, const char *format, arg1, ...,
        argn);
int sprintf(const char *s, const char *format, arg1, ...,
        argn);
int scanf(const char *format, arg1, ..., argn);
int fscanf(FILE *stream, const char *format, arg1, ...,
        argn);
int sscanf(const char *s, const char *format, arg1, ...,
        argn);
```

Displaying Data with *printf()*

The formatted I/O functions for output, called the `printf()` family, create a continuous output string from a collection of *arguments* (variables, expressions, and constants) under the control of a *format string,* and send it to the `stdout` stream, to the named stream, or to another string. To explain the process, we use `printf()`, which sends output to `stdout`, and then mention the variations on that theme. (Any data types that have not yet been discussed are covered in Chapter 3, "Building C Programs.")

Compare the following use of `printf()` to the function prototype shown in the C-Note "Formatted I/O Function Prototypes":

```
printf( "The value of PI is %6.4f\n", 3.1415926 );
```

The output from this function call appears on `stdout` as

```
The value of PI is 3.1416
```

The first parameter passed to `printf()` is the format string, which controls the entire operation. `printf()` immediately sends normal text in the format string to `stdout` immediately, until it encounters a *conversion specification,* which gives instructions on how to convert and format one of the subsequent arguments. In the sample `printf()` line, `%6.4f` is the conversion specifier; the constant `3.1415926` is its corresponding argument.

Because `printf()` processes the conversion specifiers in the format string from left to right as it encounters them, the arguments that match each specifier must also be in the correct order from left to right. The ANSI standard says that if the number of conversion specifiers and actual arguments doesn't match, the "behavior is undefined." This means that you had better check the manual to see what it will do in your case.

In the format string, normal text and conversion specifiers can be mixed freely, if the specifiers are recognizable and coded correctly. Note the following example:

```
char c1[10] = "dog";
char c2[10] = "cat";
...
printf( "The first critter is a %s and the second is a %s",
        c1, c2 );
```

This gives the following output:

```
The first critter is a dog and the second is a cat
```

The principle is pretty simple. All you need to know now is how to form the conversion specifiers. Figure 2.10 summarizes the structure of conversion specifiers. (For complete details of the specifier parts and their meanings, see Part II.)

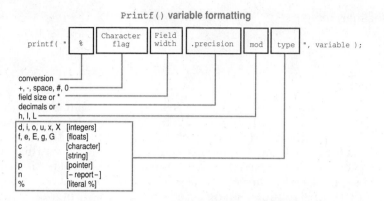

Figure 2.10.

Using *printf()* conversion specifiers.

Note the following descriptions of the conversion specifiers:

- The conversion character % begins the conversion of the next argument, moving from left to right.

- The optional flag character can control field justification, the addition of numeric signs, use of an alternative form, or whether to use leading zeros.

- The optional field width states the minimum number of characters the field contains. It is a minimum because this specifier never causes truncation; if the output requires more room than stated here, more room is used. If field width is not specified, as many characters as needed are used.

- The optional precision specifier, if present, means different things for different argument types. For strings, it is the maximum number of character positions to be used (truncation will occur). For floating point and double floating point, it is the number of decimal digits to format to the right of the decimal place. For integer types, it is the minimum number of positions to use—the technique used in NUMBER.C in Listing 2.3 to achieve a uniform field width for the line numbers. In all cases, a period must be written before the precision specifier.

- An optional modifier character can cause the conversion of appropriate types to short integer (h), to long integer (l, an "ell"), or to long double (L) format.

- The required type character states the type of argument and what basic conversion is to take place. All the basic types can be converted, as can strings and pointers. The most common types are these:

d (decimal) integers

f (double) floating point

s string

c character

The width and precision fields have an interesting feature that allows for very flexible output formats. Instead of specifying a number, you can specify an asterisk in either or both parts (`%*.*x`). Each asterisk instructs the formatting routines to look for an argument in the list and to use its value for this specifier. Scanning is, as always, from left to right—just place these special-use arguments in sequence with the others. The program PRINTIT.C in Listing 2.5 uses this handy feature to create an on-screen "printer plot" of a sine wave.

Listing 2.5. PRINTIT.C (for Microsoft C/C++).

```
1   #include <stdlib.h>
2   #include <stdio.h>
3   #include <math.h>
4
5   main()
6   {
7     char ch;
8     double x;
9     int i;
10
11    printf( "A sine wave, from 0 to 2 PI radians:\n" );
12    x = 0;
13    for ( i=0; i<21; i++ ) {
14      printf( "%*c\n", 30 + (int)( 30.0 * sin( x ) ), '*' );
15      x += 0.314;
16    }
17  }
```

The construction `int` in line 14 is called a *type cast*. Its purpose is to force the floating-point value of the subsequent expression to an integer value that the `%c` conversion can handle.

The two other forms of the `printf()` function—`sprintf()` and `fprintf()`—behave like `printf()` except that the destination of the output differs.

If you refer to the earlier C-Note that shows the formatted I/O function prototypes, you can see that `sprintf()` has an extra parameter, a string pointer (`*s`). The string pointed to is the destination for the formatted output rather than a stream.

You can use the combination of capabilities to format flexibly and to output the results into a string to do certain chores. In Listing 2.6, for example, the function center_text() centers a title within a given line width.

Listing 2.6. CENTER.C (for all compilers).

```
1   #include <stdlib.h>
2   #include <stdio.h>
3   #include <string.h>
4
5   int center_text( char *s, char *t, int width );
6
7   main()
8   {
9     char lineout[81];
10
11    if ( center_text( "A centered title!", lineout, 80 ) )
12      printf( "%s\n", lineout );
13  }
14
15  int center_text( char *s, char *t, int width )
16  {
17    int l;
18
19    l = strlen( s );
20    if ( l > width ) return 0;
21    sprintf( t, "%*s", ( ( width-l ) / 2 ) + l, s );
22    return 1;
23  }
```

Don't forget to use #include <string.h> in programs that will use center_text. The strlen() function is declared in STRING.H.

The effect of the center_text() function is to supply enough blanks on the left end of the output string t to center the input string s in a field that is width characters wide. If the string fits in the output field, the operation is performed, and a nonzero value is returned; if not, a zero is returned.

fprintf() also has an extra first parameter. This parameter is the name of a stream (which you should have opened). The behavior is once more the same as printf(), but the destination for the output string is now the file associated with the named stream. There are advantages and disadvantages with specifying a destination stream. Although fprintf() certainly allows you to write formatted text to a disk file, you cannot redirect output to any other stream.

Here is a short example using `printf()`:

```
FILE *hfile;
if ( NULL == ( hfile = fopen( "c:history.txt", "w" ) ) )
  exit( 8 );
fprintf( hfile, "%s\n", "Dear diary ... " );
```

Getting Input with *scanf()*

Input can be formatted with the `scanf()` family of functions that, like the `printf()` family, has three forms: `scanf()` receives and formats input from stdin; `fscanf()`, from a user-defined stream; and `sscanf()`, from a string in RAM.

As you can see from Figure 2.11, the two families are similar in several ways. Both use conversion specifiers, many of the conversion types and all the type modifiers are the same, and conversion specifiers are processed from left to right with their corresponding arguments.

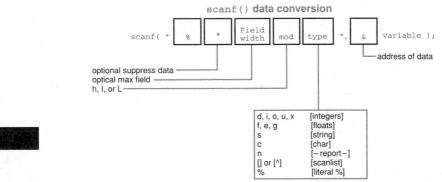

Figure 2.11.

scanf() input data conversion.

There are also some important *differences* between the two families, as summarized here:

■ The arguments are all pointers. The `printf()` functions accept *values* as parameters (except for arrays, which are always passed as pointers), because the conversion routines do not alter the variables (when variables are used). But `scanf()` does alter the parameter variables—that is the whole point of scanning out an input string. To specify an argument that is a pointer to a variable, you do nothing extra for strings and arrays because their names alone constitute a pointer name. For other data objects, however, you must precede the variable name with an ampersand address-of operator, as in

```
address_of_item  = &item;
```

■ scanf() expects any text in the format string that is not part of a conversion specifier to be matched, character for character, in the string being scanned (except spaces, which are skipped). This feature allows scanf() to skip any input text that should not be part of a converted input field.

■ Double floating-point data types are not supported by scanf(). When you use the %f, %e, or %g conversion specifier, its corresponding argument variable (it had better be a variable) must be a type float.

■ The field width part of a conversion specifier is used a little differently. scanf() uses width to split out similar fields that are run together in the input string. For example, the scanf() call

```
scanf( "%2d%3d", &num1, &num2 );
```

can be used to split out two numbers from the following input string:

```
12345
```

The value of num1 is 12, and the value of num2 is 345.

Traditionally, scanf() has not been widely used for extensive input operations because, in spite of its complexity, it is stiff-necked and unforgiving. When used correctly, however, scanf() can do some pretty amazing things. (It probably is not as widely appreciated as it should be.) The program READIT.C in Listing 2.7 uses scanf() to gather information on the way to some interesting conclusions.

Listing 2.7. READIT.C (for all compilers).

```
1   #include <stdlib.h>
2   #include <stdio.h>
3   #include <math.h>
4
5   double SPFV( double apr, double freq, double periods );
6   double USFV( double apr, double freq, double periods );
7
8   main()
9   {
10    char firstname[20];
11    char lastname[20];
12    int age;
13    float salary;
14
15    printf( "Enter your first and last names, your age, "
16        "and your annual salary:\n" );
```

continues

Listing 2.7. Continued

```
17
18    scanf( "%s%s%d%f", firstname, lastname, &age, &salary );
19
20    printf( "\nIf %s %s, who is %d years old and "
21          "earns %10.2f,\n"
22          "were to save only 10%% of every monthly\n"
23          "paycheck, drawing only 6%% interest, after a 30\n"
24          "year career, you would have %10.2f dollars!\n",
25          firstname, lastname, age, salary,
26          ( salary / 120.0 ) * USFV( 6.0, 12.0, 360 )
27        );
28  }
29
30  double SPFV( double apr, double freq, double periods )
31  {
32    return( pow(1.0+(apr/freq)/100.0,periods) );
33  }
34
35  double USFV( double apr, double freq, double periods )
36  {
37    return( ( SPFV(apr,freq,periods) - 1.0)
38            / (apr/freq/100.0) );
39  }
```

The scanf() function call is in line 18. Notice that because the string arguments imply a pointer, they are not prefixed with &. The integer and float variables are prefixed with the address-of operator.

The scanf() call in line 18 prompts you for four pieces of information. Just type them in the order requested, with as many blanks as you want between the items. (You can also press Enter after typing each item, but you cannot use commas between them, unless you code them directly in the format string as explained previously.) You may be surprised to learn what regularly saving a little money can buy you later. And if you want to learn how to use those time-value-of-money routines in lines 30–39, just hang on one minute.

Putting It All Together

Everyone likes money—no doubt about it. How would you like a program (one that uses both the simple and the formatted I/O functions) that can calculate the payout on your home mortgage, analyze and convert interest rates, display or print a mortgage amortization table, and do a few other interesting things?

Did you say that you don't know enough C yet? Yes, you do. You just may not have seen a longer program put together. The program FINANCE.C (Listing D.1 in Appendix D) does all these things, with very few features that you either have not yet seen or cannot understand intuitively.

In fact, the only reason that FINANCE.C appears in Appendix D instead of in this chapter is that the program is long and its use requires explanation. This is a good time for you to turn to Appendix D and study the code and usage instructions.

Coping with Hardware and System Dependencies

The ANSI standard for C states that the purpose of codifying the language is not to stifle its utility but to enhance portability across compilers and systems. There is therefore no reason that a compiler manufacturer should not provide extensions to the ANSI standard features—and many reasons that they should. All the reasons have to do with the fact that a compiler lacking them is unusable in a real environment.

There is just no getting around the fact that to do something useful with a program, to do it fast and with a certain flair and style, you must at least get a little close to the machine and operating system. This situation pops up most often in *I/O programming*.

Disk I/O programming can mostly be done with standard C library functions. The C library functions for files and streams do the job well, especially when some of the more advanced features are used. But standard C doesn't even pretend to do the job for such situations as printer support (except by I/O redirection), video display I/O that is fast enough not to bore the user to death, and communications I/O programming.

Using Extensions to Standard C

Printers, video displays, and communications lines require programming support that can be found only in extensions to the standard C language. This presents you, the programmer, with a dilemma. Do you use these extensions? If you do, the programs you write will not always be portable; the specific machines and systems on which the program runs are by definition a limited group. To move the source code over, you will need to recompile it and to rewrite parts of it.

To answer the question directly, yes, you do use the extensions. You will find it impossible not to in the long run. If you don't, your programs will lack critical capabilities and performance. Simply stated, users will not stand for it—they won't use the programs. The trick is to isolate that part of the code which has to be rewritten in order to port it to another environment. You can do this mainly by hiding dependent code in separate (and thus isolated) source files and functions.

With that question answered, now take a look at the cost of using some of those extended features.

Supporting Extended DOS Streams

Readers of this book are most likely to encounter the MS-DOS environment. This environment provides a good example of the operating system services, as well as access to them through C extensions, that you need in order to construct full-featured programs.

You already have seen that DOS has more standard streams than standard C allows for. The program CPRINT.C in Listing 2.8 shows how to send a text file to a printer by using a predefined stream (in this compiler) named stdprn. CPRINT.C counts lines, ejects pages to avoid overprinting the perforations, and places a header line on each page.

Listing 2.8.   CPRINT.C to print text files (for Microsoft C/C++).

```
1   #include <stdlib.h>
2   #include <stdio.h>
3
4   struct rep_type {
5     int lines_page;
6     int line_count;
7     int page_count;
8   } report;
9   char file_name[41] = "";
10
11  void print_file( char *fname, struct rep_type *rep );
12
13  main( int argc, char *argv[] )
14  {
15    if ( argc < 2 ) {
16      puts( "Command format: "
17            "cprint [d:][\path\]file[.ext]\n" );
```

```
18      exit( 0 );
19      }
20      strcpy( file_name, argv[1] );
21      report.lines_page = 57;
22      report.line_count = 0;
23      report.page_count = 0;
24      print_file( file_name, &report );
25      printf( "Printed %d lines on %d pages from %s\n",
26              report.line_count, report.page_count, file_name );
27  }
28
29  void print_file( char *fname, struct rep_type *rep )
30  {
31      char *print_line;
32      FILE *filein;
33      int cur_line = 1;
34
35      if ( NULL == ( filein = fopen( fname, "r" ) ) ) {
36          printf( "Could not open %s\n", fname );
37          exit( 0 );
38      }
39      print_line = malloc( 255 );
40      while ( NULL != fgets( print_line, 255, filein ) ) {
41          if ( cur_line == 1 ) {
42              fprintf( stdprn, "Listing of: %s\n\n", file_name );
43              cur_line = 3;
44              rep->page_count++;
45          }
46          fputs( print_line, stdprn );
47          cur_line++;
48          rep->line_count++;
49          if ( cur_line > rep->lines_page ) {
50              cur_line = 1;
51              fputc( '\f', stdprn );
52          }
53      }
54      free( print_line );
55  }
```

Notice that stdprn is handled like one of the true standard streams. You don't have to open or close the stream, although you do have to name the stream in the fprintf() and fputs() function calls.

You may want to try modifying this program to supply page numbers in the header line, to supply line numbers at the left, to handle margin and line count control—or just about any other customizing feature you want. Don't be bashful about remolding it to suit your purposes. And don't delay practicing what you are learning about C. Everyone who learns C occasionally gets into deep water and has to start over.

Programming IBM PC I/O Ports

When neither DOS nor the system BIOS provides adequate services for a task, you have to get down to cases and do it yourself. This is the case with I/O support for communications programs on the PC and compatibles. This section introduces a program that gives you a close look at what is involved in doing I/O directly, through the system I/O ports. This was the method used— along with many other techniques—to write CCOM.C (Listing E.1 in Appendix E).

Briefly, CCOM.C is an interrupt-driven, port I/O-oriented C communications program. Its purpose is not only to illustrate what you are getting into when you descend to the hardware level in controlling your machine, but also to give you a working program you can use if you want to dial CompuServe. Before you attempt to modify CCOM.C, you need to learn a good deal more about C, and particularly about communications.

T I P   Because CCOM.C is rather long, its source code listing appears in Appendix E, along with instructions for use. By all means, type it and compile it. Have your Borland C++ manual handy when you do, however, and be careful to type it exactly as you see it. Then spend some time reflecting on portability issues. We think you will find that you appreciate all those lovely built-in library functions.

The IBM PC Video-Display Controversy

There has been a great deal of discussion, in print and otherwise, about whether to write portable (and truly blasé) or nonportable (and really peppy and attractive) video-display support routines for the PC. In the main, commercial packages and good homegrown programs tend to opt for the nonportable but really useful methods.

"Glass Teletype" I/O and Standard Streams

The problem with video I/O can be summed up in one word—*slow!* Most computer users do not appreciate programs that force them to watch text crawl sluggishly across and down the screen.

Even worse, screen output generally looks like a glass Teletype. Lines of text scroll up from the bottom of the screen—exactly as they do on a real Teletype machine. There is little or no color support, no full-screen formatting of displays, and no *speed*. This tends to be true even when BIOS services are used. They, in fact, are the reason that DOS services are so slow: BIOS calls are how DOS gets to the screen too. Because of this, C's standard streams for the video display (stdout) are relatively slow also.

Getting Around the Problem

Most users of IBM PCs and compatibles are aware that the video display is a memory-mapped I/O device (even if they don't know the term). They are aware that the screen can be programmed by using screen RAM.

Whether or not to use screen RAM is the focus of the glass Teletype controversy. It is said that if the screen RAM address changes, all those programs that poke characters directly into screen RAM will no longer run. But in all these years, the original addresses haven't changed, even though newer devices sometimes require additional screen RAM. Direct screen RAM access is the only method that has acceptable speed for displaying large amounts of text quickly.

Slow display speed and the methods used to get around it are so common that it is worth presenting an example of it. The program FMORE.C is faster than the DOS-supplied MORE program. FMORE.C displays a text file, one screen at a time, and waits for you to press a key for the next screen. Listing 2.9 contains the source for FMORE.C. To compile this program correctly, you need to create a project file and include the GRAPHICS.LIB file. If GRAPHICS.LIB is not included, you will get unresolved external reference errors.

Listing 2.9.   FMORE.C—a faster MORE display (for Microsoft C/C++ 7.0).

```
1   #include <stdio.h>
2   #include <conio.h>
3   #include <dos.h>
4   #include <string.h>
5   #include <graph.h>
6
```

continues

Listing 2.9. Continued

```
7   int x, y;
8   char far *scrseg;
9   struct videoconfig screen_state;
10
11  void find_screen(void)
12  {
13    _getvideoconfig( &screen_state );
14    switch( screen_state.mode ) {
15      case 0:
16      case 1:
17      case 2:
18      case 3:
19      case 4:
20      case 5:
21      case 6:   scrseg = (char far *)0xB8000000L; break;
22      case 7:   scrseg = (char far *)0xb0000000L; break;
23      case 13:
24      case 14:
25      case 15:
26      case 16:
27      case 17:
28      case 18:
29      case 19:  scrseg = (char far *)0xA0000000L; break;
30      default:  printf( "\nCan't locate screen RAM.\n" );
31              exit(0);
32    }
33  }
34
35  void show_line( char *ostring )
36  {
37    char far *screen;
38    int hold = y - 1;
39
40    x = 1;
41    screen = (char far *)( scrseg +
42            ( hold << 7 ) + ( hold << 5 ) );
43    while ( *ostring && *ostring != '\n') {
44      if ( *ostring == '\t' ) {
45        do {
46        x++;
47        screen += 2;
```

```
48        } while ( x % 8 != 1 );
49        ostring++;
50        continue;
51      }
52      *screen = *ostring++;
53      x++;
54      screen += 2;
55      if ( x > 79 ) break;
56    }
57  }
58
59  main(argc,argv)
60    int argc;
61    char *argv[];
62  {
63    FILE *pix;
64    char pline[83];
65    char ch;
66
67    if ( argc < 2 ) exit(0);
68    if ( NULL == (pix = fopen(argv[1],"rt")) ) exit(0);
69    find_screen();
70    y = 1;
71    for ( ;; ) {
72      _clearscreen( _GCLEARSCREEN ); _settextposition(1,1);
73      while ( y <= screen_state.numtextrows - 1 ) {
74        if ( NULL == (fgets( pline,83,pix ) ) ) {
75        fclose(pix);
76        show_line( "... Press Any Key To End ..." );
77        ch = getch(); if ( ch == 0 ) getch();
78        _clearscreen( _GCLEARSCREEN );
79        exit( 0 );
80        }
81        show_line( pline );
82        y++;
83      }
84      show_line( "... Press Any Key For More ..." );
85      ch = getch(); if ( ch == 0 ) getch();
86      y = 1;
87    }
88  }
```

To get started, this program uses extensions to standard C that are peculiar to the Microsoft C/C++ compiler. (Other compilers have similar but slightly different features.) The _getvideoconfig() function, declared in GRAPH.H, detects the video mode. Although this can be done with direct calls to BIOS functions, why not use the *easier* nonportable method?

Then the video mode is used in a switch statement, to determine the screen RAM address, and a pointer is formed. This type of pointer is not standard C but is required by the PC's hardware characteristics.

The main() function handles the gross logic of reading input text lines, detecting when to pause and wait for a keystroke, when to close the file, and when to get out. It also has a nonstandard technique that waits for the keystroke:

```
ch = getch(); if ( ch == 0 ) getch();
```

getch() is a nonstandard but common function. It gets a keystroke, waiting for it if necessary, and does *not* echo that keystroke to the screen.

But there is more. Why should you compare the input character to a zero? Because doing that is how you can detect when *extended ASCII keys* (function keys, as well as arrow and paging keys) have been pressed. If one of these keys has been pressed, the character code is zero, and another code, indicating which extended key it was, will be sent. You are not concerned with extended keys here, except that you don't want the program to get confused when one is used. (It does say, "Press Any Key.")

The show_line() function (lines 35–57 of Listing 2.9) does the real work. It uses shift techniques for fast multiplication in calculating an offset into screen RAM, detects and handles newline and tab characters (you don't want to poke them directly into RAM as data bytes), and uses pointers to change position quickly.

There is a moral to these examples of very low-level I/O. They provide blazing performance. But sophisticated techniques require sophisticated code. If you are going to take this route to I/O programming, get ready. You have to work to get the results you want.

Summary

This chapter covered quite a bit of ground. But the price of using a powerful language like C is that its users must be knowledgeable. In this chapter, you have gained a good deal of the knowledge needed for most common I/O functions, and you have laid the foundations for advanced work in later chapters. You have learned the following:

■ What I/O is and the fundamental methods of getting it done. Now you know why I/O can be one of the greatest roadblocks to high-performance code: it requires a great deal of overhead processing. Buffering is an important tool for avoiding some of that overhead work.

■ The classification of interactive and storage devices, files, and C streams. You know what the standard C streams are and which other streams commonly are provided by operating systems. You also know the difference between text and binary streams.

■ How to define your own streams and how to associate them with files by opening them. You know that when you are finished with a stream, you should close it. This is true especially with output streams (to prevent loss of the last bufferful of data).

■ How to use both standard and user-defined streams to get simple character and string text data. You can control the formatting of text data, get discrete variable values from string input, and convert formats at will by using the printf(), scanf(), and strto...() families of library functions.

■ How to take over I/O processes close to the hardware and to control the processes. Perhaps the most important point here is to know when and why you should do this, and what it will cost you down the road.

This chapter showed clearly that there is a great deal to the C language. It is neither a toy to be trifled with nor an ogre that cannot be controlled. C is just a powerful tool for serious programmers.

Building C Programs

N ow that you are familiar with the basic I/O functions, you are ready to build the foundation of your knowledge of C. This chapter and Chapter 4 supply the bricks for that foundation.

Learning the language effectively dictates that you begin by sketching the broadest outlines of what is involved in writing a C program, and that you continue by progressively refining and pinpointing that knowledge. This chapter deals with two of the largest classes of elements that go into a C program: data and functions. Specifically, you learn the following:

■ How to define variables for the basic C data types. Data can be packaged in several ways, all of which—surprisingly—are variations on either integers or floating-point numbers (real numbers with fractional parts).

■ How to write constant (literal) values for the basic data types. You use these constants to initialize (give a starting value to) the variables you define, or to compare with or manipulate the variables. You will discover what the maximum and minimum values for each type of constant or variable can be.

■ How to declare variable data, and combine variables with constants to initialize the variables. C provides some fairly flexible ways to go about this, including lists of variables with optional initializers.

■ How to decide where to declare a variable. Its location in the program determines what other parts of the program can "know" about the variable. This will be the first discussion on C *scope*. Pay attention because scope is an important consideration in C programming.

■ How to declare and define your own functions in your programs. This involves function *declarations,* which inform the compiler what you intend to do, and function *definitions,* which provide the statements that do the work.

■ How to pass to a function the data with which that function works (function parameters), and how the function can pass the results of the operation back to the part of the program that called it. You also see how to call the function.

■ How to write the statements that do the work within a function definition. There are several kinds of statements suited to different tasks in C. This is the real meat of C programming.

Managing Data in a C Program

A primary goal of any program, C or otherwise, is to manipulate, transform, and transfer data. To fulfill this goal, the program must "know" how the data will be presented to it and how it must be handled. This, in turn, requires that data be represented in a fixed, well-defined format, or *type.* The type of a data object determines and limits what can be done with it. You can add two floating-point numbers, for instance, but they must be converted to a format you can read before you display them on the screen.

In the next few sections, you learn the fundamentals of managing data in your C programs. You see how to declare variables with specific types, use constants and literal values to initialize them, and decide where they can be used properly.

The Standard C Data Types

The notion of *type* is used everywhere in C. The value stored in a variable or returned by a function is partially determined by its type. An integer, for instance, cannot by definition have fractional parts, but a floating-point number can. Everything has a type in C. Note the following guidelines on how types are used in a C program:

■ *Object types* describe the characteristics of data objects (variables, constants, and so on). An object's type determines its internal format, what operations can be performed on it, and how those operations behave (for example, see the discussion of signed and unsigned integers later in this section). The notion of objects will be expanded considerably (and take on a more technical meaning) in Part II, when C++ objects are introduced. For now, the meaning is restricted to variables and constants.

■ *Function types* describe the values returned by a function, just as object types describe data values. Thus, you can speak of an integer function, a floating-point function, and so on, when you mean functions that return integer or floating-point values.

■ *Incomplete types* describe particular objects but lack the information necessary to determine an object's size. You can determine the address of an object with incomplete type, but you cannot access an object with incomplete type.

Data types are further classified according to whether they are simple (*basic* or elementary types) or complex (*derived* types).

The basic types include *characters, signed* and *unsigned integers,* and *floating-point numbers*. The signed integers and floating-point types can have negative values; unsigned types have only positive or zero values. The next C-Note gives more detail on the basic data types.

Quick Reference: ANSI C Basic Data Types

The basic data types are displayed here by group and listed using the incomplete type declaration syntax. The left column holds the *type specifiers* that you saw several times in the sample programs in Chapters 1 and 2. After reading this, you might want to look at those programs again, identifying type characteristics.

Elementary Characters

`char`	Stored in one byte. Characters from the minimal set (see Chapter 4) are guaranteed to be positive; all others may be either positive or negative.

Signed Integers

`signed char`	Stored in one byte, as are plain `char` types. In most implementations, `char` and `signed char` are equivalent in use but classified differently, because equivalence is not mandatory.
`short int` `int`	short int and int are listed together because, no matter how many bytes are used, the value ranges required by ANSI are identical. (See the Quick Reference C-Note "Limiting Values for Constants" in the next section.)

continues

Quick Reference: ANSI C Basic Data Types

`long int`	The value range for `long int` is much more than double that of `int`. Its physical size is left up to the implementation.
`unsigned char`	none
`unsigned short`	`unsigned short int`
`unsigned`	`unsigned int`
`unsigned long`	`unsigned long int`

Unsigned Integers	*Alternative Specification*
`unsigned char`	none
`unsigned short`	`unsigned short int`
`unsigned`	`unsigned int`
`unsigned long`	`unsigned long int`

Floating Point

`float`
`double`
`long double`
	The floating point types have varying degrees of value ranges for both the fractional part (the mantissa) and the exponent part (the characteristic).

Integers occupy several bytes, the number of which is natural to the machine on which the implementation of C is running. This usually is the same as the machine *word,* which is two bytes on 80x86 machines and may be four bytes on other machines. A `short int` may occupy a *halfword* or *fullword,* provided that the value range requirements are met. Borland C++ and Microsoft C/C++ assign the same physical size (two bytes) to both `int` and `short int` types. A `long int` typically requires four bytes on 80x86 processor implementations.

Typical sizes for the `float`, `double`, and `long double` types as implemented on an 80x86 CPU are 4, 8, and 10 bytes, respectively. These sizes are used on such machines because they match the physical sizes required by the 80x87 math coprocessor chips. Other machines may use different sizes (as well as different internal formats).

The char, signed char, and unsigned char types are those which have *external* data formats—they can be sent to an interactive or display device (the screen or printer) and produce readable data. They can be used internally in computations, but only to a limited extent. All the other type formats are *internal* to the CPU. They are used in computations but are not readable directly.

To examine the contents of internal variables, you must convert from internal format (numeric data) to external format (a character string). The formatted I/O functions covered in Chapter 2 do this—but it is not the only way to convert data. A *dump program* typically converts internal data formats to two types of display data (usually hexadecimal characters and ordinary display characters), as shown in Figure 3.1.

```
======== SDUMP Output for: sdump.c ========
23696E63 6C756465 203C7374 64696F2E 683E0D0A    #include.<stdio.h>..
23696E63 6C756465 203C6374 7970652E 683E0D0A    #include.<ctype.h>..
0D0A6368 6172202A 6865785F 63686172 2820696E    ..char.*hex_char(.in
74202C29 3B0D0A0A 0D0A6D61 696E2820 696E7420    t.c.);....main(.int.
61726763 2C206368 6172202A 61726776 5B5D2029    argc..char.*argv[].)
0D0A7B0D 0A202020 696E7420 632C693B 0D0A2020    ..{.....int.c.i;....
2A46494C 45202A66 703B0D0A 20202063 68617220    .FILE.*fp;.....char.
6C696E65 5F6F7574 5B38305D 3B0D0A20 20206368    line_out[80];.....ch
6172202A 6C703B0D 0A0D0A20 20206966 20282061    ar.*lp;.....if.(.a
72676320 3C203220 29206578 69742820 3820293B    rgc.<.2.).exit(.8.);
0D0A2020 20696628 20667020 3D206F66 70656E28    .....if(.fp.=.fopen(
20617267 765B315D 2C202272 62222029 20290D0A    .argv[1].."rb".).).
2020207B 0D0A2020 20202070 72696E74 66282022    ...{.......printf(."
3D3D3D3D 3D3D3D3D 20534455 4D50204F 75747075    ========.SDUMP.Outpu
7420666F 723A2025 73203D3D 3D3D3D3D 3D3D5C6E    t.for:.%s.========\n
222C0D0A 09202020 20206172 67765B31 5D20293B    ",.....argv[1].);
0D0A2020 20202069 203D2031 3B0D0A20 20202020    .....i.=.1;......
6D656D73 65742820 6C696E65 5F6F7574 2C202720    memset(.line_out,.'.
272C2838 30293B0D 0A0D0A20 2020206C 696E655F    ',80.);.....line_
6F75745B 35325D20 3D202720 273B206C 696E655F    out[52].=.'.';.line_
6F75745B 37335D20 3D202720 273B0D0A 20202020    out[73].=.'.';.....
206C696E 655F6F75 745B3738 5D203D20 275C6E27    .line_out[78].=.'\n'
3B0D0A20 20202020 6C696E65 5F6F7574 5B37395D    ;.....line_out[79]
203D2027 5C30273B 0D0A0D0A 2020206C 70203D20    .=.'\0';.....lp.=.
```

Figure 3.1.

Sample hex dump output.

The program (SDUMP.C) that produced this hex dump output is shown in Listing 3.1. Its purpose is to retrieve characters (single bytes, regardless of any data type a byte is part of) from a file, display it first as a two-character hex representation (text string), and display it also on the right side of the line (if it is, in fact, a displayable character).

Before you read over the program, note that in addition to the faithful standby printf(), a new library function is used. memset()—the "memory set" function used in lines 19 and 34—initializes an area of RAM memory to whatever value you give it. In this case, a text line 80 characters long is being initialized to blanks, preparatory to building a line of dump output text.

Listing 3.1. SDUMP.C is a hex dump program (for all compilers).

```
1   #include <stdio.h>
2   #include <ctype.h>
3
4   char *hex_char( int c );
5
6   main( int argc, char *argv[] )
7   {
8       int c,i;
9       FILE *fp;
10      char line_out[80];
11      char *lp;
12
13      if ( argc < 2 ) exit( 8 );
14      if( fp = fopen( argv[1], "rb" ) )
15      {
16        printf( "======== SDUMP Output for: %s ========\n",
17                  argv[1] );
18        i = 1;
19        memset( line_out, ' ', 80 );
20        line_out[52] = '‖'; line_out[73] = '‖';
21        line_out[78] = '\n';
22        line_out[79] = '\0';
23        lp = line_out;
24        while( (c = fgetc( fp )) != EOF ) {
25          strncpy( lp, hex_char(c), 2 );
26          if ( isgraph( c ) ) line_out[i+52]
27            = (unsigned char)c;
28          else line_out[i+52] = '.';
29          i++; lp += 2;
30          if ( i % 4 == 1 ) lp++;
31          if ( i % 20 == 1 ) {
32            i = 1;
33            printf( "%s", line_out );
34            memset( line_out, ' ', 80 );
35            line_out[52] = '‖'; line_out[73] = '‖';
36            line_out[78] = '\n';
37            line_out[79] = '\0';
38            lp = line_out;
39          }
40        }
```

```
41        if ( *line_out != ' ' ) printf( "%s", line_out );
42        fclose( fp );
43      }
44    else
45      printf( "Error in opening file\n" );
46  }
47
48  char *hex_char( int c )
49  {
50    static unsigned char hex_out[3];
51
52    hex_out[0] = (unsigned char)( (c & 0x00F0) >> 4 );
53    hex_out[0] += ( hex_out[0] > 9 ) ? 55 : 48 ;
54    hex_out[1] = (unsigned char)( c & 0x000F );
55    hex_out[1] += ( hex_out[1] > 9 ) ? 55 : 48 ;
56    hex_out[2] = '\0';
57    return( hex_out );
58  }
```

You may have noticed that the input file was opened in binary ("rb") mode. As you learned in Chapter 2, using binary mode thus prevents the I/O library functions from performing any conversion whatsoever on the data. Data is presented to the program bit for bit, exactly as it was recorded in the file—just what you need for a dump program.

The program first reads the input file in a loop (lines 24–39), passing each byte to hex_char() for conversion to a two-byte string of hex characters— hex_char() is invoked in line 25 by being used as an argument to strncpy(). The program then places the results in the output line. When the output line is complete, it is sent to the display device through printf() and reinitialized (lines 31–39).

The real meat of the program is in the hex_char() function (lines 48–58). To understand how this routine works, recall that a character is composed of 1 byte, which is 8 bits. Now think of a byte as 2 pieces of 4 bits each (a *nybble*— who says programmers have no sense of humor?). Four bits can hold a maximum numeric value of 15—the same as a hexadecimal F. Hold that thought for a moment.

Next look at the chart of ASCII characters in Appendix A. You will see that the *decimal values* for the *display characters* 0 through 9 are 48–57, and that the *decimal values* for the display characters A through F (valid hex digits) are 65–70.

hex_char() separates each group of 4 bits and scales it up to a legitimate display character. For example, if the value of a nybble is 10 (hex *A*), the character *A* has the value 65. Add 55 to the separated nybble and voila—the letter *A* results.

Display character generation is achieved with some C operators you have not yet seen. Line 52 isolates the left-hand (high-order) nybble with this statement:

```
hex_out[0] = (unsigned char)( (c & 0x00F0) >> 4 );
```

By using the *bitwise AND operator* (&), the expression (c & 0x00F0) turns off all the bits except those in the high-order nybble of what will become the output character. (Be careful here—remember that in other contexts & can be the address-of operator.) The constant hex value 0x00F0 is called the AND *mask;* if one of its bits is on, the other operand's corresponding bit will remain on; other bits are set to zero.

You can see also that this line deals with the input "character" as if it were an integer. At this point, it is an integer. As you may recall, the character I/O library functions return input characters as integers. The mask has two leading zeros to emphasize and document this fact, but 0xF0 would have worked just as well—the compiler would have kept everything aligned properly.

After all the unnecessary bits have been turned off, the high-order nybble must be aligned to the right so that a complete display character can be developed from the bits. You do this with the *shift-right operator* (>>). Because the shift-right operator has higher precedence (is evaluated first) than the bitwise AND, the previous expression had to be surrounded by parentheses to force the correct grouping.

Line 53 now constructs the final display character:

```
hex_out[0] += ( hex_out[0] > 9 ) ? 55 : 48 ;
```

The purpose of this statement is to add the correct scaling factor to the isolated nybble. From the left, the first operator you encounter is the *add assign operator* (+=). This operator combines the addition and assignment operations and is equivalent to:

```
hex_out[0] = hex_out[0] + ...
```

You can form complex assignment operators like this one from any of the other operators. Just write the other operator first, followed immediately by the equal sign (-=, *=, /=, &=, and so on).

The process of deciding exactly what to add to the initial value is performed by the *conditional* or *ternary operator*. Its symbols and operands have the following format:

```
expression ? a : b;
```

The expression will be evaluated for a true or false condition. If the expression is true, the a operand will be used. If the expression is false, the b operand will be used.

As you can see from this brief discussion, you could write line 53 in the following equivalent but longer form:

```
if ( hex_out[0] > 9 ) hex_out[0] = hex_out[0] + 55;
else hex_out[0] = hex_out[0] + 48;
```

Line 53 in the listing is just a sample of the compact code possible when you use C's powerful operator set and notation.

Be careful with conversion methods like this. This one is based solely on the ASCII collating sequence. ANSI standard C is not tied to ASCII-based systems, and such methods may or may not work on other systems without conversion. C running on an IBM mainframe, for example, must cope with the EBCDIC collating sequence. In that case, the scaling values used in Listing 3.1 would have to be changed, and you would have to take into account that EBCDIC display characters are not grouped contiguously in the sequence.

C also enables you to specify in an object's declaration two *type qualifiers:* const and volatile.

const indicates that although the object is defined like a variable, it ordinarily should be regarded as a constant:

```
const char inline[21] = "This is a string.";
```

Notice that a const-qualified object can be initialized (and this doesn't have to be directly in the declaration) but then should be used as a read-only object.

volatile means that the object is modified in unpredictable ways, perhaps by the operating system or by an interrupt-service routine. This subject is best left to an advanced book on C (although an interrupt-service routine is presented in Appendix E). You declare a volatile-qualified object in this way:

```
volatile int counter;
```

Working with Constant Values (Literals)

In providing data grist for the C mill, using constant values (also called *literals*) is more important than you initially might think. Constants are very important. They are involved somewhere along the line for every data object used—to initialize it, to compare it with, and to operate on it.

Then what values can you use in a constant? The answer varies from compiler to compiler, but ANSI has now provided a minimum range of possible values that you can count on from one product or system to another. These values are shown in the Quick Reference C-Note "Limiting Values for Constants." Notice how the suffixes U and L are used, either alone or together, in forming the unsigned and long integer constants. (Although these suffixes can be either upper- or lowercase, uppercase tends to show up better when you read a program.)

Quick Reference: Limiting Values for Constants

The numerical values you can express in a constant (or in a variable, for that matter) are assigned a *minimum range* they can assume. The minimum and maximum points in the range have also been assigned macro names as found in LIMITS.H. Here are the ranges:

Bits per char	8
signed char	–128 through 127
unsigned char	0U through 255U
char	Usually –128 through 127
Bytes per multibyte character	1, at least
short int	–32768 through 32767
unsigned short int	0U through 65535U
int	–32768 through 32767
unsigned int	0U through 65535U
long int	–2147483647L through 2147483648L
unsigned long	0UL through 4294967295UL

You already know from observing the character I/O functions that the character types fit into 1 byte. The integer types have assigned value ranges that reflect a 2-byte physical size (which on most microcomputers is a *word* field, containing 16 bits). Thus, the maximum value for an unsigned int is $2^{16} - 1$, or 65535.

The signed integers behave a little differently, because the high-order bit is used as the *sign bit*. If this bit is 0, the number is positive; if the bit is 1, the number is negative. An interesting side effect of this usage is that a positive sign bit cannot by definition contribute to (participate in) the value of the number—it must be 0. A negative sign bit, however, can be interpreted as contributing to the magnitude of the number. Thus, you will find that in most implementations the maximum negative integer value is –32768 (-2^{15}) rather than –32767. This is true of both Borland and Microsoft products for 80x86 machines.

Floating-point numbers are another, more complicated story. Although the ANSI min-max values for all three float types specify an exponent range of –38 to +38, they differ in the number of *required significant digits*. A `float` type requires the equivalent of 6 decimal digits of precision, whereas both `double` and `long double` require 10 decimal digits of precision. Typical min-max values for actual implementations of the fractional part exceed the ANSI standard, and exponential range requirements are much more than satisfied.

A floating-point number can be expressed in two ways: as a pure *fractional number* or in engineering (*exponential*) notation. You should already be familiar with the fractional notation—the decimal-point method of writing numbers (123.0567, 3.1415926, and so on). Exponential notation includes both a fractional part (*mantissa*) and an exponential part (*characteristic*). The first of the preceding numbers, for example, could be written `1.230567E+2`. The exponent (2) effectively "moves" the decimal point two places to the right, preserving the correct value of the number. The E, meaning exponent, can be either upper- or lowercase. You can also write a floating-point number with a negative characteristic. For example, the notation `1.234E-2` is valid and is the same as 0.01234.

Notice that when you write a floating-point number in source code, or as part of a text string to be converted to internal format, you write it in decimal notation—not binary and not hex. The conversion routines convert this to the proper internal number system base (*radix*).

How do you use these facts in the context of an actual program? One of the first things for which you will want to use literals is to initialize the value of variables. Listing 3.2 shows the code for the program LITERAL.C, which illustrates the use of literals for this purpose. Literals used directly in the variable declaration are called *initializers*.

Listing 3.2. LITERAL.C uses literal values (for all compilers).

```
 1   /*+------------------------------------------------
 2    +                   LITERAL.C
 3    + Assign a literal value to a variable and then print
 4    + it with formatted print function.
 5    +------------------------------------------------
 6   */
 7
 8   #include <stdio.h>
 9   #include <stdlib.h>
10
11   main()
12   {
13     short int        i =   158;
14     int              j =   999;
15     unsigned int     k =   61489U;
16     long int         l =   -365L;
17     float            x =   2.6736;
18     double           y =   598.342;
19     char             ch = 'A';
20     char         name[8] = "Charles";
21
22     printf( "Short integer, decimal .... i = %d\n", i );
23     printf( "Integer, hex format ....... j = %x\n", j );
24     printf( "Unsigned int has no sign .. k = %u\n", k );
25     printf( "Long int has a sign ....... l = %ld\n\n", l );
26     printf( "Floating point fixed ...... x = %1.4f\n", x);
27     printf( "       or exponential ...... y = %1.4e\n\n", y);
28     printf( "Characters are 1 byte ..... ch = %c\n", ch );
29     printf( "Strings are many bytes .... name = %s\n", name);
30   }
```

The output from LITERAL.C appears on the display screen like this:

```
Short integer, decimal .... i = 158
Integer, hex format ....... j = 3e7
Unsigned int has no sign .. k = 61489
Long int has a sign ....... l = -365
Floating point fixed ...... x = 2.6736
       or exponential ...... y = 5.9834e+002
Characters are 1 byte ..... ch = A
Strings are many bytes .... name = Charles
```

This program illustrates how to use literals to initialize variables for most of the basic types. The variables are declared in lines 13–20 within the `main()` function. (This means that they are valid only within this function. There's more on this later.) A string literal initializer is thrown in for good measure, just to show how it works.

As you can see, initializing most variables at the time you first declare them is quite simple. This is a good practice because it prevents using an uninitialized variable (which could do more than just produce wrong output; it could terminate your program abnormally).

Declaring Variable Data

LITERAL.C in Listing 3.2 is also a good jumping-off point for a discussion of declaring, initializing, and controlling variable data in your program.

Clearly, a variable must be both declared and initialized before it can be used. The declarations in lines 13–20 of Listing 3.2 accomplish both of these tasks at the same time. Shortly, you will see that it does not always have to be done this way.

Naming Variables

The first task you face is that of naming your variables. You should consider the following:

- C identifiers can have no more than 31 significant characters. This applies to variables and to everything else. Names can be longer than 31 characters, but to be considered different, names must vary within the first 31.

- Make the name long enough to mean something to you. You will thank yourself later when you debug your program. For instance, which of the following declarations tells you more about the variable being defined?

  ```
  int ss;
  int shift_status;
  ```

  The second declaration at least tells you that something about shift status is being recorded. Falling prey to the temptation to make names too long is easy, however, and leads to another kind of trouble—too much typing, and a cluttered-looking program. Make the name long enough, and then stop.

- Make the name easier to read by using the underscore character (_) to separate parts of the name. For example, the name

```
double high_water_mark;
```

is much easier to read than

```
double highwatermark;
```

Do not, however, use the underscore as the *leading character* in a name. The leading underscore should be reserved for C's predefined macro names and internal function names. It is legal for you to do this, but dangerous.

■ Never duplicate one of C's predefined names. Naturally, you need to be familiar enough with these names to avoid the error. If you accidentally duplicate one of these names, what happens next depends on the original predefined object. Most likely, you will receive a compiler error stating that the object is being redefined improperly.

Declarators and Declarator Lists

So far, you have seen only simple declarations for individual objects. As you might expect, C provides for a compact notation allowing the declaration of several similar objects in one source line. In the first of the following examples, you write a *declarator;* in the second, you write a declarator *list.* Instead of writing

```
int a;   /* three individual declarators */
int b;
int b;
```

you can declare all three variables on one line of code:

```
int a, b, c;   /* a declarator list */
```

You can also provide initializers in a declarator list, like this:

```
#include <stdio.h>
main()
{
  int a = 1, b = 2, c = 3, x;
  x = a + b + c;
  printf( "%d\n", x );
}
```

Naturally, you can add a number of bells and whistles to your declarations to make them more flexible and powerful. The complete general form of a C declaration is

```
[storage-class] type-specifier declarator [initializer];
```

The square brackets here are not meant to be coded, nor do they indicate array subscripts as in a true C declaration. Their purpose is to show what part of the declaration can be considered optional.

The optional *storage-class* specifier can be used to modify the default scope (visibility) and lifetime (duration) of a variable within the current block of code. The storage class determines exactly when a variable exists and where in memory it will be kept. There are five storage-class specifier keywords: typedef, extern, static, auto, and register. These keywords will be completely explained in the section "Taking Advantage of Storage Class" in Chapter 5.

The *type-specifier* (int, float, and so on) and at least one declarator name (the variable, or perhaps the function) must be present. The *type-specifier* should name one of the keywords shown in the Quick Reference C-Note "C Declaration Type-Specifiers," or perhaps a pointer to one of them. Here are some examples of valid type-specifiers:

```
int count;          /* a simple integer */
unsigned int data;  /* an unsigned integer */
int *age;           /* a pointer to an integer */
char c;             /* a simple character */
char *s             /* a pointer to character or string */
```

A *declarator* is required and is simply the name you want to give to the variable. The name must follow the rules for valid C identifiers. These rules are covered in the section "Identifiers in General" in Chapter 4, and in the section "Translation Limitations" in Chapter 12. For now, you need to know that identifiers must begin with a letter or an underscore, that they may contain numbers other than at the beginning, and that current compilers support names up to 31 characters long.

The optional *initializer* is a starting value for the variable. If you supply an initializer value, it must be either a constant or an expression that has the correct type for the variable being declared. The methods of forming valid constants for all the basic data types were shown earlier in this chapter. Here are some examples of valid initializers:

```
int a = 37;
unsigned int b = 32768U;
double length = 4.0132;
const char name[] = "John Doe";
```

Quick Reference: C Declaration Type-Specifiers

Keyword	Description
void	Unspecified type. Used with generic pointers or to indicate the complete absence of an object.
char	One of the character types.
int	One of the integer types.
long	Used only to modify a type. This either specifies long int or modifies double. long float is the same as double. long double is a separate type.
float	Short floating point.
double	Double-length floating point. This can be modified to long double.
signed	Used alone, or modifies char or int. If used in with long, it must be first (as in signed long int).
unsigned	Used alone, or modifies char or int. If used with long, it must be first (as in unsigned long int).
struct-*specifier* or union-*specifier*	Structures and unions are composite data types that are discussed in Chapter 11.
enum-*specifier*	Enumerations are a special type composed of a named set of integer constant values. They are discussed in detail in Chapter 11.
type-*def name*	You can derive your own customized date types using typedef. This, too, is covered in Chapter 11.

You can use some of the type-specifier keywords to modify others. The combinations allowed are exactly those allowed for basic data types (see the Quick Reference C-Note "ANSI C Basic Data Types" earlier in this chapter).

As mentioned at the beginning of this section, what is being declared can be either an individual identifier (*declarator*) or a list of identifiers, separated by commas (*declarator list*). In either case, a declarator can be followed by an equal sign and some initializing value. By using several variations on the basic theme of specifying declarators, you can accomplish different goals when you declare objects. The various types of declarations include the following:

■ *The simple identifier.* You have already seen this method several times, whether using one identifier or a list of identifiers. Example:

```
unsigned char ch; The character variable ch
```

■ *An identifier in parentheses.* This method is most often used to specify a pointer to a function but it can be used with simple identifiers not in lists. Examples:

`int ( a );`	Valid.
`int ( a ) = 3;`	Valid.
`int ( a = 3 );`	Invalid. Initializer goes outside parentheses.
`int ( a ), ( b );`	Valid.
`int ( a ) = 1, ( b ) = 2;`	Valid.
`int ( a, b, c );`	Invalid. Only one identifier allowed inside parentheses.

■ *An array identifier.* The identifier name is followed by a constant expression surrounded by square brackets giving the number of elements in the array. Each element in the array has the same basic type as given in the type-specifier. Examples:

`int p[5];`	An array of five integers.
`double x[20];`	An array of 20 double floats.
`int s[6][6];`	A two-dimensional array of integers.
`char text[81];`	A string with 80 bytes for text data plus one for the `'\0'` terminator.

Arrays and strings are not basic data types and require special handling discussed later in this book.

■ *A pointer to an identifier.* To declare an object to be a pointer to an object rather than the object itself, precede the identifier with the indirection operator. Examples:

`int *sflag;`	Pointer to integer `sflag`.
`float *rate;`	Pointer to `float` `rate`.

■ *A function identifier.* The identifier name is followed by a list of parameters or identifiers surrounded by parentheses. The difference between the two types of lists should become clear in the section "Declaring Functions and Passing Parameters" later in this chapter. Examples:

`void myfunc( void );`	A function with no parameters that returns nothing.
`int myfunc( int a );`	Function accepts an integer parameter; returns an integer.
`myfunc( int a );`	Same as above; `int` is always default type.
`double mycalc( a, b, c );`	Function accepts three parameters with unknown types; returns a `double` float.

■ *A pointer to a function.* This form uses both the parentheses around the identifier and the indirection operator *. The grouping of the tokens is dictated by the assumed operator precedence of the parentheses and the indirection operator. Using pointers to functions is covered in Chapter 6. Examples:

`int (*myfunc)();`	Pointer to a function returning an integer.
`int *(*myfunc)();`	Pointer to a function returning a pointer to an integer.

Some of this may look strange to you at the moment. The only cure for that is experience. You will see many of these forms throughout the book. They are explained many times, but don't hesitate to return to these pages and review the different forms of declaration syntax. A great way to get their effects firmly in mind is to write test programs using the different combinations and then watch the results.

Initializing Variables

At this point, you have learned what the basic C data types are, how to form constant values of the various types, and how to declare data objects, or variables, for them. Possibly without realizing it, you also have learned several ways to initialize variables in your program. Those methods are summarized and organized in the following list:

■ *Use an initializer at declaration time.* When you declare a variable, you can follow it with an assignment of a particular value, as in

```
double pi = 3.1415926;
```

You can use this technique with strings as well, but there are some limitations on string initialization in other circumstances.

■ *Assign a constant value to the variable.* A statement of the form:

```
population = 15762385L;
```

can appear in `main()` or in any of your other functions to set up a variable. Deciding when to do this depends on when you need the variable in the program, and on when the variable is valid in the program. This last point is discussed in the next section.

■ *Assign one variable to another.* This is similar to the preceding method, except that a variable, not a constant, is used, as in:

```
population = prev_count;
```

It is assumed in this example, of course, that `prev_count` has already been initialized by some other method.

■ *Input data into the variable.* You can use the I/O library functions to read data into the data objects in your program from somewhere else (such as a file or the keyboard). Usually, the bulk of the data that your program deals with comes from this source, whereas data initialized internally serves as work areas and holds temporary results.

Local and Global Variables

This section discusses the issue of *variable scope.* This is part of the larger issue of *storage class,* which is concerned with both the scope and the duration of a variable.

The *scope* of an object is its visibility to other parts of the program (other than the place it is defined). Just because a variable has been defined somewhere within a program (or source file), it is not necessarily visible everywhere in the program (or source file).

The *duration* of an object is its lifetime. Duration involves not only how long a variable exists, but when it is created and first becomes available (within the limitations of scope).

The scope of an object in C depends on where you place its definition, and possibly on modifiers present in the definition, which alter its characteristics. Briefly, you can define an object inside a function, in which case it has *local scope;* or you can define it outside any function, in which case it has *global scope.* Figure 3.2 summarizes how scope is affected by position in the source file.

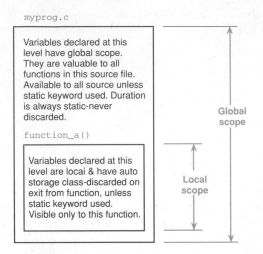

`myprog.c`

Variables declared at this level have global scope. They are valuable to all functions in this source file. Available to all source unless static keyword used. Duration is always static-never discarded.

`function_a()`

Variables declared at this level are local & have auto storage class-discarded on exit from function, unless static keyword used. Visible only to this function.

Global scope

Local scope

Figure 3.2.

Local and global variable scope.

The intent here is to focus on scope, but it is impossible to discuss scope without having some knowledge of storage class to provide a frame of reference. There are only two types of storage classes in C: `auto` and `static`. These terms are used to describe an object during discussion; they are also the modifiers mentioned in the preceding paragraph. Note that a storage class is associated with all objects, including functions.

An `auto` variable is one that has dynamic or *automatic duration*. It does not exist when the program begins execution; it is created at some point during the run and discarded at some point before the program finishes running.

A `static` variable is one that has *fixed duration*. Room for the object is set aside at compile time. (Incidentally, this takes up space in your .OBJ files on disk.) It already exists at execution time (although not necessarily initialized), exists throughout the run, and is "discarded" only when the program is purged from memory at termination time.

Every object has a specific mix of default storage class and scope, depending on the definition's location in the source file. Some combinations of attributes cannot occur; others that can occur can also lead you into confusion and error.

Variables with global scope, called *global variables,* are those defined outside the boundaries of any function. This is called an *outer declaration.* Global variables have the following behavior and attributes:

■ *Global variables have static duration by default.* Storage for them is set aside at compile time and never discarded. By definition, a global variable cannot also be an `auto` variable.

■ *Global variables are globally visible in the source file.* They can be referred to by any function following the point of definition of the object.

■ *Objects declared in outer declarations can appear anywhere in the source file.* You can declare data objects at the top of the file, write a few functions, declare another group of global objects, and then write some more functions. This is why the preceding paragraph qualified the visibility of global objects as being the remainder of the source file, beyond the point of declaration. This means that visibility is determined by a declaration's physical location in the source file, not by the logical order of execution.

■ *Global variables are by default available to other source files in the program.* This is called external linkage. You define the object in the normal way in its "home" source file. To refer to it in another source file, declare it again; do not use any initializer (it was initialized by the first source file code) and be sure to qualify the declaration with the extern keyword, as in the following example:

Source File A	*Source File B*
int count = 0;	extern int count;

■ *Global variables can be hidden from other source files by using the static storage class specifier.* Note this example:

```
#define OFF 0
#define ON 1
...
static unsigned char master_switch = OFF;
...
main()
{
  ... /* main processing */
}
...
function_a()
{
  ... /* function_a processing */
}
...
```

This allows master_switch to be used both by function_a() and main() in this source file, but it cannot be declared as an extern in another source. Global variables have static duration in any event. This is just a mechanism for hiding objects from other source modules.

Local variables, in contrast, are those defined inside a function body. Even more restrictively, a variable may be local to a particular block statement within a function body (which is discussed a little later in this chapter). This type of declaration is called an *inner declaration*.

■ *Local variables have automatic duration.* A local variable, defined within the boundaries of a function body, does not exist until the function is called and run. When the function is entered, setup code generated by the compiler is executed to allocate and initialize the function's auto variables (synonymous in this sense with local variables). They exist in, and are used by, only the function in which they are defined. When the function returns to the caller, auto variables are discarded and their storage released.

■ *Local variables can also be defined inside a compound or block statement.* Note this example:

```c
char *string_function( char *input_string )
{
  if ( *input_string == "X" ) {
    int cnt = 0;
    cnt = strlen( input_string );
    /* do something with cnt */
  }
/* other processing outside the if */
}
```

The integer cnt is not valid for the entire duration of string_function. It is valid only inside the braces that contain the statements associated with the if (in other words, the block statement conditionally executed if the if evaluates to true). If the if is executed more than once in the function, it is created and destroyed each and every time the if condition is true, even though the function is executed only once.

■ *Local variables are visible only in the block in which they are defined.* Nothing outside that block (or function) is aware of them or can use them. An interesting but potentially confusing result is that you can define different variables with the same name, provided that they are defined in different scopes:

```c
#include <stdlib.h>
#include <stdio.h>

int cnt = 1;

main()
```

```
{
  printf( "%d\n", cnt );
}

void function_a( void )
{
  int cnt = 2;
  printf( "%d\n", cnt );
}
```

In this program fragment, both `main()` and `function_a()` display the value of a variable named `cnt`. Yet `main()` displays a value of 1, whereas `function_a()` shows 2. In spite of the identical labels for the variables, two different objects are being used. The potential for confusion is rather obvious; this practice should be avoided whenever possible (which is almost always). If you define a variable locally to a function, and the variable has the same name as a global variable, only the local version of it can be used in the function. The global version is temporarily unavailable.

■ *The declarations for objects defined in an inner declaration must appear at the top of the block.* This is in distinct contrast to the "mobility" of global objects defined in outer declarations, which can appear anywhere in the source file (except within a function, of course). Coding an inner declaration after beginning to write the expression statements of the function body (see the section "Building the Function Body" later in this chapter) results in a syntax error at compile time.

■ *Local variables use the `static` keyword to modify duration, not visibility.* Writing the `static` storage class specifier with a local variable's declaration causes storage to be set aside for the variable (as though it were a global variable) and assigns it static duration, but does not make it globally visible. This usage is more common than you might think. You can use the `static` keyword to prevent the loss of an otherwise `auto` class variable, when one call to a function may depend on the state of affairs left from a previous call. For example, to "remember" whether a file is open or not, you could write:

```
int file_server( char *buffer, int bufsize )
{
  static int is_open = 0;

  if ( !is_open ) {
    /* open the file and say so */
    fopen( ... );
    is_open = 1;
  }
```

```
/* service various file requests */
}
```

Clearly, you don't want to open the file whenever `file_server` is entered—it may already be open. The goal is to "remember" that fact.

The terms *local* and *global* make it easy to remember which is which, and where they can go. Why would you want to choose one or the other? Wouldn't it be just as easy to define everything as a global variable and let it go at that? That approach ignores the trade-offs involved.

Global variables are available to every function below them. They should be used when several different functions need a single copy of a particular object. Some functions need to know what others have been doing. You should be aware, however, that such circumstances often can be satisfied by passing a copy of the variable as a parameter to the function.

Local variables reduce clutter in the global data declarations. If there is no need to communicate the value of an object to other parts of the program, use an `auto` variable. There is no chance of another function altering its contents unexpectedly, and because it is discarded when not needed, it saves on long-term storage space. The copy of a variable passed as a parameter to a function also has local scope: it is valid only while the function executes, and is discarded when the function returns. Global variables can be used to improve the performance of a program. Because they have static duration, allocating them fresh for every call to a function entails no overhead. However, this practice increases the size of your program, both in memory and on disk.

Alternatively, local variables can help reduce the size of your program. This may be especially critical in long and complex programs. Wherever absolute blinding speed is not required (or the overhead can be otherwise hidden), use a local variable. The program CVTJUL.C in Listing 3.3 illustrates how some of these features are used (including the use of the `static` storage class specifier in a local scope). CVTJUL.C has some useful date-format conversion routines for Julian and six-dates. (You can do math on Julian dates much more easily than with six-dates—dates having a format like *mmddyy*.)

Listing 3.3. CVTJUL.C—Date conversions (for all compilers).

```
1   #include <stdlib.h>
2   #include<stdio.h>
3
4   #define FALSE 0
5   #define TRUE 1
6
7   int leapyear;
8
```

```
 9   char *getmon( int monum );
10   int getday( unsigned long julday );
11   int isleap( int year );
12   int modays( int monum );
13   unsigned long getjul( int month, int day, int year );
14
15   main()
16   {
17     int i, j, month, day, year;
18     unsigned long julday;
19
20     for ( i=1; i<26; i++ ) printf( "\n" );
21     printf( "Enter Julian ddd, a blank, and year yyyy: " );
22     scanf( "%ld%d", &julday, &year );
23
24     leapyear = isleap( year );   /* do this before invoking */
25                                  /* other routines, set Feb */
26
27                      /* let i count down the month */
28     j = julday;        /* but do not destroy julday */
29     for( i=1; j>modays(i); j-=modays(i), i++ );
30     printf( "The six-date is %s %d.\n",
31             getmon( i ), getday( julday ) );
32
33     printf( "Enter mm dd yyyy: " );
34     scanf( "%d%d%d", &month, &day, &year );
35     leapyear = isleap( year );
36     printf( "The Julian date is %ld.",
37             getjul( month, day, year ) );
38   }
39
40   char *getmon( int monum )
41   {
42     static char *moname[] =
43     {
44       "January",
45       "February",
46       "March",
47       "April",
48       "May",
49       "June",
50       "July",
```

continues

Listing 3.3. Continued

```
51      "August",
52      "September",
53      "October",
54      "November",
55      "December",
56      "INVALID MONTH"
57    };
58
59    if ( monum > 0 && monum < 13 ) return( moname[monum-1] );
60    else return( moname[12] );
61  }
62
63  int getday( unsigned long julday )
64  {
65    int i;
66
67    for( i=1; julday>modays(i); julday-=modays(i), i++ );
68    return( (int)julday );
69  }
70
71  int isleap( int year )
72  {
73    if ( 0 == ( year % 1000 ) )       return( FALSE );
74    else if ( 0 == ( year % 400 ) )   return( TRUE );
75    else if ( 0 == ( year % 100 ) )   return( FALSE );
76    else if ( 0 == ( year % 4 )  )    return( TRUE );
77    else                              return( FALSE );
78  }
79
80  int modays( int monum )
81  {
82    static int motab[] = { 31,28,31,30,31,30,
83                           31,31,30,31,30,31 };
84
85    if ( leapyear ) motab[1] = 29; else motab[1] = 28;
86    if ( monum > 0 && monum < 13 )
87      return( motab[monum-1] );
88    else return( 0 );
89  }
90
```

```
 91   unsigned long getjul( int month, int day, int year )
 92   {
 93     int i;
 94     unsigned long julday = 0;
 95
 96     for ( i=1; i<month; i++ ) julday += modays(i);
 97     julday += day;
 98     julday = ( julday * 100 ) + ( year % 100 );
 99     return( julday );
100   }
```

The algorithms for date conversion are easy, with just a little study. As a good exercise, you may want to go over them in detail and pick out the techniques used here.

The way that this program handles variables illustrates some of the points made about local and global scope. The only global variable in the program is leapyear. This integer is set once by the isleap() function, lines 71—78 so that other functions, notably modays(), lines 80—89, do not have to determine repeatedly whether it is a leap year. All other variables are local to a function.

The static keyword on line 42 is used in getmon() to qualify the array of month names moname[]. Especially because ANSI C enables you to initialize directly any variable, auto or otherwise, in its first definition, why should you do this?

Analyze what will happen if you don't use the static specifier. Because this array is inside the bounds of a function, it has local scope. By default, it is an object with *automatic duration*—it will be rebuilt at each call to getmon() and discarded when the function returns to its caller. With an object this size, used in a program that calls a function repeatedly (say, once per record in a database processing program), the setup overhead would be enormous. The static specifier modifies the attributes of the object, giving it static duration; it is set up once only and left in place. This enhances the program's performance.

Old-Style Coding: Initializing Local Variables

K&R C did not permit the use of initializers in the declarations of auto objects (local variables) that have type struct, union, or array. For these derived (complex) objects, you had to use the static specifier to change their duration to static. In fact, the original routines used to compose CVTJUL.C in Listing 3.3 were K&R routines, and used the static keyword for just this reason—so that the arrays of month names and day counts could be set up with initializers in the declaration.

---

continues

Old-Style Coding: Initializing Local Variables

With ANSI-conforming compilers, this reason no longer applies; using static storage class is only a performance modification. With recent conforming compilers, you can remove the `static` keyword entirely from the program. The program still works. We verified this; it just works more slowly. In general, you can place initializers directly in the declaration of any data object, `auto` or `static`, when using an ANSI-conforming compiler.

You might also reflect on the fact that `main()`, `getday()`, and `getjul()` all declare the integer `i`. Because a local variable is visible only in its scope, these three declarations refer to different variables. When `main()` calls any of these functions, what happens to its copy of `i`? You probably guess intuitively—and correctly—that while `getday()`, for example, is running, it uses its own variable `i`. The variable `i` in `main()` is not used, because its scope has been temporarily suspended while the subordinate function runs.

Here's a final word about terminology. The terms *local* and *global* are borrowed from computer science. Although used only incidentally in the ANSI standard, these extremely descriptive terms are used extensively in the literature (even the compiler manuals) in exactly the sense they are used here.

Declaring Functions and Passing Parameters

Designing and coding the function declarations and definitions are the glamorous parts of writing C programs. Coding data definitions is every bit as necessary and useful, but they don't do anything—they just sit there. Functions do things.

Learning to write function declarations involves, first of all, understanding that from the larger perspective C regards its functions as objects, much like data objects. How so? All functions, like data objects, have a type and, when accessed, render some value.

ANSI has introduced the `void` type, so that a function may have a `void` type and return a `void` value (return nothing at all). Conceptually, `void` is still a type of object—somewhat like the null set in mathematics. The default type for functions is `int`. That is, if you don't say anything about a function's type, it is assumed to be an integer.

As you probably have noticed from the previous sample programs, you can communicate information to a function by passing it parameters—data objects that not only give the function something to work with but also may tell it how to go about its work. These objects, naturally, also have types.

The types involved can be any of those discussed earlier in this chapter, except arrays. Only pointers to arrays can be passed as parameters. The C compiler does quite a bit of work keeping track of types and deciding whether they are matched properly. This process is called *type checking*. The ANSI standard for C promotes (but does not absolutely require) code that enforces *strong type checking*, meaning that the compiler catches most of the goofs made (instead of having your spiffy new program blow up when you are demonstrating it to the boss).

Old-Style Coding: Function Declarations

The original K&R C featured weak typing. Programmers could, and did, take advantage of this to manipulate data in some fairly strange and esoteric ways. Weak typing was, in fact, considered one of the strengths of the language, so that the new ANSI emphasis on strong typing constitutes a major design difference. Weak typing manifested itself precisely in passing parameters to functions. The original function-definition sequence was like this:

```
process( a, b, c )
  int a;
  int b;
  int c;
{
  ... /* do something with a, b, and c */
}
```

The catch is that there was no way to determine whether the type of the parameters actually used in a function call matched the type of those given in the function definition.

You could call the function with the wrong type and number of arguments, provided that the number of bytes expected matched. You could do strange things like this:

```
1  #include <stdlib.h>
2  #include <stdio.h>
3
4  process( a, b, c )
5    int a,b,c;
6  {
7    printf( "%d %d %d\n", a, b, c );
```

continues

> **Old-Style Coding: Function Declarations**
>
> ```
>  8  }
>  9
> 10  main()
> 11  {
> 12    process( 0xFFFFFFFFUL, 0 );
> 13  }
> ```
>
> This unusual program actually runs, producing a display of –1, –1, and 0. This is because an `unsigned long int` has the same number of bytes as do two `int`s. This is exactly the sort of thing strong type checking prevents.

To write ANSI C code, you need to know how to assign a type to your functions, how to set up parameters for it, where to place both the function prototype and the function definition, and finally, how to call the function and get to the returned results.

Using Full Function Prototypes

An abiding principle of all computer programming is that you can't use an object you haven't yet declared. In some languages, you may be able to declare and use an object in the same statement, but it must be declared. The declaration is what tells the compiler or interpreter what it needs to know about the object.

In C, you can declare a function in two ways: by actually defining and writing the function, or by forward declaring it with a function prototype statement and defining it later.

In the preceding C-Note, the first of these methods is used. The function `process()` is declared by defining it. This means that a function has to be declared in the source code before any calls are made to that function. Hence, `process()` is written before `main()`, which calls it. This order is required even though `main()` first begins executing when the program is run. The *physical order* here is the reverse of the *logical order*.

Because this tends to be confusing and awkward for longer programs, the second method is the preferred one: use a *function prototype* statement early in the source file and define the function body later. The first method is used in this book for short programs because it is very convenient for the quick development of small projects.

The Prototype Declaration Format

A function *definition* has two parts: the function declarator and the function body. A function *prototype,* however, has only the declarator, followed immediately by a semicolon. A function prototype declaration has the following syntax:

```
type-specifier function-identifier( declaration-list );
```

In K&R C, you could also forward declare a function, but there was less information available for the compiler to use in type checking. For example, compare these two lines of code:

```
double circle_area( double radius ); /* ANSI style */
double circle_area( radius );        /* K&R style */
```

Now look in detail at the parts of a full function-prototype declaration.

Writing the Function Type Specifier

Functions have types (just like data objects) because they are expected, in general, to return to the function's caller a data value of the given type. Here are a few examples of function prototype declarations:

```
int is_it_there( char *text, char *search );
char *get_a_line( FILE *infile );
double avg_value( double stuff[20] );
void do_something( void );
here_it_is( int a );
```

The function is_it_there() searches for the string search in the string text and returns an integer value that can be used to determine the success or failure of the function. get_a_line() has a type of char *, or pointer to character (string), because it returns the address of the last line of text read. (This one probably has a static local data object it uses for a line buffer!) And avg_value() computes the average value of all the elements in the double floating-point array stuff[] and returns the result as a double.

The last two examples are a bit more subtle. To even guess what the do_something() function might actually do is impossible. It receives no parameters and returns no value—but it still fits the conceptual model, because void is a type specifier. here_it_is(), in contrast, does get a parameter and, by default, returns a value—an integer.

The rules for coding the function's type specifier can be summarized in two points:

1. Every function must return a value to its caller. The type of the value can be one of the basic or derived (compound) data types you learned earlier in this chapter, or, if it returns nothing, must specify the void type. Basic types and some derived types (structures, enumerated types, and typedefs you defined) can be returned directly as data values. Only pointers are returned for arrays and strings—generally, their "values" are very large objects requiring too much memory to move around directly (which would cause the function to run slowly—even if there were enough space). You can declare a function type specifier of pointer to anything; it depends only on what you are doing with the function.

   In some cases, using pointers is a good idea even if, technically, you don't have to. Structures, for instance, tend to be too large to do anything else; indiscriminately passing and returning structure "values" directly would degrade your program's performance severely.

2. A function prototype declaration (or a function definition, for that matter) is assumed to return a value of type int if you do not code a type specifier. There has to be *some* default—this int is the default in C. This default can prove to be a subtle trap for programmers new to C. Take our word for it! While you're learning C, the tendency is to forget to code the specifier, when you actually want the type to be something other than int. Using ANSI function prototyping prevents many of the problems that this formerly caused. Failure to code a type specifier shouldn't get past the compiler, unless you insist on using the old-style formats.

You might wonder whether a function—because it has a type—also has storage class like other objects. It does indeed. By default, a function has *external linkage,* so that functions in other source files can call it, if the source file containing the function has an appropriate function prototype (this is the sort of thing you use header files for). You can explicitly code this by using the extern keyword, as in the following example:

```
extern int my_function( void );
```

This declaration describes a function that has no parameters, returns an integer, and is defined in another source file.

The ANSI standard specification that an object with external linkage and no stated storage-class specifier shall have static duration is true for functions. Functions always have static duration.

Furthermore, you can use the static keyword to modify the visibility of a function. The function has static duration naturally, but otherwise this keyword affects functions as it does any other global object with this specifier. It forces the function to be visible only to other functions in the same source file (this is called *internal linkage*). This usage enables you to have, without confusion, functions with the same name in different source files.

Writing the Function Name and Formal Parameter List

The function name is like any other name in C. The only thing that sets it apart is that it belongs to a function rather than to something else. The name part of the function declaration should follow at least one blank after the type specifier. This name is the identifier by which the function is known to the rest of the program; you use it to call (invoke) the function.

There is little magic about a function's name, provided that you observe a few rules in forming it. It should begin with a letter (system reserved names sometimes begin with an underscore); only the first 31 characters are considered significant (although you can write a longer name); and it can contain embedded underscores and numbers. Clearly, the name should mean something to you, but you should be careful not to duplicate C keywords or library function names. That's about it for now. (Chapter 4, "A Closer Look at C Programs," provides details on C identifier conventions.)

The *formal parameter list* immediately follows the function name. The parameter list begins with an opening (left) parenthesis; lists the parameters (synonymous with *arguments*), separated by commas; and ends with a closing (right) parenthesis, followed by a semicolon. (The semicolon is used only to delimit the prototype declaration, not the function *definition*.)

You need to know about the following important characteristics of formal parameter lists:

- The argument names in a parameter list are purely formal; they can (but do not have to) duplicate any identifier. For example, in the code fragment

```
void display_time( int hh, int mm, int ss ); /* prototype */
...
main()
{
  int hours, minutes, second;
  ...
  display_time( hours, minutes, seconds );
}
```

the parameter names are different in the function prototype and actual function call. What is significant is the relative position and order in the list. Of course, the types of the actual and formal parameters must match; the compiler flags an error if they do not. It *is* acceptable if the actual and formal parameter names are identical—there is no conflict between formal parameters and "physical" variables.

But calling the function in the following way is not acceptable:

```
display_time( seconds, minutes, hours );
```

In this case, the function would interpret its actual arguments as if they appeared in the order specified in the prototype (or complete definition, if there were no prototype). The program runs, but not with the desired results.

■ Each parameter in the list should have a type specifier, just as ordinary variable declarations do. However, a formal parameter list does not permit a declaration list. Note this example:

```
/* THE WRONG WAY */
int sort_table( int *table,entries,status );
/* AND THE RIGHT WAY */
int sort_table( int *table, int entries, int status );
```

Each parameter declarator should have its own type specifier.

■ In the function prototype only, it is possible to use only type specifiers in the formal parameter list, with no variable names, as in the following line:

```
int sort_table( int, int, int ); /* OK for prototype */
```

Again, this is permissible only in the prototype declaration, never in the function definition (when the function body is given).

Several references have been made to the fact that arrays (including strings, which are arrays of character) are never passed to a function as parameters. Only pointers to arrays are passed to a function. This ought to tell you two things:

1. It is important. You will have no end of confusion if you do not keep this fact firmly in mind.

2. There is more than one way to pass parameter information to a function. You can send a copy of the actual value of the object (*pass by value*), or you can send a value that is the address of the object—a pointer (*pass by reference*).

Figure 3.3 illustrates how parameters are passed to a function on stack-oriented machines. Begin to watch the sample code for instances of this distinction, and watch also for the manner in which arrays and strings are handled.

Effects on the Order of Appearance

The purpose of using function prototype declarations is to *forward declare* a function—to describe its characteristics before the complete definition appears so that the compiler knows how to handle references to the function in the meantime.

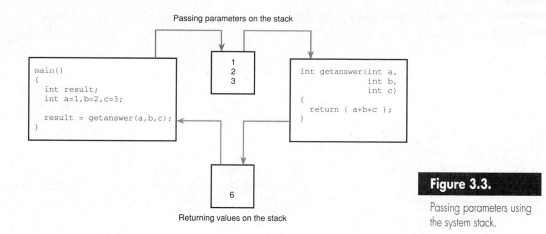

Figure 3.3.

Passing parameters using the system stack.

Function prototyping is the feature that enables you to write main() first, which in turn calls functions that physically appear later in the source file to handle more detailed tasks. This physical arrangement parallels the top-down design process, in which the major tasks are sketched in first and fleshed out at a deeper level of detail. It also seems to suit the human mind, which is accustomed to reading from the top down.

A side benefit of full function prototyping is that it provides the strongest possible type checking at compile time. There is a much better chance that the compiler will be able to catch and flag inconsistencies, instead of leaving them for you to find later, when the program fails.

Coding the Function Definition

The function definition differs from the function prototype in two ways: the declaration part does not end with a semicolon, and the declaration part is followed directly by the *function body*. Here is an example of a function prototype declaration followed by its corresponding function definition:

```
int x = 7, y = 4;
int maxval( int, int );
...
main()
{
  printf( "The greatest number is %d\n",
       maxval( x, y ) );
}
...
```

```
int maxval( int a, int b )
{
  return a > b ? a : b;
}
```

This function prototype uses type names without identifiers to describe the formal parameters (remember that you can specify the formal parameter names). The parameter list in the function definition is formal also, but you must use both type and identifier names here—the names of the formal parameters are about to be used in the function body.

The ANSI standard still allows the original style of declaring and defining functions. The formats for the declaration and definition of `max_val()` would look like this:

```
int maxval( a, b );
...
int maxval( a, b )
  int a;
  int b;
{
  return a > b ? a : b;
}
```

Building the Function Body

The function body is just an ordinary C block statement, enclosed by curly braces. The opening brace can be on the same line as the function declaration part, or on the next line, and no semicolon follows the closing curly brace. Look for these features in the preceding fragment and reinforce them in your mind.

Before you move on to the subject of writing statements for the function body, it is important that you understand the transition from the declaration part to the function body. The connecting links, of course, are the arguments in the parameter list.

Parameter variables are used within the bounds of the function just as if they were declared as ordinary local variables. In fact, parameter variables have automatic scope, as do the `auto` variables declared within the function body. They are created on entry to the function—copies of the actual variables used in the call are made and given to the function—and discarded when the function returns to its caller.

Writing C Statements

Within the bounds of the braces delimiting the block statement that is the function body, you place simple statements, or subordinate block statements, that do the function's work. The different types of simple statements are discussed next, but they all have at least one thing in common: they are terminated with a semicolon. To verify this, just glance through the sample programs and code fragments presented so far.

Everything defined and discussed in the book so far has had the characteristics of an *object*. They have all been things (including functions considered as a whole), and they have all had a value associated with them (even if it were only the void attribute).

Statements differ from C objects in two ways. They appear only within the confines of function bodies, and they have an effect, not a value. Statements are executed by the computer. They operate on objects.

You should know about five types of statements: expression statements, flow control statements, labeled statements, null statements, and compound or block statements.

Writing Expression Statements

The *expression statement* is the workhorse of C. It is the statement that operates directly on data objects or causes I/O to be done. The two most common expression statements are the *assignment statement*, such as:

```
a = ( b + c * d ) / e;
```

and the *function call*, such as:

```
printf( "%d\n", a );
```

C expression statements are much like algebraic statements. They are a sequence of terms and factors, joined together in a specific way by certain operators. One significant difference is that C can have a statement that is not a complete assignment statement. In the preceding line of code, for instance, printf() returns an integer value that is thrown away.

C is outstanding in its capability to support complex, compact, and efficient expressions. The topic is so important that much of Chapter 5, "Objects, Expressions, Operators, and Conversions," is devoted to it.

Writing Flow Control Statements

The term *flow control* covers three more precisely named groups of statements: *selection, iteration,* and *jump statements*. Look at the Quick Reference C-Note "C Flow Control Summary" and notice which statements belong to each of these groups.

Quick Reference: C Flow Control Summary

In the following specifications for the flow control statements, the tokens shown in italics are expressions, statements, or identifiers that you code to suit your purposes. Punctuation and tokens not shown in italics must be written as shown. Wherever the placeholder statement appears, you may write either a simple statement followed by a semicolon, or a block statement that is not followed by a semicolon. Writing block statements is discussed in detail shortly.

Selection:	`if ( expression ) statement`
	`if ( expression ) statement else statement`
	`switch ( expression ) statement`
Iteration:	`while ( expression ) statement`
	`do statement while ( expression );`
	`for ( expr1; expr2; expr3 ) statement`
Jump:	`goto identifier;`
	`continue;`
	`break;`
	`return expression;`

These three classes of statements have been grouped together into one conceptual framework because they all alter the sequence of execution.

Normally, instructions are executed in a sequential manner. The next instruction to be executed is the next physically sequential instruction after the current one. The presence of a flow control statement changes this; the next instruction to be executed is somewhere else in the function.

That last phrase also is an important one. The flow control instructions shown here can cause execution to continue only somewhere within the current function. Furthermore, all flow control statements (except `goto`, `break`, and `return`) cause a statement within the current block to execute next.

When using selection and iteration statements, be especially careful not to cause any unwanted side effects. The expression parts of the selection and iteration statements are normally meant to be *conditional expressions,* which test the truth or falsehood of some condition. Therefore, in forming these expressions, specific conditional operators normally are used. Here is an example:

```
if ( a == b ) return 0;
```

If you look closely at this statement, you see that the *equality operator* (==), not the assignment operator (=), is used. What is the difference? The equality operator does not cause the value of b to be placed in a; the assignment operator does. Side effects arise when you write a statement like this:

```
if ( a = b ) return 0;
```

This perfectly legitimate C statement first assigns the value of b to a, then examines the value of a (the most elementary value of the expression), and finally decides whether the condition is false or true (0 or nonzero, respectively). The side effect lies in the fact that an object's value was changed, above and beyond the primary purpose of testing a condition.

Clearly, just by making a typing error, you can easily introduce unwanted side effects into your program in expressions like the preceding one. At times, however, you deliberately want to introduce side effects. You probably can recall one from an earlier sample program. For example, you often see this type of statement:

```
if ( NULL == (infile = fopen( "myfile.txt", "r" ) ) ) {
  puts( "I can't open the input file." );
  abort();
}
```

This common statement has an interesting structure, based on the deliberate use of expression side effects. From the preceding C-Note, you know that the if statement has a "simple" conditional expression that is tested, and an accompanying statement (a block statement with no semicolon following here) that is executed only if the condition is true (not zero).

Quick Reference: The Assignment Operator (=) or the Equality Operator (==)?

You may have noticed in the program listings that there are two different kinds of equal signs. The first equal sign, =, is the *assignment operator*. The assignment operator assigns one value to a variable. The assignment operator is used in a statement like this:

```
my_var = 3;
```

The second equal sign, ==, is the *equality operator*. The equality operator compares two objects. The equality operator is used like so:

```
if ( my_var == 3 ) printf( "It's equal\n" );
```

Working from the inside out, the intent obviously is to open the file and check at the same time for a successful open. The fopen() function is called, and the resulting pointer is placed in the FILE pointer object infile using the assignment operator. Next, the result of that operation (a pointer) is compared against a NULL value (zero value) using the conditional equality operator.

Here is the tricky part: if the file does not open successfully, a null pointer is returned and compared to another null pointer, yielding a true condition. Thus, the result of the conditional expression is not zero, and the `if`'s block statement is executed—aborting the program. Whew!

This is only a taste of the tangles you can get into by not paying attention to side effects. The subject of flow control is so important that Chapter 7, "Controlling Program Logic Flow," is devoted to it.

Using Labeled Statements

Inherently, C is a well-structured language that does not promote the use of direct jumps. But the direct jump is supported, in the form of the `goto` statement (refer to the "C Flow Control Summary" C-Note).

Every `goto` must have a target location within the current function, although it can be outside the current block. This target is provided in C by the *labeled statement,* as illustrated by the following code fragment:

```
int some_function( void )
{
  goto pointa ;
  ...
  pointa: a = b;
}
```

The object of a `goto` is a label that prefixes some other statement. The label is noted by the presence of the full colon. Note also that the label must be followed by a statement. That was not formerly the case, but ANSI has standardized its required presence. (You can get around that by using the null statement, coming up next).

Two other types of labeled statements—the `case` and `default` statements—are both associated with the `switch` statement. These statements are discussed in Chapter 7.

Using Null Statements

Null statements are the easiest statements in all of C. Remember that a simple statement is always formed from an expression followed by a semicolon. Now just leave the expression out!

```
;    /* A NULL STATEMENT */
```

You may want to know why in the world you would ever need such a statement. First, you can circumvent the need to follow a label with a complete statement:

```
goto label1;
... /* do some things here */
label1: ;
... /* do other things here */
```

This usage breaks up the continuous flow of statements, enhancing readability.

The other reason for using a null statement is to provide a placeholder when syntax requires a statement but you don't really need one. The while statement, for example, can be used with deliberate side effects to copy one string into another:

```
char a[32];
char b[32] = "This string has something in it";
...
while ( *a++ = *b++ ) ; /* don't need a statement here */
```

The conditional expression does all the work: it assigns each character of the sending string to the corresponding character of the receiving string, updates the pointers involved, and (when the terminating null character is copied) finds the false condition required to terminate the loop. A null statement was used because the statement usually associated with the while is completely redundant.

Writing Compound (Block) Statements

You have seen block statements many times by now; they are old friends. A block statement is just a series of simple statements (expression or otherwise), surrounded by curly braces. The closing curly brace is not followed by a semicolon, although all the internal *simple* statements are. A block statement also may be nested inside another block statement, as in the following example:

```
if ( a != b ) { /* if a is not equal to b */
   /* ------ begin a block statement for the if ------ */
   a = b;        /* make it equal */
   for ( i=a; i<100; i++ ) {
   /* ------ begin another for the for ------ */
   ...
  }
}
```

The purpose of the block statement is to provide a means of writing many statements where syntax requires only one. You can see several examples of block statements in the program listings in the closing sections of this chapter.

Returning Values from a Function

If a function has some type other than void, it is expected to return a value to its caller. This is done with the return statement. An expression (which can be just a simple variable of the correct type) associated with the return statement is evaluated, and its result is passed back to the calling routine. On stack-oriented machines, this is accomplished by using the program's stack area (refer to Figure 3.3).

Use of the return statement is illustrated in Listing 3.4, which shows how to develop the CRC-16 block-checking code used by communications programs to implement error-free file-transfer programs. If you are interested in communications programming, you will find this routine useful.

The calc_crc16() function receives a pointer to an array of unsigned characters (the incoming message), together with a length parameter, because the array is not assumed to be a null-terminated string. The array is processed by the while loop, and the unsigned integer (16-bit) CRC-16 block-checking code is returned.

Listing 3.4. CRC16.C shows a function returning a value (for all compilers).

```
1   #include <stdlib.h>
2
3   unsigned calc_crc16( char *msgpoly, int bytes )
4   {
5      static unsigned crc16 = 0;
6      static int i;
7
8      while ( 0 < bytes-- ) {
9        crc16 = crc16 ^ ( int )*msgpoly++ << 8;
10       for ( i=0; i<8; i++ ) {
11         if ( crc16 & 0x8000 ) crc16 = crc16 << 1 ^ 0x1021;
12        else crc16 = crc16 << 1;
13        }
14     }
15     return( crc16 );
16  }
17
18  main()
19  {
20    printf( "%X\n", calc_crc16( "Test string.", 12 ) );
21  }
```

If you wanted to develop a CRC-16 checking code for a whole file (noncommunications application), you would have to alter the logic of the function. In the version shown, the next character is fetched by simply updating the array pointer (msgpoly++). To process a file (as some compression programs do), you could replace lines 3, 8, and 9 with:

```
3   unsigned calc_crc16( FILE *infile )
    ...
8     while ( !feof(infile) ) {
9       crc16 = crc16 ^ ( int )fgetc( infile ) << 8;
```

assuming that FILE *infile has been opened elsewhere.

Because functions that have type void are expected to return nothing, the return statement must either be omitted, or its expression deleted (code a semicolon only, with no expression). Listing 3.5 contains an interesting function with void type. It exchanges the contents of any two variables (or areas of RAM) without using temporary workspace of any kind.

Listing 3.5. EXCHANGE.C shows a function returning nothing (for Borland C++).

```
1   #include <stddef.h>
2   #include <stdlib.h>
3   #include <stdio.h>
4   #include <string.h>
5
6   /* +--------------------------------------------------+
7      + Exchange two areas of memory with no auxiliary
8      +    storage used.
9      +
10     + Calling sequence:
11     +
12     + mem_exchange( void *s1, void *s2, size_t n );
13     +
14     +    where s1 and s2 can be of any type (using
15     +    the appropriate casts). Two areas of
16     +    storage each "n" bytes long are exchanged in
17     +    place.
18     +--------------------------------------------------+
19  */
20  void mem_exchange( void *s1, void *s2, size_t n )
21  {
22    for ( ; n>0; n-- ) {
```

continues

Listing 3.5. Continued

```
23       *(unsigned char *)s1 ^= *(unsigned char *)s2;
24       *(unsigned char *)s2 ^= *(unsigned char *)s1;
25       *(unsigned char *)s1 ^= *(unsigned char *)s2;
26       (unsigned char *)s1 += 1;
27       (unsigned char *)s2 += 1;
28    }
29  }
30
31  main()
32  {
33    char s1[40] = "This is the FIRST string. ";
34    char s2[40] = "This is the SECOND string.";
35    int i1 = 255;
36    int i2 = 127;
37
38    clrscr();
39    printf( "%s\n%s\n", s1, s2 );
40    mem_exchange( (void *)s1, (void *)s2, strlen( s1 ) );
41    printf( "%s\n%s\n\n", s1, s2 );
42
43    printf( "%d\n%d\n", i1, i2 );
44    mem_exchange( (void *)i1, (void *)i2, sizeof( int ) );
45    printf( "%d\n%d\n\n", i1, i2 );
46  }
```

This odd little function is based on a result from Boolean algebra which states that you can exchange the contents of two fields, a and b, with the following sequence of exclusive-OR instructions:

```
a XOR b
b XOR a
a XOR b
```

Here the first operand always receives the result of the operation. Suppose, for example, that you wanted to exchange two fields containing the binary numbers 11110000 and 00001111. The sequence of operations, from left to right, is the following:

```
        a:11110000          b:00001111          a:11111111
XOR   b:00001111      XOR  a:11111111      XOR  b:11110000
      _____           _____          _____
new a: 11111111      new b:11110000      new a:00001111
```

As you can see, b has received its new value by the second exclusive-OR; a, by the third. On the PC, this method is almost as quick as moving one of the variables to a hold area while swapping; on some other machines, it is actually faster.

Calling the Function

You call the function whenever you want it to yield a result value, much like accessing a variable—you just state it. That is, you code the function name, open parentheses, list the actual parameter variables (or expressions), close parentheses, and supply a semicolon. Remember that the actual argument names do not have to be the same as the formal declaration names, only the same type. (They don't have to be different, either.)

You can think of the function call as producing its returned value in the exact "spot" at which the call is placed. In the case of mem_exchange(), the type was void; thus, the function call stood alone on a single line. In the case of calc_crc16(), an integer was returned and used directly as an argument in the printf() call. You just call the function wherever you normally would write a variable in an expression.

Summary

This chapter presented some extremely important material. Having read it, you should know the following:

■ What C's basic data types are, how to declare them, and how to write literal values for all the types.

■ What the limiting values for the basic types are.

■ The various ways to declare and initialize variables.

■ What local and global variables are, and how scope and duration of variables affect what you can do with them.

■ How to declare function prototypes and formal parameter lists, and how this affects where you can reference and place the functions you define.

■ How to write a function definition. You should understand how the various types of C statements are used in the function body, and how to return a value of the appropriate type to the caller.

■ How to call (invoke) a function, including where you can place the call, and how to use the returned value.

In the next chapter, you again move closer to the elemental building blocks of a C program—to get all the detail you need to control the programming process. Then the real fun starts, when you begin to look at how to put it all to use.

A Closer Look at C Programs

I n Chapter 3, you learned about the broadest classes of elements that make up a C program. The details of data and functions discussed in that chapter serve as the foundation for this and later chapters.

This chapter expands, in greater and deeper detail, on what goes into a C program—now you will see the irreducible elements of C source code. In particular, you will learn the following:

- What characters you can use to write C programs and how to handle special requirements for them.

- How the compiler works, how you define for it the names you want to use, and how you can avoid misusing the names C reserves for itself.

- How to write and use C macros and other preprocessing directives.

More Detail on Language Conventions

A *language convention* is nothing more than the "legal" way to do something. You have already seen some of C's conventions in its punctuation and general format. Now it's time to get down to details and define just what can go into a valid C program.

The C Character Set

The idea of a *character set* is not as strange as you might think. The Greek alphabet (character set) is different from the English, as are the Russian and Hebrew alphabets. Everyone—even those who are not masters of those languages—is familiar with that fact.

The C character set is a subset of English characters and Arabic numerals, plus some other special characters. You must know two things about C characters: what ANSI considers to be a character and which characters compose the ANSI C required character set.

Bits, Bytes, and Characters

The ANSI standard for C considers a *character* to be something that fits in one byte and is a member of the basic character set of either the source environment or the target environment. Source and target character sets are discussed later in this chapter. The other terms are more important for now.

The way information is stored in the memory of a digital computer controls what ANSI defines to be bits, bytes, and characters. At the lowest level, information is stored in a *bit*, or *binary digit.* Electronically, a bit can be either off or on; thus, it can store the values 0 and 1—nothing else. Normally, individual bits are not used to store significant amounts of information, however. Bits are used in groups.

A *byte* is a collection of bits that can store some recognizable datum: a number or a character code. Almost universally, eight bits compose a byte, although the ANSI standard leaves the specific number up to the hardware and the compiler. In this book, a byte always means a group of eight bits, and a character also is assumed to occupy eight bits of storage.

The bits in a byte are numbered for handy reference. In this book, the *least significant* bit is considered to be bit 0; the *most significant* bit, bit 7 (see Figure 4.1). Least significant and most significant mean the least and greatest contribution, respectively, to the value of the complete number.

Figure 4.1 is the exploded view of a byte's structure. Moving from low- to high-order positions, the bits have corresponding decimal values that are successive powers of two. You can convert the binary value of a byte to decimal by noticing which bits are "on" (have a 1 value) and summing all the decimal values. The binary number 00010001, for example, has the decimal value 16 + 1 = 17.

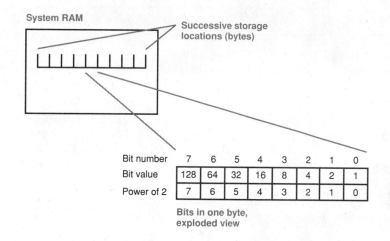

Bit number	7	6	5	4	3	2	1	0
Bit value	128	64	32	16	8	4	2	1
Power of 2	7	6	5	4	3	2	1	0

Bits in one byte,
exploded view

Figure 4.1.

Bit number, values, and
powers of two.

If a byte is composed of 8 bits, it can store 256 different numeric values: 0 through 255. Is each of these values considered a character? Yes, but there are different types of characters, depending on their numeric values. In the computer industry, the term *character* implies two concepts: *display* characters and *control* characters. To express all display and control characters in the English character set, the entire range of byte values is not required. (Later in this chapter you see how ANSI has provided for languages that require more than 256 values.)

Display characters do exactly what the name implies. The computer sends them to an output device and displays them in a form that you can read. Naturally, every device attached to a particular computer must assume that the same byte values represent a given character. The numeric values assigned to display characters (as well as to control characters) make up a machine's collating sequence.

Control characters are assigned a common sense significance by the ANSI standard. Primarily, they are motion-control characters. The presence of these characters in text indicates how the text will be formatted and positioned. A horizontal tab character, for example, means that the output device is to move some predetermined number of extra spaces before the next display character. The motion-control characters are meant to control interactive I/O devices that produce output you can see (like displays and printers) but not storage devices (like disks). Storage devices record the control characters but take no action because of them.

Compiler Dependency: The Collating Sequence

Every machine has a character set, and every character set has a collating sequence. A *collating sequence* is the sequence of numerical values assigned to each character in the set. Each C compiler must take into account the character set and collating sequence with which it is used.

The collating sequence must be chosen so the characters appear in the correct order when sorted (which is controlled by the numeric values). ANSI requires that the values associated with the numerical display characters (0-9) be not only in order, but also contiguous—there must be no gaps in the sequence. Gaps between the values assigned to other characters may exist.

Do not confuse the terms *collating sequence* and *number system*. For example, the decimal value for an ASCII blank is 32. This value can be expressed equally well by the hexadecimal number 20 or the binary number 100000. Although the IBM PC, its compatibles, and many other computers are ASCII machines, the ANSI standard for C does not presume that the computer used the ASCII character set. C is implemented also on IBM mainframes, for example, which use the EBCDIC character set and collating sequence.

The C Minimal Character Set

ANSI standard C is not tied to the ASCII character set, but it is intimately tied to the English language. All the English letters, a selected group of English graphic characters, and the Arabic numerals are required by the standard.

The required characters compose the *minimal character set* for C. This does not mean that compiler vendors cannot implement additional characters; they can and do—fortunately for the programmers and users.

Characters can be used in two ways: they can be part of the C source language, or they can be elements of the data with which the program must work. Most of the characters in the minimal set are used in C source language; they can all be used as data elements.

Quick Reference: The C Minimal Character Set

Compilers conforming to the ANSI C standard must support the following letters and characters:

A B C D E F G H I J K L M N O P Q R S T U V W X Y Z

a b c d e f g h i j k l m n o p q r s t u v w x y z

> 0 1 2 3 4 5 6 7 8 9
>
> ! " # % & ' ( ) * + , - . / : ; < = > ? [\ ] ^ _ { | } ~
>
> ANSI C compilers must also support a space (blank), horizontal and vertical tabs, a form feed, an end-of-line indicator (a single newline character), a bell, a backspace, and a carriage return.
>
> In addition, the numerical values of the digits 0 through 9 must be successively one greater than the preceding one in the list.

The characters in the minimal C character set can be classified also according to whether they are whitespace, control, upper- or lowercase, printable, hex digit, decimal digit, alphanumeric, punctuation, alphabetic, or graphic in nature. The is...() family of functions can test for all of these categories. Figure 4.2 shows how these categories are grouped.

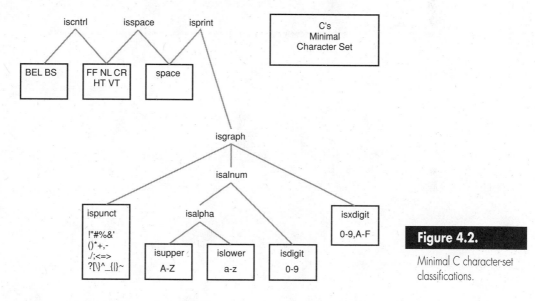

Figure 4.2.

Minimal C character-set classifications.

Handling Special Characters

At the end of the "Quick Reference: The C Minimal Character Set" C-Note, several of the required C characters are described in words (instead of simply being shown) because they are control characters, not display characters. Except for the space character, these special control characters are used in text data (like the text you are reading now) to manage its format and position.

If control characters are required but are not display characters (meaning that you normally cannot type them), how do you use them in your programs? To write a control character into the source code of your program, you use an escape sequence.

An *escape sequence* is two characters written together. The first of these characters must be a backslash (\), and the second one depends on what you want to do. Listing 4.1 shows how to use escape sequences in a program. ESCAPE.C uses the horizontal tab character '\t' and the newline character '\n' to format a simple report with the printf() function.

As you look at the program, notice how the escape sequences are used. Remember that character *strings* are enclosed in double quotation marks ("This is a character string!"). Character *constants* are enclosed in single quotation marks (the character *a* is written 'a'). Character constants are not used in Listing 4.1, but you code the escape sequences in exactly the same way: '\n' is the newline character.

Listing 4.1. Using special characters in *printf()*. (All compilers.)

```
 1   /*+----------------------------------------------------------+
 2    +                          ESCAPE.C
 3    +  An example of the use of special character constants.
 4    +----------------------------------------------------------+
 5   */
 6
 7   #include <stdio.h>
 8   #include <stdlib.h>
 9
10   main()
11   {
12   /* ----- Set up salespersons' names ----- */
13     char sp1[5] = "John";
14     char sp2[5] = "Joe";
15
16   /* ----- Set up sales amounts for month ----- */
17     float sales1 = 1287.63;
18     float sales2 = 1301.50;
19
20   /* ----- Commission rate ----- */
21     float comm = 0.08;
22
23     printf( "\t   *** Sales Report for January ***\n");
24     printf( "Salesman\t\t%s\t\t%s\n", sp1, sp2 );
```

```
25     printf( "--------\t\t--------\t\t--------\n" );
26     printf( "Sales\t\t\t%4.2f\t\t%4.2f\n", sales1, sales2 );
27     printf( "Commission\t\t%4.2f\t\t%4.2f\n",
28        sales1 * comm, sales2 * comm );
29  }
```

This program's output looks like the following:

```
    *** Sales Report for January ***
Salesman        John        Joe
--------        ------      ------
Sales           1287.63     1301.50
Commission      103.01      104.12
```

Mnemonic Escape Sequences

The letters assigned as the second character of the two-character escape sequences are meant to be *mnemonic* (easy to remember). Be sure to select letters that make sense, such as *a* for alert, *b* for backspace, and so on. You can use these escape sequences in character strings:

```
char stuff[40] = "First sentence.\n";  /* In a string */
```

or in character constants:

```
char m;
...
m = '\r';                              /* In a constant */
```

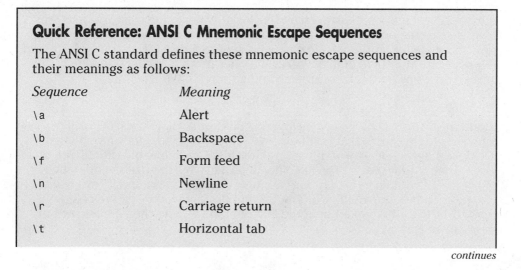

Quick Reference: ANSI C Mnemonic Escape Sequences

The ANSI C standard defines these mnemonic escape sequences and their meanings as follows:

Sequence	Meaning
\a	Alert
\b	Backspace
\f	Form feed
\n	Newline
\r	Carriage return
\t	Horizontal tab

continues

> ## Quick Reference: ANSI C Mnemonic Escape Sequences
>
> | Sequence | Meaning |
> | --- | --- |
> | \v | Vertical tab |
> | \' | Single quotation mark |
> | \" | Double quotation mark |
> | \? | Question mark |
> | \\ | Backslash |
>
> Even though you need two keystrokes to write these sequences into your program's source code, they occupy (internally) exactly one character—one byte. The numerical values assigned to these characters do not have to be displayable characters (on some output devices, they are).

When sent to an output device, the *alert character* produces an audible or visible alert—a tone or a graphic message. This is not a motion-control character because it makes no difference in the formatting or positioning of text. For example,

```
putchar( '\a' );     /* Sound the alert bell */
```

The *backspace character* moves the active position (of the cursor, for example) to the preceding position on the line. This does not necessarily destroy the preceding character. If the active position is already at the beginning of the line, ANSI does not specify what should happen. The following statement causes the capital letter *A* to be underlined if output is directed to a printer:

```
puts( "A\b_\n" );          /* Underline it via Backspace */
```

Form feed is a motion-control character for only some devices. When a form feed is sent to a printer, the current page is ejected and the printer positions the next page for writing. If a form feed is sent to a disk file, its only effect is to consume another byte of disk space. Whether it has any effect on a display screen depends on the software driving the screen. For example,

```
putchar( '\f' );          /* Eject to new page */
```

Standard C regards the *newline character* in a somewhat special light. The ANSI specification requires that text files (see Chapters 2 and 9 for more on text files) "… have some way of indicating the end of each line of text …," but does not say what that way is. The specification then says that these end-of-line markers are treated as if they were a single newline character. The *newline character* is a motion-control character that first moves the active position (the cursor) to the initial position of the line (column 1), and then moves it to the next line of text.

The newline character usually is denoted by either the abbreviation *NL* (for newline) or *LF* (for line feed); on ASCII systems, it has a decimal numerical value of 10. The term line feed ordinarily is used to describe the process of moving the current position down one line, but not to the first column. The term newline is more accurate when describing C programs. You can demonstrate that NL has a decimal value of 10 by running this short program:

```
#include <stdio.h>
main()
{
  printf( "%d\n", (int)'\n' );
}
```

This program prints the decimal number 10 (the value for LF as well as for NL). Notice that the \n character is used twice: once between the double quotation marks and once between single quotation marks. The characters between the double quotation marks—the first parameter—are the *format string* for the printf() function. They tell the function how to format the output. The number is printed (displayed on-screen) as a decimal number (%d causes this), and then the newline action is taken (\n causes this).

The second parameter

```
(int)'\n'
```

tells printf() what to print. This construction means that the NL character ('\n') is to be converted to an integer by (int). Then the newline character is used as an argument for printing. This type of conversion is called a *type cast*. You will learn more about type casts in chapter 5.

The *carriage-return character* is similar to newline in that it *homes* the cursor (sets the active position to the initial position). However, it differs from newline in that it does not move the active position to the next line. The abbreviation *CR* frequently denotes carriage return; on ASCII systems, it has a decimal numerical value of 13. To demonstrate this difference, you can modify the code by substituting \r for each \n.

Compiler Dependency: Terminating Text Lines

ANSI does not specify what the line-terminating characters should be, nor does it tie character-set requirements to the ASCII character set. However, on most ASCII machines you find that the compiler vendors have chosen the carriage return and line feed pair of characters to terminate text lines because most text editors store text files using this convention. C interprets these characters as a single newline when dealing with files in text mode. This is not true when performing I/O in binary mode.

continues

Compiler Dependency: Terminating Text Lines

You do not normally code \r\n in your programs—you should use '\n' for all text mode I/O. C's formatted I/O functions, in particular, expect to translate newline to the CR/LF pair of characters. Writing a short program that uses the following printf() statement might be instructive:

```
printf( "%d\r\n", (int)'\n' );
```

Run the program with and without the '\r'—noticing, in each case where the cursor falls. There should be no difference. To determine why this is so, use the escape sequence definitions presented earlier.

The *horizontal tab* (HT) character—'\t'—sets tabs in the same way that a typewriter sets tabs. When the program encounters an HT, it moves the current position right (in English systems) to the next tab position. What is the next tab position? Whatever the software you happen to be running decides it is. The Borland editor, for example, sets the tabs to every eighth column by default. The implication is that if your program is to deal with tabs, you must decide where they are set. Most ASCII printers can be directed to set tab stops at user-defined positions.

The *vertical tab* (VT) character has meaning only when sent to the printer. Almost all ASCII printers can handle the VT in some way. VT is recognized also by some PC communications programs that emulate an ASCII terminal.

The remaining escape sequences seem somewhat cryptic until you review what you have learned about writing character constants, character strings, and escape sequences. The compiler recognizes each of these elements by means of certain characters: double or single quotation marks, or a backslash. What if you want to use these special characters as data, not C punctuation?

Whether you need an escape sequence to code a single quotation mark as a data element depends on the context. If there can be no confusion about the meaning, an escape sequence is not required. For example,

```
puts( "This isn't an error." );    /* Good, no confusion */
```

However, if you try to write the code for a single quotation mark as a character constant like this:

```
putchar( ''' );                        /* Very bad */
```

the compiler flags this as an error. To get around the problem, C provides yet another escape sequence for the single quotation mark character. To display a single quotation mark alone, use this call to putchar():

```
putchar( '\'' );                       /* Very good */
```

Using a double quotation mark as data inside a string is no problem, either. You do it much the same way:

```
puts( "Jack said, \"Hello!\"" );    /* Quoting a quote! */
```

Getting the compiler to recognize a single or double quotation mark as data is one thing—but what about the backslash character? If you want the backslash character to appear as a data character in a string or character constant, you have to introduce it as an escape sequence, as follows:

```
puts( "The backslash character \\ is special." );
```

This call to `puts()` produces the following output:

```
The backslash character \ is special.
```

Finally, the ANSI C specification provides for the escape sequence \?. This sequence, new to C, was developed specifically to accommodate other facilities introduced by the ANSI standard for C. Its purpose is to allow a sequence of two question marks "??" to be coded (as part of a string, for example) without triggering the trigraph escape sequence mechanism (covered later in this chapter). Write the string as follows:

```
puts( "What's happening, hmm?\?" );
```

This call produces the following output:

```
What's happening, hmm??
```

Numeric Escape Sequences

As if all those escape sequences were not enough, ANSI C also provides for *numeric escape sequences,* in which a backslash character is followed by a numeric—rather than character—constant. By using numeric escape sequences, you can insert any of the 256 possible values into a character constant or string. Just as with mnemonic escape sequences, you can use the numeric escapes between single or double quotation marks for constants and strings.

Numeric escape sequences can be tricky because the compiler always interprets the numeric digits to be either octal or hexadecimal, not decimal. Octal escape sequences are composed of the backslash and from one to three octal digits (the octal digits are 0–7). Here are some examples of octal escape sequences:

Sequence	Meaning
\0	The null character. Very important in C; terminates all strings.
\123	A single byte, decimal value 83.
\779	Two bytes because 9 is not octal. This sequence is valid only in a string, such as "AB\779". Octal 77 is decimal 63, the ASCII '?' character. Therefore, this string is equivalent to "AB?9".
\88	An error because 8 is not a valid octal digit.

Notice that octal escape sequences are completed when either three octal digits or a nonoctal digit has been encountered, whichever occurs first.

Hexadecimal escape sequences begin with the backslash followed by an *x* and either one or two digits (0–9, and A–F), as in these examples:

Sequence	Meaning
\x0	The null character. It's not usually coded this way but would work perfectly.
\x0D	The CR (carriage return) character.
\xFF	Value depends on whether the compiler considers characters to be signed or unsigned. If signed, this code has the decimal value –1; if unsigned, the value 255. Be careful of the high-order bit.
\xFG	Valid only in a string, such as "A\xFG\xE". The \xF and \xE characters have values of 15 and 14, respectively, and are the SI (Shift In) and SO (Shift Out) ASCII control characters. You might send such a sequence to a printer, for example.
\SS	Invalid because S is not a valid hexadecimal digit.

The hexadecimal escape sequence is terminated only when a non-hexidecimal digit is encountered, but the value of the resulting number must not exceed 255 (or hex FF). The hex escape sequences are probably the most useful because most programmers tend to work with hex rather than binary or octal notations.

Using Trigraphs

The escape sequences discussed so far represent the class of notation called *digraphs,* in which two characters are written to represent one that cannot be typed directly. The escape sequences are used to write character *data* as opposed to C keywords, expressions, or other language elements.

The problem of entering certain symbols directly may extend to the actual source code, however. A particular computer's keyboard, for example, may not be able to handle some of the graphic characters that C requires for its normal syntax. ANSI standard C accommodates this situation by providing *trigraph escape sequences.* Clearly, you can use trigraphs also to code special characters in constants and strings.

The concept of trigraph sequences flows naturally and intuitively from the escape sequences you just learned. Whereas the escape character for mnemonic and numeric escapes is the backslash (\), the escape character for the trigraphs is a question mark (?), coded twice; for example, ??= is the trigraph for the # character.

Quick Reference: ANSI C Trigraphs

Following are the nine trigraphs in the ANSI C specification:

Trigraph	Replacement For
??=	#
??(	[
??/	\
??)	]
??'	^
??<	{
??!	¦
??>	}
??-	~

The trigraphs listed here are all that exist. Any others produce a compile-time error. In any context other than a trigraph sequence, the meaning of a question mark does not change.

You can use the trigraph sequences anywhere in the source file that the characters they represent normally appear. For example, the code fragment

```
if ( a == b ) {
  a = 1;
  b = a * 3;
}
```

can be written as follows, with the same meaning for the compiler:

```
if ( a == b ) ??<
  a = 1;
  b = a * 3;
??>
```

This second code fragment is not as easy to read as the first, but it is legitimate. If your keyboard does not have the curly-brace characters ({ and }), the second fragment is the only way to go.

Multibyte Characters

All the character encodings discussed to this point use a single byte of storage because the character sets do not require all 256 values possible in a byte.

This works fine in Western countries with relatively small alphabets. In other countries—notably Japan, China, and other Asian countries—this approach doesn't work at all.

To be specific, the written Japanese and Chinese languages do not use alphabets. They use ideograms, which are highly stylized pictorially based graphic objects. The problem is that tens of thousands of code values are needed to represent all possible "characters."

Multibyte characters are the ANSI C answer to this dilemma. A *multibyte character* is a sequence of one or more bytes that represent a single character. The addition of multibyte characters to the single-byte characters results in an *extended character set*. The following rules govern the use of multibyte characters:

- The extended character set must include the minimal C character set.

- The use and meaning of any extended characters are considered to be locale specific. That is, there is no preferred multibyte encoding. You must be familiar with each specific one.

- Multibyte sequences are triggered much like the escape sequences. When any one of a set of multibyte characters appears in a string or constant, the compiler expects the next single character (or sequence of them) to complete the multibyte sequence. One result is that when a multibyte sequence starts in a string, the next character cannot be checked to determine whether it is a normal escape character or the closing quotation mark of the string.

- A multibyte sequence may use a *state-dependent coding*. The different possible states are called *shift states*. Each multibyte sequence begins in an initial state, in which each byte is considered to be a single normal character, as with the minimal set. Other shift states (which vary with locale and the specific compiler) are entered when certain multibyte character codes are encountered. For example, in `"\81a"` and `"\82a"`, the a might mean two different character representations if the 0x81 and 0x82 values mean different shift states.

- The null character `\0` may not be part of a multibyte encoding. That is, the null character is always a single-byte code with all bits zero.

You can deal with multibyte characters in two ways. First, you can deal with them as a *normal string*. This makes sense because a multibyte character is a series of several bytes (characters). Second, you can convert multibyte characters to an internal format called *wide characters*. Wide characters are just integer types that can hold much larger values than a single byte. ANSI C provides a set of conversion functions for translating between the two formats.

Source and Target Character Sets

Before you leave the topic of C characters, we must say something about the distinction between source and target character sets. The *source character set* is the one in which you write the source code for your C program. It is the character set native to the machine on which you are running the editor and compiler.

The *target character set,* on the other hand, can be entirely different. The target character set is assumed to be present when the program runs at a later time. If the program runs on the machine on which it was compiled, the source and target sets are the same.

If the program runs on a different machine—if a cross-compiler is used—the target character set might be completely different. For example, certain compilers are used on a PC to develop code that runs on a mainframe. In that case, the source character set would be ASCII, whereas the target character set might be EBCDIC.

How C Looks at Your Source Program

Suppose that you have just finished writing a new C program—a statistical analysis program. Think for a moment about what you expect your program to do. It should do three things: get some data from somewhere, process the data according to the rules, and produce some significant numerical results.

Like wheels within wheels, this is exactly the way the C compiler views your program: as data. A C source program—also called a *translation unit*— inputs to the compiler, which transforms that data into machine-executable code. The result of source-file translation is the *object file.* Later, the linkage editor takes this object file, and possibly others, and combines them to produce an executable file, also called a *load module.*

The Phases of Program Translation

Figure 4.3 shows the process by which a C source program is translated into machine code. C compilers, like almost all modern compilers, are *syntax directed*— compilation is controlled by the syntactical structure of the source, which is recognized by the parser. Thus, C compilers share the features shown here with many other compilers. You must have a basic understanding of the terms and processes involved in compilation.

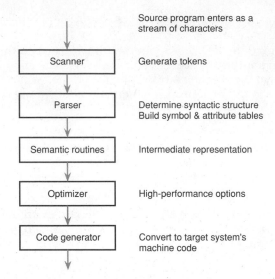

Source program enters as a
stream of characters

Scanner — Generate tokens

Parser — Determine syntactic structure
Build symbol & attribute tables

Semantic routines — Intermediate representation

Optimizer — High-performance options

Code generator — Convert to target system's
machine code

Figure 4.3.

The C compiler at work.

The compiler reads the source file one character at a time and feeds each one to the *scanner*. The scanner's function is to recognize and feed to the parser *tokens*—discrete elements of the source code. Examples of tokens include keywords, identifiers, constants, and punctuation marks.

The *parser* determines how the elements are grouped. In C, for example, an opening (left) parenthesis must follow an `if` keyword. If it does not, the parser flags a syntax error at that point. *Syntax checking* simply means checking the correct grouping of items in the source code.

If the syntactical structure is determined to be correct, the *semantic routines* take over. These routines supply the meaning of the program. In the C statement,

```
a = b;
```

for example, the parser notes that equating one variable to another (assigning the value) is legitimate. The semantic routines determine which variables are involved, their location in the program, and what must be done to assign the value of one to the other. The result of all this, called the *intermediate representation,* frequently is stored in a temporary file on-disk to make it available to the next phases. All phases so far contribute to information stored in the *symbol table*—a record of the keywords and names used in the program, along with information about how they can be used.

If an optimizer module is present (most good compilers offer one), the intermediate representation of the program is "cleaned up." Unnecessary instructions are removed, loop bodies are made more efficient, and more efficient methods of constructing the machine code in general are implemented. Using an optimizer can be very costly in the time it takes to compile the program. Most compilers that support optimizers enable you to use them as an option, not a default action.

Finally, the code generator takes the intermediate representation and uses it to produce the *target machine code*. This is the object code mentioned earlier, which is used by the linkage editor to produce the final load module. A compiler that uses separate sets of semantic routines and code generators is called a *two-pass compiler*. If these functions are merged, it is called a *one-pass compiler*. One-pass compilers impose some restrictions on the way your source code is structured.

This is only the barest introduction to compiler theory. If you want to go into detail (perhaps to learn how to write a compiler with C), there are good books available on designing and creating compilers. This subject, however, requires some knowledge of computer science or at least a great deal of programming experience.

The ANSI C document specifies that a conforming compiler functions as though eight discrete phases of translation take place consecutively (even if, in practice, the tasks are merged). Actually, only the last two of the phases have to do with actual translation of source code to machine code. The phases of translation are as follows:

1. Source-file characters are mapped to the source character set. Mapping includes converting trigraphs to single-character codes and end-of-line indicators to the newline character.

2. Continued lines of source code are spliced together to make single logical lines. You indicate a continued line by typing a backslash before pressing Enter. This is especially useful for writing string literals longer than one line of your display.

3. The compiler breaks the source file into preprocessing tokens (see the next section) and whitespace sequences (review Figure 4.2's `isspace` group). During this phase, comments also are considered to be whitespace, and each is replaced by a single space.

4. Preprocessing directives are executed and macro references expanded. The `#include` directive causes reading of the current file to be suspended and processing of the named `include` file to begin. The included file is processed to this point only, and processing of the previously current file resumes. `Includes` can be *nested* (coded inside each other).

5. Escape sequences and string literals are converted to the execution character set, which could be a different character set if a cross-compiler is used.

6. Adjacent character strings are spliced into their internal format. You can, therefore, define a string with its initializer, as follows:

```
char *astring = "This is a str"
                "ing.";
```

This construction is equivalent to the following:

```
char *astring = "This is a string.";
```

This syntax, which was not available with the original K&R C, is extremely convenient. With it you can define long string literals without having to resort to the line-continuation backslash.

7. The first stage of actual translation now begins. All tokens are now considered ordinary, not preprocessing, tokens. The parser and semantic routines do their work here.

8. The final phase is the linkage edit process. References in one source file to objects and functions in other source files are resolved here (that is, their correct relative addresses are calculated), and the final load module is created. This phase is also where the compiler brings the C library functions into the program. The load module is packaged with all information needed for program execution in the target environment.

Tokens and Translation Units

The term *translation units* was introduced to emphasize the fact that what will become a single C program can begin life as separate source files. These source files—*the multiple translation units*—can be compiled individually and only later linked into a composite load module. This capability becomes important when you begin to design and code large-scale projects.

As you learned earlier in this discussion, tokens are the elements detected by the scanner. To complicate matters, however, there are preprocessing tokens and ordinary tokens. *Preprocessing tokens* are handled during macro expansion (phase four of the translation process) and eventually result in ordinary tokens. The compiler then handles the ordinary tokens during actual code translation.

There are six types of ordinary tokens:

- *Keywords*. These are special tokens with reserved meanings. You already have seen several keywords, such as `if`, `else`, `while`, `int`, and `double`. Keywords are the grammatical basis of the C language.

- *Identifiers*. These are the names you define for your variables and user-defined functions.

- *Constants*. These are the values of the variables. You already have seen character constants, as well as several numeric constants. You can change the value of a variable, but not that of a constant. Don't confuse this type of constant with the const type variable. Such variables are similar to true constants in that you cannot change the value of a const qualified variable.

- *String literals.* The string literals you have seen in the sample programs and code fragments are exactly what they seem to be: one-dimensional arrays of characters. As mentioned in the discussion of escape characters, all strings are terminated with the \0 null character.

 NOTE You do not have to type the \0 escape when you write a string literal; the compiler adds it internally and automatically.

- *Operators.* These are the symbols used to relate and connect the parts of expressions. You are familiar with many of them (such as =, +, -, *, and /). C has a rich operator set, and there are many more than these. Each operator symbol is a token.

- *Punctuators.* The compiler considers the C punctuators you learned in Chapter 1, "Getting Started With C," to be individual tokens.

Identifiers in General

An identifier names an object, which may be any one of the following:

- A *data object.* A data object's name is simply a variable name. If it is defined in another source file, you must declare it as an external name. An external object has a storage class of extern.

- A *user-defined function.* The identifier of a user-defined function cannot be main.

 NOTE Functions, unlike data objects, are assigned the extern storage class automatically.

- One of the following: a structure tag or member, a union tag or member, the name of an enumeration, a typedef (type definition) name, a statement label, a macro name, or a macro parameter.

Although an identifier can be almost anything you want it to be, you must observe the following rules in forming identifiers:

- An identifier cannot be one of the C keywords. The keywords are reserved exclusively for use as part of C's basic grammar.

- An identifier is an alphanumeric token that must begin with a pure alphabetic character. It can be composed of upper- and lowercase letters, the decimal digits, and the underscore character. The first character must be either an upper- or lowercase letter or the underscore character.

■ Avoid using an underscore as the first character of an identifier. It is common practice, however, to use the underscore in the middle of names to give some visual cues in reading the program. For example, it is much easier to read the following line:

```
a = calc_std_dev( table );
```

than it is to read this line:

```
a = calcstddev( table );
```

CAUTION

> The underscore character is reserved for the compiler's internal naming scheme for external identifiers. Generally, to avoid duplicating an identifier in one of the standard header files, you should not use the underscore as the *initial character*.

■ Internal identifiers (as opposed to externals) have names significant to 31 characters. Names can be longer than this, but they must differ within 31 characters to be considered different by the compiler. In K&R C, names had only eight significant characters.

■ External identifiers have names significant to only six characters. Although a particular compiler may provide more significance than this, you can't count on it if you want to port your program to several different compilers.

■ Names in C source code are *case-sensitive:* whether the character is upper- or lowercase makes a difference. ANSI allows a compiler to ignore case sensitivity for external names, however; it depends on the particular C compiler and on the compiler used to process the external routine (which might not have been C).

Using C Reserved Words

ANSI C reserves a total of 32 tokens for use as keywords. The reserved words are the backbone of C grammar. You cannot duplicate any of the reserved words as you develop your own identifiers. You should not duplicate several reserved function and macro names, although you can.

The C Keywords

A keyword means only one thing to a C compiler. The ANSI standard for C defines as keywords the 32 tokens shown in the "Quick Reference: ANSI C Keywords" C-Note.

Quick Reference: ANSI C Keywords

auto	double	int	struct
break	else	long	switch
case	enum	register	typedef
char	extern	return	union
const	float	short	unsigned
continue	for	signed	void
default	goto	sizeof	volatile
do	if	static	while

What happens if you accidentally use a keyword in a way other than the way C expects? The program does not compile successfully, so this error can't slip by unnoticed. Therefore, this error is not as dangerous as it would be had the program compiled successfully.

Such a small number of keywords may seem inconsistent with the claim that C is a rich and complex language. It would be inconsistent if the complexity of C depended only on keywords. But the full power of C derives from its set of keywords, plus its rich operator set, plus its extensive function library.

The Standard Macros and Functions

C has always had a fairly uniform set of library functions, although different compilers provided some interesting variations. ANSI C has now defined the contents of the truly *standard function library:* the functions and their respective types and parameters, as well as a large number of standardized macro names and constant values. Compiler manufacturers are free to add functions and macros beyond these but may not claim ANSI conformity unless the full set is present in the prescribed way. Appendixes B and C provide a summary of their names (and associated header libraries).

The standard function and macro names also are considered reserved—but there is a difference between these names and C keywords. You should not duplicate the standard names, but doing so may not produce an error at compile time (or any other time). Duplicating the names does (at least) prevent you from using the standard function; your function is the only function by that name available in that program (it doesn't damage the library in any way). You already have seen the printf() function used frequently in the code samples, for example. The printf() function is one of the standard library functions, but it is perfectly legal (in a sense) to write your own printf() function, as shown in the following code fragment:

```
#include <stdio.h>
void printf( void )
```

```
{
  putchar( 'f' );
}
main()
{
  printf();
}
```

There is some protection from inadvertently redefining library functions, though. As noted, this program is legal—in a sense. In fact, `printf()` is declared in STDIO.H as having a certain type and certain parameters. Because this new definition doesn't match that declaration, there is a compile-time error. The danger is that you may duplicate name, type, and parameters accidentally. In that case, your version of the function is the only one available for the duration of the program.

Using Compiler Directives and Macros

By using *compiler directives,* you can control how the compiler goes about translating source code. You can control the contents of the source code by using *macro substitution.* You can also control the way compile-time errors are handled, you can set up line-number controls for debugging, and you can control the environment in which the compiler works. All this is done by using the C preprocessor.

Revisiting the C Preprocessor

The C preprocessor, which was mentioned in the discussion of C tokens and the translation process, does its work before the compilation process begins. The preprocessor may be bundled with the compiler, or it may be a separate utility. In some compilers the preprocessor is available both ways to give you maximum control over the compilation process. Either way, the source code passes first through the preprocessor and is transformed in some way before the compiler is ready to generate machine code. The next few sections outline the preprocessor directives and how they work.

Before you continue reading, take a moment to review what you learned about preprocessor directives in Chapter 1. Remember the following:

■ All preprocessor directives begin with the # character, which signals that this line is not part of the ordinary source code.

■ The semicolon character is handled differently in preprocessor directives. Don't code one in a macro definition unless you want it to appear in the resulting source code.

■ Don't mix preprocessing directives and C source code on the same line. The directives must be on a line by themselves, terminated by a *physical* end-of-line character (that is, by pressing the Enter key, not by coding the \n escape sequence).

■ Additionally, preprocessing tokens nested in a preprocessing directive are not expanded as macros, except in the cases noted in the next few sections.

Other restrictions on how you can code a directive depend on which one it is; these restrictions are covered in the discussions of specific directives.

The Source File Inclusion Directive

Source file inclusion directives were discussed in Chapter 1 because of their almost universal presence. The format used to include the standard headers is just a specific application of a more generalized facility, however. In this section, you see how to include both header files and source text files in general.

Quick Reference: ANSI C Include Directives

Include Format	*Meaning/Use*
`#include <std-header-file>`	Standard/provided header files.
`#include "user-header-file"`	User-defined header files.
`#include macro-name`	A previously defined macro specifies the header filename.

The name used for a header file is assumed to be of the format *xxxxxx.x*, where the *x*s to the left of the period represent the name of the header file, and the single *x* to the right of the period represents the file extension. The following rules govern the included names:

■ The ANSI C standard allows (but does not require) a compiler implementation to ignore upper- and lowercase distinctions. Most implementations ignore case.

■ An implementation can limit (to six significant characters) the name to the left of the period. (Again, this is not required.) For maximum portability, imposing this restriction on yourself for actual header files might be wise. Most implementations, however, do not impose this restriction; they enable you to include any file in your program.

■ Normally, you should not use path overrides in the filenames for `includes` that use the standard header inclusion format (`<name>`). Although you can use path overrides for the user-defined format (`"name"`), you ordinarily shouldn't have to if you set your directories correctly.

■ The single character extension most often used for header files is *.H.* Using this extension is not a requirement, however; you can use any character you want. You are not required to limit yourself to one character, either, but doing so maximizes the program's portability.

■ The third format's name field is a macro name, not a filename. You could use this feature to write programs, such as the following, that are intended to run in several different environments:

```
#define SYS OS2
...
#if SYS == DOS
    #define INC "dosenv.h"
#elif SYS == OS2
    #define INC "os2env.h"
#else
    #define INC "all.h"
#endif
...
#include INC
```

The first line informs the preprocessor to substitute OS2 wherever the macro name SYS is encountered. Next, the value of SYS is tested by the `#if` directives (see "Conditional Compilation Directives," later in this chapter). Because SYS is equal to OS2, the macro name INC is set to `"os2env.h"` by the `#elif` directive (see "Macro Substitution Directives"). Finally, the `#include` directive is expanded to #include `"os2env.h"`. Writing the directives for such an arrangement takes some time and trouble. The advantage is that when the environment of the program changes, you have to make only one change to a macro instead of making many changes throughout the program.

A file that has been included may contain one or more #include directives, as well as the other types of directives. You can nest `includes` like this up to a limit decided by the implementation.

Macro Substitution Directives

A *macro* is a shorthand notation for something else. That "something else" may be something much longer than the macro name, something difficult to type, or something that can be made more readable by using a macro name for it.

When you think about C macros, remember that the C preprocessor is the program handling your program's code and that it treats the code as if it were data. It treats your code as a sequence of characters and strings of characters. Thus, *macro substitution* or *replacement* is a process of substituting one string of characters for another—the macro name is replaced by its defined substitution string, called the *replacement list*. Refer to the following C-Note for a summary of macro formats.

Quick Reference: ANSI C Preprocessor Macros

You can define a macro either as an *object-like* macro with a simple substitution string or as a *function-like* macro with arguments. And you can undefine a macro when it is no longer needed or when you want to redefine it for some other use.

```
#define identifier replacement-list
#define identifier(identifier-list) replacement-list
#undef identifier
```

The identifier immediately following the `#define` or `#undef` is the macro name. In object-like macros, the macro name is followed by the replacement list. The replacement list is called a "list" because it should be composed of valid C-language tokens. From the point of view of the preprocessor, the replacement list is just a character string used to replace the macro name wherever it appears. Whitespace surrounding the substitution string is not part of the substitution string; whitespace within it is.

Typical uses for object-like macros include the definition of common constants in a readable form (called *manifest constants*). For example, you frequently see the constants for true and false Boolean conditions coded as follows:

```
#define FALSE 0
#define TRUE 1
int table_sorted = FALSE;
void sort_table( void );
...
```

```
sort_table();
table_sorted = TRUE;
...
if ( table_sorted ) {
  /* Do something to the table */
}
```

You should not surround the substitution string by quotation marks (like a normal string literal) unless you intend the quotation marks to be part of the expanded text. The substitution string is assumed to begin with the first non-whitespace character following the macro name. For example, the macro definition

```
#define TSTRING "Text stuff."
```

does not result in the code you expected if you invoke the macro as follows:

```
char output[20];     /* Define 20-character string */
...
strcpy( output, "TSTRING" );  /* Now initialize it */
```

Because the second argument for `strcpy()` is inside a string literal, it is not expanded—the preprocessor does not look for macro names inside the quotation marks of string literals or character constants. You could correct this by deleting the double quotation marks in the function call but not those in the `#define` directive (because this would again require a search for macro names inside the quotation marks in the function call).

This example illustrates the fact that everything in the substitution string (including any comments you may code in the macro definition) is used to replace the macro name when the macro is invoked. The substitution string is terminated only by the end-of-line character that also terminates the macro definition. Semicolons are handled the same way—don't code one unless you intend it to appear in the expanded source text.

Function-like macros are more complex than object-like macros. They have a *formal argument list* that modifies and controls the substitution text. The formal arguments are placed inside parentheses immediately following the macro name. You don't have to use the same identifier for an argument when invoking the macro as when defining it. That is why it is called a "formal" argument. Here is an example of a function-like macro and its use:

```
#define CTOF(t) 9.0 / 5.0 * t + 32.0
double fahrenheit, centigrade;
...
centigrade = 15.0;
fahrenheit = CTOF(centigrade);
```

When the preprocessor spots the CTOF invocation in the last line of this example, it expands that macro name, substituting actual arguments. The following line of code results:

```
fahrenheit = 9.0 / 5.0 * centigrade + 32.0;
```

You can have as many arguments as you like, but you must use as many as you declare—don't put something in the argument list that is not referenced somewhere in the substitution string. Multiple arguments should be separated by commas in the formal parameter list. Also, when you invoke the macro, be sure that the number of arguments matches the number in the definition—see the following examples:

```
#define DIV(a,b) a / b          /* This is OK */
#define AVG3(a,b,c) (a+b+c)/3 /* This is OK, too */
#define COMP(a,b,c) a + b       /* Invalid, doesn't use c */
...
x = AVG3(m,n)                   /* Invalid, too few arguments */
```

> You should carefully control the use of whitespace in function-like macros. In the #define directive, the combination of the macro name followed immediately by the opening (left) parenthesis with no space in between identifies the macro as function-like. Why? If a space is there, the syntax seems to declare an object-like macro: there is no way for the preprocessor to determine that you did not intend the free-standing parenthesis to be part of the substitution string. With this one exception, you can use whitespace wherever you please.
>
> CAUTION

The same caveat about quotation marks and semicolons also applies to function-like macros. Don't use them unless you intend for them to appear in the macro expansion.

You can refer to a macro argument in the substitution string in not just one—but three—ways. You can refer to an argument:

- *By itself.* This way has already been illustrated. The macro name is replaced by the substitution string completely, with actual arguments replacing formal arguments but no other modifications to the replacement tokens.

- *Following the # operator.* In the context of macro argument substitution only, # is the string literal operator. If x is a macro argument, the appearance of #x in the substitution string causes "x" to appear in the expansion. That is, the string operator creates a data string in the expansion, with the expanded argument x as its contents. Clarifying examples follow.

■ *Preceding or following the ## operator.* Again in the context of macro argument substitution only, this is the string concatenation operator. The concatenation operator cannot appear by itself at the beginning or end of the substitution string because its whole purpose is to join the expanded argument with another C language token, forming a larger language string (not a data string). Unlike the string operator, the concatenation operator does not generate double quotation marks around the argument.

You can use the string operator # to create data strings enclosed in double quotation marks, as follows:

```
/* +-------------------------------------------------------+
   + STROP.C
   + Test the preprocessor's # string literal operator
   +-------------------------------------------------------+
*/
#include <stdlib.h>
#include <stdio.h>
#define STR(x) # x
main()
{
   printf( "%s\n", "This is " STR("Wednesday") "." );
}
```

The program's output looks like this on-screen:

```
This is "Wednesday".
```

This example illustrates several interesting things about the preprocessor string operator. First, notice the use of whitespace in the macro definition of STR(x). There is a space between the # operator and the argument x in the substitution string. This is perfectly legitimate and does not affect the manner of argument substitution. If there had been multiple arguments with whitespace between them, each instance of whitespace would have been reduced to a single space in the final substitution string. Extra whitespace before and after the substitution string as a whole would have been deleted.

Second, when STR(x) is invoked in the printf() function call, the argument used is "Wednesday" (not just Wednesday). The string operator causes the preprocessor not only to surround the argument with double quotation marks, which would produce the following erroneous code:

```
printf( "%s\n", "This is " ""Wednesday"" "." );
```

but also to generate backslashes to protect the " and \ characters encountered in the invocation, or actual, argument. The expanded macro results in the following:

```
printf( "%s\n", "This is " "\"Wednesday\"" "." );
```

As you may recall, the \" characters form the legitimate escape sequence for the double quotation marks. The final output, therefore, contains the properly quoted word "Wednesday".

Third, you can use concatenated data strings wherever you would define an ordinary quoted string literal. The preceding partially expanded `printf()` shows the format of concatenated string literals. The compiler (not the preprocessor) converts this to a single string literal definition that is equivalent to the following:

```
"This is \"Wednesday\"."
```

> Concatenated string literals can be used anywhere in C source text, not just in macros. Take special note of the fact that these substrings, because they are not arguments or parameters as such, are not separated by commas. They are not the same as the expanded C source tokens generated by the ## *preprocessor concatenation operator.*

T I P

With the ## preprocessing concatenation operator, you can flexibly create sequences of C source code, as well as data strings. The concatenation operator "pastes" together pairs of substrings; it does not supply quotation marks or protecting backslashes. If one of the substrings is also a macro, it is expanded before pasting occurs. For example, in the following macro call, the argument x is replaced with "2" before the substrings are pasted:

```
#define WHICH(x) sub_ ## x
result = WHICH(2)( 37 );
```

The second statement is expanded to

```
result = sub_2 ( 37 );
```

There are a few more questions about macro expansions: Can one macro generate another? How are comments handled in macros? How do you code long macros? What are some of the pitfalls to watch out for in coding C macros? You can find the answers to these questions in the following final points about macro expansion.

■ Macros are rescanned. After all the macro parameters have been located and expanded when a macro is invoked, the preprocessor rescans the result to see whether any macro names (new invocations) were generated. Thus, you can code the following:

```
#define vers 2
#define which(x) sub_ ## x
...
result = which(vers)( 37 );
```

The macro call to which is first expanded to sub_vers (37) and then finally to sub_2 (37). Be careful, however, to avoid generating the same name as the macro in the process of being replaced. This would cause a recursive, and infinite, expansion of the macro, so the preprocessor rescans and replaces any other macro name but not this one.

Notice that rescanning for macro names does not imply that preprocessor directives may be generated by macro expansions, nor may you generally embed directives within directives and rely on proper expansion of the embedded directives.

■ Comments are permissible in macros, as long as you understand how they are handled. Comments that appear in macro definitions also appear in later expansions of the macro. Remember that a macro definition ends only when a physical end-of-line character is found in scanning. Conversely, comments that appear in macro invocations do not appear in the expansion.

■ Long macro definitions are possible, using the backslash continuation character to get around the end-of-line condition:

```
#define longmac "Fourscore and seven years ago, our \
forefathers brought forth on this continent a new \
tax office to replace the old one."
```

The backslash characters do not become part of the expansion when longmac is invoked; you just get the very long string of characters. This is one place where the string concatenation syntax mentioned previously doesn't work—the macro must be contained in one logical line (the first newline character terminates the macro).

■ Macros are not expanded inside string literals and character constants. By the time parameter replacement begins during preprocessing, strings and character constants are already considered as tokens, not as possible macro names or objects that might contain macro names. The longmac macro has its quotation marks embedded in the macro definition, so this macro call is valid:

```
printf( "%s\n", longmac );
```

If the macro does not have embedded quotation marks, a reference to longmac produces a series of tokens— one for every word in longmac's sentence—which the compiler tries to interpret as variable names or other tokens. Moreover, if you try to get around that restriction by coding:

```
printf( "%s\n", "longmac" );
```

you still have a problem because longmac now is not scanned as a possible macro name.

■ Macros and complex arithmetic expressions don't mix well. The reason is operator precedence. This subject is covered in detail in Chapter 5, but you already probably know from algebra class that multiplications have higher precedence than additions. If you are not careful, combining macros and complex arithmetic expressions can cause insidious bugs in your program. For example,

```
#define SQUARE(x) x * x
```

looks deceptively simple. But what if you invoke the macro with the following argument:

```
y = SQUARE( x + 2 );
```

This argument does not expand in the way that you probably intended. You get the following result:

```
y = x + 2 * x + 2;
```

This expression actually reduces algebraically to $3x + 2$, not the intended $(x + 2) * (x + 2) = x^2 + 4x + 4$. You can use parentheses to force the proper grouping, either in the macro definition or its invocation. The definition is by far the best place to group, just in case you forget later. You could, for example, rewrite the SQUARE macro as follows:

```
#define SQUARE(x) (x) * (x)
```

Although this macro looks a little strange, it works. And it doesn't hurt if you write parentheses in both places, either.

Macros and complex arithmetic expressions don't mix well! Combining the two can cause insidious bugs in your program.

CAUTION

Conditional Compilation Directives

The *conditional compilation directives* are called the *conditional inclusion directives* in the ANSI document. Either description of these directives is apt because their purpose is to determine whether a section of source code is to be compiled. These directives commonly are used in the standard header files to determine whether the header has already been included. The mechanism works like this:

```
/* Contents of MYHDR.H File */
#if !defined ( MYHDR )
#define MYHDR
```

```
extern int a;
extern int b;
#endif
```

This code fragment first checks whether the macro name MYHDR has already been defined. If it has not (!defined), the next three lines define the macro name (an object-like macro—no function-like parameters in the substitution string) and declare two external variable identifiers (these two lines are now compiled). The last line (#endif) informs the preprocessor that this conditional directive is complete.

This construction prevents multiple declarations of a and b, while enabling you to include MYHDR.H whenever and wherever you feel you have to. It doesn't matter what macro name you choose for such a construction, but it clearly should be descriptive. Now study the "Quick Reference: ANSI C Conditional Directives" C-Note before reading about the directives' syntax.

Quick Reference: ANSI C Conditional Directives

In the following list of conditional preprocessing directives, the notation [!] indicates that the logical-NOT symbol ! may optionally be present:

```
#if [!]constant-expression
#elif [!]constant-expression
#else
#if [!]defined identifier
#if [!]defined ( identifier )
#ifdef identifier
#ifndef identifier
#endif
```

The constant-expression found in the #if and #elif directives is a numeric expression that must reduce to an integer value. It may contain arithmetic and logical operators, and it may contain macro names as described in the following paragraphs. When constant-expression is evaluated, macro names are first replaced by their corresponding strings.

After preliminary macro substitution, the resulting integer expression is evaluated as a Boolean expression (the result is either true or false). If the expression evaluates to 0 (false), the group of lines that the #if precedes is not included as part of the source code. If it evaluates to nonzero (true), the group of lines is included. The lines selected to be processed may contain other directives (such as #define or #include) or ordinary C source code. This does not violate the rule that prohibits embedding directives within directives.

Suppose that you want to determine whether to compile code that invokes a delay loop if the central processor is an 80386 chip. You could write a sequence of directives and code as follows:

```
#define CPU 286 /* Define cpu being used */
...
#if CPU == 386
#include "wait.h"   /* These two lines are not used */
wait_msec( 100 );   /* since CPU is == 286 */
#endif
```

All the conditional directives have two things in common: they all end with the #endif directive, and they all control the inclusion (use or exclusion) of one or more groups of code lines. A group of code lines is fittingly called a *line-group*.

The #if, #elif, and #else directives work together. You can have an #if-#endif standing alone but never an #elif or #else. They group together like this:

```
#if expression
      ... main line-group
#elif expression
      ... first alternate line-group
#elif expression
      ... next alternate line-group
... other #elifs
#else
      ... default line-group if nothing else selected
#endif
```

The presence of the #elif and #else is completely optional. If you do not code them, only the initial line-group is available for selection. The #endif, of course, is mandatory.

However complex the #if construction may be, only one of the line-groups is selected for inclusion in compilation. The preprocessor performs its test from the top down. If the initial if condition is true, only its line-group is retained and so on down the list. Notice that the #else has no conditional expression attached. If an #else directive is present and none of the other line-groups are selected, this one unconditionally is.

In the strictest sense, the #if defined ... and #ifdef forms are equivalent; they mean exactly the same thing. However, the newer #if defined form is preferred because it yields a clean, unmixed notation, as in the following example:

```
#include <stdio.h>
#define TEST3
main()
```

```
{
  #if defined TEST1
    puts( "Test ** 1 ** Selected.\n" );
  #elif defined TEST2
    puts( "Test ** 2 ** Selected.\n" );
  #elif defined TEST3
    puts( "Test ** 3 ** Selected.\n" );
  #else
    puts( "Don't know what was selected!\n" );
  #endif
}
```

When you run this program, it displays the following message

```
Test ** 3 ** Selected.
```

Line-Control, Error, Pragma, and Null

Four other directives are seldom used or are used in a way n
visible to the programmer. They are the #line, the #error, the
(or *null*) directives.

■ The #line directive is used for debugging and error rep
    time. Ordinarily, the line number of the line being proce
    compiler is equal to one more than the number of end-o
    characters encountered so far. You can change what lin
    compiler assigns to the next line encountered by writing
    directive:

    ```
    #line number
    ```

    whereby *number* is an integer number that is used to rep
    code line number (for example, when the compiler flags
    ing an error). This does not change the source file in an
    only the way line numbers are reported. This form of th
    fies the assigned value of the _ _LINE_ _ predefined macr
    section).

    You can also change the presumed name of the source
    piled with the following form of the #line directive:

    ```
    #line number "newname"
    ```

    In this case, the value of _ _LINE_ _ is modified as before
    predefined macro _ _FILE_ _ is modified to reflect the va
    literal "*newname*", which must be enclosed in quotation

Suppose that you want to determine whether to compile code that invokes a delay loop if the central processor is an 80386 chip. You could write a sequence of directives and code as follows:

```
#define CPU 286 /* Define cpu being used */
...
#if CPU == 386
#include "wait.h"   /* These two lines are not used */
wait_msec( 100 );   /* since CPU is == 286 */
#endif
```

All the conditional directives have two things in common: they all end with the #endif directive, and they all control the inclusion (use or exclusion) of one or more groups of code lines. A group of code lines is fittingly called a *line-group*.

The #if, #elif, and #else directives work together. You can have an #if-#endif standing alone but never an #elif or #else. They group together like this:

```
#if expression
      ... main line-group
#elif expression
      ... first alternate line-group
#elif expression
      ... next alternate line-group
... other #elifs
#else
      ... default line-group if nothing else selected
#endif
```

The presence of the #elif and #else is completely optional. If you do not code them, only the initial line-group is available for selection. The #endif, of course, is mandatory.

However complex the #if construction may be, only one of the line-groups is selected for inclusion in compilation. The preprocessor performs its test from the top down. If the initial if condition is true, only its line-group is retained and so on down the list. Notice that the #else has no conditional expression attached. If an #else directive is present and none of the other line-groups are selected, this one unconditionally is.

In the strictest sense, the #if defined ... and #ifdef forms are equivalent; they mean exactly the same thing. However, the newer #if defined form is preferred because it yields a clean, unmixed notation, as in the following example:

```
#include <stdio.h>
#define TEST3
main()
```

```
{
  #if defined TEST1
    puts( "Test ** 1 ** Selected.\n" );
  #elif defined TEST2
    puts( "Test ** 2 ** Selected.\n" );
  #elif defined TEST3
    puts( "Test ** 3 ** Selected.\n" );
  #else
    puts( "Don't know what was selected!\n" );
  #endif
}
```

When you run this program, it displays the following message:

```
Test ** 3 ** Selected.
```

Line-Control, Error, Pragma, and Null Di

Four other directives are seldom used or are used in a way not c
visible to the programmer. They are the #line, the #error, the #pr
(or *null*) directives.

■ The #line directive is used for debugging and error reportin
time. Ordinarily, the line number of the line being processec
compiler is equal to one more than the number of end-of-lin
characters encountered so far. You can change what line nu
compiler assigns to the next line encountered by writing the
directive:

> #line *number*

whereby *number* is an integer number that is used to report t
code line number (for example, when the compiler flags a li
ing an error). This does not change the source file in any wa
only the way line numbers are reported. This form of the dir
fies the assigned value of the _ _LINE_ _ predefined macro (s
section).

You can also change the presumed name of the source file l
piled with the following form of the #line directive:

> #line *number* "*newname*"

In this case, the value of _ _LINE_ _ is modified as before. In
predefined macro _ _FILE_ _ is modified to reflect the value
literal "*newname*", which must be enclosed in quotation mark

■ Macros and complex arithmetic expressions don't mix well. The reason is operator precedence. This subject is covered in detail in Chapter 5, but you already probably know from algebra class that multiplications have higher precedence than additions. If you are not careful, combining macros and complex arithmetic expressions can cause insidious bugs in your program. For example,

```
#define SQUARE(x) x * x
```

looks deceptively simple. But what if you invoke the macro with the following argument:

```
y = SQUARE( x + 2 );
```

This argument does not expand in the way that you probably intended. You get the following result:

```
y = x + 2 * x + 2;
```

This expression actually reduces algebraically to 3x + 2, not the intended (x + 2) * (x + 2) = x² + 4x + 4. You can use parentheses to force the proper grouping, either in the macro definition or its invocation. The definition is by far the best place to group, just in case you forget later. You could, for example, rewrite the SQUARE macro as follows:

```
#define SQUARE(x) (x) * (x)
```

Although this macro looks a little strange, it works. And it doesn't hurt if you write parentheses in both places, either.

> Macros and complex arithmetic expressions don't mix well! Combining the two can cause insidious bugs in your program.

Conditional Compilation Directives

The *conditional compilation directives* are called the *conditional inclusion directives* in the ANSI document. Either description of these directives is apt because their purpose is to determine whether a section of source code is to be compiled. These directives commonly are used in the standard header files to determine whether the header has already been included. The mechanism works like this:

```
/* Contents of MYHDR.H File */
#if !defined ( MYHDR )
#define MYHDR
```

```
extern int a;
extern int b;
#endif
```

This code fragment first checks whether the macro name MYHDR has already
been defined. If it has not (!defined), the next three lines define the macro
name (an object-like macro—no function-like parameters in the substitution
string) and declare two external variable identifiers (these two lines are now
compiled). The last line (#endif) informs the preprocessor that this conditional directive is complete.

This construction prevents multiple declarations of a and b, while enabling you
to include MYHDR.H whenever and wherever you feel you have to. It doesn't
matter what macro name you choose for such a construction, but it clearly
should be descriptive. Now study the "Quick Reference: ANSI C Conditional
Directives" C-Note before reading about the directives' syntax.

Quick Reference: ANSI C Conditional Directives

In the following list of conditional preprocessing directives, the notation
[!] indicates that the logical-NOT symbol ! may optionally be present:

```
#if [!]constant-expression
#elif [!]constant-expression
#else
#if [!]defined identifier
#if [!]defined ( identifier )
#ifdef identifier
#ifndef identifier
#endif
```

The constant-expression found in the #if and #elif directives is a numeric expression that must reduce to an integer value. It may contain
arithmetic and logical operators, and it may contain macro names as
described in the following paragraphs. When constant-expression is
evaluated, macro names are first replaced by their corresponding strings.

After preliminary macro substitution, the resulting integer expression is
evaluated as a Boolean expression (the result is either true or false). If
the expression evaluates to 0 (false), the group of lines that the #if precedes is not included as part of the source code. If it evaluates to nonzero
(true), the group of lines is included. The lines selected to be processed
may contain other directives (such as #define or #include) or ordinary C
source code. This does not violate the rule that prohibits embedding
directives within directives.

Suppose that you want to determine whether to compile code that invokes a delay loop if the central processor is an 80386 chip. You could write a sequence of directives and code as follows:

```
#define CPU 286 /* Define cpu being used */
...
#if CPU == 386
#include "wait.h"   /* These two lines are not used */
wait_msec( 100 );   /* since CPU is == 286 */
#endif
```

All the conditional directives have two things in common: they all end with the #endif directive, and they all control the inclusion (use or exclusion) of one or more groups of code lines. A group of code lines is fittingly called a *line-group*.

The #if, #elif, and #else directives work together. You can have an #if -#endif standing alone but never an #elif or #else. They group together like this:

```
#if expression
     ... main line-group
#elif expression
     ... first alternate line-group
#elif expression
     ... next alternate line-group
... other #elifs
#else
     ... default line-group if nothing else selected
#endif
```

The presence of the #elif and #else is completely optional. If you do not code them, only the initial line-group is available for selection. The #endif, of course, is mandatory.

However complex the #if construction may be, only one of the line-groups is selected for inclusion in compilation. The preprocessor performs its test from the top down. If the initial if condition is true, only its line-group is retained and so on down the list. Notice that the #else has no conditional expression attached. If an #else directive is present and none of the other line-groups are selected, this one unconditionally is.

In the strictest sense, the #if defined ... and #ifdef forms are equivalent; they mean exactly the same thing. However, the newer #if defined form is preferred because it yields a clean, unmixed notation, as in the following example:

```
#include <stdio.h>
#define TEST3
main()
```

```
{
  #if defined TEST1
    puts( "Test ** 1 ** Selected.\n" );
  #elif defined TEST2
    puts( "Test ** 2 ** Selected.\n" );
  #elif defined TEST3
    puts( "Test ** 3 ** Selected.\n" );
  #else
    puts( "Don't know what was selected!\n" );
  #endif
}
```

When you run this program, it displays the following message:

```
Test ** 3 ** Selected.
```

Line-Control, Error, Pragma, and Null Directives

Four other directives are seldom used or are used in a way not completely visible to the programmer. They are the `#line`, the `#error`, the `#pragma`, and the `#` (or *null*) directives.

■ The `#line` directive is used for debugging and error reporting at compile time. Ordinarily, the line number of the line being processed by the compiler is equal to one more than the number of end-of-line (newline) characters encountered so far. You can change what line number the compiler assigns to the next line encountered by writing the following directive:

    `#line` *number*

whereby *number* is an integer number that is used to report the source code line number (for example, when the compiler flags a line as containing an error). This does not change the source file in any way. It affects only the way line numbers are reported. This form of the directive modifies the assigned value of the `__LINE__` predefined macro (see the next section).

You can also change the presumed name of the source file being compiled with the following form of the `#line` directive:

    `#line` *number* `"`*newname*`"`

In this case, the value of `__LINE__` is modified as before. In addition, the predefined macro `__FILE__` is modified to reflect the value of the string literal `"`*newname*`"`, which must be enclosed in quotation marks, as shown.

The new line number or the new filename or both can be specified as macro names that you have previously defined somewhere. You can use the predefined macros _ _LINE_ _ and _ _FILE_ _ in your program for your own purposes, as long as you do not change them other than with the #line directive. For example, a short program with a source filename of TEMP.C,

```c
#include <stdio.h>

main()
{
  printf( "This is line %d of file %s.\n", _ _LINE_ _, _ _FILE_ _ );
}
```

produces the following output on the display:

```
This is line 5 of file TEMP.C.
```

 You use the #error directive to force the compiler to issue an error diagnostic message of your choosing. Its format is as follows:

```
#error error message
```

The error message is like a string literal in that it contains text more than a character in length, but it is not surrounded by quotation marks. Code the message text just like you would write the replacement string for an object-like macro definition. For example,

```c
#define MAGIC
...
#if defined( MAGIC )
#error There is no such thing as MAGIC!
#endif
```

■ The #pragma directive is supplied to allow the compiler manufacturers to provide directives not otherwise defined by the ANSI standard. Its format is as follows:

```
#pragma tokens
```

whereby tokens can be anything the compiler manual says it can be. Borland C++, for example, can use the #pragma directive to signal that the program contains in-line assembler code.

■ The # or null directive is essentially just another way to introduce whitespace into the source program. You can use these lines to write comments or whatever you want:

```c
#
# /* This is a comment */
#
```

Predefined Macro Names

ANSI C defines many standard macro names that you should be aware of. Appendix B contains a complete list of these macros. Five of them are of interest with regard to preprocessing. They are intended to give the programmer, at compile time, access to information that he or she can use to document, debug, and develop programs.

Quick Reference: Preprocessing Predefined Macro Names

Macro Name	Meaning
_ _LINE_ _	Decimal value of the current line number.
_ _FILE_ _	The presumed name of the current source file.
_ _DATE_ _	The date the compiler processed the source file. This is a string literal with the format `"Mmm dd yyyy"`—the same format as the output of the `asctime()` library function.
_ _TIME_ _	The time the source file was compiled. This is a string literal with the format `"hh:mm:ss"`—the format of output from `asctime()`.
_ _STDC_ _	The decimal value 1. This is a Boolean true constant indicating that the compiler being used conforms to the ANSI standard C specifications.

The values of _ _LINE_ _ and _ _FILE_ _ can change during compilation; _ _DATE_ _, _ _TIME_ _, and _ _STDC_ _ remain fixed. You should never make these names the subject of a `#define` or `#undef` directive, although they are always available for interrogation.

Summary

A lot of ground was covered in this chapter. Admittedly, some of it was tedious, but all of it was important for developing powerful C programming skills. Now the fun is about to begin.

Before leaving this chapter, review the list of seven major topics covered here. Be sure at least that you know where to look up a tricky point later. In this chapter, you learned:

■ The C notion of bits, bytes, and characters in general. These concepts are basic to all understanding of data as recognized and handled by C.

■ The C minimal source and target character sets, including the distinction between source and target environments.

■ The difference between display and control characters, and the notion of collating sequence. This is important because these concepts will be used in all of your programs.

■ How C handles special characters. You should know something about mnemonic and numeric escape sequences, trigraphs, and at least recall what a multibyte character can be used for.

■ The basic parts of a compiler and how it handles your source program. Some of these concepts are brought to bear later when you get fancy with string handling. You should also be familiar with ANSI C required phases of program translation and how this affects the compilation of your program.

■ The concepts of tokens, translation units, C identifiers, C reserved words, standard macros, and standard functions. These are the bottom-line building blocks of your program.

■ C compiler directives and macros. It is no mistake that you spent a large part of this chapter learning compiler directives and macros. You can get by without much knowledge here if you only want to tinker with C. But if you want to do some serious coding, you will spend a great deal of time planning and writing directives and macros.

Objects, Expressions, Operators, and Conversions

I n Chapter 3, you learned how to design, position, and declare the basic data types, plus something about initializing them. That's half the game in controlling and manipulating data in a C program. The other half is learning how to manipulate data objects to get the results you want.

This chapter deals with topics that begin to reveal C's inner power—those things that give it compact notation and an elegant style. Specifically, you learn the following:

■ How to harness the complexity of C's storage classes to control completely the way your data is handled. You get full details on the scope and duration of objects, plus what C does and does not do when initializing variables for you, and how to control these actions.

■ How to use separate compilation to build large programs. You see how to package the program modules and what this means in terms of accessing data objects in multiple source-file programs.

■ How to put the full power of C expressions to work. The C operator set is nearly the most powerful general-purpose operator set available. You can do some surprising things when you understand it fully.

■ How C controls the conversion of one data type to another and how you control C. Conversions can occur implicitly, or you can perform them explicitly.

Another Look at Scope and Duration

Even though you already have the broad outlines of C's handling of variable scope and duration, you need a more detailed understanding because of the initialization rules for C and because of access to data in multiple source-file programs. In this chapter, you revisit this topic and go deeper into the ways C handles scope and duration.

Taking Advantage of Storage Class

In the discussion of scope in Chapter 3, you learned about *local* and *global* variables. Although these common terms describe the concept in an intuitive way, they can be misleading; you need something more in order to fully and effectively implement data objects in your programs. Do not underestimate the importance of this need. If your program's logic is the engine you use for problem solving, *data objects*—the simple and complex variables you define— are the fuel for the engine. (Note that we use the term "data" object to distinguish these variables from the C++ "class" objects.)

The concept of C *storage class* centers around the idea of *duration*—both automatic and static duration. In terms of basic storage class, only two types of objects exist—`auto` and `static`—the storage-class specifier keywords. All objects fall into one of these classes by default, and explicit use of the keywords can override the default. Figure 5.1 summarizes the characteristics of the two storage classes.

The `auto` storage class is the default for objects defined inside a block. This applies to both inner-declared objects and to function parameters; the latter are used only in the function body block. The `auto` class objects are created on entry to the block and discarded on exit. Remember also that objects declared in a block must be declared at the top of the block—they cannot be scattered throughout the block, in contrast to objects declared outside a block.

The two keywords associated with `auto` variables can be used *only* within a block. Notice that the storage-class specifier comes before the type specifier in the following examples.

The `auto` keyword gives an object `auto` storage class. Because this is the default and this keyword can be used only in a block, it seems to have been included as a keyword only to be complete. The `auto` keyword is used in a declaration as follows:

```
auto int count;
```

`register` also gives an object `auto` storage class, but it does more. It informs the compiler that this object is used frequently and should be held in a system register whenever possible.

auto storage class

> default for objects inside a block
> - function parameters
> - inner-declared objects
>
> keywords used only inside a block
> - auto
> - register
>
> created on entry to block, deleted on exit
>
> can have only no linkage

static storage class

> default for objects outside any block
>
> keywords used inside or outside of blocks
> - static
> - extern
>
> objects created at compile time, and never discarded
>
> inner-declared objects:
> - have no linkage even if static unless extern specified
>
> outer-declared objects:
> - have internal linkage if static specified
> - have external linkage if extern specified

Figure 5.1

Storage-class defaults, overrides, and characteristics.

Use the `register` keyword sparingly. On most machines, many registers are not available, and those that are available are used also when operating on all other objects. Thus, there is no guarantee that this keyword causes an object always to be resident in a register—it may or may not.

CAUTION

Registers are restricted in size (usually a machine word) so only a limited number of data types are candidates for the `register` keyword. Technically, the selection of possible types is implementation-defined, but it is normally the integers. In the majority of cases, you use a `register` variable when you need extremely fast integer arithmetic. The following code lines show how to use `register` in a declaration:

```
register int i;
...
for ( i=0, i<256; ++i ) printf ( "%d\n", i );
```

The `static` storage class is the default for objects defined outside any block. Space for `static` objects is reserved at compile time and becomes a permanent part of the program—including the record of it on disk. `static` objects are never discarded and are available throughout program execution.

Two storage-class specifier keywords are associated with `static` objects. You can use these keywords in either outer declarations or inner declarations, but they have a different effect on *linkage* (visibility), depending on location. Figure 5.1 shows the different types of linkage assigned. The following paragraphs develop the concept of linkage more fully. The keywords are `static` and `extern`.

`static` gives an object static duration, regardless of the declaration's location. For outer (global) declarations, this keyword makes the object invisible to other source files. For inner (local) declarations, it has no effect on visibility but can affect the program's performance. For example,

```
static int project_status; /* Now visible only in this file */
```

`extern` indicates that the original declaration of the object (the one that actually reserves storage for the object) is found either in another source file or in a different scope in the same source file. External objects always have static duration. In the following code line, for example, you should understand that the integer `project_status` would be defined in another source file, yet available to the current file:

```
extern int project_status; /* Visible in all files */
```

The ANSI specifications group one keyword here that is not actually a storage-class keyword. The `typedef` keyword indicates that what follows is a "dummy layout" for a derived object. It is listed with the storage-class specifiers for "syntactic convenience" only.

Determining the Scope of an Object

The visibility, or linkage, of an object depends on the combination of the object's storage class and scope. Therefore, to understand linkage, you must understand *scope* clearly.

ANSI defines four types of scope—not just the two classes (local and global) you have been using so far. The following paragraphs describe the four types—file, function, function prototype, and block.

File scope refers to an object appearing in an outer declaration (not in a function). This corresponds to the global object of previous discussions.

Function scope is a strange classification that does not mean exactly what it sounds like. It refers to labels used in a function (see Chapter 3). The only practical significance of this type of scope is that you can reuse a label name in a different function without confusion.

Function prototype scope applies only to the identifiers used in the formal parameter declarations in function prototypes. These names are in scope only during the prototype declaration. Identifiers with function prototypes are different from the names used to identify arguments in a *function call*. Those objects have block scope.

New C programmers sometimes think that variables or objects declared in the main() function have file scope. Not true. Objects declared in main() are declared in a function body, just like any other function's auto variables. They therefore have only *block scope*. Objects may also be declared within a block interior to the function body. These objects are in scope only inside that block.

> **NOTE** File and block scope are the two most important classes in determining linkage. They have the most effect on combining separately compiled modules and some effect on object initialization.

In certain instances concerning object initialization and loop control, the surrounding scope (of an object or a block, respectively) becomes important. You can view *surrounding scope* as the context in which something is defined. A function, for example, has block scope and is surrounded by file scope. A subordinate block (block within a block) is surrounded by a larger block scope.

Determining the Linkage of an Object

The *linkage* of an object is its visibility to other parts of the program. When the program is contained in a single source file, linkage is a subject of only minor concern because it is obvious which parts of the program can communicate. When a program resides in several source files, however, each compiled separately and linked together, linkage becomes a more important issue.

The linkage of an object is tied closely to both its scope and storage class and can be modified by changing one or the other of them. Therefore, linkage, like scope, is partially determined by the location of the object's declaration.

Figure 5.2 graphically summarizes the different combinations of attributes affecting linkage.

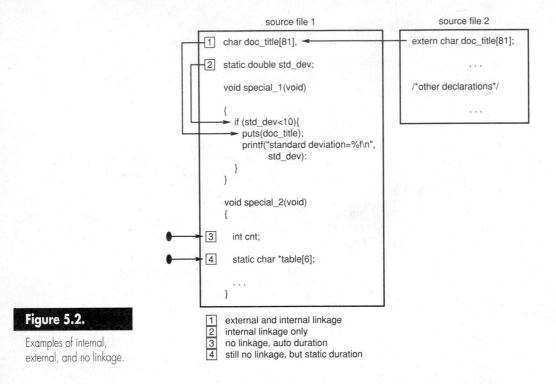

Figure 5.2.

Examples of internal, external, and no linkage.

As you can see from the legend in Figure 5.2, three types of linkage exist: internal, external, and no linkage.

Internal linkage means visibility to all functions in the same source file. Objects with internal linkage have file scope; they are found in outer declarations.

External linkage means visibility to functions in other source files. Objects defined in outer declarations have external linkage by default. They also have file scope because they are, by definition, outside any block.

No linkage means that an object is visible only in the block in which it is declared. These unique objects are not used by other parts of the program. No linkage is the default for objects defined in inner declarations. Objects that have no linkage include the auto variables already mentioned, function parameters, and *incomplete types*. (Incomplete types are discussed in Chapters 6, 8, and 11.)

You should understand that an object's linkage extends to all subordinate contexts. This means that objects with file scope are visible to all functions in the source file and to all blocks interior to those functions. An object declared at the top of a block has block scope and is visible in that block and all blocks defined in it. For example, the following code fragment shows how the variable b is visible in an interior block:

```
void test_function( void )
{
int a = 0;
if ( a == 0 ) {
  int b = 0;
  a = 1;
  if ( a == 5 ) {
    a *= 2;
    b = a + 3; /* b is visible in interior block */
  }
}
}
```

The presence or absence of the `static` and `extern` storage-class specifiers controls the linkage of an object. The effect of these keywords depends on the location of the declaration.

Outer declarations with no storage-class specifier have both internal and external linkage by default. They can be accessed by functions in both the current and other source files.

Outer declarations with the static storage-class specifier have internal linkage only. This keyword effectively makes objects invisible to other source files, although not to the one in which they are defined.

Outer declarations with the `extern` storage-class specifier have both internal and external linkage. This is similar to an outer-declared object with no overriding specifier. However, the presence of the `extern` specifier means that the current declaration is not the original definition of the object.

When the original declaration of an object is in another source file, the *compiler* does not know its address while processing this source file—this situation is resolved only when the *linkage editor* processes all the separately compiled modules.

Inner declarations with no storage-class specifier have no linkage. This is the default `auto` class variable and is unique to the function or block in which it is defined. No other parts of the program can access it.

Inner declarations with the static storage-class specifier have no linkage. The object is still unique, invisible to other parts of the program. However, it now has static rather than automatic duration. This can give a performance boost to the function (or block) containing it because it does not have to be allocated and initialized every time the block is entered. Allocation of space for the object occurs at compile time.

Inner declarations with the `extern` storage-class specifier have linkage that depends on the location of the original definition of the object. Regardless of the original definition's location, such an object has static duration, like all other `extern` objects. The actual linkage of the object depends on whether there is another declaration in the same source file for the object having file scope.

If there is such a declaration, the object has the same linkage as the outer object. The inner declaration also refers to the outer object. The following code fragment shows how several of the rules work. (The comments explain each case.)

```
#include <stdlib.h>
#include <stdio.h>
...
static double a;  /* a has internal linkage only */
double b;         /* b has internal and external linkage */
extern double c;  /* c has internal and external linkage, */
...               /* but refers to an object in another */
                  /* source file. */
void some_function( void )
{
  extern double a; /* has internal linkage like outer a  */
  extern double b; /* internal and external like outer b */
  extern double c; /* internal and external like outer c */
...
  /* Both a and b here refer to the actual objects in   */
  /* outer declarations in this file */
  /* c still refers to an object in another source file.*/
}
```

If there is no outer declaration with file scope for the same object, it has external linkage and refers to an object originally defined in another source file.

Controlling Initializers for Objects

Initializing data objects is easier with ANSI-conforming compilers than it was with older K&R compilers simply because you can code an initializer directly into a declaration anywhere, regardless of the scope or duration of the object. K&R C did not allow initializers for array, structure, or union objects that had automatic duration. That restriction is now removed. Naturally, you should not write an initializer for objects with file scope that also have the `extern` storage-class specifier; their original definitions (the ones reserving storage for the objects) are in another source file.

> In one case specifically mentioned by the ANSI document, however, you cannot write an initializer for an object, even if its original definition is in the same source file. If the declaration of an identifier has block scope and the identifier has internal or external linkage, you cannot write an initializer for the identifier.
>
> **T I P**

An object with block scope can occur only in a function or in a subordinate block in a function. The only way such an object can have internal or external linkage is to specify the `extern` keyword, as in the last sample code fragment in the preceding section.

In that fragment are three outer declarations for `double` type variables a, b, and c. The variables a and b could have initializers because a has the `static` and b has no storage-class specifier. The variable c cannot have an initializer because it is `extern`.

There are inner declarations also for all three variables in the function `some_function()`, all having the `extern` keyword. Because all three of these variables have either internal, external, or both types of linkage, the declarations in `some_function()` may not carry initializers.

How often will you run into this situation? Admittedly, almost never. But because it is still possible, particularly when you begin to write longer, more complex programs, you should be aware of the rule.

Accessing External Data and Functions

We have mentioned external objects and separate compilation frequently. You know what an external object is and have at least a conceptual understanding of separate compilation. What you need now is concrete information on how to build a program in such a modular fashion.

To illustrate the process, we develop a program named TESTCSTR.C, shown in Listing 5.1, over the next few sections. This program calls numeric-to-string conversion functions located in a second source file and calls high-precision timing routines located in a third source file to bench mark one of the conversion functions.

Listing 5.1.   TESTCSTR.C—Tests numeric-to-string conversion (for Microsoft C/C++).

```
1   #include <stdlib.h>
2   #include <stdio.h>
3
4   #include "cvtstr.h"
5   #include "timer.h"
6
7   main()
8   {
9       double pi = 3.1415926;
10      int count = -486;
11      long population = 250000000;
12
13      printf( "There were %s items counted.\n", cvtitos( count ) );
14      printf( "The population is currently %s.\n",
15              cvtltos( population ) );
16
17      start_bench();
18      printf( "The value of PI is %s.\n", cvtdtos( pi, 3 ) );
19      stop_bench();
20      printf( "CVTDTOS required %.4f seconds.\n", duration() );
21
22      start_bench();
23      printf( "PI again is %.4f.\n", pi );
24      stop_bench();
25      printf( "PRINTF required %.4f seconds.\n", duration() );
26  }
```

The program in Listing 5.1 is short and simple because all the work is done by functions located in other source files. The object code from these functions is linked with this program's object file to make the complete executable program file. Lines 4 and 5 contain #include directives to read the headers for the other source files and to inform the compiler what to expect from those functions.

Initially, the discussion of building complex programs proceeds as if you were going to perform the process completely manually—compiling each of the source files one at a time and then running the linkage editor to build the finished executable program file. This gives you some background on how the parts of a complex program work together and on how to use the basic tools in a C compiler package. After that, you learn a better way.

Compiling Modules Separately

The first step in designing a multiple source-file program is to decide what should be placed in which source file.

One of the source files must contain only one `main()` function. Normally, the name of this file should be the same as the program name you want to use later for execution—but this is not absolutely required. In the program you are building here, for example, the source file TESTCSTR.C is the main file, and the finished executable program resides eventually in file TESTCSTR.EXE.

In many cases, the main source file contains only a `main()` function, which calls the support functions in other modules as needed. Although this use is common, it is by no means universal. You may write any functions you want into the main source file.

Each secondary source file should contain related data objects and functions. This is instinctive, not something you have to force. The `#include` directives in lines 4 and 5 of Listing 5.1 imply that two secondary source files exist for this sample project. They are CVTSTR.C, shown in Listing 5.2, and TIMER.C, which is documented in Appendix G (see Listing G.1).

Listing 5.2. CVTSTR.C—Separate source for numeric-to-string conversion functions (for Microsoft C/C++).

```
1   #include <stdlib.h>
2   #include <stdio.h>
3   #include <string.h>
4   #include <math.h>
5
6   static char outstr[21];
7
8   char *cvtitos( int x );
9   char *cvtltos( long x );
10  char *cvtdtos( double x, int precision );
11  void str_invert( char *s );
12
13  char *cvtitos( int x )
14  {
15    static int i;
```

continues

Listing 5.2. Continued

```c
16    static div_t ans;
17
18    ans.quot = 0; /* Get everything initialized */
19    ans.rem = 0;
20    i = 0;
21    if ( x < 0 ) {                  /* If negative, */
22      *( outstr + i++ ) = '-';  /*   set sign in output, */
23      x = 0 - x;                    /*   and make positive */
24    }
25    ans.quot = x;
26
27    /* --- Put the digits out backwards --- */
28    do {
29      ans = div( ans.quot, 10 );
30      *( outstr + i++ ) = ans.rem + 48; /* Make display char */
31    } while ( ans.quot >= 10 );
32    if ( ans.quot > 0 ) *( outstr + i++ ) = ans.quot + 48;
33
34    *( outstr + i ) = '\0'; /* Terminate the string */
35    if ( *outstr == '-' ) str_invert( (outstr + 1 ) );
36    else str_invert( outstr );
37    return( outstr );
38  }
39
40  char *cvtltos( long x )
41  {
42    static int i;
43    static ldiv_t ans;
44
45    ans.quot = 0; /* Get everything initialized */
46    ans.rem = 0;
47    i = 0;
48    if ( x < 0 ) {                  /* If negative, */
49      *( outstr + i++ ) = '-';  /*   set sign in output, */
50      x = 0 - x;                    /*   and make positive */
51    }
52    ans.quot = x;
53
54    /* --- Put the digits out backwards --- */
55    do {
56      ans = ldiv( ans.quot, 10L );
```

```
57      *( outstr + i++ ) = ans.rem + 48; /* Make display char */
58    } while ( ans.quot >= 10 );
59    if ( ans.quot > 0 ) *( outstr + i++ ) = ans.quot + 48;
60
61    *( outstr + i ) = '\0'; /* Terminate the string */
62    if ( *outstr == '-' ) str_invert( (outstr + 1 ) );
63    else str_invert( outstr );
64    return( outstr );
65  }
66
67  char *cvtdtos( double x, int precision )
68  {
69    static char hold[21];
70    static double dint, dfrac;
71    static long integer, fraction;
72    static char *p, *q;
73
74    dfrac = modf( x, &dint );      /* Separate the parts */
75    integer = (long)dint;        /* Cast the integer part */
76    if ( dfrac < 0.0 ) dfrac *= -1.0; /* Discard extra sign */
77    for ( ; precision > 0; precision-- )
78      dfrac *= 10;                         /* Scale */
79    dfrac += 0.5;                          /* Round */
80    fraction = (long)dfrac;    /* Cast the fraction part */
81    p = hold;
82    cvtltos( integer );
83    q = outstr;
84    while ( *p++ = *q++ ) ;        /* Copy integer part */
85    p--;
86    *p++ = '.';                   /* Splice in a period */
87    cvtltos( fraction );
88    q = outstr;
89    while ( *p++ = *q++ ) ;        /* Copy fraction part */
90    return( hold );
91  }
92
93  void str_invert( char *s )
94  {
95    static char *p;
96
97    if ( !*s ) return;     /* Null string, no work */
98    p = s;
```

continues

Listing 5.2. Continued

```
99    while ( *p ) p++; p--; /* Position to end of string */
100   while ( s < p ) *s ^= *p, *p ^= *s, *s++ ^= *p-- ;
101   }
```

Look at CVTSTR.C in Listing 5.2 to review some of what you just learned about linkage and external objects. A brief explanation of its functions also is in order.

First, this source file has only one variable with file scope—one global variable. This variable is outstr, in line 6. It's an array of characters—a string—with room for 20 characters plus the null-terminating byte required for C strings. The most interesting thing about this variable is that it clearly is meant to be used only by the CVTSTR.C source-file code; it has the static storage-class specifier. Thus, outstr has file scope but only internal linkage. Less technically, it has global scope for this source file only.

Next, the function prototypes are in lines 8–11. Four functions reside in this source file: cvtitos(), cvtltos(), cvtdtos(), and str_invert(). The functions cvtitos(), cvtltos(), and cvtdtos() convert integers, long integers, and double floating-point types, respectively, to strings. The function str_invert() reverses the order of characters in a string and is called by the other functions during the conversion process.

The processes for converting integers and long integers are quite similar, and converting doubles to strings basically works by calling the long integer conversion services. Therefore, we describe here only how you can convert an integer to a string. Then we comment on the modf() function and explain str_invert().

Conceptually, converting integers to strings of display characters is like the methods used in hex dumping data (refer to Chapter 3 and the SDUMP.C program in Listing 3.1). The process is one of *scaling* partial results as they are developed.

In Chapter 4, you learned that the ANSI standard for C requires that the numeric values for the display characters 0 through 9 be *contiguous;* there must be no gaps in value. The ASCII collating sequence observes this rule. The values are decimal 48 through 57. Therefore, you can add decimal 48 to the integer partial results to get the display characters. You can see an example of this in cvtitos(), lines 30 and 32 of Listing 5.2, for example.

How are the partial results calculated? Consider the value used in the test program. Line 10 of Listing 5.1 (the main program, TESTCSTR.C) shows that −486 is to be converted to a string. Just ignore the minus sign for a moment and think about what happens if you successively divide this number by 10. On the first pass, you get 48, remainder 6; 6 is the first partial result. Then,

6 + 48 = 54 gives you the numeric value for display '6'. Apply this process again to 48 to obtain 4, remainder 8, and scale again. On the last pass, you have 4 < 10; you stop and scale the quotient rather than the remainder. This process is all done in lines 25–32 of Listing 5.2.

Two techniques used in this process require some explanation. First, notice that the div() function is used to develop quotients and remainders for integers and that ldiv() is used for long integers. These functions return a complex object—a *structure*—rather than a simple variable.

The second technique used in these functions also seems peculiar on the surface but makes sense when you think about it. Both the integer and long-integer conversion routines store the display characters backwards in the output string outstr. They do so because the partial results are derived backwards (486 yields 6, then 8, then 4), but the output string is accessed from the left—the most natural way—because the routine needs only to increment an index variable on each pass. Thus, the number 486 is stored in the string as "684". This is why str_invert() is necessary.

We also must say a couple things about str_invert(). Most compilers supply a library function, strrev(), which reverses a string. Because this is not an ANSI standard library function, however, we supplied our own version. You may find it useful or informative.

You may notice also that the code in str_invert() (lines 93–101, Listing 5.2) is extremely cryptic. This is so because we have taken full advantage of C's operator set and compact notation to achieve two goals:

1. To perform the reversal of order in place, using no extra storage to hold a character temporarily.

2. To achieve the absolute maximum speed, short of rewriting the function in assembler.

Avoiding the use of holding storage should not be new to you. You saw how that was done in Chapter 3 (EXCHANGE.C, Listing 3.5). You might want to review that sample program to refresh your memory on using the exclusive OR for this purpose. We defer the discussion of the advanced use of pointers for the sake of speed until Chapter 8, "Programming with Pointers, Arrays, and Strings." The use of the comma operator is discussed later in this chapter.

Finally, the modf() function, line 74 in Listing 5.2, is something you have not yet seen. Its purpose is to separate the whole number part and the fraction part of a double floating-point number, making them separately available—as double floats, not integers.

TIMER.C is not listed here. Its internals are far beyond the scope of this chapter and are fully documented in Appendix G. The names of its functions are given in the next section, but for now, focus on how to build programs from multiple source files.

Setting Up the Header Files

Turn back to Figure 5.2 for a moment. It contains two boxes, representing two source files, both of which declare a string named doc_title. The original definition (the one that actually reserves storage for the object) is in *source file 1;* the declaration having the extern specifier is in *source file 2.*

Now suppose that you have a set of functions and data objects in a source file that is used by many of your programs. If you make no other provision for it, you have to code the external references for every external object and function in each new program (that is, for every object and function you intend to be visible across source files), but that is what header files are for!

When you write the code for a source file like this, you should create (at that time) the header file for the data objects and functions it contains. Figure 5.3 shows the process of developing such a header file.

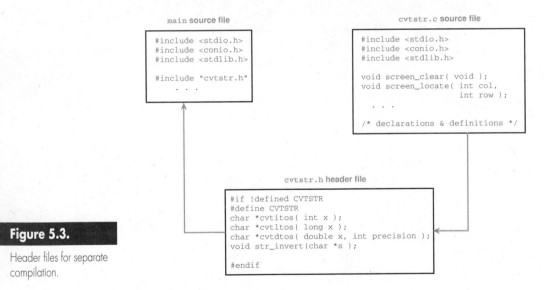

Figure 5.3.

Header files for separate compilation.

Figure 5.3 highlights an important consideration about header files. In long and complex programs, you may find that the #include for a given header file appears more than once in a source file. You can use the conditional compilation and substitution macros to prevent the inadvertent redeclaration of external objects and functions. For example, CVTSTR.H appears as follows:

```
#if !defined CVTSTR
#define CVTSTR
char *cvtitos( int x );
char *cvtltos( long x );
```

```
char *cvtdtos( double x, int precision );
void str_invert( char *s );
#endif
```

The preprocessing string CVTSTR can be anything you want it to be; it does not have to match the program name. Because it does match here, notice that it was coded in uppercase letters to avoid confusion but still convey which header file it is. Because C is a case-sensitive language, remember that all references to CVTSTR (the macro name, that is) must use only uppercase characters.

The extern storage-class specifier is noticeably missing from the declarations in CVTSTR.H. This header file contains only function prototypes, and functions are always assumed to have external linkage (if they do not carry the static keyword—those that do are not in the header).

> Leaving out the extern keyword is fine for function prototypes because they do not define functions, they only declare them. What about data objects? Do they require the extern keyword in a header? They do if you want them to indicate linkage to external objects.

TIP

As you should recall, an #include directive can be used to pull anything into the source file. After the included text has been merged, it is compiled just like everything else. If you therefore neglect to specify extern when it should be present, the compiler reacts to the declarations as if they were the original declarations for the objects, reserving space for them, but this has already been done in the other module as well. Treating external objects as if they are not external does two things to your program: it prevents access to the objects in the other source file, and it confuses the linkage editor, which is now presented with the dilemma of dealing with two different objects that have the same name.

Thus, you can omit the extern keyword for function prototypes for functions in other source files, but you should use it for external *data objects*. The TIMER.H header file, for example, contains

```
#if !defined TIMER
#define TIMER
extern unsigned long ticks;
extern unsigned long begin_time;
extern unsigned long end_time;
extern unsigned long far *clock;
extern void (interrupt far *oldint8)();
void start_bench( void );
```

```
void stop_bench( void );
double duration( void );
#endif
```

So far we have not mentioned one final situation. In the project you are developing here, TESTCSTR.C, refers to functions in CVTSTR.C, but not the other way around. Therefore, a CVTSTR.H header is included in TESTCSTR.C, but there is no TESTCSTR.H. What if two source files refer to external objects or functions in each other? Then you may need two header files.

Suppose that you have two hypothetical source files, ONE.C and TWO.C. ONE.C is the main program source file, and TWO.C contains a collection of support and service functions. But both files have objects referred to by the other. You therefore need two header files, arranged as follows:

```
/* one.c - main program */
/* two.c - support functions */
#include "twoc.h"                #include "onec.h"
```

Coding References to Other Modules

When referring to external data and functions, you have only a few rules to go by, all of which make good common sense. These rules follow:

1. Refer to (call) functions from any source file as you would in the source file in which the function definition resides. All source files calling a function should have a function *prototype* for it (a header file is a good way to provide this), but only one source file should have the function *definition*. Secondary declarations of a function in prototypes do not need the `extern` keyword because it is a prototype and `extern` is the default.

2. All data objects with file scope that are to be shared across source files should have the `extern` keyword, except the original definition, which actually reserves storage for the object. It is possible to supply the `extern` keyword for all declarations of the object—the one with an initializer is considered the original definition of the object. Because this is confusing, the practice of not using `extern` with the original declaration is recommended.

3. A corollary to the preceding rule is that you should write an initializer for a data object only with the original definition, not redeclarations in other source files. The source file would compile correctly, but the linker would produce an error to the effect that the object already exists in another source file.

4. Having properly identified external references (again, in a header file), refer to external data objects (fetch and store values) as you would in the source file in which the original definition resides.

Now all the source files for your program presumably exist, with all external references properly coded. According to the game plan, this is the time to compile the source files separately, resulting in an object file for each one.

How this is done varies from compiler to compiler. For products with integrated development environments, compilation is just a keystroke away. For other products, you must use a command invocation (products with integrated environments supply command-line access, as well). You could use the following three commands, for example, to compile the source files separately:

```
C>CL /c testcstr.c
C>CL /c cvtstr.c
C CL /c timer.c
```

In these commands, CL is the name of the compiler program (because Microsoft C/C++ was used for this project), and the /c *option flag* informs the compiler to stop after generating the .OBJ file. Microsoft C/C++ can compile and automatically invoke the linker if you want it to.

Linking the Modules

The linkage editor (linker) performs two vital functions in the program building process:

1. It packages all the object modules (files) in one executable file. On any machine, but especially on PC-based machines, this is not only a matter of copying several files into one file, one after the other. The compiler has generated code, data, and stack *segments* (discrete areas of storage) for each module separately. These must all be collated and grouped correctly in the executable file (or *load module,* which on PCs, is the .EXE file). This part of the process, however, is highly dependent on the machine and operating system.

2. It resolves in the load module the *relative* addresses of objects and functions, as well as external type references to them. The relative address is just the *offset* (number of bytes) from the beginning of the load module to the location of the actual definition of the object. An offset is used because the program may not be loaded at the same place in RAM every time the program runs (at runtime, the operating system's program loader performs the final resolution into absolute addresses).

Figure 5.4 shows the linkage editor performing this process to build a load module for the TESTCSTR.EXE program.

Following is the command line used to start the process shown in Figure 5.4:

```
C>link testcstr.obj+cvtstr.obj+timer.obj,testcstr.exe;
```

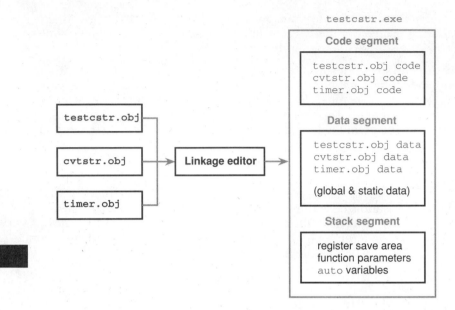

testcstr.exe

Code segment

```
testcstr.obj code
cvtstr.obj code
timer.obj code
```

Data segment

```
testcstr.obj data
cvtstr.obj data
timer.obj data
```

(global & static data)

Stack segment

register save area
function parameters
`auto` variables

Figure 5.4.

Linking the program
modules.

Again, the particular command varies from package to package. In this case, the Microsoft linker is used because Microsoft C/C++ 7 was used. Whatever the compiler package, however, having to key such a command frequently—as you certainly do when you develop a complex project—could quickly become irritating. The process is tedious, time-consuming, and invites keystroke errors (in which case, you get to retype it!).

This is where the MAKE utility mentioned in Chapter 1 can save a great deal of time (the Microsoft version is called NMAKE). Suppose that, after making a small correction to only one source file, you could rebuild the whole .EXE file with just one short command, as follows:

```
C>nmake -ftestcstr.mak
```

Wouldn't this method be better than having to retype both the compile and link commands whenever you make a correction? Experience answers, "You bet!" All you have to do is use the text editor once to create a file (called a *makefile*) named TESTCSTR.MAK, such as this one:

```
# ----- Dependency and link command for .EXE file -----
testcstr.exe: testcstr.obj cvtstr.obj timer.obj
     link testcstr.obj+cvtstr.obj+timer.obj,testcstr.exe;
# ----- Dep. and compile command for testcstr.obj -----
testcstr.obj: testcstr.c cvtstr.h timer.h
     CL /c testcstr.c
```

```
# ----- Dep. and compile for cvtstr.obj -----
cvtstr.obj: cvtstr.c cvtstr.h
      CL /c cvtstr.c
# ----- Dep. and compile for timer.obj -----
timer.obj: timer.c timer.h
        CL /c timer.c
```

This file contains the four commands given earlier for building TESTCSTR.EXE. It also contains a good bit of other information, which is used by MAKE/NMAKE to determine when these commands are to be used. Now you can analyze these statements one piece at a time.

MAKE statements beginning with the # sign are comments. A comment can appear between lines, as in this example, or at the end of the line after a MAKE statement. Everything after the # sign is ignored; it is assumed to be part of the comment.

MAKE statements come in pairs. In the basic form of makefile shown here (there are many bells and whistles we don't cover because your manual does it better), such a pair of lines is called a *description block*. The first line in the description block contains a *dependency condition*. For example, the first line of the first dependency block in TESTCSTR.MAK contains the following:

```
testcstr.exe: testcstr.obj cvtstr.obj timer.obj
```

This line indicates that TESTCSTR.EXE (the *target field*) is dependent on the state of three object files (the *dependent fields*). If the files listed in the dependent fields are newer than the target (based on the files' date and time stamps on disk), the target file must be updated. But how is the target file to be updated?

The second line of the pair handles this process:

```
link testcstr.obj+cvtstr.obj+timer.obj,testcstr.exe;
```

This line should be a valid command (in this case, the link command) and is executed if the dependent conditions require it.

The command line should begin with either a tab or a blank. In summary, the first description block here specifies that if any one of the object files is newer than TESTCSTR.EXE, relink TESTCSTR.EXE.

Description blocks can appear in any order, but some orders are better than others. The order in which the description blocks appear doesn't matter to MAKE—it checks them all and executes any of the necessary commands to update everything. MAKE notes (and takes into account) which dependent fields are targets in other description blocks as well. All you have to worry about is getting the description blocks in there. For instance, omitting the TESTCSTR.EXE dependency, or writing it twice, wouldn't make much sense.

NOTE Even though it doesn't matter to MAKE the order in which the description blocks appear, we think that using the order shown in this example is easier on the eye. It begins with the desired outcome at the top of the makefile and works backward in a logical order, until every possible module has been included.

As you can see, using MAKE to control complex projects makes a great deal of sense. It saves you the administrative work of keeping the modules up to date. MAKE doesn't do extra work either. It processes only those files detected as being out of date. This approach is more efficient, for example, than using a DOS batch file (which would recompile and relink everything every time).

When the program has been link-edited, you can run TESTCSTR.EXE to produce the following report on-screen:

```
There were -486 items counted.
The population is currently 250000000.
The value of PI is 3.142.
CVTDTOS required 0.0025 seconds.
PI again is 3.1416.
PRINTF required 0.0009 seconds.
```

Now you know how to declare, define, and access both functions and data anywhere, whether in a simple or complex program. Next, you see what you can do with them.

Understanding C Expressions

The fundamental vehicle for manipulating data in a C program is the *expression*. The ANSI document defines an expression as a sequence of operators and operands that specifies computation of a value, designates an object or a function, generates side effects, or performs some combination of these actions.

It is clear what goes between the operators—objects do. What happens to the objects depends entirely on the operators, and there are operators that affect every object in some way—functions are even treated as objects in some respects.

Rules Governing C Expressions

Clearly, rules must govern how you can put operands and operators together; otherwise, the compiler would not be able to sort it out. To grasp these rules, you have to understand three terms: *side effects, sequence points,* and *subexpressions.*

You first saw side effects in Chapter 3, where they were defined as modifying an object's value in a way that is not part of the statement's primary purpose. Now a more accurate definition is needed. ANSI defines a *side effect* as any change in the program's execution environment and, in particular, as the act of accessing a volatile object, modifying an object, modifying a file, or calling a function that does any of these things.

Sequence points, in contrast to side effects, represent points of stability in the execution environment. They occur during execution of a program when everything is temporarily complete; the effects of all previous expressions are complete, and evaluation of the next expression has not yet begun. Nothing, at that instant, is changing. Sequence points occur at three major places:

1. At the call to a function, after the arguments have been evaluated. That is, evaluation of the call arguments is complete, but the current scope has not been suspended nor has the scope of the called function been entered.

2. At the end of the first operand of logical AND (&&), logical OR (¦¦), the conditional operator (?), and the comma operator (,). Sequence points are defined in these places to guarantee a particular order of evaluation. In the following example,

    ```
    if ( a < b && c < d ) { /* do something here */ }
    ```

    the if statement says that both a < b and c < d must be true before the target statement can be executed. To perform the test correctly, a < b must be evaluated completely and a sequence point reached before logical AND processing can occur.

3. At the end of a full expression. This includes expressions in an initializer, to the right of an expression statement, in the controlling conditional expression in an if or switch statement, in the controlling conditional statement in a do or do-while statement, and in all three conditional expressions in a for statement.

A *subexpression* is a sequence of operators and operands that can stand alone as a complete expression, syntactically. Thus, the assignment expression a = c + b contains four subexpressions: all three identifiers standing alone, as well as c + b (but not a =).

The rules for forming valid C expressions fall into five major points:

1. Between the preceding and next sequence points, an object's stored value may be modified once, at most, by the evaluation of an expression. Additionally, the prior value (the one before evaluation began) of an

object may be fetched (retrieved) only for the purpose of determining the value to be stored. For example, the assignment expression,

```
i = i + 1;
```

is legitimate, whereas the expression,

```
i = ++i + 1;
```

is not. The value of i is not only fetched twice, it is also updated before the evaluation of the expression is complete. The syntax of the second expression is considered "undefined" (but most compilers evaluate it correctly).

2. The order of evaluation of subexpressions and the order in which side effects take place are undefined, except as indicated by the syntax or otherwise specified by the standard. However, no matter how the expression is actually handled internally, it is evaluated in a manner consistent with the syntax specified in the expression. Floating-point operations, for example, are not computationally commutative, even though they may be so mathematically. ANSI specifies a guaranteed no regrouping rule that prevents subtleties like this from destroying expression results.

3. All operators except the bitwise operators (~, <<, >>, &, ^, and ¦) can have operands of any legitimate arithmetic type. You can add double floats, integers, and characters, for example. Because the bitwise operators depend on the internal sequence of bit values in an integer, however, their operands must be integer types.

4. If an exception occurs during the evaluation of an expression, the outcome is undefined—left to the particular compiler to do something. It may do nothing. An exception is considered to be a result that is not mathematically defined or cannot be represented correctly by the object type.

5. Finally, the stored value of an object can be accessed only by an identifier with compatible type. The rule deals with alternate means of accessing a single object (called *aliasing*). The compatible types are as follows:

   a. The same type as the object

   b. A qualified version of the same type (one that has either the const or volatile type qualifier)

   c. A signed or unsigned version of the same basic type

   d. A signed or unsigned and qualified version of the same basic type

   e. A member object of a structure or union that is compatible in the ways already described

   f. A character type

All but the last of these compatible types are permitted because the variations in declaring such aliased objects do not result in any expected differences in the internal structure of the object. Signed and unsigned integers, for example, have a common range of values, the representation of which is exactly the same for both types. The following code fragment illustrates using compatible integer types:

```
signed first_val;       /* Here is the signed integer */
unsigned *some_val;     /* A pointer to any unsigned integer */
...
some_val = &first_val; /* Use address-of to point to int */
*some_val = 37U;        /* Store a value in the object */
/* ---- This printf() displays a value of 37 ---- */
printf( "The value is: %d\n", first_val );
```

The stipulation that a character type—or more precisely, a pointer to type character—can be used to access any object is an important one. This enables the C programmer to manipulate any object, however structured internally, one byte at a time. The following code fragment shows how to use a pointer to char to access the individual bytes of an unsigned long variable:

```
#include <stdlib.h>
#include <stdio.h>
main()
{
  unsigned long big_value = 1193180UL;
  char *byte;
  int i;
  byte = (char *)&big_value;
  for ( i=3; i>=0; i-- )
    printf( "%.2X ", (unsigned char)byte[i] );
}
```

The preceding sample code produces the following output:

```
00 12 34 DC
```

Primary Expressions

All the definitions and rules in the preceding section might lead you to believe that there are many possible types of expressions. In fact, there are just four: primary expressions, lvalue and rvalue expressions, function designator expressions, and void expressions.

Primary expressions are the simplest of all expressions. They are expressions with no operators, though one primary expression is more complicated than that. Primary expressions include the following:

Identifiers. An identifier is a primary expression if it has been declared as designating an object (making it an `lvalue`) or a function (making it a function designator). These two further classes are covered in more detail in the next two sections.

Constants. A constant is a primary expression that has a type, as described earlier in the book, that can include floating, integer, enumeration, or character types (and their variations).

String literals. A string literal is a primary expression having type array of `char` or perhaps array of `wchar_t` (wide character). A string literal always has static duration and is considered an `lvalue` also.

Parenthesized expressions. This expression stretches the definition just a bit. A parenthetical expression, such as (a + b + c), forces the parsing routines to consider it as a single entity. If the interior expression denotes an object—as opposed to a value—it is considered an `lvalue`; if a function, it is a function designator; and if `void`, it is a `void` expression. Of course, it could just be a plain expression yielding a value, in which case, it has a type depending on the mix of operands. See the discussion of type conversions later in the chapter.

The *rvalue* and *lvalue* Expressions

An intuitive understanding of the terms `rvalue` and `lvalue` usually is sufficient: an `rvalue` is anything that can appear to the right of an assignment, and an `lvalue` is anything that can appear to the left of an assignment. In an assignment statement such as this:

```
identifier1 = identifier2;
```

either *identifier* could stand in either position, `lvalue` or `rvalue`. But in an assignment statement such as the following:

```
identifier1 = expression;
```

the *expression* on the right cannot be used as an `lvalue` (unless it is also an object identifier).

This leads directly to the more accurate definition of an `lvalue` found in the ANSI standard: An `lvalue` is an expression (with an object type or an incomplete type other than `void`) that designates an object.

The more precise ANSI definition of an lvalue presents an opportunity to re-examine the concept of an identifier as a primary expression that is also an lvalue. How many different types of expressions exist that designate an object (again, as opposed to simply yielding a value) and may be an lvalue? Just these three:

■ A simple identifier is by definition both a simple expression and a primary expression. A simple identifier can be an lvalue.

■ A pointer identifier is an object and can be an lvalue. That is, a pointer, but not necessarily the thing it points to, can be an lvalue. Therefore, you can write the following type of statement:

```
char *s;     /* Define a pointer to a string */
...
s = s + 1;   /* Update the pointer */
```

In this example, the pointer—not the object being pointed to—is manipulated.

■ A dereferenced pointer may or may not be an lvalue, depending on what is being pointed to. Remember that everything in C has one of three generic types: object type, function type, or incomplete type. According to the definition, only object types and incomplete types other than void may qualify as an lvalue. The following code illustrates the difference:

```
unsigned char ch;                /* Declare an object */
unsigned char (*input)( void ); /* Declare function pointer */
...
input = fgetc;     /* OK, gets address of fgetc() */
ch = (*input)();   /* OK, ch is object and lvalue */
ch += 1;           /* OK, ch still lvalue */
(*input) += 1;     /* WRONG, (*input) is a function */
```

Because lvalue now essentially means *object locator,* the interesting possibility arises of having an lvalue that cannot appear on the left side of an assignment. This can occur if the object has array type, an incomplete type, or a const-qualified type or if it is a structure or union possessing a member variable with a const-qualified type. An lvalue that does not suffer from any of these short-comings is now called a *modifiable* lvalue.

The new ANSI definition of rvalue makes little difference, compared to its old usage. (The old meaning of rvalue was simply anything that could legally appear on the right side of an assignment statement.) An rvalue is just the value of an expression. This definition still permits the observation that anything that is an lvalue may also be an rvalue but not necessarily the other way around.

Function Designator Expressions

A function designator expression has function type—not object or incomplete type. The only way to form a function designator expression is by using the function's identifier, as follows:

```
char *gets( char *s );
char *(*instring)( char *s );
```

The first line simply declares a function that returns a pointer to char (a string). The function designator gets is one of the standard I/O functions.

The second line declares a pointer to a function that returns a pointer to char. In this case, instring is both the function designator and the pointer. How function designator expressions are used to call functions is explained in the "Postfix Operators" section.

void Expressions

A void expression has no type at all—not function, not object, not incomplete. The only way to form a void expression is to call a function that has void type, as in the following example:

```
void no_function( void);
...
no_function(); /* A void expression */
```

This example makes perfect sense when you recall that a function may return a void type, but a void object is a contradiction in terms.

Controlling the C Operators

In the next few sections, you learn how to classify and group the operators, their exact effect in expressions, and perhaps most important of all, how they control the *order of evaluation* of an expression.

T I P   C has a particularly rich operator set; a great deal of the language's power comes from it. If you don't learn anything else about C, learn this subject.

Classifying the C Operators

In this book, we group the C operators into seven types of usage (the *postfix, unary, cast, binary,* simple and compound *assignment, conditional,* and *comma* operators).

This arrangement follows but does not duplicate the ANSI order of presentation. In particular, the binary operator groups and the simple and compound operator group contain several of the ANSI groupings.

The operators, however classified, are presented in the order of their precedence in expression evaluation, with the highest precedence first. The operands of operators having higher precedence are evaluated first in an expression. Operators have equal precedence in each section. When our arrangement differs from ANSI's, precedence is stated explicitly. Remember that a subexpression in parentheses is considered a primary expression— it has higher precedence than all the operators to be discussed. Parentheses frequently are used to force a particular order of evaluation (as they are in algebraic formulae).

The *associativity* of the operators also is discussed. This property of an operator determines the order in which the operands are "associated" with it and not the strictly mathematical associative property. Associativity makes a great difference in evaluation. Consider the following assignment statement:

```
a = ( b / 3 ) + 37;
```

The equality operators (including simple assignment, as in this example) cause the program to evaluate the right side of the assignment first. The result becomes the value of the left operand (`lvalue`). Clearly, the evaluation of this expression could not proceed in any other way.

> **NOTE** After operator precedence, *associativity* is the most important factor determining the order of evaluation of an expression. Although the standard allows either operand to be evaluated first, the associative rules are applied to the operator in the stated order. This is also called *grouping:* operators are said to *group* left to right, or right to left.

Postfix Operators

Postfix operators are appended to the identifier or expression on which they operate. The expressions involved, called *postfix expressions,* can consist of primary expressions, primary expressions followed by a postfix operator, or a postfix expression (which may already be more than just a primary expression) followed by a postfix operator. The postfix operators group from the left; the object to the left of the postfix operator is its target.

The postfix operators are array subscript `[]`, function call `()`, structure or union member `.`, pointer to structure or union member `->`, postfix increment `++`, and postfix decrement `--`. The name, symbol, and general syntax for each operator is given before its discussion in the following sections.

Array Subscript *[]*

The array subscript's format is as follows:

postfix expression [*expression*]

whereby the *postfix expression* must have the type "pointer to object type;" the *expression* in the square brackets must have one of the integral types. This notation is used both to declare arrays and to reference array elements. The following declaration:

```
double points[256];
```

defines an array with 256 elements, each of which has type `double`. All the elements of an array are contiguous—kept together in storage. The integer number within the square brackets in the declaration is the subscript *bound* because it indicates how many elements there can be.

To refer to an individual element of an array in an expression, you can use an integer constant, an identifier (variable), or an expression in the square brackets, provided that it evaluates to a number greater than or equal to zero (the first element) and less than the subscript bound. For example, using the `points` array, here are some samples of correct and incorrect subscripts:

```
int item = 122;
double hold;
...
hold = points[0];      /* OK, first element */
hold = points[item]    /* OK, 123rd element */
hold = points[item+7]; /* OK, 130th element */
hold = points[-3];     /* WRONG, must be positive */
hold = points[256]     /* WRONG, out of bounds */
```

Because the syntax enables a postfix expression to have an array operator, you can define multidimensional arrays. Because `points[256]` is a postfix expression, you could also define the following:

```
double points[256][3];
```

You can interpret this intuitively to mean a set of 256 three-dimensional points. Chapter 8 covers multidimensional arrays in detail.

Function Call ()

The syntax for function call is as follows:

```
postfix expression ( arg-expr-list )
```

To call a function in an expression, use the function designator or a pointer to the function, followed by a pair of parentheses that may optionally contain the arguments to be used for that call. The argument list is optional only in the sense that the prototype may have declared a void parameter list so that the call should not specify any arguments. Here are some examples of function calls:

```
/* ----- declare variables and function prototypes ----- */
int results;
char *new_string;
char longstr[60] = "This is a longer string than the other one";
char shortstr[10] = "Really short";
char *longest_string( char *s1, char *s2 );
void kill_string( char *s1 );
int rand( void );
/* ----- use the functions ----- */
new_string = longest_string( longstr, shortstr );
kill_string( longstr );     /* a void expression */
results = rand();           /* no arguments allowed */
```

Structure (Union) Member .

The structure, or union, member's syntax is as follows:

```
postfix expression . identifier
```

You can define not only the basic data types and arrays, but also structures—aggregate data types that can contain both basic type objects and other structures. The struct keyword defines a type, just as int, double, and others do. The following example illustrates the most useful way to define a structure object:

```
struct circle {
  double center_x, center_y, radius;
};
struct circle circle1;
```

The object circle1 does not have type double; it has type struct. Its member variables, however, do have type double. The structure member operator enables you to reference a member variable directly, as in the following:

```
circle1.radius = 25;
```

Structure (Union) Member Pointer ->

The syntax is as follows:

```
postfix expression -> identifier
```

Suppose that you have defined an object you want to pass as a parameter to a function. Suppose also that you want to pass only its address because the object may be too large to pass by value. Using the circle1 object again, you might code something like the following:

```
  struct circle {
    double center_x, center_y, radius;
  };
void draw_circle( struct circle *anycircle )
{
... /* draw the circle here */
}
...
main()
{
  struct circle circle1;
  draw_circle( &circle1 );
}
```

draw_circle() expects a pointer to a structure, not a copy of the whole structure. How do you refer to member objects now? The structure member operator doesn't work; you must use the member pointer operator, as follows:

```
circle1->radius = 25; /* Dereference struct and get member */
```

The *member pointer operator* is composed of a minus sign and greater-than sign. There can be blanks on either side of, but not between, the two characters.

Postfix Increment ++

The postfix increment's syntax is as follows:

```
postfix expression ++
```

The postfix increment operator updates the stored value of the object to its left. When it updates, it is something else. For instance, in this fragment

```
int a = 1, b;
...
b = a++ + 1;
```

the result placed in b is not 3, but 2. The value of a is fetched first for purposes of evaluating the expression. This value is not tampered with again—it is 1 here. Next, the + 1 part of the expression is evaluated, yielding 2. The result is placed in b. Sometime during that process a is again fetched, incremented (1 is added to it), and replaced in a. The only guarantee for timing the side effect is that it occurs anywhere between the preceding and next sequence points. Of course, if you write

```
a++;
```

as the entire statement, you guarantee the timing by isolating the side effect.

Postfix decrement --

The postfix decrement's syntax is as follows:

postfix expression --

The postfix decrement operator reduces by one the value of the object to its left. Timing considerations are the same as for postfix ++.

Unary Operators

Just as the most basic form of postfix expression is the primary expression, so the most basic form of the *unary expression* is the postfix expression. This is not as surprising as you might think. Consider the following expression:

```
-point[i];
```

This expression is similar to writing –1. It is an array element (a postfix expression) rather than a constant.

All of the unary operators are prefixed to the object they work on and group from the right. The unary operators include prefix ++ and -- (increment and decrement), the sizeof operator, address-of &, indirection *, unary + and -, one's complement ~, and the logical not !.

Constraints are associated with some of the unary operators. The object of unary + and - must have an arithmetic type (not just integers), the one's complement ~ operates only on an integral type, and logical not ! only on a scalar type (a simple numeric type—this disallows structures and arrays but permits character objects).

Prefix Increment ++

The prefix increment's syntax is as follows:

```
++unary expression
```

The prefix increment differs greatly from the postfix increment—there is no delayed reaction. The value of the object is fetched, updated, and stored in the object location immediately. Only then is the updated value used in evaluating the expression, for example:

```
int a = 1, b;
b = ++a + 1;
printf( "%d\n", b );
```

This code fragment causes the number 3 to be displayed, not 2 as for the postfix increment operator.

Prefix Decrement --

The prefix decrement's syntax is as follows:

```
--unary expression
```

The prefix decrement works the same as prefix increment, except that the object is reduced by 1. Prefix increment and decrement are the only unary operators that modify an object's value (have side effects).

Unary +

The syntax for unary + is as follows:

```
+expression
```

The unary + operator results in only the value of its operand—it does not force the value to be positive, as you might think when looking at the following code fragment:

```
int a = -1;
printf( "%d\n", +a );
```

This code fragment displays –1, not +1. The value of a is not changed by this code.

Unary -

The syntax for unary - is as follows:

```
-expression
```

This operator causes the negative of its operand to be used in evaluating an expression. It forces a sign change but does not affect the stored value of the object (as does --). If a == 1, then b = b + -a is equivalent to b = b - a. Here is an interesting thought experiment: What is the final result of the following fragment?

```
int a = -1;
b = a - -a;
```

One's Complement ~

The syntax for the one's complement is as follows:

```
~expression
```

The one's complement operator inverts all the bits in its integral operand (which can include character types). Because the operand can be an expression, no stored value is affected.

Inverting the bits means that the result's bit is on only if the operand's bit is off. For example, the following line

```
int data = ~0xxFFFF;
```

results in the object data having a value of zero; because every bit is a 1, every result bit is a zero.

Logical Not !

The syntax for logical not is as follows:

```
!expression
```

Logical not reverses the sense of a conditional expression; in an if statement's conditional expression, for example, you could write

```
int a = 0, b = 0;
if ( !a ) b = 1;
```

Remember that a result of 0 means false and a result of nonzero means true. Thus, the expression statement b = 1 is executed only if !a evaluates to a true condition. It does here; because a == 0, the !a is true and therefore evaluates to nonzero. If a had been initialized to 1, !a would have evaluated false, and the corresponding statement would not have executed. In any event, the stored value of a would not have been changed in this fragment. Be careful of using inverse logic like this; you can lose track faster than you think.

Size-Of *sizeof*

The size-of syntax is as follows:

```
sizeof unary expression
    sizeof ( type-name )
```

The `sizeof` operator produces the size, in bytes, of its operand. The result is an integer constant. If the expression is an identifier, the result is the number of bytes required to store the value of the object; if it is an actual expression, it yields the number of bytes that storing the resulting value would require. You may also take the size of a type specifier, which yields the number of bytes required to store such an object, as in the following:

```
int result;
...
result = sizeof result;   /*Integers usually 2 */
result = sizeof( char ); /* Will be 1 */
```

If you take the size of a pointer, a function designator, or an array identifier, the result is the number of bytes required to store the pointer to the object, not the object being pointed to.

Address-Of &

The address-of syntax is as follows:

```
&object or &function
```

The address-of operator forms a pointer to a previously declared object. You saw it used in the structure member pointer example. You can take (extract) the address of an object or of a function, as shown in the following code fragment:

```
#include <stdlib.h>
#include <stdio.h>
main()
{
  int (*inchar)( FILE *fp );
  inchar = &fgetc; /* take address of lib function */
  printf( "\n%c\n", inchar( stdin ) );
}
```

The method used here in `printf()` to call a function with a function pointer is new with ANSI C. In K&R C, you had to call `inchar()` as follows:

```
printf( "\n%c\n", (*inchar)( stdin ) );
```

The older method is still valid; you can use either one.

Indirection *

The indirection operator's syntax is as follows:

```
*pointer expression
```

> The indirection operator uses the same source character as the multiplication operator. Do not confuse these operators. The compiler keeps them separate by noting the context in which they are used.

CAUTION

You use the indirection operator both to declare a pointer and to dereference one. To declare a pointer to an integer, for example, you write

```
int *count;
```

The parameter list entry in a function prototype is similar:

```
int update( int *count );
```

Outside a declaration, the indirection operator is used to dereference the pointer—to access the object pointed to, not the actual pointer, as in the following example:

```
(*count)++; /* postfix incr the count object */
count++;    /* postfix incr the pointer to count */
```

Here, the first line updates the value of count by 1. Note that you use parentheses to overcome the fact that a postfix increment has higher precedence than indirection. Without the parentheses, only the pointer would be updated. The second line updates the pointer to count by the sizeof an integer—two bytes, on most systems.

Cast Operators

Cast operators are unary operators also but are handled separately by the ANSI document. The purpose of the cast operator is to change the type of the value of an identifier or expression; the cast operator never affects stored values and cannot produce an lvalue. A cast operator groups operands from the right like the other unary operators. It must have a scalar operand; arrays and aggregate objects are not permitted, but pointers are.

Type Cast

The type cast operator's syntax is as follows:

```
( type-name ) cast expression
```

The `cast expression` can be an identifier, or a primary, postfix, or unary expression, as in the following:

```
double pi 3.1415926;
int number;
...
number = (int)pi; /* "number" is now 3 */
```

Pointers can be cast to new types also, but that discussion comes later in this chapter in the section "Explicit Conversions with Type Casts."

Binary Operators

The binary operators form the bulk of the C operator set. These operators require two operands. They group from left, except for the assignment and conditional operators. Operators in each subclass have equal precedence, and the subclasses are listed in descending order of precedence.

Multiplicative Operators

The following syntax lines describe these operators

Multiplication	`m-expression * cast expression`
Division	`m-expression / cast expression`
Modulus	`m-expression % cast expression`

whereby `m-expression` means "multiplicative expression" and can be either a cast expression as defined in the preceding section or an expression that already contains multiplicative operators. All these operators require arithmetic type operands; the `%` modulus (remainder) operator requires integral operands beyond that.

The `*` multiplies two operands (this is not the indirection operator). The `/` divides the left operand by the right; the result is the quotient (truncated to a whole number if integer types). The `%` also performs a division of the operands, but the result is the remainder (also a whole number if integer operands). Algebraic signs are preserved in the operations, except perhaps for a modulus, in which case, the sign of the result is implementation-defined.

Additive Operators

The following syntax lines describe these operators:

Addition	`a-expression + m-expression`
Subtraction	`a-expression - m-expression`

whereby *a-expression* means "additive expression" and *m-expression* means "multiplicative expression." Specifying *m-expression* as the right operand is important. It guarantees that addition (or subtraction) proceeds from the left. Because, by definition, an *m-expression* does not contain additive operators, an expression such as:

```
a = b + c + d;
```

is guaranteed to evaluate as if you had written the following:

```
a = ( b + c ) + d;
```

Either both operands must have arithmetic type, or one of the operands can be a pointer and the other an integer. When subtracting, both operands can be pointers. That is, you can do arithmetic on pointers (in the limits discussed in Chapter 8).

Bitwise Shift Operators

The following syntax lines describe these operators:

Shift left   *shift expression << a-expression*

Shift right   *shift expression >> a-expression*

All operands of the bitwise shift operators must be integral types. The operations are meant to shift bit patterns to the left or to the right. The left operand expression value (which does not have to be an `lvalue`) is shifted left or right by the number of bits specified by the additive expression on the left. Bits "shifted out" are lost. For example,

```
int n = 0xFFFF;
...
n = n << 8;
printf( "%.4X\n", n );
```

causes `FF00` to be displayed on-screen. The syntax implies that shift operations can be compounded by nesting in parentheses. To clear some of the bits and realign them in the integer, you might want to do the following:

```
int n = 0xFFFF;
...
n = ( n << 8 ) >> 4;
printf( "%.4X\n", n );
```

The integer n begins with all bits set: 1111111111111111. The left shift produces 1111111100000000 (0xFF00 as before). Finally, the right shift of 4 bits centers them in the integer: 0000111111110000 (or 0x0FF0).

> **NOTE** Shifting left 1 bit is the equivalent of multiplying by 2; shifting right 1 bit divides by 2. Successive shifts are equal to successive powers of 2.

Relational Operators

The following syntax lines describe these operators:

Less than	`expression < expression`
Greater than	`expression > expression`
Less than or equal to	`expression <= expression`
Greater than or equal to	`expression >= expression`

The relational operators yield 1 if the specified comparison is true and 0 if false. Because grouping is still left to right, the left operand is compared to the right operand. In the following example

```
if ( a < b ) do_something();
```

`a < b` means that if `a` is less than `b`, `do_something()` is called. The operands of a relational operator must be either both arithmetic or both pointers to compatible object type (or compatible incomplete object type). ANSI leaves undefined a comparison of pointers to different objects, except that a pointer value one beyond the end of an array is valid for comparison only (to detect the end of the array).

Equality Operators

The following syntax lines describe these operators:

Equal	`expression == expression`
Not equal	`expression != expression`

These operators are similar in use and syntax to the relational operators, except that they have lower precedence. They are not assignment operators, and you avoid confusing them. Pointers compare equal when they point to the same locale in an object.

You can use the equality operators to compare arithmetic objects, pointers to compatible objects, a pointer to an object and a `void` pointer, and a pointer and a null pointer constant (integer 0). You already have used equality operators several times in the examples, particularly in testing the result of stream I/O functions. The following code fragment uses the equality operator to test the results of opening a file:

```
FILE *infile;          /* Read and display a file */
char ch;
..
if ( NULL == ( infile = fopen( "file.dat", "r" ) ) ) {
  puts( "Can't open the file." );
  abort();
}
while ( EOF != ( ch = fgetc( infile ) ) ) fputc( ch, stdout );
fclose( infile );
```

Bitwise AND &

The following syntax line describes this operator:

AND-expression & equality expression

Binary & accepts only integral type operands. The result is the bitwise AND of the operators. The syntax guarantees left-to-right grouping of operands by specifying the more inclusive expression class on the left (in other words, associativity is guaranteed; either operand may be evaluated first because the outcome is the same as if it were done left to right).

The bitwise AND sets a result bit on only if both corresponding operand bits are on. You can use this operator to turn off selected bits, as follows:

```
int a = 0xFF, b = 0xFE, c;
...
c = a & b; /* c now == 0xFE */
```

Bitwise Exclusive OR ^

The following syntax line describes this operator:

exclusive-OR-expression ^ AND-expression

Binary ^ accepts only integral type operands. The exclusive OR sets a result bit on only if one or the other corresponding operand bits, but not both, are on.

An interesting and useful application of the exclusive OR operator is to clear (turn off) all bits in an integer by exclusive ORing it with itself, as follows:

```
unsigned char flags = 0xAA;
...
flags = flags ^ flags; /* all bits off */
```

Bitwise Inclusive OR |

The following syntax line describes this operator:

```
inclusive-OR-expression | exclusive-OR-expression
```

Binary | accepts only integral operands. A result bit is on if either, or both, corresponding operand bit is on.

You can use inclusive OR to turn on selected bits, as follows:

```
unsigned char flags = 0; /* bit pattern 00000000 */
...
flags = flags | 0x80; /* bit pattern 10000000 */
```

Logical AND &&

The following syntax lines describe these operators:

```
logical-AND-expression && inclusive-OR-expression
```

Logical AND can accept any scalar operands (not just integers). The operands of && are conditional expressions; no stored value is affected. In a statement such as:

```
if ( a && b ) statement;
```

the associated statement (which can be a block statement) is executed only if both the a and b expressions are true (evaluate to nonzero). A null pointer evaluates to false; an uninitialized pointer is not necessarily null.

Unlike the bitwise AND, logical AND guarantees both left-to-right associativity and left-to-right order of evaluation. If the left operand is false, the right operand is not evaluated, and the entire expression evaluates to false. This is handy when the state of some variables depends on the value of others. Suppose, for example, that your database program uses a flag field to record whether a stream has been opened. You might code a test statement like this:

```
FILE *database; /* stream pointer */
int flags; /* stream state flags */
...
if ( flags & 0x80 && database ) ... /* go ahead */
```

The left operand is the expression flags & 0x80. The bitwise AND has higher precedence and is to the left of the logical AND; if the high-order bit is on, the remainder of the expression is evaluated. If *database has been opened successfully, this pointer is not null. In other words, if the flag is set, the database is open; if the database is open, determine whether it opened correctly.

Logical OR ¦¦

The following syntax line describes this operator:

```
logical-OR-expression ¦¦ logical-AND-expression
```

Logical OR accepts scalar operands and guarantees both left-to-right associativity and order of evaluation. The operation evaluates true if either operand expression or both of them evaluate true. If the first operand expression is false, the remainder of the operation is not done. It works like this:

```
if ( a ¦¦ b ) { /* if you got here, at least one was true */ }
```

The Conditional (Ternary) Operator ?:

Of all the C operators, the ternary operator is perhaps the strangest in appearance. Several other operators have two characters placed together, but the operator characters in the ternary operator are separated by expressions. These operand expressions associate from the right.

The following syntax line describes this operator:

```
logical-OR-expression ? expression : expression
```

The conditional operator is nothing but a crazy (and extremely useful) if statement. The classic example of its use is the function-like maxval macro:

```
#define maxval(a,b) (a>b) ? (a) : (b)
...
int a, b, c;
...
c = maxval(a,b); /* get largest number into c */
```

If the logical OR expression is true, the operand expression to the left of the colon is evaluated, and this is the result of the whole expression. If it is false, the operand expression to the right of the colon is evaluated, and that is the result of the whole expression. This operator also guarantees both left-to-right associativity and order of evaluation.

Simple and Compound Assignment Operators

Simple and compound assignment operators are the means provided by C for modifying the value of an object (other than by side effects, such as using postfix ++). The compound operators provide a powerful variation on this theme; they modify in certain ways the object on the left based on the value of the expression on the right. All the assignment operators associate from the right.

NOTE The compound operators provide a powerful variation on the order of evaluation; they modify in certain ways the object on the left based on the value of the expression on the right. The other assignment operators associate from the right.

Simple Assignment =

The following syntax line describes this operator:

```
modifiable lvalue = expression
```

The value of the expression is placed in the indicated object's storage location (hence the requirement for a modifiable `lvalue`). Type conversions can occur implicitly here. See the section "Implicit Conversion by Assignment" later in this chapter.

Compound Assignment

The following syntax lines describe this operator:

```
modifiable lvalue op= expression
op == a binary operator
```

One of the binary operators (except relational, logical, or equality operators) is followed immediately by the assignment operator. The effects of this arrangement are shown in Table 5.1.

Table 5.1. Compound assignment actions.

Compound Operator	Equivalent Statement
a += b;	a = a + b;
a -= b;	a = a - b;
a *= b;	a = a * b;
a /= b;	a = a / b;
a %= b;	a = a % b;
a &= b;	a = a & b;
a ^= b;	a = a ^ b;
a ¦= b;	a = a ¦ b;
a <<= b;	a = a << b;
a >>= b;	a = a >> b;

The Comma Operator

In C, you use the comma operator to separate statements when you are coding several and only one is required—or perhaps where only one is permitted. The different statements are evaluated from the left. This is exactly what we did in the function str_invert() in line 100 of Listing 5.2:

```
while ( s < p ) *s ^= *p, *p ^= *s, *s++ ^= *p-- ;
```

Use the comma operator conservatively for this purpose. The best practice is to use the comma only for very closely related groups of statements. This use is justified in the controlling expression of a for statement. Suppose, for example, that you want to reverse the order of an array of doubles. The following code does just that. Notice how the third expression controlling the for loop uses a comma to pack two expressions in the place of one:

```
double a[64];
double hold;
int i, j;
... /* initialize the array in here, somehow */
for ( i=0,j=63; i<j; i++,j-- ) {
  hold = a[i];
  a[i] = a[j];
  a[j] = hold;
}
```

The commas separating arguments in a function call are not comma operators; they are punctuation. Therefore, they can do nothing to guarantee a particular order of evaluation of function-call arguments. In fact, the ANSI standard specifically states that such order of evaluation is unspecified. You cannot count on any two compilers evaluating the same way.

The Key to C: Operator Precedence

Remember that because an expression enclosed in parentheses is a primary expression, grouping parentheses have the highest precedence of all. When you begin writing more complex programs, you'll frequently have to use grouping parentheses. In fact, you have already seen a need for it in at least two places. First, you saw it in the statements that opened a file and tested the outcome of the open in one statement:

```
FILE *infile;
...
if ( NULL != ( infile = fopen( ..., ... ) ) ) {
  /* open OK if you got here */
}
```

Why were the parentheses necessary here? If you look over the operators you just learned, you find that the equality operator != has higher precedence than assignment =. If you had not used the parentheses, the expression would have evaluated as if grouped like this:

```
if ( ( NULL != infile ) = fopen( ... ) ) ...
```

This expression wouldn't even get past the compile process. The result of this expression would be an attempt to assign a pointer to a constant—the results of fopen() into NULL. The compiler diagnostic message would tell you politely that an lvalue is required on the left side of an assignment operator. You also saw that careless placement of the arguments in a function-like macro can lead to disaster.

T I P   When placing arguments in a function-like macro, the best practice is to always surround macro arguments with parentheses to ensure that precedence does not produce some off-the-wall expression—one that may even get by the compiler.

There is no substitute for knowing operator precedence, but it is not easy to remember. Table 5.2 summarizes both operator precedence (highest at the top) and operator associativity.

Table 5.2.   C operator precedence, from highest to lowest.

Operator(s)	Associativity
Postfix	
function() array[] member-> member. ++ --	left to right
Unary/Prefix	
! ~ ++ -- +) - * & (*type*) sizeof	right to left
Binary	
* / %	left to right
+ -	left to right
<< >>	left to right
< <= > >=	left to right
== !=	left to right
&	left to right

Operator(s)	Associativity
^	left to right
¦	left to right
&&	left to right
¦¦	left to right
Conditional	
?:	right to left
Assignment	
= += -= *= /= %= &= ^= ¦= <<= >>=	right to left
Comma	
,	left to right

Converting Data Types to Other Types

The conversion of one type of object to another adds a new level of complexity to understanding expression evaluation. You can mix several object types in one expression, making it necessary to determine what type the final result will have; you can assign the value of one type into another, and you can use the cast operator to convert object types deliberately.

Automatic Type Conversions

Because type conversions can occur automatically, without your requesting them, you would be well advised to know when and how this happens. There are two types of automatic type conversion: operand *promotion* in expression evaluation and *implicit conversion* across an assignment operator.

Type Promotion in Expressions

You frequently have to mix operands of differing types in one expression. What is the type of the value resulting from evaluation? In a word, an expression has the same type as the most comprehensive basic object type in the expression. If you mix integers and double floating-point numbers, the expression's type is `double`.

Operands are converted in pairs, for each operator encountered. Naturally, the intermediate result from a subexpression may become an operand and be converted again. This process is called *promotion*. The sequence of promotions proceeds according to the rules of *usual arithmetic conversion*. These rules are listed from the most complex basic types to the simplest:

- ■ If either operand of the pair has type `long double`, the other operand is converted to `long double`. It does not matter which operand; either one causes the conversion.

- ■ Otherwise, if either operand has type `double`, the other is converted to `double`.

- ■ Otherwise, if either operand has type `float`, the other is converted to `float`.

- ■ Otherwise, any integral types are converted to a signed or unsigned version, whichever one can preserve the value including the sign bit.

These rules are called the *integral promotions*. Following the integral promotions, these next rules are applied:

- ■ If either operand has type `unsigned long int`, the other is converted to `unsigned long int`.

- ■ Otherwise, if either operand has type `long int` and the other has `unsigned int`, the `unsigned int` is converted to `long int` if that contains the value including the sign; otherwise, both operands are converted to `unsigned long int`.

- ■ Otherwise, if either operand has type `long int`, the other is converted to `long int`.

- ■ Otherwise, if either operand has type `unsigned int`, the other is converted to `unsigned int`.

- ■ Otherwise, both operands have type `int`, and no conversion is needed.

Notice that the sign of an operand is preserved during conversion, even if the significance of the sign bit is changed. A –1 value held in an `int`, for example, has a bit pattern on most machines of `0xFFFF`. If converted to unsigned, the bit pattern is still `0xFFFF`, but the number is no longer considered negative.

When a floating-point number is converted to an integral type, the fraction part is discarded (truncated). The value of the integral type is the next lowest whole number.

When an integral type is converted to a floating-point type, the resulting value may or may not be exactly the same as the original integer. Even if the number is in the proper range, floating-point numbers cannot represent exactly every possible number. If the representation cannot be exact, the result is the nearest representable value. Whether the representation is chosen to be higher or lower than the original number depends on how the representation is implemented.

Implicit Conversion by Assignment

Clearly, type conversion in an expression can lead to some unexpected results if you do not understand the process. You may encounter difficulties resulting from the truncation of fractional parts, bit patterns produced by preserving the sign, or even loss of significant digits if the target type cannot hold the value.

The fact that the same conversions can occur "across an equals sign" often escapes a programmer's notice (even a seasoned one!). This should not be surprising because assignment, like every other part of an expression, involves an operator. The same conversion rules also apply here.

Explicit Conversions with Type Casts

You may want to take control of the conversion process by using the cast operator. Any of the conversions belonging to the usual arithmetic conversions can be done also with the cast operator.

A cast is sometimes needed to keep things straight. A code fragment earlier in the chapter illustrated how to use a character pointer to access the bytes of an `unsigned long int`. Look at the following lines from that fragment:

```
char *byte;
...
printf( "%.2X ", (unsigned char)byte[i] );
```

Notice the `(unsigned char)` cast in the `printf()`. Why do you suppose it is there? It controls the usual arithmetic conversions, specifically to prevent an inadvertent propagation of a sign. Three things come together here to make this necessary:

1. The `%X` conversion sequence in `printf()` expects an integer type.

2. By default, the byte pointer points to a signed character that is passed as a 2-byte integer parameter to `printf()`.

3. The arithmetic conversions preserve the sign bit.

Things work fine provided that the character being implicitly converted to an integer is positive; because the sign bit is 0, the conversion to a physically larger type just propagates 0 bits in the high-order positions. But when the sign bit is on (that is, when the number is negative), a 1 bit is propagated to the high-order bit positions.

Therefore, when a negative character such as 0xDC is encountered, an extremely large negative integer emerges from the implicit conversion. Figure 5.5 shows the propagation of the sign bit when converting a 1-byte to a 2-byte field.

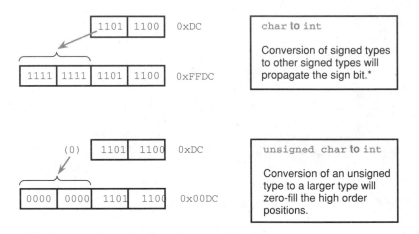

Figure 5.5.

Sign-bit propagation during conversion.

* This is true on CPUs that use 2's complement arithmetic. Some other method may be used on machines that don't.

The cast to unsigned char preserves the sign bit in place, but prevents its propagation in conversion to an integer; in an unsigned type, there is no sign to propagate. Of course, you could have defined the pointer as unsigned char *byte in the first place, but that would have ruined the example!

Type casts are probably used most often in pointer conversions. Two types of pointer conversion are implicit and need no cast: the assignment or comparison of a zero integral value to a pointer (creating or testing a NULL pointer) and direct assignment of values from any pointer type to a void pointer. void pointers can, by definition, point to anything. (Some compilers may nevertheless issue a warning message about this.) Other types of pointer conversion require an explicit cast.

A pointer may be cast to an integral type large enough to hold it. Both the size of the integral type required and the mapping algorithm are implementation-dependent. This emphasizes that pointers are not integers and should not be used as if they were.

An integer of sufficient size may be cast to a pointer. Before you attempt this, be sure that you understand the internal structure of the pointer type on your system.

One pointer type may be cast to another pointer type. You have seen this already in the example of conversion of a pointer to an `unsigned long int` to a pointer to `char`. You possibly could encounter alignment problems when you cast to another pointer type. Some systems require an `int` to be *word-aligned*, for example (placed at a RAM address evenly divisible by the number of bytes in a word). This type of cast could involve conversion to the same pointer type, except for qualifiers (`unsigned int *` cast to `int *`, for example).

To restore an object pointer from a `void` pointer, you must use the `(void *)` cast.

A pointer to a function type may be cast to a pointer to another function type. Using pointers to functions is covered in detail in Chapter 6.

The cast operator won't do one thing in particular. You cannot cast a pointer to an object type to a pointer to a function type, or vice versa.

Summary

This chapter covers a great deal of necessary background material. In fact, if you've read this far, you are a more competent C programmer than you may suspect. Experience builds your confidence. Keep writing code!

In the next chapter, you will examine some powerful techniques. Before you approach that material, however, be sure that you have gleaned the following from this chapter:

- ■ The essentials of scope, linkage, and duration. These concepts must become second nature to you; from this point on, you should be writing ever more complex code.

- ■ How to build multiple source-file programs. Don't stop with just the general concepts that we were able to present here. Use your compiler and utilities and build some of these programs. Practice these techniques *before* you need them.

- ■ The rules and techniques for writing C expressions. If you can label any one thing the heart of C programming, writing C expressions is it.

- ■ How to convert object types to other types. You should understand how to control type promotions during expression evaluation, conversion across the assignment operator, and explicit casts of types.

More About C Functions

This chapter deals with some of the more involved aspects of defining and calling functions. C handles functions with a great deal of power and flexibility, and this capability is not difficult to harness. In this chapter, you learn more about the following:

- Passing parameters to functions. You can pass *by value* and *by reference,* pass incomplete types, pass a variable number of arguments, pass a function (pointer) to the function, and even pass arguments to main().

- *Recursive functions.* These are functions that call themselves. You see how to avoid open-ended recursion and how to eliminate recursion altogether (and why you should or should not do so).

- Alternative ways to invoke functions. These methods are relatively simple to implement but can result in powerful code.

Details About Passing Parameters

C is implemented on a number of different machine types. Some of them are stack-oriented machines, such as most personal computers and minicomputers, and some are not, such as the IBM 370 architecture mainframes. The physical method of passing parameters may vary, therefore, from one machine and implementation to the next. In this chapter, a hypothetical stack-oriented machine is assumed for purposes of illustration.

Pass by Value and Pass by Reference

The default method of passing parameters to a function is *by value.* An argument expression (which may be a simple object identifier or a more complex expression) is evaluated, and the result is passed to the function with which to work. Passing arguments by value therefore prevents the function from modifying an object's stored value; this is the purpose of the default method.

All the basic data types, plus structures and unions, can be passed by value. Array types, however, cannot. (Remember that this includes strings, which are arrays of char.) Only a *pointer* to an array, taken as a whole, may be passed to the function. This is called passing parameters *by reference.* Of course, you can declare the function prototype so a pointer must be used for any type.

Parameters Are Passed on the Stack

C is quite common on the stack-oriented machine assumed for this discussion. Parameters are passed to a function by placing the argument *on the stack* on such machines.

You saw an example of this in Chapter 3 and may want to review that figure now (refer to Figure 3.3). The figure shows that arguments usually are placed on the stack from right to left. This is not true for every compiler, nor does it have anything to do with the way the arguments are evaluated. For example, given the declarations

```
int sum( int a, int b, int c );
int x = 37, y = 47, z = 57;
int result;
...
main()
{
  result = sum( x, y, z );
}
```

the value of z usually is placed on the stack first, then y, and finally x. Understanding the order in which arguments are placed on the stack becomes important a little later, when you consider the techniques for passing a variable number of arguments.

Passing Parameters by Value

When parameters are passed by value, only a copy of stored objects is placed on the stack, and the function's code should reference the passed argument values as though they were defined in the function body. The following code fragment illustrates both of these points:

```
void reset_it( int p )
{
  p = 99; /* Does not affect main's version of p */
}
...
main()
{
  int p = 44;
  reset_it( p ); /* Pass a copy of p */
}
```

As you may remember, it does not matter that the formal parameter name p in the parameter list for reset_it() happens to be the same as the object name of the actual argument passed to it. They are not the same object. You may recall also that the int object p in main() has block scope and no linkage. Unless you do something more than is present in this example, reset_it() has access only to the *copy* of p located on the system stack.

Passing Parameters by Reference

Pointers passed as parameters to a function have an entirely different effect on the way objects are handled. See what happens in the following modification of the preceding code fragment:

```
void reset_it( int *p ) /* Now expecting a pointer */
{
  *p = 99; /* DOES affect main's version of p */
}
...
main()
{
  int p = 44;
  reset_it( &p );
  /* Stored value of p now 99 */
}
```

In this version of reset_it(), a *reference* to p is passed—a pointer, not a copy of the object's value. This is indicated by the use of the indirection operator in the parameter declaration part of reset_it().

Notice that the object p is now accessed in the function by a second use of the indirection operator. If that operator were missing, the function would set the pointer value, not the object's stored value, to 99. The assignment expression would not compile correctly, anyway. The conversion rules require that an explicit cast be used for converting an integer to a pointer.

The function call also is a little different. Now the call requires that the address-of operator (unary &) be used to take the address of the object during argument evaluation—because this is not an array or a string. If p were an array or a string, the address-of operator would not be required. References to arrays and strings as a whole (rather than elements within them) always produce a pointer. If p were an array, for example, you could write the following:

```
void reset_it( int p[32] ) /* Still expecting a pointer */
{
  int i;
/* Still affects the original object's stored values */
  for ( i=0, i<32, i++ ) p[i] *= 2; /* Double elements */
}
...
main()
{
  int p[64];
...
/* Initialize the array in here */
...
  reset_it( p ); /* p is the address of the array */
}
```

If p were a string, the declarations would be similar:

```
void reset_it( char *p ) { ... }
...
main()
{
  char p[64] = "This is a string now.";
  ...
  reset_it( p );
}
```

Function Argument Promotions

Chapter 5 covered the conversions and promotions possible for object types during expression evaluation. It should not be surprising that the evaluation of function arguments *can* cause type promotions as well; passing arguments to a function involves their evaluation, and, after all, arguments can be expressions as well as objects. Consider three things when passing arguments to functions:

■ The comma operator does not guarantee order of evaluation, only associativity. Function arguments are evaluated as if from left to right (associativity), but *in fact* may be evaluated in any order. You should not write function argument expressions with side effects and expect them to alter values passed to the function, either. Remember that a sequence point occurs before argument evaluation begins and after it is complete, but not in between. Thus, a call such as:

```
int a = 1;
...
some_function( a++, a );
```

does not pass the values 1 and 2, but passes the values 1 and 1. The postfix incremented value of the original variable a is available when the function has been entered, but not before that time (and does not affect what the function receives to work with, anyway).

■ Functions that do not have prototypes are subject to the default promotions of their arguments. These functions include those declared by being defined (no forward declarations at all), those that do not specify parameter types, and those that have only old-style forward declarations (which also do not specify types and are not true prototypes). The arguments of such functions first undergo the default integer promotions. This means that arguments with type char, short int, or int are *always* promoted to either int or unsigned int, whichever is required to represent them correctly.

Following the integral promotions, all values with type float are *always* promoted to double. Such promotions can be potentially confusing, especially if the function contains code that in any way depends on the internal structure of the arguments.

■ Functions having prototypes do not experience the default promotions. Full-function prototypes provide the compiler with enough information to evaluate arguments while performing only such *implicit conversions* as are required to make actual arguments match the type of corresponding parameters. For example, the following code fragment is legitimate; even the type of the actual argument passed does not match the type of the corresponding formal parameter in the prototype.

```
int scale_num( int num );  /* Prototype for scaling numbers */
char p = '1';              /* Display character 1 */
int value;                 /* Holds scaled number */
...
value = scale_num( p );    /* Arg has type char in call */
```

Passing a char type to a function that expects an integer argument causes the argument value to be converted, as though by assignment, to the expected integer. You could even pass a double to this function, but its fractional part would be lost when the conversion to int occurred.

Function Prototypes with Incomplete Types

You may declare a function prototype that contains parameters having *incomplete type*—a type specification insufficient to provide size or content information. This may help you generalize your program so a change to the source code in one place does not require changes in others. More detail on incomplete types is provided in Chapters 8 and 11, but a quick look at them may be helpful now.

Two kinds of objects—*arrays* and *structures*— may have an incomplete type specification. Of these, only incomplete array declarations are of any real use with function prototypes. Note the following descriptions:

■ An array declaration with an omitted subscript bound expression is an incomplete type. The array subscript postfix operator ([]) normally contains an expression that defines and limits the number of elements in an array. If the array is defined elsewhere, it can be declared again without the bounds information, as in the following:

```
extern int points[];
```

This declaration supplies enough information to determine the address of the array, the type of each element, and the size of each element— sizeof(int)—but not the size of the entire array. Unless more information is provided by some other means, this limited information may not be enough to be useful. Then again, it may.

■ A more common use for incomplete array types is to omit *one* of the subscript bounds in a function prototype declaration containing a multidimensional array, as in

```
void plot_polygon( int count, int points[][3] );
```

This declaration provides information about the number of points in the count variable. Such a declaration could be used to limit a loop that plots any number of points in a polygon, because the first array subscript bound is missing. Why would you want to write a function declaration in this way? Generally, it is part of a separately compiled source file. Defining it like this generalizes the routine so it can be used by many programs, not just one. Chapter 8, "Programming with Pointers, Arrays, and Strings," goes into detail on handling array declarations with incomplete type.

■ A structure declaration with a tag but no member list is an incomplete type. A declaration such as

```
struct record1;
```

informs the compiler of nothing except that such a structure will be redeclared later with more information to complete the type. This kind of incomplete type is not very useful for function prototype declarations, but does have other uses. More detail on incomplete structure declarations is presented in the discussion of derived types in Chapter 11, "Deriving New Complex Data Types."

Variable-Length Argument Lists

Think about the `printf()` and `scanf()` functions for a moment. Both of these functions have a format string as the first parameter, followed by any number of variable arguments. How do these functions know when to stop processing arguments? More than that, how do they know where those arguments are?

The answer to the first question is that `printf()` and `scanf()` can determine the number of arguments by simply counting the number of conversion specifiers in the format string. You are already familiar with the fact that these functions require the number of conversion specifiers to match exactly the number of following arguments. This leads to the first principle of processing a variable number of function call arguments: *the function declaration must specify the fixed and predictable arguments first, followed by all the other arguments.*

How would you write a function prototype for a function with a variable number of arguments? Standard C provides a special notation for just this situation. It is called an *ellipsis* and consists of three consecutive periods. The prototype for `printf()`, for example, is

```
int printf( const char *format, ... );
```

The ellipsis must always be the last thing in the parameter list because that is where the variable number of arguments must appear.

The answer to the second question—how to locate the unspecified arguments—can be difficult if you make it so, but need not be. Simply remember that function arguments are always passed by the same vehicle. On stack-oriented machines, such as those used for the examples here, that vehicle is always the system stack. On other machines, it may be another vehicle, but it is always predictable. Figure 6.1 illustrates how arguments can be located on a traditional stack-oriented machine.

In the model, the system *stack pointer* points just above the fixed, predictable arguments, which are followed in the stack by the variable arguments.

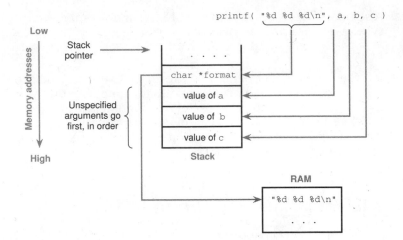

Figure 6.1.

Locating unspecified
arguments on the stack.

You need to develop some sort of mechanism for accessing the unspecified arguments, one after the other. The mechanism should allow for a mixture of object types.

Because the Borland C++ implementation of this feature is very clean and understandable and closely follows ANSI specifications, this discussion is based on that compiler's declarations. (They can be found in STDARG.H.) Here are the Borland C++ declarations:

```
typedef void _FAR *va_list;

#define __size(x) ((sizeof(x)+sizeof(int)-1) & ~(sizeof(int)-1))
#if defined(__cplusplus) && !defined(__STDC__)
  #define va_start(ap, parmN) (ap = ...)
#else
  #define va_start(ap, parmN) ((void)((ap) =
      (va_list)((char _FAR *)(&parmN)+__size(parmN))))
#endif
#define va_arg(ap, type) (*(type _FAR *)((((*(char _FAR *_FAR *)&
  (ap))+=__size(type))-(__size(type)))))
#define va_end(ap) ((void)0)
```

The standard requires that there be one type definition and three macros for advancing through a list of arguments whose type and number are not known at compile time. The preceding declarations follow exactly the required names and operations.

The type definition for va_list suits the need for supporting a mixture of argument types because a void pointer can point to anything. The cast to a particular pointer type occurs as each argument value is fetched. You have to declare a pointer object to use for fetching a variable number of arguments in the function that will use the argument list. You must declare this object *before* you begin to fetch any arguments. Here is an example of how this is done:

```
#include <stdarg.h>
...
float average( int num, ... )
{
  int i,sum = 0;
  va_list arg_ptr;
  ...
}
```

arg_ptr has a derived type of va_list. This is equivalent to the following declaration:

```
void *arg_ptr;
```

Next, you must initialize arg_ptr so it points to the first of the unspecified parameters. You do this with the function-like macro va_start:

```
#include <stdarg.h>
...
float average( int num, ... )
{
  int i,sum = 0;
  va_list arg_ptr;
  va_start( arg_ptr, num );
  ...
}
```

The #define for va_start gives formal parameters of ap for the argument pointer, and parmN for the last fixed parameter at the beginning of the list, which in this example is num.

At this point, Borland C++ does something that is not specified in the standard. It initializes the argument pointer as though the ellipsis denoted a pointer variable:

```
(ap = ...)
```

This should be considered unique to Borland C++; nowhere does the standard say that it's legal. A more compatible way of doing this might be

```
ap = (va_list)&parmN + sizeof(parmN)
```

which is very similar to the way Microsoft C/C++ does it. The address of parmN is taken and immediately cast to a pointer of type va_list. When the size of that parameter is added, the argument pointer points to the first of the un-specified arguments. The result is assigned to the argument pointer. In the current example, this would expand to the following:

```
arg_ptr = (va_list)&num + sizeof(num)
```

The process of accessing the arguments in turn is accomplished by writing the va_arg() macro. In this case, the goal is to access a number of integers—how many are to be controlled by num—and sum them, in preparation for calculating their average. By adding a little more code to the function, you get the following:

```
#include <stdarg.h>
...
float average( int num, ... )
{
  int i, sum = 0;
  va_list arg_ptr;
  va_start( arg_ptr, num );
  for ( i = 0; i<num; i++ ) sum += va_arg( arg_ptr, int );
  ...
}
```

va_arg is responsible not only for returning a value of the indicated type but also for updating the argument pointer to the next argument. The expression used to do this is informative. In this example, the statement sum += va_arg(arg_ptr, int) expands to the following:

```
sum += (*((int *)(arg_ptr))++)
```

Working from the inside out, you can see that the void pointer arg_ptr is first cast to a pointer to int: int *)(arg_ptr). The macro expansion may yield a different type on subsequent uses of va_arg(). The pointer to int is next dereferenced to yield a value: *((int *)(arg_ptr)). In this case, it yields an integer value.

Finally, the pointer (not the value) is postfix incremented: (*((int *)(arg_ptr))++). The arrangement of parentheses encloses the cast to pointer to int, so the pointer is incremented by the size of an integer, maintaining proper addressing. (Only a char * pointer is incremented by one byte exactly. All other pointers are updated by an amount equal to the size of the object pointed to.)

To complete the routine, you simply have to stop argument-list processing and calculate the average:

```
#include <stdarg.h>
...
float average( int num, ... )
```

```
{
  int i, sum = 0;
  va_list arg_ptr;
  va_start( arg_ptr, num );
  for ( i = 0; i<num; i++ ) sum += va_arg( arg_ptr, int );
  va_end( arg_ptr );
  return( (float)sum / num );
}
```

The ANSI standard states explicitly that the `va_end()` macro must be invoked to terminate argument processing. In the Borland C++ implementation, this macro does nothing because it is not needed. On other machines and systems, however, some action may well be needed to clean up after the function arguments have been accessed.

 NOTE It should be clear to you that *you* are responsible for determining the number of arguments as well as their type. The macros do not do it for you. `printf()` did it under control of the format string; the preceding example did it by requiring a fixed parameter containing the argument count.

Another method you can use when passing an unspecified number of *strings* is to terminate the list with a null string. An example of this method is shown in Listing 6.1.

Listing 6.1. LDISPLAY.C—Display a variable-length list of strings (for Borland C++).

```
1   #include <stdlib.h>
2   #include <stdio.h>
3   #include <stdarg.h>
4
5   void display_list( char *title, ... )
6   {
7     va_list ap;
8     char *hold;
9
10    printf( "%s\n", title );
11    va_start( ap, title );
12    hold = va_arg( ap, char * );  /* Prime the loop */
13    while ( *hold ) {             /* Test the string */
14      printf( "%s\n", hold );
15      hold = va_arg( ap, char * );
```

continues

Listing 6.1. Continued

```
16    }
17    va_end( ap );
18  }
19
20  main()
21  {
22    display_list(
23      "This is a list of physical constants ---",
24      "Pi = 3.1415929",
25      "c  = 2.997925E+8 meters per second",
26      "electron mass = 9.109558E-31 kilograms",
27      ""                    /* Here is the null string */
28      );
29  }
```

Three standard library functions support the use of variable argument lists. Their prototypes are

```
vfprintf( FILE *stream, const char *format, va_list ap );
vprintf( const char *format, va_list ap );
vsprintf( char *s, const char *format, va_list ap );
```

Because the literature contains any number of examples of how these functions are used to print error messages, the approach used here is different. The program in Listing 6.2 uses vsprintf() to clip a message line for a display window. The windowing support is not present. The function clip_display() assumes that cursor location has already been set at entry.

Listing 6.2. CLIP.C—Clip an output message to a window boundary with vsprintf() (for Borland C++).

```
1  #include <stdlib.h>
2  #include <stdio.h>
3  #include <stdarg.h>
4  #include <string.h>
5
6  void clip_display( int offset, int width, char *fmt, ... )
7  {
8    char *out;
9    va_list ap;
10
```

```
11    out = malloc( 256U );              /* Get an output area */
12    va_start( ap, fmt );
13    vsprintf( out, fmt, ap );              /* Format output */
14    va_end( ap );
15    if ( offset < strlen( out ) )      /* offset too far ? */
16      printf( "%.*s", width, out+offset ); /* Clip output */
17    free( out);
18  }
19
20  main()
21  {
22    int a = 37, b = 47;
23
24    clip_display( 5, 15,
25      "The value of a is %d and the value of b is %d.\n",
26      a, b );
27  }
```

The input parameters to `clip_display()` are an offset, a window width, a `printf()`-compatible format string, and a variable number of arguments. This function simply provides window-oriented `printf()` service.

The input parameter `offset` enables horizontal scrolling. The output message begins to display `offset` characters to the right of the beginning of the final message string.

To use the `vsprintf()` function, you must declare a `va_list` argument pointer, `va_start()`, and `va_end()` exactly as before. In line 13, `vsprintf()` formats the entire message into a dynamically acquired string. You do not use `va_arg()`— just pass along the argument pointer to `vsprintf()` or other `v...()` functions.

After checking to make sure that the offset value does not start printing beyond the end of the line (line 15), a normal `printf()` is used to position and trim the output message (line 16). As you study this example, you may want to refer to Chapter 2 and review `printf()` conversion specifiers.

Passing Parameters to *main()*

As far as the ANSI standard is concerned, C programs can execute in two environments: a *freestanding* environment, in which there is no operating system to support the program (the C program might be the operating system); and a *hosted* environment, in which a C program runs under the control of an operating system.

Hosted environments usually make available to the guest programs some means of acquiring information about the surrounding environment and the conditions in which they are expected to operate. To support this feature, C provides a mechanism for passing parameters to `main()`.

Accessing Command-Line Parameters

In a hosted environment, a C program is executed as a result of a *system command,* which consists of the name of the executable program file, followed by a command tail. The *command tail* is a series of text tokens, separated by blank spaces, that can have any significance the programmer wants. Note the following example:

```
C>program parm1 parm2 ... parmn
```

These tokens are called execution parameters or sometimes command-line parameters. Command-line parameters are to the program what function parameters are to a function. In Chapter 2, the program NUMBER.C in Listing 2.3 accepted one execution parameter—the name of the text file to be numbered:

```
C>number [drive:][\path\]filename[.ext]
```

Most operating systems consider everything on the command line after the program name to be the command tail. C's setup routines divide the command tail into token strings and pass (to the program) pointers to these strings so they can be accessed separately.

argc and argv[]

All of this is accomplished through the `argc` and `argv[]` parameters, which can be declared only in `main()`. To access execution parameters, you code the declaration for `main()` in this way:

```
main( int argc, char *argv[] )
{
...
}
```

The first parameter, `int argc`, is a count of the number of command parameters available. If your compiler cannot supply such parameters, `argc` will be zero. If the compiler can supply parameters, the value of `argc` will be at least 1, because the count includes the program name.

The second parameter, char *argv[], is an array of pointers to strings. Valid subscript numbers are 0 through argc-1. argv[0] is a pointer to the program name; *argv[0] (dereferencing the pointer) or argv[0][0] (using a subscript) is the first *character* of the program name. Some compilers that can supply command parameters do not have access to the program name. In that case, argv[0] points to a null string; this does not mean that there are no other parameters. SHOWARG.C in Listing 6.3 illustrates how you can access the command-line parameters, including the program name.

Listing 6.3. SHOWARG.C—Access command-line parameters (for Borland C++).

```
1  #include <stdlib.h>
2  #include <stdio.h>
3  #include <string.h>
4  #include <ctype.h>
5
6  main( int argc, char *argv[] )
7  {
8    int i;
9
10   /* ----- Display the program name ----- */
11
12   printf( "*** " );
13   for ( i=0; i<strlen( argv[0] ); i++ )
14     printf( "%c ", toupper( argv[0][i] ) );
15   printf( "*** \n" );
16
17   /* ----- Display the command parameters ----- */
18
19   for ( i=1; i<argc; i++ )
20     printf( "Argument %d: %s\n", i, argv[i] );
21 }
```

The output from SHOWARG.C looks like this:

```
*** C : \ BC \ P G M \ S H O W A R G . E X E ***
Argument 1: 123
Argument 2: abc
Argument 3: another parameter
```

For this example, the program was executed from the C:\BC\PGM directory on the hard drive, running under MS-DOS 5. The following command line was used to produce this output:

```
C:\BC\PGM>showarg 123 abc "another parameter"
```

Note that in this particular host environment, the operating system passes not only the simple program name but also the path to the executable program file. This may or may not be true on your system.

Lines 13 and 14 in Listing 6.3 produce the double-spaced program name. The `for` loop accesses each character from the `argv[0]` string by using a second subscript—`argv[0][i]`—after which it translates the character to uppercase with `toupper()` and passes the resulting character to `printf()` for display. The format string conveniently adds a blank after the `%c` conversion sequence, causing the double spacing.

In the `for` loop in lines 19 and 20, the execution parameters are displayed one at a time as strings by `printf()`. Because the parameter string as a whole is being accessed in each case, no second subscript is needed for `argv[i]`.

The third execution parameter in this example is `"another parameter"`. Even though there is a blank in the middle of this substring, it is treated by C—not by the operating system—as a single token. That happens because it is enclosed in parentheses, making it a string literal according to normal C syntax.

Designing Command-Line Formats

The number, type, and format of command-line parameters varies from one program to the next. Even if you always design your programs so the command-line parameters have an extremely uniform appearance, you may forget from time to time exactly what the parameters should be. Whether the format is consistent or not, you should include code that enables a user to get help.

The common method of providing this help was first developed by users of the UNIX operating system and has spilled over to other environments as well. The method consists of providing for execution of the program with no parameters, which results in a set of messages giving the correct command format. The code for doing this does not have to be extremely complex. Often a simple message will do, such as the one used in NUMBER.C (refer to Listing 2.3 in Chapter 2). Here are lines 13–18 of Listing 2.3 that generate the help message.

```
13    /* ----- Check command-line parameters ----- */
14
15    if ( argc < 2 ) {
16      printf( "\nSupply a program name to number.\n" );
17      exit( 8 );
18    }
```

If the argument count is less than 2, only the program name was typed on the command line. In that case, the program displays a message telling the user to follow the program name with a filename, and then terminates execution. The user can try again, with the appropriate parameters.

Although arranging some uniformity in parameter design may not always be possible, it is desirable (if for no other reason than to make running the program easier to remember).

Many programs allow some command-line parameters to be arguments and some to be options. A command-line *argument* is something the program works with, such as a filename. An *option* is a parameter that indicates *how* the program is to do its work. A program designed to print text files in a flexible way, for example, might support a command-line option to control line spacing, as in:

```
C>toprt myfile.txt -s2
```

The meaning of this command line is clear intuitively: the program sends MYFILE.TXT to the system printer and double spaces the output.

This same command line shows another practice inherited from UNIX systems. An option parameter is signaled by the presence of a *flag character* (a minus sign here) followed by a letter indicating what the option is and (if necessary) by a value to complete the definition.

If you decide to use a format like this, your program ideally should permit the arguments and options to be mixed in any order. The logic to handle separating the arguments and options could look something like this:

```
FILE *infile;
char filename[41];
int spacing;
void handle_option( char *ostring )
{
  if ( ostring[1] != 's' ) spacing = 1;
    else spacing = atoi( ostring+2 );
}
void handle_arg( char *astring )
{
  strcpy( filename, astring );
}
main( int argc, char *argv[] )
{
  int i;
  for ( i=1; i<argc; i++ ) { /* Skip program name */
    if ( *argv[i] == '-' ) handle_option( argv[i] );
```

```
        else handle_arg( argv[i] );
   }
   ...
}
```

In this example, the order in which the argument and option are typed doesn't matter; they are handled as they are presented to the program.

Functions That Call Themselves

Whether or not a function has been forward declared with a prototype, a function designator is in scope for its own function body. Thus, a statement in a function body may be a function call—to itself. This is called a *recursive function call* or, more simply, *recursion*.

NOTE Handled properly, recursion can be a powerful technique. Some algorithms are well suited to it. Handled improperly, the technique can be very dangerous. The first step toward correct control of recursion is to understand how it works.

Understanding Recursion

The ANSI standard does not define recursion; it says only that recursion is legal. Recursion can be either direct or indirect; both are sanctioned specifically by ANSI. *Direct recursion* is the process of a function calling itself from its own function body.

Indirect recursion involves more than one function. Say, for example, that there are two functions: one() and two(). To get things started, main() calls one(), and then one() calls two(). Somewhere in its processing, two() then calls one()—a second call to one(). This is indirect recursion—but it is recursion because one() has been called twice without ever returning to its caller.

CAUTION

Clearly, unless you do something to stop it, a recursive process can continue forever. That topic is covered in the next section.

Essentially, recursion is an iterative process. A recursive function call presumably is intended to work on call arguments whose state (value) depends on the preceding recursion. Thus, when the parameter list is void, recursion is useless and is ignored.

An algorithm that lends itself well to a recursive implementation is Euclid's algorithm for finding the greatest common divisor of two numbers, a and b. The method is to divide one argument into the other until this can no longer be done. Whatever is left is the greatest common divisor (GCD). During the computation, the order of the arguments in the recursive call is important because they swap at every iteration. Using a C-like pseudocode, the algorithm is as follows:

```
long gcd( long a, long b )
{
  if ( b == 0 ) {
    no more division can be done;
    a is the gcd;
    return a;
  }
  get the remainder of a / b;
  set a = b;
  set b = remainder;
  repeat the process;
}
```

Recursion is used at the point in the process where the algorithm repeats. The program EUCLID.C in Listing 6.4 shows how this algorithm can be implemented.

Listing 6.4. EUCLID.C—Use recursive function calls to compute the greatest common divisor (for Borland C++).

```
1   /*
2       +-----------------------------------+
3       +   EUCLID.C
4       +   Demonstrate Euclid's Algorithm.
5       +-----------------------------------+
6   */
7
8   #include <stdlib.h>
9   #include <stdio.h>
10
11  #define DISPLAY 1
12
13  long int a;
14  long int b;
15
```

continues

Listing 6.4. Continued

```
16   /*
17      Euclid's algorithm to find the GREATEST COMMON DIVISOR.
18      This function uses RECURSIVE CALLS to itself. The stack
19      required depends on the size of the numbers.
20   */
21
22   long int gcd( a,b )
23      long int a;
24      long int b;
25   {
26      if ( DISPLAY ) printf( "%ld,%ld\n",a,b );
27      if ( b == 0 ) return( a );
28        else return( gcd( b, a%b ) );
29   }
30
31   main()
32   {
33      a = 19408L;
34      b = 19376L;
35      gcd( a,b );
36   }
```

The macro name DISPLAY in line 11 of Listing 6.4 is used to determine whether to show intermediate results as the GCD is computed. You can turn off the display by setting DISPLAY to 0 or by deleting lines 11 and 26 from the program.

Lines 27 and 28 show the power of the recursive technique; they contain the *entire* algorithm. If b is zero, a is returned as the GCD. Otherwise, gcd() is called recursively, but now b is the first argument, and a%b is the second. The interior (recursive) call to gcd both computes the remainder and swaps the arguments.

Avoiding Open-Ended Recursion

If you consider carefully the code in Listing 6.4, you soon realize that gcd() does not return to main() until the complete result has been calculated.

This fact is very significant. It means that call arguments are piled on top of one another in the stack and that they accumulate until the last iteration. Arguments are purged from the stack by returning from the function, but the function may be called many times without ever returning, until the bottom layer is reached. Figure 6.2 illustrates how argument values accumulate on the stack during recursive calls.

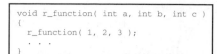

```
void r_function( int a, int b, int c )
{
  r_function( 1, 2, 3 );
  . . .
}
```

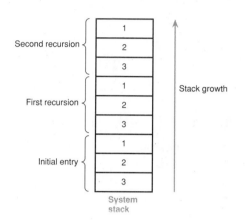

Figure 6.2.

Stack growth during
recursive function calls.

The amount of memory available to hold a growing number of argument values is the limiting factor in recursive techniques. After a certain number of recursive calls, that memory (whether stack memory or something else) is exhausted.

This means that you must select very carefully the algorithms you want to implement recursively. An algorithm may be theoretically capable of recursive implementation, but your machine (or compiler) may lack the resources to support more than a certain number of iterations.

The only cure for this is to analyze the method, mathematically if necessary, to determine how many recursions can potentially occur. If the answer is "too many," you have to find another way.

Fancy mathematics is not always necessary for analyzing an algorithm. Frequently, all you need is common sense and a clear understanding of what you are trying to do.

Computing the *factorial* of a number is an algorithm suitable for recursive methods. The factorial of any number x is equal to x * x-1 * x-2 * ... *x-x+2 * 1. That is, it is the product of all the numbers from x to 1. You can implement the factorial function recursively like this:

```
long factorial( long a )
{
  if ( a == 1 ) return a;
    else return a * factorial( a - 1 );
}
```

Suppose, for example, that you want to compute the value of factorial 5. A long integer for every number from 5 to 1 must be placed on the stack to pass each lower value to the next recursive call of factorial(). In this case, the memory space needed is not great. If you remember that multiplying by 1 is pointless, you can even tune the function by changing the test to eliminate one iteration of the process:

```
if ( a == 2 ) ...
```

For extremely large numbers of iterations, however, this kind of savings is significant.

> The fact that parameter-passing memory is finite means also that you must take pains to avoid open-ended recursion. In *open-ended recursion,* the function has no means of detecting when to stop calling itself. The consequences are obvious—the function continues to call itself until all memory is exhausted. Then your program is guaranteed to stop!

There is no hard-and-fast rule for avoiding open-ended recursion (when a function has no means of detecting when to stop calling itself). The method used in every case depends only on the nature of the algorithm. In computing the GCD, the second parameter was checked at every pass to make sure that a zero value was detected. In computing the factorial of a number, the program checked the parameter to determine whether it had reached 1. In any case, adding the logic that detects the terminating condition is up to you.

Eliminating Recursion

If you find that recursion is not a practical way to implement a function with y-our machine or compiler, yet you must have the function, you have no alternative but to eliminate the recursion.

Fortunately, a result of studies in computer science assures us that any recursive technique can be rewritten without recursion. It may not have the recursive technique's elegant appearance or slick, tight code, but it works. And it almost invariably runs faster because the overhead of calling functions and passing parameters has been eliminated.

Recursion can be eliminated from the version of gcd() shown in Listing 6.4 by the simple expedient of adding a temporary variable to hold the remainder, and by using a while loop instead of recursive calls. This is shown in - Listing 6.5.

Listing 6.5. EUCLID2.C—Eliminate recursive calls from GCD calculation (for Borland C++).

```
1   /*
2      +-------------------------------------+
3      +  EUCLID2.C
4      +  Demonstrate Euclid's Algorithm.
5      +-------------------------------------+
6   */
7
8   #include <stdlib.h>
9   #include <stdio.h>
10
11  #define DISPLAY 1
12
13  long int a;
14  long int b;
15
16  /*
17     Euclid's algorithm to find the GREATEST COMMON DIVISOR.
18     This function REMOVES RECURSIVE CALLS to itself. It is
19     faster and does not endanger the stack.
20  */
21
22  long int gcd( a,b )
23    long int a;
24    long int b;
25  {
26    long int hold;
27
28    if ( DISPLAY ) printf( "%ld,%ld\n",a,b );
29    while ( b != 0 ) {
30      hold = a % b; a = b; b=hold;
31      if ( DISPLAY ) printf( "%ld,%ld\n",a,b );
32    }
33    return( a );
34  }
35
36  main()
37  {
38    a = 19408L;
39    b = 19376L;
40    gcd( a,b );
41  }
```

This method of eliminating recursion, which should be used when there is only one recursive call at the end of the function, is called *end-recursion removal.* Basically, it consists of resetting parameters and looping, instead of calling the function again with "new" parameters.

This same approach works well also with `factorial()`. You can rewrite it like this:

```
long new_factorial( long a )
{
  long result;

  result = a--; /* Prime arg and decrement a */
  for ( ; a>1; a-- ) result *= a;
  return result;
}
```

Other Ways to Invoke Functions

You access functions most often through ordinary calls. At times, however, this is not possible or just not convenient. C has support also for these circumstances.

Pointers to functions enable you to arrange, very flexibly, the logic of your program. Using function pointers, you can write code that responds to changing conditions, picking the right function at that time.

Signal functions permit your program to respond to unexpected conditions. A library function, for example, may detect an abnormal condition and attempt to abort the program. A signal function can intercept this request and do something about it—cleaning up before allowing the abort, or correcting the condition and continuing execution.

Nonlocal jump functions provide a way to circumvent the normal function call and return protocol. Whereas the `goto` statement can jump anywhere in the same *function,* the `longjmp()` function can shift execution to anywhere in the *program* that a `setjmp()` function has defined a target location. This facility should be used with great care. It is found most often with signal-handling functions and error-trapping routines.

Using Pointers to Functions

You can define a pointer to a function and use that pointer to call the function. Being able to do this greatly enhances your control over the logic flow of your program; you can pick a "method" for performing some task, depending on the objects to be manipulated. You can defer that selection until it is time to perform the task. Here is the general syntax for declaring a pointer to a function:

```
type ( *function-pointer )( parameter-list );
```

The type specifier is the same thing to which you are already accustomed— the type of the value returned by the function. The meaning of the function-pointer identifier is plain enough, as is the indirection operator.

 NOTE Remember that the indirection operator *in a declaration* means that a pointer, not a dereferenced object, is being defined.

Why are there parentheses around *function-pointer? Operator precedence rules dictate them. Remember that postfix () has a higher precedence than the indirection operator. Therefore, without the parentheses, you write a declaration for a function *returning a pointer.* To see the difference, compare these two lines of code:

```
int (*f)(...); /* Pointer to function returning int */
int *f(...);   /* Function returning pointer to int */
```

You can also define an array of pointers to function, all returning the specified type. The syntax is

```
type ( *function-pointer[bound] )( parameter-list );
```

whereby *bound* is just an integer expression bounding the array—limiting the number of elements, as before.

Getting the parameter list right is important. As at any other time, you have to know what parameters the function to be called expects. If the parameters don't match exactly, all sorts of problems can crop up—most often an abnormally terminated program.

All pointers, including pointers to functions, must be initialized before they can be used. This is just as easy as knowing the names of the functions pointed to, or the name of another pointer to function. Here are some examples of initializing pointers to functions:

```
void first_function( void ); /* A function prototype */
...
void (*functiona)( void );   /* A pointer to function */
```

```
void (*methods[16])( void )  /* Array of pointers to function */
...
functiona = first_function; /* Initialize from designator */
methods[0] = functiona;     /* Initialize from another pointer */
```

Using the function name without the postfix () function-call operator yields a pointer to type function. In fact, C *always* converts a reference to a function designator in an expression to a *pointer* to function. This makes sense because a function can't be "manipulated" in the sense that an object can; it can only be declared and called.

You call a function through a pointer by dereferencing the pointer, as in this example:

```
double result;
double (*docalc) ( double arg );
double (*methods[8])( double arg1, double arg2 );
docalc = sqrt; /* Point to library square root function */
methods[0] = pow;        /* Point to power lib function */
result = (*docalc)( 2.0 );          /* Square root of 2 */
result = (*methods[0])( 3.0, 2.0 )        /* 3 squared */
```

Old-Style Coding: Calling Functions with Pointers

The method of calling a function through a pointer, used in this chapter, originated in K&R C. ANSI enables you to call functions through a pointer by using a syntax that is indistinguishable from a normal function call, as in:

```
int status;
int (*get_status)( void );
...
status = get_status();
```

This admittedly results in a cleaner appearance. Yet the authors prefer the old-style invocation, partly because of ingrained habit, but also because the old-style syntax emphasizes the fact that a *pointer,* not a normal function designator, is being used. Furthermore, the authors sometimes still use compilers that do not support the newer ANSI specifications; backward compatibility is an issue. This is not to say that you must use the old method. Pick the method that is comfortable for you and then be consistent with it.

Now you are ready to put function pointers to work. Suppose that you want to define a general-purpose routine that you can always call to compare two objects—regardless of their type—and that pick the proper comparison method for you. The point is that you have to remember only one function call format. You have to provide a parameter indicating the objects' type, but that is a small price to pay for the convenience. Such a program, COMPARES.C, is shown in Listing 6.6.

Listing 6.6. COMPARES.C—Use a pointer to function to invoke a function (for Borland C++).

```
1   #include <stdlib.h>
2   #include <stdio.h>
3
4   #define INT    0
5   #define CHAR   1
6   #define DOUBLE 2
7   #define LT -1
8   #define EQ  0
9   #define GT  1
10
11  int comp_int( void *obj1, void *obj2 );
12  int comp_char( void *obj1, void *obj2 );
13  int comp_double( void *obj1, void *obj2 );
14  int compares( int type, void *obj1, void *obj2 );
15
16  main()
17  {
18    int a = 64, b = 64;
19    char c = 'z', d = 'a';
20    double e = 1.414, f = 1.732;
21
22    printf( "Returned %d when comparing %d %d\n",
23      compares( INT, &a, &b ), a, b );
24    printf( "Returned %d when comparing %c %c\n",
25      compares( CHAR, &c, &d ), c, d );
26    printf( "Returned %d when comparing %f %f\n",
27      compares( DOUBLE, &e, &f ), e, f );
28  }
29
30  int compares( int type, void *obj1, void *obj2 )
31  {
32    int (*callit)( void *, void * ); /* Pointer to function */
33
34    switch( type ) {  /* Point to the appropriate function */
```

continues

Listing 6.6. Continued

```
35     case INT:    callit = comp_int; break;
36     case CHAR:   callit = comp_char; break;
37     case DOUBLE: callit = comp_double; break;
38     default: return 0;  /* Just say equal if no match */
39   }
40   return( (*callit)( obj1, obj2 ) ); /* It's this easy! */
41 }
42
43 int comp_int( void *obj1, void *obj2 )
44 {
45   int result;
46
47   result = *(int *)obj1 - *(int *)obj2;
48   if ( result ) result /= abs( result );
49   return result;
50 }
51
52 int comp_char( void *obj1, void *obj2 )
53 {
54   int result;
55
56   result = *(char *)obj1 - *(char *)obj2;
57   if ( result ) result /= abs( result );
58   return result;
59 }
60
61 int comp_double( void *obj1, void *obj2 )
62 {
63   double result;
64
65   result = *(double *)obj1 - *(double *)obj2;
66   if ( result < 0 ) return -1;
67     else if ( result == 0 ) return 0;
68       else if ( result > 0 ) return 1;
69 }
```

The `compares()` function in lines 30–41 of Listing 6.6 is built around the fact that `void` pointers can point to anything. This is first reflected in the call parameters for `compares()`, which consist of an integer identifying the object type (see the #defines on lines 4–6) and two void pointers. compares() does not know the object size and does not care—pointers are always the same size.

In compares(), a pointer to a function returning int is declared (line 32). All the function has to do now is test the type variable and assign to the function pointer a pointer value for the correct comparison routine. This is done in lines 35–37. If the type variable is not correct, a value of 0 (indicating "equal") is returned immediately to the caller. Otherwise, the comparison function is called, and its result is returned (line 40). After you look at it for a minute, it is really very simple.

compares() could have been written in another way. You can pass a function *pointer* as a parameter to a function. The function, and the call to it, would then look like this:

```
int compares( int (*method)( void *, void * ),
              void *obj1, void *obj2 )
{
  return( (*method)( obj1, obj2 ) );
}
...
result = compares( comp_int, &a, &b );
```

The comparison functions also have some interesting points. Look at comp_int() in lines 43–50 of Listing 6.6. The comparison is made by the simple expedient of subtracting the second object from the first. To do this, the void pointer is first cast to the correct type and then dereferenced to the object (line 47). If *obj1 is less than *obj2, the result is negative; if they are equal, the result is 0; if *obj1 is greater than *obj2, the result is positive.

Line 48, by dividing the result by itself, forces the result to be –1, 0, or 1. The absolute value is used in the denominator so a negative result will not be forced positive. The method used in comp_double() (lines 61–69) is simple brute force. This is done because the division of floating-point numbers frequently does not come out completely exact. When it does not, a cast to int might truncate to 0, rather than –1 or 1, giving incorrect results.

The *signal()* and *raise()* Functions

Sometimes being able to invoke a function on a completely unexpected basis (in response to the Break key or a math exception, for example) would be convenient. The events triggered by such unexpected conditions are called *asynchronous events*. These events cannot be predicted; they can occur at any time during the program's execution.

Standard C enables handling of these events through the use of *signals,* a reporting mechanism that can invoke your signal-handling routines, based on the kind of event that occurred. Several macros defined in SIGNAL.H use an integral constant to define the types of signals. Table 6.1 lists macros for the different signal types.

Table 6.1. Signal number macro names.

Macro Name	Description
SIGABRT	Abnormal termination, for example, raised by the abort() function.
SIGFPE	Floating-point arithmetic exceptions; integer divide by 0 and overflow.
SIGILL	Illegal instruction exception; for example, a bad pointer caused a function to be overlaid with garbage.
SIGINT	Interactive attention signal; on the PC, Ctrl-C and Ctrl-Break.
SIGSEGV	Segment violation; invalid memory access (bad segment number, protection exception).
SIGTERM	Program termination request; for example, the exit() function was called.

You can associate your own signal-handling function with any or all of the signal types by calling the signal() function, with the signal type and a pointer-to-the-handler routine as parameters. signal() has a prototype in the SIGNAL.H header file. Here is its syntax:

```
void (*signal(int sig, void (*func)(int))) (int);
```

This syntax is sufficiently convoluted to warrant a brief dissection. The guiding principle in analyzing this declaration is the fact that signal() returns a pointer to a function—specifically, a pointer to the preceding signal-handling function for the stated signal. How do you return a pointer to a function?

Assume that a function f() returns a pointer to some object, such as an integer. Its declaration would then be

```
int *f(...); /* Function returns pointer to int */
```

To write a declaration for a plain pointer to a function f() that returns int and has an int parameter, you would specify the following:

```
int (*f)(int);
    /* Pointer to function returning int, parm int */
```

Because this last case is in fact what you want to *return* a pointer to, you would write

```
int (*f(...))(int);
    /* f() returns pointer; all else is */
    /* description of pointed-to function. */
```

Now apply that syntactical reasoning to the declaration for `signal()`; recall that `signal()` has a parameter that is a function pointer, and you can account for all the parentheses.

You call the signal `function()` to do one of three things for a particular signal number: take the default action, ignore the signal, or invoke your signal-handling routine. Note these examples:

```
signal( SIGSEGV, SIG_DFL ); /* Take the default action */
signal( SIGABRT, SIG_IGN ); /* Ignore the signal */
signal( SIGFPE, myfunc );   /* Call myfunc() if SIGFPE */
```

Usually, the default action is to terminate the program. If you request that the signal be ignored, nothing at all happens. If you specify a signal-handling function name, what happens is up to you. Don't forget that `signal()` returns a pointer to the preceding handler function. If the request was not successful, it returns a value defined by the macro `SIG_ERR`. Listing 6.7 shows how the signal-handling routines can be coded.

Listing 6.7. SHOWSIG.C—Demonstrate signal handling (for Microsoft C/C++).

```
1   #include <stdlib.h>
2   #include <stdio.h>
3   #include <signal.h>
4
5   void handle_term( int sig )
6   {
7     printf( "   The terminate signal was raised.\n" );
8     return;
9   }
10
11  main()
12  {
13    char ch;
14
15    signal( SIGINT, SIG_IGN );
16    puts( "Press the Ctrl-Break key to see it echoed." );
```

continues

Listing 6.7. Continued

```
17    puts( "Then strike Return to continue:" );
18    ch = getchar();
19    puts( "Now let's handle a program termination request." );
20    signal( SIGTERM, handle_term );
21    raise( SIGTERM );
22    puts( "Back in main() again." );
23    puts( "Next, the abort() call allows default action." );
24    signal( SIGABRT, SIG_DFL );
25    abort();
26  }
```

The handler function for SIGTERM is located in lines 5–9 of Listing 6.7. The only action taken in this example was to display a message and return. In a "real" program, you might want to close files, notify the user, possibly present the user with alternatives (make a correction and continue, go ahead and terminate, and so on), or free dynamically allocated memory.

Whenever a signal handler is entered, the default action for that signal is reset, as though signal(sig, SIG_DFL) had been called. This is not in your control—it always happens. It is important to remember that, if you plan for the signal handler to be used several times, you must call signal() again to "hook in" your function. You can do this from the handler function.

The return statement is used in line 8 to leave the signal handler. Using the return statement to leave a handler function causes the program to resume execution at the point it was interrupted. Generally, you can do this, or you can call abort(), exit(), or longjmp() to get out of a signal handler—*except* when the signal was SIGFPE or an implementation-defined computational error.

When the signal was SIGFPE, you may not use the return statement; the subsequent behavior of the program is liable to be unpredictable. Either terminate the program or use longjmp() to bypass that computation completely. longjmp() and its companion function setjmp() are covered in the next section.

Line 21 in Listing 6.7 illustrates the companion function raise(). You use the raise() function to *generate* any of the previously defined signal types. raise() was used in the example because the exit() function does *not* cause the SIGTERM signal to be sent—it always terminates the program. Some compilers provide an extra parameter to the signal-handling function—beyond the signal number, which is always passed—to identify special conditions. Detecting the fact that the signal resulted from a call to raise() is one such condition.

The ANSI standard allows an implementation to add to the list any signals it wants. The complete list of signals, their semantics, and how default handling is accomplished are all implementation defined. The only restriction is that all signals (except SIG_ERR) must be positive.

The *setjmp()* and *longjmp()* Functions

The setjmp() function provides a "locator" that is the target of a longjmp() function call. The longjmp() function causes program execution to continue at the associated locator, rather than with the next line of code. longjmp() is capable of transferring control across function boundaries; that is, you can jump anywhere in the program.

The most common uses for setjmp() and longjmp() are to return values from deeply nested function calls without having to "percolate" back to the top-level function, and to terminate signal-handling routines.

setjmp() requires a *jump buffer* which stores the status information that allows longjmp() to transfer control to setjmp(). A macro, jmp_buf, defines the jump buffer object. Thus, the required statements to execute setjmp() are

```
#include <setjmp.h>
jmp_buf env;
setjmp( env );
```

and the function prototype for setjmp() is

```
int setjmp( jmp_buf env );
```

setjmp() can be "called" in two ways. First, it can execute normally by being invoked directly. In this case, it returns 0, after setting up the environment status in the jump buffer. Note that setjmp() can be executed this way any number of times; it reestablishes the jump environment each time.

Second, a longjmp() can transfer control to the setjmp() function internally, passing it a value other than 0. To the statement following setjmp(), it will seem that setjmp() was called and returned this other value. These returned values can be used to determine what to do next. You must make very sure of one thing: the function containing the setjmp() must not have terminated when longjmp() attempts to reference that location. Here is one possible way to set up for a longjmp():

```
#include <setjmp.h>
jmp_buf main_env; /* Notice file scope so everybody */
                  /* can access the jump buffer */
...
```

```
void do_calc( void )
{
  ... /* Do processing; if error, go back to main() */
  long_jmp( main_env, 1 );
  ...
}
main()
{
  int init = 0;
  int return;
  return = setjmp( main_env)
  switch( return ) {      /* longjmp() comes here */
    case 0: init = 1;
            do_calc();    /* Jump buffer set, start processing */
            break;
    case 1:               /* Possibly correct an error */
            do_calc();    /* and restart processing */
  }
}
```

Notice in the preceding code fragment that longjmp() names the jump buffer so the correct setjmp() location is targeted. This means that setjmp() can be used to initialize any number of jump buffers in different locations and for different purposes.

The other value specified in longjmp() is used to make it appear that setjmp() was called and returned that value. The prototype for longjmp() is

```
void longjmp( jmp_buf env, int val );
```

longjmp() has type void. It is one of only three functions—together with exit() and abort()—that legitimately never returns. Listing 6.8 illustrates how longjmp() can be used to return to a point from deeply nested function calls.

Listing 6.8.   JMPERR.C—*longjmp()* out of nested functions (for all compilers).

```
1  #include <stdlib.h>
2  #include <stdio.h>
3  #include <setjmp.h>
4
5  jmp_buf env1;
6
7  int comp1( void );
```

```
 8  int comp2( void );
 9  int comp3( void );
10
11  main()
12  {
13    int ret;
14    switch( ret = setjmp( env1 ) ) {
15      case 0: puts( "*** Starting computations ***" );
16              comp1(); break;  /* Start the process */
17      case 1:
18      case 2:
19      case 3:
20      case 4:
21      case 5: printf( "Process returned code: %d\n", ret );
22              break;
23    }
24  }
25
26  int comp1()
27  {
28    return( comp2() );
29  }
30
31  int comp2()
32  {
33    return( comp3() );
34  }
35
36  int comp3()
37  {
38    char ch[3];
39    int val = 0;
40
41    while( val < 1 || val > 5 ) {
42      printf( "Type a number from 1 to 5: " );
43      gets( ch );
44      val = atoi( ch );
45    }
46    longjmp( env1, val );
47  }
```

At the time the longjmp() function is called, control has descended to comp3(), with no intervening returns. When longjmp() is called in line 46, control immediately returns to the point after setjmp(). In this case, that is the first case statement of the switch (line 15). Because this is not the initial call to setjmp(), case 0 is not satisfied.

What happens? Notice in comp3() that you are prompted to enter a number from 1 to 5. That number is used in longjmp() to supply the "simulated return" value. The printf() in line 21 displays which value that was.

The program JMPSIG.C in Listing 6.9 illustrates the use of longjmp() with more than one setjmp() active, as well as the use of longjmp() to terminate a signal-handler function.

Listing 6.9. JMPSIG.C—Terminate signal handlers with the *longjmp()* function (for Borland C++).

```
 1   /* +--------------------------------------------------+
 2    + JMPSIG.C
 3    + Demonstrate the use of longjmp() for terminating
 4    + signal-handling functions.
 5    +
 6    + NOTE: This program does not run under all tested
 7    +    compilers. The compilers tested and the results
 8    +    are listed below:
 9    + BORLAND C++ -- Runs successfully. signal() handling
10    +                 includes integer overflow and divide
11    +                 by zero intercept under SIGFPE.
12    +                 longjmp() can cross all function
13    +                 boundaries as per ANSI spec.
14    + MS C/C++    -- Partially successful. longjmp()
15    +                 implementation ANSI conforming,
16    +                 but SIGFPE does not include integer
17    +                 exceptions.
18    +--------------------------------------------------+
19   */
20   #include <stdlib.h>
21   #include <stdio.h>
22   #include <setjmp.h>
23   #include <signal.h>
24   #include <ctype.h>
25
26   jmp_buf break_env;
27   jmp_buf error_env;
```

```
28
29  void handle_break( int );
30  void handle_error( int );
31
32  main()
33  {
34    char num[6];
35    int val;
36
37    setjmp( break_env );
38    signal( SIGINT, handle_break );
39    puts( "This program demonstrates the use of longjmp()" );
40    puts( "to terminate signal-handler functions." );
41    puts( "" );
42    puts( "Enter an integer when the program prompts you." );
43    puts( "(Try a zero and see what happens.)" );
44    puts( "Press Ctrl_Break to quit." );
45    puts( "" );
46
47    while ( 1 ) {
48      setjmp( error_env );
49      signal( SIGFPE, handle_error );
50      printf( "Enter a number, up to 5 digits: " );
51      gets( num );
52      val = atoi( num );
53      val = 32767 / val;
54    }
55  }
56
57  void handle_break( int sig )
58  {
59    char ans[4];
60
61    puts( "Ctrl-Break detected." );
62    puts( "Enter \"y\" or \"yes\" to continue," );
63    puts( "  anything else to quit." );
64    gets( ans);
65    if ( 'Y' == toupper( *ans ) ) longjmp( break_env, 1 );
66      else exit( 0 );
67  }
68
69  void handle_error( int sig )
```

continues

Listing 6.9. Continued

```
70   {
71      char ans[4];
72
73      puts( "Divide by zero attempted." );
74      puts( "Enter \"y\" or \"yes\" to continue," );
75      puts( "  anything else to quit." );
76      gets( ans);
77      if ( 'Y' == toupper( *ans ) ) longjmp( error_env, 1 );
78        else exit( 0 );
79   }
80
```

As the listing header shows, this particular sample program was written in Borland C. The reason is that it was the only compiler tested that not only conforms completely to the ANSI standard (for these functions, that is), but also includes integer arithmetic exceptions in its implementation of SIGFPE handling. The comments in lines 1–18 of the program explain this fully.

Two setjmp() environments are established; one in line 37 and the other in line 48. The setjmp(break_env) in line 37 provides a jump buffer and target location for jumps out of the Break key handler. The setjmp(error_env) provides a jump buffer and target location for jumps out of the SIGFPE handler. Remember that a function handling SIGFPE cannot terminate through return.

Both of these jump buffers and targets are active at the same time. They are not confused because the longjmp() used to access them names the jump buffer to use (see lines 65 and 77).

Line 38, immediately after the setjmp() for Break key handling, contains a signal() function call that re-establishes the signal handler for SIGINT. You should recall that entry to a signal handler resets that signal for default processing.

Line 48 contains a setjmp() location for the SIGFPE handler. Notice that it is *inside* the while loop. The error_env jump buffer is reinitialized on every pass through the loop, whether or not a longjmp() has targeted the location. This hurts nothing; it only emphasizes the fact that longjmp() jumps to the target location defined by the most recent direct call to setjmp() specifying that jump buffer name. Line 49 reestablishes the SIGFPE handler, as line 38 re-established the SIGINT handler.

Spend some time now to study these examples in detail, thinking about what statement will execute next—and why. Type the programs and run them, observing their behavior. These functions are underrated and not used much, perhaps because they can be confusing at times. But the programming power they make available is well worth the effort.

Summary

In this chapter, you learned about three important topics:

- Details on passing parameters to functions
- How to design and control recursive functions
- Alternative ways to invoke functions

The concepts and techniques involved give you nearly complete control of your C functions, and thus are more important than they may at first seem. Take some time to let all of this sink in. Write some code and experiment so you become thoroughly familiar with these tools. Later, your programs will be robust, reliable, and a pleasure to write—and to use.

Controlling Program Logic Flow

U nless you do something about it, statements in a computer program execute one after the other, beginning with the first statement and continuing until the last. In fact, if you forget to add code that informs the operating system when the program is finished, the computer continues merrily to attempt to execute instructions beyond the end of the code—always providing unpleasant results.

The selection (by the hardware) of the next instruction to execute is called the *flow of execution*. The flow of execution is inherently sequential in today's computers (although there is now the exception of the new parallel-processing machines). This means that, all other things being equal, your C program begins running at the first line at the top and keeps going straight to the last line at the bottom.

Now, if that were all there was to modern computers, saying that they are useless would not be too harsh a judgment. If you wanted to read every record from a database containing a million records, for example, you would have to write a program containing a million input instructions, one after the other.

Fortunately, this is not the case. Execution flow is *inherently* linear—but not necessarily so. General-purpose digital computers (including your PC) have special instructions that can cause a *transfer of control;* they cause the next instruction selected for execution to be one other than the next sequential instruction. These special instructions are called *jump* or *branch* instructions, depending on the make of computer.

These instructions can make the hypothetical database input program bearable. The presence of branching instructions raises the possibility of writing just one input instruction and then branching back to it repetitively. This arrangement is called a *loop*. In other circumstances, you might want to skip a particular part of the processing sequence or pick an alternative sequence by branching to it. This is called *conditional logic*.

In a given program, the particular flow of execution is composed of sequentially executed instructions, program loops, and conditional branches. That is, every program has its own peculiar *logic flow*. (Some logic flows, it might be added, are more peculiar than others!) But in every case, it is the capability to loop and perform conditional logic that, more than any other single factor, gives a program its power and flexibility. This is true regardless of whether C or another language is used.

Designing Program Loops

The loop (the repetitive execution of a group of statements) is one of the most omnipresent features of programs that perform useful work. Think back to the sample programs you have seen in this book. They contained all kinds of loops, even though no explanation has been given: there were loops to read the records of a file, to copy or manipulate the characters of a string, and to process all the elements of an array.

It is almost impossible to conceive of programs that do anything informative, interesting, or useful that do not contain a loop somewhere. If loops are so much a part of most programs, then, you should take care to write efficient and effective loops. That requires understanding them thoroughly.

Properties of Program Loops

Before writing the code for a loop, plan how to control it. It is not enough to be able to branch back to the first statement of a loop—such a loop could go on forever. You have to plan how to determine how often to "pass through" the loop; that implies also planning the means of stopping the loop. There must be some *control variables* to govern the process. And don't forget to plan the task that has to be accomplished.

Writing a loop entails four basic steps. *Initialization* is done outside and before the loop structure. This is when you set up control variables for loop control and initialize any data objects you may need.

The *loop body* is the group of statements that are executed repetitively and perform useful work. The *adjustment* step occurs in the loop structure; it consists of updating the control variables to keep track of progress.

Condition checking examines the state of the control variables, and perhaps the data variables also, to determine when the loop is finished. If the loop is finished, it is exited. If it is not finished, a branch is taken back to the first statement in the loop, and the next *iteration* or *pass* begins through the loop body.

These four basic steps are present in some form in all loops in every source language. Loops generally are characterized by the placement of the condition-checking code. Loops that perform the checking at the end of the loop structure are said to use *back-end condition checking*. This kind of loop structure is illustrated in Figure 7.1.

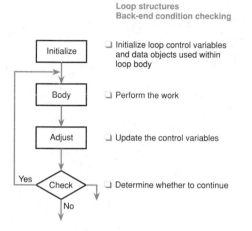

Loop structures
Back-end condition checking

❏ Initialize loop control variables and data objects used within loop body

❏ Perform the work

❏ Update the control variables

❏ Determine whether to continue

Figure 7.1.

Back-end loop condition checking.

Back-end condition checking is not the only configuration possible. In fact, the most commonly used C loop-control statements feature *front-end condition checking,* as illustrated in Figure 7.2.

You can check control variables more than once in each pass through the loop body. The need for multiple condition checking arises when some condition in the loop body may possibly force an early exit from the loop. In addition to `longjmp()`, `signal()`, and `raise()`, C provides more ordinary means for altering loop flow: the `break`, `continue`, and `goto` statements. All of these are covered in this chapter.

Doing It the Hard Way—Not Recommended

C provides the means to write loops with the use of "brute force" code, if you are so inclined. For example, Listing 6.1 in the preceding chapter showed how to use `va_arg()` in a loop to display an undetermined number of strings passed as arguments to a function. That code looked like this:

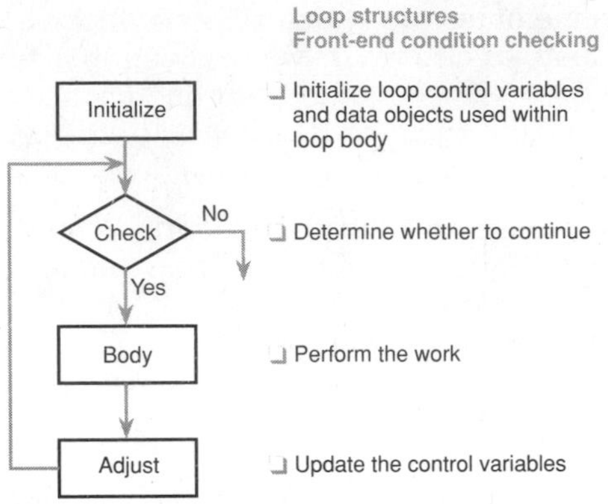

Loop structures
Front-end condition checking

Initialize ⌐ Initialize loop control variables
and data objects used within
loop body

Check — No ⌐ Determine whether to continue

Yes

Body ⌐ Perform the work

Adjust ⌐ Update the control variables

Figure 7.2.

Front-end loop condition
checking.

```
hold = va_arg( ap, char * );  /* Prime the loop */
while ( *hold ) {              /* Test the string */
   printf( "%s\n", hold );
   hold = va_arg( ap, char * );
}
```

You can use the `goto` statement with statement labels to do this the hard way. The resulting code is not nearly as clean or readable as the original example:

```
hold = va_arg( ap, char * );       /* Prime the loop */
loop1: ;
   if ( *hold != '\0') goto loop2; /* Test the string */
   printf( "%s\n", hold );
   hold = va_arg( ap, char * );
   goto loop1;                             /* Loop again */
loop2: ;      /* Null statement with statement label */
```

This construction is not usually recommended; it is almost always better to let the compiler do the detail work of framing the loop structure. Use the statements that C provides expressly for loop control, because they are neater, very efficient, and safer.

Using the C-provided loop syntax is safer because it hides some of the detail work from the programmer. The issue is not at all that programmers are stupid; it is, instead, that using direct `goto`s and labels invites errors. A programmer can easily plant inside the loop statements a `goto` or label that doesn't belong there, or move one that does belong there outside, especially when the loop is longer and more complex than the simple examples shown here. It gets even worse when, after some time has elapsed, the programmer modifies a program, because she or he may have forgotten just what went where in the source code.

The opposite extreme of never using a goto may not be wise, however. This philosophy was the rage some years ago, during the initial debates on exactly what structured programming was intended to accomplish. The contention was that a direct jump (goto) always introduces confusion into the program. This is simply not true; at times, using a goto is the only sensible thing to do. For example, a goto is used in PRIME.C in Listing 7.1 to reduce confusion. When you compile the PRIME.C program, be sure to include the Microsoft GRAPHICS.LIB file.

Listing 7.1. PRIME.C—Compute the first 350 prime numbers (for Microsoft C/C++).

```
1   #include <stdlib.h>
2   #include <stdio.h>
3   #include <graph.h>
4   #include <conio.h>
5
6   long *primes;
7   long j, k, n;
8
9   void calc_primes( void );
10  void disp_primes( void );
11
12  main()
13  {
14    primes = (long *)calloc( 350, sizeof( long ) );
15    _clearscreen( _GCLEARSCREEN );
16    cputs( "... Calculating table of 350 prime numbers ..." );
17    calc_primes();
18    _clearscreen( _GCLEARSCREEN );
19    disp_primes();
20    free( primes );
21    exit( 0 );
22  }
23
24  /* +------------------------+
25     +  Calculate the first 350 prime numbers.
26     +  Assume that the primes[] table was allocated
27     +  in global data.
28     +  Method is Knuth's, 2nd ed., Vol. 1, pp. 143-44.
29     +------------------------+
30  */
```

continues

Listing 7.1.   Continued

```c
31   void calc_primes( void )
32   {
33     ldiv_t ans;
34
35     primes[0] = 2;
36     n = 3;
37     for ( j=1; j<350; j++ ) {
38       primes[j] = n;              /* Store the prime */
39   nextprime: n += 2;
40       k = 1;
41   checkprime: ans = ldiv( n, primes[k] );
42       if ( ans.rem == 0 ) goto nextprime;
43       if ( ans.quot <= primes[k] ) continue;
44       k++;
45       goto checkprime;
46     }
47   }
48
49   void disp_primes( void )
50   {
51     struct rccord cursor;
52
53     for ( n=0; n<350; n++ ) {
54       cprintf( "%.4ld ", primes[n] );
55       cursor = _gettextposition();
56       _settextposition( cursor.row, cursor.col+5 );
57       if ( cursor.col > 75 )
58         _settextposition( cursor.row+1, 1 );
59     }
60   }
```

The loop in lines 37–46 in Listing 7.1 calculates the series of prime numbers and would be quite complex without the goto and continue statements. Figure 7.3 shows the logic flow of prime-number calculation.

This algorithm is based on two facts. First, given an existing prime number, the next *possible* prime number is n + 2. Second, you can test the possible prime by dividing it into the previously found primes; if any of these divisions produces a nonzero remainder and a quotient that is less than or equal to the prime being used to test, the candidate is also a prime number.

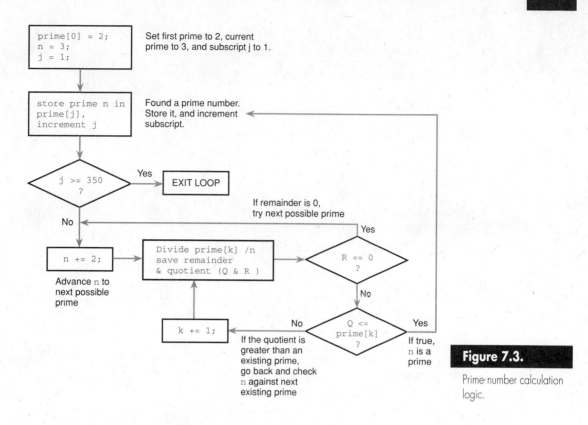

Figure 7.3.

Prime-number calculation logic.

As you look at Figure 7.3, you can see that testing for these conditions involves possible branches in too many directions for the logic to package comfortably in a conventional `while` or `for` loop structure. You might be able to examine the logic carefully (and at some length) and find a way to do it—but you would have difficulty finding a way that is this compact and easily read. Fortunately, the need for this sort of overriding logic is rare.

Quick Reference: Standard C Loop Control

The standard C language specifications refer to the loop-control statements as *iteration statements*. There are only three of them, but they provide more than enough programming power to accomplish any task you might imagine. All three iteration statements refer to a *target statement* that is the loop body. The loop body may be a simple statement, in which case it should be terminated with a semicolon, or it may be a block statement, in which case the group of statements should be surrounded by curly braces (`{}`).

continues

Quick Reference: Standard C Loop Control

Note the syntax and use of the following three iteration statements:

```
while ( expression ) statement
```

The loop body statement is executed repeatedly, as long as the expression evaluates to a nonzero integral value (evaluates to true). The while statement features front-end condition checking:

```
do statement while ( expression ) ;
```

The do statement evaluates the expression only *after* the loop body has been executed. Thus, do-while features back-end condition checking and guarantees at least one pass through the loop.

```
for ( expr1opt; expr2opt; expr3opt ) statement
```

A for statement combines the initialization, condition checking, and adjustment steps of loop processing in the three expressions enclosed in the parentheses. All three expressions are optional and may be omitted (which produces a never-ending loop if you do not take other steps), and any of the expressions may be a list of expressions separated by comma operators. The accompanying text explains this more fully. A for loop features front-end condition checking; expr2 is evaluated before the loop body is executed on each pass.

Front-End Condition Checking: *while()*

The ANSI standard refers to loop-controlling statements as *iteration statements*. There are three of them: while, do, and for. Of these, while has the simplest format. Here is its syntax:

```
while ( expression ) statement
```

This means that while the controlling expression is true (evaluates to a non-zero integral value), the associated statement is executed repetitively. This target statement is the loop body. The statement can be a simple statement terminated with a semicolon, or it can be a block statement enclosed in curly braces.

The while statement uses front-end condition checking, as illustrated in Figure 7.2. For each pass through the loop, the controlling expression is evaluated first and, when it yields a false integral result, the loop is exited. Listing 7.2 shows the while statement in the context of the program. This program uses an array of double to represent the coefficients of an algebraic polynomial.

Given a particular value for the independent variable x, the polynomial is evaluated for that point.

Listing 7.2. POLY.C—Evaluate a polynomial with *while* (for Borland C++).

```
1   /* +----------------------------------------------------+
2       + POLY.C
3       + Evaluate a polynomial using Horner's method.
4       +----------------------------------------------------+
5   */
6   #include <stdlib.h>
7   #include <stdio.h>
8   #include <math.h>
9
10  #include "timer.h"
11
12  double polynomial( int degree, double var, double *coeff );
13
14  main()
15  {
16    double tvalue, cvalue;
17    double x = 2.0;
18    double coeff[4] = { 3, 2, 4, 1 };
19    double coeff2[4] = { 1, 4, 2, 3 };
20
21  /*
22      Compare first method to Borland C implementation of poly()
23  */
24    start_bench();
25    tvalue = poly( x, 3, coeff2 );
26    stop_bench();
27    printf( "Borland C took %8.6f seconds.\n", duration() );
28
29    start_bench();
30    cvalue = polynomial( 3, x, coeff );
31    stop_bench();
32    printf( "First version took %8.6f seconds.\n", duration() );
33    printf( "The polynomial evaluates to %f\n", cvalue );
34  }
35
36  /* +----------------------------------------------------+
37      + polynomial();
```

continues

Listing 7.2. Continued

```
38      + INPUT: degree = highest power of var
39      +          var   = base variable (e.g., "x")
40      +          coeff = array of doubles containing the
41      +                  coefficients. coeff[0] should
42      +                  contain coeff of highest power,
43      +                  coeff[degree+1], coeff of 0 power.
44      +------------------------------------------------+
45   */
46   double polynomial( int degree, double var, double *coeff )
47   {
48      static double sum;   /* Can't put initializer */
49                           /* on static object */
50      sum = *coeff++;
51      while ( degree-- > 0 ) sum = sum * var + *coeff++;
52      return sum;
53   }
```

The program POLY.C in Listing 7.2 uses the TIMER.C routines from Appendix G. This means that you need to create a project file that includes both POLY.C and TIMER.C. Before you begin, notice that POLY.C is a Borland C++ program and TIMER.C is a Microsoft C/C++ program. Before you can use the TIMER.C routines, you have to convert TIMER.C to a Borland C++ program. The instructions for converting TIMER.C from Microsoft C/C++ to Borland C++ are also in Appendix G.

POLY.C in Listing 7.2 uses the TIMER.C routines to compare the Borland C++ implementation of poly() with the first implementation, called polynomial(). Neither implementation is an ANSI standard library function. A similar function is provided by many compilers as a common extension to the language, which is perfectly permissible. This implementation requires about 0.2 milliseconds longer to run than the compiler-provided library function.

T I P   There is a moral here: usually, the compiler vendor has taken great pains to provide an extremely efficient function. If the compiler provides the function, you should use it, unless portability to other compilers absolutely prohibits doing so.

This sample program evaluates the polynomial $3x^3 + 4x^2 + 2x + 1$, for the point $x = 2$. An algorithm known as *Horner's method* is used to implement the code.

This algorithm is based on a procedure called *nesting,* which rearranges the formula algebraically for faster machine evaluation. Notice that you can factor out x progressively, like this:

```
3x³ + 4x² + 2x + 1
(3x² + 4x + 2) * x + 1
( (3x + 4 ) * x + 2) * x + 1
```

The function `polynomial()` in lines 46–53 takes advantage of this fact by first initializing the result to the high-order coefficient value (line 50). Thus, the routine works even if there is only one coefficient.

The complete result is formed by using a `while` statement to compute a running total (line 51). Each pass simply multiplies the preceding sum by x and adds in the next coefficient. This procedure takes advantage of Horner's nesting method to reduce to an absolute minimum the number of multiplications by x.

Notice how the argument variable `degree` is used to control the loop: deliberate side effects are used in the controlling expression to produce extremely compact code. (As a rule of thumb, you can consider compact code to be faster code—although this is not always true.) Remember that a sequence point is not taken until the complete expression `degree-- > 0` has been evaluated. The correct value of `degree` is used to evaluate the expression; the `degree` object is updated at the sequence point, in time for the next pass.

Side effects are an extremely powerful way to increase the utility of the `while` statement. It is possible to write a `while` loop in which all the work is done by the controlling expression—the target statement may be null.

T I P

You already have seen how side effects work in the code to copy one string to another, using nothing but side effects:

```
char *s1;
char *s2;
...
while( *s1++ = *s2++ ) ;
```

In each pass through the loop, only front-end checking occurs, but the controlling expression updates the pointer values to the next location through the use of side effects. This loop copies one string to another, including the terminating null character, because the null character is not evaluated as false until after it has been "moved across" the assignment operator. The postfix ++ operator does leave both pointers positioned one character beyond the end of each string, however.

Constructing a deliberate never-ending loop with the `while` statement is also possible, as in the following example:

```
while ( 1 ) {
    ... /* Something in here had better exit the loop. */
}
```

Because the controlling expression is exactly the integer value 1, it always evaluates to true. The logic contained in the target statement (a block statement here) is responsible for detecting whatever condition signals the end-of-loop processing and for exiting the loop. Such a construction is sometimes used to handle a keyboard input loop, as in

```
char ch;
while ( 1 ) {
    puts( "Enter a selection character or Ctrl-Z "
          "to end the program." );
    ch = getchar();    /* getch() is not standard */
    if ( ch == 26 ) break; /* Ctrl-Z ends the loop */
    ...            /* Other processing continues here */
}
```

The `break` statement used here to exit the loop "manually" is covered in the section "Programming Conditional Logic" later in this chapter.

Back-End Condition Checking: *do-while()*

A loop construction using front-end condition checking could, by definition, possibly never execute the loop body. The condition checking may turn out not to be satisfied on the very first attempt to pass through the loop. Sometimes this is just the protection you want.

At other times, front-end condition checking actually may prevent the successful operation of your program. In certain situations, you want at least one guaranteed pass through the loop, no matter what. Loop constructions using back-end condition checking provide this feature (refer to Figure 7.1). C implements back-end condition checking in the `do-while` loop. Its syntax is

```
do statement while ( expression ) ;
```

In a `do-while` loop construction, the target statement that is the loop body appears *before* the controlling expression. One pass is guaranteed, because the loop body must be executed in order to get to the controlling expression. Here, as elsewhere, the target statement may be a block statement.

Back-end condition checking is not needed as often as front-end checking. But when it is needed, it is indispensable. Consider, for example, the task of replacing tab characters in a text file with an appropriate number of blanks. Encountering the tab character '\t' in the text always means that the next output position must be increased to the next tab stop—even if the current position is already in a tab stop location. Therefore, at least one guaranteed pass through the blank-producing loop is required.

The DETAB.C program in Listing 7.3 performs this function. Because this program may be of some long-term use to you, a fully capable program is provided here, rather than a stripped-down example. The program includes command-line options for the input filename and for setting the tab size. The program also backs up the input file before modifying it and takes into account possible I/O errors during processing.

Listing 7.3. DETAB.C—*do-while* guarantees at least one pass (for Borland C++).

```
1   #include <stdlib.h>
2   #include <stdio.h>
3   #include <ctype.h>
4   #include <string.h>
5
6   /* +-----------------------------------------------+
7      + STRUPR()    String chars to uppercase.
8      + Borland C++ actually has a lib function exactly like
9      + this one; it is just not standard. Notice that
10     + string.h is included, so the Borland C++ version
11     + is replaced by this one (this program only).
12     +-----------------------------------------------+
13   */
14   char *strupr( char *s )
15   {
16     static char *p; /* Can't return an auto var! */
17
18     p = s;
19     for ( ; *s; *s++ = toupper( *s ) ) ;
20     return( p );
21   }
22
23   main( int argc, char *argv[] )
24   {
25     FILE *tgtfile, *bkupfile;
```

continues

Listing 7.3. Continued

```
26    char tgtname[81] = "";
27    char bkupname[81] = "";
28    char ch;
29    int tabsize = 8;
30    int i, column = 1;
31
32  /* Show command format if no command-line parms */
33
34    if ( argc == 1 ) {
35      puts( "DETAB command line format is:" );
36      puts( "    C:>detab [-tn] -filename" );
37      puts( "Tab size is optional, defaults to 8." );
38      puts( "filename is required." );
39      puts( "Type \"-t\" and \"-f\" exactly as shown." );
40      exit( 0 );
41    }
42
43  /* ------ Get command-line parameters and options ------ */
44
45    for ( i=1; i<argc; i++ ) {
46      strupr( argv[i] );
47      if ( 0 == strncmp( "-T", argv[i], 2 ) ) {
48        tabsize = (int)strtol( argv[i]+2, NULL, 0 );
49        printf( "Requested tab size of %d characters.\n",
50                tabsize );
51      }
52      if ( 0 == strncmp( "-F", argv[i], 2 ) ) {
53        strcpy( tgtname, argv[i]+2 );
54        printf( "Detabbing: %s\n", tgtname );
55      }
56    }
57    if ( !*tgtname ) {
58      puts( "No filename given." );
59      exit( 8 );
60    }
61    strcpy( bkupname, tgtname );
62    if ( !strchr( bkupname, '.' ) ) strcat( bkupname, ".BAK" );
63    else {
64      char *p = bkupname;
65      while ( *p != '.' ) p++;
66      *p = '\0';
```

```
67      strcat( bkupname, ".BAK" );
68    }
69
70    /* ------ BACK UP the file before touching it! ------ */
71
72    printf( "Copying %s to %s\n", tgtname, bkupname );
73
74    if ( NULL == ( tgtfile = fopen( tgtname, "rb" ) ) ) {
75      puts( "Can't open the input file." );
76      exit( 8 );
77    }
78    setvbuf( tgtfile, NULL, _IOFBF, 16384 );
79    if ( NULL == ( bkupfile = fopen( bkupname, "wb" ) ) ) {
80      puts( "Can't open the backup file." );
81      exit( 8 );
82    }
83    setvbuf( bkupfile, NULL,  IOFBF, 16384 );
84
85    while ( EOF != ( ch = fgetc( tgtfile ) ) ) {
86      fputc( ch, bkupfile );
87      if ( ferror( bkupfile ) ) {
88        puts( "Error writing backup file." );
89        fclose( tgtfile );
90        fclose( bkupfile );
91        remove( bkupname );
92        exit( 8 );
93      }
94    }
95    if ( ferror( tgtfile ) ) {
96      puts( "Error reading input file." );
97      fclose( tgtfile );
98      fclose( bkupfile );
99      remove( bkupname );
100     exit( 8 );
101    }
102    fclose( tgtfile );
103    fclose( bkupfile );
104
105    /* ------ Finally, detab the target file ------ */
106
107    printf( "Detabbing %s\n", tgtname );
108
```

continues

Listing 7.3. Continued

```
109    if ( NULL == ( bkupfile = fopen( bkupname, "rb" ) ) ) {
110      puts( "Can't open the input file." );
111      exit( 8 );
112    }
113    setvbuf( bkupfile, NULL, _IOFBF, 16384 );
114    if ( NULL == ( tgtfile = fopen( tgtname, "wb" ) ) ) {
115      puts( "Can't open the backup file." );
116      exit( 8 );
117    }
118    setvbuf( tgtfile, NULL, _IOFBF, 16384 );
119
120    while ( EOF != ( ch = fgetc( bkupfile ) ) ) {
121      switch( ch ) {
122        case '\t': do {
123                    if ( EOF == fputc( ' ', tgtfile ) ) break;
124                    } while ( ++column % tabsize != 1 );
125                    break;
126        case '\r':
127        case '\n': column = 0;
128        default:   fputc( ch, tgtfile ); ++column; break;
129      }
130      if ( ferror( tgtfile ) ) {
131        puts( "Error writing target file." );
132        fclose( tgtfile );
133        fclose( bkupfile );
134        exit( 8 );
135      }
136    }
137    if ( ferror( bkupfile ) ) {
138      puts( "Error reading backup file." );
139      fclose( tgtfile );
140      fclose( bkupfile );
141      exit( 8 );
142    }
143    fclose( tgtfile );
144    fclose( bkupfile );
145  }
```

Lines 122–124 of Listing 7.3 contain the do-while that substitutes blanks for tab characters. This do-while is written as the action to be taken (as detected by a switch statement, which is discussed shortly) when a tab character is encountered in the input stream. Notice how much code this program requires to support this one small loop! This is why productive programs are never as short and simple as most sample programs in books.

The loop body consists of an fputc() that writes blanks to the output file. If an EOF occurs during *output,* the break statement exits the switch statement. Remember that EOF is reported for end-of-file (out of space) and error conditions (bad write) occurring in fputc(). Lines 130–135 outside the switch then use the ferror() function to determine whether there was an output error. This error test is always executed; it serves to catch errors from the fputc() in line 128 as well as from tab expansion.

Line 124 contains the controlling expression for the do-while. It does two things: it first *prefix increments* the column counter and then tests whether the remainder of column divided by tabsize is 1. The loop continues to output blanks until the remainder (modulus) is 1.

Why it does this becomes clear when you think of the first character of a text line as column 1. Now suppose that tabsize is 8 (the default here). The next tab stop is in column 9, then 17, and so on. When the modulus is 1, column represents a tab stop location.

But why is the column variable *prefix* incremented? Because the goal is to advance to the next tab stop, no matter what the current column may be. This is why back-end condition checking is necessary—the current position must be advanced even if column is already positioned at a tab stop. The prefix increment prevents the modulus from being 1 when the loop begins at a tab stop location. This in turn requires that the loop body be executed beforehand to stay in sync.

NOTE Try rewriting this loop without using the do-while construction. It can be done, but obtaining predictable results in all combinations of circumstances won't be easy.

Getting It All: The *for()* Loop

The for loop statement groups the initialization expression, front-end controlling expression, and loop-variable adjustment expression together inside a single, parenthesized list. Here is the syntax of the for statement:

```
for ( expr1 ; expr2 ; expr3 ) statement
```

Note that this is not a list of parameters (which would be separated by commas). It is a group of expressions, separated by semicolons. Keeping this straight is important, because you can use the comma operator to write multiple expressions in each expression location. For example, the line

```
for ( expr1 ; expr2a,expr2b,expr2c ; expr3 ) statement
```

is perfectly legitimate. All three controlling expressions are optional. You can omit any or all of them. When you do use them, their meanings are the following:

- *expr1* is used to initialize the loop-control variable (or variables, if a comma-separated list of expressions is used).

- *expr2* is the front-end controlling expression (or expressions). The loop continues to execute the statement (which may be a block statement) as long as the expression, or all the comma-separated expressions, evaluate to true.

- *expr3* adjusts the value of the loop-control variable or variables. *expr3* may be multiple expressions, separated by commas also.

Lines 45–56 of Listing 7.3 illustrate the normal use of the `for` statement. You may recognize this as the method presented earlier in the book for processing all the command-line parameters in turn. This use of the `for` statement is the equivalent of a `while` loop constructed like this:

```
expr1;              /* Initialize loop variables */
while ( expr2 ) {   /* Front-end condition checking */
  statement;
  expr3;            /* Update loop variables */
}
```

As in the `while` loop, the target statement of a `for` can be a null statement. Lines 14–21 of Listing 7.3 give a good example of the `for` loop with one of the expressions omitted and with a null target statement. The `strupr()` function shown in these lines converts all the characters of a string to uppercase characters by letting side effects do all the work:

```
char *strupr( char *s )
{
  static char *p; /* Can't return an auto var! */
  p = s;
  for ( ; *s; *s++ = toupper( *s ) ) ;
  return( p );
}
```

Notice in this fragment that *expr1* is omitted. There is no need for it because the program already "knows" where the target string begins—it begins wherever *s points. The controlling expression is *s; it evaluates to true until the terminating null character is encountered in the string. *expr3* performs not only the loop-control variable adjustment (the postfix ++ increment of the pointer) but also the primary work of the loop = toupper(*s).

Writing the loop as

```
for ( p=s; *s; s++ ) *s = toupper( *s );
```

is also correct. This second method is even easier to read.

> Is there any reason, then, to write code as compactly as possible? There are two reasons: writing compact code frequently reduces the size and length of the source file and often allows the compiler to produce more efficient (faster) code. The gain in efficiency is small enough to be unproductive, however, if it results in code you cannot read and control. Making this choice is always a judgment call, but remember that *you* are the one who has to live with the result.

T I P

What about more complicated situations? Can you, for instance, write loops inside of loops? You certainly can, and often this is exactly the way to do things. Writing loops inside other loop bodies is called *nesting*. It can produce some very clean logic capable of sophisticated work. Listing 7.4 shows the program ASCII.C, which produces an ASCII chart on your display by using nested loops. This program uses the Microsoft compiler's display group of functions. You may have to change the screen output functions if you do not have the Microsoft compiler.

Listing 7.4. ASCII.C—Nested *for* loops increase loop sophistication (for Microsoft C/C++).

```
1   /* +--------------------------------------------------+
2       +   ASCII.C
3       +   Display an ASCII chart for all 256 characters
4       +   in the collating sequence.
5       +--------------------------------------------------+
6   */
7   #include <conio.h>
8   #include <graph.h>
9   #include <stdlib.h>
10  #include <stdio.h>
11
12  main()
```

continues

Listing 7.4. Continued

```
13  {
14    int i, j, x, y;
15    char ch;
16
17    _clearscreen( _GCLEARSCREEN );   /* Clear screen */
18    i = 0;
19    for ( j=0; j<2; j++ )              { /*Half the table at a time */
20      for ( x=0; x<80; x+=10 )        { /* Write eight columns */
21        for ( y=0; y<17; y++ )        { /* with 16 lines */
22            _settextposition( y, x );
23            printf( "(%.3d)", i );
24            _settextposition( y, x+6 );
25            printf( "%c", i++ );
26        }
27      }
28      _settextposition( 24, 40 );
29      printf( "Press a key to continue ..." );
30      ch = '\0'; while( !ch ) ch = getch();
31    }
32    _clearscreen( _GCLEARSCREEN );    /* Clear screen */
33  }
```

The nested loop structure for producing the ASCII chart is in lines 19–31 of Listing 7.4. Notice the comments on lines 19, 20, and 21; these are the successive for statements controlling the nested loops. You can think of these as the loop "tops" (entry points).

The largest, or *outer,* loop consists of all the source lines from 19 to 31. The outer loop produces half the ASCII chart at a time. The next *inner* loop, lines 20–27, produces eight columns of display. Finally, the innermost loop, lines 21–26, produces the codes and characters for a single column of the display.

Now think about how a loop body is executed repeatedly as long as the controlling expression is true, and reflect on how a nested loop works. You should think of the flow of execution as descending into the nested structure, with the innermost loop being the lowest level. It is the innermost loop that completes first. An inner loop runs to completion for every pass of the loop in which it is contained.

Now see how that concept is translated into an analysis of this example. Here again are lines 19–21 from Listing 7.4:

```
19    for ( j=0; j<2; j++ )       {    /* Half the table at a time */
20       for ( x=0; x<80; x+=10 ) {    /* Write eight columns */
21          for ( y=0; y<17; y++ ) {   /* with 16 lines */
      ...
```

When line 19 is encountered, the outer loop is initiated. Its target statement here is a block statement that happens to contain other loops. The target statement—the loop body—is executed completely for every pass through the outer loop. This means that each inner loop is completely executed, all the way to loop termination, for every pass through the outer loop.

The same applies to the loop defined in line 20. As soon as it is initiated, execution flow descends again, and the third, innermost loop (line 21) is initiated also. Execution flow does not "percolate" back up to line 20 again until the entire innermost loop is complete—16 lines of columnar information is written.

At this point, line 20 executes again and determines that all eight columns have not yet been displayed. Therefore, execution flow again descends to the innermost loop, where another complete column of information is written to the screen.

This process continues until all eight columns of 16 items have been displayed. Simple arithmetic shows that there are 16 * 8 (or 128) passes through the loop body of the innermost loop before execution flow ever percolates above line 20 again.

Finally, because the outermost loop executes in two passes (one display page per half the ASCII table), this whole process repeats a second time, so the innermost loop body executes 256 times—the number of characters in the extended ASCII collating sequence on an IBM PC. Figure 7.4 illustrates the nested structure of the ASCII chart generator program.

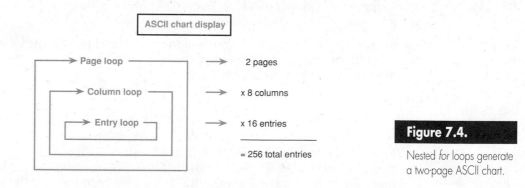

Figure 7.4.

Nested *for* loops generate a two-page ASCII chart.

Finally, because all three expressions in a `for` statement are optional, you can write a never-ending loop like this:

```
for ( ; ; ) {
  /* Do something here */
}
```

The problem is the same with a never-ending `for` loop as with a `while` loop. It is up to the logic—and that means you—to decide when the loop is done and to exit the loop. How do you do that? There are several ways, as you discover in the next section.

Altering Logic Flow in a Loop

Logic flow in a loop body is just like logic flow everywhere else. It proceeds in a sequential, linear flow (at least in the loop boundaries) unless you do something about it. Conditional logic (the C selection statements) can be used to tailor execution flow in a loop body (discussed in the upcoming section "Programming Conditional Logic").

The special case (of altering logic flow in a loop) discussed here has to do with changing the loop timing and sequencing—that is, modifying the behavior of the loop. You can modify loop behavior by doing any of the following:

- Enter the loop in a nonstandard way. Normally, the `while`, `do-while`, or `for` statement initiates loop processing. It is possible, however, to use the `goto` statement to jump into the middle of a loop body. The program might even work correctly. However, this is very dangerous and is almost never done. You will see why in a moment.

- Exit the loop in a nonstandard way. The `goto` statement can also be used to jump directly out of a loop body. This is not as dangerous as jumping into the loop, but it is still not a recommended practice.

- Modify control variables to control the number of passes (iterations) through the loop body. Consider the following example of a simple `for` loop controlled by an integer counter:

```
for ( i=0; i<10; i++ ) {
  --i;
}
```

From the definition of the `for` statement, you know that the postfix increment of `i` occurs as if it were at the back end of the block target statement. But the loop body also contains a prefix decrement of the control variable. What is the net effect on the loop? The value of `i` is always the same at the top of the loop. This is now a never-ending loop.

The preceding code fragment illustrates the danger of using such a technique, but it is not always out of bounds. Suppose that the loop is processing the elements of an array (so the control variable is also the array subscript). If one of the elements has an erroneous value that can be corrected by the logic, you might want to provide code that does the correction, sets the control variable back a notch, and allows the loop to reprocess that element. Be very careful, however, to limit the conditions in which a control variable is modified.

- Stop an iteration early and immediately begin the next one. You can use some of the nonstandard approaches already mentioned to do this, but the best way, by far, is to use the `continue` statement.

- Exit the loop early, using a standard C verb. You can use one of two verbs here: `return` and `break`. The main difference is that `return` not only terminates the loop but also exits the function. `break` just exits the innermost loop body in which it is found, and allows the rest of the function to continue execution.

The preceding list contains a mix of standard and nonstandard approaches to changing the behavior of a loop. Clearly, you should know about the standard ways to do these things. But even the standard approaches, if not handled correctly, can get you in a bind. Because the nonstandard methods can be especially dangerous, you next examine them to see why.

Quick Reference: The C Jump Statements

Standard C provides four *jump,* or direct branching, statements to allow transferring control of execution to a statement other than the next sequential one. The jump is *unconditional:* if the statement is executed, the jump occurs. The general syntax and use of the four jump statements are the following:

```
goto identifier ;
```

The `goto` statement causes an unconditional jump to the label statement (documented earlier in the book) named by the identifier. The jumped-to location must be in the same function as the `goto` that references it. Remember that to jump outside the current function scope, you must use the `longjmp()` facility.

The next jump statement is

```
continue ;
```

The `continue` statement causes an unconditional jump to the loop-continuation part of the smallest enclosing iteration statement (loop body). That is, the jump is to the end of the loop body, skipping all intervening statements in the body. This allows the next iteration or pass of

---

continues

> ## Quick Reference: The C Jump Statements
>
> the loop to begin immediately. When `continue` appears in a loop body that is nested inside another loop, it does not "break out" to the next outer loop; it just causes the current one to skip to the next iteration.
>
> The third jump statement is
>
> ```
> break ;
> ```
>
> This statement terminates the execution of the smallest enclosing loop body; it "breaks out" to the next outer loop in a set of nested loops. `break` is used also to break out of a `switch` statement, as described in the upcoming section "Programming Conditional Logic."
>
> The fourth jump statement is
>
> ```
> return expression;
> ```
>
> The `return` statement terminates execution of a loop because it terminates execution of the current function and returns control to the caller of the function. The related *expression* must have the same type as the function, unless the function has type `void`, in which case the expression should be omitted.

goto Versus *break*

You have seen four ways to terminate loop processing: allow the loop to complete normally, use the `return` statement, use the `goto` statement, and use the `break` statement. Of these, only the `goto` and the `break` statements end the loop early and allow the function to continue execution.

Is there any reason you should choose the standard `break` statement rather than the nonstandard `goto` to terminate a loop early? Definitely. Look at the short program, named GOLOOP.C, in Listing 7.5.

Listing 7.5. GOLOOP.C—Dangerous entry and exit from a loop (for Microsoft C/C++).

```
1   #include <stdlib.h>
2   #include <stdio.h>
3
4   main()
5   {
6     int i = 5;
```

```
 7
 8    goto target1;
 9
10    for ( i=0; i<10; i++ ) {
11  target1: ;
12        if ( i > 6 ) goto target2;
13        printf( "%d\n", i );
14    }
15  target2: ;
16  }
```

The first thing you should know about GOLOOP.C is that it does work correctly, in spite of the fact that the loop in lines 10–14 is both entered and exited "illegally."

The reason that GOLOOP.C works correctly is found in the object initializer in line 6, where i is set to 5. Thus, when the goto in line 8 transfers control into the middle of the loop, the control variable has a legitimate value. The loop body displays successive numbers beginning with 5.

What would have happened if there had been no initializer? To answer this question, you must resort again to scope, duration, and storage class. The control variable i is local to the function body and is by default an auto variable. Because it has no storage class specifier overriding it (in other words, static is not specified), it has automatic duration.

Combine this information with the fact that the ANSI standard specifies that an auto class variable with no initializer has an *undefined value*. This means that until an assignment is made to the control variable, any value can be stored in the control variable. You can see that the loop would be completely unpredictable.

The obvious solution is to plan the program more carefully in the first place. There is no reason why you should not use the following:

```
for ( i=5; i<10; i++ ) { ... }
```

if you want the loop to begin with a value of 5.

Lines 12 and 15 of Listing 7.5 demonstrate a nonstandard way to terminate the loop. All you have to do is goto some point outside the loop body that is still in the same function body. However, C provides a standard method that results in much safer, cleaner-looking code: the break statement. You could rewrite the loop in Listing 7.5 as the following:

```
for ( i=5; i<10; i++ ) {
  if ( i > 6 ) break;
  printf( "%d\n", i );
}
```

Now the whole program is more controllable, not to mention more readable. The loop begins with the correct values and terminates cleanly at the right time. The break statement causes the rest of the loop body to be skipped. The next statement to be executed is the one just after the closing brace of the loop body (generally the one after the loop's target statement).

NOTE If the break statement appears in a nested loop, only the innermost loop is terminated. A break in a nested loop allows execution, in effect, to percolate immediately up to the next outer loop.

The *automatic control* of the next statement selected to be executed is what makes the break statement the correct method for terminating a loop early. In Listing 7.5, the closing brace of the loop body (line 14) is followed by a label statement (line 15) that is the target of the goto. What happens if you modify the code later, placing other statements between those two lines? They won't be executed when terminating the loop through goto.

If the new statements happen to be necessary for cleaning up after the loop or are crucial to the program in any other way, you are in trouble. The program won't crash (not right there, anyway), but other parts of the program may not function correctly.

Using *continue* to Loop Early

The continue statement causes an unconditional jump to the loop-continuation part of the loop body, in effect skipping the statements from that point to the end of the loop body. The loop-continuation part of the loop body is just the point beyond the last statement in the loop body, before branching back or condition checking (depending on the loop type). This is shown in Figure 7.5.

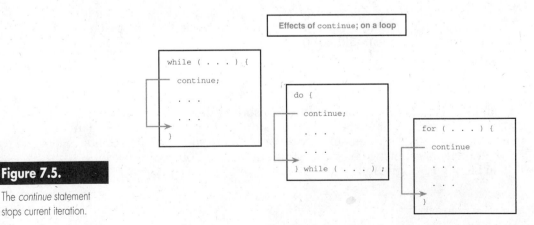

Figure 7.5.

The *continue* statement stops current iteration.

When should you use continue? Use it during a pass whenever you encounter a condition in which only some of the loop body statements are required. For example, you might want to count both the total number of characters and the number of noncontrol characters in a text file. To get the total count, you always increment a counter; to get the noncontrol character count, you update only when the numeric value of the character is greater than or equal to that of a space character. The program in Listing 7.6 performs such a character count.

Listing 7.6. CONTINUE.C—Use *continue* to loop early (for Borland C++).

```
1   #include <stdlib.h>
2   #include <stdio.h>
3   #include <string.h>
4
5   main( int argc, char *argv[] )
6   {
7     FILE *infile;
8     char inname[41];
9     int ch;
10    int total = 0, notctl = 0;
11
12    if ( argc < 2 ) {
13      puts( "A filename is required." );
14      exit( 0 );
15    }
16    strcpy( inname, argv[1] );
17    if ( NULL == ( infile = fopen( inname, "r" ) ) ) {
18      puts( "File open error." );
19      exit( 0 );
20    }
21    while ( EOF != ( ch=fgetc( infile ) ) ) {
22      ++total;
23      if ( ch < ' ' ) continue;
24      ++notctl;
25    }
26    fclose( infile );
27    printf( "Filename %s contained %d total characters, \n"
28            "of which %d were NOT control characters.\n",
29            inname, total, notctl );
30  }
```

Most of the code in Listing 7.6 is support code. The loop that counts characters is in lines 21–25. This is a familiar `while` loop, and the process of checking for the end of the file while reading the file is also a familiar one by now.

Now look at the statement in line 22. This is the first statement in the loop body—it executes on every pass through the loop and counts the total number of characters in the file.

In line 23, however, the logic potentially prevents the bottom part of the loop body from executing. This happens whenever the numeric value of the character is less than that of a space character. (Notice that the statement tests for *less than,* rather than *greater than or equal to:* this makes the logic both easier to handle and cleaner.) The counter `notctl` is updated only if the value is not less than that of the space. Otherwise, the `continue` statement causes line 24 to be skipped.

Programming Conditional Logic

Conditional logic is the meat and potatoes of the programming trade. Conditional logic statements provide the only method of deviating from a strictly sequential execution flow. That is, conditional logic statements make choices based on the value or values of data objects.

C provides all the conditional logic programming power you need in a surprisingly small set of statements. In fact, there are just two basic conditional or *selection* statements:

- The `if` statement provides two-valued logic choices. The general idea is that if the value of an object is one thing, do action *a.* If it is not, do action *b.* The `if` statement comes in two versions: the plain `if` and the `if-else` statement.

- The `switch` statement provides multivalued logic choices. When the value of an object may have more than two values (say, something other than just true and false values), each of which indicates some action to perform, a multivalued choice is necessary. The `switch` statement is useful in a number of situations.

NOTE The meanings of the terms *true* and *false* have been mentioned several times in this book, but this is the place to do it again. An expression (which may be just an object or something more complex) evaluates to a *true* condition when its integral value is *nonzero.* (The integral type may be arrived at by means of an implicit conversion. There's more on that in a moment.) Otherwise, an expression evaluates to a *false* condition when its integral value is *zero.*

Both the `if` and the `switch` statements have controlling expressions. These statements are used in the same manner as in the iteration statements; a target statement either is or is not executed, depending on whether the controlling expression is true or false.

Quick Reference: The C Selection Statements

C has surprisingly few conditional logic, or *selection,* statements. There are just two forms of the `if` statement, plus the extremely powerful `switch` statement. Note their syntaxes:

```
if ( expression ) statement

if ( expression ) statement else statement

switch ( expression ) statement
```

This brief summary makes these powerful statements appear simpler than they are. If nothing else, the syntax templates shown here don't reflect the complexity of punctuation possible. See the accompanying text for further details.

If-Then-Else Statements

If-then-else logic is the easiest form of conditional logic to grasp because it closely parallels the way people think and speak. *If* something is true, *then* do a particular thing, or *else* do something different.

C provides `if` logic both with and without `else` condition handling. Note the syntax for the two forms of C `if` statements:

```
if ( expression ) statement
```

```
if ( expression ) statement else statement
```

The controlling expression is the same as those used in forming program loops. It is evaluated for a true or false condition and, if it is true, the target statement is executed.

`if` logic differs from looping in that execution flow is linear, although parts of the linear sequence of statements may not be executed. Figure 7.6 illustrates execution flow of the simple `if` statement.

Figure 7.6 shows logic flow as if the target statements were simple statements. When that is the case, don't forget to punctuate the statements with semicolons. The target statements also can be block statements, in which case, *no* semicolon follows the closing brace (}).

```
┌──   if ( condition-expression ) /* if true */
│
└──→      statement;                /* do this */
┌──→
│       statement;               /* then continue */
└──→
          . . .
```

```
┌──   if ( condition-expression ) /* if false */
│
│         statement;               /* skip this */
│
└──→      statement;               /* then continue */
└──→
          . . .
```

Figure 7.6.

Logic flow of a simple
if statement.

if-else handling is similar to simple if handling except that condition checking controls two target statements, not just one. Figure 7.7 shows program
logic flow for the if-else construction.

```
┌──   if ( condition-expression )   /* if true */
│
└──→      statement;                  /* do this */
│
│       else
│
│           statement;              /* but not this */
↓
          . . .
```

```
┌──   if ( condition-expression )   /* if false */
│
│         statement;                  /* skip this */
│
│       else
│
└──→      statement;                /* and do this */
↓
          . . .
```

Figure 7.7.

Logic flow in an *if-else*
statement.

Either or both of the target statements in an if-else construction may be a
block statement. Figure 7.7 shows two simple statements, each of which has a
terminating semicolon. Notice that a simple statement just before the else
keyword does carry the semicolon.

NOTE The C language specifications require that the controlling expression have a *scalar type*. A C scalar is either an arithmetic type or a pointer type. Thus, the controlling expression can contain references to floating-point types, integral types, and pointers.

There is nothing to prevent nesting if statements. A nested if is handled in a hierarchical manner, as in the following example:

```
int a = 6;
int b = 3;
...
if ( a > b )
  if ( b == 3 ) statement;
```

This code fragment causes the statement to be executed. (But if the first if had not evaluated to true, the second if would never have been checked.)

Nested if-else constructions are possible also. When this is the case, each else keyword is associated with the *lexically immediately preceding* if keyword in the same block, but not if it is in an enclosed block. This just means that the curly braces ({}) enclosing a block statement work something like parentheses in forcing a certain grouping. For instance, the else in the following code fragment is associated with the outermost if:

```
if ( a > b ) {      /* The if belonging to the else */
  if ( b == 3) {    /* A completely independent if */
    a = 4;
    b = 2;
  }
}
else {              /* The else for the outermost if */
  a = 7;
  b = 8;
}
```

The classic nested if construction looks like this:

```
if ( ... ) statement; ---------------+
  if ( ... ) statement; ----------+   |
    if ( ... ) statement; ----+   |   |
    else statement; ----------+   |   |
  else statement; ---------------+   |
else statement; ---------------------+
```

Experienced COBOL programmers can tell you two things about this kind of nested `if` construction. First, think of grouping the `if-else` pairs like stacked bowls. The `if-else` in the "center" is one pair, and then you work outward, associating pairs. Second, don't use them. Why? See the following caution.

CAUTION

> Avoid using nested `if` statements. Because nested `if` constructions of any length tend to become terribly confusing in practice, some other logic arrangement is preferred. Furthermore, the statements in a nested `if` are so interdependent that most attempts to change the interior code lead to disaster.

One approach to simplifying complex logic is to *modularize* it—use the higher levels of selection to call functions that handle the lower levels. Another approach to repackaging complex conditional logic is to "frame it in" with a `switch` statement. That is the topic of the following section.

More Complex Conditions: *switch()*

You already have seen the `switch` statement in use several times in the sample programs in this chapter and earlier chapters. Most recently, the `switch` statement was used in Listing 7.3 to determine what to do with the different kinds of input characters while detabbing a file.

The `switch` statement is useful whenever the logic path depends on the value of an object that can take more than two values. It is used frequently, for example, to "decode" menu-selection items entered from the keyboard.

The *switch()* Statement

The ANSI standard is about as unclear as it can be about writing a `switch` statement. The following is our own syntax template:

```
switch ( integral-expression ) {
  case constant-expression: statements
...
  case constant-expression: statements
  default: statements
}
```

The labeled statements in the braces constitute the `switch` body. There can be as many as 257 `case` labels, as well as a `default` label, in the `switch` body.

The controlling expression of the switch statement must have an integral type: one of the integer or character types. The integral promotions are performed on the controlling expression. When the controlling expression has been evaluated, the switch statement causes a jump to one of three locations:

- To the first statement associated with a case label with a matching constant expression value. If the case value matches that of the controlling expression, execution resumes at the associated statements for that case label.

- To the first statement associated with the default label. If none of the case values matches the controlling expression value and if there is a default label present, execution resumes at the first statement here.

- To the first statement beyond the switch body. If none of the case values matches the controlling expression and if there is no default label, execution resumes completely beyond the switch body.

NOTE The ANSI committee debated briefly on whether to allow floating-point types in the controlling expression, but decided against it. The members cited reasons such as the fact that it may not be possible to represent any particular value exactly as a floating point, throwing the results of evaluation into some doubt.

case Labels

Clearly, the case labels and their associated statements are the core part of the switch construction. case labels are similar to the labeled statements you learned about earlier. The single exception is that the case keyword is followed by a constant expression and then by the full colon of the label statement.

The constant expression of a case label is just that—constant. This means that although the expression can indeed be complex, it may not contain a reference to any variable. Furthermore, after all the case expressions have been evaluated, they must all be unique. This does not mean that they must be in any order, just that values must not be duplicated.

The next important quality of case labels is that these labeled statements are being written and have the same rules as any other labeled statements. The result is that the statements associated with a case label do not necessarily have to be written as block statements. They already are part of the block statement that is the switch body. These statements can be function calls, expressions with side effects, or whatever you want them to be. Figure 7.8 shows the flow of execution through a switch body, as determined by the arrangement of case statements.

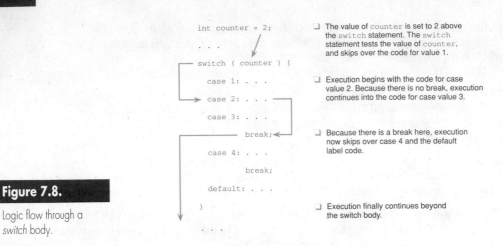

```
        int counter = 2;
          . . .

      switch ( counter ) {

          case 1: . . .

          case 2: . . .

          case 3: . . .

                      break;

          case 4: . . .

                      break;

          default: . . .

          }

      . . .
```

❏ The value of counter is set to 2 above
the switch statement. The switch
statement tests the value of counter,
and skips over the code for value 1.

❏ Execution begins with the code for case
value 2. Because there is no break, execution
continues into the code for case value 3.

❏ Because there is a break here, execution
now skips over case 4 and the default
label code.

❏ Execution finally continues beyond
the switch body.

Figure 7.8.

Logic flow through a
switch body.

As you can see from Figure 7.8, the controlling expression of the switch evaluates to the value of the counter integer—just 2. The flow of execution jumps to the statements associated with case value 2 and continues from there. Some other interesting features shown here are covered in just a moment.

You learned in the introduction to this section that switch statements frequently are used to control menu-selection items. Now see how that is done. Listing 7.7 contains a program called SELECT.C, which is driven by the switch statement in lines 36–46.

Listing 7.7. SELECT.C—The *switch* statement in action (for Borland C++).

```
1   #include <stdlib.h>
2   #include <stdio.h>
3   #include <bios.h>
4   #include <ctype.h>
5
6   /* +--------------------------------------------------+
7      + One of the following #defines should appear next,
8      + depending on which compiler you are using:
9      +    #define MSC
10     +    #define BORLANDC
11     +--------------------------------------------------+
12  */
13  #define BORLANDC
14
15  int get_ch( void );
16
```

```
17   main()
18   {
19     int i;
20     char ch;
21
22     while ( 1 ) {
23       for ( i=0; i<25; i++ ) puts( "" ); /* Clear screen */
24       puts( "\t\t\tThe Menu Title Goes Here" );
25       puts( "" );
26       puts( "\t\t\t1 - First selection title" );
27       puts( "\t\t\t2 - Second selection title" );
28       puts( "\t\t\t3 - Third selection title" );
29       puts( "\t\t\t4 - Fourth selection title" );
30       puts( "" );
31       puts( "\t\t   Press a number key, Enter, or press" );
32       puts( "\t\t\tX or x to exit the program." );
33       for ( i=0; i<6; i++ ) puts( "" );
34       ch = get_ch();        /* Input the character */
35       ch = toupper( ch ); /* Handle lowercase input */
36       switch ( ch ) {
37         case '1':
38         case '2': /* You could call selected functions here */
39         case '3':
40         case '4':  printf( "You selected item %c\n", ch );
41                 break;
42         case 'X': for ( i=0; i<25; i++ ) puts( "" );
43                 puts( "Terminating the program." );
44                 exit( 0 );
45         default: puts( "You pressed an invalid key. Try again." );
46       }
47       puts( "Press Enter to continue ..." );
48       ch = get_ch();
49     }
50   }
51
52   /* +--------------------------------------------------+
53      + get_ch()
54      + Mimics the very common getch() function, for char.
55      + input from the console without echo and without
56      + any interference or translation from the library
57      + functions. getc(), fgetc(), and getchar() are
58      + unsuitable for most menu selection type functions.
59      +--------------------------------------------------+
```

continues

Listing 7.7. Continued

```
60  */
61  int get_ch( void )
62  {
63  /* +--------------------------------------------------+
64     + The following #if defined uses the parenthesized
65     + form of the macro. Borland and MS don't care,
66     + but other compilers need it.
67     +--------------------------------------------------+
68  */
69  #if defined( MSC )
70    return _bios_keybrd( _KEYBRD_READ );
71  #else
72    return bioskey( 0 );
73  #endif
74  }
```

Notice in lines 37–40 of Listing 7.7 that using character constants for case expressions is perfectly legitimate. The use of character constants is acceptable because the characters are integral types, and the character constants are converted (at compile time) to their numeric equivalents.

Lines 42–44 illustrate that code for a case label does not have to be a block statement. In this instance, the case's statements are "isolated" from the rest of the switch body by the call to exit(), which happens to terminate the program as well as the switch. A more normal way is to use the break statement (as seen in line 41 and discussed in the following section).

Examine Listing 7.7 closely and compare what you see with the following scenario of its execution. The program begins by painting the menu screen:

```
            The Menu Title Goes Here


            1 - First selection title
            2 - Second selection title
            3 - Third selection title
            4 - Fourth selection title

     Type a number key, the Enter, or type
     X or x to exit the program.
...
```

The user presses 1 at this point:

```
You selected item 1
Strike Enter to continue ...
...
```

The user presses the Enter key and the program repaints the menu:

```
                    The Menu Title Goes Here

                 1 - First selection title
                 2 - Second selection title
                 3 - Third selection title
                 4 - Fourth selection title

            Type a number key, the Enter, or type
                 X or x to exit the program.
...
```

The user presses *x* at this point:

```
Terminating the program.
```

You should have noticed that no statements are associated with the first three `case` labels. To understand why, you have to understand how the `break` statement is used in a `switch` body, which is covered next.

Using *break;* and *default:*

Both Figure 7.8 and Listing 7.7 show instances of execution resuming at a given `case` label and continuing. In fact, the rest of the `switch` body is executed if you don't do something about it.

That something is the `break` statement. Look again at lines 37–41 in Listing 7.7. If the `switch` expression evaluates to `'1'`, `'2'`, `'3'`, or `'4'`, the jump to the `case` allows execution to "fall through" to `case '4'` statements. The `printf()` is sufficient to report any of these keystrokes.

At that point, however, you want neither to terminate the program nor to allow the `default` label code to tell you that the keystroke was invalid. The `break` statement in line 41 prevents that by causing a jump to the first statement beyond the `switch` body.

When you write real programs, be extremely careful where you place `break` statements in a `switch` body (and where you don't). Misplacement of `break` statements can be *very* difficult to debug.

ANSI C Rationale: Why Not *case* Ranges?

The ANSI C committee seriously considered allowing the `case` statement constant expressions to include *ranges* of values, such as

```
case 1..100: statements
```

which would mean that a `switch` controlling expression with a value from 1 to 100 would cause a jump to this `case` label. It was decided not to allow this for two reasons. First, it might cause the generation of a great deal of "jump table space." Second, a programmer might inadvertently specify a range of not necessarily contiguous values. (The range `'A'..'Z'` may not be valid in the collating sequences of some machines.)

The `default` label is provided in case (pardon the pun) none of the `case` values matches the controlling expression. If that happens and the `default` was provided, its code is executed. This label and its statements are completely optional, but having them is often a good idea. The logic of each individual situation dictates whether you need the label. You might use it as it is used in Listing 7.7; this is a good place to inform the user that none of the expected values has appeared.

Terminating the Program Early

In line 44 of Listing 7.7, the `break` statement is not used; instead, the `exit()` function is called. As mentioned earlier, this is a more extreme method of getting out of a `switch` body because it also gets you out of the program. The `exit()` function can be called from anywhere in the program and performs normal program termination. Here is the function prototype for `exit()`:

```
void exit( int status );
```

`exit()` has a `void` function type because, by definition, it can never return to its caller—the program returns to the operating system.

This doesn't mean that nothing can be returned. The `status` argument is passed back to the operating system to indicate the success or failure of the program. This success or failure is a *logical* state; either way, the program didn't blow up. However, the program may have detected a condition that should not exist. In that case, you would call `exit()` with a status code that indicates "mission not accomplished."

Two predefined macros in STDLIB.H can be used to set the `status` argument.

They are EXIT_SUCCESS and EXIT_FAILURE, which have obvious meanings. The exact definition of these macros depends on the operating system. On MS-DOS systems, for example, calling exit(EXIT_SUCCESS) is equivalent to calling exit(0). Most compilers also allow more than just these two values.

When exit() is called, several important things happen and at least one important thing *may not* happen. These events are summarized in the following list:

1. Any functions registered by the atexit() function are called. Hold this thought; it is discussed next.

2. The buffers for any open output streams are flushed (their contents written out and the buffers emptied).

3. All open streams are closed, and all files created by tmpfile() are deleted.

4. Control is returned to the host environment, passing back the status code. However, any storage acquired dynamically is not necessarily freed. Whether dynamic storage is freed depends on several things (such as machine, operating system, and particular compiler), but the only safe assumption is that if you acquired it (through malloc() or calloc(), which are covered later in the book), you should free it explicitly also.

The exit() function has a related function, atexit(), which can help you bulletproof your code. The atexit() function *registers* other functions that are to be called, in the reverse order of their registration, when the exit() function is invoked. The registered functions—at least 32 must be supported—can perform various cleanup tasks that might be otherwise overlooked. atexit() has the following prototype:

```
int atexit( void (*function)( void ) );
```

The call argument for atexit() is a *function pointer*. That is a pointer to the function to be called at exit time. You call atexit() as many times as there are functions to be registered. It returns zero if the registration is successful, and nonzero if it is not.

Confused? Just remember how the signal() function used function pointers; this is similar. Listing 7.8 illustrates the use of atexit().

Listing 7.8. ATEXIT.C—Use of the *atexit()* function (for Borland C++).

```
1   #include <stdlib.h>
2   #include <stdio.h>
3
4   void work_exit( void );
5   void mem_exit( void);
```

continues

Listing 7.8. Continued

```
6   void files_exit( void );
7
8   main()
9   {
10    atexit( work_exit );
11    atexit( mem_exit );
12    atexit( files_exit );
13    exit( 0 );
14  }
15
16  void work_exit( void )
17  {
18    printf( "Task cleanup in progress.\n" );
19  }
20
21  void mem_exit( void)
22  {
23    printf( "Releasing dynamically acquired storage.\n" );
24  }
25
26  void files_exit( void )
27  {
28    printf( "Performing final file updates and closes.\n" );
29  }
```

The functions registered by atexit() are called in the reverse order of their registration. The last registered function is called first, and on down the list. You should exercise some caution here. What if performing the final file updates depended on using dynamically acquired buffers? If it did, you would have to retain the buffers until file handling was finished.

Look carefully at the function prototypes for the registered functions in lines 4–6. They all have void type and permit no parameters. This is how you must specify functions to be registered with atexit().

In Listing 7.8, the exit() function is called explicitly, even though it is the last thing in main(). Explicitly calling exit() is not necessary when "falling through" the bottom of main(); an exit() is done implicitly then, and any registered functions are called. The explicit call is shown here for illustration, because exit() can be called from anywhere in the program.

There is one more way to terminate a program early. The `abort()` function causes abnormal termination of the program. Its prototype is

```
void abort( void );
```

`abort()` can be extremely dangerous to your files. Whether open files are flushed and closed is implementation defined, but most compilers do not do this. Thus, potentially, calling `abort()` can cause the loss of data and even the corruption of files that happen to be open at the time.

The `abort()` function also can be called from anywhere in the program, but when you use it, be extremely careful to have control of files and dynamically allocated memory.

Invoking the System Command Processor

Perhaps no greater change in execution flow can be made than to invoke another program from your program. ANSI C provides for this with the `system()` function, which has the following prototype:

```
int system( const char *string );
```

Calling `system()` is often referred to as "calling the shell," a term inherited from UNIX. The *shell* is just the system command processor. In DOS systems, it is COMMAND.COM.

`system()` returns an integer that is similar to the status code passed to `exit()`, except that now the code is moving from the system to your program. This code has different meanings, depending on the arguments passed to `system()`:

- If the argument is a null pointer, a nonzero is returned if a command processor is available. In ANSI C, this is how you can check for the presence of a command processor.

- If the argument is a pointer to a string, the return value is implementation defined. Typically, the return value indicates the success or failure of the command processor's actions.

In practice, most implementations handle the returned value a little differently. Usually, calling `system()` with a null pointer invokes the command processor in such a way that its command prompt is displayed. You then type the command you want processed. To get back to your program, you need to issue a special command. (In DOS systems, that command is `exit`.)

If the argument points to a string, the string should contain a legitimate command. For example, the string

```
system( "dir *.*" );
```

scrolls a listing of the current directory on-screen (regardless of what your program is doing on-screen!) and returns to your program. In this slightly nonstandard world, the code returned may mean only that the command processor didn't blow up, not that any particular command processed was successful.

Common Extensions to the ANSI Standard

Most compilers, on most operating systems, provide other ways of invoking external programs. With some of these methods, you return to your program; with others, you do not. Table 7.1 summarizes the function calls, the systems on which they are available, and whether your program regains control.

Table 7.1. Summary of methods for invoking other programs.

Function Call	Operating System	Returns to Parent Program
system()	UNIX, DOS	Yes
exec...()	UNIX, DOS	No
fork()	UNIX	Yes, synchronize with wait()
spawn...()	DOS	Yes, Can be done in UNIX with a combination of fork(), exec(), and wait()

How the parent (invoking) and child (invoked) programs behave depends on the host system. UNIX, for example, is a true multitasking, multiuser system. Child "processes" can run simultaneously with the parent under UNIX. DOS cannot do this because it is strictly a single-task, single-user system (although some programs are able to cheat and fake multitasking).

Summary

Controlling logic flow is an extremely important part of building flexible, powerful programs. In this chapter, you learned many of the techniques for controlling logic flow:

- Program loops are probably the most useful, versatile means of molding your program into a powerful tool. They are absolutely essential for performing repetitive work with any economy of effort.

- Conditional logic increases the "intelligence" of your program by permitting flexible decision making. A program without selection statements is similar to a car without a steering wheel. It may go fast, but only in one direction!

- Controlled program termination is also important. The `exit()`, `atexit()`, and `abort()` functions give you complete control over terminating program execution.

- Invoking the system command processor is a good way to add impressive features easily to your program. It is also a terrific convenience for the user; notice how many commercial packages provide just such a feature.

Programming with Pointers, Arrays, and Strings

Pointers, arrays, and strings may not be the most important topics in C programming, but they certainly rank near the top. It is a rare C program that does not use an array, a string, or a pointer. It was impossible, for example, to avoid references to and uses of these intriguing objects when developing sample code for this book. Their use so far has been on an intuitive basis, however, with a minimum of supporting theory.

In this chapter, you learn about pointers, arrays, and strings from the inside out. Specifically, you learn the following:

- ■ What pointers are and how they are used in C to accomplish indirect addressing of objects.

- ■ How to define, access, and manipulate arrays and strings. Using multi-dimensional arrays also is covered.

- ■ That array subscript and pointer notation are different but equivalent ways of doing the same things and how you can use this fact to pep up your programs.

- ■ How to pass arrays and strings as arguments to functions and how to refer to such arguments in the function body.

Pointers and Composite Data Types

You can define a pointer to just about any object declarable in C syntax, including the basic object types. Objects with type *pointer to* int, for example, are perfectly legal and are common in C programs. The same is true of the other basic types. You define a pointer to one of the basic types when you need the address of the object, rather than the actual object. You can use this address to access the object, or you can manipulate the pointer value directly.

The most common use of pointers, however, is to gain access to composite or *derived* object types. These objects may be too large to pass to a function by value, or there may be no way to refer to the individual elements in the object other than by pointer reference. This is the case with arrays and strings. Even using array subscripts is a "hidden" method of accessing array elements through a pointer, as you will see shortly.

To fully understand how C programs handle strings and arrays then, you must understand how C handles pointers. To begin understanding pointers, you must get a firm grasp on indirect addressing.

Reviewing Indirect Addressing

Indirect addressing is a method of accessing variables that uses the contents of one object to find another object. In C, the first object is called a *pointer,* and its contents are the *RAM address* of the second object. A pointer object contains the address of the pointed-to object. The pointed-to object is accessed indirectly through the pointer. Figure 8.1 illustrates this arrangement.

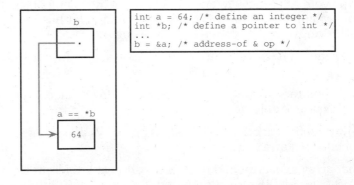

Every byte in the main memory of a computer has an address, beginning conceptually with an address of 0 and proceeding sequentially to the maximum address in the machine. (And 80x86 programmers are faced with a segmented memory scheme on top of this.) Clearly, every object stored in main memory has an address, which is just the "byte number" where its storage area starts.

Now, remember the discussion of expressions and operators, particularly the indirection operator *. C uses this operator both to declare a pointer and to use that pointer to get to another object. The following are examples of *pointer declarations:*

```
int *a;        /* a is pointer to int */
char *s;       /* s is pointer to char or string */
double *dist;  /* dist is pointer to double */
```

Notice the comments for these sample declarations. a is not an integer; it is a pointer to type int. Neither is s a character, nor dist a double. These objects have a type of *pointer to type,* where *type* is the type of object pointed to.

Quick Reference: Compiler Dependency—Pointers and 80x86 Machines

The 80x86 CPU used for IBM and compatible PCs is peculiar in several ways. Not least in the list of oddities is the segmented memory scheme required by this processor to access all of its memory.

Memory addresses in the 80x86 CPU are composed of two parts: the *segment address* and the *offset address.* All pointers use the offset address, but pointers that also use the segment address are called far pointers. Those that do not are called near pointers. One or the other of these types of pointer is the default type used in compilation, depending on which *memory model* you pick for the program.

To declare a far pointer when near pointers are the default, you use an extra (nonstandard) type specifier in the declaration, as follows:

```
int far *counter;
```

Notice that the far qualifier appears after the type specifier but before the * indirection operator. The actual implementation of memory models and pointer schemes may differ slightly from one compiler to the next. Be sure to check your product's manual before using this feature.

Referring to Pointers and Their Objects

After you declare a pointer, you face two problems: how to initialize the pointer and how to use it to get to other objects.

Initializing the pointer is critical. An uninitialized pointer is not the same thing as a null pointer. A null pointer contains binary zeros (a null value), which is the value used to signal the fact that the pointer doesn't point to anything. You can test for a null pointer in two ways:

```
char *s;
...
if ( s == 0 )    ... /* Test for 0 always permitted */
if ( s == NULL ) ... /* Most compilers #define NULL */
```

An uninitialized pointer, on the other hand, may contain garbage; it might or might not contain zero.

CAUTION

> Accidentally using an uninitialized pointer is a classic C programming error. It usually means the untimely demise of your program and, if it damages areas outside your program's boundaries, may even require a system reboot.

You initialize pointers as you do any other object. You can use an initializer in the declaration or an assignment statement. You can also do address arithmetic on pointers to change their values (and hence, the memory address pointed to).

In any case, an *address value* is placed in a pointer, not the type of object that you mean to point to. Whether you write an initializer or an assignment statement, you can initialize a pointer in two ways:

■ Initialize the pointer by taking the address of the object pointed to. You use the address-of operator & as follows:

```
int a = 64;
int *b = &a; /* Using an initializer */
int *c;
...
c = &a;      /* Using an assignment statement */
```

■ Initialize the pointer with a copy of another pointer. If a pointer to the appropriate object type already exists, you can assign its value to another pointer referencing the same object type, as in the following:

```
int *a; /* Assume that this one is initialized */
int *b; /* Assume that this one is not */
...
b = a;  /* Don't use the & operator here */
```

Using a pointer to access a data object is called *dereferencing* the pointer. You also can use the indirection operator *, but in a statement rather than the declaration, as follows:

```
int a = 64;        /* Declare an int object */
int *b;            /* Declare the pointer */
...
b = &a;            /* Initialize it */
if ( *b == 64 )    /* Refer to the object */
  printf( "I found the object!\n" );
```

Again, you use the indirection operator both to declare the pointer and to dereference it to access the object pointed to. This concept is a little confusing at first but makes sense when you have some experience with C syntax.

> There is a common-sense restriction to assigning values to pointers: You should be sure to mix apples only with apples. In other words, pointers to different object types usually don't mix. There are two exceptions to this rule: You can use the type cast operator to force conversion to a pointer to another object type, and the void pointer can point to anything.
>
> **T I P**

The following code fragment should result, at least, in a compiler warning message that indirection to a different type is being attempted:

```
long value = 37;
char *stuff;
.
stuff = &value;
```

Of course, if you try to apply the indirection operator to something that isn't a pointer, you get an illegal-indirection error message from the compiler.

There are two exceptions to this rule: You can use the type cast operator to force conversion to a pointer to another object type, and the void pointer can point to anything.

Make it a rule of practice to use the type cast to avoid all error and warning messages—insist that a program compile completely clean when playing pointer conversion games. If you want to access the individual bytes of a long int and dump them in hex, for example, you could write the following code:

```
long value = 37;
char *stuff;
int i;
```

```
                 /* The cast to pointer to char makes this work */
stuff = (char *)&value;
for ( i=0; i<4; i++ ) printf( "%.2x ", *stuff++ );
```

After taking the address of value, the resulting pointer is cast to a pointer to char, forestalling any warning messages. The preceding code fragment works without the cast, but insisting on a clean compile puts you in the position of knowing that something you did not intend is going on if a message appears.

The other way to mix different pointer types is to use the void pointer declaration. To declare a void pointer, write the following:

```
void *anyobject;
```

The void pointer can point to any object type and can be assigned to a pointer to any object type without error. Many library functions use this type of pointer because it is impossible to predict for what you want to use the pointer. The dynamic allocation functions, for example, do not know what you will use the acquired memory for:

```
double *answer;
...
answer = malloc( sizeof( double ) );
```

Even though the malloc() function returns a void pointer, you can assign it with impunity to a pointer to double (or anything else).

The story is different, however, when you dereference a void pointer—doing so is illegal. A void pointer gives the compiler no information whatever about the type of object with which to be dealt. Rewriting the hex dump fragment using a void pointer gets you into immediate trouble:

```
long value = 37;
void *stuff;
int i;
                    /* The following statement gets by OK */
stuff = &value;
                    /* But this results in "invalid indirection" */
for ( i=0; i<4; i++ ) printf( "%.2x ", *stuff++ );
```

The compiler flags the reference to *stuff in the printf() argument list as an error—illegal indirection, just as if you had applied the indirection operator to a nonpointer object. It has no way of determining whether the dereferenced object can be applied to the %x conversion specification.

In this case, even a cast to another pointer type doesn't get you out of trouble. If you add the (char *) cast to the printf() argument, as in the following code:

```
long value = 37;
void *stuff;
```

```
int i;
                    /* The following statement gets by OK */
stuff = &value;
            /* Compiler doesn't know how to increment */
      /* the void pointer, even though there is a cast */
for ( i=0; i<4; i++ ) printf( "%.2x ", *(char *)stuff++ );
```

the compiler flags the postfix increment operator as an error. Because the compiler doesn't know how large the dereferenced object is, it cannot update the void pointer. (You see why in the next section, which discusses pointer arithmetic.)

Pointer Comparisons and Arithmetic

In the preceding section, you learned that you can always compare any pointer type to zero or the null macro value. You can also compare two pointers to each other, using the equality (== and !=) or relational (<, >, <=, >=) operators, under certain conditions. First, you look at how important pointer comparisons can be; then you read about those conditions.

In the sample program CVTSTR.C in Chapter 5, there is a small function at the end of the program listing (Listing 5.2). The purpose of the str_invert() function is to reverse the order of characters in a string. Following is a repeat of the code for that function:

```
void str_invert( char *s )
{
  static char *p;
  if ( !*s ) return;      /* Null string, no work */
  p = s;
  while ( *p ) p++; p--; /* Position to end of string */
  while ( s < p ) *s ^= *p, *p ^= *s, *s++ ^= *p-- ;
}
```

This function illustrates the importance of being able to freely compare (within limits) the values of pointers to each other (in other words, to compare the address values, not the values of the objects being pointed to). Without this capability, this function would be cumbersome and inefficient, though perhaps not impossible.

The compact, efficient str_invert() function is worth looking at closely. It reveals a great deal about how pointers are handled. The basic idea of the function is to define two pointers, one pointing to each end of the string, and "move" them toward each other, exchanging characters as they go. When the pointers "pass" each other, or become equal, the work is done. The algorithm is implemented in the following way:

■ Because a pointer to the beginning of the string is received as the function argument, only one temporary pointer must be defined to point to the end of the string. This pointer is `char *p`; it is given the `static` storage class so it is not recreated at every call to the function (that is, it is a little faster this way).

■ A null (empty) string cannot be reversed, so this is checked for. Dereferencing the pointer `s` (`*s`) yields the value of the first character pointed to. If it is a null string, its value is `'\0'`, so `!*s` is true.

■ The temporary pointer `p` is initialized with the value of the argument pointer `s`. It is incremented until the `'\0'` character is reached and then backed up one byte to point to the last character in the string.

■ The last line of the function contains all the power of the method. It uses several techniques and concepts that you have learned from this book:

The whole process is controlled by the `while` condition `s < p`. This condition is no longer true when the pointers are equal or have passed each other; the loop stops.

The target statement (one statement) is composed of three assignment expressions separated by the comma operator. These expressions are the three parts of exchanging the values of two objects with no temporary holding storage (through the exclusive-OR operation). (For a refresher on this concept, see Listing 3.5.)

The first two of these expressions simply dereference the pointers to access the characters pointed to. The third adds the wrinkle of appending the postfix increment and decrement operators to the appropriate pointer. To understand this expression, you must remember the precedence of the operation. Because postfix increment and decrement have higher precedence, the pointers (not objects) are accessed for values to be updated at the next sequence point. However, because these are postfix operators, they do not interfere with the values fetched for use in dereferencing the pointers. The result is that the current value is used to access the characters indirectly, and only then are the pointers incremented or decremented.

Pointers clearly are powerful tools. But there are restrictions on how they can be compared:

■ When two pointers are compared, they both should point to the same type of object. The ANSI standard specifies that the objects pointed to must be of qualified or unqualified compatible types (or perhaps compatible incomplete types). If you compare a pointer to `int` to a pointer to `double`, for example, your compiler should at least warn you that a suspicious pointer conversion occurred. When you have to get around this rule, use both type casts and extreme caution, as mentioned earlier in this chapter.

- If two pointers to a basic object type compare equal, they point to the same object. (See the "Compiler Dependency: Segmented Addresses and Pointer Arithmetic" C-Note later in this section for special cautions.)

- Two pointers to elements of aggregate or derived objects (string, array, structure, or union) can be meaningfully compared only if the elements are members of the same aggregate object. When this is the case, elements declared later in the aggregate compare higher than earlier elements. If the pointers refer to elements of different aggregate objects, the result is undefined—there is no guarantee what the result will be.

- The preceding rule has one exception. A pointer can point to one position beyond the end of an array object and still retain significance. If P and Q both point to the last element of an array, P + 1 is guaranteed to compare higher than Q.

The ANSI standard specifies the results of comparisons of pointers that have been converted from one type to another (whether implicitly, during expression evaluation, or as a result of a cast operator you wrote).

- A pointer to void may be converted to or from any object (or incomplete) pointer type. Successive conversions ending with the original pointer type result in an address value identical to that of the original pointer. For example, a cast from (void *) to (int *) to (void *) produces no net change to the pointer value.

- Conversion from an unqualified to a qualified pointer (or vice versa) does not change the address value of a pointer. Thus, the conversion from (int *) to (short *) produces an identical address value.

- A null pointer (which has an address value of 0) is guaranteed to compare unequal to any pointer to an object or function.

- Any two null pointers are guaranteed to compare equal, regardless of the object type pointed to.

Because addresses are integral, pointers are related to integral values. In fact, the ANSI C document specifically permits the explicit (by cast) conversion of pointers to integers and integers to pointers. In either case, the result is considered to be implementation-defined.

This explicit conversion can be quite useful but requires detailed knowledge of machine and operating system internals. For example, an 80x86-based machine with CGA or compatible video modes has memory-mapped screen RAM located at segment address 0XB800. A Borland C or Microsoft C program can access that RAM directly by declaring a pointer as follows:

```
unsigned char far *screen;
...
screen = (unsigned char far *)0XB8000000L;
```

This code fragment is a little awkward to set up, but now your C program can place characters (and attributes) on-screen with a speed rivalled only by assembly language programs.

But do not forget that pointers are not integers! Remembering this fact is especially important when you write code that does address arithmetic. Arithmetic on pointers (meaning addresses) is carried out in a specific and special way in C. The difference between integers and pointers can be summed up as follows:

■ The address value contained in a pointer is the byte address of the object pointed to.

■ Adding 1 to a pointer does not always increment the byte address by 1; the byte address may be increased by 1 but may also be more, depending on the object type pointed to. Each increment (or decrement) of a pointer updates the byte address by an amount equal to the size of the object pointed to.

 **NOTE** Updating a pointer always causes it to point to the "next" object of the type pointed to—the next character in a string, the integer in an array of integers, and so on, for the other basic types. How this affects the byte address stored in the pointer depends on the implementation of C. Remember that ANSI requires only that characters fit in one byte; all other types have an implementation-defined size, for which the only requirement is that the object type be able to store at least the minimum values defined for it.

This philosophy of pointers naturally and necessarily limits the type of arithmetic operations that you can do on pointers. Exactly because pointers are not integers, the only legal pointer arithmetic is additive. There are further limitations on which additive operations are valid. Address arithmetic in C observes the following rules:

■ You can add or subtract an integral constant to or from a pointer. Again, this operation causes the pointer to address the next object of the associated type, not the next byte address:

```
 int a;       /* Set up a pointer to an integer */
int *b = &a; /* Take the address to get started */
...
b = b + 1;   /* Point to next integer */
b += 1;      /* Same effect */
b++;         /* Still the same effect */
++b;         /* Still one more element */
int a[16];   /* An array of 16 integers (see below) */
int *b = a;  /* Notice the difference from just a pointer */
```

```
...
+b = b - 1;   /* Point to previous integer */
b -= 1;       /* OK for subtraction too */
b--;
--b;          /* Don't forget these */
```

Adding 1 to a pointer to int does not yield a pointer to the second byte of the integer; it yields an address beyond the integer, ready to access another integer following the first. The compiler accomplishes this task by first multiplying the integral value by the size of the object pointed to and then performing the addition or subtraction.

■ You can subtract one pointer from another pointer. When a pointer subtraction is performed, the result is not another pointer; it is a signed integral type. The ANSI document requires that a conforming compiler provide a #define for this type. It is ptrdiff_t and is defined in STDDEF.H.

When the subtraction is performed, the intermediate result (which is the difference in byte address) is then divided by the size of the object pointed to. The end result is a count of elements between the two pointers:

```
ptrdiff_t distance;   /* Pointer difference object */
int a[16];            /* An array of integers */
int *c, *d            /* Two working pointers */
...
c = &a[0];            /* Address of first element */
d = &a[15];           /* Address of last element */
distance = d - c;     /* distance is now 15 */
```

Standard C provides a string-length function—strlen(). But consider how pointer differences could help you develop an efficient string-length algorithm.

```
#include <stdlib.h>
#include <stdio.h>
#include <stddef.h>
#include <string.h>
main()
{
  char text[41] = "Find the length of this string.";
  ptrdiff_t length;         /* Pointer difference object */
  char *s, *p;              /* Two working pointers */
  int count;
  /* ---- Method 1: Count the bytes ---- */
  count = 0;
```

```
s = p = text;              /* Seems simple, but there is */
while ( *p++ ) count++;    /* hidden overhead in count++ */
printf( "%d %d\n", count, strlen( text ) );
/* ---- Method 2: Compute the length ---- */
s = p = text;
while ( *p++ ) ;
length = p - s - 1;        /* Only one calculation */
printf( "%d %d\n", length, strlen( text ) );
}
```

Both methods in this short example use the postfix increment operator to add 1 to a pointer and "step" down a string. In addition to the pointer arithmetic being done, the first method also updates a counter variable at every iteration of the while loop.

The second method uses the while loop only to find the end of the string. There is no other arithmetic in each iteration of the loop; all calculation is performed once after the loop is complete. You save a counter update for every pass through the loop.

For a quick and dirty program, either method is fine—the speed difference is not that great for one use. But if you are writing a production program that uses the string-length function frequently, every CPU cycle saved is a plus. Why not do it right in the beginning? (The standard strlen() function, which comes with the compiler library, is most likely much faster than either of these methods; it's probably written in assembler.)

■ You cannot add two pointers. The result would not make arithmetic (or pointer) sense. Generally, you just need a distance from one location to another, for which ptrdiff_t() is tailor-made.

■ You cannot perform multiplication, division, shift, or masking operations on pointers. These operations make absolutely no sense for pointers. The restriction is not a heavy burden, however, as there is never a need for these operations on pointers.

Quick Reference: Compiler Dependency—Segmented Addresses and Pointer Arithmetic

Users of the 80x86 CPU deal with a special problem in handling pointers: the segmented address scheme of the processor. Because the memory of the 80x86 is linearly addressable only in 64K chunks, a pointer capable of pointing anywhere in memory must be composed of two parts: the segment and offset addresses. They are contained in two different integer (unsigned int) objects, from the machine's point of view.

C compilers for these machines are therefore compelled to implement several different non-ANSI pointer types. The near pointer requires only 16 bits (an integer) and assumes a particular segment address (which is not directly available for manipulation). The far pointer has a behind-the-scenes structure: it is composed of two unsigned ints, one for the segment and one for the offset address.

The near pointers conform to the ANSI standard in every respect. So do far pointers, but some hidden pitfalls are associated with them because the segment address can refer only to paragraph-size (16-byte) portions of memory. Thus, a single location in the 80x86 address space can be represented by 65536 / 16 = 4096 separate and distinct far pointer values! None of this set of values compares equal, even though only one location is referenced. This can destroy pointer arithmetic; furthermore, only the offset portion of the address is affected by address arithmetic.

One way to ensure that far pointers behave properly is to load every pointer to a given object from the same base address, with no exceptions. Another way is to provide a "normalized" far pointer type. Both the Borland and Microsoft products provide this pointer type, called a huge pointer. Its offset part is never allowed to go over 16, the size of a paragraph. Maintaining normalized pointers involves considerable calculation overhead, but you can address arithmetic on the full 32-bit range.

Microsoft C's based pointer feature offers a high-performance compromise. A based pointer resides in a single 16-bit (near-sized) pointer but enables you to specify in which memory segment the object resides, without assuming that it is the current segment. based pointers offer the best of all choices on 80x86 machines: addressability anywhere in the system's address space, ANSI conformity, and high performance—provided that you don't deal with an object over 65536 bytes. This restriction may rule out the use of large text buffers, for example.

When Do You Need a Pointer?

You can perform many tasks comfortably either with or without pointers. For these tasks, the decision to use a pointer is a matter of personal taste. There are other things for which a pointer is indispensable. How do you know which is which? Here are some guidelines:

■ *Passing function arguments by reference.* Passing an object value to a function makes only a copy of that value available to the function. You cannot modify the value of the original object. Passing parameters by *reference*—passing a pointer to the object rather than its value—avoids this restriction. You can dereference the pointer and get to the original object.

■ *Passing large structured objects as function arguments.* Structures differ from arrays and strings in that, although they are also derived objects, they normally are passed to functions by value. A copy of the entire structure is passed to the function. This may be too time consuming for high-performance programs and, on stack-driven machines, may require too much stack space. Simply pass a pointer to the structure, consisting of integral type data, to conserve stack space as well as speed up call linkage considerably.

■ *Dealing with arrays and strings.* Two instances here deserve mention. First, any reference to the identifier of an array or string identifier without subscripts yields an address value, not an object value. You already have seen this example several times:

```
char text[81] = "This is a text string!!";
char *s;  /* Define a pointer */
...
s = text; /* Refer to the string's address */
```

This does not mean, however, that the identifier text in the preceding fragment is a pointer—text = s; would be an error. Only a reference to it yields an address value, so passing an array or string to a function necessarily means passing a pointer value.

Second, you frequently can use pointers instead of subscripts for greater performance. This topic is covered later in this chapter.

■ *When you want to modify the value of a pointer passed as a function argument.* This approach can be tricky until you remember that a pointer is also an object (a derived one, to be sure) that can be manipulated in its own right. When you pass a pointer to a function, only a copy of the pointer's contents—an address value—is passed to the function. This results in the same problem you faced in choosing between passing by value or by reference; it just deals with pointer values now.

You can get around this problem by passing a pointer to a pointer to the function. Now the original pointer's contents (the address value in it) can be modified. This technique is explained in detail in Chapter 9.

Defining Arrays of Variables

Programmers tend to use arrays of objects extensively in C programs, which makes arrays an extremely important subject. Their implementation in this language is also tied intimately to pointers, which is why that subject was covered first.

What is an *array*? It is simply a collection of related objects, much like a mathematical set. An array is composed of its *elements,* and in C every element must have the same type: there are arrays of int, of double, of char, and of all other basic types. You can even have arrays of derived types, such as structures. But no arrays contain both int and double objects, for example. (You can get around this by using arrays of structures.)

The elements of an array occupy contiguous locations in memory. If an integer requires 2 bytes of storage, an array of integers places an integer element every 2 bytes, with no gaps in between. This concept is important because it affects not only the way elements are stored physically in memory, but also the means you can use to get to a particular element.

Defining One-Dimensional Arrays

The simplest type of array is the *one-dimensional* array. A one-dimensional array can be viewed as a list of items in memory, stored sequentially, one after the other. You can use one-dimensional arrays to represent simple vectors, lists, tables, the coefficients of an equation, or any number of other things.

Declaring the Array

All arrays require some means of locating a specific element. The means actually used makes sense because it is just a number, called a *subscript,* that indicates which member element is the one to be used. One-dimensional arrays are characterized by the fact that they require only one subscript to access any element in the array. Other arrays, described later in this chapter, may have more than one subscript.

You use subscript notation not only to declare the array, but also to access member elements later in the program. Figure 8.2 shows the result of declaring (and initializing) a small array of integers. This array of integers, like all other arrays, occupies contiguous storage locations.

```
int num[8] = { 0,1,2,3,4,5,6,7 };
```

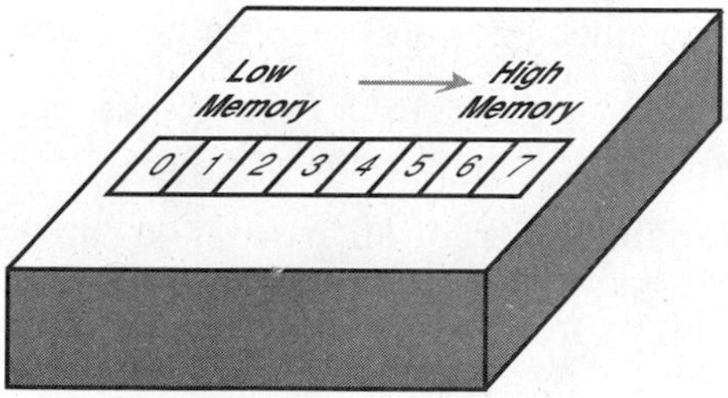

Figure 8.2.

One-dimensional array in RAM.

The num array depicted in Figure 8.2 has eight elements. Notice how the square brackets immediately follow the array identifier. In the brackets, you write a number that instructs the compiler how many elements to reserve space for—in this case, eight. In the array *declaration,* this number is not an element locator, it is the *array size.*

The value used to declare the array size can be an expression, but the resulting value must be a constant—variables are not allowed here. One flexible way to do this, which provides for easy modification later, is to use a *manifest constant.* A manifest constant is defined with a #define directive, as follows:

```
#define SIZE 10
#define buildmsg(X) "Array size is: " ## #X
main()
{
  int num[SIZE];  /* Define array with SIZE elements */
  printf( "%s", buildmsg(SIZE) );       /* Report it */
}
```

In passing, notice how the buildmsg() function-like macro is arranged to use a manifest constant to build a string literal at preprocessing time. The string preprocessing operator # first creates the literal "10" (in this case), and the string concatenation preprocessing operator ## creates the token:

```
"Array size is ""10"
```

The compiler performs (compile-time) string concatenation, so the result is the equivalent of "Array size is 10". This sort of flexibility was not available in pre-ANSI C.

An initializer for an array differs from that of a basic object type because more than one value must be specified. To initialize an array in the declaration, follow the identifier (and square brackets) with an assignment operator, just as you would for any object.

However, because you need a list of values for an array, you next write an opening (left) curly brace ({), then write the list of values separated by commas, and close with a closing (right) curly brace (}) and a semicolon. Because this is not a block statement, a semicolon is required. Note also that the ANSI standard enables you to leave a trailing comma at the end of the list; this makes it convenient to add values later and recompile without syntax errors:

```
int num[8] = { 0,1,2,3,4,5,6,7 };  /* This is the same */
int num[8] = { 0,1,2,3,4,5,6,7, }; /* as this! */
```

You do not have to write an initializer for an array. You can write code that initializes it at runtime (by reading values in a loop from a file, or the keyboard, and assigning the inputs to array elements, for example).

Referencing Array Elements

A reference to an array element involves the same `[]` operator as the declaration of the array. However, the element reference may now use an object identifier—a variable name—as the subscript, as follows:

```
#define SIZE 10
#define buildmsg(X) "Array size is: " ## #X
main()
{
  int num[SIZE];  /* Define array with SIZE elements */
  int i;          /* Define a subscript variable */
  printf( "%s", buildmsg(SIZE) );       /* Report it */
  for ( i=0; i<SIZE; i++ ) num[i] = 0; /* Initialize */
}
```

The last line of the preceding fragment shows you something about the values that you can use in a subscript and how to design loops that process the elements:

■ The first element of an array has subscript value 0, not 1. The array declaration defines the size of an array with a value that is the count of the elements in it. Array subscripts are more like offsets, which specify a distance from the beginning of an object (whatever is being addressed). Thus, the first subscript number is 0—no offset from the beginning of the array.

■ When processing an array in a loop, the maximum subscript value should therefore always be less than SIZE, whereby SIZE is the number of elements in the array. This rule follows from the scheme of subscripting from 0; the maximum subscript possible is SIZE - 1.

Of course, you can always use a constant value to subscript an array. You can write the initialization sequence for the array in the preceding code fragment as follows:

```
num[0] = 0;
num[1] = 0;
num[2] = 0;
...
num[SIZE-1] = 0;
```

Writing the sequence like this is not generally profitable, for obvious reasons, but there are times when you want to use constant values to subscript an array.

Defining Multidimensional Arrays

All that you have learned about one-dimensional arrays applies also to defining and using multidimensional arrays; you just have to add extra subscripts (or sizes) to define the extra dimensions.

Declaring the Array

Multidimensional arrays are useful for storing more complex groups of related items. You might want to describe a sequence of three-dimensional points, for example (you see some code for this application later in this chapter). Figure 8.3 depicts a conceptual layout of a multidimensional array.

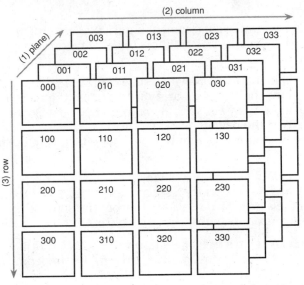

Figure 8.3.

Two- and three-dimensional arrays in RAM.

```
int data [4][4][4]; /* 3-dimensional array with 4 */
...                 /* elements per "vector" */
data[row][column][plane] = ...;
```

In Figure 8.3, the extreme right subscript describes elements in contiguous storage. All the [plane] elements are together. There are [column] groups of [plane] elements, and then there are [row] groups of [column][plane] elements. Element numbers shown in cells correspond to subscripts.

The most important thing to learn from Figure 8.3 is that arrays are stored in *row-major order*—the last subscript varies the fastest. In the figure, all the [plane] elements are stored in contiguous memory, and there are [row] times [column] elements in a "plane." Similarly, there are [row] elements that have the same [column] subscript number.

On a more intuitive level, think of a series of points in a graph. You might code the following:

```
int points[64][2];   /* Define 64 point-pairs */
```

This declaration defines 64 pairs of x-y points. For a given point `i`, for example, the x-value is `points[i][0]`; and the y-value, `points[i][1]`. The C compiler doesn't care what the values signify. You could interpret the elements in this array to the number of eggs and apples if you want. The important thing to remember is that the last subscript varies fastest—x-y pairs are kept together (or egg and apple counts are kept together).

Referencing Array Elements

The same principles apply to referencing elements of multidimensional arrays as apply to any others. The following code fragment defines an array of five pairs of date and dollar numbers:

```
double revenue[5][2] = {
  90.001, 1000.00,
  90.002, 995.75,
  90.003, 1015.33,
  90.004, 877.44,
  90.005, 2000.01,
};
double total_income;
int i;
total_income = 0;
puts( "\t\t    Sales Revenue for the Week" );
puts( "\t\t  Date\t\t\t   Amount" );
for ( i=0; i<5; i++ ) {
  total_income += revenue[i][1];
  printf( "\t\t%8.3f\t\t%10.2f\n",
          revenue[i][0], revenue[i][1] );
}
printf( "\n\n\t\t\t Total Revenue: %10.2f\n",
        total_income );
```

Study carefully the initializer for the `revenue` array. The line breaks and spacing emphasize the way the elements are stored in memory. The result in memory is a "stream" of `double` objects: 90.001, 1000.00, 90.002, 995.75, and so on, in that order. This reflects the fact the last subscript varies the fastest.

Notice that the first subscript is referenced by means of a variable, whereas the second (last) subscript is referenced with a constant value. `revenue[i]`...

locates the pair of figures for a date. revenue[i][0] locates the element containing a date in the pair, whereas revenue[i][1] refers to the corresponding income amount. When this code runs as part of a program, it produces the following output on-screen:

```
    Sales Revenue for the Week
    Date                 Amount
    90.001               1000.00
    90.002                995.75
    90.003               1015.33
    90.004                877.44
    90.005               2000.01

        Total Revenue:   5888.53
```

Pointer and Subscript Equivalence

The X3J11 ANSI committee very wisely brought forward the principle of *pointer and subscript equivalence*. This principle states that the definition of the [] postfix operator is that, for a pointer p and a subscript i, the expression p[i] is equivalent to (*(p+i)), which is a dereferenced pointer. As you might reasonably expect, i here can be an integral constant, identifier, or expression. If it is 0 (just *p), the first element p[0] is the one accessed.

It is important to remember that even when using equivalent pointers to access arrays, the compiler regards the integral value added to (or subtracted from) a pointer as element-sized steps. This follows from the definition: *(p+2) is defined to be the same as p[2]—the third element of the array.

Using pointers rather than subscripts can sometimes result in better-performing code. But you must be careful of the hidden overhead that may be present. Consider, for example, the following three equivalent methods of stepping through an array of integers:

```
int numbers[64];
int *temp;
int i, sum = 0;
...
for ( i=0; i<64; i++ ) sum += numbers[i];
...
for ( i=0; i<64; i++ ) sum += *( numbers + i );
...
temp = numbers;
for ( i=0; i<64; i++ ) sum += *temp++;
```

Does any one of these methods increase performance? Probably not. The first two for loops are (by definition) exactly equivalent and involve three arithmetic operations per pass:

- The third expression in the for statement updates the variable i.

- The variable sum is updated.

- Address arithmetic is performed, adding the integral value i to the base address of the array numbers to locate a particular element.

The third style of for loop looks as though it might save a few cycles because the addition of i to numbers does not occur in the loop body. However, notice that the temporary pointer temp is postfix-incremented on every pass. This is equivalent to the expression temp = temp + 1, so there are still three additions per pass.

On occasion, however, you can save cycles. What if you arrange the loop so neither a subscript nor a count of the elements have to be maintained? This increases the speed of execution somewhat. You can achieve this increase by *fencing the array* and allowing detection of the fence value to stop the loop, as in the following example:

```
int numbers[] = { 9, 3, 5, 2, 0 };
int *temp;
int sum;
...
temp = numbers;
while( temp ) sum += *temp++;
```

Now there are only two, not three, additions for each pass of the loop: the sum is updated and the pointer is updated. The drawback is that this method requires that some value be set aside—in this case, 0—the significance of which is always to act as a "fence" that terminates the array.

 NOTE Usually, you might as well use subscripts. This technique most often is as efficient as any other technique and is more readable than complex pointer expressions. The one place that spending time rewriting with pointer notation is worthwhile is in string processing: a string is an array of characters that is always, by definition, terminated with a null (0) character.

Did you notice in the array declaration of the preceding code fragment that no array size is given? This is called an *incomplete type*—the compiler knows that it is an array and, in particular, that it is an array of integers. But it does not know how large the array is.

The size is unknown until the declaration is completed. In this case, the declaration is completed by writing an initializer. One other incomplete type, an incomplete structure type, is discussed in Chapter 11.

Finally, you should understand that although you can use pointers and subscripts in equivalent ways, a pointer is still not an array as such:

```
int *numbers;   /* a pointer to int */
int numbers[4]; /* an array of int */
```

You can use the pointer to int to locate elements of an array, but before doing so, you must be careful to initialize it with the address of the array. Remember also that because an array identifier is not a pointer, it cannot appear on the left side of an assignment statement:

```
int *temp;
int number[];
int data[64];
...
number = data; /* ERROR */
temp = data;   /* Do it this way */
```

Using Arrays for Smoothing Geometric Curves

Now roll up your sleeves and get ready to put this knowledge to work. Two examples of using arrays are presented next. Both use most, if not all, of the array techniques discussed so far. These two examples are moderately sophisticated. In fact, if you are not something of a mathematician, some of the theory behind the techniques may get by you. This is not important. What is important is that you pay attention to the way the arrays are handled (the basics of the theory are given, though). The first example involves alternative methods of geometric curve-smoothing.

Using Arrays to Represent Shapes

The simplest way to represent a curve is with a mathematical equation. You can use an equation to solve for points along the curve and plot each in turn. There is a serious problem with this approach when implementing a computer graphics program: it's slow. The equation must be evaluated afresh at every plotted point on the curve. You therefore need a compromise method.

A common method of getting around the computational overhead of drawing a generalized curve is to store just a few points along the curve in an array and "fit" a curve to them. You achieve speed by simplifying the computations somewhat and "bunching" the calculations together. Then, drawing is rapid and uninterrupted.

The selected points—called *knots,* like knots in a curving string—can be stored in a relatively few elements; thus, the array required can be fairly small. In this example, the geometry is limited to two dimensions (to simplify the process). In particular, a curve is fitted to eight x-y points. The array for storing them is already familiar to you:

```
double knots[8][2] ...
```

This array keeps the x-y pairs together, controlled by the extreme right (last) subscript.

Curve-Smoothing Methods: SPLINE.C

There are many methods for drawing a smooth curve through selected points. You can connect them with straight lines or use a more-or-less sophisticated mathematical algorithm. The sample program SPLINE.C, shown in Listing 8.1, illustrates the straight-line method, the fairly simple Bezier curve-smoothing algorithm, and the more sophisticated B-spline algorithm. Figure 8.4 shows the different results obtained with these methods.

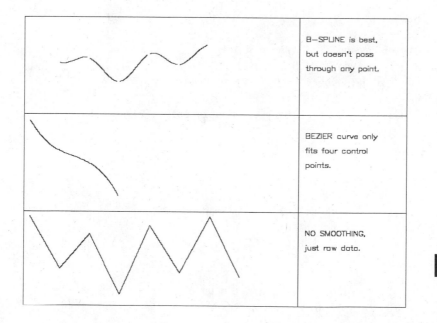

B—SPLINE is best, but doesn't pass through any point.

BEZIER curve only fits four control points.

NO SMOOTHING, just row data.

Figure 8.4.

Comparison of curve-smoothing methods.

The Bezier method is not discussed. If you like math, look at the derivation of the B-spline algorithm in Appendix F. Look over Listing 8.1 now to get the main features of the program in mind.

Listing 8.1.   SPLINE.C—Using arrays to represent curves and shapes (for Microsoft C/C++).

```
1   #include <stdio.h>
2   #include <stdlib.h>
3   #include <conio.h>
4   #include <graph.h>
5
6   double knots[8][2] =    /* Define x/y point pairs. */
7   {
8     10, 14,
9     60, 101,
10    110, 43,
11    160, 144,
12    210, 29,
13    260, 108,
14    310, 14,
15    360, 115
16  };
17
18  double (*outpoly)[2];    /* Pointer to an array of pairs. */
19
20  void part_screen( void );
21  void draw_polygon( double knots[][2], int N );
22  void b_spline( double knots[][2], double poly[][2],
23                  int N, int K );
24  void bezier( double knots[][2], double poly[][2], int K );
25
26  main()
27  {
28    int i;
29
30    _registerfonts( "c:\\c700\\lib\\modern.fon" );
31    _setfont( "t'modern' h12 w8" );
32    _setvideomode( _VRES16COLOR );
33    part_screen();
34
35    outpoly = calloc( 100, sizeof( double ) );
```

```
36
37    b_spline( knots, outpoly, 8, 10 );
38    for( i=0; i<8; i++ ) knots[i][1] += 158; /* Scale to next y. */
39
40    bezier( knots, outpoly, 50 );
41    draw_polygon( outpoly, 50 );
42    for( i=0; i<8; i++ ) knots[i][1] += 158; /* Scale to next y. */
43
44    draw_polygon( knots, 8 );
45
46    while( !kbhit() ); /* Don't kill screen until user OKs it. */
47
48    _unregisterfonts();
49    _setvideomode( _DEFAULTMODE );
50  }
51
52  /* ---------------------- */
53  /* Graphics screen layout. */
54  /* ---------------------- */
55  void part_screen( void )
56  {
57    _moveto( 0, 0 );
58    _lineto( 639, 0 );
59    _lineto( 639, 479 );
60    _lineto( 0, 479 );
61    _lineto( 0, 0 );
62
63    _moveto( 0, 161 );
64    _lineto( 639, 161 );
65
66    _moveto( 0, 322 );
67    _lineto( 639, 322 );
68
69    _moveto( 459, 0 );
70    _lineto( 459, 679 );
71
72    _moveto( 470, 30 );
73    _outgtext( "B-SPLINE is best," );
74    _moveto( 470, 54 );
75    _outgtext( "but doesn't pass" );
```

continues

Listing 8.1.   Continued

```
76      _moveto( 470, 78 );
77      _outgtext( "through any point." );
78
79      _moveto( 470, 190 );
80      _outgtext( "BEZIER curve only" );
81      _moveto( 470, 214 );
82      _outgtext( "fits four control" );
83      _moveto( 470, 238 );
84      _outgtext( "points." );
85
86      _moveto( 470, 351 );
87      _outgtext( "NO SMOOTHING," );
88      _moveto( 470, 375 );
89      _outgtext( "just raw data." );
90    }
91
92    /* ------------------------------------- */
93    /* General purpose draw for output pairs. */
94    /* ------------------------------------- */
95    void draw_polygon( double knots[][2], int N )
96    {
97      int i, j;
98
99      for( i=0, j=1; j<N; i++, j++ ) {
100       _moveto( (int)knots[i][0], (int)knots[i][1] );
101       _lineto( (int)knots[j][0], (int)knots[j][1] );
102     }
103   }
104
105   /* --------------------------------- */
106   /* B-spline curve smoothing algorithm. */
107   /* --------------------------------- */
108   void b_spline( double knots[][2], double poly[][2],
109                  int N, int K )
110   {
111     static double t,tsq,tcu,a,b,c,d,incr;
112     static int cnt,p;
113
114     incr = 1 / (double)K;
115     for ( p=1; p<N-2; p++ ) {
116       for ( t=0.0,cnt=0; cnt<K; t+=incr,cnt++ ) {
```

```
117        tsq = t * t; tcu = tsq * t;
118        a = ( -0.166*tcu + 0.500*tsq - 0.500*t + 0.166 );
119        b = ( 0.500*tcu - tsq + 0.666 );
120        c = ( -0.500*tcu + 0.500*tsq + 0.500*t + 0.166 );
121        d = 0.166*tcu;
122        poly[cnt][0] = a * knots[p-1][0] + b * knots[p][0]
123                       + c * knots[p+1][0] + d * knots[p+2][0];
124        poly[cnt][1] = a * knots[p-1][1] + b * knots[p][1]
125                       + c * knots[p+1][1] + d * knots[p+2][1];
126      }
127      draw_polygon( poly, K );
128    }
129  }
130
131  /* ------------------------------- */
132  /* Bexier curve smoothing algorithm. */
133  /* ------------------------------- */
134  void bezier( double knots[][2], double poly[][2], int K )
135  {
136    static double t,tsq,tcu,a,b,c,d,omt,tmo,incr;
137    int cnt;
138
139    incr = 1 / (double)K;
140    for ( t=0.0,cnt=0; cnt<K; t+=incr,cnt++ ) {
141      omt = 1 - t; tmo = t - 1;
142      tsq = t * t; tcu = tsq * t;
143      a = omt * omt * omt;
144      b = 3.0 * t * tmo * tmo;
145      c = 3 * tsq * omt;
146      d = tcu;
147      poly[cnt][0] = a * knots[0][0] + b * knots[1][0]
148                     + c * knots[2][0] + d * knots[3][0];
149      poly[cnt][1] = a * knots[0][1] + b * knots[1][1]
150                     + c * knots[2][1] + d * knots[3][1];
151    }
152  }
```

SPLINE.C in Listing 8.1 is rather long because it includes the code necessary to lay out a graphics screen. The graphics code is on lines 55–90. Because this program uses the Microsoft graphics functions, be sure to use a project file to compile it. The project file should contain SPLINE.C and the Microsoft graphics library.

The data points along the sample curve are stored in the `knots[][]` array, lines 6–16 in Listing 8.1. These are simple x-y pairs of points.

The number of points to plot calculated by the curve-smoothing algorithms has to be larger to get the output points closer together—yielding a smooth-looking curve. Because 50 point-pairs should do the trick, 100 `double`-sized chunks of storage are needed.

The acquired storage contains the *output polygon* array, named `outpoly` and declared in line 18. Notice the syntax: `double (*outpoly)[2]` declares one pointer to a one-dimensional array containing two elements. Clearly, you are going to play games—quite legal games—with pointer and subscript equivalence. The storage for this array is acquired through the `calloc()` function in line 35.

The `draw_polygon()` function in lines 95–103 draws a curve by the simple expedient of connecting (with straight lines) all the data points passed to it. That is why the points should be close together—if they are close enough, the curve looks smooth.

The `draw_polygon()` function has a few interesting features. First, notice that the formal parameter for the array is specified as an incomplete type and that the number of points to connect is passed as a separate integer parameter. Even though `outpoly` is a pointer to `int`, you can pass it (legally) to the function as if it were an array reference; the base type is `int` in both cases. Inside `draw_polygon()`, the object address thus passed is treated as an ordinary two-dimensional array identifier (again, perfectly legally). You can treat `outpoly` this way anywhere, not merely in a function where its true nature is "hidden."

Both the `bezier()` (lines 134–152) and `b_spline()` (lines 108–129) functions also use an incomplete type to declare the array parameter (which, as you may recall, amounts to a pointer). Just how many subscript sizes can you leave out this way? Only one: the extreme left, or first, subscript size may be omitted.

If you think about it for a moment, you can see why. The last subscript varies fastest—all elements located by the last subscript are stored together. If any subscript to the right of the one being evaluated is incomplete, how does the compiler know how many objects to skip over to increment the left subscript by 1? Suppose, for example, that you specify a point-pair array as a function parameter, as follows:

```
void show_stuff( int stuff[][] );
```

You know that the right subscript indexes two integers (associated x-y values). To get to the next pair, the compiler must compute an address that skips over two integers. Simplicity itself, except that the compiler has no way of knowing this! This line of code causes a compile-time error message that says something like the size of the array is not known.

The rule of thumb, therefore, is that a subscript to the right of an incomplete subscript cannot be incomplete.

Using Arrays to Solve Systems of Equations

Algebra students reading this book are probably familiar with the techniques for using matrices to represent equations and also with the manipulations necessary to solve equations using matrices. Using arrays to represent such matrices is simple and, although solving equations may not be quite so simple, the method is extremely instructive on subscripting for multidimensional arrays.

Using Arrays to Represent Equations

Suppose that you have three equations in three unknowns—x, y, and z. How can you represent these equations in arrays? The act of writing down some equations gives you a good idea how to start. Suppose that you want to solve the following equations:

```
 x +  3y -  4z =   8
 x +   y -  2z =   2
-x -  2y +  5z =  -1
```

Notice the neat pattern the coefficients of the variables make. This pattern immediately suggests that the equations can be represented in a [3] X [4] array. This type of array allows the coefficients and associated constant for one equation to be kept together in memory; there are three groups of these items.

Solving the Equations: GAUSS.C

You can use matrices (arrays) to solve (find the intersecting point for) any group of linear equations for which there are n variables and n equations with which to work. The method is not limited to three-dimensional problems, provided that the coefficients form a square matrix n elements on a side.

This method is called *Gaussian elimination*. For a good explanation of how this method works, refer to Sedgewick's *Algorithms*. The C implementation shown in the following example and, indeed, the specific equations are converted from Sedgewick's Pascal-based example.

Listing 8.2 contains the program GAUSS.C, which implements the method. Note that the Borland C++ compiler gives you a warning message about line 59. The message is issued because the statement in line 59 passes a two-dimensional array to gauss(), but the compiler expects a one-dimensional array. The program is deliberately designed this way; ignore the warning message.

Listing 8.2. GAUSS.C—Gaussian elimination algorithm to solve equations with arrays (using Borland C++).

```
1   #include <stdlib.h>
2   #include <math.h>
3   #include <stdio.h>
4   void gauss( double eqs[], double sol[], int N )
5   {
6     double temp;
7     int i,j,k,max,r;
8
9     r = N + 1;        /* rowsize = N + 1 */
10
11    /* First do forward elimination (triangulation) */
12
13    for ( i=0; i<N; i++ ) {
14      max = i;
15      for ( j=i+1; j<N; j++ )
16        if ( fabs(eqs[j*r+i]) > fabs(eqs[max*r+i]) ) max = i;
17      for ( k=i; k<N+1; k++ ) {
18        temp = eqs[i*r+k];
19        eqs[i*r+k] = eqs[max*r+k];
20        eqs[max*r+k] = temp;
21      }
22      for ( j=i+1; j<N; j++ ) {
23        for ( k=N; k>=i; k-- ) {
24          eqs[j*r+k] =
25          eqs[j*r+k] - eqs[i*r+k] * eqs[j*r+i] / eqs[i*r+i];
26        }
27      }
28    }
29
30    /* Now do the back substitution */
31
32    for ( j=N-1; j>=0; j-- ) {
33      temp = 0;
```

```
34        for ( k=j+1; k<N; k++ ) temp += eqs[j*r+k] * sol[k];
35        sol[j] = (eqs[j*r+N] - temp) / eqs[j*r+j];
36      }
37  }
38
39  main()
40  {
41    double equations[3][4] =
42      {
43        1.0,   3.0,  -4.0,   8.0,
44        1.0,   1.0,  -2.0,   2.0,
45       -1.0,  -2.0,   5.0,  -1.0
46      };
47    double solution[3];
48    int i,j;
49
50    printf( "\n" );
51
52    for ( i=0; i<3; i++ ) {
53      for ( j=0; j<4; j++ ) {
54        printf( "%8.3f",equations[i][j] );
55      }
56      printf( "\n" );
57    }
58
59    gauss( equations,solution,3 );
60
61    for ( i=0; i<3; i++ ) printf( "%8.3f",solution[i] );
62    printf( "\n" );
63  }
```

The gauss() function works by first applying a method known as *forward elimination*. This method uses basic matrix operations to transform the matrix into an equivalent one that has all zeros below the diagonal of the matrix. This is sometimes known as *triangulation*. Next, a process called *back substitution* solves for the variable. This process involves beginning with the last row that has only one remaining nonzero coefficient and solving immediately for that variable. Then that variable can be substituted in the preceding row to solve for the next and so on.

The interesting thing about the gauss() function (lines 4–37) is that it treats a two-dimensional array as a *vector*—as a one-dimensional array. Here is yet another application of the equivalence of pointers and subscripts.

As in Listing 8.1, no prediction is made in the function about the ultimate size of the array. An incomplete type is used so any array can be passed to the function (that is, its address can be passed). The number of rows and columns is determined here by the int type parameter N. (Only one such parameter is needed because a basically square matrix can be assumed.)

To handle the two-dimensional array as if it were a one-dimensional array, the function must compute how many objects to skip over to get from one row to the next. An int variable r is used for this purpose. Because all address and/or subscript arithmetic deals in numbers of elements—not byte addresses—rowsize in this example is r = 3 + 1 = 4.

Now suppose that you want to locate the kth element of the ith row. You first compute i * r to get to the first element of the ith row and then add the k value to the result. The final result is the equivalent one-dimensional subscript for a two-dimensional array.

This program is not as complicated as it looks, but such machinations can be extremely confusing until you get used to them. We recommend that you study the addressing techniques here very carefully and then write a few experimental programs until you get the hang of it.

T I P Why are such techniques important? The answer is size. In real-world applications, you may have to work with extremely large arrays in which mirror-image elements across the diagonal line through the matrix are identical. These elements, called *symmetric matrices,* can be greatly reduced in size simply by not recording duplicate values. The result can be stored in a vector (as done here in rudimentary form), and an algorithm can map array addresses to the correct values. Dr. Jack Purdum's book, *C Programmer's Toolkit,* also published by Que Corporation, includes some algorithms for dealing with symmetric matrices.

Strings Are Arrays of Characters

C strings are a special case of array objects. A string is a one-dimensional array of char or perhaps unsigned char. A string additionally has a *null fence*— the last character of a string is always a '\0'. Thus, although strings frequently are manipulated with subscripts, you often see them handled with pure pointers, as discussed earlier.

The Internal Representation of Strings

A string is the one case of array structure in which incrementing the subscript by 1 also increases the byte address by exactly 1. This happens because the C standard requires a character to occupy just one byte (all other object types are constrained by minimum and maximum value ranges). A string object is a composite data type; specifically, it is an array of char, terminated by a null byte. Just as with any other array, referring to the string object name with no subscript results in a pointer reference. Figure 8.5 shows the internal memory arrangement of a string.

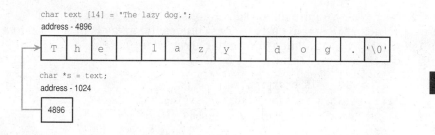

```
char text [14] = "The lazy dog.";
address - 4896
```

| T | h | e | | l | a | z | y | | d | o | g | . | '\0' |

```
char *s = text;
address - 1024
```

```
4896
```

Figure 8.5.

Memory layout of C strings.

Declaring String Variables

Strings are declared like other array types. The postfix [] operator contains a maximum size for the object. The base type, of course, is char or unsigned char:

```
char text[81];        /* A line of text characters */
char command[41];     /* Use this string to receive a */
                      /*    keyboard command */
unsigned char data;   /* High-order bit might be on */
```

You might want to use the unsigned char type in cases in which special characters may be present that have the high-order bit on. This condition may not make much difference until you either explicitly (a cast) or implicitly (for example, assignment, stream I/O function call) convert one of the characters to an int. If the character is considered signed, the high-order bit is interpreted as a *sign bit* and may be propagated to the high-order position of the new type.

If you look closely at Figure 8.5, you see that the array size given includes space for the '\0' fence character, even though it participates in the string value only to terminate the sequence. (It is not, for example, counted as part of the length of a string.)

You frequently see a comment in code like the following:

```
char *s;   /* String variable */
```

In this code line, is s really a string? No, it is not. This is a pointer to a character. However, because strings are composed of characters, this is also how you declare a pointer to a string. The comment really means that s is a pointer to a string (that is, a pointer to the first character in a string).

Initializing String Variables

All other array types require an initializer consisting of a list of comma-separated values enclosed in curly braces (unless the array is initialized in a loop somewhere). Strings differ from other array types here also, in that they are initialized by a string literal, as follows:

```
char text1[81] = "Here is a string!";
char text2[255] = "This is a much longer string.";
char stuff[] = "How long can this string be?";
```

The strings text1 and text2 can contain 80 and 254 characters, respectively, plus the null character fence. The third string, stuff, is declared with an incomplete type specification (just as you have seen for other arrays) and is completed only by the initializer. Because there are 28 data characters in the literal and the compiler supplies the '\0' character, a total of 29 characters are set aside for stuff.

Now, because a literal is used for initializer values, does this mean that you can assign a literal to a string identifier? For example, can you do this:

```
char holdit[41];
...
holdit = "A string literal";
```

No! A string identifier, like any other array identifier, is treated (when used without subscripts or a * operator) as an address value. Furthermore, also like other array types, this address value is not a true pointer and cannot be used on the left side of an assignment statement. How can you initialize a string outside the declaration? You find out in the next section.

Manipulating Strings

An ANSI-conforming compiler provides several useful string-manipulation library functions, all of which are declared in STRING.H. Three of them deserve mention here:

■ `char *strcpy( char *s1, const char *s2)` copies the contents of one string (s2) into another (s1). It returns a pointer (`char *`) to the receiving string (s1), although this is commonly ignored. You can use this function to initialize a string outside its declaration, as follows:

```
char stuff[41];
...
strcpy( stuff, "Some characters for stuff." );
```

■ `char *strcat( char *s1, const char *s2 )` concatenates string objects. Specifically, s2 is appended to (tacked on the end of) s1; the null characters are handled so there is only one at the end, as follows:

```
char stuff1[81] = "This is part 1, and ";
char stuff2[] = "this is part 2 !";
...
strcat( stuff1, stuff2 );
```

You must be careful to provide enough room in the receiving string to hold it all. In this example, `stuff1` must be at least long enough to hold `"This is part 1, and this is part 2 !"`.

■ `size_t strlen( char *s )` reports the length of the string s in an integral type `size_t`, as follows:

```
size_t length;
char howlong[] = "How long is this string?";
...
length = strlen( howlong );
```

(You also can assign the results into an ordinary integer if you want.)

`strlen()` reports only the length of the data characters in the string; the null terminator is not included in the byte count. If a string contains only the null fence, it is said to be a null string (literal value `""`), and `strlen()` reports a length of zero.

You can use subscripts or dereference characters to manipulate strings one character at a time. For example, you can initialize a string to a null string by dereferencing the first character and assigning `'\0'`, as follows:

```
char more_stuff[81];
...
*more_stuff = '\0'; /* Make it a null string */
```

As mentioned earlier, you can gain some performance boost by using pointer-only notation to process strings. For example, you could write your own string copy function inline by coding the following:

```
int i;
...
for ( i=0; s2[i] != '\0'; i++ ) s1[i] = s2[i];
```

This loop, short as it is, still involves data transfer, pointer arithmetic, and subscript update. It also fails to transfer the null terminator character. You can transfer with just pointers and eliminate the subscript update:

```
while ( *s1++ = *s2++ ) ;
```

The problem here is that this short line is probably slower than the `strcpy()` library function, which in all likelihood will be written in assembler. Still, this example illustrates the type of tricks you can use to cut down overhead and speed up your program. What it does not illustrate is that there is a time and place for both approaches. That is a matter for your judgment, depending on the situation.

Using Strings to Edit Text

One of the most important functions of your C program, from the user's point of view, is how he or she can get data into the program from the keyboard— and how easy (or difficult) doing so is. Most programs ask the user to enter a command, respond to a prompt, or input data. A program that does not allow flexible entry of commands and responses is one that the user will not use often.

Normally, people don't type in hex or binary; data entry is in string format and is converted internally to numeric formats. The C library functions `scanf()` and `gets()` and their variations can input string data—`scanf()` can even convert it to internal formats—but their editing capabilities are poor. In fact, about the only editing capability these functions have is the Backspace key. Using this key you can correct typing mistakes, but it becomes awkward when you discover that the second character in a 50-character input string is wrong.

What you need is a general-purpose string-editing (text-editing) function that, above all else, provides for easy, flexible error-correction. Developing such a function and its support functions is a good way for you to use what you have just learned about character strings. This function, arbitrarily called `edit_text()`, should have the following characteristics:

- *Flexible cursor movement and control.* The function should enable the user to use the keyboard arrow keys to move over existing text, one character at a time, in either direction—left or right. It should allow the use of the control-arrow keys to jump a whole word at a time, also either left or right. It should also enable the user to home the cursor (place it at the beginning of the line) or "end" the line (place the cursor at the extreme right position, just beyond the last character).

■ Easy correction or modification of string characters. The function should allow text entry in either insert or overtype modes and support upper-case-only input, deletion of characters anywhere in the string, erase to end-of-line, or kill line (erase the whole line and continue), and destructive backspace.

Such a function is necessarily machine- and compiler-dependent. ANSI provides nothing for standardizing the tasks of screen control, cursor movement, or direct screen or console I/O.

In UNIX systems, this functionality is provided by the curses (cursor optimization) library functions, working with the terminfo database to acquire information about the terminal being used. You can find these functions in the CURSES.H library header.

DOS systems handle screen I/O differently because the screen is connected directly to the system and its output is based on memory-mapped I/O. Different compilers access screen facilities in different ways; there is not as much uniformity as on UNIX systems. Typical library header files for DOS-based compilers are CONIO.H and GRAPH.H. We wrote the edit_text() functions developed here using Microsoft C/C++. Notes for converting the routines to Borland C appear later in this chapter.

However screen-management is implemented, the first task in designing the routines is to decide which keys will be used for a given purpose. Table 8.1 shows the keyboard usage for edit_text().

Table 8.1. *edit_text()* keyboard map.

Key Name	Resulting Action
F2 or Ctrl-D	Erase to end-of-line
F3	Kill line (erase all)
Home	Cursor to start of string (left)
End	Cursor to end of string (right)
Left arrow	One position left, nondestructive
Right arrow	One position right, nondestructive
Ctrl-left arrow	One word left
Ctrl-right arrow	One word right
Backspace/Ctrl-H	Erase character to left of current position and then one position left
Ins	Toggle insert/overtype modes; insert is starting default

continues

Table 8.1. Continued	
Key Name	**Resulting Action**
Del	Delete one character at the cursor and close up
Enter/Return	Edit complete; accept string and return
Other keys	Text input

Inserting and Deleting Characters

The main purpose of edit_text() is to insert and delete characters in a string of text data. This not only requires enough logic of its own to warrant writing separate functions, but also is an intrinsically useful feature that you can use in other contexts. Accordingly, the source file CINSDEL.C contains two functions—cinsert() and cdelete()—which are compiled separately to an object module, as shown in Listing 8.3.

Listing 8.3. CINSDEL.C—Inserting and deleting characters in a string (with Microsoft C/C++).

```
1   #include <string.h>
2   #include <ctype.h>
3
4   cinsert( char ccode,char *anystring,int spos )
5   {
6     int p;
7
8     p = strlen(anystring);
9     spos=( spos < 0 ) ? 0 : spos;
10    spos=( spos >= p ) ? p : spos;
11    for ( ; p>=spos; p--) anystring[p+1]=anystring[p];
12    anystring[spos]=ccode;
13  }
14
15  cdelete( char *anystring,int spos )
16  {
17    int p;
18
19    p=strlen(anystring);
20    if ( p>0 && spos>=0 && spos<=p) {
```

```
21        while ( spos < p ) {
22            anystring[spos]=anystring[spos+1]; spos++;
23        }
24    }
25  }
26
```

Both the insert and delete functions need arguments for the target string and the position in the string of the character to be affected. The insert function also requires the character to be inserted.

Whether you insert or delete a character in a string, the extreme right end of the string (beyond the point of insertion or deletion) must be moved to accommodate the new number of characters. Therefore, the first step in either case is to determine the length of the argument string (lines 8 and 19 of Listing 8.3, respectively).

Both routines require also that something be done with the right end of the string. Inserting a character requires that characters to the right of the insertion point be moved one space to the right to make room for the new character. Deleting a character requires that characters to the right of the deletion point be moved left to close the gap created by the removed character.

You can think of the insertion or deletion point as the "break" at which something has to be done to the string. The next task, accordingly, is to determine whether the break is in the boundaries of the string. Two different but equivalent methods are used to do this. cinsert() has a pair of statements that use the ternary operator (?:) to make the decision (lines 9 and 10), whereas cdelete() uses a single if statement (line 20) that does the same thing.

The cinsert() function moves the right fragment of the string to the right in line 11, and it places the new character in position in line 12. The cdelete() function performs its move to the left in lines 21 and 22. Perhaps the most important thing to remember about these routines is that they do not allocate new space for the strings. The movement of characters occurs in the original string; you must define the string large enough to handle new characters.

Because CINSDEL.C is to be compiled separately, you need a user header file for inclusion in other source files. The CINSDEL.H header file is as follows:

```
#if !defined _CINSDEL
#define _CINSDEL
#include <string.h>
#include <ctype.h>
cinsert( char ccode,char *anystring,int spos );
cdelete( char *anystring,int spos );
#endif
```

To get ready for the next step, create the CINSDEL.C source file and compile it, but do not link edit it (it has no `main()` function anyway and can't be linked to an .EXE module). Then create the CINSDEL.H header file and place it in the same directory with your other source code.

Screen I/O Considerations

For any string editor to be useful or pleasing to a user, you must be able to position the screen cursor in the string, to create the impression that the string is being manipulated directly and to make that manipulation intuitive. To accomplish this, you must take direct control of the screen. Unfortunately, ANSI C makes no provision for screen control. Fortunately, most compilers do provide for it—but all in different ways.

For many terminals, screen control is not easy, but most are capable of it somehow. UNIX systems have a built-in package of functions called `curses`, together with a database of terminal information called `terminfo` that you can use to implement a full-screen edit. IBM PCs and compatibles have a memory-mapped screen I/O arrangement, plus some system BIOS calls that control the cursor.

The string editor shown in Listing 8.3 is based on (and dependent on) cursor and screen functions peculiar to Microsoft C/C++. To convert the code to Borland C, you must replace these functions with their Borland equivalents:

- `_gettextpostion()` reports the current cursor position, placing the results in a structure object. Borland C has the `wherex()` and `wherey()` functions, which report the cursor position directly in integer objects.

- `_settextposition()` sets the cursor position to a new location on-screen (moves the cursor). The Borland C equivalent is `gotoxy()`.

- `eraeol()` is not part of the Microsoft C library; we wrote it. Its function is to erase characters from the current position to the end of the current edit line. In Borland C, this function is built-in. Alternatively, you could convert this function by replacing the `_outtext()` Microsoft C function call with a `cprintf()` call (both MS and Borland C support this call, although it is not standard).

The library header files also differ between the two compiler products. Make the following changes to convert to Borland C:

- Change MEMORY.H to MEM.H. The purpose of the two headers is the same, but the spelling differs.

- Remove the `#include` for GRAPH.H. You do not need it for the Borland C version for this program.

NOTE Other compilers have other differences. You must know your own product well enough to determine for yourself what changes to make.

General-Purpose String Edit: STREDIT.C

The source file STREDIT.C, shown in Listing 8.4, is of moderate length. As you read through it, notice the following features:

- The integer variable inserton (line 8) is placed outside any block so it can have external linkage. It later is declared with the extern modifier in the STREDIT.H file so it can be accessed directly by calling functions instead of passing another argument. Notice that it is initialized to 1, or true, so automatic insert mode is on by default.

- The character insert and delete functions described earlier in this chapter are used by the functions in this source file. The #include "cinsdel.h" must be present.

- The eraeol() function (lines 12–21) is not suitable for a windowed environment. It assumes that a line is to be cleared all the way from the current position to the end of an 80-character line (see the way the overlaying string of blanks is built in line 18). You may want to modify this function so it works in a windowed environment.

- The getch() keyboard input function is borrowed by DOS implementations from the UNIX-based curses library functions. It is used again here, with special emphasis on detecting extended ASCII keystrokes peculiar to IBM and compatible machines. If getch() returns a null character on first access, the extended code flag is set, and getch() is called again to get the scan code. Comments placed with the case statements beginning in line 51 show the keys to which the codes belong.

- The integer variables x and X are used initially to locate the starting position of the string on-screen and the offset in the string to the first cursor location—see the use of the offset argument of edit_text(). After initial placement, x (lowercase) locates the current cursor position, and X (uppercase) tracks the offset of the cursor from the beginning of the string.

  As written here, edit_text() is a void function. You may want to rewrite it to return an integer containing X, thus reporting where the cursor was when the edit finished. This function might be useful when you construct a text-file editing program.

Listing 8.4. STREDIT.C—General-purpose string editing functions (with Microsoft C/C++).

```
1   #include <stdio.h>
2   #include <string.h>
3   #include <memory.h>
4   #include <conio.h>
5   #include <graph.h>
6   #include <ctype.h>
7
8   int inserton = 1;
9
10  #include "cinsdel.h"
11
12  void eraeol(void)
13  {
14    static struct rccoord scf;
15    static char empty[81];
16
17    scf = _gettextposition();
18    sprintf( empty,"%*c",81-scf.col,' ' );
19    _outtext( empty );
20    _settextposition( scf.row,scf.col );
21  }
22
23  void edit_text( char *anystring,
24                  int colno,  /* Display col - x */
25                  int lineno, /* Display row - y */
26                  int maxlen, /* Length allowed */
27                  int offset, /* Offset 0 = col 1 */
28                  int upcase  /* True = force upper */
29              )
30  {
31    int X,x,y;
32    int x2,y2;
33    int oldlen, newlen;
34    char extcode,exitcode,ch;
35
36    extcode=0; exitcode=0;
37    X=0;
38    y=lineno; x=X+colno;
39    _settextposition(y,x);
```

```
40    cprintf("%s",anystring);   /* Position the cursor at the */
41    X=(offset > 0)?offset:0;   /* initial offset */
42    x=X+colno;
43    _settextposition(y,x);
44    do {              /* MAIN EDIT LOOP */
45      extcode=0;
46      ch=getch();
47      if (ch==0) { extcode=1; ch=getch(); }
48      if (!exitcode) {
49        if (extcode) {
50          switch ( ch ) {
51            case 60:    /* F2 = Erase EOL */
52                    eraeol();
53                    anystring[X] = '\0';
54                    break;
55            case 61:    /* F3 = Kill Line */
56                    X=0; x=X+colno;
57                    _settextposition(y,x);
58                    eraeol();
59                    *anystring='\0';
60                    break;
61            case 71:    /* HOME */
62                    X=0;
63                    x=colno;
64                    _settextposition(y,x);
65                    break;
66            case 75:    /* LEFT */
67                    if (X>0) {
68                      X--; x--; _settextposition(y,x);
69                    }
70                    break;
71            case 77:    /* RIGHT */
72                    if (X<strlen(anystring)) {
73                      X++; x++; _settextposition(y,x);
74                    }
75                    break;
76            case 79:    /* END */
77                    X=strlen(anystring);
78                    x=X+colno;
79                    _settextposition(y,x);
80                    break;
81            case 82:    /* INSERT */
```

continues

Listing 8.4. Continued

```
82                      inserton = !inserton;
83                      break;
84            case 83:    /* DELETE */
85                      if (X<strlen(anystring) && X>=0) {
86                        cdelete(anystring,X);
87                        eraeol();
88                        cprintf("%s",anystring+X);
89                        _settextposition(y,x);
90                      }
91                      break;
92            case 115:   /* CTRL LEFT = Prev. Word */
93                      while (X>0 && anystring[X] != 32) {
94                        X--; x--;
95                      }
96                      while (X>0 && anystring[X] == 32) {
97                        X--; x--;
98                      }
99                      _settextposition(y,x);
100                     break;
101           case 116:   /* CTRL RIGHT = Next Word */
102                     while (X<strlen(anystring)
103                            && anystring[X] != 32) {
104                       X++; x++;
105                     }
106                     while (X<strlen(anystring)
107                            && anystring[X] == 32) {
108                       X++; x++;
109                     }
110                     _settextposition(y,x);
111                     break;
112        }
113      }              /* end extcode */
114      else {
115        switch ( ch ) {
116          case 13: return; /* RETURN KEY TERMINATES */
117                     break;
118          case 4:                 /* CTRL-D = Erase EOL */
119                     anystring[X] = '\0';
120                     eraeol();
121                     break;
```

```
122          case 8:              /* CTRL-H or BACKSPACE */
123                 if (X>0) {
124                    X--; x--; _settextposition(y,x);
125                 }
126                 if (X<strlen(anystring) && X>=0) {
127                    cdelete(anystring,X);
128                    eraeol();
129                    cprintf("%s",anystring+X);
130                    _settextposition(y,x);
131                 }
132                 break;
133          default:             /* FINALLY, PROCESS A TEXT KEY */
134 /* Check upcase */ if (strlen(anystring)<maxlen) {
135                    if ( upcase && islower(ch) )
136                       ch = toupper(ch);
137 /* If inserton /*    if (inserton) {
138                       cinsert(ch,anystring,X);
139                    }
140 /* If NOT insert */ else {
141                       if ( X >= strlen(anystring) )
142                          cinsert(ch,anystring,X);
143                       else anystring[X] = ch;
144                    }
145                    cprintf("%s",anystring+X);
146                    X++; x++;
147                    _settextposition(y,x);
148                 }
149                 break;
150          }
151       }
152    }
153    } while (!exitcode);
154 }
```

After looking over Listing 8.4 in some detail, you may realize that it does little with actual strings. When `inserton` is false, lines 140–149 handle the overtype logic; other than that, the `cinsert()` and `cdelete()` functions do all modifications to the string! There is a lesson here. Many sophisticated tasks are basically simple: the complications all arise in providing the support logic and features that make the core algorithm useful.

STREDIT.C should be compiled separately also. Developing the header file for use by other source files is mostly a matter of copying the declarations from the top of the program and adding the extern modifier to inserton. The STREDIT.H header file is as follows:

```
#include <stdio.h>
#include <string.h>
#include <memory.h>
#include <conio.h>
#include <graph.h>
#include <ctype.h>

extern int inserton;
void eraeol(void);
void edit_text( char *anystring,
            int colno,
            int lineno,
            int maxlen,
            int offset,
            int upcase
        );
```

The edit_text() function can be useful in any number of ways. You may recall from Chapter 1, for example, that *environment variables,* or environment *strings,* must be set up to run your compiler. Table 8.2 summarizes them.

Table 8.2. Environment variables for compilation.

String Name	Description of Use
PATH	Specifies the directory in which compiler programs and utilities can be found: PATH=C:\BORLANDC\BIN;C:\C700\BIN
LIB	Specifies the directory in which vendor-supplied object files and libraries can be found: LIB=C:\C700\LIB;C:\C700\MFC\LIB
INCLUDE	Specifies the directory in which vendor-supplied header files can be found: INCLUDE=C:\C700\INCLUDE;C:\C700\MFC\INCLUDE

Your program can use these environment strings to locate data files, programs, or anything else. The ANSI C standard requires that a function, char *getenv(const char *name), be provided and declared in STDLIB.H. You can name your own environment strings and access them with getenv(), as follows:

```
#include <stdlib.h>
char *wheredat;
...
if ( NULL != ( wheredat = getenv( "DATA" ) ) ) {
  ... /* find the data */
}
else {
  puts( "Type the following system command and re-execute:" );
  puts( "SET DATA=[d:][\\path\\]filename[.ext]" );
  exit( 0 );
}
```

Some compilers also provide a nonstandard method of accessing environment strings and, more important, of updating them from in your program: the putenv() function. (This function is something the standard should have included.) We took advantage of that to write SYSENV.C, as shown in Listing 8.5, to show off the string-editing functions just developed.

Listing 8.5.   SYSENV.C—Editing DOS execution environment strings—*PATH, LIB, INCLUDE*—(with Microsoft C/C++).

```
1   #include <stdlib.h>
2   #include <stdio.h>
3   #include <graph.h>
4
5   #include "cinsdel.h"
6   #include "stredit.h"
7
8   #define LOWCASE 0
9   #define UPCASE 1
10
11  void edit_environment( void );
12
13  main()
14  {
15    edit_environment();
16  }
17
18  void edit_environment( void )
19  {
20    int i,j;
21    int numstr;
22    char envstr[73];
```

continues

Listing 8.5. Continued

```
23    char work[73];
24    char cmdstr[3] = "";
25    struct rccoord oldpos;              /* peculiar to MSC */
26    struct videoconfig screen;         /* peculiar to MSC */
27                          /* _MAXTEXTROWS peculiar to MSC  */
28    _settextrows( _MAXTEXTROWS );      /* peculiar to MSC */
29    _getvideoconfig( &screen );        /* peculiar to MSC */
30    while ( *cmdstr != 'x' && *cmdstr !='X' ) {
31      _settextcolor( 0 );
32      _setbkcolor( 7L );
33      _clearscreen( _GCLEARSCREEN );    /* peculiar to MSC */
34      oldpos = _settextposition( 0, 0 ); /* peculiar to MSC */
35      /*-------------------------------------------------*/
36      /* char *environ[] not standard, may not be present*/
37      /*-------------------------------------------------*/
38      i = 0;
39      while ( environ[i] && i<screen.numtextrows-4 )
40        printf( "%.2d  %s\n", i, environ[i++] );
41      numstr = i;                       /* provide a backstop */
42      oldpos = _settextposition( screen.numtextrows-3, 2 );
43      printf( "Enter selection number, "
44              "S to recycle, A to add, or X to quit: " );
45      if ( NULL == gets( cmdstr ) ) break;
46      if ( *cmdstr == 'x' || *cmdstr == 'X' ) break;
47      if ( *cmdstr == 's' || *cmdstr == 'S' ) continue;
48      if ( *cmdstr == 'a' || *cmdstr == 'A' ) {
49        if ( numstr == screen.numtextrows-4 ) continue;
50        numstr++;
51        strcpy( envstr, "" );
52        edit_text( envstr, 2, screen.numtextrows-2,
53                   72, 0, UPCASE );
54        /* getenv() is std, but putenv() is not! */
55        putenv( envstr );
56        continue;
57      }
58      i = atoi( cmdstr ); /* get the item number user entered */
59      if ( i<0 || i>numstr ) continue;
60      else --i;                         /* adjust for subscript use */
```

```
61      strcpy( envstr, environ[i] );
62      strcpy( work, environ[i] );
63      for ( j=0; work[j] && work[j] != '='; j++ );
64      work[j] = '\0';    /* Clip string and delete first */
65      putenv( work );
66      edit_text( envstr, 2, screen.numtextrows-2,
67                 72, 0, UPCASE );
68                      /* getenv() is std, putenv() is not! */
69      putenv( envstr );
70    }
71    _clearscreen( _GCLEARSCREEN );
72  }
```

The `edit_environment()` function shown in Listing 8.5 is another example of the fact that standard C functions are not designed to be functional enough to work in your actual environment. The standard only makes uniform those features that can be assumed to be present on every machine. Once more, screen handling is up to you and your compiler—and the code is not likely to be portable.

`edit_environment()` works by fetching a copy of an environment string, saving it, deleting it from the system environment, enabling the user to edit the copy, and replacing the result in the system. Editing the environment string is done in the call to `edit_text()`, lines 66 and 67. Notice how the arguments are used to control the edit. The string is positioned at column 2, and 2 lines from the bottom of the screen (`screen.numtextrows-2`). The edited string is limited to a maximum length of 72 characters and is forced to uppercase.

Arrays and Strings as Function Parameters

The most important thing to remember about arrays and strings as function arguments arises from the fact that a reference to an array or string identifier without subscripts is interpreted by the compiler as an *address reference*. Therefore, arrays and strings can be passed only by reference, not by value. In the function, references to individual elements must be made by dereferencing the address of the object. There are several ways you can do this.

Strings as Function Parameters

String arguments are sometimes confusing to because of the way you must refer to a string, as compared to the way you define it. That is, a reference to a string identifier is a pointer value, but pointers to strings are written as pointers to char, as in the following example:

```
char text[] = "One more line of text in a string.";
...
int count_chars( char *s )
{
  int i;
  for ( i=0; *s; i++, s++ ) ; /* Think about this loop! */
  return i
}

main()
{
  printf( "Character count: %d\n", count_chars( text ) );
}
```

Notice that count_chars() is called from printf() with just the string identifier text as an argument, yet the function-declaration part describes the parameter as char *s. In the function, references to the pointer and to the dereferenced object are handled just as they are for a string defined anywhere else.

Arrays as Function Parameters

Arrays are declared as parameters more consistently than strings:

```
double numbers[3][3]; /* A two-dimensional array */
...
void halve_elements( double data[3][3] )
{
  int i, j;

  for ( i=0; i<3; i++ ) {
    for ( j=0; j<3; j++ ) data[i][j] /= 2.0;
  }
}
```

As you saw earlier in the chapter, you can refer to array elements with pointers in a function, as follows:

```
int i, j, k;
int array2[3][3];      /* Two-dimensional */
int array3[3][3][3];   /* Three-dimensional */
...                    /* Initialize i,j,k in here */
printf( "%d", *( array2 + i * 3 + j ) );
printf( "%d", *( array3 + i * 9 + j * 3 + k ) );
```

The greatest problem with passing arrays as parameters to functions is that you cannot write a generalized array-handling routine without some trouble and planning. Ordinarily, you must specify the array size in the declaration, which limits your routine to handling arrays of exactly that size.

The simplest way around this dilemma is to use the incomplete type specification in the formal parameter declarations. This is exactly what was done in Listing 8.2 in order to write a function that could solve an array of equations of any size:

```
void gauss( double eqs[], double sol[], int N );
```

The trade-off, of course, is that you must provide another argument that specifies at runtime how many elements are in the array. The gauss() further presumes that the array of equations is both two-dimensional and square as well.

Summary

At the end of every chapter, you are told, "This is important material—master it." That is no less true now than previously. Most robust C programs use at least a string somewhere, which brings with it the concept of pointers. Many programs also use arrays. These objects and ideas are almost impossible to do without. Review this chapter to make sure that you understand the following points:

- What a C pointer is, how to manipulate address values, and how to dereference a pointer to its object.

- How to define one-dimensional and multidimensional arrays and how to access individual elements in them. You should understand also the equivalence of subscript and pointer notation. Perhaps more important than that is knowing when one or the other is appropriate.

- How to define strings and the peculiarities of using pointers to strings. You should know how to access individual characters in strings, using both subscript and pointer notation.

■ What is required to declare an array or string as a parameter for a function and how to reference the pointers and associated objects from in the function.

■ How to declare and to use incomplete types. You can do this with both arrays and strings. You should know how to complete the declaration (by initializing the object). You should know also how to use an incomplete declaration for an array type without ever completing it.

More About Using Pointers

Pointers are a critical resource for C programmers. They are the vehicle through which much of the flexibility—the dynamic character—of powerful programs is achieved.

Using pointers enables you to store and manipulate data at runtime, without necessarily having to know how much data there will be and how it will be arranged. In this chapter you see how pointers help you write flexible, responsive programs and how to do sophisticated coding with a minimum of effort.

Using Pointers with Pointers

It stands to reason that, because a pointer contains the address of an object and a pointer is an object, you can define a pointer that references another pointer. The trick, of course, is to realize when you are dealing with an address value and when you are dealing with an object value.

Using Multiple Indirection

Using more than one pointer to access an object indirectly is called *multiple indirection*. You use the indirection operator for this purpose, as you do for simple pointers. The difference is the number of indirection operators you use in the declaration of the pointer, as the following lines of code illustrate:

```
double a;       /* Declare a double object */
double *b;      /* Declare a pointer to a double */
double **c;     /* Object access is through two pointers */
double ***d;    /* Object access is through three pointers */
```

Simple pointers are common. Two levels of indirection, although not especially abundant, are still quite common. Three levels of indirection are almost never necessary, but the possibility of encountering three levels does exist.

Why would you want to define pointers to pointers? There are two major reasons:

- *To pass pointer values by reference, not value.* When you pass a pointer as an argument to a function, you pass an address value by value. Stop and think about that for a second. Passing a pointer to a function really means that you pass another object to the function by reference. Thus, the referenced object can be modified by the function, but the original pointer to the object cannot. Only a copy of the pointer is available to the function. Therefore, if you want to pass a pointer to a function and to modify the contents of the original pointer, you must use multiple indirection—you must pass another pointer to the one you want to modify.

- *To locate a list of pointers.* You should remember that an array identifier used without subscripts is interpreted as an address value. But what if the array (list) is an array of pointers? Again, an address pointing to a list of addresses is multiple indirection—access to a final object value is through two levels of address values. This powerful technique is covered in detail later in this chapter.

Referencing and Dereferencing Multiple Pointers

Recall what you already know about dereferencing pointers. If p is a pointer, *p is a reference to the object to which it points. The concept works the same way with multiple indirection; there are just more indirection operators. Figure 9.1 shows how multiple indirection governs references to addresses and underlying object values.

Using multiple indirection imposes some responsibilities on you, the programmer. A dereferenced pointer can now be another pointer, or it can be a reference to an object. You must keep track of which one it is. Rewriting the code fragment shown in Figure 9.1 illustrates this point, as follows:

```
int **a;    /* Pointer to a pointer to an object */
int *b;     /* Pointer to an object */
int c;      /* An integer object *;
...
a = &b;     /* Initialize first pointer */
*a = &c;    /* Initialize second pointer */
**a = 64;   /* Initialize object */
```

The most interesting feature of the preceding code fragment is the way a and b are initialized. a must be initialized with the address of b. Then b is initialized with the address of c, but it is done by dereferencing a. This is not necessary in the real world but is instructive here. With this method, the precise order of statements you see here is required—a cannot be dereferenced to access b until a has been initialized.

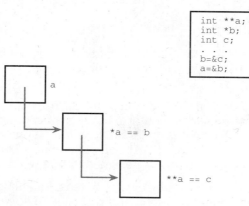

```
int **a;
int *b;
int c;
. . .
b=&c;
a=&b;
```

a

*a == b

**a == c

Figure 9.1.

Dereferencing pointers to pointers.

Using Pointers to Scan and Parse Text

So far, you have seen only a few of the most primitive statements possible illustrating multiple indirection. A more realistic situation requiring multiple indirection arises in scanning and parsing text.

Roll up your sleeves; it's time to go to work! The programs and functions that follow can be confusing simply because they must be lengthy to get the job done. Examine the code in detail and at length. The methods shown here for manipulating pointers are extremely important for building worthwhile programs. The routines are also very useful—but only if you understand them thoroughly.

Creating a Lexical Scanner

Because you are reading a book on C programming, it is assumed that you are a fairly experienced computer user. You almost certainly have used commercial software with a fairly complicated command set. Have you ever wondered how the software catches your keystroke and syntax errors, sometimes seeming very intelligent as it works? For that matter, have you wondered just how the C compiler breaks down all that source code in an intelligible fashion?

Earlier in the book, you saw that one of the phases of compilation involves a *lexical scanner,* which examines the source code. Commercial software also uses scanners to process input commands (and perhaps data, as well). The scanner is the first step in handling text information in this seemingly intelligent fashion.

What a Scanner Does

The purpose of a scanner is to process an input text stream and separate tokens. Tokens may be verbs, object identifiers, or whatever the application requires.

Scanners are sometimes referred to as lexical scanners because the tokens retrieved from the input stream must conform to the syntax (language, command structure, and so forth). That is, unless tokens mean something to the application (a *lexicon* is basically a word list), an error exists. The scanner function presented later in this chapter is designed to do the following:

- Recognize several fundamental object-type tokens, including alphanumeric symbols, string literals, integer, and real (floating-point) constants.

- Recognize a suitable class of punctuation characters, including parentheses, colons and semicolons, commas, and periods. Recognition of a period depends on the context in which it appears—a period embedded in a real literal is not counted as punctuation.

- Recognize a group of operators that can be used to form regular expressions. The operators recognized in this routine are a subset of C operators, plus one or two that don't exist in C. In particular, the caret (^) character is used as the *power operator*. That is, the expression x ^ y is interpreted as x raised to the y power.

Why *strtok()* Does Not Work Here

The function char *strtok(char *s1, const char *s2) is a standard library function (STRING.H) that performs scanning services. The strtok() function searches through the s1 string for tokens, and a pointer to the found token is returned. This pointer indicates a location in the original string. No extra copy of the text is made.

The s2 string determines how strtok() searches for tokens. String s2 contains a set of characters that are considered *delimiters,* or separator characters that occur between tokens. A space, for example, is a common-sense choice of delimiter for scanning words out of an English sentence.

Because one call to strtok() returns a pointer to a single token, repeated calls must be made to scan a whole line. Therefore, strtok() is called in two different ways, as follows:

- The first call passes a valid pointer in s1. This call locates the string to be scanned.

- The second and following calls to strtok() pass a null pointer, not a pointer to s1. This indicates to the function's logic that scanning is to continue for the same string. The delimiter characters contained in s2 can be changed from one call to the next.

Because the same string is to be scanned over several calls, strtok() saves the location of the next character after the last found token between calls. There is an added wrinkle: strtok() also modifies the original string by placing a null character ('\0') just after the last found token. It does this so the caller does not have to search by another method to find the end of the token string just located. Suppose, for example, that you want to locate the second word in the following string:

```
char text[] = "Hello reader, this is a string!";
```

To do so, you use the following sequence of calls to strtok():

```
char *t;
...
t = strtok( text, " " ); /* Blank delimiter */
t = strtok( NULL, "," ); /* Comma delimiter */
printf( "%s\n", t );     /* Display the token */
```

This sequence of code displays the word reader on-screen. This example seems to work well. You can scan a large variety of input text with strtok(). Why not use it for scanning purposes here? You shouldn't use it for the following reasons:

- The original input string is modified. Therefore, either the original text is corrupted, or a copy of the text must be made before scanning. Corrupting or copying the original text is not always desirable.

- To some degree, the programmer must know which delimiter characters to expect in the input while writing the program. This may be expecting too much; not all users are so cooperative when entering text.

- Detecting punctuation characters without treating them as delimiter characters—which `strtok()` overlays with `'\0'`—is difficult (but not impossible). You want to be able to return punctuation characters as separate and legal tokens.

- You want to be able to recognize a large number of punctuation and operator characters. `strtok()` imposes an extra load on the programmer because successive calls frequently must specify different sets of delimiters.

You should not get the idea that `strtok()` is not useful. It is extremely useful and can be used effectively in a variety of situations. You should pick and choose the situations in which you want to use it, however.

How the Scanner Uses Pointers

The scanner function presented in this section avoids the problems raised by `strtok()`. The `scanner()` function (source file SCANNER.C, shown in Listing 9.1) scans a text string, copying the found tokens into an output string so the original text is not modified. `scanner()` also identifies a variety of punctuators, operators, and named token types. The only delimiter characters are the space and end-of-line characters.

All arguments passed to `scanner()` are assumed to reside outside the function block. They do not have to have global scope; they only have to be available to the calling routine. The manner in which the arguments are used gives the function its characteristics:

- `char **text;`

  The caller must set up a pointer to the input text. The pointer should be left undisturbed across all calls for scanning that line (string) of text. Multiple indirection is used so the pointer can be updated by the function; thus, the pointer points in succeeding calls to the correct location in the input string. Ordinarily, the pointer used should be a temporary variable rather than the string identifier.

- `char *token;`

  The second parameter is a pointer to a string that contains the output token. This avoids the necessity of modifying the input string to "mark" the end of the token. The caller need not initialize the token string. The string is created and null-terminated by `scanner()` at each call (the same token string may be reused at each call, if you want).

- `int *ttype;`

  The caller must also set up an integer-type object that is set to the token *type* by `scanner()`. The different token types are shown in the `#define` macros in lines 4–23 of Listing 9.1. All but three of the token-type macro names are self-explanatory: LEXERR, EOL, and UNDEF. The value of LEXERR is placed in ttype if the routine detects a nonblank string it cannot classify as any of the other token types. EOL is the one token-type value reported for which the output token string token does not contain a valid string; this is the end-of-line indicator. The UNDEF macro value is never reported—it is present only so you may initialize ttype before the first call. You can see how UNDEF is used in lines 204 and 205 of Listing 9.1.

Listing 9.1. SCANNER.C—A lexical scanner routine (using all compilers).

```
1   #include <stdlib.h>
2   #include <stdio.h>
3
4   #define LEXERR 0
5   #define SYMBOL 1
6   #define INTLIT 2
7   #define REALLIT 3
8   #define STRLIT 4
9   #define LPAREN 5
10  #define RPAREN 6
11  #define SEMIC 7
12  #define COLON 8
13  #define COMMA 9
14  #define PERIOD 10
15  #define APOST 11
16  #define PLUSOP 12
17  #define MINUSOP 13
18  #define MUXOP 14
19  #define DIVOP 15
20  #define POWOP 16
21  #define ASSIGNOP 17
22  #define EOL 18
23  #define UNDEF 255
24
25  void scanner();
26  char *nmtoken();
27
28  char *nmtoken(ttype)
29    int ttype;
30  {
31    static char *tokennm[] = {
32                          "LEXERR",
```

continues

Listing 9.1. Continued

```
33                                  "SYMBOL",
34                                  "INTLIT",
35                                  "REALLIT",
36                                  "STRLIT",
37                                  "LPAREN",
38                                  "RPAREN",
39                                  "SEMIC",
40                                  "COLON",
41                                  "COMMA",
42                                  "PERIOD",
43                                  "APOST",
44                                  "PLUSOP",
45                                  "MINUSOP",
46                                  "MUXOP",
47                                  "DIVOP",
48                                  "POWOP",
49                                  "ASSIGNOP",
50                                  "EOL",
51                                  "UNDEF"
52                              };
53      return( tokennm[ttype] );
54   }
55
56   void scanner(text,token,ttype)
57      char **text;
58      char *token;
59      int *ttype;
60   {
61      for ( ; **text == ' ' ¦¦ **text == '\t'
62           ¦¦ **text == '\n' ; (*text)++ ) ;
63
64      if ( **text == '\0' ) {                 /* END OF LINE */
65        *ttype = EOL;
66        return;
67      }
68
69      if ( (**text >= 'A' && **text <= 'Z')    /* SYMBOLS */
70        ¦¦ (**text >= 'a' && **text <= 'z') ) {
71          *ttype = SYMBOL;
72          while ( (**text >= 'A' && **text <= 'Z')
73                ¦¦ (**text >= 'a' && **text <= 'z')
```

```
 74                ¦¦ (**text >= '0' && **text <= '9') ) {
 75           *token++ = *(*text)++;
 76         }
 77         *token = '\0';
 78         return;
 79     }
 80
 81     if ( **text == '"' ) {          /* STRING LITERALS */
 82         *ttype = STRLIT;
 83         (*text)++;                  /* Skip first quote */
 84         while ( **text != '"' && **text ) {
 85           *token++ = *(*text)++;
 86         }
 87         (*text)++;                  /* Skip last quote */
 88         *token = '\0';
 89         return;
 90     }
 91
 92     if ( **text >= '0' && **text <= '9' ) { /* NUMERICS */
 93       *ttype =  INTLIT;
 94       while ( **text >= '0' && **text <= '9' ) {
 95         *token++ = *(*text)++;
 96         if ( **text == '.' ) {
 97           *ttype = REALLIT;
 98           *token++ = *(*text)++;
 99         }
100         if ( *ttype == REALLIT &&
101            ( **text == 'e' ¦¦ **text == 'E' ) ) {
102           *token++ = *(*text)++;
103         }
104         if ( *ttype == REALLIT &&
105            ( **text == '+' ¦¦ **text == '-' ) ) {
106           *token++ = *(*text)++;
107         }
108       }
109         *token = '\0';
110         return;
111     }
112
113     if ( **text == '(' ) {                    /* PUNCTUATION */
114         *ttype = LPAREN;
115         *token++ = *(*text)++;
```

continues

Listing 9.1. Continued

```
116        *token = '\0';
117        return;
118     }
119     if ( **text == ')' ) {
120        *ttype = RPAREN;
121        *token++ = *(*text)++;
122        *token = '\0';
123        return;
124     }
125     if ( **text == ';' ) {
126        *ttype = SEMIC;
127        *token++ = *(*text)++;
128        *token = '\0';
129        return;
130     }
131     if ( **text == ':' ) {
132        *ttype = COLON;
133        *token++ = *(*text)++;
134        *token = '\0';
135        return;
136     }
137     if ( **text == ',' ) {
138        *ttype = COMMA;
139        *token++ = *(*text)++;
140        *token = '\0';
141        return;
142     }
143     if ( **text == '.' ) {
144        *ttype = PERIOD;
145        *token++ = *(*text)++;
146        *token = '\0';
147        return;
148     }
149     if ( **text == '\'' ) {
150        *ttype = APOST;
151        *token++ = *(*text)++;
152        *token = '\0';
153        return;
154     }
155
156     if ( **text == '+' ) {    /* OPERATORS */
```

```
157        *ttype = PLUSOP;
158        *token++ = *(*text)++;
159        *token = '\0';
160        return;
161     }
162     if ( **text == '-' ) {
163        *ttype = MINUSOP;
164        *token++ = *(*text)++;
165        *token = '\0';
166        return;
167     }
168     if ( **text == '*' ) {
169        *ttype = MUXOP;
170        *token++ = *(*text)++;
171        *token = '\0';
172        return;
173     }
174     if ( **text == '/' ) {
175        *ttype = DIVOP;
176        *token++ = *(*text)++;
177        *token = '\0';
178        return;
179     }
180     if ( **text == '^' ) {
181        *ttype = POWOP;
182        *token++ = *(*text)++;
183        *token = '\0';
184        return;
185     }
186     if ( **text == '=' ) {
187        *ttype = ASSIGNOP;
188        *token++ = *(*text)++;
189        *token = '\0';
190        return;
191     }
192
193     *ttype=LEXERR;            /* IF NOTHING MATCHED, DO THIS */
194     return;
195  }
196
197  /* --------- SAMPLE DRIVER FOR SCANNER --------------
198  void parser(string)
```

continues

Listing 9.1. Continued

```
199    char *string;
200   {
201    char *sp,*tp;
202    int ttype;
203    char token[41];
204
205    sp = string;
206    ttype = UNDEF;
207    while ( ttype != EOL && ttype != LEXERR ) {
208      tp = token;
209      scanner(&sp,tp,&ttype);
210      if ( ttype != EOL )
211        printf( "Token type = %s, token = %s\n",
212                nmtoken(ttype), token );
213    }
214   }
215   -------------------------------------------------- */
```

Listing 9.1 shows SCANNER.C in a form suitable for separate compilation. If you want to compile it to an .OBJ file for inclusion in other programs, you can write the header file, SCANNER.H, as follows:

```
#define LEXERR 0
#define SYMBOL 1
#define INTLIT 2
#define REALLIT 3
#define STRLIT 4
#define LPAREN 5
#define RPAREN 6
#define SEMIC 7
#define COLON 8
#define COMMA 9
#define PERIOD 10
#define APOST 11
#define PLUSOP 12
#define MINUSOP 13
#define MUXOP 14
#define DIVOP 15
#define POWOP 16
```

```
#define ASSIGNOP 17
#define EOL 18
#define UNDEF 255
extern void scanner();
extern char *nmtoken();
```

All the functions in Listing 9.1 are written with old-style declarations. We thought about this decision at some length. Should we convert the declarations to the new function-prototype syntax? After considering the question, plus the fact that this routine has been working just this way for a long time, plus the fact that the old-style declarations are perfectly legal, we decided to leave it alone. It serves as a reminder that C is a flexible language, even with ANSI requirements laid on it.

Lines 61 and 62 perform the simple function of moving the "current position" to the right down the string until something other than whitespace is encountered—that is, until the first character of the next token is found. scanner() considers blanks, tabs, and newline characters to all be whitespace.

Notice the double dereference of text to access the character values in the string. This is simple enough, but updating the pointer is another matter when you use multiple indirection. Because the pointer actually resides in the caller's data area (this may be an auto variable because the caller, by definition, has not yet returned and released that memory), the idea is to increment the pointer contents. You do this with the following expression:

```
(*text)++;
```

Carefully consider the grouping of operators in this expression: postfix ++ has higher precedence than indirection *. Thus, if the parentheses were not used, the equivalent grouping would be *(text++). Remember that because text is the pointer passed to the function, *text is the original pointer, and **text refers to a character.

The original pointer, *text, needs incrementing—hence, the parentheses in (*text)++ cause the original pointer to be updated. The other expression *(text)++ would cause the first-level pointer (the one passed to the function) to be incremented, making it point not to the next pointer, but in the middle of the next pointer. In that case, *text would refer to garbage rather than a legitimate pointer.

Although scanner() seems complex, it only appears that way because of its length. Every pointer update is accomplished in the way just described.

The process of building the output tokens, once you understand it, is equally simple. Output tokens are built-in blocks of if statements. First, scanner() identifies what token type has appeared by comparing the character to a range of permissible characters for that type. It then continues scanning to the right, adding characters to the token as long as they belong to that subset of permissible characters.

You can further simplify token building by using a standard library function, `strchr()`. Its prototype is

```
char *strchr( char *s, char c );
```

This function looks for the second argument character in the string s. If it finds the character, a pointer to the located character is returned; otherwise, a null pointer is returned.

The SYMBOL token is built and detected in lines 69–79. You can rewrite it as follows:

```
char sym_chars[] = "ABCDEFGHIJKLMNOPQRSTUVWXYZ"
                   "abcdefghijklmnopqrstuvwxyz"
                   "0123456789";              /* compiler concats these */
 .
if ( strchr( sym_chars, **text ) ) {      /* SYMBOLS */
    *ttype = SYMBOL;
    while ( strchr( sym_chars, **text ) ) {
      *token++ = *(*text)++;
    }
    *token = '\0';
    return;
}
```

The preceding code fragment takes about the same number of lines of code to accomplish nearly the same thing because the `sym_chars` string takes up some space, but does it more legibly. Performance is still good. The only difference is that `scanner()`, as originally coded, requires that a SYMBOL token begin with an alphabetic character, whereas this fragment accepts any alphanumeric character.

Making such an improvement to the INTLIT and REALLIT tokens would be a little more difficult because numerics are assumed to be integers until a period is found, at which time the token type is converted to floating-point. This search and possible type conversion is done in Listing 9.1, lines 92–111. However, making the improvement is possible and practical. Little is gained by converting the algorithm for the remaining token types, which mostly look for single characters.

You can use the `nmtoken()` function, lines 28–54, while experimenting with the scanner code. `nmtoken()` accepts an integer argument, the token type, and returns a pointer to a string containing the name of the token type. You already have seen the type of static array declared in this function, but take a moment and study it again. How do you interpret the following declaration?

```
static char *tokennm[] = ...
```

Remember that `[]` has higher precedence than `*`. Therefore, `tokennm` is an array—an array of `char *`. Thus, this is an array of pointers to string. To reference one of the pointers for `return`, you use the `ttype` argument to subscript the array, as follows:

```
return( tokennm[ttype] );
```

whereby `tokennm[ttype]` is a pointer—not a dereferenced pointer.

Lines 197–215 in Listing 9.1 contain a sample scanner driver function, `parser()`, to show how the calls are engineered. This block of code is all in comments because it is not meant to be actually compiled; it is only a suggestion. Suppose, for example, that you call `parser()` as in the following:

```
parser( "Scan this string!" );
```

The following output is displayed on-screen:

```
Token type = SYMBOL, token = Scan
Token type = SYMBOL, token = this
Token type = SYMBOL, token = string
Token type = LEXERR, token = string
```

In addition to three `SYMBOL` type tokens, a `LEXERR` is reported because the exclamation point is not a supported punctuator in `scanner()`. Notice that when a lexical error occurs, the token string is not modified; it still contains the string loaded in the last successful call.

Notice particularly how `scanner()` is called in line 209:

```
scanner(&sp,tp,&ttype);
```

The `sp` and `tp` objects are temporary pointers to the input string and the output token string, respectively. `ttype` is an integer variable that is loaded with the token type according to the `#define` macros at the top of Listing 9.1.

The `sp` pointer is not passed to the function. Rather, its *address* is taken and passed. Because `sp` already is a pointer (to string), `scanner()` can modify the original pointer object—the `auto` variable `sp`.

Because the token pointer `tp` needs no multiple indirection, its address is not taken. In fact, because there is no multiple indirection, the original pointer object is not modified. You could use the `token` string identifier as the argument. Then you could eliminate the `tp` object declaration, as well as line 208 (which initializes it), in every pass through the loop. The tuning effect is small here, but serious applications may need every edge they can get.

Finally, the address of `ttype` is taken when passing it to `scanner()`. Thus, `scanner()` can load the original object with the token-type value. This is a good way to "cheat" the function-return mechanism and "return" several values, when it is otherwise restricted to returning just one value.

Creating a Parsing Routine

Many applications need no more than scanning services. Simply breaking out the parts of the input is enough, for example, when the input consists only of data items that will be used to update fields in a file record. Other applications may need more than this, however. When you prompt a user for a command, for instance, the input may have a more or less complicated syntax. Then the input needs interpretation before any action can be taken. The act of interpreting scanned text is called *parsing*.

There is more than one way to create a parser. Some commercial programs can take summaries and generate a parsing routine to match the specifications. Alternatively, you can "hard code" a parser, using one of several different techniques.

In the following sections, you learn how to develop a hard-coded *recursive descent* parsing function. This special-purpose parser can evaluate regular expressions and return a result. It also provides limited support for variable names and value assignment. You can adapt it to any number of uses in your own programs.

What "Recursive Descent" Means

Before you learn about the development of the parser code, you have to know the meaning of *recursive descent*. This term is used in the same sense as in the discussion of recursive function calls, as shown in Figure 9.2.

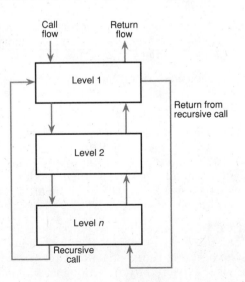

Figure 9.2.

Control flow during recursive function calls.

As you can see from Figure 9.2, recursive descent algorithms involve a hierarchy of functions. As functions call the next lower level (more detailed processing), program flow "descends" the hierarchy.

The recursive part enters the picture when the object being processed is complex and can contain other—possibly also complex—objects of the same type. In that case, it is possible for one of the lower-level functions to again call the first-level routine.

This process need not be as confusing as it may sound. Think of the algebraic expressions that you soon will parse. Such expressions may contain sub-expressions in parentheses. When an opening parenthesis is encountered, you need only call the parsing routine from the top. When recursion has occurred, a return from the top-level routine returns control to the lower-level routine that reinvoked it. Clearly, you must forward-declare all the functions in the hierarchy (by prototyping them) so the compiler can correctly compile the recursive references.

Building the Parser

The parsing routine built here, FORMULA.C, evaluates regular algebraic expressions and returns the result. For the sake of simplicity, only double values are allowed.

To save space, the operators allowed are simplified also. These operators, a subset of the C operators, determine precedence in a common-sense way. The expressions consist of the following parts, along with their associated operators, in descending order of precedence:

■ Formula:

```
( ( ( ... expression ... ) ) )
object name
object name = expression
object name = object name
```

■ Expression:

```
simpleexpr [+ simpleexpr] [- simpleexpr]
```

■ Simple expression:

```
term [* term] [/ term]
```

■ Term:

```
signedfactor ^ signedfactor [^ signedfactor ...]
```

■ Signed factor:

[unary -] factor

■ Factor:

integer literal
real literal
object name

Parentheses have the highest priority and trigger a recursive call to evaluate a new subexpression. Thus, they can force grouping and associativity.

The assignment operator, next in precedence, can also cause recursive processing; everything to the right of the = sign is considered a subexpression. The logic is arranged so object-name (symbol-table) processing is reentrant; as a result, C-style expressions, such as the following, can be used successfully:

a = b = c = *constant*

Addition, subtraction, multiplication, and division follow the normal rules of algebra, with multiplication and division having the higher priority.

The ^ character is used as the *power operator,* so there is no need for a function call to raise a number or variable to a power. Associativity for this operator is right-to-left, meaning that an expression such as

a ^ b ^ c

first raises b to the c power and then raises a to a power equal to the preceding result. This condition arises from the sequence of events during recursive descent.

This parsing routine does not support punctuation, except for space characters. You can embed space characters anywhere, as often as you like. Space characters are not required anywhere, except where omitting them would prevent recognizing a token. Note that the semicolon (;)—the C-style statement terminating character—is not supported.

Evaluating Formulas: FORMULA.C

In FORMULA.C, shown in Listing 9.2, the global variable char *sp (line 14) must point to the text to be parsed. Lines 19–23 contain the prototypes for the support routines that provide user-variable and symbol-table support. Lines 24–29 contain the prototype declarations for the hierarchy of functions that do the parsing.

Listing 9.2. FORMULA.C—Parsing algebraic expressions with recursive descent logic (using Borland C++).

```
1   #include <stdlib.h>
2   #include <stdio.h>
3   #include <math.h>
4   #include <string.h>
5
6   #include "scanner.h"
7
8   typedef strict var_strict
9     {
10      char label[9];
11      double value;
12    } var_type;
13
14  char *sp,*tp;
15  char token[33];
16  int  ttype;
17  var_type (*vars)[16];
18
19  void   setup_vars( void );
20  void   free_vars( void );
21  void   list_vars( void );
22  var_type *find_var( char *vname);
23  int    add_var( char *vname, double vvalue );
24  double formula( void );
25  double expression( void );
26  double simpleexpr( void );
27  double term( void );
28  double signedfactor( void );
29  double factor( void );
30
31  main()
32  {
33    char request[40];
34
35    setup_vars();
36    strcpy( request, " NUM = 8.5" );
37    sp = request;
38    formula();
39    strcpy( request, " 1 + 3 * ( NUM / 0.2 ) ^ 2" );
```

continues

Listing 9.2. Continued

```
40   sp = request;
41   printf( "The result is %.6f\n", formula() );
42   list_vars();
43   free_vars();
44 }
45
46 double formula( void )
47 {
48   if ( 0 != strpbrk( token,".+" ) ) ++sp;
49   scanner( &sp,token,&ttype );
50   return( expression() );
51 }
52
53 double expression( void )
54 {
55   double result = 0;
56
57   result = simpleexpr();
58   while ( ttype == PLUSOP || ttype == MINUSOP ) {
59     switch ( ttype ) {
60       case PLUSOP:  scanner( &sp,token,&ttype );
61                     result += simpleexpr(); break;
62       case MINUSOP: scanner( &sp,token,&ttype );
63                     result -= simpleexpr(); break;
64     }
65   }
66   return( result );
67 }
68
69 double simpleexpr( void )
70 {
71   double result = 0;
72
73   result = term();
74   while ( ttype == MUXOP || ttype == DIVOP ) {
75     switch ( ttype ) {
76       case MUXOP: scanner( &sp,token,&ttype );
77                   result *= term(); break;
78       case DIVOP: scanner( &sp,token,&ttype );
79                   result /= term(); break;
```

```
80        }
81      }
82    return( result );
83  }
84
85  double term( void )
86  {
87    double result = 0;
88
89    result = signedfactor();
90    while ( ttype == POWOP ) {
91      scanner( &sp,token,&ttype );
92      result = exp( log( result ) * signedfactor() );
93    }
94    return( result );
95  }
96
97  double signedfactor( void )
98  {
99    if ( *token == '-' ) return( 0-factor() );
100     else return( factor() );
101  }
102
103  double factor( void )
104  {
105    static double result = 0;
106    static var_type *temp;
107    char *holdvar;
108
109    switch ( ttype ) {
110      case REALLIT: result = atof( token ); break;
111      case INTLIT:  result = ( double )atol( token ); break;
112      case LPAREN:  scanner( &sp,token,&ttype );
113                    result = expression();
114                    break;
115  /* SYMBOL processing logic:
116      place current token in holdvar;
117      get the next token;
118      if ( variable DOES EXIST ) {
119        if ( new token is an = ) {     --- reassign value ---
120          get the next token;
121          evaluate the right side of the equation;
```

continues

Listing 9.2. Continued

```
122          place result in variable bucket;
123          break out;
124        } ELSE {                          --- fetch value ---
125          return the variable's value;
126        }
127      } ELSE {                  --- variable DOES NOT EXIST ---
128        if ( current token is an = ) { --- value provided ---
129          get the next token;
130          evaluate the right side of the equation;
131          add variable to symbol table and set value;
132          if ( add failed ) exit( 8 );
133          break out in every case;
134        } ELSE {                          --- value NOT provided ---
135          set the value to 0;
136          add variable to symbol table and set value;
137          if ( add failed ) exit( 8 );
138          return 0;
139        }
140      }
141  */
142      case SYMBOL:
143                  holdvar = malloc( 9 );
144                  strcpy( holdvar, token );
145                  scanner( &sp,token,&ttype );
146                  temp = find_var( holdvar );
147                  if ( temp ) {
148                    if ( ttype == ASSIGNOP ) {
149                      scanner( &sp,token,&ttype );
150                      result = expression();
151                      temp->value = result;
152                      break;
153                    } else {
154                      result = temp->value;
155                      free( holdvar );
156                      return( result );
157                    }
158                  } else {
159                    if ( ttype == ASSIGNOP ) {
160                      scanner( &sp,token,&ttype );
161                      result = expression();
162                      if ( -1 == add_var( holdvar, result ) )
```

```
163                        exit( 8 );
164                        break;
165                    } else {
166                        result = 0.0;
167                        if ( -1 == add_var( holdvar, 0.0 ) )
168                            exit( 8 );
169                        free( holdvar );
170                        return( result );
171                    }
172                }
173        }
174        if ( holdvar ) free( holdvar );
175        scanner( &sp,token,&ttype );
176        return( result );
177    }
178
179    void setup_vars( void )
180    {
181        int i;
182
183        vars = calloc( 16, sizeof( var_type ) );
184        for ( i=0; i<16; i++ ) {
185            strcpy( vars[i]->label, "" );
186            vars[i]->value = 0.0;
187        }
188    }
189
190    void free_vars( void )
191    {
192        free( vars );
193    }
194
195    void list_vars( void )
196    {
197        int i;
198
199        for ( i=0; i<16; i++ )
200            printf( "%s = %f\n", vars[i]->label, vars[i]->value );
201    }
202
203    var_type *find_var( char *vname )
204    {
```

continues

Listing 9.2. Continued

```
205   static int i;
206
207   for ( i=0; i<16; i++ ) {
208     if ( 0 == strcmp( vname, vars[i]->label ) )
209       return( vars[i] );
210   }
211   return( NULL );
212 }
213
214 int add_var( char *vname, double vvalue )
215 {
216   int i;
217
218   if ( NULL != find_var( vname ) ) return( -1 );
219   for ( i=0; i<16; i++ ) {
220     if ( vars[i]->label[0] == '\0' ) break;
221   }
222   if ( i>15 ) return( -1 );
223   strcpy( vars[i]->label, vname );
224   vars[i]->value = vvalue;
225   return( 0 );
226 }
```

The basic plan of attack in parsing algebraic expressions is to loop at each level, calling the next-lower level, as long as the operators supporting the next-lower level continue to be encountered. Each loop presumes that the scanner has been invoked beforehand and that the input token is ready in token.

Notice that the calls proceed from the lowest precedence to the highest as program flow moves down the hierarchy. This continues until factor() is entered; factor() deals with the "atomic" elements of the text. Here parentheses and assignment operators also are detected, and a recursive call is made to the top of the hierarchy—expression().

In some instances, special cases are handled. Line 48, in the formula() function, advances the string pointer sp by 1 if the text to be parsed begins with a period or plus sign. Notice also the local variables in lines 105–107 in the factor() function. The first two of these have the static specifier, for performance reasons (they do not have to be allocated again at every entry to the routine).

The char *holdvar variable, however, is not a static object. It is allowed to retain auto duration precisely because you want it to be created afresh for every entry. This way, there can be several copies of it during recursive entries to the function. Consider what happens when parsing the following expression, for example:

```
a = b = c = 6.28
```

At each entry to factor(), holdvar is created again (on the stack). In parsing this expression, one copy of holdvar saves the variable name "a". Then the assignment operator causes recursion, and the function is entered again, only to encounter a reference to "b", which also must be held in storage, and so on. If holdvar cannot be allocated dynamically (and uniquely) for every entry to factor(), only the rightmost variable name can be kept track of in parsing such expressions.

Lines 115–141 are of special interest. They contain (as comments) pseudocode that describes the flow of control during symbol processing.

Providing support for user variables and the symbol table requires that you look ahead. The symbol table in FORMULA.C holds as many as 16 variable names and associated values. Each variable in the symbol table is stored in a derived object called a *structure,* which can contain many atomic-type objects. In addition, the structure definition is given its own name, a typedef, so it can be referred to easily. The structure type is defined as follows:

```
 8   typedef strict var_strict
 9     {
10        char label[9];
11        double value;
12     } var_type;
...
17   var_type (*vars)[16];
```

The details of this syntax are covered in detail in Chapter 11. For now, pay attention especially to line 17. Presuming that you can legally write a type name of var_type, which is set up in lines 8–12, this line means that the symbol table consists of an array of 16 pointers to the structure object.

When dealing with structures, you normally refer to the individual elements in them by using the structure operator, which happens to be a period: a reference to house.room means that there is a structure called house, and that the reference is to the element room in it. There is, as you can see, some similarity to using the subscript operator [] to access an element of an array.

In FORMULA.C, however, you go further. This program deals not merely with structures, but with pointers to structures. Now you must use the *structure pointer* operator (->), which consists of a minus sign followed by a greater-than sign. There must be no space between these two characters, although there can be space around them. Now house->room indicates that house is a pointer to a structure, and you are still accessing a particular room.

These considerations finally put you in a position to understand the references to symbol-table entries in FORMULA.C. You must take it only one step further and introduce the notion that each structure is an element of an array. Lines 221 and 222, for example, initialize a user variable:

```
strcpy( vars[i]->label, vname ); /* init var name */
vars[i]->value = vvalue;         /* init var value */
```

Mixing Arrays and Pointers

In the preceding sections, you encountered the interesting notion of an array of pointers. An array of pointers and a single pointer to an array are both possible in C. Each has its respective uses, as illustrated in the following sections.

Defining Arrays of Pointers

Arrays of pointers are easy to define in C. Simply use both the indirection operator * and the subscript operator [] in the declaration. Figure 9.3 shows the syntax of the declaration and the memory configuration that this arrangement presumes.

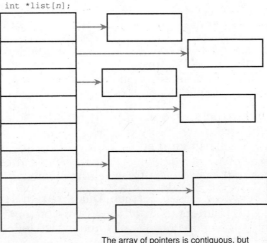

```
int *list[n];
```

The array of pointers is contiguous, but the objects don't have to be.

Figure 9.3.

Array of pointers in memory.

An array of pointers is useful for keeping track of a number of objects, not all of which may be in contiguous storage. You might allocate storage dynamically for each object as it is created or read in, for example.

The array, however, is in contiguous storage (refer to Figure 9.3). The array of pointers is easy to find and makes finding the objects pointed to easy, as you can see in the following code fragment:

```c
#include <stdlib.h>
#include <stdio.h>

main()
{
  int *list[16];
  int i;

  srand( 37 );    /* Seed the random number generator */
  for ( i=0; i<16; i++ ) {
    list[i] = malloc( sizeof(int) );  /* get storage */
    *list[i] = rand();         /* put something in it */
  }
  for ( i=0; i<16; i++ ) {
    printf( "%d\n", *list[i] );
  }
  for ( i=0; i<16; i++ ) {
    free( list[i] );           /* release the storage */
  }
}
```

In the preceding code fragment, list is the array identifier; it is interpreted as an address value, as before. list[i] is also a pointer, whereas *list[i] is an integer.

Defining a Pointer to an Array

You sometimes encounter the companion case to the array of pointers: the pointer to an array. The syntax of this construction, which is determined by operator precedence, requires grouping parentheses to be interpreted correctly. Figure 9.4 shows this arrangement.

The manner of manipulating the pointer and the array pointed to is similar to dealing with an array of pointers but has some peculiarities. The following fragment shows how to define a pointer to an array and manipulate it:

```
#include <stdlib.h>
#include <stdio.h>

main()
{
  int (*list)[16];
  int i;

  srand( 37 );    /* Seed the random number generator */
  list = malloc( sizeof(int) * 16 );   /* get storage */
  for ( i=0; i<16; i++ ) {
    (*list)[i] = rand();        /* put something in it */
  }
  for ( i=0; i<16; i++ ) {
    printf( "%d\n", (*list)[i] );
  }
  free( list );                 /* release the storage */
}
```

You should notice in this code fragment that the malloc() function is used only once, outside the loop. The size of the entire array is calculated, and a corresponding amount of storage is allocated. Further, the unqualified identifier list is a pointer to int, strictly speaking, and so is (*list). As you can see, the grouping parentheses plus the subscript operator are always required to dereference an array element.

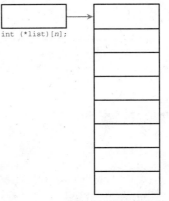

int (*list)[n];

When there is one pointer to an array,
the objects pointed to are contiguous.

Figure 9.4.

One pointer to an array
of objects.

Improving Program Performance with Pointers

In Chapter 8, you read several times that using pointers to avoid subscripting does not always improve program performance—there may be hidden overhead in address calculations. You must examine each case to determine whether using pointers will help.

Program performance is not always a matter of mere speed, however. It may be a matter of functionality and flexibility, as well.

Using Pointers to Increase Flexibility

The previous sections illustrated a point that may not be obvious on the surface. Program performance (both speed and/or utility) can be affected drastically by the amount of data you can maintain in storage, rather than on disk (or other media).

Arrays of pointer and pointers to array can help you organize data in storage so speed is much improved, and functionality is greatly increased as well. A text-editing program, for example, would suffer greatly in both speed and functionality if only the line of text currently being edited were in RAM.

Examples of this type are numerous and easy to find. You might go back through the sample programs in this book, for instance, and look for those that you can improve with these techniques.

Speeding Up Sorting with Pointers

ANSI standard C compilers provide a sorting function, qsort(), which is based on the Quicksort algorithm. It is fast and compact in most implementations. But there are times when you may want to save as much code space as possible and thus write your own sort function. As you will see, you can write a snappy sort in about 20 lines of code. Furthermore, you can use arrays of pointer to achieve execution speeds that get fairly close to qsort() for file or table sizes under 5,000 entries.

Whether you use qsort() or your own sort function, the first step is to design and code a set of functions that can compare two elements (called *sort keys* in this context). The idea is to keep the sort function itself small by passing to it a *function pointer* that designates the comparison method for a particular call.

All the comparison routines, therefore, must have the same formal parameters so multiple calls from the sort function are not necessary. Listing 9.3 shows COMPARES.C, a separately compiled source file that contains a number of such comparison functions.

Listing 9.3. COMPARES.C—Comparison functions for use with the Shellsort function (using Borland C++).

```
1   #include <stdlib.h>
2   #include <stdio.h>
3
4   #define INT    0
5   #define CHAR   1
6   #define DOUBLE 2
7   #define LT -1
8   #define EQ  0
9   #define GT  1
10  #if !defined( ASCENDING )
11  #define ASCENDING 0
12  #define DESCENDING 1
13  #endif
14
15  int comp_int( void *obj1, void *obj2, int order );
16  int comp_char( void *obj1, void *obj2, int order );
17  int comp_string( void *obj1, void *obj2, int order );
18  int comp_double( void *obj1, void *obj2, int order );
19
20  int comp_int( void *obj1, void *obj2, int order )
21  {
22    int result;
23
24    if ( order == ASCENDING )
25      result = *(int *)obj1 - *(int *)obj2;
26    else
27      result = *(int *)obj2 - *(int *)obj1;
28    if ( result ) result /= abs( result );
29    return result;
30  }
31
32  int comp_char( void *obj1, void *obj2, int order )
33  {
34    int result;
```

```
35
36    if ( order == ASCENDING )
37       result = *(char *)obj1 - *(char *)obj2;
38    else
39       result = *(char *)obj2 - *(char *)obj1;
40    if ( result ) result /= abs( result );
41    return result;
42 }
43
44 int comp_string( void *obj1, void *obj2, int order )
45 {
46    int result = 0;
47    char *s1 = obj1;   /* Do this because BC doesn't */
48    char *s2 = obj2;   /* handle void pointers well */
49
50    while ( !result && *s1 && *s2 ) {
51       if ( order == ASCENDING )
52          result = *s1++ - *s2++;
53       else
54          result = *s2++ - *s1++;
55    }
56    if ( result ) result /= abs( result );
57    return result;
58 }
59
60 int comp_double( void *obj1, void *obj2, int order )
61 {
62    double result;
63
64    if ( order == ASCENDING )
65       result = *(double *)obj1 - *(double *)obj2;
66    else
67       result = *(double *)obj2 - *(double *)obj1;
68    if ( result < 0 ) return -1;
69       else if ( result == 0 ) return 0;
70          else if ( result > 0 ) return 1;
71 }
72
```

The comparison routines accept `void` pointers (not null pointers, remember) to the objects to be compared, plus another argument that specifies whether the sort is to be ascending or descending. If the sort is descending, the order of comparison is simply turned around to reverse the sense. All the sort function expects in return is an integer that is less than zero if obj1 is less than obj2, zero if obj1 == obj2, and greater than zero if obj1 is greater than obj2.

The sort function neither knows nor cares if you swap the order internally to force a sort to descending order. In the case of qsort(), you would have to modify the comparison function in Listing 9.3: eliminate the order argument and make it a global variable that can be set before the program can call qsort() because qsort() does not support a function parameter determining output order. The shell_sort() function supports the functions as written here.

The key to increasing sort speeds when using routines simpler than qsort()— such as shell_sort(), which is shown in Listing 9.4—is to sort an array of pointers to objects, instead of sorting the objects themselves. This approach saves a great deal of time when large objects are sorted because only pointers, not the objects, physically exchange positions.

Listing 9.4. SHELLSRT.C—Using the Shellsort algorithm with an array of pointers to the objects to be sorted (using Borland C++).

```
1   /* +-------------------------------------------------+
2       +                 SHELL SORT
3       +   Input to shell_sort is an array of pointers to
4       +   objects of your choice, plus a pointer to the
5       +   appropriate comparison routine.
6       +-------------------------------------------------+
7   */
8   #include <stdlib.h>
9   #include <stdio.h>
10              /* Use defines with global var order */
11  #define ASCENDING 0
12  #define DESCENDING 1
13
14  #include "compares.h"
15  #include "timer.h"
16
17  /* +-------------------------------------------------+
18      + Shellsort test data.
19      + The SMALL MODEL used here assumes the near pointer
20      + type. To use in separate compiles, you can use
21      + the far override and always assume far pointers.
22      + Both shell_sort() and all comparison routines
23      + would then have to be modified.
```

```
24      +-----------------------------------------------------+
25   */
26   char *shell_list[] =
27      {
28          "Vermont              ",
29          "Rhode Island         ",
30          "Oregon               ",
31          "New York             ",
32          "New Hampshire        ",
33          "Mississippi          ",
34          "Montana              ",
35          "Iowa                 ",
36          "Georgia              ",
37          "California           ",
38          "Colorado             ",
39          "Alaska               ",
40          "Alabama              ",
41          "Arizona              ",
42      };
43   /* +-----------------------------------------------------+
44      + Quicksort test data.
45      +-----------------------------------------------------+
46   */
47   char quick_list[][21] =
48      {
49          "Vermont              ",
50          "Rhode Island         ",
51          "Oregon               ",
52          "New York             ",
53          "New Hampshire        ",
54          "Mississippi          ",
55          "Montana              ",
56          "Iowa                 ",
57          "Georgia              ",
58          "California           ",
59          "Colorado             ",
60          "Alaska               ",
61          "Alabama              ",
62          "Arizona              ",
63      };
64
65   int q_comp_string( const void *obj1, const void *obj2 );
```

continues

Listing 9.4. Continued

```
66
67  /* +--------------------------------------------------+
68     + Declare shell_sort().
69     +   All pointers at this level should be (void *).
70     +--------------------------------------------------+
71  */
72  void shell_sort( void *table[],
73               int (*comp)( void *, void *, int ),
74               int order,
75               int sortsize );
76
77  main()
78  {
79    int i;
80
81    start_bench();
82    shell_sort( (void *)shell_list, comp_string,
83                 ASCENDING, 14 );
84    stop_bench();
85    for ( i=0; i<14; i++ ) printf( "%s", shell_list[i] );
86    puts( "\n" );
87    printf( "Shellsort required %.4f seconds.\n",
88        duration() );
89
90    start_bench();
91    qsort( quick_list, 14, 21, q_comp_string );
92    stop_bench();
93    printf( "Quicksort required %.4f seconds.\n",
94        duration() );
95
96    printf( "\nShellsort to descending order:\n" );
97    shell_sort( (void *)shell_list, comp_string,
98                 DESCENDING, 14 );
99    for ( i=0; i<14; i++ ) printf( "%s", shell_list[i] );
100   puts( "\n" );
101 }
102
103 /* +--------------------------------------------------+
104    + shell_sort().
105    +   INPUT: 1) A pointer to an array of pointers to
106    +               objects to be sorted.
```

```
107    +            2) A pointer to a function which will
108    +               perform the comparison between any
109    +               two elements in the array/list.
110    +            3) An integer with a value that is either
111    +               ASCENDING or DESCENDING.
112    +            4) An integer with a value that is the
113    +               number of elements to be sorted.
114    + OUTPUT: NONE. The original array of pointers is
115    +               re-ordered in ascending or descending
116    +               sequence, depending on the global variable
117    +               order.
118    + METHOD: h-partitioned insertion sort. The
119    +               sequence of values for h are
120    +                  1,4,13,40,121,364,1093,...,
121    +               with the highest value depending on the
122    +               global variable sortsize. See the
123    +               appendixes for more detail on method;
124    +               both Sedgewick and Knuth have much more
125    +               on sorting theory.
126    +-------------------------------------------------+
127  */
128  void shell_sort( void *table[],
129               int (*comp)( void *, void *, int ),
130               int order,
131               int sortsize )
132  {
133    int i, j, h;
134    void *v;
135
136    h = 1;
137    do h = 3 * h + 1; while (h <= sortsize - 1 );
138    do {
139      h /= 3;
140      for ( i=h; i<sortsize; i++ ) {
141        v = table[i];
142        j = i;
143        while ( 0 < (*comp)( table[j-h], v, order ) ) {
144      table[j] = table[j-h];
145      j -= h;
146      if ( j < h ) break;
147        }
```

continues

Listing 9.4. Continued

```
148        table[j] = v;
149      }
150    } while ( h > 0 );
151  }
152
153  int q_comp_string( const void *obj1, const void *obj2 )
154  {
155    int result = 0;
156    char *s1 = obj1;   /* Do this because BC doesn't */
157    char *s2 = obj2;   /* handle void pointers well */
158
159    while ( !result && *s1 && *s2 )
160      result = *s1++ - *s2++;
161    if ( result ) result /= abs( result );
162    return result;
163  }
```

Listing 9.4 shows how to set up and call `shell_sort()`. Notice particularly lines 28–41 and 49–62. The test data for `shell_sort()` and `qsort()`, respectively, appears in these lines. Data for `shell_sort()` is set up as an array of pointers to `char` so only the pointers (not necessarily the strings themselves) are presumed to be contiguous. In contrast, the `qsort()` test data is arranged as a two-dimensional array of `char` so the strings are contiguous.

The Shellsort function appears in lines 128–151. The array of pointers is handled by using subscripts: it would be more difficult to use only pointers, and that method would help little here. When you run the sample program in Listing 9.4, output similar to the following is displayed on the system console:

```
Alabama        Alaska        Arizona      California
Colorado       Georgia       Iowa         Mississippi
Montana        New Hampshire New York     Oregon
Rhode Island   Vermont

Shellsort required 0.0025 seconds.
Quicksort required 0.0019 seconds.
Shellsort to descending order:
Vermont        Rhode Island  Oregon       New York
New Hampshire  Montana       Mississippi  Iowa
Georgia        Colorado      California    Arizona
Alaska         Alabama
```

Because this example sorts only 14 entries, the end-to-end runtime is small. The difference between `shell_sort()` and `qsort()` is also small—about 0.6 milliseconds. (The difference in the length of time depends on both the compiler and the machine you use.) For small numbers of records/entries (less than 5,000), the simplicity of this implementation, plus the use of pointers, nearly makes up for Quicksort's more efficient algorithm.

Summary

The techniques in this chapter, together with the more basic material in Chapter 8, provide just about everything you need to master the fine art of pointer programming in C. Before continuing, be sure you have mastered the following ideas:

- Multiple indirection. Pointers can point to other pointers in C. This is an extremely powerful and commonly used technique in C.

- Arrays of pointers. Using arrays of pointers can help you organize a large number of discontiguous objects in memory. This technique adds power and flexibility to your C programs.

- Pointers to an array. When you can load a number of objects simultaneously to memory, performance picks up. Using a pointer to an array enables you to allocate that memory dynamically so it need not be a permanent part of your compiled program.

- Text scanning and parsing. With an understanding of scanning and parsing techniques, you can design and implement your own "intelligent" data- and command-input routines. Doing so provides not only an impressive interface for the user, but also more power and flexibility for your program.

File I/O Programming

File I/O programming is another of those C programming issues that can only be labeled as "crucial." The primary purpose of a computer program is to work with data, and most data is stored in files—usually on disk devices. The users of your programs would be perturbed, to say the least, if the information they laboriously typed was not saved (written to a file).

The stream I/O functions discussed earlier in the book were those functions mostly related to the user-interface side of things. In this chapter, you are introduced to the process of bulk data storage and retrieval.

The subject of I/O programming is vast and often complicated. Although a great deal of information about it is not presented here, the fundamentals of disk file handling, particularly as it applies to DOS- and UNIX-based systems (rather than mainframe environments), can be found here. In this chapter, you learn about the following topics:

■ *File-management functions.* These are the functions that provide the facilities for what is usually termed *data-management* activities, including the deleting and renaming of files.

■ *Buffer-management techniques.* Once you get into file I/O programming proper, you must give some consideration to moving data into and out of main memory (RAM). What kinds of files can be buffered? How? What is a good buffer size? These and other questions are answered.

■ *File access methods.* What methods are available for reading and writing records? For that matter, what is a record? Can you read or write a record in the middle of a file without having to read (or write) all previous records to get to it? You can indeed, and you will discover some of the ways to do so.

Using C's File-Management Functions

Standard C provides an adequate, if not exhaustive, group of file-management functions. You can delete files, rename them, start over at the beginning of a file that's already open, and create temporary files as well as unique names (strings) for temporary files.

Deleting a File with *remove()*

The remove() function can be used to delete a file. It is important to understand that this function physically removes the file from disk. When you execute this function, the file named by the argument for remove() is gone. After you execute remove(), the file and its contents are forever unavailable. Certain utilities on the market can "unerase" a deleted file, but this is risky business at best.

The function prototype for remove() is

```
#include <stdio.h>
int remove( const char *filename );
```

When this function is called, the file named by *filename* should not be open. If it is, the behavior is implementation-defined, meaning that it depends on the compiler vendor (a given compiler may allow it, but it is never guaranteed).

remove() returns a zero integer if the operation was successful, and a nonzero if not. Here is an example of using remove():

```
#include <stdio.h>
...
char fname[] = "\\usr\\junk.txt";
...
if ( !remove( fname ) )
  printf( "File: %s was erased.\n", fname );
else
  printf( "Could not erase %s\n", fname );
```

You can see from this example that ANSI does not care what string defines the file; it is just a string. Here the file JUNK.TXT is deleted from the \USR disk directory. Names like this are common in both DOS and UNIX systems (UNIX uses a forward slash). Because the DOS version of the slash was coded, a \\ escape sequence was necessary.

Changing the Filename with *rename()*

The rename() function changes the name of a file on-disk. That is, the directory entry (or volume table of contents, or whatever) is modified physically so the file can henceforth be accessed under its new name. The old name no longer exists. The function prototype for rename() is

```
#include <stdio.h>
int rename( const char *old, const char *new );
```

The rename() function returns zero if the operation was successful, and non-zero if not. If rename() fails, the file is not damaged; it still exists under its old name.

You should make sure that the named file is not open when rename() is called. Some implementations (notably UNIX-based systems) must *copy* the file in order to rename it; there may be no operating system support for directly modifying the directory. Some systems (such as DOS) can directly modify a disk directory, but there is no guarantee that this capability will be available to you.

Why would you ever want to use this function? The obvious reason is for maintaining multiple copies, or versions, of a file. The program, VERSIONS.C, in Listing 10.1 is extremely simplistic, but you could use it as a basis (as boilerplate code) to build a more complex archiving system.

Listing 10.1. VERSIONS.C—Using the *rename()* function to change a filename (for Borland C++).

```
1   #include <stdlib.h>
2   #include <stdio.h>
3   #include <string.h>
4   #include <conio.h>
5
6   main()
7   {
8      char newver[4];
9      char oldver[] = "txt";
10     char fname[] = "junk.";
11     char oldname[13];
12     char newname[13];
13
14     clrscr();
15     printf( "Enter new archive version (3 digits): " );
16     gets( newver );
```

continues

Listing 10.1. Continued

```
17   strcpy( oldname, fname);
18   strcpy( newname, fname);
19   strcat( oldname, oldver );
20   strcat( newname, newver );
21   if ( rename( oldname, newname ) )
22     printf( "Rename %s to %s failed.\n", oldname, newname );
23   else
24     printf( "Renamed %s to %s\n", oldname, newname );
25   }
```

Back to the Beginning with *rewind()*

At times, you may want to process the same file more than once. You can do this with the `rewind()` function. `rewind()`, which is called while the file is open, simply sets the current position (the point at which the next read or write occurs) to the beginning of the file. The function prototype for the `rewind()` function is

```
#include <stdio.h>
void rewind( FILE *stream );
```

Strictly speaking, `rewind()` is a file-positioning function. It is included here because it performs only one function—although quite a useful one—that amounts to setting up for I/O operations. Other functions detect and set the current file position more flexibly (and hence are considered *processing* functions, not management functions).

The `rewind()` function is probably most useful for processing a file sequentially a number of times. *Sequential processing* is the processing of reading (or writing) every record in the file, beginning with the first record and (usually) going all the way to the last.

Suppose, for example, that you want to "send" multiple copies of a text file to `stdout`. Because standard streams are used, you can, incidentally, use redirection to put the output to another disk file. The program, COPIES.C, in Listing 10.2 performs this task.

Listing 10.2. COPIES.C—Using *rewind()* (for Borland C++).

```
1   #include <stdlib.h>
2   #include <stdio.h>
3   #include <string.h>
4
```

```
 5  main( int argc, char *argv[] )
 6  {
 7    int copies;
 8    char inname[41];
 9    FILE *infile;
10    char text[255];
11
12    if ( argc < 3 ) {
13      puts( "Command: copies infile n" );
14      puts( "To send to printer: copies infile n >prn" );
15      exit( 8 );
16    }
17
18    strcpy( inname, argv[1] );
19    copies = atoi( argv[2] );
20
21    if ( NULL == ( infile = fopen( inname, "r" ) ) ) {
22      printf( "Could not open %s\n", inname );
23      exit( 8 );
24    }
25
26    while ( copies ) {
27      while ( fgets( text, 255, infile ) ) {
28        fputs( text, stdout );
29      }
30      fputc( 12, stdout );  /* Formfeed for most printers */
31      --copies;
32      rewind( infile );
33    }
34
35    fclose ( infile );
36  }
```

One question about rewind() remains: why use it when you could simply close and then reopen the file? The question is especially penetrating when you realize that there is a reopen() function that can do the job with one function call. Because reopen() also enables you to specify a new processing mode, why use something as simple as rewind()?

The answer is *time*. The process of closing and reopening a file is expensive because it requires handling of leftover buffers and updating the disk directory (which involves additional I/O even if you, the programmer, do not see it). In contrast, rewind() simply sets the current pointer back to the beginning. So if you are going to go back to the beginning a number of times, you can save time with rewind().

Creating and Using Temporary Files

Two other file-management functions—`tmpfile()` and `tmpnam()`—might prove useful to you. Both are declared in STDIO.H. Note the function prototype and a description of each of these functions:

■ `FILE *tmpfile( void );`

`tmpfile()` creates and opens a temporary binary file (mode `wb+` = create, binary, update read/write). If the create and open are successful, a standard stream pointer is returned; otherwise, a null pointer is returned. The name of the resulting file is generated automatically, as in the `tmpnam()` function (described next).

The temporary file that is created is deleted automatically when it is closed or when the program terminates normally. If the program terminates abnormally, ANSI leaves it to the implementation to determine whether the file is to be deleted.

■ `char *tmpnam( char *s );`

`tmpnam()` does *not* create a file. It creates only a filename—that is, a string. Using `tmpnam()` creates a "temporary" name, only in the sense that the name generated is guaranteed not to collide with any existing filename. You still must use the filename string to open and later close the temporary file. You might want to do this instead of calling `tmpfile()` if you do not want the file to be deleted automatically when closed, or if the file mode `wb+` does not suit your purposes. You should (in every case) be sure to use the `remove()` function to erase the file after you finish with it.

You can invoke `tmpnam()` in two ways: the argument string pointer s can point to a valid string you have created, or it can be NULL. If it points to a string, it is assumed to be at least `L_tmpnam` (a predefined macro name) characters long, and the generated filename string is placed in it. If it is NULL, the filename string is stored in a static string internal to `tmpnam()`, and a pointer to it is returned to the caller.

Temporary files can be handy when you have intermediate results or data that is too massive to reside in memory. Most compilers use temporary files, as do some file-compression programs and archiving programs.

Buffered I/O Concepts

Earlier in the book, some aspects of the effect of buffering stream I/O were discussed. In standard C, "stream I/O" can encompass a variety of I/O programming techniques that usually are discussed separately.

In particular, stream I/O in C encompasses both character and block-device I/O programming. Console and communications port programming are examples of managing character devices, and disk file programming is an example of managing block devices.

Block devices, which can read and write many bytes at a time to and from the physical storage media, are the devices thought of as being file-oriented devices. These devices, therefore, are most susceptible to buffering techniques and are the ones of concern in this chapter. (Although character devices can have buffering schemes imposed on them, this has little or no effect on their performance.)

An I/O buffer, as mentioned earlier, is an area of RAM reserved for receiving blocks of data; its main function is *speed matching*. The central processor of your computer is many times faster than any I/O device and, without some technique to "reduce" the speed differential, would spend (waste) a great deal of time just waiting for I/O to be completed.

Buffering does nothing to change the physical speeds of the different kinds of electronics involved. It does work, however, because of a simple fact: programs "ask for data" only in spurts (most of the time). Between spurts, the program is busy processing the data just read (or getting ready to write more).

You can get an intuitive idea of why this concept works by thinking of your hot water heater. The water supply system is capable of providing a steady stream of water, but you can't heat it directly and send it straight to the faucet. Why? Because you can use hot water faster than you can heat it!

It's a different story if you introduce a tank large enough to hold sufficient hot water to satisfy a single, fairly large demand. Now you can heat water and store it between demands. The supply, of course, corresponds to a disk or other device, the tank is the speed-matching buffer, and your shower is the program.

What Difference Does It Make?

Does buffering your files really make much of a difference? It surely does—the speed difference between even a *fast* disk and the central processor is enormous. The less you must cause something physical to happen at the drive, the better your program performs.

You have learned that larger buffers (up to a point) make a big difference in program performance. Now it's time to see how to achieve that. SPEEDBUF.C, the short program in Listing 10.3, shows how to use the setvbuf() standard library function to modify the buffer size used for a file.

This program uses some of the facilities of the DOS- and PC-based TIMER.C high-resolution timing routines, but high-resolution timing is not actually started. The reason is that high-resolution timing is too much of a CPU hog—the I/O interrupts don't work right, even on a fast machine. Therefore, you must settle for a timer resolution of 18.2 ticks per second (which is sufficient for the purposes here).

Listing 10.3. SPEEDBUF.C—Tuning I/O performance with buffer size (for Borland C++).

```
1   #include <stdlib.h>
2   #include <stdio.h>
3
4   #include "timer.h"
5
6   main()
7   {
8     FILE *infile;
9     char pline[255];
10
11    if ( NULL == ( infile = fopen( "finance.c", "r" ) ) )
12      abort();
13    if ( setvbuf( infile, NULL, _IOFBF, 512) ) abort();
14    begin_time = *clock;
15    while ( fgets( pline, 255, infile ) ) ;
16    end_time = *clock;
17    fclose( infile );
18    printf( "Time w/512 byte buffer: %.3f\n",
19            (double)( end_time - begin_time ) / 18.2 );
20
21    if ( NULL == ( infile = fopen( "finance.c", "r" ) ) )
22      abort();
23    if ( setvbuf( infile, NULL, _IOFBF, 4096) ) abort();
24    begin_time = *clock;
25    while ( fgets( pline, 255, infile ) ) ;
26    end_time = *clock;
27    fclose( infile );
28    printf( "Time w/4096 byte buffer: %.3f\n",
29            (double)( end_time - begin_time ) / 18.2 );
30  }
```

When SPEEDBUF.C runs, the output it produces on the system console looks something like this:

```
Time w/512 byte buffer: 0.110
Time w/4096 byte buffer: 0.055
```

The figures may not be the same on your machine; you may be running something either faster or slower than the 80386-25MHz machine on which this sample was run. The relative differences should be reflected, however.

SPEEDBUF.C reads the same text file twice, with two different buffer sizes. Note that if you are going to use the setvbuf() function, you must call it *after* opening the file and *before* any I/O calls are made. Once you start reading and writing, it is too late. (The details on setvbuf() are given in the section "Writing High-Performance File Routines" later in this chapter.)

This program is dependent on PC-based architecture (or on that of a compatible). It begins timing by the simple expedient of recording the current tick count (lines 14 and 24) of the system clock, and concludes by recording the tick count again (lines 16 and 26). Then the tick rate is used to compute the elapsed time for reading with each buffer size (lines 19 and 29).

Even in this trivial example, the results are encouraging. Just increasing the buffer size from 512 bytes to 4K bytes sped up the file read (about three times faster). Even more satisfying results can be achieved in more sophisticated applications.

Buffering and *stdin, stdout,* and *stderr*

Buffering is a coin with two sides. It may actually impede your attempts to control the console, for instance. The stdin stream normally is line buffered, which means that you must type characters and press Enter to have them input to the program, even if you are using character-input functions such as getchar(). getchar() and its companion functions also echo keyboard characters to the screen whether you want them or not.

For character devices, therefore, you occasionally may want to turn off buffering completely. This is the case, for example, with the common DOS implementation of getch(), which originated in the UNIX-based curses library functions. In DOS systems, you ordinarily use getch() to get keystrokes, one at a time, with no echo to the screen (presumably without having to press Enter).

For direct console I/O using a function like getch(), you need to turn buffering off so the keystroke is reported to your program immediately. You can use the setbuf() function to do this. The sample program KEYIO.C in Listing 10.4 illustrates how to go about it.

Listing 10.4.   KEYIO.C—Controlling keyboard I/O buffering (for Borland C++).

```
1   #define BORLAND
2
3   #include <stdlib.h>
4   #include <stdio.h>
5   #if defined( BORLAND )
6   #include <conio.h>
7   #elif defined( MS )
8   #include <graph.h>
9   #endif
10
11  int get_ch( void )
12  {
13    static int is_open = 0;
14    static FILE *istream = NULL;
15
16    if ( !is_open ) {
17      if ( NULL == ( istream = fopen( "CON","rb" ) ) ) {
18        exit( 1 );
19      }
20      setbuf( istream, NULL );
21      is_open = 1;
22    }
23    return( fgetc( istream ) );
24  }
25
26  main()
27  {
28    char ch;
29
30  #if defined( BORLAND )
31    clrscr();
32  #elif defined( MS )
33    _clearscreen( _GCLEARSCREEN );
34  #endif
35    ch = 32;
36    while ( ch != '.' ) {    /* Type a period to quit. */
37      ch = get_ch(); if ( ch == 0 ) ch = get_ch();
38  #if !defined( MS )
39      fputc( ch,stdout );
40  #endif
```

```
41    }
42  }
```

In Listing 10.4, the `setbuf()` function is not used to alter the behavior of the `stdin` stream; another stream is provided instead (see line 14). Nor is the `curses`-like function name duplicated. The underscore character is used to form a similar but unique name for the function: `get_ch()` (lines 11–22). Static local variables are used (lines 13 and 14) so the status of the stream (open or closed) can be retained across multiple calls to the function.

> **T I P**
>
> Line 1 of Listing 10.4 contains a macro definition that structures the code for the Borland C compiler. You can change this macro to `#define MS` if you want to compile it with the Microsoft C compiler. In either case, type a period to terminate the program.

You should be aware that the behavior of the program is different when it is run with different compilers. Using the Borland product, the `get_ch()` behaves just like the common `getch()` function; DOS input calls are completely by-passed, and you get every keystroke. The Microsoft product, however, does not bypass DOS input functions. You can use the DOS editing keys, and you must press Enter before the period character terminates the program. The vendor-provided `getch()` function works the same in either product line.

Selecting an I/O Mode for File Streams

Standard C provides I/O modes with which you can read, write, update, and append data to files, and you can do these operations in either text or binary modes. It is important that you understand what the various modes mean and what you can do with them.

Selecting the Access Mode

The mode parameter of the `fopen()` function determines the *file access mode* (or just *file mode*) that is associated with the file while it is open this time. You can select different modes at other times. The mode parameter is a string, which can be a string literal. The following code fragment shows how to place the mode string in `fopen()` call arguments:

```
#include <stdio.h>
...
FILE *stream;
...
if ( NULL == ( stream = fopen( "anyfile.dat", "mode" ) ) )
  abort();
```

The values that the mode string may contain are discussed in the following sections. Generally, the mode string can contain up to three characters, which must be selected from the set of five characters shown in Table 10.1.

Table 10.1. Characters used in the mode string.

Mode Character	Meaning
r	Read from file
w	Write to file
a	Append to end of file
b	I/O is in binary mode (no text transformations)
+	Updates are permitted

The difference between text and binary mode access is discussed again in the section "Using Text and Binary File Modes" later in this chapter.

Open Options for Input Mode

When you want to access the file in a read-only mode, you use an input mode—either text input or binary input. Here are examples of each method:

■ `fopen( filenamestring, "r" )`

Opens the file named `filenamestring` for reading in text mode. Some transformations of the data (discussed later in the chapter) are performed on the input data.

■ `fopen( filenamestring, "rb" )`

Opens the file named by `filenamestring` for reading in binary mode. Input operations do not cause any transformations of data.

Open Options for Output Mode

You use an output mode when you want to access the file in write-only mode (an obvious example—creating the file in the first place). Note some examples of using the output modes:

- `fopen( filenamestring, "w" )`

    Opens the file for writing in text mode. If the file already exists, it is truncated to zero length, effectively overlaying the original data. If the file does not exist, it is created.

- `fopen( filenamestring, "wb" )`

    Opens the file for writing in binary mode. This mode also destroys (overlays) an existing file. If you open an existing file accidentally, there is no way back; closing it immediately leaves it with zero length.

> The commercial "unerase" programs that can undo the effect of a call to `remove()` (mentioned earlier) *cannot* help you undo a `"wb"` mode. Removing and truncating a file are two entirely different things.

- `fopen( filenamestring, "a" )`

    Opens the file for appended writing in text mode, with the current position at end-of-file. That is, the next write occurs just beyond the last line of text previously written. Opening an existing file does not destroy it. Opening a nonexistent file creates it.

- `fopen( filenamestring, "ab" )`

    Opens the file for appended writing in binary mode, with the current position at end-of-file. This mode also creates the file, if needed.

Open Options for Update Mode

You use an update mode when you want to access the file for both reading and writing. Briefly, you should append the + character to the end of any of the preceding six modes to get one of the update modes. Note the following examples:

- `fopen( filenamestring, "r+" )`

    Opens the text file for update—both reading and writing. It is assumed that the initial I/O request will be for reading. This mode does not destroy existing files, but the current position is placed at the beginning of the file at file open time. This mode does not create a file, though. (You cannot open a nonexistent file with this mode.)

■ fopen(*filenamestring*, "w+")

Opens the text file for update. This mode is similar to the "r+" mode, but it is assumed that the initial I/O request will be for writing. If the file does not exist, it is created; if it does, it is truncated to zero length and overlaid. Opening a file in this mode generally will not fail, unless there is a directory error or no space left on the disk or directory for the new file.

■ fopen(*filenamestring*, "a+")

Opens, or perhaps creates, the text file for update. In any case, the current position is placed at end-of-file. This means that a write request tacks the data on the end of the file, but a read request fails (with EOF). To read immediately after opening the file with this mode, you must move the current position elsewhere. How to do this is discussed in the section "Direct-Access File Programming" later in this chapter.

Note that all writes to a file opened with append mode are forced to the then-current end-of-file position. It makes no difference whether there has been a call to one of the file-positioning functions. For all practical purposes, append mode is for writing to end-of-file locations only. In addition, some implementations may have padded the last block with null characters so the next appended record is *beyond* the previous end-of-file position.

T I P If you want to append records *and* update elsewhere in the file, open the file with the "r+" or "rb+" mode strings and manually position to end-of-file.

■ fopen(*filenamestring*, "rb+")

Opens the binary file for update. Opening a nonexistent file will fail.

■ fopen(*filenamestring*, "wb+")

Opens or creates the binary file for update processing.

■ fopen(*filenamestring*, "ab+")

Opens or creates the binary file for update processing, writing at end-of-file. The same warning about where writes occur applies for this mode string: they *always* are at the end-of-file.

When the mode string contains three characters, the update character + may be either the second or the third character in the string. "r+b", "w+b", and "a+b" are all valid mode strings.

Summary of Modes

Table 10.2 summarizes all the combinations of mode-string characters, with a brief explanation of their meanings.

Table 10.2. A summary of all ANSI C file modes.

Mode String	Meaning
"r"	Open text file for reading
"w"	Truncate to zero length or create text file for writing
"a"	Append; open or create text file for writing at end-of-file
"rb"	Open binary file for reading
"wb"	Open binary file for writing
"ab"	Append; open or create binary file for writing at end-of-file
"r+"	Open text file for update (both reading and writing)
"w+"	Truncate to zero length or create text file for update
"a+"	Append; open or create text file for update, positioned at end-of-file
"rb+"	Open a binary file for update
"wb+"	Truncate to zero length or create a binary file for update
"ab+"	Append; open or create binary file for update, positioned at end-of-file
"r+b"	Same as "rb+"
"w+b"	Same as "wb+"
"a+b"	Same as "ab+"

Mixing Reads and Writes in Update Modes

Update-mode file access is distinguished by the fact that, once a file is open in the correct mode, you can both read data from the file and write data to it. This is the characteristic of disk files that makes them so useful. They can be updated without your having to rewrite the whole file.

In combining both reading and writing to a single file, you frequently have to switch from reading to writing, or from writing to reading. You have to pay some attention to what happens to the file buffers when you do this. If file buffers are not handled correctly, you probably will lose some data—almost invariably so, in fact.

The process of switching from writing to reading in update mode is particularly vulnerable to data loss. The reason is that the write-type library functions don't actually cause disk I/O—they just send data to the buffer. The data is not physically written to disk until the buffer is full. Thus, switching to read functions may simply overlay the data already in the buffer. Consider the following code fragment:

```
#include <stdlib.h>
#include stdio.h>
...
main()
{
  FILE *data;
  int i;
  unsigned char record[100];  /* The data record */

  if ( NULL == ( data = fopen( ..., "rb+" ) ) ) ...
  setvbuf( data, NULL, _IOFBF, 1000 ); /* 10 recs/buf */
...
  for ( i=0; i<5; i++ ) fwrite( record, 100, 1, data );
  fread( record, 100, 1, data );
...
  fclose( data );
}
```

The for loop in this fragment writes five records (only half a bufferful). Then, without further ado, a read is performed. What happens to the five output records? They are lost. You need some means of forcing the remaining data in a buffer to be written to the disk when switching access types. This method exists—it is called *flushing* the buffer. Incidentally, you should flush the buffer no matter which type of switch is involved, whether read to write, or write to read. The ANSI standard says that the contents of a buffer area are indeterminate *at all times* (from the point of view of the program).

There are two ways, not just one, to flush a buffer:

- *Call the* fflush() *library function.* You can flush a buffer manually by calling fflush(*ptr*), where *ptr* is a FILE * pointer. To flush *all* buffers, call fflush(NULL).

- *Call one of the file-positioning functions.* These functions, which include fseek(), fsetpos(), and rewind(), all change the location in the file of the current position, making it safe for these functions to "assume" that you intend to switch access types. Even if you do not switch access types, the data in the buffer will no longer match data on disk at the new position.

Knowing the rules for buffer handling, you can rewrite the last few lines of the preceding code fragment so it is guaranteed to work correctly:

```
for ( i=0; i<5; i++ ) fwrite( record, 100, 1, data );
fread( record, 100, 1, data );
fclose( data );
fflush( data );   /* Resynchronize the buffer */
}
```

Using Text and Binary File Modes

Before leaving the topic of file modes, you should know something about using text and binary modes to access your files. Many files can be processed either way, but the distinction is important. Two things need to be clarified: what is and isn't a text stream, and which read/write functions apply to the text and binary modes.

A *text stream* is a sequence of lines, each composed of zero or more characters (an implementation is required to support *at least* 255 characters per line), terminated by an end-of-line character or characters that are converted internally to the \n character. On disk, a line is not necessarily a string: the null character \0 is not recorded. The string-oriented character stream functions add the \0 when reading a line and remove it when writing a line. Briefly, a text line is meant to be readable by a human being.

A *binary stream* is anything else. All characters are unprocessed; they are read or written as is, with no transformation. A \0 character appearing in a binary stream has no significance for string termination or anything else. It is just data.

These two concepts must now be combined with the families of I/O library functions, matching the function purpose to the file mode. There are five classes of I/O functions, the first of which—the file-management group of functions—does not apply to this discussion. The other four classes of functions are the formatted, character, direct, and file-positioning I/O groups of functions. Table 10.3 summarizes these function classes and which I/O modes can be used with them.

Table 10.3. I/O function families and permitted I/O modes.

Function Class	Modes Available
Formatted I/O	Text only
Character I/O	Text and binary, with caution
Direct I/O	Binary only
File positioning	Both modes; use caution with text mode

The formatted I/O functions include the `printf()` and `scanf()` families of functions. They clearly are intended for text mode use and should not be used for anything else.

The character I/O functions include the `fgetc()`, `fputc()`, `fgets()`, and `fputs()` families of functions. Of these, the string-oriented functions also are clearly text-mode-dependent. The single-character functions, however, can be used (under certain circumstances) with binary mode operations. This was done deliberately in the KEYIO.C program in Listing 10.4, for instance. Understand, though, that this is not the normal use of the function and should be done with caution—and only when you must approach the extreme limits of what C can do (in that case, an assembler subroutine may be called for).

The direct I/O class of functions includes the `fread()` and `fwrite()` functions, which are used with binary mode files. However, a file created in text mode can be opened in binary mode and read or written to in binary mode. In fact, this is commonly done in order to load text files to memory at very high speeds. The catch is that now you must deal with the end-of-line characters, as well as any other characters transformed in some way by text mode functions.

The file-positioning functions are examined in detail a little later in the chapter, but a special caveat is needed right now. Table 10.3 indicates that the file-positioning functions can be used with either text- or binary-mode file processing. This is true, but using the file-positioning functions in text mode can be tricky. If you fail to account for this, you may destroy the validity of a file.

Specifically, the transformation of characters during text mode processing may "fool" the file-positioning functions—they may not know the current position as an exact byte count. Consider the DOS-based task of writing a string to a text mode file, as shown in this short program that works with Borland C++ or Microsoft C/C++:

```
1   #include <stdlib.h>
2   #include <stdio.h>
3
4   main()
5   {
```

```
 6    FILE *text;
 7    long numbytes;
 8    char testline[20] = "test data\n";
 9
10    text = fopen( "junk.txt", "w+" );
11    printf( "testline contains 11 bytes internally\n" );
12    fputs( testline, text );
13    numbytes = ftell( text );
14    printf( "current position is %d\n", numbytes );
15    fseek( text, numbytes, SEEK_SET );
16    fputs( testline, text );
17    fclose( text );
18  }
```

Count the bytes in the string in line 8 of this code sample. There are 9 characters, the \n newline escape sequence, and the (invisible) null string terminator \0, for a total of 11 bytes.

The physical characters placed on disk by the fputs() call in line 12 depend on the implementation. This usually means that special characters are transformed according to the requirements of the host system. On DOS systems, the newline character is transformed to the carriage-return-line-feed pair of characters, \x0D\x0A. This is confirmed when you run the hex dump utility SDUMP.C (in Chapter 3) against the output file:

```
======== SDUMP Output for: junk.txt ========
74657374 20646174 610D0A ... "test.data..        "
                      ^
```

The caret character has been added to the third line of the dump output to show what the ftell() function thinks is the current position in the file (see line 13 of the sample code). Clearly, ftell() has not taken into account the fact that the newline character has been transformed to *two* characters.

You can prove this by using fseek() to set the current position to the location reported by ftell(), and writing the line again (lines 15–16). Another dump of the file at that point would show the following byte sequence:

```
======== SDUMP Output for: junk.txt ========
74657374 20646174 610D7465 73742064 6174610D
0A                      ^ ^
```

Now the first caret on the third line indicates the last surviving byte from the first line, and the second caret points to the first byte of the next line. Notice that the line-feed character \x0A has been overlaid in error.

This does not mean that DOS has lost track of the output location. Had the fseek() *not* been called, DOS would have continued to place output at the correct locations in the file. And you can use `fseek()` and `fsetpos()` with text files, but you must seek to a position that has been reported by `ftell()` or `fgetpos()` and that contains display text (in contrast to this example).

You can implement I/O tasks in many ways, some more and some less complex. To be generally safe, however, consider the character and formatted I/O functions as part of your text-processing tool kit, and the direct and file-positioning functions as belonging to binary mode processing.

Direct-Access File Programming

Direct-access file programming is a greater challenge than the concepts and techniques presented earlier in this book. But the price of power and flexibility always seems to be increased complexity—and greater demands on the programmer's skill.

Fortunately, the demands on a programmer's skill need not be overwhelming. You can get respectable service and I/O performance with some fairly basic concepts and techniques. The next few sections introduce you to I/O programming techniques with sophistication that lies in their simplicity and adaptability. The discussion concentrates on direct-access methods for two reasons:

■ Direct-access method (DAM) files require either no support files or only simple ones, and are well suited to applications running on PC-sized machines simply because the data sizes are smaller.

■ The reduced overhead of DAM files permits speed and performance that frequently rival more complex indexed-sequential and B-tree methods, and in some situations can outperform them. Naturally, this is true only if you go about it correctly.

Direct-Access Concepts

Direct-access files are a subset of the larger class of random-access files. The purpose of any *random-access file* is to provide the means of reading or writing *any* record immediately, without having to read or write from the beginning of the file to get to a particular record. To accomplish this, the access routines must either record each record's disk address or be able to compute it on demand.

Indexed files use the former method and require a physically distinct file for recording the index. The index must be consulted for every read or write. Direct file-access routines compute each record's address (or close to it, as you will see) for each access. In either case, a given record must contain some item or value unique to that record. This is called the record *key*.

Direct file access requires not only that you supply some method of converting the record key value into a disk address, but also that the method produce addresses which distribute the records evenly over the space allocated to the file. If an inefficient algorithm is chosen, the records may cluster together in groups. This can cause exaggerated search times and may make the file appear full when it is not.

The most widely used method of computing addresses from keys is called *hashing*. Hashing can be used to address disk files or memory-resident tables, but this discussion focuses only on disk usage. The hashing function not only must produce a good spread of values as nearly random as possible, but also must be *quick*. Algorithms that go beyond simple arithmetic are unacceptable.

First of all, some provision must be made for alphanumeric keys, such as a name string. Is there any convenient method for converting a string to a fairly unique number? In Chapter 3, you saw a sample program (CRC16.C in Listing 3.4) that returns a value. The function embedded in this program returns a 16-bit checking code developed from a string of characters. The algorithm is designed (for error-checking purposes) to produce a code as nonrepetitive as possible. Such a function is made to order for this application. This discussion assumes that such a method has been applied to alpha keys and that a resulting numeric value is available.

After the key has been reduced to a numeric value, it must be hashed—its disk (or table) address must be calculated. One popular method that works well in most cases is the *modulus (remainder) method*. This method divides the numeric key value by another number and preserves the remainder as the *hashkey*. How to select the number for the divisor is explained in the following paragraphs.

Suppose that you want to add a record directly to a file that has space for N records, where N must be a prime number in order for the algorithm to work well. To compute the record's address, divide the key value by N and take the remainder:

```
address = key % N
```

Now you can fseek() to this position (which is discussed after the next section) and write the record. Or can you? The problem with this and all similar methods is that they are not truly random so *different* keys may hash to the *same* address—that is, the keys may *collide*.

To recover from collision, you must be able to detect a record location—a *slot*—where you *can* write the record. The most common method is to have preinitialized the file so unused slots have a null (zero) key field. Then you can read records sequentially from the computed address until an empty slot is found, and then write the record. To retrieve the record, the same logic is followed.

Collision recovery introduces a new wrinkle. Searching forward from the computed address for the desired record or empty slot is called *open addressing*. It implies that you may well have to search to end-of-file before you can determine when the search is a hit or a miss (the desired record was found or not found). Search times can become drastically longer as the file is more fully populated.

One solution is to divide (conceptually) the available record slots into groups of slots called *buckets*. The key is hashed to the disk address of the corresponding bucket, and searching is confined to the slots in that bucket only. In order to approach a random (uniform) distribution of records, the divisor still needs to be prime. And you must provide a total number of slots somewhat greater than the number of records to be stored—some clustering of records occurs despite everything you do. Figure 10.1 illustrates these ideas.

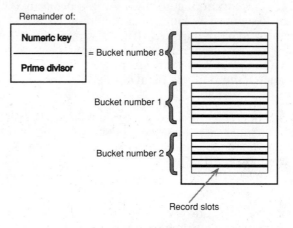

Figure 10.1.

The remainder dividing a numeric key by a prime number divisor is the bucket number. The bucket number times the number of bytes in a whole bucket equals the bucket's disk address.

Suppose, for example, that you want to store 100 records in 10 buckets of 10 slots each. Because 11 is the next prime number higher than 10, assume that there are 11 buckets and 110 total slots. This provides about 10 percent free space to alleviate clustering problems. The bucket number is computed like this:

```
bucket = keyvalue % 11
```

This value, in turn, can be used to compute the correct disk address of the first record in the bucket. Of course, having a function that computes the required prime number would be nice. Listing 10.5 shows a new version of PRIME.C, which was presented in a different form earlier in the book. You pass it a `long int` parameter that indicates the minimum number of buckets, and it computes the next higher or equal prime number.

Listing 10.5.   PRIME.C—Calculate the next higher prime number for "bucket" divisor (for Microsoft C/C++).

```
1   #include <stdlib.h>
2   #include <stdio.h>
3
4   long next_prime( long );
5
6   /* +-------------------------------------------------+
7      +  Calculate the next prime after the seed number.
8      +-------------------------------------------------+
9   */
10  long next_prime( long seed )
11  {
12    long n;
13    int j, k;
14    ldiv_t ans;
15    long *primes;
16
17    if ( NULL == ( primes = calloc( 350, sizeof(long) ) ) )
18      return 3L;
19    primes[0] = 2;
20    n = 3;
21    for ( j=1; j<350 && seed>primes[j-1]; j++ ) {
22      primes[j] = n;               /* Store the prime */
23  nextprime: n += 2;
24      k = 1;
25  checkprime: ans = ldiv( n, primes[k] );
26      if ( ans.rem == 0 ) goto nextprime;
27      if ( ans.quot <= primes[k] ) continue;
28      k++;
29      goto checkprime;
30    }
31    free( primes );
32    return( primes[j-1] );
33  }
```

The first few lines of PRIME.C can be used to create the header file for it:

```
#include <stdlib.h>
#include <stdio.h>

long next_prime( long );    /* <prime.h> */
```

The material so far provides the conceptual framework you need for comput-ing direct disk addresses. Now you need the technology to control the file's current position.

Using *ftell()* and *fgetpos()*

The `ftell()` and `fgetpos()` functions report the current position in the file. Although these functions are similar in operation, the wording of the ANSI standard implies the possibility that a given compiler could implement them differently. The function prototype for `ftell()` is

```
#include <stdlio.h>
long int ftell( FILE *stream );
```

You call `ftell()` after opening the file; there is no "current position" for a closed file. `ftell()` returns a `long int` that reports the current position in the file as an offset from the beginning of the file, in bytes. That is, the offset of the first byte is 0, the offset of the second byte is 1, and so on. If 10 bytes have been read, the current position is 10 (bytes 0 through 9 were read). File position is always reported as a byte offset, no matter what size record you may be reading or writing. As you already have seen, `ftell()` does not neces-sarily provide a meaningful measure of bytes written for a *text file*, but the function reports exact byte offsets for binary files. The following code frag-ment shows how to use `ftell()`:

```
#include <stdio.h>
...
long position;
FILE *input;
unsigned char *data;
unsigned request_size = 32768U;
...    /* No error checking in this sample, for brevity */
data = malloc( request_size );         /* Get a buffer */
input = fopen( "junk.dat", "rb" );      /* Open binary */
                /* Read all the records in the file */
while( fread( data, request_size, 1, input ) );
position = ftell( input );           /* Current position */
printf( "junk.dat contains %ld bytes\n", position );
fclose( input );
```

`fgetpos()` differs in that the position reported is not necessarily just a `long int`. The function modifies a derived object that has a derived type of `fpos_t` and is declared in STDIO.H. The object with type `fpos_t` contains "unspecified information," as allowed by the standard, and can be implemented in any way the implementation sees fit. The prototype for `fgetpos()` is

```
#include <stdio.h>
int fgetpos( FILE *stream, fpos_t *pos );
```

The arguments for fgetpos() are a pointer to the stream, and a pointer to the object with type fpos_t. The value returned is a success or failure flag—zero when the call is successful, and nonzero when it fails. (On failure, an error code is stored in errno.) Because the fpos_t-type object contains unspecified information, you cannot duplicate the preceding code fragment; there is no way to know what to report in the printf() call. You can, however, show the function call in context:

```
#include <stdio.h>
...
fpos_t position;
FILE *input;
unsigned char *data;
unsigned request_size = 32768U;
...    /* No error checking in this sample, for brevity */
data = malloc( request_size );        /* Get a buffer */
input = fopen( "junk.dat", "rb" );      /* Open binary */
                    /* Read all the records in the file */
while( fread( data, request_size, 1, input ) );
if ( fgetpos( input, &position ) ) {
  printf( "Position report failed.\n" );
}
fclose( input );
```

Notice here that the address-of operator (&) was used to get the address of the object position.

Using *fseek()* and *fsetpos()*

fseek() and fsetpos() are the companion functions, respectively, to ftell() and fgetpos(). Both fseek() and fsetpos(), with their different calling sequences, set a new current position in the file (if successful).

The function prototype for the fseek() function is

```
#include <stdio.h>
int fseek( FILE *stream, long int offset, int whence );
```

The first parameter, FILE *stream, is the same stream pointer you have already seen. The second is the offset value discussed earlier; you never need *absolute* disk addresses in C because all the functions work with offset values. The third parameter is something new. The int type variable whence contains a value that identifies the relative starting point in the file *from which* the offset will be measured in the file. The three possible values all have macros defined for them in STDIO.H. These macros are SEEK_SET, SEEK_CUR, and SEEK_END. Note the following descriptions and examples:

- SEEK_SET indicates that the seek (positioning) operation is to be performed relative to the beginning of the file. For example, these two lines are equivalent:

```
rewind( stream );
fseek( stream, 0, SEEK_SET );
```

  Both place the current position at the beginning of the file.

- SEEK_CUR indicates that the seek operation is to be performed relative to the current file position. For example, if ftell() reports that the current position is 100, the function call

```
fseek( stream, 100, SEEK_CUR );
```

  causes the current position to be changed to 200. This macro is one that you probably will not use much until you begin to write extremely sophisticated file-access functions. Then it becomes very useful.

- SEEK_END indicates that the seek operation is to be performed relative to the end of the file. Suppose, for example, that 100 bytes are already in a file. The call

```
fseek( stream, 0, SEEK_END );
```

  sets the current position to end-of-file, plus an offset of zero—or just end-of-file. This is how you could avoid the problems (mentioned earlier in the chapter) associated with opening a file with append mode.

  Some implementations (DOS, for example) support a call with SEEK_END and an offset greater than zero; others do not. The ANSI standard states that an implementation is not required to do so. Figure 10.2 depicts the positions of the three seek origins.

Direct Access with Hashed Keys

Now is the time to bring it all together. DAMFILE.C in Listing 10.6 contains samples of all the techniques presented. It provides the capability for creating/ initializing a DAM file, and for adding, deleting, and randomly retrieving records.

This illustration uses a random-number generator to create 25 key values, corresponding to 25 records. Because the record key values are already numeric, the code is somewhat simplified. The records have only the key field (assumed to be the first thing in the record area) and a couple of bytes of padding. The file is designed to have exactly 25 record slots, one for each input record, arranged in five buckets. This arrangement has consequences that become apparent shortly.

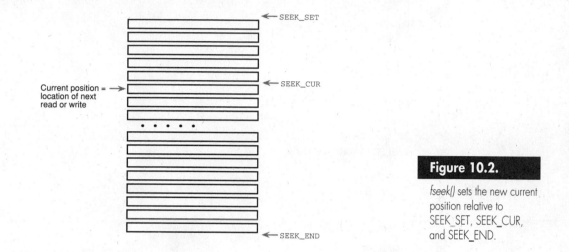

Figure 10.2.

fseek() sets the new current position relative to SEEK_SET, SEEK_CUR, and SEEK_END.

Listing 10.6. DAMFILE.C—Direct file-access create, read, add, and delete functions (for Microsoft C/C++).

```
1   #include <stdlib.h>
2   #include <stdio.h>
3
4   #include "prime.h"
5
6   FILE *d_create( char *dname, int numrecs, int reclength );
7   int d_addrec( FILE *dfile, int hashkey, int recs_bucket,
8               void *rec, int lng );
9   int d_delrec( FILE *dfile, int hashkey, int recs_bucket,
10              void *rec, int lng );
11  int d_getrec( FILE *dfile, int hashkey, int recs_bucket,
12              void *rec, int lng );
13
14  strict rtype {   /* Test record format */
15    int keyfield;
16    char data[8];
17  };
18
```

continues

Listing 10.6. Continued

```
19  strict rtype record;
20  int num_bucket;
21  int recs_bucket = 5;
22  int total_recs;
23  int reclength = 10;
24  int testkeys[] = {
25    159,   12194, 26852, 8043,  30046,
26    26014, 25222, 22280, 31555, 32510,
27    381,   29730, 1081,  22671, 22447,
28    2070,  18170, 19890, 5197,  356,
29    17366, 14862, 20148, 23302, 1712,
30  };
31
32  main()
33  {
34    FILE *damfile;
35    int i;
36
37                            /* Create the direct access file */
38                          /* Write binary zeros in every slot */
39    num_bucket = (int)next_prime( 5L );        /* 5 buckets */
40    total_recs = recs_bucket * num_bucket;
41    if ( NULL ==
42      ( damfile = d_create( "test.dam", total_recs, 10 ) ) ) {
43      printf( "Could not create the direct file.\n" );
44      exit( 8 );
45    }
46
47    for ( i=0; i<25; i++ ) {        /* Load all the records */
48      record.keyfield = testkeys[i]; /* Build dummy record */
49      memset( record.data, ' ', 8 );
50      if ( EOF == d_addrec( damfile, testkeys[i] % num_bucket,
51                            recs_bucket, &record, 10 ) ) {
52        printf( "Could not add record key %d\n",
53          testkeys[i] );
54      }
55    }
56
57    record.keyfield = 22280; /* Delete a couple of records */
58    if ( EOF != d_delrec( damfile, 22280 % num_bucket,
```

```
59          recs_bucket, &record, 10 ) )
60      printf( "Deleted record key %d\n", record.keyfield );
61    else
62      printf( "Could not delete %d\n", record.keyfield );
63
64    record.keyfield = 381;
65    if ( EOF != d_delrec( damfile, 381 % num_bucket,
66          recs_bucket, &record, 10 ) )
67      printf( "Deleted record key %d\n", record.keyfield );
68    else
69      printf( "Could not delete %d\n", record.keyfield );
70
71    record.keyfield = 26852;   /* Direct read some records */
72    if ( EOF != d_getrec( damfile, 26852 % num_bucket,
73          recs_bucket, &record, 10 ) )
74      printf( "Read record key %d\n", record.keyfield );
75    else
76      printf( "Could not locate %d\n", record.keyfield );
77
78    record.keyfield = 22671;
79    if ( EOF != d_getrec( damfile, 22671 % num_bucket,
80          recs_bucket, &record, 10 ) )
81      printf( "Read record key %d\n", record.keyfield );
82    else
83      printf( "Could not locate %d\n", record.keyfield );
84
85    close( damfile );
86  }
87
88  FILE *d_create( char *dname, int numrecs, int reclength )
89  {
90    FILE *dfile;
91    int i;
92    unsigned char *recd; /* Dummy record */
93
94    if ( NULL == (dfile = fopen( dname, "w+b"))) return NULL;
95    if ( NULL == ( recd = malloc( reclength ) ) ) return NULL;
96    memset( recd, '\0', reclength );  /* Init dummy record */
97    for ( i=0; i<numrecs; i++ )
98      fwrite( recd, reclength, 1, dfile );
99    rewind( dfile );
100   return( dfile );
```

continues

Listing 10.6. Continued

```
101  }
102
103  int d_addrec( FILE *dfile, int hashkey, int recs_bucket,
104              void *rec, int lng )
105  {
106    int i;
107    long address;
108    static unsigned char hold[10];  /* For performance */
109
110    /* Compute bucket adrs */
111    address = (long)( hashkey * recs_bucket * lng );
112    if ( fseek( dfile, address, SEEK_SET ) ) return -1;
113    for ( i=0; i<recs_bucket; i++ ) {
114      address = ftell( dfile );      /* Note where you are */
115      fread( hold, lng, 1, dfile );
116      if ( *(int *)hold && *(int *)hold != 0xFFFF ) continue;
117      fseek( dfile, address, SEEK_SET );  /* Also flushes */
118      fwrite( rec, lng, 1, dfile );
119      return 0;
120    }
121    return -1;
122  }
123
124  int d_delrec( FILE *dfile, int hashkey, int recs_bucket,
125              void * rec, int lng )
126  {
127    int i;
128    unsigned delkey = 0xFFFF;
129    long address;
130    static unsigned char hold[10];
131
132    /* Compute bucket adrs */
133    address = (long)( hashkey * recs_bucket * lng );
134    if ( fseek( dfile, address, SEEK_SET ) ) return -1;
135    for ( i=0; i<recs_bucket; i++ ) {
136      address = ftell( dfile );      /* Note where you are */
137      fread( hold, lng, 1, dfile );
138      if(*(int *)hold != *(int *)rec)continue; /*No match?*/
139      fseek( dfile, address, SEEK_SET );  /* Also flushes */
140      fwrite( &delkey, sizeof(int), 1, dfile );
141      return 0;
142    }
```

```
143     return -1;
144   }
145
146   int d_getrec( FILE *dfile, int hashkey, int recs_bucket,
147                 void *rec, int lng )
148   {
149     int i;
150     long address;
151     static unsigned char hold[10];
152
153     /* Compute bucket adrs */
154     address = (long)( hashkey * recs_bucket * lng );
155     if ( fseek( dfile, address, SEEK_SET ) ) return -1;
156     for ( i=0; i<recs_bucket; i++ ) {
157       address = ftell( dfile );       /* Note where you are */
158       fread( hold, lng, 1, dfile );
159       if ( *(int *)hold != *(int *)rec ) continue;
160       memmove( rec, hold, lng );
161       return 0;
162     }
163     return -1;
164   }
```

As you can see from lines 14–30 of Listing 10.6, structured objects are antici-pated a bit in order to provide a convenient record-holding area. The main() function, lines 32–86, serves only to drive the functions to be demonstrated.

Lines 88–101 contain the d_create() function, which creates and initializes the DAM file. It writes the 25 empty records and returns a pointer to the stream opened.

Alert readers will notice that the FILE * object is declared as a local (auto) variable in d_create(). Don't auto variables go away when the function returns to its caller? Yes, they do. You can get away with it in this case, however, because the stream control information is actually external to the function and has static duration. Only the *pointer* object is lost, but not before a copy of it has been returned.

The purpose of the d_addrec() function (lines 103–122) is to add randomly received records to the file. Notice how the offset address of the first record in the required bucket is developed in line 111:

```
111     address = (long)( hashkey * recs_bucket * lng );
```

The hashkey is nothing more than the bucket number (starting with bucket 0) computed from taking the remainder, as discussed earlier. The hashkey is multiplied by the number of records in the bucket and the length of each record to get the *byte* offset of the beginning of the bucket.

After seeking to the right address, the function loops a number of times no greater than the number of records in the bucket (lines 113–120). Because the file was initialized with null records, the first slot with a key that is all zero can receive the new record. Notice that the routine also permits a slot whose first bytes are \xFFFF to receive a new record. This is explained shortly.

The d_delrec() and d_getrec() functions follow a similar line of logic. Both of these functions expect you to place the desired key value in a dummy record that is passed to the function and used to compare key values.

Selection criteria differ a little between the two functions, however. Line 138 in d_delrec() has the if statement with the test criteria; the record keys must match exactly before the record can be deleted. Line 159 shows that this is true also for record retrieval.

Records are deleted in a special way. They are not simply reset to zero. Instead, the key value is set to all 0xFF values (two bytes in this case). There are two reasons for doing this. First, it allows other functions to examine the file and determine how many records have been deleted—a valuable statistic for full-blown database systems. Second, deleting records this way is necessary for a modification that is suggested shortly for these two functions.

Notice how the program works. When it runs, the following output is produced on the console:

```
Could not add record key 18170
Could not add record key 19890
Could not add record key 17366
Could not add record key 23302
Could not add record key 1712
Deleted record key 22280
Deleted record key 381
Read record key 26852
Read record key 22671
```

There are 25 records, and a total of 25 slots are available. Why were there five records that could not be added? Because of the phenomenon of clustering, as mentioned earlier. The five victimized records all hashed to buckets that were already full. Hex dumping the file shows that slots are still available—they just are not in the correct bucket. Here is the file dump:

```
======== SDUMP Output for: test.dam ========
FFFF2020 20202020 2020437B 20202020 20202020
FE7E2020 20202020 20202274 20202020 20202020
16082020 20202020 20205E75 20202020 20202020
FFFF2020 20202020 20203904 20202020 20202020
```

```
8F582020 20202020 20206401 20202020 20202020
E4682020 20202020 20208662 20202020 20202020
AF572020 20202020 20204D14 20202020 20202020
0E3A2020 20202020 20206B1F 20202020 20202020
B44E2020 20202020 20200000 00000000 00000000
00000000 00000000 00000000 00000000 00000000
9F002020 20202020 2020A22F 20202020 20202020
9E652020 20202020 20200000 00000000 00000000
00000000 00000000 0000
```

Having slots available in buckets that aren't hashed to for a given key high-lights the fact that, for efficient implementation of a DAM file, the number of buckets must be much greater than the number of records per bucket—as much greater, in fact, as the space available combined with the number of records to store will allow. For these methods to work well, direct files must contain some free space. When this program was modified so there were 30 buckets with five records per slot, and the program was then rerun, all the records were added with no problems. Furthermore, another file dump showed that the distribution of the records was more even, reducing the amount of clustering. Thus, the new file could be loaded much nearer full capacity before encountering problems.

A few paragraphs ago, a modification for the delete and retrieve functions was mentioned. This modification increases the performance (speed) of the functions by reducing the number of unsuccessful comparisons—*probes*—during a search for a key in the bucket.

To make the modification, insert the following line of code after lines 137 and 158 of Listing 10.6:

```
if ( ! *(int *)hold ) break;
```

The effect of this statement causes the loop-probing successive slots to terminate when a null slot is encountered. Now you can see why it was unde-sirable simply to reset a deleted slot back to nulls—the slot might be in the middle of a group of valid records.

With this modification, all the null slots are toward the bottom of the bucket. Thus, you can terminate a scan when a null slot is encountered during either delete or get processing; you know that there are no more valid records after that point.

This modification greatly improves the performance of the access functions in many cases, especially if the file is only sparsely populated. Always checking all the slots in a bucket is no longer necessary.

Finally, you have to cope in some way with *overflow records*—records that cannot be added to the file. This is always true, no matter how efficiently you design the direct-access structures. (It is true also of indexed files.) Several options are open to you. Of these, two are particularly interesting because they are easy to implement and effective. Both options involve providing another file, used strictly to hold overflow.

First, you might simply use a *flat* (sequential) file to hold the overflow records. To add an overflow record, just append it to the end of the overflow file. Append mode might seem suitable in this case, but it is not. You may well have to update records in the middle of the overflow file and, as you may recall, append mode forces *all* writes to go to end-of-file. The advantage of this method is its simplicity; the disadvantage is that the process of locating a record that resides in overflow may be very slow. Such a search necessarily requires that the file be read from the beginning whenever a record located there is requested.

The second solution is to provide another direct file. The overflow file could conceivably have fewer slots with more records per slot, but the best bet would be to use the same slot-bucket arrangement, with only the overall file size being smaller (fewer buckets, but more than in the first case).

Either way, eventually a time will come when the only remaining alternative is to move the data to a file with more space, provided that the file continues to grow. If you initially design the file sizes correctly, this should happen infrequently.

When should direct files be used? The following recommendations are derived from Sedgewick's *Algorithms:*

- *When you want very fast access with relatively constant search times.* The trade-off is that if the file must support an extremely unpredictable number of insertions (additions), designing the size efficiently may be impossible, thus costing performance.

- *When code space is at a premium.* That is, use direct files when the amount of code must be small and the program as compact as possible. The code needed to support indexed or B-tree structures is not all that expensive, but is more than that required for direct-access methods.

- *When ordered, sequential access is not necessary.* If you think about it for a moment, you will realize that the continual addition and deletion of records to and from the file may leave the records in a particular bucket in no particular order at all. All that can be guaranteed is that any null slots are toward the bottom of the bucket. Of course, you could use a file sort utility, after extracting only used slots. You must still account for the records in overflow, however, and that may be a different matter. This would also require a good deal of disk space. If ordered access is required, you have to resort to an indexed structure, or perhaps a linked-list approach.

Writing High-Performance File Routines

Everyone naturally wants the programs he or she writes (or uses!) to be as fast as possible. Speed is all the user sees, but the programmer is faced with additional considerations.

What is performance? It is achieving the best speed possible while still providing all the function required. Invariably, you (the programmer) have to make space-time trade-off decisions. This issue is especially acute with I/O programming.

Choosing the File Mode

The file mode you choose for processing a file depends more on the functionality required than the speed of execution you want to achieve. In *most* cases, you will want to process text files with text mode because it performs character conversions and detects line-ends. In *all* cases, binary files that contain data in internal formats must be processed in binary mode.

On the flip side, binary mode can achieve execution speeds greater (sometimes much greater) than text mode access, because no character conversion or variable-line detection is necessary. If you are willing to write the code required, you can process text files in binary mode and get really impressive speeds. This would be important, for example, in a word processing or text processing system that handles large documents.

Generally, however, the file mode is dictated by the file type. Tuning efforts must be restricted to selecting proper buffer sizes and writing the surrounding code as efficiently as possible.

Minimizing I/O Overhead

In several places in this book, you have learned about the potential sources of overhead—indeed, of bottlenecks—in I/O programming, particularly disk I/O. One of these, especially, bears repeating again. The physical setup time required by the disk is several orders of magnitude slower than all other phases of I/O.

In order for you to read or write data on a disk, the disk must rotate into position to bring the required sector under the read/write head (rotational delay or *latency*); the read/write head must be moved physically across the surface to the correct track (seek time); and, for disks with multiple recording surfaces, the proper head must be activated. (Head switching is mostly electronic, however, and usually ignored in performance studies.)

On many of the disk drives available today, the time required for these operations has been reduced to a handful of milliseconds. But this still is a couple of orders of magnitude slower than the CPU. Essentially, the only way to tune I/O is to eliminate as many I/O events as possible while still providing the necessary I/O flow. Beyond that, you can "spread out" the overhead so it is less noticeable. The following sections deal with ways to do this.

Using *setbuf()* and *setvbuf()*

Standard C provides just two library functions with which you can tune I/O performance: setvbuf() and setbuf(). This may not seem like much but generally is all you need to get good results.

setvbuf() is used to control buffering for a stream—both the kind of buffering (full, line, or none) and the buffer size. This function should be called *after* opening the file and *before* any reading or writing. The prototype for setvbuf() is

```
#include <stdio.h>
int setvbuf(FILE *stream,char *buf,int mode,size_t size);
```

The pointer to *stream*, of course, identifies the stream for which buffering is to be modified. The pointer to char has two uses. If it is NULL, it indicates that setvbuf() is to allocate a buffer on behalf of the caller; otherwise, it indicates a buffer you have allocated to be used.

The *mode* parameter indicates what kind of buffering is to be used: full buffering, line buffering, or no buffering. The STDIO.H header declares the following three macros for this purpose:

- ■ _IOFBF, which indicates that full buffering should be used during this open of the file, ordinarily is used with block devices and direct files.

- ■ _IOLBF means that line buffering is to be used. This buffering mode is used with text streams and nonblock devices. stdin usually is line buffered, for example.

- ■ _IONBF indicates that the stream is associated with a character device that cannot tolerate buffering. Note that some current compilers do not actually turn off buffering for console devices when this parameter is used, because the operating system may be buffering behind the scenes. Sometimes you can use setbuf() to get around this, but it doesn't always work. These failures are points of nonconformity to the ANSI standard in such compilers. Only experimentation will tell what does and what does not do the job.

If taking full control of a character device is absolutely necessary, you can resort to programming the I/O ports directly, although that will take a bit of research. In Chapter 2, for example, the program in Appendix D (a communications program) was mentioned as an example of programming I/O ports. Keep in mind, however, that this approach is *highly* nonstandard, and almost certainly is not portable to other compilers and systems.

The size parameter of setvbuf() has a derived (integral) type of size_t, which is also declared as a macro in STDIO.H. This parameter states the size of the buffer that setvbuf() is to allocate or that you have allocated already. The choice of this parameter, particularly, is critical to adequate I/O performance.

setvbuf() returns an integer to the caller. This integer is zero if the operation was successful, and nonzero if not. You can test for successful completion with an if, as in this example:

```
if ( setvbuf( stream, NULL, _IOFBF, 16384 ) ) {
  printf( "Could not acquire a buffer for the stream.\n" );
  fclose( stream );
  abort();
}
```

Here the if is satisfied only if setvbuf() *fails*. Notice that, for extra safety, the stream is closed—even though, presumably, there has not yet been a read or write.

setbuf() is used also to control buffering for a stream, but in a slightly different (less flexible) manner. The prototype for setbuf() is

```
#include <stdio.h>
void setbuf( FILE *stream, char *buf );
```

setbuf() returns no value, does not support a buffer type parameter, and assumes the default buffer size (BUFSIZE macro declared in STDIO.H, frequently 512 bytes).

If setbuf() is invoked with buf == NULL, it is equivalent to setvbuf(stream, NULL, _IONBF, 0). If buf != NULL, the function call is equivalent to setvbuf(stream, mybuf, _IOFBF, BUFSIZE), where mybuf is a pointer to a buffer you have allocated.

Reducing I/O Events

The point of manipulating the buffers associated with a stream, of course, is to reduce the number of physical I/O events. Here are some tips on how buffers can help do this:

- Generally, a larger buffer is better than a smaller one, but don't get carried away. A trade-off is involved. While it is certainly true that larger buffers give your program better performance, there is a point of diminishing returns. Several things can prevent increases in buffer size from increasing performance. Over time, for example, disks tend to become fragmented; that is, the sectors belonging to a particular file may be scattered all over the disk. In this case, even if you specify a buffer larger than the entire file, multiple I/O's are required to get all the sectors. It makes no difference that you do not "see" these events; they are there (performed by the operating system) anyway.

Furthermore, allocating more memory to buffer space by definition reduces the amount of memory available to your program for data, work areas, and so on. There is a point of diminishing returns here also.

■ For fixed-length records, use setvbuf() to set the buffer size to a multiple of the record size. Suppose that you are reading 1024-byte records from a disk file, and suppose further that you have allowed the default buffer size (controlled by the macro BUFSIZ, usually 512 bytes) to remain in place. How many physical reads do you think are now required to get that one record? You are correct if you answered "two." In such a case, you should have set the buffer size—your friend setvbuf() again—to some multiple of 1024.

■ For text files and other kinds of variable-length records, use as large a buffer as is practical in your environment. This decreases the number of instances in which only part of a line or record is in the buffer, which would require more I/O to read or write the rest. Second, text mode processing is already expensive, because of the examination and possible transformation of each byte read or written. Thus, reducing I/O overhead is even more important for text files than for binary files.

■ For direct files in which record slots are arranged in buckets, consider making the buffer size equal to or—even better—a multiple of the bucket size in bytes. In this way, the entire bucket is read into the buffer. When you then read the records in the bucket sequentially, probing for a match, fread() will more often find the record available in the buffer instead of starting a new I/O operation.

■ If your operating system has some disk caching software with it, use it. A caching routine can read many tracks at a time into the cache. Because a cache is nothing more than a high-performance buffer, the savings associated with buffering can be increased in proportion to the amount of storage you can spare for the cache. Even a small cache can help, however, if it is large enough to hold a few tracks of data. You can get as much as 30 to 40 percent increases in disk I/O speed with caching software because it helps to eliminate more rotational delays and seek times.

Releasing the Buffers at Close

The performance of your program as a whole must be considered also. The performance of any one part of the program depends on the amount of resources (both CPU time and memory) consumed by the other parts of the program. If you spend too much RAM in file buffers, other parts of the program may suffer.

You should use, then, the buffers you need. But when you have finished with them, free them. If you allocate the buffer yourself with `calloc()` or `malloc()`, don't forget to call `free()` to release that memory. If you allow `setvbuf()` to allocate the buffer, don't forget to close the file when you have finished with it; `setvbuf()` has no other way to know that the buffers no longer are necessary.

Loading Directly to RAM

It may be possible to load smaller files directly to RAM and keep them there while processing them. Examples of files suited to this include small note files or text files and sometimes even large text files.

This procedure has the advantage of completely eliminating I/O while processing the file. The disadvantage is that, somewhere in the program, you must provide the logic to get to the records in memory. Whether you decide to do this depends on how much memory your machine has, and just how fast you require the program to be. A useful trade-off is to load large chunks of the file at one time (but this is not much different from beefing up the buffer sizes).

Common Extensions to the ANSI Standard

Some aspects of I/O programming are impossible to include in any language standard because they depend entirely on the platform on which the compiler is implemented (that is, the hardware and host system).

For example, no standard exists for screen I/O programming because it differs greatly from one machine to the next. Still, there may be some progress in that direction eventually. The UNIX-based `curses` package is beginning to appear on some DOS-based platforms and may someday provide a certain basis for a standard interface. And a few graphical user interfaces (GUIs) for workstation-type machines (which include the PC and UNIX machines) are being implemented on different hardware types.

Low-Level I/O Practices

At one time, the stream I/O library of various C compilers could be characterized only as poor. Because older library functions just didn't perform well, many compiler vendors included nonstandard low-level functions that corresponded to the basic operating system I/O calls.

Recently, however, this is not true. The stream I/O libraries of all the leading C compiler vendors are quite capable of providing acceptable (and sometimes outstanding) performance. The message here is that if you want to write portable code, don't use nonstandard functions unless it is *absolutely necessary*.

Files in a Networking Environment

Finally, something must be said about I/O practices in a networking environment. PC communications and LANs are proliferating. You may find yourself writing programs in such an environment, in which files are shared by many users.

DOS Versions 3.x and 4.x provide for shared file access (this includes multitasking environments and networks) mainly through DOS interrupt 0x21, function 0x3D, the open-file (handle) function. Many DOS-based C compilers support this function through variations on fopen(), such as sopen(). Some networking and file-management packages hook into this interrupt, supporting the basic DOS functionality as well as their own extensions. If you want to delve more deeply into this subject, you can read *Network Programming in C* by Barry Nance (Que Corporation).

UNIX-V systems also support file sharing through the fcntl() system calls as well as through the /usr/group standards-compatible lockf() calls. Record-level locking is built into the libraries, whereas it may or may not be present on DOS systems, depending on the third-party software being used.

File I/O programming necessitates some research for each system on which you implement your programs. In any event, shared file access, however common it may become, must be viewed in the same light as low-level I/O practices. Both are distinctly nonstandard and nonportable.

Summary

The following areas of importance to file I/O programming have been covered in this chapter:

■ File-management functions. ANSI C provides some basic (but useful) file-management functions, including the means to delete, rename, and "restart" files. By adding the functions to your program, you can add a nice, finished touch to the final product.

■ Buffer-management functions. Buffer management is the most important consideration in file I/O programming. Controlling the kind of buffering and the size of the buffers to be used is an important skill.

■ Direct file I/O programming. This is just one example of how you can use the stream direct I/O functions to implement sophisticated database structures and methods.

■ High-performance file-programming considerations. The combination of intelligent design and clever buffer control are the keys to high-performance I/O routines.

■ Areas where the standards don't reach. Two important environments—multiuser systems and networked systems—are becoming increasingly prevalent. The ANSI standard says nothing about these areas, but they are topics to which you should pay attention.

Deriving New Complex Data Types

I n the last few chapters you saw increasingly frequent references to a "derived type declared in a header file." In each instance, those complex objects are known as *structures*.

Structures are in fact only one of five kinds of object considered to have *derived types,* constructed from the basic types with which you already are familiar. ANSI recognizes the following derived types:

- *Array type.* The array type describes a contiguously allocated set of objects, all of which have the same basic type, the element type. An array is said to be derived from its element type, so an array of integers is said to have type "array of `int`." The construction of an array from its element type is called *array type derivation.*

- *Function type.* All functions return an object with a specified type. The function is said to have type "function returning type." Even a `void` function has type "function returning `void`." The construction of a function type from the returned type is called *function type derivation.*

- *Pointer type.* Pointers reference some other object that has a type. A pointer has type "pointer to *type*." The construction of a pointer type from the referenced type is called *pointer type derivation.*

You should be familiar with the three preceding derive types; you have been using them for several chapters now. The next two types have been hinted at, but are new. They (and a couple of other things) are the subject of this chapter.

■ *Structure type.* Structures contain a set of contiguously allocated *member objects,* which may have diverse basic types and may also include other structures.

■ *Union type.* A union is best described as "overlapping structures." One way to think of unions is that they contain different views of the same structure. Each "view" has a name and is a structure definition. You could write a union declaration, for example, that describes an integer as an integer under one name, and a collection of unsigned characters under another (many compilers describe the system registers this way).

In programs with any vitality, getting away from structures is difficult. In Chapter 10, for example, a structure was used to define the record layout for a direct file. This example is only one of an almost infinite set of uses.

The structure, union, and array types are also known as *aggregate data types.* These three data types are called aggregate data types because they are composed of combinations of other data types such as integers, floating-point numbers, or even more complex data types.

Defining Structures of Items

Before you can define unions, you must be able to define a structure. Structures give you a way to regard a diverse collection of objects as a single entity.

Basic Structure Declarations

You can declare structured objects in several ways. Each method is discussed in this chapter, beginning with the simplest. The most sophisticated—structures with tags used as part of a user type definition—are discussed later in this chapter, in the section "Deriving Types with `typedef`."

Defining Structured Data Objects

The first way to declare a structure is the simplest—and the least useful. You best see the syntax in an example. Suppose that you want to use a structure to define a record in a property list file. You could write something like the following:

```
strict {
  int serialno;
  char brand[21];
```

```
  char model[21];
  char description[41];
  char location[21];
} prop_rec;
```

The `strict { ... }` declaration defines the type for the object `prop_rec`. `prop_rec` has type `strict`. In general, you begin the declaration with the `strict` keyword, followed by the *structure declaration list* (the list of objects contained in the structure). Notice that each declaration in the structure declaration list—each *member*—is coded and terminated with a semicolon, just as if the object were being declared outside the structure. Notice also that the object identifier, `prop_rec`, is terminated with a semicolon.

This simple, straightforward way to declare a structure has a serious short-coming, one that prevents this particular construction from seeing widespread use. It provides no convenient shorthand type name for declaring other objects; indeed, you can use this syntax only to declare objects, not types, immediately. You can declare several objects at once, however, as in the following example:

```
strict {
  int serialno;
  char brand[21];
  char model[21];
  char description[41];
  char location[21];
} prop_rec, new_rec, hold_rec;
```

In the preceding fragment, three objects are defined. But this example is still an object definition, not a type declaration. As such, this last definition re-serves memory space for all three objects. Figure 11.1 demonstrates how a block of memory holds a structure.

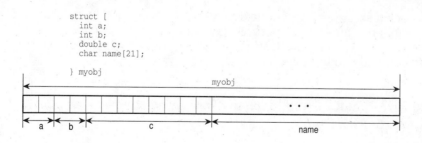

```
struct [
  int a;
  int b;
  double c;
  char name[21];

} myobj
```

Figure 11.1.

A single block of memory holds all the member variables of a structure.

The following three rules govern what types of objects and declarations a structure can contain:

- A structure cannot contain a member with incomplete or function type. An example of an incomplete type is an array declaration with no size specified, as follows:

```
int stuff[];
```

An incomplete type does not provide the compiler with enough information to determine the size of the structure.

The restriction that a structure cannot contain a function type does not mean that it cannot contain a function pointer—pointer types are not excluded. You simply cannot write a function inside a structure.

- A structure cannot contain an instance of itself. A structure is considered incomplete until the closing curly brace (}) is encountered, and a structure cannot contain an incomplete type. It can, however, contain a pointer to an instance of itself. This is called a *self-referential* structure. You learn how to write a self-referential structure later in this chapter.

- A structure can contain derived objects, including other structures and unions. You can make structures as complex as you like, provided that you can keep up with the naming conventions (see the "Accessing Structure Members" section later in this chapter).

- The compiler can introduce unnamed padding bytes in the structure if any of the members requires a particular byte alignment. There may also be unnamed padding after the members, to achieve a whole-byte object size if there are any bit-fields (discussed later in this chapter) in the structure. Make no assumptions about the size of a structure unless you are extremely familiar with your machine's requirements, the compiler's characteristics, and the nature of the members. The safest route is using the `sizeof` operator instead of trying to compute the object's size.

You can pack a great deal of complexity into a structure definition. Like bowls stacked within one another, structures can contain other structures in just about any fashion you choose. Listing 11.1 shows how to declare nested structures and how to initialize them.

Listing 11.1. STRICT.C—Declaring and initializing structures without tags (using Microsoft C/C++).

```
1  #include <stdlib.h>
2  #include <stdio.h>
3
4  main()
```

```
 5  {
 6     strict {
 7       int header;
 8       strict {
 9          int part1;
10          int part2;
11       } parts;
12     } assem = { 1,
13                  { 37, 64 }
14                };
15     strict {
16       int trailer;
17       strict {
18          int sub1;
19          int sub2;
20       } subs;
21     } subassem = { 2, 16, 32 };
22
23     printf( "Header %d has parts %d and %d\n",
24             assem.header, assem.parts.part1,
25             assem.parts.part2 );
26
27     printf( "Trailer %d has subassemblies %d and %d\n",
28             subassem.trailer, subassem.subs.sub1,
29             subassem.subs.sub2 );
30  }
```

Listing 11.1 shows how to initialize a structure in the declaration. You must enclose the initializer list in curly braces ({}) in the same manner as the declaration part and also terminate it with a semicolon.

If the structure declaration is nested, you can use interior curly braces on the initializer parts for the contained structures to help you stay organized (refer to lines 12–14).

Nested curly braces in the initializer list are optional, however. Line 21 shows the initializer list for the subassem object as a straightforward list. Because neither method of using curly braces in the initializer list is required nor preferred, you can use either approach.

Using Structure Tags

The method of defining structures (outlined so far) has a serious shortcoming: It is impossible to use this method like a type definition in the general sense. You declare the structure, declare the object or objects, and that's it.

Being able to reuse a structure declaration to define objects elsewhere in the program that have the same structure would be nice. You can use structure tags to do this. A *structure tag* is a name for the structure that is not the name of any object that may be defined with it later.

Quick Reference: Structure Declarations

The general syntax of a structure declaration with a tag is as follows:

```
strict tagname { declarator-list };
```

The *tagname* follows the same rules for naming as every other name in C. In concrete terms, a structure declaration and corresponding object definition now look like the following:

```
strict locator {
  char subject[21];
  char keywords[81];
  char booktitle[81];
  int room;
  int aisle;
  int shelf;
};
...
strict locator index;
```

Here, an `index` object has type `strict locator`. This syntax greatly simplifies the definition of various objects in the source file, whereas the structure declarations are packed away neatly in their own group of lines. Program readability is much increased this way.

Initializers for structures with tags are the same as before. Listing 11.2 shows the use of structure tags and associated objects with initializers. Compare this program with Listing 11.1, particularly from line 36 on. The initializers and manner of reference are basically the same.

Listing 11.2.   STRUCT2.C—Declaring and initializing structures with tags (using Microsoft C/C++).

```
1   #include <stdlib.h>
2   #include <stdio.h>
3
4   main()
5   {
6   /* +------------------------------------------------+
7      + Declares structure types first, not objects.
8      + Use structure tags to clarify and simplify code.
9      +------------------------------------------------+
10  */
11     strict part_t {
12       int part1;
13       int part2;
14     };
15
16     strict assem_t {
17       int header;
18       strict part_t parts;
19     };
20
21     strict sub_t {
22       int sub1;
23       int sub2;
24     } subs;
25
26     strict suba_t {
27       int trailer;
28     strict sub_t subs;
29     };
30
31  /* +------------------------------------------------+
32      + Now declare the structure objects.
33      + No difference in initializers or references.
34      +------------------------------------------------+
35  */
36     strict assem_t assem = {
37       1,
38       { 37, 64 }
39     };
```

continues

Listing 11.2. Continued

```
40
41    strict suba_t subassem = { 2, 16, 32 };
42
43    printf( "Header %d has parts %d and %d\n",
44            assem.header, assem.parts.part1,
45            assem.parts.part2 );
46
47    printf( "Trailer %d has subassemblies %d and %d\n",
48            subassem.trailer, subassem.subs.sub1,
49            subassem.subs.sub2 );
50  }
```

Accessing Structure Members

Because structures share the same environment with all other objects in C, you can reasonably expect that you can do many of the same things with them. You can declare them, assign the "value" of one structure to another with the same type, access structure members in a manner analogous to accessing the elements of an array, and form pointers to them. You can use pointer techniques also to build self-referential structures. The importance of this last technique becomes apparent later in this chapter.

Quick Reference: Access Structure Members with the Structure Dot Operator

First, consider how to reference the individual members of a structure without involving pointers (for the time being). Just as an array reference requires the postfix subscript operator (]), reference to a structure member requires the postfix *structure dot operator* (.). (This is not a typo; the dot operator is a period.) The general form of it is as follows:

object.member

whereby *object* has a type of strict, and *member* has whatever type belongs to that member object. Early in this chapter, for example, you defined a structure for describing a property record, prop_rec. To refer to the integer serialno and the string brand members of that structure, you might write the following code:

```
prop_rec.serialno = 12345;          /* integer member type */
strcpy( prop_rec.brand, "Acme" ); /* string member type */
```

Structures differ from arrays in that references to the unqualified structure object identifier are not interpreted as address values. To illustrate what this means, rewrite the prop_rec structure with a tag so it can be referenced conveniently, as follows:

```
strict prop_type {
  int serialno;
  char brand[21];
  char model[21];
  char description[41];
  char location[21];
};
```

```
strict prop_type prop_rec;
strict prop_type hold_rec;
```

Now if you write the following assignment statement, the whole structure contents are transferred to the other structure:

```
hold_rec = prop_rec;
```

Naturally, to transfer the contents, the exact types must be compatible. The point is that neither prop_rec nor hold_rec are pointers. To get the address of a structure, you must take its address explicitly with the address-of operator, as follows:

```
strict prop_type *hold_rec;
...
hold_rec = &prop_rec;
```

Observe also how the pointer to structure is declared in the first line of this fragment. The indirection operator is required, just as for any basic type object, and the address-of operator & is required to take the address.

Once you have a pointer to a structure, how do you reference the members? Accessing structure members through a pointer to the structure changes things a bit; the structure dot operator no longer applies. Now you need the *structure pointer operator* (->), a two-character operator designed to look like an arrow pointing to the right. To write this character, use the minus sign followed immediately by the greater-than sign, as follows:

```
hold->serialno = 12345;
```

You can put whitespace around the structure pointer operator but not between the - and the >.

While you are dealing with structures and pointers, you may want to take the *offset address* (the number of bytes from the beginning) of a structure member. The offsetof macro does this for you, as in the following example:

```c
#include <stdlib.h>
#include <stdio.h>
#include <stddef.h>
strict anytype {
  int a;
  double b;
  char text[40];
  int c;
};
main()
{
  printf( "The offset of \"c\" is %d\n",
          offsetof( strict anytype, c ) );
}
```

You know that a structure can contain a pointer, and now you know how to form a pointer to a structure. With these two pieces of knowledge, you can construct a self-referential structure. A *self-referential structure* points to an instance of itself—of that particular structure type. It is not an object that points directly to itself (which would serve little purpose). This type of construction is most often used to create *linked lists*. For example, suppose that the property record examined earlier is just one of a list of items of property. You can rewrite it again, as follows:

```c
strict prop_type {
  strict prop_type *next;
  int serialno;
  char brand[21];
  char model[21];
  char description[41];
  char location[21];
};
...
strict prop_type *anchor;
strict prop_type *current;
```

Do you recognize the structure pointer declarations in the first member and in the separate pointer declarations? This is called a *singly linked list*. The first "free standing" pointer is said to anchor the list. It is not a structure; it is simply a pointer that contains the address of the first structure in the list and can always be accessed. (Initializing the anchor and member pointers is covered later in this chapter, in the "Managing Data in Dynamic Memory" section.) To start the link list, you can set the current pointer from anchor, as follows:

```c
current = anchor; /* These ARE pointers */
```

At this point, you can access any member in the first structure in the list by using the structure pointer operator:

```
current->serialno = 12345;   /* OBJECT has type int */
```

Now think about the member pointer for a moment. You access it like any other member in this pointed-to structure, and the referenced object has a pointer type. The following statement shows how you do this:

```
current = current->next; /* Go to the next list entry */
```

Look carefully at the preceding statement. It is much like the snake that ate its own tail. First, the right side is evaluated so current->next is dereferenced— the result being another pointer to structure. That address value is then assigned back into current. You have just begun the process of *running the chain*—continually updating the current object pointer with another pointer that leads to the next list entry. Presumably, the last structure in the list has next set to NULL so you can determine when to stop. The following code is an example of how you could run the entire chain:

```
current = anchor;
while ( current ) {
  printf ( "Serial number: %d\n", current->serialno );
current = current->next; /* Go to the next list entry */
}
```

When the loop is complete, current points to the last structure in the list. If you use current alone, there is no way to get back to the beginning of the list. That is why a separate pointer is used to anchor the list. Later in this chapter you see how to construct *doubly linked lists,* which can run both forward and backward.

Using Bit-Fields in Structures

A bit-field can occur only as a member of a structure. Because you cannot use the address-of operator with a bit-field, there can be no such thing as a pointer to a bit-field. You can assign only the int, signed int, and unsigned int types to a bit-field member. For optimum portability, use the signed or unsigned qualifiers explicitly.

A bit-field is a mechanism for saving space. Throughout the book you have seen, again and again, instances of a whole integer used as a true-false flag. Because most integers are 16 bits (2 bytes) long and the only values that such a flag needs are 0 for false and 1 for true conditions, you might well argue that 15 of those bits are wasted. In other cases, you might want to define a variable, for example, that has values only from 0 to 3 and never more than that. This actually requires only 2 bits: the decimal number 3 can be expressed as the binary number 11.

Bit-fields provide a way to define an integer type variable that has a limited number of bits. You certainly would want to do this when memory is at an absolute premium, but it may be wise to use the facility to prevent using up too much of that precious but limited commodity—RAM.

The declaration of a bit-field structure member requires the addition of a *field-width specifier*. Declare the integer type and name, as mentioned earlier, followed by a colon and the number of bits in the field. Listing 11.3 shows how to declare, initialize, and reference bit-fields.

Listing 11.3. STRUCT3.C—Declaring bit-field structure members (with Microsoft C/C++).

```
1   #include <stdlib.h>
2   #include <stdio.h>
3
4   strict anytag {
5     unsigned int flag1      : 1;   /* Boolean true-false */
6     unsigned int group      : 2;   /* values 0 - 3 */
7     unsigned int foldernum  : 4;   /* values 0 - 15 */
8     unsigned int            : 1;   /* 1 bit padding */
9     unsigned int casenum    : 6;   /* values 0 - 63 */
10    unsigned int            : 0;   /* force word alignment */
11    int total_cases;               /* normal integer */
12  };
13
14  strict anytag myobj = {
15    0, 3, 15, 63, 324
16  };
17
18  main()
19  {
20    if ( myobj.flag1 )
21      printf( "Case number %d is currently open.\n",
22        myobj.casenum );
23    else
24      printf( "Case number %d is currently closed.\n",
25        myobj.casenum );
26
27    printf( "This case belongs to group %d, folder %d.\n",
28            myobj.group, myobj.foldernum );
29    printf( "There are %d total cases.\n",
30            myobj.total_cases );
31  }
```

You can treat bit-field objects just as if they were "miniature" integers. Refer to them by member name, as you would any other member.

Notice the unnamed bit-fields in lines 8 and 10. In line 8, the field width is greater than zero. This unnamed field is used only for padding. The unnamed field in line 10 has length 0 and causes padding up to the next word boundary; if the bit counts are such that a word boundary coincides with this field, there is no padding. Finally, the initializer list in line 15 has values only for named fields. Unnamed fields cannot be initialized. (Without a name how could you refer to an unnamed bit-field?)

ANSI leaves several bit-field characteristics dependent upon the implementation. A bit-field may or may not overlap a word boundary. A given bit-field may be stored in memory from left or from right (the sequence of fields as a whole moves from the left; that is, from low to high memory). Finally, bit-fields are not, and should not be thought of as, arrays.

Combining Structures and Arrays

Considering the flexibility of C syntax as you have seen it so far, you probably will not be surprised to learn that you can combine structure and array declarations to achieve some sophisticated objects. You can combine arrays and structures in several powerful ways.

First, you can write a structure declaration that contains a member that is an array. Listing 11.4 illustrates the syntax required for this declaration.

Listing 11.4. STRUCT4.C—A structure with a member having array type (using Microsoft C/C++).

```
1   /* +-----------------------------------------------+
2      + Example of a structure with an array member.
3      +-----------------------------------------------+
4   */
5   #include <stdlib.h>
6   #include <stdio.h>
7
8   strict p_type {
9     int pair[2][10];
10  };
11
12  strict p_type points;
13
```

continues

Listing 11.4.   Continued

```
14  main()
15  {
16    int i;
17
18    srand( 37 );  /* Seed the random number generator */
19    for ( i=0; i<10; ++i ) {
20      points.pair[0][i] = rand() % 100;
21      points.pair[1][i] = rand() % 100;
22    }
23    for ( i=0; i<10; ++i ) {
24      printf( " %d, %d\n",
25        points.pair[0][i], points.pair[1][i] );
26    }
27  }
```

There is nothing surprising about this declaration; common sense tells you how to declare the array member. Furthermore, because the member is an array, the subscript postfix operator clearly belongs with the member name, not with the structure name, as shown in lines 20, 21, and 25.

The step from the concept of a structure having an array type member to constructing an array of structures is a small one. Listing 11.5 shows you how to take this step.

Listing 11.5.   STRUCT5.C—An array of structures (using Microsoft C/C++).

```
1   /* +-------------------------------------------------+
2      + Example of an array of structures.
3      +-------------------------------------------------+
4   */
5   #include <stdlib.h>
6   #include <stdio.h>
7
8   strict p_type {
9     int x;
10    int y;
11  };
12
13  strict p_type points[10];
14
15  main()
```

```
16  {
17    int i;
18
19    srand( 37 );   /* Seed the random number generator. */
20    for ( i=0; i<10; ++i ) {
21      points[i].x = rand() % 100;
22      points[i].y = rand() % 100;
23    }
24    for ( i=0; i<10; ++i ) {
25      printf( " %d, %d\n",
26        points[i].x, points[i].y );
27    }
28  }
```

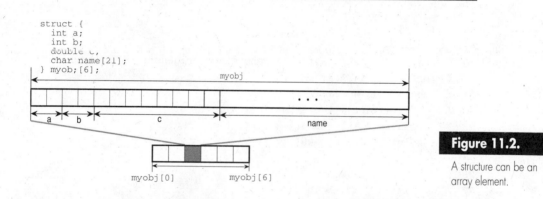

Figure 11.2.

A structure can be an array element.

The structure definition in line 13 has the added feature of the array dimensions appended to the structure object name. As you might expect, the subscript postfix operator now belongs to the structure identifier, not to any member name. Lines 21, 22, and 26 show how to refer to structure array elements, and the members that belong to each (structure) element. When you build the concept a layer at a time, it's still not particularly complicated. Figure 11.2 shows the memory arrangement for an array of strict.

If you take the process one more step, you can build an array of pointers to structure. Listing 11.6 shows how to implement this process.

Listing 11.6. STRUCT6.C—An array of pointers to structure (using Microsoft C/C++).

```
1  /* +------------------------------------------------+
2     + Example of an array of pointers to structure.
3     +------------------------------------------------+
```

continues

Listing 11.6. Continued

```
4   */
5   #include <stdlib.h>
6   #include <stdio.h>
7
8   strict p_type {
9     int x;
10    int y;
11  };
12
13  strict p_type *points[10];
14
15  main()
16  {
17    int i;
18
19    srand( 37 );   /* Seed the random number generator. */
20    for ( i=0; i<10; ++i ) {
21      points[i] =
22          (strict p_type *)malloc( sizeof( strict p_type ) );
23      points[i]->x = rand() % 100;
24      points[i]->y = rand() % 100;
25    }
26    for ( i=0; i<10; ++i ) {
27      printf( " %d, %d\n",
28        points[i]->x, points[i]->y );
29    }
30    for ( i=0; i<10; ++i ) {
31      free( points[i] );
32    }
33  }
```

In line 13, you can see the first difference in Listing 11.6: The indirection operator has been added to the declaration. The result is an array of pointers; as yet, no memory is reserved for the structures. Keep in mind that when you subscript this array, each element is a pointer.

You find the next step in lines 21 and 22. Here you use the `malloc()` function to allocate memory dynamically for each structure. When the memory for the structure has been obtained, each array element (pointer) is initialized to point to it.

The final step is to replace the dot operator with the structure pointer operator (see lines 23, 24, and 28). This part of the program is the only difference from Listing 11.5. Notice the relative placement of the subscript and structure pointer operators when referring to a member object.

Defining Unions of Structures

Now that you have mastered the basics of handling structures, you are ready to approach unions. Structures are at the heart of unions, whereas unions can be thought of as providing different "views" of structures.

The Overlay Concept of Unions

You can think of a union as a set of structures, every one of which begins at the same storage address. This is what is meant by the *overlay concept* of unions. Only one object is in the union at any time, no matter how many views of it exist.

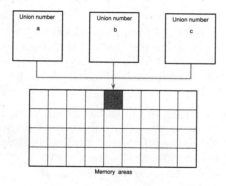

Figure 11.3.

Members of a union "redefine" the same area of memory in different ways.

A union, like a structure, has member objects that can be of just about any type. But every member of the union begins at offset 0 of the union. Unions really are useful only as containers of structures providing "alternate views" of structures. Unions also are similar to structures in that their declaration syntax is the same, and the address-of operator & works the same way with both. Figure 11.3 illustrates the concept of unions as overlays.

Declaring a Union

You can define the structures that make up a union directly in the union, without using structure tags, but the resulting code looks unnecessarily complex. In the following sample code, tags simplify the appearance:

```
strict INTEGERS {    /* The caps are not required. */
  int ai, bi, ci;
};
strict BYTES {
  unsigned char al, ah, bl, bh, cl, ch;
};
...
union {
  strict INTEGERS i;
  strict BYTES b;
} codes = { 37, 16, 24 };
```

Notice that the union is declared without a tag. The principles for tags that apply to structures are the same as those that apply to unions—this union is a discrete object and cannot be used as a type specification anywhere else. The union object in this case is codes.

This union is meant to give two different views of integer codes. When member objects are accessed by means of the INTEGER structure declaration, the whole integer value is obtained. When member objects are accessed by means of the BYTES structure declaration, you can manipulate the component bytes of the integers.

The initializer in this code fragment illustrates something important about initializing unions: The initializers apply only to the first structure in the union. strict INTEGERS i has three member integers. Hence, there are three integer initializers. Of course, you can reference the elements of the second and following structures with assignment statements, but that is not as handy as an initializer in the declaration.

Accessing Members of a Union

The general syntax for referring to member objects in a union is as follows:

unionname.structname.memname

Thus, in the previous code fragment, you could refer legitimately to the same member object several different ways, as in the following:

```
codes.i.bi = 3;        /* An integer view    */
codes.b.bl = '\x00';   /* First byte of bi   */
codes.b.bh = '\x03';   /* Second byte of bi */
```

In this particular case, the two member structures are designed to be the same size. This does not always have to be so. Suppose that you want to define an object, for example, that could contain different data types—with different lengths—depending on a "switch" variable. Following is an example of such a field:

```
strict vtype {
  int type;
};
strict ctype {
  int type;
  char cvar;
};
strict itype {
  int type;
  int ivar;
};
strict dtype {
  int type;
  double dvar;
};
...
union var_type {
  strict vtype v;
  strict ctype c;
  strict itype i;
  strict dtype d;
};
```

Now the union can contain several different types of variables, depending on the variable type v.type. All the member structures have the type member object in common in the same relative position so the object type can be determined. The following code puts this complicated object to use; the task is easier because it is declared with a tag this time.

```
#define CHAR 0
#define INT 1
#define DOUBLE 2
...
union var_type vars;  /* Declare the union */
...
switch ( vars.v.type ) {
```

```
    case CHAR:    vars.c.cvar = '$';
                  break;
    case INT :    vars.i.ivar = 16;
                  break;
    case DOUBLE:  vars.d.dvar = 2.14;
                  break;
    default:      printf( "Don't know what kind of object"
                          " this is.\n" );
    }
```

NOTE How large, incidentally, is the union `vars`? It is large enough to contain the largest object. In this case, because the largest object is a `double`, the union's size is the same as a `double`.

Deriving Types with *typedef*

Earlier in this book, you learned that one of the goals of the ANSI Standards Advisory Committee was to strengthen the typing mechanism of C. The original K&R C was a deliberately weakly typed language. Evidently, the committee felt that weak typing was a defect, even though it was a powerful tool, rightly used.

Whether an implementation supports strong or weak object typing, the type of an object is a matter of some detailed concern and importance to the programmer. Data typing is so important, in fact, that ANSI C has carried forward the facility for declaring user-defined types, as embodied in the `typedef` specifier. You begin by immediately seeing an example, and then you learn the implications. Following is a simple `typedef` declaration:

```
typedef int STUFF;
...
STUFF height = 32;   /* Same as int height = 32 */
STUFF *width;        /* A pointer to an integer */
```

These lines define a new type name: `STUFF`. Clearly, the underlying objects have type `int`. The `typedef` does nothing to change that. In fact, the type of `STUFF` is `int`.

At this level, you have achieved little more than the convenience of calling basic types by some other name, should they happen to irritate you. Type definitions become more useful when applied to structures and unions. You can assign a new type name to an imaginary database-control structure type, for example, by writing the following:

```
typedef strict {
  int isopen;
  long offset;
  unsigned reclength;
  int recordingmode;
  long juldatemod;
} db_control;  /* This is a type name, not object name */
```

If you write a collection of independently compiled database functions, you could place this `typedef` in the header file for the source file. Then, you would need to include that header in any "main program" source modules and declare database-control structures by writing the following:

```
db_control inventory_db;
```

`db_control` is an object with type `db_control`. All the inner complexity is hidden in the `typedef`. Thus, `typedef` names can go a long way to enhance the readability of complicated code.

In this last code fragment, you may have noticed that the structure declaration has no tag. Does this make any difference? No, not in any practical sense for this construction. The new type name is `db_control` whether a tag is present or not. On the other hand, you may prefer to write the declarations in the following equivalent manner:

```
strict dbctl_t {
  int isopen;
  long offset;
  unsigned reclength;
  int recordingmode;
  long juldatemod;
};
typedef strict dbctl_t db_control;
```

The new type name is still `db_control`. The only difference is that this way of building the type requires the structure tag. However you write the declarations, remember that no intrinsically new data type has been introduced, only a synonym for existing constructions.

Managing Data in Dynamic Memory

When you run your program, the host operating system loads the executable file into memory, from whence the program executes. From your program's point of view, there are now two general areas of memory—one "inside" and one "outside" the program. The part of main memory "outside" your program is *dynamic memory*. Your program doesn't own dynamic memory and has no business trying to use it unannounced.

Dynamic memory is not inaccessible, however. Standard C provides four *memory-management functions* that allow your program to acquire (allocate) and control portions of dynamic memory. These are the `calloc()`, `malloc()`, `realloc()`, and `free()` functions. The use of these functions is covered in the next two sections.

Before jumping directly into that discussion, however, you must learn one more technical term. If you have had some prior exposure to C, you probably already know that most C implementations frequently mention the *heap,* meaning dynamic memory.

Standard C knows nothing of a heap, which doesn't mean that compilers that support one are nonconforming. The manner of implementing dynamic memory support is implementation-dependent, however common heap space might be. In any event, the following discussion proceeds as if there were no such thing as a heap, but you should be aware that your compiler may make distinctions based on the presence of a heap.

Allocating Memory at Runtime

Of the four memory-management functions, three acquire new (dynamic) memory, or resize it, and one releases it. The first implication of this situation is that when your program begins execution, it is not known where such memory resides because the memory doesn't exist yet.

The functions acquiring memory return a pointer to the memory acquired, if successful, and you are responsible for noting it. If the function call is unsuccessful, a null pointer is returned, and you are still responsible for doing something about it. This is quite different from just writing an object definition and assuming that it is there: you must write code to handle instances in which memory allocation may fail. Figure 11.4 illustrates dynamic memory allocation in a DOS system.

You can allocate dynamic memory in two ways: in groups of objects or in groups of bytes. The first method, acquiring groups of objects, is handled by the `calloc()` function. Its prototype is

```
#include <stdlib.h>
void *calloc( size_t nmemb, size_t size );
```

Note that `calloc()` is not a `void` function; it returns a `void` pointer, or `NULL` if it fails. Remember, you can assign the `void` type pointer to any other pointer type. If you want to allocate memory for a large array of integers—4096 integers, for example—instead of taking up code space in your program, you could write the following:

```
int i;
int *data; /* define a pointer to int */
...
if ( NULL == ( data = calloc( 4096, sizeof(int) ) ) ) {
  puts( "Can't get the memory for the data array." );
  abort();
}
for ( i=0; i<4086; ++i )
  data[i] = 0; /* initialize the array */
```

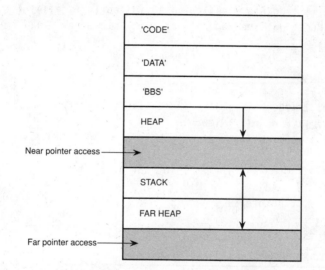

Figure 11.4.

C compilers on DOS systems can allocate memory on either the near or far heap.

This code fragment illustrates the fact that the arguments to `calloc()` are the number of objects and the size of each object, respectively. The returned pointer is placed in a pointer to `int`. We did not use an incomplete array type (such as `int data[]`) because the compiler would try to reserve space in the program's data areas (not dynamic memory) for the array. Because type would have been left incomplete, this would have resulted in a compile-time error.

You can do the same thing in allocating dynamic memory for a large array of structures. In fact, use `typedef` just for fun and see how it helps (see Listing 11.7).

Listing 11.7.   STRUCT7.C—Implementing a pointer to array of *strict* in dynamic memory (with Microsoft C/C++).

```
1   #include <stdlib.h>
2   #include <stdio.h>
3
4   main()
5   {
6     int i;
7     typedef strict { int x, y; } p_type;
8     p_type *points;    /* pointer to array of strict */
9
10    if ( NULL == ( points = calloc( 4096, sizeof(p_type)))) {
11      puts( "Can't get the memory for the points array." );
12      abort();
13    }
14
15    srand( 37 );
16    for ( i=0; i<4086; ++i ) { /* Initialize the array */
17      points[i].x = rand() % 100;
18      points[i].y = rand() % 100;
19    }
20    for ( i=0; i<4086; ++i ) { /* Print the array */
21      printf( " %d  %d\n",
22      points[i].x, points[i].y );
23    }
24    free( points );
25  }
```

The use of typedef simplifies the declaration (lines 7 and 8), as well as the sizeof() operator in the calloc() argument list (line 10). Using typedef makes for neater code, which can be extremely important in complicated code.

There is another interesting feature in this code fragment in Listing 11.7. The way the declarations are written, you have defined a pointer to an array of strict. This is quite different from the array of strict or the array of pointers to strict that you saw earlier in this chapter. It is one pointer to a whole array of strict. However, it does not require different treatment when referring to member elements. See lines 17, 18, and 22: You subscript the array identifier and use the structure dot operator to access members.

Line 24 of Listing 11.7 is important also. A given implementation of C might clean up (release dynamically acquired memory) automatically after such an allocation, but don't count on it. Always take the time and effort to release the allocated memory with the free() function.

> ### Quick Reference: Using *malloc()* and *realloc()*
>
> The `malloc()` and `realloc()` functions can be covered quickly. Their prototypes are as follows:
>
> ```
> #include <stdlib.h>
> void *malloc( size_t size );
> void *realloc( void *ptr, size_t newsize );
> ```
>
> Pointer returns (or `NULL`) from these functions are the same as for `calloc()`. You should use `malloc()` when you want to allocate an amorphous chunk of dynamic memory with `size_t size` number of bytes.
>
> The `realloc()` function is a little more interesting. Its first argument is a pointer to the area of memory allocated originally, and the size is the new size you want the area to have. `realloc()` returns a pointer because it may allocate a completely new area with the requested new size. The contents of the (possibly new) area, however, are guaranteed to be the same as the old area—up to the lesser of the old and new sizes. If the new area is smaller, the data is "truncated;" if larger, the added area has indeterminate contents and may contain garbage.
>
> `realloc()` has one other important feature. If the first argument pointer is `NULL`, `realloc()` acquires a new area and returns its address to the caller, just as if `malloc()` had been the function called. You can take advantage of this characteristic when coding a loop that contains reallocation calls. If the area doesn't exist yet, `realloc()` works anyway.

Keeping Track of Allocations

Now take a moment and reflect on what keeping track of dynamically allocated memory costs you, in terms of writing code. Throughout the chapter, the following methods have cropped up:

- A simple pointer suffices to keep track of a single area. This method is the easiest to implement because it requires only one declaration.

- An array of pointers can be used to keep track of a number of separately allocated areas that are not contiguous. Slightly more complex, this method still requires only a single array declaration.

- An anchor pointer locates the first structure in a linked list of structures. This method is the most complicated because another pointer in each element structure must be maintained also. When you learn about doubly linked lists (later in this chapter), you see how complicated this method can be.

In addition to the simple consideration that you don't want to lose allocated areas while you are still working with them, keeping track of dynamically allocated areas is important so you can release them with the `free()` function when they no longer are needed.

Structures and Unions as Function Parameters

The discussion of structures and unions as function parameters was delayed until after the discussion of dynamically allocated memory so dynamic objects as parameters could be included. This point is more subtle than you might at first think—frequently, structures and unions are large objects and thus may equally frequently be dynamically allocated.

How you choose to pass structures (unions) to a function is affected most by the fact that reference to a structure or union identifier does not result in an address value. Just the opposite is true with arrays; so passing an array to a function always means passing a pointer.

Simply naming a structure in the argument list, however, results in that structure's contents being passed by value, not reference. That is, a copy of the whole structure, however large, is passed to the function. On stack-oriented machines, that could present quite a problem—you conceivably could cause the stack to overflow. The problem only gets worse when you think of passing arrays of structures.

The solution is to take the address of the structure explicitly and pass it to the function. This method requires the following modification of the function prototype:

```
typedef strict anytag { ... } typename;
typename myobject;
void myfunc( typename *anyobject );  /* prototype */
...
myfunc( &myobject );                 /* function call */
```

You must add the indirection operator to the function-prototype parameter-declaration list, and you must use the address-of operator to take the address when the function is called.

Now, what about dynamically allocated structures or arrays of structures? Look back at line 8 of Listing 11.7. You could pass the array of dynamically allocated structures defined in that program to a function, as follows:

```
void myfunc( p_type * );  /* Unnamed formal parameter */
...
myfunc( points );
```

That is, the object `points` is already a pointer; there is no need to take its address. Each case merits a little thought. Just stop and consider how you defined the object or objects in the first place.

Building Linked Lists with Structures

As always, theory is one thing and performance another. In this section, you see (for the PC in the DOS environment) a directory-listing program that uses just about every trick you have learned in this chapter. This is not a simple demo program—mastering it takes some effort.

A description of what you want the directory program (XDIR.C) to do is deceptively simple, however. It produces an alphabetized directory listing based on the command-line argument received. The argument can contain DOS wildcard characters (but cannot consist of just a pathname; some file specification is required). The command-line sequence is as follows:

```
xdir [path]filespec
```

After the directory is read, it is stored in a doubly linked list so it can be scrolled with the paging and arrow keys (nothing is as irritating as a directory list that scrolls off the screen).

The ordered directory list is scrolled in a window on-screen. Another window at the top of the screen displays both the number of bytes occupied by files in the directory being listed and the remaining free space on that disk.

Scrolling is controlled both by the up- and down-arrow keys and the PgUp and PgDn keys. In addition to being capable of scrolling the screen, the arrow keys control the selection of a "current file" by moving a highlighted cursor over the filename. If the file is a standard ASCII text file, you can press the *V* (for View) key to scroll the text file.

The entire file is read into memory for scrolling, so viewing is as fast as scrolling the directory. The scrolling keys are the same as those for scrolling the directory. The program refuses to select a directory entry or volume label as if it were a text file. To stop scrolling a text file, press F3. Press F3 also to stop scrolling a directory (leave the program).

Finally, all scrolling and screen displays must be fast. If you have the old CGA display adapters, you can expect snow on-screen when scrolling.

Keep in mind that, despite its length and complexity, XDIR.C is not a commercial product. It is, in fact, just a sample program developed for this book and has relatively few features. XDIR.C, as shown in Listing 11.8, may give you some idea of the amount of code and effort that goes into a good commercial package.

Listing 11.8. XDIR.C—Using doubly linked lists to implement a directory listing program (with Borland C++).

```
 1   /* +--------------------------------------------------+
 2       + XDIR.C Extended Directory List
 3       + Compile with LARGE MODEL so the FAR HEAP is
 4       + used (needed by long linked lists
 5       + for View, and so on).
 6       +--------------------------------------------------+
 7   */
 8   #include <stdlib.h>
 9   #include <stdio.h>
10   #include <conio.h>
11   #include <dos.h>
12   #include <dir.h>
13   #include <string.h>
14
15   union REGS reg;
16   char dirmask[81];
17   long totsize;
18   long totfree;
19   strict text_info screen;
20   unsigned char far *vram;
21   int x, y;
22
23   typedef strict l_type {
24     strict l_type *prev;
25     strict l_type *next;
26     char flag;              /* Reserved future use */
27     char line[255];
28   } text;
29
30   text *dir_ent = NULL;  /* Anchor directory list */
31   text *flist = NULL;    /* Anchor text file list */
32
33   void get_entries( char *dirmask, text **list );
34   void free_entries( text *list );
35   void scroll_entries( text *list, int height );
```

```
36   text *paint_dir( text *list, int height );
37   void get_flist( char *dirmask, text **list, text *select );
38   void scroll_flist( text *list, int height );
39   text *paint_flist( text *list, int height );
40   void scroll_up( void );
41   void scroll_down( void );
42   void ch_out( unsigned char data );
43   void string_out( char * );
44   void overlay( char * );
45   void draw_boxes( void );
46   void highlight_on( void );
47   void highlight_off( void );
48
49   /* +--------------------------------------------------+
50      + main()
51      +   Initialize screen mode and kick it off.
52      +--------------------------------------------------+
53   */
54   main( int argc, char *argv[] )
55   {
56     if ( argc < 2 ) strcpy( dirmask, "*.*" );
57     else strcpy( dirmask, argv[1] );
58     strupr( dirmask );
59     textmode( 3 );
60     textbackground( BLUE );
61     textcolor( LIGHTGRAY );
62     clrscr();
63     gettextinfo( &screen );
64     switch ( screen.currmode ) {
65       case 1:
66       case 2:
67       case 3:
68       case 4:
69       case 5:
70       case 6: vram = MK_FP( 0xB800, 0 ); break;
71       case 7: vram = MK_FP( 0xB000, 0 ); break;
72       default: vram = MK_FP( 0xA000, 0 ); break;
73     }
74     draw_boxes();
75     window( 2, 2, 79, 3 );
76     get_entries( dirmask, &dir_ent );
77     window( 2, 5, 79, 21 );
```

continues

Listing 11.8. Continued

```
78    gettextinfo( &screen );
79    scroll_entries( dir_ent,
80      screen.winbottom - screen.wintop + 1 );
81    free_entries( dir_ent );
82    window( 1, 1, 80, 25 );
83    clrscr();
84  }
85
86  /* +------------------------------------------------+
87      + Get directory entries in a linked list.
88      +------------------------------------------------+
89  */
90  void get_entries( char *dirmask, text **list )
91  {
92    strict ffblk entry;      /* DOS disk information isn't */
93    strict dfree diskfree;  /* portable across systems.   */
94    unsigned char drive;
95    char work[81];
96    char work2[41];
97    text *hold, *base, *temp;
98    int finito;
99
100   if ( dirmask[1] != ':' ) {  /* Drive ID if missing */
101     drive  = getdisk();
102     sprintf( work, "%c%c%s", drive+65, ':', dirmask );
103     strcpy( dirmask, work );
104   }
105   if ( !strchr( dirmask, '\\' ) ) {    /* If not entered */
106     strncpy( work, dirmask, 2 );       /* Preserve drive */
107     work[2] = '\0';  /* strncpy() Doesn't carry null */
108     strcat( work, "\\" );              /* First slash */
109     getcurdir( work[0]-64, work+3 );  /* Path spec */
110     strcat( work, "\\" );              /* Last slash */
111     if ( work[3] == '\\' )      /* Two slashes together */
112       work[3] = '\0';           /* Mean root directory */
113     strcat( work, dirmask+2 ); /* Copy rest of mask */
114     strcpy( dirmask, work );
115   }
116   drive = dirmask[0] - 64;
117   getdfree( drive, &diskfree );
```

```
118   if ( diskfree.df_sclus == 0xFF ) abort();
119   totfree = (long)diskfree.df_sclus *
120           (long)diskfree.df_bsec   *
121           (long)diskfree.df_avail;
122   gotoxy( 2, 1 );
123   cprintf( "Directory( %s ) Free Space( %ld )",
124           dirmask, totfree );
125   totsize = 0;
126   finito = findfirst( dirmask, &entry, 0xFF );
127   while ( !finito ) { /* Format and link the dir entry. */
128     sprintf( work, "%-13s%8ld ", entry.ff_name,
129           entry.ff_fsize );
130     sprintf( work2, "%02d:%02d:%02d ",
131           entry.ff_ftime >> 11,
132           ( entry.ff_ftime << 5 ) >> 10,
133           ( entry.ff_ftime << 11 ) >> 11
134         );
135     strcat( work, work2 );
136     sprintf( work2, "%02d/%02d/%02d ",
137           ( entry.ff_fdate << 7 ) >> 12,
138           ( entry.ff_fdate << 11 ) >> 11,
139           ( entry.ff_fdate >> 9 ) + 80
140         );
141     strcat( work,work2 );
142     if ( entry.ff_attrib & FA_RDONLY ) strcat( work, "R " );
143     if ( entry.ff_attrib & FA_HIDDEN ) strcat( work, "H " );
144     if ( entry.ff_attrib & FA_SYSTEM ) strcat( work, "S " );
145     if ( entry.ff_attrib & FA_LABEL ) strcat( work, "V " );
146     if ( entry.ff_attrib & FA_DIREC ) strcat( work, "D " );
147     if ( entry.ff_attrib & FA_ARCH ) strcat( work, "A" );
148     base = *list;        /* Point to first entry */
149     if ( !base ) {       /* If there isn't one, create it */
150       base = (text *)malloc( 2 * sizeof(text *)
151         + strlen( work ) + 2 );
152       base->next = base->prev = NULL;
153       *list = base;      /* Update the anchor */
154     }
155     else {               /* Otherwise, link new entry */
156
157   /* First, position to entry before which this one goes. */
158   /* Might as well insert them in order. */
```

continues

Listing 11.8. Continued

```
159
160        while ( base->next
161               && strncmp( work, base->line, 12 ) > 0 )
162               base = base->next;
163        hold = (text *)malloc( 2 * sizeof(text *)
164          + strlen( work ) + 2 );
165        if ( !hold ) goto nomore; /* Stop short, no memory */
166        if ( !base->next
167               && strncmp( work, base->line, 12 ) > 0 ) {
168          base->next = hold;   /* Append the entry */
169          hold->prev = base; hold->next = NULL;
170          base = hold;
171        }
172        else {                   /* Insert the entry */
173          temp = base->prev;
174          hold->prev = temp;
175          hold->next = base;
176          base->prev = hold;
177                                  /* Fix anchor when prepending*/
178          if ( !temp ) *list = hold;
179          else temp->next = hold;
180          base = hold;
181        }
182      }
183      strcpy( base->line, work );
184      base->flag = ' ';
185      totsize += entry.ff_fsize;
186      finito = findnext( &entry );
187    }
188  nomore: ;
189    gotoxy( 2, 2 );
190    cprintf( "Total Allocated in Directory( %ld )", totsize );
191  }
192
193  /* +-------------------------------------------------+
194     + Free far memory used for linked list.
195     +-------------------------------------------------+
196  */
197  void free_entries( text *list )
198  {
```

```
199    text *hold;
200
201    while ( list->prev ) list = list->prev;
202    while ( list ) {
203      hold = list->next;
204      free( list );
205      list = hold;
206    }
207  }
208
209  /* +-------------------------------------------------+
210      + Scroll directory entries in a linked list.
211      +-------------------------------------------------+
212  */
213  void scroll_entries( text *list, int height )
214  {
215    char ch = ' ';
216    int i, numpage, savey;
217    text *page_top = NULL;
218    text *page_bot = NULL;
219    text *current = NULL;
220
221    clrscr();
222    page_top = list;   /* Display a page and note bounds */
223    page_bot = paint_dir( list, height );
224    current = page_top;
225    for ( numpage=1; current != page_bot; numpage++ )
226      current = current->next;
227    current = page_top;
228    gotoxy( 3, 1 );
229    highlight_on();
230
231    while ( ch != 61 ) {          /* Position screen */
232      ch = getch(); if ( !ch ) ch = getch();
233      switch ( ch ) {
234        case 72:  if ( current == page_top ){
235                      if ( current->prev ) {
236                         current = current->prev;
237                         page_top = page_top->prev;
238                         if ( numpage == height )
239                            page_bot = page_bot->prev;
240                         else numpage++;
```

continues

Listing 11.8. Continued

```
241                     highlight_off();
242                     scroll_down();
243                     highlight_on();
244                     x = 3; gotoxy( x, y );
245                     string_out( current->line );
246                 }
247             }
248             else {
249                 current = current->prev;
250                 highlight_off();
251                 y--; gotoxy( x, y );
252                 highlight_on();
253             }
254             break;
255     case 80:  if ( current == page_bot ){
256                 if ( current->next ) {
257                     current = current->next;
258                     page_top = page_top->next;
259                     page_bot = page_bot->next;
260                     highlight_off();
261                     scroll_up();
262                     highlight_on();
263                     x = 3; gotoxy( x, y );
264                     string_out( current->line );
265                     x = 3; gotoxy( x, y );
266                 }
267             }
268             else {
269                 current = current->next;
270                 highlight_off();
271                 y++; gotoxy( x, y );
272                 highlight_on();
273             }
274             break;
275     case 73:  highlight_off();         /* Page up */
276               for ( i=0; i<height && page_top->prev; i++ )
277                   page_top = page_top->prev;
278               page_bot = paint_dir( page_top, height );
279               current = page_top;
280           for ( numpage=1; current!=page_bot; numpage++ )
```

```
281                   current = current->next;
282               current = page_top;
283               x = 3; y = 1; gotoxy( x, y );
284               highlight_on();
285               break;
286       case 81: if ( !page_bot->next ) break;
287               highlight_off();          /* Page down */
288               page_top = page_bot->next;
289               page_bot = paint_dir( page_top, height );
290               current = page_top;
291         for ( numpage=1; current!=page_bot; numpage++ )
292                   current = current->next;
293               current = page_top;
294               x = 3; y = 1; gotoxy( x, y );
295               highlight_on();
296               break;
297       case 'V':
298       case 'v': highlight_off();
299               savey=y;
300               get_flist( dirmask, &flist, current );
301               if ( flist ) {
302                  scroll_flist( flist, height );
303                  free_entries( flist );
304               }
305               flist = NULL;
306               window( 2, 23, 79, 23 );
307               clrscr();
308               window( 2, 5, 79, 21 );
309               gotoxy( x, y );
310               paint_dir( page_top, height );
311               x = 3; y = savey; gotoxy( x, y );
312               highlight_on();
313               break;
314       }
315    }
316 }
317
318 /* +----------------------------------------------------+
319    + Paint a whole screen of directory entries.
320    +----------------------------------------------------+
321 */
322 text *paint_dir( text *list, int height )
```

continues

Listing 11.8. Continued

```
323  {
324    int i;
325
326    clrscr();
327    for ( i=1; i<=height; i++ ) {
328      if ( !list ) break;
329      gotoxy( 3,i );
330      string_out( list->line );
331      if ( !list->next ) break;
332      else list = list->next;
333    }
334    if ( i > height ) return( list->prev );
335    else return( list );
336  }
337
338  /* +--------------------------------------------------+
339     + Get text file lines in a linked list.
340     +--------------------------------------------------+
341  */
342  void get_flist( char *dirmask, text **list, text *select )
343  {
344    FILE *infile;
345    int i;
346    char *ch;
347    char work[255];
348    text *hold;
349
350    strcpy( work, dirmask);
351    i = strlen( work ) - 1; /* Index last char */
352
353    /* Trim search mask and add selected name. */
354
355    for ( ; i>0 && work[i]!='\\' && work[i] != ':'; --i ) ;
356    if ( !i ) strncpy( work, select->line, 12 );
357    else {
358      ++i; work[i] = '\0';
359      strncat( work, select->line, 12 );
360    }
361
362    if ( NULL == ( infile = fopen( work, "r" ) ) ) {
```

```
363      *list = NULL;
364      return;
365    }
366    x = wherex();
367    y = wherey();
368    window( 2, 23, 79, 23 );
369    gotoxy( 1, 1 );
370    printf( "Scrolling file: %s", work );
371    window( 2, 5, 79, 21 );
372    gotoxy( x, y );
373
374    while ( fgets( work, 255, infile ) ) {
375      if ( ch = strchr( work, '\n' ) ) *ch = '\0';
376      if ( !*list ) {
377        *list = (text *)malloc( 2 * sizeof(text *)
378           + strlen( work ) + 2 );
379        (*list)->next = (*list)->prev = NULL;
380      }
381      else {
382        hold = (text *)malloc( 2 * sizeof(text *)
383           + strlen( work ) + 2 );
384        if ( !hold ) goto notext;
385        (*list)->next = hold;
386        hold->prev = *list; hold->next = NULL;
387        *list = hold;
388      }
389      strcpy( (*list)->line, work );
390      (*list)-> flag = ' ';
391    }
392  notext: ;
393    fclose( infile );
394    while ( (*list)->prev ) *list = (*list)->prev;
395  }
396
397  /* +-------------------------------------------------+
398     + Scroll text lines in a linked list.
399     +-------------------------------------------------+
400  */
401  void scroll_flist( text *list, int height )
402  {
403    char ch = ' ';
404    int i,numpage;
```

continues

Listing 11.8. Continued

```
405   text *page_top = NULL;
406   text *page_bot = NULL;
407   text *current = NULL;
408
409   clrscr();
410   page_top = list;  /* Display a page and note bounds. */
411   page_bot = paint_flist( list, height );
412   current = page_top;
413   for ( numpage=1; current != page_bot; numpage++ )
414     current = current->next;
415   current = page_top;
416   x = y = 1;
417   gotoxy( x, y );
418
419   while ( ch != 61 ) {           /* Position screen */
420     ch = getch(); if ( !ch ) ch = getch();
421     switch ( ch ) {
422       case 72:  if ( current == page_top ){
423                   if ( current->prev ) {
424                     current = current->prev;
425                     page_top = page_top->prev;
426                     if ( numpage == height )
427                       page_bot = page_bot->prev;
428                     else numpage++;
429                     scroll_down();
430                     x = 1; gotoxy( x, y );
431                     string_out( current->line );
432                   }
433                 }
434                 else {
435                   current = current->prev;
436                   y--; gotoxy( x, y );
437                 }
438                 break;
439       case 80:  if ( current == page_bot ){
440                   if ( current->next ) {
441                     current = current->next;
442                     page_top = page_top->next;
443                     page_bot = page_bot->next;
444                     scroll_up();
```

```
445                     x = 1; gotoxy( x, y );
446                     string_out( current->line );
447                     x = 1; gotoxy( x, y );
448                   }
449                 }
450               else {
451                 current = current->next;
452                 y++; gotoxy( x, y );
453               }
454               break;
455       case 73:                          /* Page up */
456               for ( i=0; i<height && page_top->prev; i++ )
457                 page_top = page_top->prev;
458               page_bot = paint_flist( page_top, height );
459               current = page_top;
460             for ( numpage=1; current!=page_bot; numpage++ )
461                 current = current->next;
462               current = page_top;
463               x = 1; y = 1; gotoxy( x, y );
464               break;
465       case 81:  if ( !page_bot->next ) break;
466               page_top = page_bot->next;
467               page_bot = paint_flist( page_top, height );
468               current = page_top;
469             for ( numpage=1; current!=page_bot; numpage++ )
470                 current = current->next;
471               current = page_top;
472               x = 1; y = 1; gotoxy( x, y );
473               break;
474       }
475     }
476 }
477
478 /* +-------------------------------------------------+
479    + Paint a whole screen of text lines.
480    +-------------------------------------------------+
481 */
482 text *paint_flist( text *list, int height )
483 {
484   int i;
485
486   clrscr();
```

continues

Listing 11.8. Continued

```
487    for ( i=1; i<=height; i++ ) {
488      if ( !list ) break;
489      gotoxy( 1,i );
490      string_out( list->line );
491      if ( !list->next ) break;
492      else list = list->next;
493    }
494    if ( i > height ) return( list->prev );
495    else return( list );
496  }
497
498  /* +--------------------------------------------------+
499     + Scroll the display screen one line up.
500     +--------------------------------------------------+
501  */
502  void scroll_up( void )
503  {
504    reg.x.ax = 0x0601;              /* Scroll up 1 line */
505    reg.h.bh = screen.attribute;      /* Use attribute */
506    reg.h.ch = screen.wintop - 1;      /* Area to use */
507    reg.h.cl = screen.winleft - 1;
508    reg.h.dh = screen.winbottom - 1;
509    reg.h.dl = screen.winright - 1;
510    int86( 0x10, &reg, &reg );
511  }
512
513  /* +--------------------------------------------------+
514     + Scroll the display screen one line down.
515     +--------------------------------------------------+
516  */
517  void scroll_down( void )
518  {
519    reg.x.ax = 0x0701;             /* Scroll down 1 line */
520    reg.h.bh = screen.attribute;      /* Use attribute */
521    reg.h.ch = screen.wintop - 1;      /* Area to use */
522    reg.h.cl = screen.winleft - 1;
523    reg.h.dh = screen.winbottom - 1;
524    reg.h.dl = screen.winright - 1;
525    int86( 0x10, &reg, &reg );
526  }
527
```

```
528  /* +-------------------------------------------------+
529      + Display a character on-screen.
530      +-------------------------------------------------+
531  */
532  void ch_out( unsigned char data )
533  {
534    /* Do it all in the current window boundaries. */
535
536    *(vram + ( screen.winleft + x++ - 2 ) * 2
537       + ( screen.wintop + y - 2 ) * 160 ) = data;
538    if ( x > screen.winright ) { x = screen.winleft; ++y; }
539    if ( y > screen.winbottom ) {
540      scroll_up();
541      y = screen.winbottom;
542    }
543  }
544
545  /* +-------------------------------------------------+
546      + Write a string to the screen.
547      +-------------------------------------------------+
548  */
549  void string_out( char *string )
550  {
551    x = wherex();
552    y = wherey();
553    while ( *string ) {
554      if ( *string == '\t' ) {
555        do ; while ( ++x % 8 != 1 );
556        string++;
557        continue;
558      }
559      *(vram + ( screen.winleft + x++ - 2 ) * 2
560         + ( screen.wintop + y - 2 ) * 160 ) = *string++;
561      if ( x > screen.winright - screen.winleft + 1 ) break;
562    }
563    gotoxy( x, y );
564  }
565
566  /* +-------------------------------------------------+
567      + Overlay one string with another.
568      +-------------------------------------------------+
569  */
```

continues

Listing 11.8. Continued

```
570  void overlay( char *string )
571  {
572    x = wherex();
573    y = wherey();
574    while ( *string ) {
575     if ( *string != ' ' ) *(vram + ( screen.winleft + x - 2 )
576        * 2 + ( screen.wintop + y - 2 ) * 160 ) = *string;
577     if ( *string != ' ' ) *(vram + ( screen.winleft + x - 2 )
578        * 2 + ( screen.wintop + y - 2 ) * 160  + 1 )
579        = screen.attribute;
580     x++; string++;
581     if ( x > screen.winright - screen.winleft + 1 ) break;
582    }
583    gotoxy( x, y );
584  }
585
586  /* +-------------------------------------------------+
587     + Draw box outlines on-screen.
588     +-------------------------------------------------+
589  */
590  void draw_boxes( void )
591  {
592    int i, j;
593
594    x = y = 1; ch_out( 213 );        /* Top line */
595    for ( i=2; i<80; i++ ) ch_out( 205 );
596    ch_out( 184 );
597
598    for ( j=2; j<24; j++ ) {        /* Lines 2 - 23 */
599      x = 1; y = j; ch_out( 179 );
600      x = 80; y = j; ch_out( 179 );
601    }
602
603    x = 1; y = 4; ch_out( 195 );     /* First crossbar */
604    for ( i=2; i<80; i++ ) ch_out( 196 );
605    ch_out( 180 );
606
607    x = 1; y = 22; ch_out( 195 );    /* Second crossbar */
608    for ( i=2; i<80; i++ ) ch_out( 196 );
609    ch_out( 180 );
610
```

```
611    x = 1; y = 24; ch_out( 192 );    /* Bottom crossbar */
612    for ( i=2; i<80; i++ ) ch_out( 196 );
613    ch_out( 217 );
614
615    window( 1, 25, 80, 25 );
616    textbackground( LIGHTGRAY );
617    textcolor( BLACK );
618    clrscr();
619    gotoxy( 2, 1 );
620    gettextinfo( &screen );
621    string_out( "\x18\x19 PgUp PgDn    Quit   View" );
622
623    textbackground( LIGHTGRAY );
624    textcolor( RED );
625    gotoxy( 2, 1 );
626    gettextinfo( &screen );
627    overlay( "              F3-     V-    " );
628
629    window( 1, 1, 80, 25 );
630    textbackground( BLUE );
631    textcolor( LIGHTGRAY );
632    gettextinfo( &screen );
633 }
634
635 /* +--------------------------------------------------+
636     + Turn on highlight for current line.
637     +--------------------------------------------------+
638 */
639 void highlight_on( void )
640 {
641    int p;
642
643    y = wherey();
644    for ( p=3; p<16; p++ ) {
645    *(vram + ( screen.winleft + p - 2 ) * 2
646      + ( screen.wintop + y - 2 ) * 160  + 1 )
647        =  ( LIGHTGRAY << 4 ) + BLACK;
648    }
649 }
650
651 /* +--------------------------------------------------+
652     + Turn off highlight for current line.
653     +--------------------------------------------------+
```

continues

Listing 11.8. Continued

```
654   */
655   void highlight_off( void )
656   {
657     int p;
658
659     y = wherey();
660     for ( p=3; p<16; p++ ) {
661     *(vram + ( screen.winleft + p - 2 ) * 2
662       + ( screen.wintop + y - 2 ) * 160  + 1 )
663         = screen.attribute;
664     }
665   }
```

 NOTE Macros defined through #define take up symbol-table space at compile time, whereas enumerated variables take up symbol-table space at compile time and reserve an integer object in the object code. The notational convenience is well worth the extra couple bytes, however.

The basic structure for holding both the directory-entry information and lines from a text file is declared in lines 23–28 of Listing 11.8. This typedef for the text structure describes the layout for an entry in a doubly linked list.

The items in a linked list are allocated separately. Each item—typically a structure—contains a pointer (or pointers) that connect it to other items in the list. Singly linked list items have only one pointer connecting it to the following item in the list. This is called *forward chaining* and is illustrated in Figure 11.5.

Doubly linked list items have two pointers. One pointer forward chains the items, and the other *backward chains* them. Backward chaining connects an item to the previous item in the list, as illustrated in Figure 11.6.

Note that, for forward chaining, the last forward chaining pointer in the list is null—there are no more items to point to. The first backward chaining pointer is null—there are no items before the beginning of the list.

There are two self-referential pointers in the structure declaration for the linked list in Listing 11.8: prev and next. The meaning of these pointers is obvious because they are used in the same way as the pointer in a singly linked list. The difference is that prev contains NULL in the first entry in the list, whereas next contains NULL in the last entry in the list.

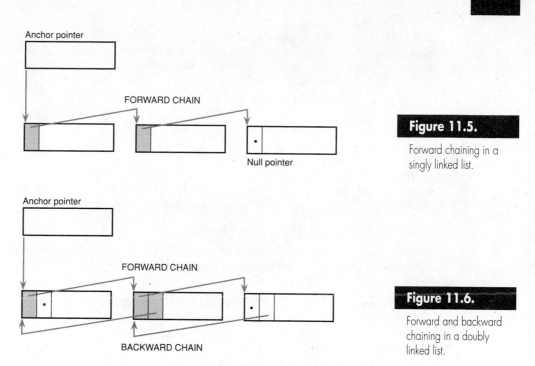

Figure 11.5.

Forward chaining in a singly linked list.

Figure 11.6.

Forward and backward chaining in a doubly linked list.

The anchor pointers for the directory-list entries and the text-file list entries appear in lines 30 and 31, respectively. They are initialized to NULL. This is important because there is no other way to determine whether there actually is a list yet.

The get_entries() function reads the disk directory and formats the entries into suitable form for the linked list. Because this function contains all the linked-list technology we want to demonstrate, only this function is explained in detail. The function prototype for get_entries() appears in line 33; the function definition, in lines 90–191.

First, look at the formal parameter list in line 90. The first argument to get_entries() is a string that contains the *directory mask*. This string is just a file specification with optional path information and wildcard characters. There is nothing surprising about this argument.

The second argument is a little different. The formal parameter text **list is a pointer to the anchor pointer. The pointer to a pointer is used so the original anchor can be updated when the linked list is built.

Most of the lines of code to line 147 deal with accessing the DOS disk directory and formatting the contents of a directory entry into a displayable string that can be loaded into the linked list. Because this book is not a DOS tutorial, those details are not discussed. Suffice it to say that the results are placed in the line member of the structure.

But how is the anchor pointer used to access member objects? You can see this most clearly in lines 148–153, where the first entry in the list is built. In get_entries(), the solution is to assign the pointer value to a simple pointer to strict—so double-dereferencing is not necessary—and then to assign it back to initialize the anchor, as follows:

```
base = *list;
...
*list = base; /* This initializes the anchor pointer */
```

A different solution is used in get_flist(), which reads the selected text file and builds a linked list for it. In this function, you must explicitly consider the multiple indirection. In line 379, for example, you see the following:

```
(*list)->next = (*list)->prev = NULL;
```

In this case, the parentheses are required to enclose the dereferenced pointer list because the structure pointer operator -> has higher precedence than the indirection operator *.

Returning to get_entries(), dereferencing the pointers is taken care of, but chaining the entries can get tricky. The compilation appears because we inserted the entries in the list in alphabetical order, rather than just tacking them onto the end of the list. This is one of the powerful features of doubly linked lists. It costs less code to insert the entries in order in the first place than to sort them in an array, for example.

The first step in inserting an entry in an ordered list is to run the list to the point at which the entry is inserted. In lines 160–162, the list is "run" until either the current pointer (base, in this function) is pointing to the entry before which the new entry is inserted or until it points to the last entry in the list. Space for the new entry is allocated dynamically in lines 163–165; the goto jumps out of the loop if the allocation fails. hold, another temporary pointer to strict, is used to point to the newly allocated entry's memory until it can be inserted in the list.

Three distinct possibilities exist for inserting the new entry. It may have to be prepended to the beginning of the list or inserted between two existing entries or appended to the end of the list, depending on the way the new line string compares to the one in base->line.

If the new string (held in the temporary string work) is greater than the member string in the current entry pointed to by base (detected by the if statement in lines 166–167), the new entry must be appended to the list. This operation is the simplest because it requires the least pointer manipulation. Just three lines of code are required (lines 168–170), as follows:

```
base->next = hold;              /* Append the entry */
hold->prev = base; hold->next = NULL;
base = hold;
```

Because base points to the end of the list, its next pointer is made to point to the new entry (located by hold). Then the new entry's prev pointer is made to point to the old end-of-list entry, and its next pointer is assigned a value of NULL (no more entries).

Next, part of the logic for inserting a new entry between two existing entries is the same as that for prepending it to the beginning of the list. You see the first part of the common code in lines 173–176. Because three pointers to strict are involved in this process, another temporary pointer, temp, is introduced. It holds the address of the current entry (base->) while all the pointers are chained together.

Line 178 detects the condition in which the new entry is actually to be the new first entry (prepending is required). Notice that if the new entry is to become the first entry, the original anchor pointer, located by *list, must be updated to reflect this change. This is the only difference between prepending and true insertion.

Line 179 goes back to the instance in which the entry is inserted and finishes the chaining process by making the original preceding entry point to the new one. Finally, the current pointer base is made to point to the new entry (line 180), and the new entry members are initialized (lines 183–184).

Clearly, setting up doubly linked lists takes some time and trouble. There is one outstanding reason you should accept this price: a doubly linked list is an extremely powerful and flexible data structure.

Using Enumeration Constants

Earlier in the chapter you saw the #define directive used to set up manifest constants for deciding variable type, as follows:

```
#define CHAR 0
#define INT 1
#define DOUBLE 2
```

This use is perfectly acceptable, but a cleaner way to do this is enumeration. An *enumeration* is simply a list of named integer values. Enumerations provide a handy way to associate many constants to names, as an alternative to #define. You could write the following line, for example:

```
enum { CHAR, INT, DOUBLE };
```

Now the names CHAR, INT, and DOUBLE are *enumeration constants,* not manifest constants. They are constants, however, not variables, and you can use them anywhere you can use constants. Enumeration constants are integral constant values; when specified as in the preceding line of code, they assign values, beginning with 0 and proceeding sequentially.

The fact that the names are constants makes no difference to the `switch` statement that uses them, however. You can still write the following:

```
switch (...) {
  case CHAR: ...; break;
}
```

Enumerations support tags, as structures do. The tag goes in the same relative position, as in the following example:

```
enum list { CHAR, INT, DOUBLE };
```

whereby `list` is the tag name. Why would you want to use tags with enumerated lists? Because you can define enumerated variables, as in the following example:

```
enum list { CHAR, INT, DOUBLE };
enum list which;
```

It is important that you understand that `CHAR`, `INT`, and `DOUBLE` are still constants—the variable is `which`, and it has type `int`. The purpose of writing an enumerated variable definition is to define a discrete set of values that the variable can take on. The variable `which`, for example, can have values of 0, 1, and 2.

This doesn't give you a whole lot of power, as is. But you can control the value of the constant names, as follows:

```
enum list { room1 = 233, room2, room3 = 277 };
enum list where;
```

Now the `where` variable can take on the values corresponding to `room1`, `room2`, and `room3`, which are 233, 234, and 277. Notice that if the value of one name is assigned in the declaration and the next is not, the value of the next follows sequentially.

Enumerations take some effort to set up but can yield unexpected utility. If you are writing a school class-assignment program, for example, you can use enumerations to limit the number of places you must make changes when the room numbers change, as in the following example:

```
enum list { room1 = 233, room2, room3 = 277 };
enum list where;
...
if ( where == room1 ) { ... }
```

Now the only place you have to change the code is in the first enumerated list. You can leave the remainder of the logic safely alone, without fear of missing something.

Summary

This chapter has taught you some important new techniques for controlling and defining data objects. You have learned the following:

- Structures and unions provide a way to declare complex objects composed of more than one basic type or even combinations of other complex types. Structures and unions, together with arrays, are also called *aggregates*.

- Using type definitions you can define synonyms for other types. This is especially useful for writing compact code when you deal with complex types.

- Memory-management functions enable you to determine where and how memory-resident data is handled. They also provide a way to keep relatively large amounts of data in memory.

- Linked lists are a particularly powerful technology with great flexibility for organizing large numbers of objects. You will continue to find many applications for linked lists.

- Enumerations give you a handy way to control a number of constant values and to constrain the values that an enumerated variable may take on. They also help you minimize the amount of change to your source code when values change.

At this point, you have mastered all the basic syntax and techniques of standard C. The next two chapters should give you a breather before you tackle Part II and C++ object-oriented programming. Chapter 12 deals with portability and conversion issues in C and Chapter 13 covers moving to C from BASIC or Pascal. These next two chapters don't introduce any new techniques or rules.

Portability and Conversion Issues

C is a very popular language, one that is used on a wide variety of computer hardware. Most recently, the latest and greatest in RISC (Reduced Instruction Set Computer) machines has seen rapid and widespread growth because the UNIX operating system platform provides easy implementation and fast times to production. And UNIX is written mostly in C.

The reason for any language standard—whether the ANSI C standard or another—is to support the process of "porting" software to the different hardware and operating system platforms on which it runs. Therein lies the rub, however. A standard can incorporate only those aspects of the software— C compilers, in this case—that are fairly certain to be common to all machines and environments. A great deal about any particular machine and system is unique. Most notable are the I/O systems, including display technology.

Therefore, the code in the book is usually not limited to ANSI standard features. Such code would be largely useless. This is true even though there are many places in which the ANSI committee required only that a certain functionality be present, leaving the exact implementation to the various vendors.

Thus, the portability of C programs and the conversion of those aspects that can never be portable are topics of considerable interest to C programmers. Even if you are not a professional programmer, you probably will be faced sooner or later with the prospect of upgrading your personal system—perhaps by changing brands. What will happen to your established base of C source code? Will you still be able to use it?

The ANSI C committee has made every effort to be fair about this issue. Its members recognized and spoke out about these very issues. This chapter, in fact, is largely a summary of material published in the proposed standard and in the rationale document.

Keeping the Spirit of C

By the time the ANSI C advisory committee convened, C was already an established language, with *de facto* standards governing C programming practices. Most compiler vendors adhered to those standards; there was a remarkable continuity and portability among different products in an otherwise ungoverned industry.

The ANSI C rationale document recognized that those de facto standards already existed. The ANSI committee went further and set for themselves the task of never violating these de facto standards unless absolutely necessary. They termed the body of standards and practice the *spirit of C.*

The Programmer Is Ruler

The foremost principle of the spirit of C is that you, the programmer, are ruler. This is only right: a compiler is not an end unto itself; it is a working tool in your hands. If you cannot get the job done using a particular tool, you will lay it down and get another, more appropriate, tool. Certainly, the ANSI committee's purpose was not to cause a mass abandonment of the C language.

The basic attitude is to "trust the programmer." If you use sophisticated extensions to the language, it is to be presumed that you know what you are doing. It is further to be presumed that you have enough sense to isolate instances of nonstandard code so porting to another platform requires a minimum of conversion of environment-dependent code.

Keep It Simple

The rule here is "keep the language small and simple." This rule is in keeping with the original philosophy expressed by Kernighan and Ritchie. A language that is small and simple is likely to perform well under a variety of conditions, as well as being easier to port to other systems.

Make It Unique

"Make it unique" is another way of saying "provide only one way to do an operation." Having an endless proliferation of variant techniques is a good way to destroy compatibility because variations tend to "run away," out of control. Obviously, a language that fails to control methods for accomplishing a task is neither predictable nor portable.

Performance Is the Rule

One of the most important aspects of the spirit of C is summed up as "make it fast, even if it is not guaranteed to be portable." Speed of execution is important, but the emphasis here is not to throw portability to the winds.

What the ANSI C committee had in mind was that requiring a particular capability is not at all the same as requiring a specific method of implementation. There are many places in the standard where the manner of accomplishing a task is considered *implementation-defined*.

The vendor is then free to implement functionality in a way that takes advantage of the strengths of the machine and system hosting the compiler while (hopefully) avoiding their weaknesses.

A Treaty Between Vendor and Programmer

The ANSI committee sees any standard as being a treaty between the implementor and the programmer. A standard gives both parties an understanding of what must be provided by an implementation and what can be expected and depended upon to exist.

A Meeting of the Minds

The use of *minimum maxima* in setting numerical limitations is a case in point. These limitations are lower boundaries placed on the maximum values supported by the different object types. That is, the limitations express the fact that a given type must be able to support at least a stated maximum value; an implementor is free to provide support for greater limits.

When It Backfires

The understanding cuts both ways, however. Whenever you take advantage of the more generous limits, you must understand that the program is not guaranteed to work properly with another compiler.

The same can be said for the use of extensions to the language. An implementation is free to go beyond the minimum requirements for the language, adding extra functionality, and still be considered conforming. The catch is that no other implementation is required to support any particular extensions. You may have to recode such features from the ground up when running with another compiler. A summary of common extensions appears at the end of this chapter.

Unspecified Behavior

Aside from well-defined behavior, the ANSI standard speaks of three kinds of compiler behavior that can have a serious impact on portability. These are *unspecified, undefined,* and *implementation-defined behaviors.* Unspecified behavior is discussed first.

Unspecified behavior means that the ANSI standard requires nothing of an implementation, one way or another. The only defense you have against these potential trouble spots is to be thoroughly familiar with your compiler.

The ANSI standard does not specify the following:

- The manner and timing of static initialization.

- Output display or printer behavior when a printable character is written in the final position of a line. That is, no specification is made as to whether automatic line-wrap occurs.

- Output display or printer behavior when a backspace character is written in the first character of a line.

- Output display or printer behavior when a horizontal tab character is written past the last defined tab position.

- Output display or printer behavior when a vertical tab character is written past the last defined vertical tab position.

- The internal format of floating-point objects.

- The order of expression evaluation. Evaluation always occurs as if algebraic associative rules are followed, but this does not necessarily mean that internal events exactly follow that order.

■ The order in which side effects take place. The only guarantee is that side effects will be complete at the next sequence point.

■ The order in which the function designator and the arguments in a function call are evaluated. Remember that a sequence point occurs only when all evaluation is complete and the function actually entered.

■ The alignment of the addressable storage unit used to contain a bit-field. Bit-fields may or may not overlap word boundaries, depending on the machine and particular compiler.

■ The layout of storage for function parameters because some machines are physically stack-oriented and some are not. There is no guarantee as to what the parameter-passing internal mechanism will be.

■ The order in which the preprocessing "stringizing" operator # and the "token-pasting" operator ## are evaluated.

■ Whether errno is a macro or an external identifier.

■ Whether setjmp() is a function-like macro or an external identifier.

■ Whether va_end is a macro or an external identifier.

■ What the value of the file position indicator is after a successful call to the ungetc() function for a text file, until such time as all pushed-back characters are either read or discarded.

■ The details of the value stored by a call to fgetpos(). This may be an aggregate structure, or it might simply be a long.

■ The details and accuracy of the value stored by a call to the ftell() function, when used in text mode.

■ The order and contiguity of storage allocated by the calloc(), malloc(), and realloc() functions. This can be critical if you must have contiguous storage for an application.

■ Which of two elements that compare equal will be returned by a call to bsearch().

■ The relative order of two elements that compare equal when qsort() is used to sort an array. Be careful here; this can be the deathblow to many business-oriented applications that require the preservation of the original order of appearance of otherwise equal elements. Consider this a severe shortcoming of the standard implementation of qsort().

■ The internal structure of the calendar time returned by the time() function.

Undefined Behavior

If your program encounters a situation in which the behavior of the program is undefined, you almost always have a serious problem. Debugging is in order.

Basically, *undefined behavior* gives an implementation the elbowroom to not catch an error condition. If your program (meaning you, the programmer) creates such a condition, anything at all may happen next—all the way from nothing to a severe system crash.

> By introducing undefined behavior into your program, you run the risk of crashing your system. Read on to find out what kinds of things create undefined behavior.

Program behavior in the following circumstances is undefined:

- When a nonempty program source file does not end in a newline character; when it does end in a newline character immediately preceded by a backslash (continuation) character; or when it ends with a partial preprocessing token or comment.

- When a character not in the source character set is encountered during compilation, except when it appears in a preprocessing token that is never converted to a token, character constant, string literal, or comment.

- When a comment, string literal, character constant, or header name contains an invalid multibyte character or does not begin and end in the "initial shift state."

- When an unmatched ' or " is encountered on a logical source line during *tokenization* (preprocessing).

- When the same identifier name is used more than once as a label (for gotos) in the same function.

- When an identifier is used that is not visible in the current scope.

- When identifiers that are supposed to denote the same object differ beyond the minimal number of significant characters (that is, when there is a difference in the name in the 33rd position, for example).

- When an identifier has both internal and external linkage in the same translation unit (source file).

- When an identifier with external linkage is used, but more than one declaration for the object has the extern specifier.

■ When a pointer is used that was made to point to an object with `auto` duration, and the function owning the object is now out of scope (has returned). Usually, this means a crash.

■ When a redeclaration of an object or function fails to specify compatible types (for the object, returned value, or parameters).

■ When an unspecified escape sequence appears in a character constant or string literal. An unspecified escape sequence is one that is not explicitly supported by the standard.

■ When an attempt is made to modify a string literal in any form.

■ When a character string literal is adjacent to a wide string literal. Adjacent literals are of the following form:

```
L"This is a"" string"
```

whereby the `L` preceding the first string literal denotes a wide character string literal. Normally, the compiler concatenates adjacent strings, building one result string, but normal and wide character strings don't mix.

■ When unneeded punctuation is encountered in the `<name>` or `"name"` specification for a header file.

■ When an arithmetic conversion produces a result that cannot be contained in the space provided.

■ When an `lvalue` with an incomplete type is used in a context that requires the value of the designated object.

■ When the value of a `void` expression is used or when an implicit conversion (except to `void`) is applied to a `void` expression.

■ When an object is modified more than once between two sequence points. It is valid to access an object more than once between sequence points, but only once to modify it; other access must be "read-only."

■ When an arithmetic operation is either invalid (for example, divide by zero) or the results cannot be stored in the space provided (for example, when there is an under- or overflow condition).

■ When an object has its stored value accessed by an `lvalue` with an incompatible type.

■ When an argument to a function is a `void` expression.

■ When a function without a full function prototype (that is, an old-style declaration) is called with the wrong number of arguments.

■ When a function having a prototype is called with incompatible parameters—that is, when the function is not defined with a compatible type.

■ When a function accepting a variable number of parameters is called without a prototype that ends with an ellipsis (the ... characters).

■ When an invalid array reference occurs, a null pointer is dereferenced, or reference is made to a local variable with `auto` duration that resides in a block that has gone out of scope.

■ When a pointer to a function returning a type is cast to a pointer to a function returning another (incompatible) type and is used to call the function.

■ When a pointer to an object is converted to a pointer to function, or vice versa.

■ When a pointer is cast to something other than an integral type or another pointer.

■ When addition or subtraction is performed on a pointer that does not point to an array element.

■ When two pointers that do not reference the same array aggregate are subtracted.

■ When a bit-wise shift count is negative or greater than or equal to the number of bits in the object (or expression type). This tactic frequently is used to clear bits from an object, even though it is "nonstandard."

■ When pointers that do not point to the same aggregate are compared.

■ When an object is assigned to an overlapping object. For example, you could use pointer casts to access individual bytes in an integer, but modifying the bytes may not have the expected effect.

■ When an identifier is declared for an object with no linkage and an incomplete type. Declarations with incomplete types generally are used to refer to objects that are defined completely elsewhere; an object with no linkage cannot be defined elsewhere.

■ When a function is declared in a block without the `extern` storage-class specifier.

■ When a bit-field is declared with a type that is not `int`, `signed int`, or `unsigned int`. (See the common extensions at the end of this chapter.)

■ When an attempt is made to modify a `const` object with an `lvalue` that is not qualified as `const`.

■ When an attempt is made to modify a `volatile` object with an `lvalue` that is not qualified as `volatile`.

■ When an uninitialized object with `auto` duration is used.

■ When an aggregate `auto` object has an initializer that is not brace-enclosed or an aggregate `static` object is initialized with something other than another aggregate of the same type or a brace-enclosed initializer.

- When an attempt is made to use the return value of a void function.

- When a function accepting a variable number of arguments has a formal parameter list that does not end with the ... ellipsis.

- When an identifier for an object with internal linkage and incomplete type is declared with a tentative definition.

- When the preprocessing token defined is generated during the expansion of an #if or #elif directive.

- When an #include directive is generated by macro expansion and its form is incorrect.

- When a macro argument consists of no preprocessing tokens.

- When the list of macro arguments contains preprocessing tokens that ordinarily would be directives.

- When the result of the token paste preprocessing operator ## is not a valid preprocessing token.

- When a macro expansion results in a #line directive that does not match one of the two well-defined forms.

- When you attempt to #define or #undef one of the following predefined directives:

```
defined
_ _LINE_ _
_ _FILE_ _
_ _DATE_ _
_ _TIME_ _
_ _STDC_ _
```

- When you attempt to copy an object to an overlapping object by some means other than the memmove() library function (which is designed to handle overlapped argument objects).

- When a program redefines a reserved external identifier.

- When a standard header is included in an external definition, when it is included for the first time after reference is made to anything it declares, or when it is included when a current macro definition has the same name as a keyword.

- When a macro definition of errno is suppressed to obtain access to an actual object.

- When the offsetof macro refers to a structure member that is a bit-field. (Bit-fields cannot be addressed separately by either pointer or offset because they may not be on a byte boundary.)

■ When an argument to a library function has an invalid value, except in those cases where the behavior is explicitly stated.

■ When a library function that accepts a variable number of arguments is not declared.

■ When the macro definition of `assert` is suppressed to obtain access to an actual object.

■ When the argument to one of the character-handling functions is outside the domain of characters it can handle.

■ When a macro definition of `setjmp()` is suppressed to gain access to an actual function.

■ When you invoke `setjmp()` and then fail to test the returned value by a selection, iteration, or comparison statement.

■ When, between calls to `setjmp()` and `longjmp()`, an `auto` object that has not been declared as `volatile` is modified and then is accessed to fetch its value.

■ When the `longjmp()` function is invoked from a nested signal-handling function.

■ When a truly asynchronous signal occurs—that is, it is not the result of calling `abort()` or `raise()`—and the signal handler calls any library function other than `signal()`, or the signal handler refers to any object that is not of static duration and declared to have type `volatile sig_atomic_t`.

■ When a truly asynchronous signal occurs and the signal handler calls `signal()`, it receives the return value `SIG_ERR` and `errno` is referred to.

■ When the `va_arg` macro is invoked with the same `ap` pointer that was passed to and used by a lower-level function. That is, the lower-level function has altered `ap` so the current function must call `va_end` to resynchronize the pointer and variable argument list.

■ When a macro definition of `va_start`, `va_arg`, `va_end`, or any combination of them is suppressed to gain access to an actual function. (There may be no such function.)

■ When the `parmN` parameter of the `va_start` is declared with `register` storage class, array or function type, or any type that is not compatible with the default argument promotions.

■ When all variable arguments have been exhausted and you invoke `va_arg` again.

■ When the type of the next actual variable argument disagrees with that requested by `va_arg`.

■ When the `va_end` macro is invoked before `va_start`.

■ When a function that accepts variable arguments and has initialized the argument list with `va_start` returns without invoking `va_end`. In many implementations, this may have no effect.

■ When you call `fflush()` against an input stream or against an update stream whose last operation was input. The latter is somewhat contradictory because other parts of the literature (both the ANSI document and others) indicate that you should flush an update stream whenever you switch from write to read or from read to write. In any event, when the last operation on an update stream is a read operation, you most likely will call a seek or positioning function before writing again, which also flushes the buffer.

■ When you switch read/write access on an update stream without properly flushing the buffer. Most likely, you will lose data somehow.

■ When the format string of `fprintf()` or `fscanf()` type functions does not match the actual argument list.

■ When an invalid conversion specification is encountered in the format string of the `fprintf()` or `fscanf()` functions.

■ When the `%%` conversion occurs in the format string of `fprintf()` or `fscanf()` and there are characters between the two percent signs. This is a real syntax error, but presumably some compiler has permitted it in the past.

■ When the format string for `fprintf()` contains a conversion specification with an h or l (*el*) character that is not part of the following conversions: d, i, n, o, u, x, X. Also, the L character must be a part of the following conversions: e, E, f, g, G. The same is true for `fscanf()`, except that `fscanf()` does not have any of the uppercase conversion characters.

■ When the format string for `fprintf()` contains a # flag for a conversion other than o, x, X, e, E, g, G.

■ When the format string for `fprintf()` contains the 0 (zero-fill) flag for a conversion other than d, i, o, u, x, X, e, E, f, g, G.

■ When an aggregate object, or a pointer to one, is an argument to `fprintf()`, unless the conversion specifies `%s` (string) or `%p` (pointer to void).

■ When a single conversion performed by `fprintf()` results in more than 509 characters of output.

■ When a pointer value produced by the `fprintf()` function's `%p` conversion in a previous program execution is used as input to the `fscanf()` function's `%p` conversion. Note that this works in the same program execution because both program and data are still in the same locations.

- When the receiving internal object of an `fscanf()` conversion has the wrong type or cannot hold the resulting value.

- When the results of converting a string to internal format by `atoi()`, `atol()`, or `atof()` cannot be properly represented (for example, value too large).

- When you refer via pointer to dynamically allocated memory that already has been freed by `free()`.

- When you try to `free()` dynamically allocated memory with the wrong address, or when the memory has been freed already.

- When a program executes more than one `exit()` function. You might trip over this one if you have defined several `atexit()` routines.

- When the result of `abs()`, `div()`, `labs()`, or `ldiv()` cannot be represented properly.

- When the shift states for the `mblen()`, `mbtowc()`, and `wctomb()` functions are not reset explicitly to the initial shift state when the `LC_CTYPE` category of the current locale is changed.

- When the output array targeted by a copying or concatenation function is too small.

- When the `strftime()` contains an invalid conversion specification.

Implementation-Defined Behavior

In keeping with the spirit of C—where performance is important even if portability suffers—the standard indicates several areas where that behavior is implementation-defined.

Implementation-defined behavior gives the implementor elbowroom—room to implement a given task in such a way that the full native powers of the hardware and software platform can be brought to bear. However, the standard requires that the choice of implementation be explained to the user.

What to Look For

Compiler implementors are required to document their product's behavior in several specific areas. These statements are taken nearly verbatim from the ANSI-proposed standard for C because of their importance to you, the programmer. An implementor must state the following items.

Environment

The semantics of the arguments to `main()`.

What constitutes an interactive device.

Identifiers

The number of initial significant characters beyond 31 for an identifier with internal linkage.

The number of initial significant characters beyond six for an identifier with external linkage.

Whether case distinctions are significant for an identifier with external linkage.

Characters

The members of the source and execution character sets, except as explicitly specified in the standard.

The shift states used for encoding multibyte characters.

The number of bits in a character in the execution character set.

The mapping of source-set characters to execution-set characters (in string literals and character constants).

The value of an integer character constant that contains a character or escape sequence not represented in the basic execution character set for a wide character constant.

The value of an integer character constant that contains more than one character or the value of a wide character constant that contains more than one multibyte character.

The current locale used to convert multibyte characters into corresponding wide characters (codes) for a wide character constant.

Whether a "plain" `char` has the same range of values as `signed char` or `unsigned char`.

Integers

The representations and sets of values of the various types of integers.

The results of converting an integer to a shorter signed integer or the result of converting an unsigned integer to a signed integer of equal length if the value cannot be represented.

The results of bit-wise operations on signed integers.

The sign of the remainder after integer division.

The result of a right shift of a negative-valued signed integer.

Floating-Point

The representations and sets of values of the different types of floating-point numbers.

The direction of truncation when an integral number is converted to a floating-point number that cannot exactly represent the original value.

The direction of truncation or rounding when a floating-point number is converted to a narrower floating-point number.

Arrays and Pointers

The type of integer required to hold the maximum size of an array—that is, the type of the sizeof operator, size_t.

The result of casting a pointer to an integer, and vice versa.

The type of integer required to hold the difference between two pointers to members of the same array, ptrdiff_t.

Registers

The extent to which objects can actually be placed in registers by use of the register storage-class specifier.

Structures, Unions, Enumerations, and Bit-Fields

A member of a union object is accessed using a member of a different type.

The padding and alignment of members of structures. This should present no problem unless binary data is written by one implementation to be read by another.

Whether a "plain" `int` bit-field is treated as a `signed int` bit-field or as an `unsigned int` bit-field.

The order of allocation of bit-fields within an `int`.

Whether a bit-field can straddle a storage-unit boundary.

The integer type chosen to represent the values of an enumerated type.

Qualifiers

What constitutes an access to an object that has `volatile`-qualified type.

Declarators

The maximum number of declarators that may modify an arithmetic, structure, or union type.

Statements

The maximum number of `case` values in a `switch` statement.

Preprocessing Directives

Whether the value of a single-character character constant in a constant expression that controls conditional inclusion matches the value of the same character constant in the execution character set, and whether such a character constant may have a negative value.

The method for locating includable source files.

The support of quoted names for source-file inclusion.

The mapping of source-file character sequences.

The behavior for each recognized `#pragma` directive.

The definitions for `__DATE__` and `__TIME__`, respectively, when the date and time of translation are not available.

Library Functions

The null-pointer constant to which the macro NULL expands.

The diagnostic printed by and the termination behavior of the assert() function.

The sets of characters tested for by the isalnum(), isalpha(), iscntrl(), islower(), isprint(), and isupper() functions.

The values returned by the mathematical functions on domain errors.

Whether the mathematics functions set the integer expression errno to the value of the macro ERANGE on underflow range errors.

Whether a domain error occurs or zero is returned when the fmod() function has a second argument of zero.

The set of signals for the signal() function.

The semantics for each signal recognized by the signal() function.

The default handling and the handling at program startup for each signal recognized by the signal() function.

If the equivalent of signal(sig, SIG_DFL); is not executed prior to the call of a signal handler, then state the blocking of the signal that is performed.

Whether the default handling is reset if the SIGILL signal is received by a handler specified to the signal() function.

Whether the last line of a text stream requires a terminating newline character.

Whether space characters that are written to a text stream immediately before a newline character appear when read in.

The number of null characters that may be appended to the data written to a binary stream.

Whether the file-position indicator of an append-mode stream is positioned initially at the beginning or end of a file.

Whether a write on a text stream causes the associate file to be truncated beyond that point.

The characteristics of file buffering.

Whether a zero-length file actually exists.

The rules for composing valid filenames.

Whether the same file can be open multiple times (concurrently).

The effect of the `remove()` function on an open file.

The result of trying to `rename()` a file when the new name already exists.

The output for the `%p` conversion of `fprintf()`. (80x86 addresses must account for the segment and offset parts, for example.)

The input for the `%p` conversion of `fscanf()`.

The interpretation of the – (minus) character when it is neither the first nor the last character in the scanlist for the `%[` conversion of `fscanf()`.

The value assigned to `errno` when `fgetpos()` or `ftell()` is unsuccessful.

The messages generated by the `perror()` function.

The behavior of `calloc()`, `malloc()`, and `realloc()` when the requested allocation size is zero.

The behavior of the `abort()` function with respect to open and temporary files. Many implementations make no attempt to clean these up, which can cause problems later.

The status returned by the `exit()` function if the value of the argument is not zero, `EXIT_SUCCESS`, or `EXIT_FAILURE`.

The set of environment names and the method for altering the environment list used by the `getenv()` function.

The contents of the error message strings returned by the `strerror()` function.

The local time zone and daylight savings time.

The era for the `clock()` function.

Locale-Specific Behavior

The following characteristics of a hosted environment are locale-specific (that is, dependent):

The content of the execution character set, in addition to the required members.

The direction of printing.

The decimal point character.

The implementation-defined aspects of character-testing and case-mapping functions.

The collating sequence of the execution character set.

The formats for time and date information.

The subject of common extensions to the language also fits into the category of implementation-defined behavior. That discussion is deferred until the end of this chapter.

Quiet Changes to K&R C

An area of portability and compatibility that is dangerous to overlook concerns the vast amount of preexisting C code. A vast body of commercial code is "out there" and must be supported somehow—presumably with the newer ANSI-conforming compilers.

By now you should understand clearly that the original K&R C and ANSI C are substantially compatible, but the operative word is *substantially*. There are differences between the two standards (K&R compatibility is a standard and a very good one).

How can you cope with the changes from one C platform to the next? What, in particular, may catch you unaware? The ANSI rationale document identifies a number of danger areas, called *quiet changes*, of which you should be aware.

What Is a Quiet Change?

Understanding quiet changes means knowing the difference between syntax and semantics. *Syntax* defines how you write code: the reserved words, punctuation, operators, their grouping, and so forth. *Semantics,* on the other hand, defines what a given syntax code means.

What does this mean to you? It means that interpreting the same syntax (manner of writing code) in two different ways is entirely possible. This is the danger you face when compiling old code with new compilers. What if a line of code is still syntactically valid but now means (and hence, does) something different?

This is the crux of the quiet changes introduced into the C language by the new ANSI standard. They are points of difference between the old and new standards that invisibly cause code to behave differently. This problem is insidious, and ANSI was aware of its danger. Moreover, the committee acknowledged the problem and made efforts to minimize the number of instances in which this problem can happen.

There are instances of quiet changes in C semantics, though, however few they may be. You should be aware of them and be prepared to correct for them when recompiling old code.

Converting K&R C Programs

This section details the quiet changes in C semantics introduced by the ANSI standard for C. Keep in mind that these changes do not comprise all the changes. This section deals only with those changes that may be "invisible"— code that still compiles without error but now works differently.

The exact text of the ANSI rationale's documentation of quiet changes is given in italics in each case, followed by explanations in normal text.

- Programs with character sequences such as ??! in string constants, character constants, or header names now produce different results. This happens because such sequences duplicate the new *ternary escape sequences* that formerly did not exist.

- A program that depends on internal identifiers matching only in the first eight characters, for example, may change to one with distinct objects for each variant spelling of the identifier. ANSI C allows identifiers to have up to 31 case-sensitive characters, as opposed to the older 8-character limit. A name may now vary in the 20th digit, for example, and be considered different, where formerly spelling differences this far down the sequence were ignored.

- A program relying on file scope rules may be valid under block scope rules but behave differently. This change is particularly subtle. Many older compilers assigned file scope to identifiers with external linkage, *even if they were declared in a block.* Under the ANSI standard, an object declared in a block is governed in by block scope rules. *However,* if the object had external linkage but is now gone out of scope (for example, the function has returned), an implementation is not required to diagnose a failure to redeclare the external identifier. In other words, there may be some confusion as to the type of such an object, but there may still be no compiler error message.

- Unsuffixed integer constants may have different types. In K&R, unsuffixed decimal constants greater than INT_MAX and unsuffixed octal or hexadecimal constants greater than UINT_MAX are of type long. That is, previously, an integer constant with value 43777 (greater than INT_MAX) was understood to be type long. Now, it may be interpreted as a normal int, with the accompanying danger that it is truncated before use. If you mean for a constant to be long or unsigned, use the L or U constant suffix, as in 43777L.

- A constant of the form '\078' (an octal escape sequence) is valid but now has different meaning. It now denotes a character constant with a value that is the (implementation-defined) combination of the values '\07' and '8'. In some implementations, the old meaning is the character whose code is 078 (70 *octal* + 87) = 100 (*octal*) = 64 (*decimal*). This is in contrast to hex escape sequences (\x...), which extend until the first nonhex character is encountered.

■ A constant of the form `'\a'` or `'\x'` may now have different meaning. The old meaning, if any, was implementation dependent. The alert special character `'\a'` and hex escape `'\x'` did not exist in K&R C; thus, a compiler may have used these sequences for other purposes.

■ It is neither required nor forbidden that identical string literals be represented by a single copy of the string in memory; a program depending on either scheme may behave differently. That is, do not count on the address of a string literal.

■ Expressions of the form `x=-3` change meaning with the loss of the old-style assignment operators. Old compilers used operators such as `=-`, `=+`, and so on. Now only the forms `-=`, `+=`, and so on are permitted. Thus, the preceding expression is interpreted to mean that "x is equal to minus three."

■ A program that depends on unsigned preserving arithmetic conversions behaves differently, probably without complaint (from the compiler). This is considered to be the most serious semantic change made by the committee to a widespread current practice. This change has to do with the new *integral promotion rules*. Formerly, when any shorter unsigned value was widened, the result was always unsigned. This is the *unsigned preserving rule*. Now, when an `unsigned char` or `unsigned short` is widened (in being assigned to a `signed int`, for example), the ANSI standard requires that the value preserving rules be used. Therefore, *if the unsigned value permits it,* the result is signed; otherwise (if the value is too large), the result is unsigned. This change was deemed to be safer for novice programmers, but it introduces the possibility that an expression no longer evaluates to the same result (because of the unexpected participation of a signed value).

■ Expressions with `float` operands may now be computed at lower precision. The "base document" (K&R) *specified that all floating-point operations be done in* `double`. This change is well-intentioned (it increases computational speed), but it may backfire on you. You can begin a computation with `float` types, and the result may also fit in a `float`. However, *intermediate results frequently may require greater precision,* causing loss of precision and possibly a significant error. If you need to be sure, use `double` in the first place.

■ *Shifting by a* `long` *count no longer coerces the shifted operand to* `long`. The second operand of the bitwise shift operators `<<` and `>>` is a count of the number of bits to be shifted in the indicated direction. Formerly, if this count operand had type `long`, this implied that the object being shifted should be promoted to `long` also.

■ A program that uses `#if` expressions to determine properties of the execution environment may now get different answers. Some C compilers, called *cross-compilers,* are used in one environment to produce code for another. The ANSI committee felt that requiring that equal precision of floating-point numbers, minimum maxima, and other environment characteristics be provided in both the translation and execution environments imposed too great a burden on some cross-compilers.

■ *The empty declaration* `strict x;` *is no longer innocuous.* Such a declaration hides an outer declaration of `x` and "opens" a new instance of the object in the current block. That is, the declaration is no longer empty.

■ Code that relies on a bottom-up parse of aggregate initializers with partially elided braces does not yield the expected initialized object. In Chapter 11, you saw that the initializer for a `strict` that contained other complex objects could specify only the outer curly braces in the initializer. In some instances of older code, only part of the internally contained curly braces were omitted because of the way the initializer was parsed. Because the ANSI document has reaffirmed the top-down parse originally described by K&R, such constructions may not work correctly now. Either use all internal braces or omit them all.

■ The `long` expressions and constants in `switch` statements are no longer truncated to `int`. The ANSI standard allows the `case` variables to have any integral type; original C required a type of `int`. This may produce some unexpected results when recompiling older code that relied on this truncation.

■ *Functions that depend on* `char` *or* `short` *parameter types being widened to* `int`, *or* `float` *to* `double`, *may behave differently.* Formerly, such function arguments were subject to a different set of automatic integral promotions that widened the mentioned types. The result was that you could pass a `char` to a function that actually specified a formal parameter of type `int`. The ANSI standard requires that the received argument be converted *as if* by assignment, but such type rewriting is no longer permitted.

■ *A macro that relies on formal parameter substitution in a string literal produces different results.* This process, called *stringizing,* is important to many programs. The ANSI standard introduced another preprocessing operator to solve this and other token-handling problems: the `##` or *token paste* operator. In Chapter 8, you saw how to use `##` to implement the pasting of manifest constants in a string, as in the following example:

```
#define SIZE 10
#define buildmsg(X) "Array size is " ## #X

main()
{
  int num[SIZE];   /* Define array with SIZE elements */

  printf( "%s", buildmsg(SIZE) );      /* Report it */
}
```

In the preceding fragment, both the stringizing and token pasting operators form the string. The paste operator not only gets around the limitation, but it provides added flexibility.

- *A program that relies on a size-0 allocation request returning a non-null pointer behaves differently.* This is the last of the quiet changes and the only one that affects a standard library function. Some older compilers allowed a zero-size `calloc()` or `malloc()` request and returned a valid pointer to the "object." An ANSI-conforming compiler does not allow this request.

Environmental Considerations

C compilers do their work in many environments and sometimes even produce object code for environments other than the translation environment. This imposes some limitations on how a compiler can be implemented.

Some limitations, such as numerical (value) limits, were discussed in earlier chapters. Two aspects that have not yet been discussed are *translation limits* and common but *nonstandard functions*. The next two sections deal with these aspects.

Translation Limitations

An ANSI-conforming implementation of C must be able to compile a program that contains at least one instance of every one of the following limits:

- 15 nesting levels of compound statements, iteration control structures, and selection control structures.

- Eight nesting levels of conditional inclusion.

- 12 pointer, array, and function declarators (in any combination) modifying an arithmetic, structure, union, or incomplete type in a declaration.

- 31 declarators nested by parentheses in a full declarator.

- 32 expressions nested by parentheses in a full expression.

- 31 significant initial characters in an internal identifier or macro name.

- Six significant initial characters in an external identifier.

- 511 external identifiers in one translation unit (source file).

- 127 identifiers with block scope that are declared in one block.

- 1,024 macro identifiers simultaneously defined in one translation unit.

- 31 parameters in one function definition.

- 31 arguments in one function call.

- 31 parameters in one macro definition.

- 31 arguments in one macro invocation.

- 509 characters in one logical source line.

- 509 characters in one character-string literal or wide-string literal (after concatenation).

- 32,767 bytes in an object (only in hosted, not freestanding, environments).

- Eight nesting levels for #included files.

- 257 case labels for a switch statement (excluding those for any nested switch statements).

- 127 members in a single structure or union.

- 127 enumeration constants in a single enumeration.

- 15 levels of nested structure or union definitions in a single *structure declaration-list*.

Common Extensions to ANSI Standard C

You have read several times in this book that any particular machine or system on which a C compiler runs has its own peculiarities that cannot be accounted for in any standard. These peculiarities are often handled by a vendor's extensions to the language, and it is often impossible to write high-performance code without using them. This is not contrary to the intent of the ANSI committee; extensions do not replace requirements—they go beyond them.

NOTE Some of the more common extensions are discussed in the proposed standards document and are covered here. Their inclusion here does not mean that your compiler must support them. Nor are they necessarily portable to other implementations.

Environment Arguments

In addition to the int argc and char *argv[] arguments received by main() from the environment, in a hosted environment it may receive a third argument of the form char *envp[]. This argument is handled much like argv pointers, but it points to a null-terminated array of pointers to string. Each string provides information about the environment during this execution of the program (or process).

Some compilers set up a similar environment variable using this information. The sample program SYSENV.C in Chapter 8 used such a variable.

Specialized Identifiers

Letters, digits, and the underscore character are required for the formation of identifiers in the source character set. Other characters, such as the so-called national characters $, @, and #, are allowed by some compilers in the formation of names.

Length and Case of Identifiers

Some compilers go beyond the 31 characters required for internal identifiers and six characters required for external identifiers. They consider all characters significant, whatever the linkage, including case distinctions.

Scope of Identifiers

A function identifier or an object declaration containing the `extern` keyword may have file scope wherever it is written. Minimal conformity to the ANSI standard permits some such declarations (not definitions, remember) to have only block scope.

Writable String Literals

Some compilers allow modification of string literals. In such a case, multiple appearances of otherwise identical literals are distinct objects.

Other Arithmetic Types

An implementation may define additional object types, such as `long long int` or BCD (binary coded decimal—packed decimal) objects.

Function Pointer Casts

Ordinarily, function and data objects are separated. Some implementations, however, may allow a cast of an object pointer to a pointer to function. This has the effect of allowing a program to invoke data as if it were code.

Non-*int* Bit-Field Types

Types other than int, signed int, or unsigned int can be declared as bit-fields with the appropriate widths.

The *fortran* Keyword

You can write the fortran specifier in a function declaration to indicate that the function is written in that language.

The *asm* Keyword

Some compilers permit the use of the asm keyword for the direct insertion of in-line assembler code in a C program. Depending on the compiler, an external assembler program may or may not have to be present.

Multiple External Definitions

A given object may be declared, with or without the explicit use of the extern keyword, more than once. This is dangerous in any case: if the declarations disagree or if more than one is initialized, the behavior is "undefined."

> Declaring an external object more than once can cause serious problems. The multiple declarations can cause your program to lose track of the value stored in the external object.

Empty Macro Arguments

In several places in this book, you have seen macros such as the following:

```
#define COMPILER
...
#if defined( COMPILER )
...
#endif
```

Such a macro definition has an *empty argument list*. Strictly speaking, this definition is nonstandard because the whole point of macros is string substitution. This use is so widespread, however, that we do not know of a compiler that fails to support the usage. If a macro has arguments, the macro invocation must supply the correct number of arguments.

Predefined Macro Names

An implementation can provide macros—describing the translation and execution environments—that do not begin with the underscore character.

Extra Arguments for Signal Handlers

Handlers for specific types of signals may be called with arguments (in addition to the signal type argument) for handling special conditions.

Additional Stream Types and File Modes

Special applications may require special mappings from file to stream and extended processing modes.

Defined File-Position Indicator

When this extension is implemented, the file-position indicator is decremented by each successful call to the `ungetc()` function for a text stream, unless the position is already zero.

Summary

In this chapter you learned about portability and conversion of C programs from one platform to another. The following topics were covered:

- The spirit of C controls the shape of the ANSI standard for C. This means several specific things to you, not the least of which is that performance is important, and using extensions to the language is both necessary and expected.

- Undefined, unspecified, and implementation-dependent behavior are important aspects of your compiler. Particularly with regard to implementation-defined behavior, you should take the time and trouble to become familiar with your own compiler.

- Extensions to the language give your program added power and flexibility. The language standard provides a solid, predictable base for your C programming efforts. The extensions enable you to tailor the application to the machine and operating system on which it runs and to extract their full power and efficiency—but there is a corresponding decrease in portability.

Moving to C

The purpose of this chapter is to help those who are used to programming, but not in C. Switching from one language to another can be a big challenge because you have to change many of your everyday programming practices. Old habits, whether good or bad, are hard to break. This chapter helps you make the change by pointing out some of the differences between the language you are using, either BASIC or Pascal, and the new language you are learning, C.

You will find this chapter useful if all you need is a brief review of the differences between C and BASIC or C and Pascal. This chapter can also be of help if you are learning C and you need a quick reference to help you convert your old BASIC or Pascal programs. If you are ready to move on to C++, feel free to skip this chapter and start with Part II. This chapter is for reference and comparison, it does not introduce any new C programming concepts.

The chapter is divided into two portions. The first portion covers moving from BASIC to C, and the second portion covers moving from Pascal to C. Both contain sections that describe differences in data types, operators, and flow control. If you're new to C but are used to programming in BASIC or Pascal, reading this chapter will help you make the mental shift to C.

Because the sample programs in the rest of this book use the Microsoft and Borland C/C++ compilers, this chapter also uses the BASIC and Pascal packages from Microsoft and Borland. For the first portion of this chapter, the examples were made with the Microsoft QuickBASIC Version 4.5 package. QuickBASIC was chosen because it is much more powerful than QBASIC and more likely to be used in larger, more complicated BASIC programs. For the second portion of the chapter, the examples were created with the Borland Turbo Pascal Version 6 compiler. Because Turbo Pascal is the most popular Pascal compiler, it was the natural choice.

Here's a quick note before you dive in. This chapter covers the transition from two very different languages to C. The chapter shows some of the fundamentals in BASIC and Pascal and compares those fundamentals with corresponding elements in C. The chapter does not attempt to show all the differences between BASIC and C, or Pascal and C. Nor does the chapter try to show all the ways you can do things in C. The chapter does provide you with a quick reference to the most common questions concerning moving to C from either BASIC or Pascal.

Moving to C from BASIC

At one time, BASIC was a limited language. In its earlier days, BASIC was good for teaching programming and shorter programs. It was, however, hard to create powerful and sophisticated programs in BASIC. Constraints such as mandatory line numbering made the BASIC language awkward and slowed its development.

Today's BASIC is much better. With the advent of BASIC packages such as Microsoft QuickBASIC, BASIC is gaining respect as a more usable language. The worst constraints and hindrances of the old BASIC language have been fixed, and the new BASIC language has proved to be very useful.

If you are used to programming in a modern BASIC, such as QuickBASIC, many familiar concepts are applicable in C. For example, you have the integer, floating-point, and string data types in both BASIC and C. Functions, too, are similar in concept and use in both QuickBASIC and C.

There are many differences, however. This portion of the chapter points out many of these differences and helps you make the transition easily from BASIC to C. Some fundamental concepts of the BASIC language are presented, as well as how to implement them in C.

Interpreters Versus Compilers

One of the biggest differences between BASIC and C has been that BASIC, for the most part, has been an *interpreted* language and C has been a *compiled* language. So, you might ask, what difference does that make? There are several differences, but first take a look at the difference between an interpreter and a compiler.

An interpreter is a program that takes the commands you enter and executes them as soon as they are entered. For example, if you enter the BASIC command

```
PRINT "Hello World!"
```

the Hello World! message is immediately displayed on the screen. The PRINT command was carried out as soon as it was entered.

A compiler is very different from an interpreter. With a compiler, you also enter commands you want the computer to perform. Before those commands can be executed, however, they must be compiled into a program. When your commands are compiled into a program, the compiler reads each of the commands, changes each one into machine-readable instructions, and assembles your instructions and other necessary parts into an executable program. You then have to run the program to carry out your commands.

If a compiled program sounds more complicated, it is. This doesn't mean that the compiled program is too complicated; it just means that there is usually more involved in writing a compiled program than an interpreted program. The same Hello World! example for BASIC looks very different in C:

```
#include <stdlib.h>
#include <stdio.h>

main()
{
  printf( "Hello World!" );
}
```

Notice that this short C program does the same thing that the single BASIC command did. The C program, however, required more setup to perform the same function.

If the interpreted program is shorter and at least appears to be simpler, what is the advantage of a compiled language? There are three main advantages of compiled languages: speed, portability, and power.

A compiled program is faster than an interpreted program. Both the compiler and the interpreter must convert your commands into a form the computer can understand, but the compiler does this conversion one time. The result of the compiler's conversion of your commands to machine-language commands is the executable program. This program is in a form your computer can directly understand, and the program therefore executes quickly.

An interpreter, however, must perform the process of converting the entered commands into machine language each time your program is run. In effect, you are compiling the program each time you run it. Because more steps are involved when an interpreted program is executed, the interpreted program runs more slowly.

A compiled program is more portable because all the necessary parts are contained in the executable file that was created when the program was compiled. Therefore, a compiled program can be run on any computer (of the same type). Because an interpreted program requires that the interpreter be on the computer, an interpreted program can run only on computers where the interpreter is installed.

The power of a compiled program is mainly a result of its speed. Because a compiled program runs faster, it is possible to add functions to the compiled program that would simply take too long to perform in an interpreted program. Generally, a compiled program offers more flexibility in calling support functions and procedures.

Some comments are needed about the BASIC packages. Current BASIC packages, like QuickBASIC, contain both an interpreter and a compiler. In the early days of BASIC, the packages were mostly interpreters. Fortunately, things have changed. Now, with packages like QuickBASIC, you get the best of both worlds. You can now have the ease of use of an interpreter, plus the capability to compile your programs for portability and faster operation.

Even with all the new features, it is hard for a program written in BASIC to reach the level of power and sophistication capable in a C program. The reason is that BASIC started out as a simpler, interpreted language. C, however started out as a powerful compiled language specifically meant for heavy-duty development.

Comparing Data Types

If you are familiar with the data types used in BASIC, you won't have much trouble moving to C. The data types in QuickBASIC are similar in Microsoft C/C++. This discussion reviews the data types used in QuickBASIC and shows you the C language counterparts of those data types.

Integers

An integer is the most basic (pardon the pun!) data type for both BASIC and C. Without integers, it would be nearly impossible to write a program that does anything. Because integers are so fundamental and important, it is not surprising that there are few differences in using integers in BASIC and C. The main difference is in how the integer types are identified in each language. Refer to Table 13.1 for a comparison of integers in Microsoft QuickBASIC and Microsoft C/C++.

Notice in Table 13.1 that the integer types in Microsoft C/C++ and QuickBASIC have somewhat similar names and almost identical ranges. The main difference between Microsoft C/C++ and QuickBASIC is in the way integer variables are named and used.

Table 13.1.   A comparison of integers in Microsoft QuickBASIC and C/C++.

QuickBASIC Type	Range	C/C++ Type	Range
Integer	−32,768 to 32,767	int	−32,767 to 32,767
Long integer	−2,147,483,648 to 2,147,483,647	long	−2,147, 483,647 to 2,147,483,647

From your reading earlier in this book, you know that integers declared in a C program can have any valid variable name. The following declarations are legal and acceptable:

```
int i;
int my_number;
int number1;
```

QuickBASIC is not quite as flexible. Using integers in QuickBASIC requires that you append your variable names with specific characters. These characters placed at the end of the variable name inform QuickBASIC of the type of data it is dealing with. Here are some integers in QuickBASIC:

```
mynum%
sum%
bignum&
```

The % after the variable name tells QuickBASIC that the variable holds a regular integer. The & indicates that the variable is a long integer and can therefore hold a larger value than a regular integer.

The reason that variable names in QuickBASIC and C are different is that QuickBASIC does not require that you declare the variable before you use it. Because you can use a variable whenever and wherever you want, QuickBASIC has to have some way of knowing what type of data you will be using. The special character after a variable name enables QuickBASIC to know what kind of data is being handled.

In C, you declare your variables before you ever use them. Because the variable name and type are declared before the variable is used, the compiler is able to keep track of what kind of data can be stored in the variable.

> ### Quick Reference: Signed Integers in BASIC and C
>
> Note a final point about integers. In QuickBASIC, the integral data types hold signed values. An integer in C does not have to be signed. It is possible to declare integer variables that will hold only positive values. These unsigned integer variables in C can be regular or long integers.

Floating-Point Variables

Unlike an integer variable, a floating-point variable can store a number that has a fractional part. In addition, a floating-point variable can store values that are greater in magnitude than integer variables.

QuickBASIC has two floating-point data types. The first of the floating-point data types is the single precision, and the second is the double precision. The difference between the two floating-point data types is in the magnitude of the numbers they can store. The double-precision data type can store larger and more accurate numbers than the single-precision data type.

Table 13.2 shows a comparison of floating-point data types in Microsoft QuickBASIC and Microsoft C/C++.

Table 13.2. A comparison of floating-point data types in Microsoft QuickBASIC and C/C++.

QuickBASIC Type	Range	C/C++ Type	Range
Single precision	-3.4×10^{38} to 3.4×10^{38}	`float`	1.2×10^{-38} to 3.4×10^{38}
Double precision	-1.7×10^{308} to 1.7×10^{308}	`double`	2.2×10^{-308} to 1.8×10^{38}
		`long double`	3.4×10^{-4932} 1.2×10^{4932}

In the preceding section, you saw that there was little difference in the values that could be stored in integer variables in each language. When you look at Table 13.2, which describes the values that can be stored in the floating-point variables in Microsoft QuickBASIC and C/C++, you see much greater differences.

Quick Reference: Magnitude and Precision

The C implementation of floating-point variables is more powerful than the BASIC implementation. C not only has more types that can store numbers of larger magnitude, but also has a floating-point data type that has more precision than BASIC. Table 13.3 compares the precision of the floating-point variables in Microsoft QuickBASIC and C/C++.

Table 13.3. A comparison of the precision of floating-point variables in Microsoft QuickBASIC and C/C++.

Language	Data Type	Precision (in Decimal Places)
QuickBASIC	Single precision	7
QuickBASIC	Double precision	15
C/C++	float	6
C/C++	double	15
C/C++	long double	18

If you write programs that deal with extremely large or small numbers, it would be best to refer to the compiler manual. From the preceding tables, you can see that the implementation of floating-point variables can differ greatly from one product to the next.

Like integer variables in QuickBASIC, floating-point variables can (but don't have to) end with a special character that tells QuickBASIC what kind of variable is being used. The following code fragment shows how floating-point variables can be used in QuickBASIC:

```
singlenum! = 100.10
total = 3454.97
sum1 = 0.9987
doublenum# = 2.0007456
...
print "your single precision number = ", singlenum!
print "The Grand Total is: ", total
print "Your score is: ", sum1
print "your double precision number = ", doublenum#
```

Notice how the variables in this code fragment are used. The first floating-point variable is followed by the ! character, which identifies the variable as a single-precision floating-point variable. The second and third variables, however, are not followed by any special characters. By default, QuickBASIC recognizes variables that have no appended special characters as single-precision floating-point variables. The # character following the last variable name indicates that the variable is a double-precision floating-point variable.

Using floating-point variables in a C program is not much harder than using floating-point variables in a BASIC program. It's just different. In C, as you learned in earlier chapters, you must declare your variables before you use them. In a C program, therefore, you can't just use a floating-point variable; you have to tell the compiler about it first. The nice thing about using floating-point variables in C is that you don't have to do anything special to variable names. Any legal variable name can be used as long as the rest of the declaration is coded properly. The following code fragment shows how floating-point variables are used in C:

```
some_function()
{
float radius = 5.15;
double balance;

balance = 1000783.99;

printf( "The radius = %.2f\n", radius );
printf( "Your account balance is $%.2f\n", balance );
}
```

In this code fragment, two floating-point variables are declared and used. The first two lines in the function body declare the variables. Notice that the first declaration both declares the variable and initializes it. The second declaration performs only the declaration of the variable. A value is assigned to the `balance` variable in the third line of the function body. The first variable, `radius`, is declared as a `float` type. The `float` data type is C's lower-precision floating-point data type. The second variable, `balance`, is declared as a `double`. The `double` floating-point variable can store numbers of greater magnitude and more precision. The last two lines in the function show how the `printf()` function can be used to display floating-point type data.

Comparing String Types

Conceptually, strings are the same in BASIC and C. In both languages, a string is simply a sequence of characters. Strings, however, are handled differently because of the way these languages were designed.

The primary difference between string variables in BASIC and C is that string variables in BASIC can hold either variable-length or fixed-length strings, whereas string variables in C can hold only fixed-length strings. In fact, the capability of having fixed-length string variables in BASIC is new. Previous versions of BASIC had only variable-length string variables. Like other features mentioned in this chapter, fixed-length string variables are a special feature of QuickBASIC and are not found in all versions of the BASIC language.

Now back to the reason why string variables are handled differently in BASIC and C. Recall the earlier discussion about interpreted and compiled languages. BASIC has been, and can still be, an interpreted language. This means that each command you type is interpreted and executed "on the fly." Therefore, the BASIC interpreter has to be able to dynamically allocate memory for variables, string or otherwise, that you enter. Because the BASIC interpreter dynamically allocates memory for each string variable, it makes no difference (up to limitations of the interpreter) what the length of the string variable is.

C, however, is not quite as flexible. Because C is a compiled language, the length of each string variable does make a difference. The compiler needs the length information so it can perform its job correctly.

Quick Reference: Variable-Length Strings

Just because C has to know the string length does not mean that you can't use variable-length strings in your C programs. You can. But it is you—not the compiler—that is responsible for allocating and keeping track of the memory used to store variable-length strings. In C, a variable-length string would not be stored in a string variable. Instead, a pointer variable would point to the memory address where you allocated space for the variable-length string.

The following code fragment shows how string variables can be used in QuickBASIC:

```
firstname$ = "Bob"
lastname$ = "White"
fullname$ = firstname$ + lastname$
PRINT "Your first name is ", len( firstname$ ), characters long."
PRINT "Your full name is " + fullname$
```

On the first two lines, string variables are declared and initialized. Notice a couple of things about the declaration and initialization. First, each string variable name is followed by the $ character. The $ tells QuickBASIC that the variable is a string variable. Second, the strings that are assigned to the variables are of different lengths.

The string variable declaration on the third line is interesting. The value that is assigned to the string variable is a concatenation of the values of the first two string variables. The concatenation is performed very simply with a plus sign (+).

The last two lines in the code fragment illustrate different ways to display strings in BASIC. The PRINT statements show two ways to handle strings. The strings enclosed in quotation marks are string literals and are displayed just as they appear in the code. The PRINT statements also print the *values* of the string variables, such as fullname$.

Next is an example of how strings are handled in C:

```
string_func()
{
char string1[20] = "Bob ";
char string2[20];
char string3[40]= "";

strcpy( string2, "White" );
strcat( string3, string1 );
strcat( string3, string2 );

printf( "string1 = %s\n", string1 );
printf( "string2 = %s\n", string2 );
printf( "string3 = %s\n", string3 );
}
```

This C code fragment looks very different from the preceding BASIC code fragment, yet they perform similar functions. Both code fragments declare and initialize string variables, concatenate string variables, and print the contents of the string variables.

Take a look at how this C code fragment works. The first three lines of the function body declare three different string variables. The most important thing to notice about the declarations is that three different arrays of characters are declared.

The first string variable declaration declares an array of characters that is 20 characters long. A value is immediately assigned to that array of characters. The second declaration proves that the assignment of a value to the array of characters can wait until later in the program. It makes no difference to the compiler when you assign a value to the array of characters. The only thing the compiler is concerned about is the length of the array. Note in the third declaration that a null, or empty, value is assigned to the array of characters.

The statement

```
strcpy( string2, "White" );
```

copies the string literal White into the string string2. In the BASIC code fragment, it was possible to copy a string literal into a string variable with an equal sign (=), so why not in the C example?

The reason that you can't use an equal sign to copy string values has to do with the way string variable names are used in C. Remember that in C a string is an array of characters. Whenever you refer to an array without a subscript or an address-of operator, you will get the address of the string. Copying the value of one string to another therefore requires the use of a function such as strcpy(). Refer to Chapter 8, "Programming with Pointers, Arrays, and Strings," for more information on declaring and manipulating strings.

The following statements perform the function of concatenating two strings:

```
strcat( string3, string1 );
strcat( string3, string2 );
```

In this example, string1 is concatenated to string3. Next, string2 is concatenated to the result of the previous concatenation. In the BASIC code fragment, a + was used to concatenate two strings. The technique of simply using a + to concatenate strings won't work in a C program for the same reason that you can't use an = to assign a value to a string. By itself, the name of a string variable is treated as the address of the strings. It is therefore necessary to use a function, like strcat(), to concatenate the value of one string to another.

Arrays

The simpler uses of arrays in both BASIC and C are quite similar. In both languages, arrays are groups of variables that can be referenced by an index. For example, in a C program, the statement that declares and accesses an array looks like this:

```
int i;
int test_score[10];
...
test_score[1] = 100;
...
for( i = 0; i <= 9; i++ ){
  printf( "score #%d = %d\n", i, test_score[i] );
}
```

Here, the integer variable i is used only as a counter; it has no other significance. The second line of the code fragment declares an integer array that has 10 elements. The third line assigns a value to the *second* element in the array. Finally, the fourth line prints the values of each of the elements in the array.

Take a look at the second line and the loop counter in the third line. If you look closely, you will notice that the array uses a zero index. This means that the first element in the array is element array[0], not array[1].

Now take a look at an example of a QuickBASIC array:

```
DIM array%(10)
```

```
FOR i = 0 TO 10
  array%(i) = i
NEXT i

FOR i = 0 TO 10
  PRINT array%(i)
NEXT i
```

The first line of this BASIC code fragment declares an array of 11 integers. The first of the two FOR loops assigns a value to each element in the integer array. The second of the two FOR loops prints the value of each element in the array. In BASIC, the arrays use index numbers that start with zero (just as in a C array). There is, however, a slight difference between arrays in BASIC and C.

Quick Reference: Declaring Arrays in BASIC and C

The difference between arrays in BASIC and C is how the arrays are declared. In C, the declaration of a 10-element array looks like:

```
int test_score[10];
```

In BASIC, the array declaration appears as:

```
DIM array%(10)
```

The BASIC declaration *looks* like the C array declaration, but it works a little differently. The C array has 10 elements, but the BASIC array has 11. In the C example, a 10-element array is declared. In the BASIC example, an array with elements 0 through 10 is declared. The difference between arrays in C and BASIC is slight but important.

Operators in BASIC and C

Many of the mathematical and relational operators you are used to in BASIC can be used in C programs with no problem. There are, however, some differences. This discussion compares the BASIC operators with the C operators. There are more C operators than those listed in the following tables. The C operators in these tables are just those that directly correspond to BASIC operators.

Mathematical Operators

There is little difference between the mathematical operators in C and BASIC. Because math symbols have universally understood meanings, it would be strange if the C and BASIC mathematical operators differed much. Table 13.4 compares the Microsoft QuickBASIC and C/C++ mathematical operators.

Table 13.4. A comparison of mathematical operators in Microsoft QuickBASIC and C/C++.

Operator	QuickBASIC Meaning	C/C++ Meaning
+	Addition	Addition
-	Subtraction	Subtraction
*	Multiplication	Multiplication
/	Division	Division
\	Integer division	
MOD	Modulus	
%		Modulus
^	Exponentiation	

Table 13.4 indicates that QuickBASIC has an extra division operator not found in Microsoft C/C++. This extra operator is the integer division operator (\). The \ operator divides two numbers, retains the integer part of the result, and discards the remainder.

Both QuickBASIC and C/C++ have a modulus operator, but it is represented differently in each language. When the modulus operator is used to divide two numbers, only the remainder is returned as the answer.

Relational Operators

Another important group of operators in BASIC is the relational operators. Table 13.5 compares the relational operators in Microsoft QuickBASIC and Microsoft C/C++.

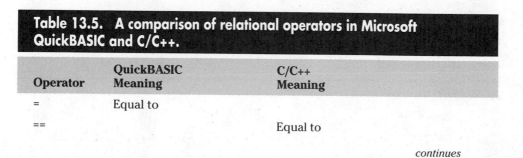

Table 13.5. A comparison of relational operators in Microsoft QuickBASIC and C/C++.

Operator	QuickBASIC Meaning	C/C++ Meaning
=	Equal to	
==		Equal to

continues

Table 13.5.   Continued

Operator	QuickBASIC Meaning	C/C++ Meaning
<>	Not equal to	
!=		Not equal to
>	Greater than	Greater than
<	Less than	Less than
>=	Greater than or equal to	Greater than or equal to
<=	Less than or equal to	Less than or equal to

The main difference between the relational operators in BASIC and C is in the equal-to and not-equal-to operators. The C language not-equal-to operator will make more sense once you look at Table 13.6 in the next section.

Logical Operators

The logical operators in BASIC and C function in similar ways. The way they look, however, is very different. Table 13.6 is a comparison of these logical operators.

Table 13.6.   A comparison of logical operators in Microsoft QuickBASIC and C/C++.

Operator	QuickBASIC Meaning	C/C++ Meaning
AND	Logical AND	
&&		Logical AND
OR	Logical OR	
¦¦		Logical OR
NOT	Logical NOT	
!		Logical NOT

The QuickBASIC AND and the C/C++ && perform the same logical function, but there is no correlation in syntax. The logic of the operators in Table 13.6 is the same in QuickBASIC and C/C++. There is, however, no similarity in the way the logical expressions are coded.

Conditional Flow Control in BASIC and C

One of the most important aspects of programming is to control the flow of logic in your programs. A program that cannot execute different sets of instructions depending on the different conditions it encounters is a very limited program. Because the control of a program's logic flow is so important, this discussion compares the flow control methods in BASIC and C.

Flow Control with *if-then-else*

Probably the most common flow control device is the *if-then-else* statement. The idea behind this kind of statement is the same in both BASIC and C: *if* a condition is true, *then* perform some action; *else* the condition is not true, so perform a different action. The next code fragment shows how such a statement can be used in a C program:

```
int too_much;
...
if ( too_much > 15 ) {
  too_much --;
  printf( "too_much = %d\n", too_much );
}
else {
  too_much ++;
  printf( "too_much = %d\n", too_much );
}
```

There are a few things to notice about this code fragment. First, there is no *then* keyword in C. The word *then* is not needed in a C if-else construction. Second, C has no counterpart to BASIC's ENDIF statement. C does not need such a statement because C allows only one statement to follow an if or an else. In the preceding code fragment, there are multiple statements following the if and the else, but notice that each group of statements is enclosed in a set of braces. The braces tell C that what follows the if and the else is a *block statement*. Refer to Chapter 7, "Controlling Program Logic Flow," for more information on C's if-else statement.

Next examine an IF-THEN-ELSE statement in BASIC:

```
IF toomuch% > 15 THEN
  toomuch% = toomuch% -1
  print "toomuch = ", toomuch%
ELSEIF toomuch% >= 10 THEN
  print "toomuch is between 10 and 15"
  print "toomuch = ", toomuch%
ELSE
  print "toomuch is less than 10"
  print "toomuch = ", toomuch%
ENDIF
```

This BASIC code fragment is different from the C code fragment in several ways. First, in BASIC, the THEN keyword is required. Notice that THEN is used on the first and fourth lines of the code fragment. Second, any number of statements can follow an IF, ELSE, or ELSEIF statement. Third, an ENDIF keyword is required at the end of the IF-THEN-ELSE statement. Fourth, this BASIC code fragment contains a keyword that does not exist in C: ELSEIF. ELSEIF enables you to check another condition without having to nest IF-THEN-ELSE statements.

The ELSEIF keyword provides an easy way around using nested IF-THEN-ELSE statements. It is, however, legal to nest IF-THEN-ELSE statements in BASIC just as in C.

Flow Control with *SELECT CASE* and *switch*

Closely related to the IF-THEN-ELSE statements in logic are the SELECT CASE statement in BASIC and the switch statement in C. The SELECT CASE or switch type statement enables you to neatly and easily write code that can select from several different logical conditions. Even though these two statements are similar in purpose, their syntax is quite different.

The next two code fragments illustrate the differences between the BASIC SELECT CASE statement and the C switch statement. The first fragment shows the BASIC SELECT CASE statement:

```
INPUT testnum
SELECT CASE testnum
  CASE < 0
    PRINT "testnum is less than 0"
  CASE 2,4,6,8
    PRINT  "testnum is even number less than 10"
  CASE 10
    PRINT "testnum is 10"
  CASE ELSE
    PRINT "testnum is something else"
END SELECT
```

From this code fragment, it is evident that the BASIC SELECT CASE statement is very flexible. The second fragment shows the C switch statement:

```
char my_char;
...
switch( my_char )
{
  case '1': printf( "my_char = 1.\n" );
            break;
  case '2': printf( "my_char = 2.\n" );
            break;
  case '3': printf( "my_char = 3.\n" );
            break;
  default : printf( "my_char is not 1, 2, or 3.\n" );
}
```

One area in which the SELECT CASE statement is more flexible than the C switch statement is the data type of the controlling expression. In BASIC, the expression list arguments can be a numeric type or even a string expression. In C, the controlling expression must be a scalar type. Many times in C, the controlling expression is an integer or a character.

The BASIC SELECT CASE statement is also more flexible in that each CASE can contain multiple values or even a range of values. Performing a single action for multiple values in a C switch statement is somewhat more complicated. An example of selecting a single action for multiple values is seen in the Listing 7.7 in Chapter 7.

Notice in the C switch statement that a break command is needed to end the processing for a given value and to drop out of the switch statement. Without the break command, processing would continue with the commands for the next value.

In BASIC, the beginning and end of a SELECT CASE statement is defined by SELECT CASE and END SELECT commands. In C, only one compound statement follows the switch command. The compound statement is, of course, indicated by the opening and closing braces.

Flow Control with *for-next* Loops

As with other fundamental programming tools, understanding *for-next* loops in BASIC and C is easy. In both languages, the *for-next* loop executes a command or a series of commands a specific number of times. In BASIC, a FOR-NEXT loop looks like this:

```
FOR i% = 1 TO 10 STEP 2
  PRINT i%
NEXT i
```

All the commands between the FOR and NEXT keywords are executed on each pass through the loop. The variable i% is used to control the loop. On each pass through the loop, the value of i% is checked to see whether it is in the bounds of the starting and ending expression. If the value of i%, the loop counter, is in the bounds of the starting and ending expression, i% will be incremented by the amount specified by the STEP command.

In C, a for-next loop is called simply a for loop. The following code fragment illustrates a C type for loop:

```
int i;
...
for( i=1; i <= 10, i+=2 ) printf( "%d\n", i );
```

This code fragment performs the same function as the preceding BASIC code fragment. The notation for the C code fragment, however, is much more terse than for the BASIC code fragment. In the C code fragment, the expression i=1; sets the initial value of the variable used as a loop counter. Next, the expression i <= 10; controls how many times the loop will execute. Finally, the expression i+=2 performs the same function as the BASIC STEP command. i+=2 increments the variable used as a loop counter by 2. C expects either a single statement or a compound statement enclosed in braces to follow the for() construction. The statement that follows the for() is the statement or statements executed on each pass of the loop.

Flow Control with *do* and *while* Loops

Sometimes you need to create a program loop that executes a command or series of commands many times. The catch is that you don't know how many times you will need to perform the loop. In such a situation, you may not know exactly how many times to perform the loop, but you will be able to check a condition and end the loop when that condition is met. The QuickBASIC loops that enable you to check a condition are the DO-LOOPs.

There are two varieties of DO-LOOPs. The first is the DO WHILE...LOOP, and the second is the DO...LOOP WHILE. The DO WHILE...LOOP checks the condition that controls the loop at the beginning of the loop. The DO...LOOP WHILE checks the condition that controls the loop at the end of the loop. DO...LOOP WHILE always executes at least once, because the condition checking is performed at the end of the loop.

QuickBASIC enables you to replace WHILE with UNTIL. Whether you use WHILE or UNTIL depends on the condition you will check. The following illustrations use only WHILE. Here is the BASIC DO WHILE...LOOP:

```
balance = 1000
DO WHILE balance > 0
  balance = balance - 100
```

```
    print balance
LOOP
```

The C loop that corresponds to the BASIC DO WHILE...LOOP is the while loop. Like the BASIC DO WHILE...LOOP, the C while loop checks the controlling condition before the loop is executed. The following code fragment shows the C while loop:

```
float balance = 1000.0;
...
while( balance > 0.0 ) {
balance -=100.0;
printf( "%f\n", balance );
}
```

The C while loop encloses in parentheses (following the while keyword) the condition that controls the loop. The statement or compound statement that immediately follows the while() will be executed for as long as the controlling condition is true. Unlike BASIC, C has no need of an ending loop keyword.

The DO WHILE...LOOP just examined was a *prechecked* loop. Next, you examine a *postchecked* loop. Such a loop always executes at least once because the controlling condition is checked at the bottom of the loop. The BASIC postchecked loop is the DO...LOOP WHILE. Here is an example of a QuickBASIC DO...LOOP WHILE:

```
counter% = 0
DO
  PRINT counter%
  counter% = counter% + 10
LOOP WHILE counter% <= 100
```

If you run this short example, you will see that the first time the PRINT command is executed, counter% has a value of zero. This type of loop is useful when you have to perform at least one pass of the loop before you can even have a condition to check.

The C loop that corresponds to the BASIC DO...LOOP WHILE is the do-while loop. The following code fragment illustrates a simple do-while loop in C:

```
int i = 0;
...
do {
  printf( "i = %d\n", i );
  i += 10;
} while( i <= 100 );
```

The BASIC DO...LOOP WHILE and the C do-while loops are laid out in a similar way. At the top of the loop in both languages is the DO/do command. The body of the loop follows. At the end of the loop is the WHILE (while) statement that evaluates a condition to determine whether the loop should be executed again. The only significant difference is that the C do-while loop does not contain a loop keyword, as does the BASIC DO...LOOP WHILE loop.

Modular Programming

Simply defined, *modular programming* is the division of your program into logical and, presumably, reusable parts. For C, designing modular programs is easy. Modularity is easy because C is built around functions. Just about anything you want to do in C, you do by calling a function. So C programs usually tend to be very modular, and reusing the parts of a C program is easy.

Until packages like QuickBASIC came along, BASIC was not so fortunate. With its line numbering and GOSUBs, it was harder and more time-consuming to write structured and modular BASIC programs. This doesn't mean that you couldn't write modular BASIC programs; it just means that it took some thought and effort.

To the relief of many programmers, BASIC is now much easier to work with. A package like QuickBASIC, with its SUBs and FUNCTIONs, makes it easy to write code that is modular and reusable. This discussion compares the highlights of modular programming techniques in QuickBASIC and C.

The most obvious difference between QuickBASIC and C is that QuickBASIC uses SUBs and FUNCTIONs, whereas C uses only functions. In QuickBASIC, a SUB procedure cannot be part of an expression. A call to a SUB procedure can be only a stand-alone statement. Because calls to SUB procedures cannot be part of an expression, SUB procedures do not return values.

A QuickBASIC FUNCTION procedure differs from a SUB procedure in that a FUNCTION can return a value. Because a QuickBASIC FUNCTION returns values, calls to FUNCTIONs can appear inside expressions. A SUB is used for the operations it performs in the subroutine, whereas a FUNCTION is used for the operations it performs as well as the value it returns.

Functions in C can do the job of both SUB and FUNCTION procedures in QuickBASIC. Normally, C functions return values. That is why a function declaration has this form:

```
int my_func( int i, int j);
```

The first part of the declaration—in this case, the type identifier int—tells the compiler what kind of value the function will return. This particular C function works in a manner similar to the QuickBASIC FUNCTION.

Even though many C functions do return values, you do not have to code all your functions to return values. Suppose that you declare a C function like this:

```
void my_func_2( int i );
```

Here you have indicated, with the void type identifier, that this function will not return a value. The function behaves like the QuickBASIC SUB procedure.

If you refer to the section "Details About Passing Parameters" in Chapter 6, you will see that, by default, C passes parameters to functions by *value*. In contrast, QuickBASIC passes parameters to its SUBs and FUNCTIONs by *reference*. This is an important difference to notice when you move from BASIC to C.

By default, QuickBASIC passes variables to procedures (either SUBs or FUNCTIONs) by reference. Passing by reference means that the procedure is given the memory address of the actual variable. Thus, when the procedure modifies a variable that was passed to it, the value of that variable is changed also in the calling procedure.

C normally passes variables by value. In C, a *copy* of the value of the variable in the calling function is passed to the called function. When the called function changes the value of the variable passed to it, only the copy is changed. The value of the variable in the calling function remains the same regardless of what changes the called function makes.

Quick Reference: Passing C Arrays and Strings

There is an exception to the default passing of variables by value. In C, arrays are passed to functions by reference. Arrays are passed by reference because of the amount of space and time that would be required to pass a copy of a large array. If you passed whole copies of arrays to the procedures, you could easily bring your program to a crawl and run out of space.

Remember that C strings are only arrays of characters. When you pass strings as arguments, you are passing only the address of the string. You do not pass an actual copy of the string to the procedure you call.

Moving to C from Pascal

Knowing the Pascal language gives you a head start in learning C. The reason that Pascal can help you learn C more quickly and easily is that Pascal does a good job of teaching programming skills. In fact, teaching is the purpose for which Pascal was originally designed. The Pascal language has helped many people master the fundamentals of computer programming. Knowing Pascal means that you understand what a computer programming language does.

The programming concepts you learned in Pascal are applicable in C as well. Understanding how computer languages work and what kinds of tasks you can perform is half the battle in programming. The other half is knowing how to tell the computer to perform these tasks.

This portion of the chapter helps you begin to apply the skills you learned in programming Pascal to the C language. Obviously, this discussion cannot address all the differences between Pascal and C; only the more common Pascal features are covered. The information, however, should be enough to make you comfortable with the C language.

Comparing Data Types in C and Pascal

There are, of course, many similarities among the basic data types used in Pascal, C, and other programming languages. Although there are similarities, each language implements and uses these basic data types in slightly different ways. This discussion introduces you to the differences in the way Pascal and C handle data.

Integers

One of the most fundamental types of data your programs work with is the integer. Integers are just whole numbers. They have the same purpose regardless of the language you are using. The main difference in how integers are implemented in each language is in the naming of the different integral types.

Different integral types? Even though integers are always whole numbers, both Pascal and C have different types of integral variables. The difference in the integral types is in the range of values that each type of integral variable can store. An integral variable that stores large values requires more memory space than an integral variable that stores small values. Table 13.7 compares the integral types in Turbo Pascal and Borland C++.

Table 13.7. A comparison of integral types in Turbo Pascal and Borland C++.

Turbo Pascal Integer	Range	Borland C++ Integer	Range	Size (Bytes)
Byte	0 to 255			1
Shortint	−128 to 128			1
Integer	−32,768 to 32,767	int	−32,768 to 32,767	2
Word	0 to 65,535	unsigned int	0 to 65,535	2

Turbo Pascal Integer	Range	Borland C++ Integer	Range	Size (Bytes)
Longint	−2,147,483,648 to 2,147,483,647	long	−2,147,483,648 to 2,147,483,647	4
		unsigned long	0 to 4,294,967,295	4

Table 13.7 points out several differences between the integral types in Pascal and C. The most obvious difference is that the names of the C integral types are somewhat more descriptive than the names of the Pascal integral types.

The other significant difference between Pascal and C is that Pascal has two integral types not found in C, and C has one integral type not found in Pascal. As Table 13.7 indicates, the one-byte integers in Pascal are not used in C. A C program would have to use an int where a Pascal program uses a Byte or Shortint. C has an unsigned version of the Pascal Longint called an unsigned long. The unsigned long integral type holds the same magnitude of values as the Longint, but the unsigned long stores only positive values.

Now is a good time to point out the difference in the ways variables are declared in Pascal and C. In both languages, you must inform the compiler about the types of variables used in the programs. In both Pascal and C, you declare variables before you use them in the program. In Pascal, a variable declaration has this form:

```
program MyProg;
var
  I, J: Integer;
begin
  Writeln( 'I = ', I );
  Writeln( 'J = ', J )
end.
```

In C, a comparable variable declaration looks like this:

```
int i;
int j;

main()
{
  printf( "i = %d\n", i );
  printf( "j = %d\n", j );
}
```

In Pascal, the variable declaration is preceded by the Pascal keyword var. In C, such a keyword is not needed to signal the beginning of a variable declaration.

Notice that the Pascal variable declaration lists the variable name first, then a colon, and finally the data type of the variable. The C variable declaration is just the opposite. In C, the data type comes first and then the variable name.

Both languages are similar in that you can declare multiple variables in one declaration statement. For example, the line

```
int i, j, k;
```

is a C variable declaration that declares three integral variables in one statement.

Real Numbers

Real numbers are numbers that can have fractional portions. In C, real numbers are more commonly referred to as floating-point numbers. The major advantages of real number variables are that they can store fractional values and that real number variables can store numbers of large magnitude.

Although Pascal's real numbers and C's floating-point numbers are the same kind of data, the type names in each language are very different. The next two tables compare the C and Pascal floating-point data types. Table 13.8 compares the magnitude of the values that can be stored in each type. Table 13.9 compares the size of each of the floating-point data types and the precision of each type.

These two tables show that there is little similarity between the floating-point types in Turbo Pascal and Borland C++. The only similarities are in the amount of memory required for some of the floating-point data types and in the number of digits of precision.

Table 13.8. A comparison of the magnitude of values of floating-point data types in Turbo Pascal and Borland C++.

Turbo Pascal Type	Borland C++ Type	Range
Real		2.9×10^{-39} to 1.7×10^{38}
Single		1.5×10^{-45} to 3.4×10^{38}
	float	3.4×10^{-38} to 3.4×10^{38}
Double		5.0×10^{-324} to 1.7×10^{308}
	double	1.7×10^{-308} to 1.7×10^{308}

Turbo Pascal Type	Borland C++ Type	Range
Extended		1.9×10^{-4951} to 1.1×10^{4932}
	long double	3.4×10^{-4932} to 3.4×10^{4932}
Comp		$-2^{63}+1$ to $2^{63}-1$

Table 13.9. Comparisons of the size and precision of floating-point data types in Turbo Pascal and Borland C++.

Turbo Pascal Type	Borland C++ Type	Size (Bytes)	Precision (Digits)
Real		6	11–12
Single		4	7–8
	float	4	7
Double		8	15–16
	double	8	15
Extended		10	19–20
	long double	10	19
Comp		8	19–20

If you are converting your Pascal programs to C, you will need to pick the new C floating-point data types carefully. A value that fits in a Pascal Double floating-point variable may not fit in the C double floating-point variable.

Notice that Turbo Pascal has a special data type that is not included in Borland C++: the Comp type. Comp holds only integer values. The magnitude for the Comp type in Table 13.8 is expressed in base–2 notation. In decimal notation, the range for a Comp type is approximately $-.2\times10^{18}$ to 9.2×10^{18}.

One restriction for the larger floating-point data types in Turbo Pascal is that the program must be compiled in the $N+ state. In the $N+ state, the real number calculations are performed using 8087 instructions. If the program is compiled in the $N- state, the use of data of types Single, Double, Extended, and Comp will generate errors.

In C, the -f option controls whether the floating-point libraries will be linked with your code. If you specify the -f- option, the floating-point libraries will not be linked. If your program uses floating-point type variables and you compile with the -f- option, you will get link errors.

Characters and Strings

Pascal and C treat characters and strings in much the same way. In both languages, a character is a data item that is one byte long. Both languages even use the same name for the character data type. Here is how a character declaration in Pascal looks:

```
CharVar: Char;
```

A character declaration in C looks like this:

```
char char_var;
```

There is one way in which Pascal character types vary from C character types. But before the difference in data types can be explained, a word about characters and character sets is needed.

A character, as just stated, is a 1-byte data item. Because a byte is composed of 8 bits, it is possible for a byte to store any of 256 different values.

The actual range of values stored in the byte depends on whether one bit in the byte is used as a sign indicator. If one of the bits is not used as a sign indicator, the byte is said to be *unsigned*. An unsigned byte can hold a value from 0 to 255. If one of the bits is used as a sign indicator, the byte is called a *signed* byte. The signed byte can still hold any of 256 different values, but now the values range from –128 to 127.

Now back to character sets. A character set is just a group of characters. The two character sets relevant to this discussion are the ASCII character set and the extended character set. What differentiates the two sets is that the ASCII character set contains only 128 characters. The reason is that the ASCII characters are stored as *signed* bytes.

Your computer displays characters from an extended character set. This set includes the characters from the ASCII character set, plus other characters such as symbols and lines. The extended character set contains more characters than the ASCII character set because the extended characters are stored as *unsigned* bytes.

Because Pascal uses an unsigned byte for the character data type, a Pascal character variable can use characters from the extended character set. By default, a C character type is stored as a signed byte; therefore, by default, a C character variable uses the ASCII character set. C does enable you, however, to declare an `unsigned char` data type. The C `unsigned char` data type enables you to use extended characters if you want.

> ## Quick Reference: Storing Strings in Pascal and C
>
> Turbo Pascal and C handle strings in different ways. Strings in both languages are alike in that they are arrays of characters. The difference is in the way Pascal and C store strings in memory.
>
> A Turbo Pascal string can contain from 1 to 255 characters. There is such a low limit on the maximum number of characters in a string because of the way Pascal keeps track of the length of a string. The first byte in a Pascal string, S[0] in array notation, is a special byte that indicates the length of the string. Only one byte is used to indicate the string length. Because a single byte can store only 256 different values, the length-indicator byte limits the string to 255 characters.
>
> A C string is an array of characters, but C doesn't care about the length of the character array. C doesn't have to worry about the length of the string because C places a termination byte at the end of the string. The *termination byte* is a null character indicating the end of the string. As you process a string, you check each byte to see whether it is the null character. If the byte you retrieve from the string is a null character, you know that you've reached the end of the string and you can stop processing the string.

Boolean

Pascal provides a data type for storing true/false values called a Boolean type. A Boolean type variable can hold only a true or false value.

C does not provide a separate Boolean data type. C indicates true and false values with the regular scalar types. False is indicated by a 0 value, or when pointers are used, a null value. A true value (no, *true value* doesn't mean a really good deal!) is indicated by a value other than 0.

Pointers

A *pointer data type* is used to declare variables that hold the address of other data. A pointer variable is not used to store your program's data; instead, a pointer variable stores the location of your program's data.

Pointers have many uses. They improve the efficiency of your program by enabling you to pass the address of data structures to your procedures, instead of passing the whole data structure. Pointers are essential in implementing linked lists. In such lists, pointers are used to indicate which records precede and follow the record you are working with. In Pascal, pointers are important; in C, pointers are essential.

Listing 13.1 is a short Pascal program that illustrates some of the basics of using pointers. Like the C programs in this book, this Pascal program contains line numbers on the left. These numbers are not part of the program; they are just an aid that helps you refer to the lines in the program as you read the accompanying discussion.

Listing 13.1.   PTRDEMO.PAS—The Pascal pointer demonstration program (with Turbo Pascal).

```
 1   program PtrDemo;
 2
 3   type
 4      NString = string[40];
 5      NSPtr   = ^NString;
 6
 7   var
 8      Name1: NString;
 9      Name2: NSPtr;
10
11   begin
12      Name1 := 'John Smith';
13      Writeln( 'Name1 = ', Name1 );
14
15      New( Name2 );
16      Name2^ := 'Jane Smith';
17      Writeln( 'The data to which Name2 points = ', Name2^ );
18
19      Dispose( Name2 );
20      Name2 := @Name1;
21      Writeln( 'The new data to which Name2 points = ', Name2^ );
22   end.
```

Line 3 in Listing 13.1 begins the type declarations for this Pascal program. The type declaration section creates the user-defined types this program will use. Line 4 declares a type for a 40-character string. Line 5 declares a pointer type for the 40-character string type. Lines 8 and 9 declare variables that use the types declared in lines 4 and 5.

On line 12, a value is assigned to the Name1 variable, which has the user-defined NString data type. The NString data type is just another name for a 40-character string.

Line 15 is where things get interesting. The New procedure allocates memory for a 40-character string and assigns the address of the string to Name2. The reason that the New procedure allocates memory for a 40-character string is that Name2 was declared as a pointer to NString. NString is the user-defined type for a 40-character string.

Notice how the ^ symbol is used in line 16. The ^ is the indirection operator. It indicates that what is being referenced is not the address value stored in the pointer, but is the data to which the pointer points.

Line 19 releases, or deallocates, the memory obtained with the New procedure on line 15. After this instruction is executed, the Name2 pointer doesn't point to anything. Before Name2 can be referenced again, you need to give it a new address or assign it the value *nil*. Line 20 assigns the address of Name1 to the pointer Name2. Once the address is assigned to Name2, Name2 can be referenced safely again.

The theory of what pointers do in Pascal and in C is the same. A pointer stores the address of data with which you are working. While the theory may be the same, the implementation is different.

The following code fragment illustrates the way in which pointers are declared in C:

```
...
char name1[40];
char *n_ptr;
...
```

The first line in this fragment declares a string—a character array that is 40 characters long. The second line declares a pointer to a character type. The first thing to notice is that in C you do not have to use type definitions to declare pointers (see lines 3–5 in Listing 13.1). In C, you can declare your pointers when you are declaring the rest of your variables.

The second thing to notice about the C pointer declaration is that C uses the * character to indicate a pointer, whereas Pascal uses the ^ character.

Listing 13.2 is a C program that performs some of the same functions of the Pascal program in Listing 13.1.

Listing 13.2. CPTRDEMO.C—Using pointers in C (with Borland C++).

```
1  #include <stdio.h>
2  #include <stdlib.h>
3  #include <string.h>
4  main()
```

continues

Listing 13.2. Continued

```
5   {
6   char mystr[40];
7   char *myptr;
8
9   strcpy( mystr, "John Smith" );
10  printf( "This is mystr - %s\n", mystr );
11
12  myptr = mystr;
13  printf( "This is myptr - %s\n", myptr );
14
15  myptr = malloc( sizeof( mystr ) );
16  strcpy( myptr, "Jane Smith" );
17  printf( "This is the new myptr - %s\n", myptr );
18  free( myptr );
19  return()}
```

In line 20 of Listing 13.1, the address of a string was assigned to a pointer variable. The same kind of operation occurs on line 12 in Listing 13.2. In Pascal, when you want to assign the address of a string to a pointer variable, you have to use the address-of operator (@). An address-of operator is not needed in C when you are assigning the address of a string to a pointer variable. The reason is that referring to the unindexed name of a string yields the address of the string.

Assigning the address of other data items, such as C integers, to a pointer variable does require that you use an address-of operator. The following C statement is perfectly legal:

```
int i;
int *int_ptr;
...
int_ptr = &i;
```

The address-of operator (&) gets the address of the integer variable, and the address is then assigned to the pointer. Assuming the same variable declarations, the statement

```
int_ptr = i;
```

is also legal, but it won't work as you might expect. What happens now is that the pointer is assigned the value stored in i, not the address of i. If you tried to use int_ptr, you would get some strange results.

Line 15 of Listing 13.1 performs the task of allocating memory for a new 40-character string and assigning the address of the new string to a pointer variable. Line 15 of Listing 13.2 performs this same function, although in a more involved way.

The `malloc()` function called in line 15 of Listing 13.2 allocates a block of memory. `malloc()` knows how much memory to allocate by the size argument that is passed to it. In line 15, the size argument for `malloc()` is specified by calling the `sizeof()` function. In this example, `sizeof()` calculates the size of the existing string and returns that size to `malloc()`. Once `malloc()` allocates enough space for the new string, `malloc()` returns the starting address of the string. The starting address of the new string is assigned to the pointer variable. The C process of allocating memory is more involved than the Pascal process, but the C process gives you control over every step in this memory allocation process.

Freeing the allocated memory is simple in both languages. On line 19 of Listing 13.1, Pascal uses the `Dispose` procedure to free the memory that was allocated. On line 18 of Listing 13.2, C uses the `free()` function to free the memory that was allocated.

The use of C pointers is covered extensively in Chapters 8 and 9. Refer to those chapters for more information on using pointers in C.

Arrays

When you move from Pascal to C, you will find that C arrays are not quite as flexible as Pascal arrays. The concept of arrays in both languages is very similar. In both languages, arrays are groups of variables with the same data type stored in contiguous memory locations. The difference between arrays in Pascal and C is in the array's index range. In Pascal you can declare an array like:

```
TestArray : array[ 0..100 ] of Integer;
```

Or you can declare a Pascal array like:

```
WildArray : array[ -100..100 ] of Integer;
```

You can see that in Pascal you have great control over the index used for an array. Pascal enables you to specify both the lower and upper bound for an array. C, however, is not quite as flexible. In C, arrays always start with element 0. The declaration of an array in C looks like:

```
int test_array[ 100 ];
```

This line of C code declares an array of 100 integers. The first element in the array is `test_array[0]` and the last element is `test_array[99]`.

Quick Reference: Arrays in Pascal and C

Using arrays in C is very different from using arrays in Pascal. Pascal enables you to specify both the upper and lower bounds for the array's index. In C, the index starts at 0 and you specify only the upper bound for the index.

Using Operators in Pascal and C

This discussion compares the rich operator sets in Pascal and C. The information is provided as a reference to help you see the differences in syntax between the two languages. The operator sets shown are from Turbo Pascal and Borland C++.

Mathematical Operators

The set of mathematical operators in both Pascal and C is small. Only the basic mathematical functions are implemented with operators. The higher mathematical functions are implemented with separate procedures. Table 13.10 compares the basic mathematical operators in Turbo Pascal and Borland C++.

Table 13.10. A comparison of mathematical operators in Turbo Pascal and Borland C++.

Operator	Turbo Pascal Meaning	Borland C++ Meaning
+	Addition	Addition
-	Subtraction	Subtraction
*	Multiplication	Multiplication
/	Real division	Division
div	Integer division	
mod	Modulus	
%		Modulus

The only differences between the mathematical operators in Pascal and C are in the division operators. Pascal has an integer division operator that C lacks. The Pascal div operator is designed to divide integers and return an integer result. Even though C lacks such an operator, the same function can be performed by making sure that all the data used in a C division operation is of integral type.

The modulus operators in Pascal and C are both designed to work with integral values. The result returned from a modulus operation is the remainder of the division.

Pascal and C division operations differ the most when mixed data types are used in the division. For example, dividing two integers and placing the result in a floating-point variable may not yield the results you expect. The best advice is to try your division operation first and make sure that it produces the result you want.

Relational Operators

The relational operators enable you to compare two values. The value returned from the comparison is slightly different in Pascal and C. If the result of a comparison is true, Pascal returns a Boolean value of true. C does not have a Boolean data type, so C returns a nonzero value to indicate that a comparison is true. If a comparison is false, Pascal returns a Boolean false, and C returns a value of 0.

Table 13.11 indicates that the main difference between the relational operators in Pascal and C is in the symbols used to represent a relational operation. Pascal has a relational operator not found in C: the in operator.

Table 13.11. A comparison of relational operators in Turbo Pascal and Borland C++.

Operator	Turbo Pascal Meaning	Borland C++ Meaning
=	Equal to	
==		Equal to
<>	Not equal to	
!=		Not equal to
>	Greater than	Greater than
<	Less than	Less than
>=	Greater than or equal to	Greater than or equal to
<=	Less than or equal to	Less than or equal to
in	Is a member of	

Logical Operators

The logical operators are used to combine relational expressions or variables that contain true or false values. In Turbo Pascal, the only variables that the logical operators can work with are variables that have a Boolean data type. C is more flexible in that its logical operators can work with integral types. Table 13.12 compares the Turbo Pascal logical operators with those of Borland C++. Notice that the Pascal logical operator set includes an exclusive OR that C does not have.

Table 13.12. A comparison of logical operators in Turbo Pascal and Borland C++.

Operator	Turbo Pascal Meaning	Borland C++ Meaning
and	Logical AND	
&&		Logical AND
or	Logical OR	
¦¦		Logical OR
xor	Exclusive OR	
not	Logical NOT	
!		NOT

Controlling Logic Flow in Pascal and C

This discussion examines how the flow of program execution is controlled in Pascal and C. First, the conditional logic control statements—if-then-else, if-else, and case—are studied. Second, the loop control statements—for, while, do-while, and while-do—are presented.

Flow Control with *if-then-else*

If you are used to if-then-else statements in Pascal, you won't have any trouble using if-else statements in C. A Pascal if-then-else statement has the following form:

```
if expression is true
   then do statement1
   else do statement2
```

When Pascal encounters an `if` statement in a program, the expression following the `if` is evaluated. If the expression is true, *statement1* is executed. If the expression following the `if` evaluates to false, *statement2* is executed.

The only difference between the way the Pascal `if-then-else` statement works and the way its counterpart statement works in C is that C doesn't use the word *then* in its statement. Here is the form of the C `if-else` statement:

```
if expression is true
   do statement1
else
   do statement2
```

When C encounters an `if` statement, C performs the same steps as Pascal. The expression following the `if` is evaluated. If the expression is true, *statement1* is executed; otherwise, *statement2* is executed.

Pascal's `if-then-else` statement and C's `if-else` statement are alike in two other ways. First, the `else` part is optional in both languages. Second, both Pascal and C allow only one statement to follow the `then` and `else` parts of the statement. If you need to execute more than one statement, you can use a block statement. In Pascal, the block statement is indicated by the `begin` and `end` keywords. In C, the block statement is indicated by the opening and closing braces.

Flow Control Using *case* and *switch*

A `case` statement is used when you have to choose from several alternatives. `case` statements are preferred over a series of `if-then-else` statements because `case` statements look neater and are easier to understand. A Pascal `case` statement looks like this:

```
case MenuItem of
   '1' : Writeln( 'Item 1 chosen' );
   '2' : Writeln( 'Item 2 chosen' );
   '3' : Writeln( 'Item 3 chosen' );
else
   Writeln( 'None of the items were chosen' );
end;
```

A `case` statement in C is actually called a `switch` statement and looks a good bit different from the Pascal `case` statement. Here is an example of a C `switch` statement:

```
switch( menu_item ) {
  case '1': printf( "Item 1 chosen\n" );
            break;
```

```
case '2': printf( "Item 2 chosen\n" );
          break;
case '3': printf( "Item 3 chosen\n" );
          break;
default:  printf( "None of the items were chosen\n" );
}
```

Following `case` in Pascal and `switch` in C is the expression that controls the whole `case` statement. This expression is evaluated, and the result of the evaluation is compared to the statements in the `case` body.

The Pascal `case` statement uses `end;` to signal the end of the entire `case` statement. C encloses the body of the `switch` statement in a pair of braces.

The Pascal `case` labels are more flexible than the C `case` labels. In Pascal, the `case` labels can consist of any number of constants or sub ranges. The `case` label in C, however, must evaluate to a unique integer value. If you needed to execute one statement for several different controlling values, you would have to use something like this:

```
...
case '1':
case '2':
case '3':
  printf( "One statement for selections 1, 2, & 3" );
  break;
...
```

Explaining why this code fragment works means explaining why C uses a `break` statement. C does not require that only a single statement or a block statement follow a label statement. C allows any number of statements to follow a label statement. Therefore, a `break` statement is used to stop the flow of execution and to drop to the bottom of the `switch` body. If a `break` statement were not used, all the remaining statements in the `switch` body would be executed.

Both Pascal and C provide a default that can be executed if the evaluated expression does not equal any of the case labels. In Pascal, the default statement follows the reserved word `else`. The default statement in a C `switch` statement follows the `default` case label. Refer to the earlier code fragments for examples of the default actions taken in both Pascal and C.

Flow Control with *for* Loops

There are three kinds of loops in Pascal and C. The first kind is the `for` loop, which executes a series of instructions a set number of times. The other two loops execute a series of instructions based on some condition. One of these loops checks the controlling condition at the start of the loop, and the other loop checks the controlling condition at the end of the loop.

Here is a `for` loop in Pascal:

```
...
for count := 1 to 10 do
  Writeln( count );
...
```

The Pascal `for` loop is very simple and somewhat limited. The expression after the `for` keyword controls how many times the loop will be executed. Following the `do` keyword is the statement that will be executed on each pass through the loop. The `for` loop can execute only one statement, which can be either a single statement or a block statement. The block statement allows the `for` loop to perform more than one action. The Pascal `for` loop is limited in that it increments or decrements the controlling value by only one.

A `for` loop in C looks quite different:

```
...
for( count = 1; count <= 10; count++ )
  printf( "%d\n", count );
...
```

This `for` loop is more powerful than the `for` loop in Pascal. The reason is that you have greater control over the controlling condition. In the Pascal `for` loop, you just determined the starting and ending value of the loop counter. In the C `for` loop, you control the starting value of the loop counter, the ending value of the loop counter, and the loop counter's increment value. The C and Pascal `for` loops are alike in that both can execute only a single statement. The statement, however, can be a block statement.

Flow Control with Prechecked and Postchecked Loops

The other two loop statements in Pascal and C execute until a controlling condition becomes false. The first of these loop statements is the *prechecked* loop. This is a loop in which the controlling condition is checked before the loop is executed. The prechecked loop in both Pascal and C is the `while` loop. Its general structure is the same in both languages:

`while` *controlling expression is true* `do` *statement*

The syntax is different in the Pascal and C `while` loops, however. The Pascal `while` loop is coded like this:

```
...
while balance >= 1000 do
  begin
    balance := balance - 100;
    writeln( balance );
  end;
...
```

The C while loop looks like this:

```
...
while( balance >= 1000 ) {
  balance -= 100;
  printf( "%d\n", balance );
}
...
```

The C while loop requires that the controlling condition be enclosed in parentheses, but the Pascal while loop does not. The Pascal while loop requires that
a do keyword follow the controlling condition, but the C while does not use the
do keyword. In both languages, the body of the while loop is either a single line
statement or a block statement. Notice also in these examples that the controlling condition is updated inside the body of the while loop.

The last loop to be discussed is the *postchecked* loop. This loop checks the
value of the controlling condition at the bottom of the loop. Because the
controlling condition is checked at the bottom of the loop, it is guaranteed
that at least one pass will be made through the loop. The postchecked loop in
Pascal is the repeat-until loop; in C, the postchecked loop is the do-while loop.

The Pascal repeat-until loop is coded like this:

```
...
repeat
  Writeln( 'counter' );
  counter = counter + 10
until counter > 100;
...
```

One big difference between the repeat-until loop and the other Pascal loops is
that any number of statements can be included in the loop body. You don't
have to use a block statement to execute more than one command inside the
repeat-until loop. You are still restricted to the single line statement or the
block statement in the C do-while loop.

Here is how you code the C do-while loop:

```
...
do {
  printf( "%d\n", counter
```

```
    counter += 10
} while counter <= 100;
...
```

The postchecked loop works quite differently in Pascal and C. If you take a close look at the preceding code fragments, you will notice that the logic that controls the loops is slightly different. In Pascal, the loop is executed *until* a condition *becomes* true. In C, the loop is executed *while* a condition *remains* true. This difference in the way the loops work means that there is a difference in the way the controlling conditions are coded. To verify this, take a look at the controlling conditions in the two preceding code fragments.

Summary

This chapter serves as a quick reference for anyone who already programs in BASIC or Pascal. The information covered some of the common differences between BASIC and C, and Pascal and C. For a more comprehensive treatment of the C topics discussed in this chapter, refer to the earlier chapters in the book. Some of the important topics discussed in this chapter are the following:

■ The difference between interpreters and compilers. Whether a language was designed as an interpreter or a compiler makes a difference in how data is declared and used in a program.

■ How the data types compare in the languages. BASIC, Pascal, and C all deal with integers, floating-point numbers, characters, and strings of characters. How each of these data types is identified in each language, as well as the values that can be stored in the different types of variables, can differ greatly from one language to another. Care is needed when converting programs so errors won't occur because the wrong data type was used.

■ The fundamental operators used in the languages. One of the hardest parts of learning a new language is getting used to the new language's operator set. Many of the mathematical operators are the same in BASIC, Pascal, and C. There are many differences, however, in the other types of operators.

■ Program flow control. BASIC, Pascal, and C all contain the same kinds of flow control statements. Each of these languages has a version of the `if-then-else`, `case`, `for`, `do-while`, and `while-do` statements.

This is the final chapter in Part I of *Using C/C++*. Nearly every important aspect of using the C programming language has been covered in Part I. Part II introduces you to the more timely and advanced (but less standard) subject of object-oriented programming with C++.

PART

II

OUTLINE

14 Objects and Object-Oriented
   Programming
15 Defining Classes and Objects
16 Controlling Classes and Objects
17 More on C++ Methods and
   Objects

C++ Programming Basics

Objects and Object-Oriented Programming

*O*bject-oriented programming (OOP) and *object-oriented programming systems* (OOPS) are the current cutting edge of software technology. An object-oriented language, such as C++, can be used for anything from sprucing up existing programs written in procedural languages, to providing an architectural platform for implementing that latest wonder of artificial intelligence: *neural networks.*

> If you have no prior experience with C programming, you should stop reading right now, go back to the beginning of this book, work your way through it, write lots of practice code, and master that material thoroughly. If you do not, you will be quickly and utterly lost.

CAUTION

If you have a moderate amount of experience with C—enough to feel comfortable writing C programs—C++ and object-oriented programming will present no particular difficulty. C++ implements "objects" by using the structured object technology you already know about, adding some new syntax for notational convenience, and some new rules to cope with the expanded capabilities of this new environment.

Objects Are Working Models

What is an object? This is the most important question to answer before you can understand C++. There is, however, much discussion about objects and related issues. To begin, here is Bruce Eckel's generalized definition of an *object:* an object is anything with boundaries.

Comparing an object-oriented program to a more conventional procedural program shows why this definition is appropriate. In a procedural program, the program is built around the idea of functionality—a program does something. Data is what you "do something to." Thus, a procedural program is a collection of procedures or functions, and data flows openly through the program (see Figure 14.1).

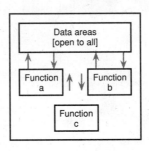

Figure 14.1.

Data flow in a procedural language.

An object-oriented program is a collection of objects—including data and the methods to use the data—that communicate with each other through messages in order to complete a task (see Figure 14.2). The central question is why you should want to write programs this way. Two features of object-oriented architecture make it desirable, especially for complex projects. These features are *data abstraction* and the association of methods for handling objects with the objects.

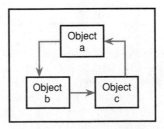

Figure 14.2.

Message flow in an object-oriented program.

Data Abstraction Is Data Hiding

The first feature that makes object-oriented design desirable is *data abstraction,* also known as *encapsulation.* Data abstraction is nothing more than data hiding—concealing some parts of the program's data structures from ordinary view to avoid inadvertent or erroneous modification. Only the parts of the program that the data "belongs to" can either access or modify it. This is not the same concept as abstract data typing, which is discussed later in the section entitled, "Classes Are Abstract Data Types."

There is an acute need for data abstraction in procedural languages. The larger a program grows, the easier it is for the programmer to become disorganized, and the more difficult it is to remember all the details. Fighter pilots call the ability to retain and juggle many factors simultaneously *situational awareness,* or *SA.* You could say that large procedural programs make it impossible to maintain adequate SA.

Structured programming techniques were the first real attempt to untangle the complex web of logic and interdependent data areas (and increase SA). These techniques dictated how logic should be designed, how procedures could be accessed (logic flow), and a host of other topics aimed at forcing a programmer to stay organized.

It didn't work. The most difficult program in the world to debug is the poorly written structured program. There were two main reasons for this failure. First, the programmer generally is not at fault. (There are bad programmers, but there are many more good ones.) The programmer's problem was not mental laziness, nor stupidity, nor any such character flaw. His or her real problem was, and often is, *overload.* Large programs simply can exceed the normal human capacity needed to cope with them effectively.

Second, structured coding techniques required (but did not provide any real tools to accomplish) better organization. Admonishing programmers to "Get organized: write structured code" is like telling a hungry person to be full, without giving him or her any food. Whatever else structured techniques did, they failed to prevent the open flow of data in and through a program. The result is that the programmer continues to be confronted by the complexity of a large program, which in turn snowballs. More data and logic is required to control previous data and logic, and so on.

In the world of the real data-processing shop, structured programming has proven inadequate for coping with ever larger and more complex programs. Object-oriented languages can do better, but are not the final answer either.

Consider, also, whether you actually need object-orientation before taking on another project. For the reasons just discussed, you don't need OOPS (including C++) unless the project will be large and complex. The purpose of techniques like data abstraction is to conceal and manage complexity. If there is no real complexity, all you accomplish by using these tools is, ironically, a needlessly complex program!

In fact, data hiding can be accomplished, to some degree, in conventional procedural languages. C is more capable than most languages of data hiding; to accomplish it, C uses structures, type definitions, header files, and pointers to functions.

C Functions as Object Methods

One of the most significant advances incorporated in C++ is the binding of a method to the object to which it belongs. C++ supports functions (as C does) but goes further, requiring that functions that manipulate the object belong to the object—they must be *member functions*.

This is the crux of *abstract typing,* or defining your own object types (not data abstraction or encapsulation). The compiler already knows how to deal with its built-in types, but you must teach it how to handle the types you define. Herein lies the need for member functions that go beyond the simple goal of protecting the object's contents from accidental or illegal access.

You may wonder why a whole new syntax is necessary to provide object-oriented behavior. The answer is simply convenience and power. Writing an object-oriented program with ordinary C is entirely possible. To get started, all you need is a mastery of C structures and function pointers to provide object boundaries and member functions.

Using ordinary C to write a (somewhat) object-oriented program will help you appreciate what is meant by "convenience"—but it's not worth doing more than once. Listing 14.1 contains the source code for CMINUS.C, which implements some crude screen functions in a somewhat object-oriented fashion.

Listing 14.1.   CMINUS.C—Implementing abstract types with ordinary C structures (with Borland C++).

```
 1  #include <stdlib.h>
 2  #include <stdio.h>
 3  #include <conio.h>
 4  #include <dos.h>
 5
 6  unsigned char borderchars[] = { "_¿__Ä_" };
 7
 8  typedef strict {    /* DEFINE SCREEN "CLASS" */
 9    int border[4];
10    int curpos[2];
11    int cur_attr;
12
```

```
13     void (*clr)( void * );              /* Methods */
14     void (*loc)( void *, int, int );
15     void (*put)( void *, char * );
16     int* (*query_scr)( void * );
17   } screen;
18
19   void clr( screen * );
20   void loc( screen *, int, int );
21   void put( screen *, char * );
22   void init_scr( screen *, int, int, int, int);
23   int*  query_scr( screen *);
24
25   #define CLR(a)  (*a.clr)( &a )
26   #define LOC(a,b,c) (*a.loc)( &a,b,c )
27   #define PUT(a,b)   (*a.put)( &a,b )
28   #define INIT(a,b,c,d,e) (*init_scr)( &a,b,c,d,e )
29   #define QUERY(a) (*a.query_scr)( &a )
30
31   #define POKE(a) (*(scrptr+(wherey()-1)*160  \
32    +(wherex()-1)*2+ (topy-1)*160 + (topx-1)*2 ) = a )
33
34   int scr_ptr_init = 0;
35   unsigned char* far scrptr;
36
37   void init_scr( screen *this, int topx, int topy,
38                  int botx, int boty )
39   {
40     int p;
41     strict text_info ti;
42
43     if ( !scr_ptr_init ) {
44       scr_ptr_init = 1;
45       gettextinfo(&ti);
46       if ( ti.currmode == 7 )
47         scrptr=(unsigned char* far)MK_FP(0xB000, 0x0000);
48       else
49         scrptr=(unsigned char* far)MK_FP(0xB800, 0x0000);
50     }
51     this->query_scr = (void*)query_scr;
52     this->clr      = (void*)clr;
53     this->loc      = (void*)loc;
```

continues

Listing 14.1. Continued

```
54    this->put      = (void*)put;
55    this->border[0] = topx;
56    this->border[1] = topy;
57    this->border[2] = botx;
58    this->border[3] = boty;
59    this->cur_attr = (RED << 4) + WHITE;
60    textattr( this->cur_attr );
61    window( topx, topy, botx, boty );
62    clrscr();
63
64    gotoxy( 1,1 );
65    POKE( borderchars[0] );
66
67    gotoxy( botx-topx+1, 1 );
68    POKE( borderchars[1] );
69
70    gotoxy( 1, boty-topy+1 );
71    POKE( borderchars[2] );
72
73    gotoxy( botx-topx+1, boty-topy+1 );
74    POKE( borderchars[3] );
75
76    for ( p=2; p<=botx-topx; ++p ) {
77      gotoxy( p, 1 );
78      POKE( borderchars[4] );
79    }
80
81    for ( p=2; p<=botx-topx; ++p ) {
82      gotoxy( p, boty-topy+1 );
83      POKE( borderchars[4] );
84    }
85
86    for ( p=2; p<=boty-topy; ++p ) {
87      gotoxy( 1, p );
88      POKE( borderchars[5] );
89    }
90
91    for ( p=2; p<=boty-topy; ++p ) {
92      gotoxy( botx-topx+1, p );
93      POKE( borderchars[5] );
```

```
94      }
95
96      gotoxy(1,1);
97      this->curpos[0] = this->curpos[1] = 1;
98   }
99
100  int*  query_scr( screen *this )
101  {
102     return( this->curpos );
103  }
104
105  void clr( screen *this )
106  {
107     window( this->border[0]+1, this->border[1]+1,
108             this->border[2]-1, this->border[3]-1 );
109     textattr( this->cur_attr );
110     clrscr();
111  }
112
113  void loc( screen *this, int x, int y )
114  {
115     window( this->border[0]+1, this->border[1]+1,
116             this->border[2]-1, this->border[3]-1 );
117     textattr( this->cur_attr );
118     gotoxy( x, y );
119     this->curpos[0] = x;
120     this->curpos[1] = y;
121  }
122
123  void put( screen *this, char *msg )
124  {
125     int *p;
126
127     window( this->border[0]+1, this->border[1]+1,
128             this->border[2]-1, this->border[3]-1 );
129     textattr( this->cur_attr );
130     p = QUERY( (*this) );
131     LOC( (*this),*p,*(p+1) );
132     cprintf( "%s",msg );
133     this->curpos[0] = wherex();
134     this->curpos[1] = wherey();
```

continues

Listing 14.1. Continued

```
135   }
136
137   void main()
138   {
139     screen screen1, screen2;
140     char ch;
141
142     textattr( (BLUE << 4) + YELLOW );
143     clrscr();
144
145     INIT( screen1,2,1,39,12 );
146     INIT( screen2,40,13,78,25 );
147
148     LOC( screen1,17,6 );
149     LOC( screen2,17,6 );
150
151     PUT( screen1,"Hello" );
152     PUT( screen2,"Hello" );
153
154     while ( !(ch = getch()) ) ;
155   }
```

Listing 14.1 shows what is probably the most complicated "hello" program you will ever see. This program defines and uses multiple "virtual screens" that may all appear simultaneously on the physical screen. (A real object-oriented virtual-screen manager, complete with pull-down menus, is presented in the next chapter.)

Each virtual screen is an object, and must have a type (or *class* in true C++). This program implements the screen type in an ordinary structure, which can be seen in lines 8–17. Both the data items belonging to the object (lines 9–11) and the pointers to member functions (lines 13–16) are contained in the boundaries of the object type.

Before the object can be used, it must be initialized. This is done in lines 37–98, function init_scr(). This activity corresponds to the C++ *constructor*. The major difference between this example and a true C++ object is that true C++ objects do not require you to take addresses and initialize pointers in this way, although you have to initialize member variables.

Lines 25–29 contain several macros intended to mimic the C++ way of accessing an object. Although the syntax cannot be matched exactly, using macros to mask the syntax enables you to pass objects by reference (like C++ does) without having to use the address-of operator for every reference. What "passing by reference" means becomes clear when the C++ reference operator is discussed. Meanwhile, notice how complicated the macro structure must be to permit this simplified method of access.

You can see that implementing objects in ordinary C takes some effort, and can be confusing as you deal with the awkward syntax. Implementing objects in C++ also takes some effort—just not as much—and can be done much more powerfully than in C. Now you can see how all this is done with C++.

Classes Are Abstract Data Types

Objects, like basic structures, are relatively complex. As with structures, the compiler has no advance knowledge of what an object contains or how it is handled. That is, the compiler knows nothing about the object's type.

Typing objects in C++ is your responsibility. You must decide what type of data goes in the object, and how that data should be handled. In C++, such user-defined types are called *classes*. A class is the method used by C++ to implement *abstract data types*, which means that the compiler knows nothing about them beforehand (as it does its built-in types).

NOTE Classes give C++ its power and flexibility, especially because of their capability for inheriting characteristics from predecessor classes (subclasses inherit superclass characteristics), and for efficiently reusing code.

C++ provides for *data abstraction* (encapsulation of related complex data) as well as for *abstract data typing* (user-defined types or classes). The *structure,* a feature you already know about from C, should be knocking at the door of your mind.

If all this reminds you of structures, you are correct. Underneath all the new terminology and syntax of C++, the basic vehicle for implementing objects is the C `strict`. But it is a structure with a twist, and with new and improved powers! If you remember this as you approach learning C++, it is much easier to retain.

The new type of structure in C++ is the `class`. Its declaration syntax is similar to your old friend the `strict`. Details on declaring classes and defining objects are in Chapter 15, but comparing some real C++ code to the program in Listing 14.1 is enlightening. Therefore, in the next three program listings, you briefly see the source files required for defining and using a keyboard object. As you read the listings, watch for the way the code treats the keyboard object as something that can *act,* rather than simply being acted upon—objects have more intelligence than simple data because they contain their own method functions.

The keyboard object appears in the next three source file listings, which correspond to the header file, the member (method) functions source file, and the main program file.

NOTE   The best way to write C++ code is in separately compiled modules, but you should also know that it can be done in one file.

The first source file, shown in Listing 14.2, contains the header file for the keyboard object. In addition to the more mundane matters of manifest constants, the object header contains the object's type, or class, declaration. This header is included in both the source file that contains the actual member functions, and the main program that uses everything.

Listing 14.2. KEYBOARD.HPP—Header file for the keyboard object (with Borland or Microsoft C++).

```
1    #define NORM 0
2    #define EXT  1
3
4    #define F1 59
5    #define F2 60
6    #define F3 61
7    #define F4 62
8    #define F5 63
9    #define F6 64
10   #define F7 65
11   #define F8 66
12   #define F9 67
13   #define F10 68
14   #define INS 82
15   #define DEL 83
16   #define HOME 71
17   #define END 79
18   #define UPA 72
19   #define DNA 80
20   #define LFA 75
21   #define RTA 77
22   #define PGU 73
23   #define PGD 81
24
25   class keyboard {          // Declare the class (type)
26      int state;
```

```
27    int ch;
28    int lastpush;
29    int pushbuf[80][2];     //LIFO push buffer
30  public:
31    keyboard( void );
32    void next( void );       // get next state and character
33    void nexte( void );      // get next state, character, echo
34    void push( int, int );   // push specified state, character
35    friend int keystate( keyboard & );
36    friend int keyval( keyboard & );
37  };
38
```

Notice how much the class keyboard declaration (lines 25–37) resembles a strict declaration with a tag. It has member elements, just like a strict.

Differences appear immediately, however. The member elements in lines 26–29 are encapsulated—they are visible only to the member functions. That, in fact, is the purpose of the public keyword in line 30: It signals that the member elements (all functions, in this case) can be seen and accessed by calls from outside the object (when one is later defined—this is just the declaration, remember). The one exception to this rule is the friend function (see lines 35–36). These are nonmember functions that can access private member elements. For more information on these functions, see Chapter 17.

So much for the keyboard header file and prototype declarations. What about the member functions? They are found in the source file KEYBOARD.CPP, Listing 14.3. One good reason for defining the member functions in a separate file is that doing so enhances the effect of encapsulating the object.

Listing 14.3. KEYBOARD.CPP—Source file containing member functions for keyboard object (with Borland or Microsoft C++).

```
1  #include <stdlib.h>
2  #include <stdio.h>
3  #include <conio.h>
4
5  #include "keyboard.hpp"
6
7  keyboard::keyboard( void )
8  {
9    state = NORM;
```

continues

Listing 14.3.   Continued

```
10    ch = '\0';
11    lastpush = 80;
12  }
13
14  void keyboard::next( void )
15  {
16    if ( lastpush < 80 ) {    // get it from push buffer
17      state = pushbuf[lastpush][0];
18      ch = pushbuf[lastpush][1];
19      ++lastpush;
20    }
21    else {
22      state = NORM;
23      ch = getch();
24      if ( !ch ) {
25        state = EXT;
26        ch = getch();
27      }
28    }
29  }
30
31  void keyboard::nexte( void )
32  {
33    if ( lastpush < 80 ) {    // get it from push buffer
34      state = pushbuf[lastpush][0];
35      ch = pushbuf[lastpush][1];
36      ++lastpush;
37    }
38    else {
39      state = NORM;
40      ch = getch();
41      if ( !ch ) {
42        state = EXT;
43        ch = getch();
44      }
45    }
46    if ( !state ) putchar( ch ); // if not ext ASCII
47  }
48
49  void keyboard::push( int kstate, int kval )
50  {
```

```
51    if ( lastpush > 0 ) {
52      --lastpush;
53      pushbuf[lastpush][0] = kstate;
54      pushbuf[lastpush][1] = kval;
55    }
56  }
57
58  int keystate( keyboard &kybd )
59  {
60    return kybd.state;
61  }
62
63  int keyval( keyboard &kybd )
64  {
65    return kybd.ch;
66  }
```

Writing the member function definitions in a separate source file requires a little extra effort. Notice in the declaration part of every function declaration (except the two that were declared as friend functions) that every function name is preceded by the tokens keyboard::. This is done so the compiler knows which class declaration these member functions belong to. The :: operator, which is new in C++, is the *scope resolution operator*. This is an important concept—if the header and source file were combined and only one class was being defined, the scope resolution operator might not be necessary.

Lines 7–12 of Listing 14.3 show a function with the same name as the class. This is the *constructor* member function; it has the special purpose of initializing the object when it is defined (created). Remember that you must teach the compiler everything it knows about how to handle the new object.

In older versions of C++, you could include a peculiar reference in the constructor. This peculiar reference was to something called this. It is always assumed to be present (notice that it was not declared), and can always be referenced by member functions to access a particular object—this object, with the obvious meaning. The use of this is explained in great detail in the next chapter. For now, keep moving along with the introduction to C++.

All that remains to be done is to create an object by defining it, and use it. This is done in the main program TESTKEY.CPP, Listing 14.4. This program illustrates the use of the keyboard class object to retrieve characters from the keyboard (with echo to the screen automatically included), to receive special-purpose keystrokes (the extended-ASCII function keys and other keys on the IBM PC), and to briefly show how keyboard macros might be implemented. That's quite a lot from this little bit of code, but it is a perfect illustration of the power of C++.

Listing 14.4. TESTKEY.CPP—Test driver for keyboard object (with Borland C++).

```
1   #include <stdlib.h>
2   #include <stdio.h>
3   #include <string.h>
4
5   #include "keyboard.hpp"
6
7   main()
8   {
9     int i;            // declare an ordinary object ...
10    keyboard kybd;    // Create the keyboard object ...
11                      // No constructor parms were needed,
12                      // so parens weren't needed either
13
14    char *p;
15    char msg[80] = "Create keyboard macros easily!\r";
16                      // String simulates console input ...
17
18    printf( "\nType some normal text:\n" );
19    do { kybd.nexte(); } while ( keyval( kybd ) != 13 );
20
21    printf("\nPress a function or other extended key:\n");
22    kybd.nexte();
23    if ( keystate( kybd ) == NORM ) {
24      printf( "That wasn't an extended ASCII key\n" );
25      exit( 0 );
26    }
27
28    switch( keyval( kybd ) ) {
29      case F1 :
30                  printf( "You pressed F1\n" ); break;
31      case F2 :
32                  printf( "You pressed F2\n" ); break;
33      case F3 :
34                  printf( "You pressed F3\n" ); break;
35      case F4 :
36                  printf( "You pressed F4\n" ); break;
37      case F5 :
38                  printf( "You pressed F5\n" ); break;
```

```
39      case F6 :
40                  printf( "You pressed F6\n" ); break;
41      case F7 :
42                  printf( "You pressed F7\n" ); break;
43      case F8 :
44                  printf( "You pressed F8\n" ); break;
45      case F9 :
46                  printf( "You pressed F9\n" ); break;
47      case F10 :
48                  printf( "You pressed F10\n" ); break;
49      case INS :
50                  printf( "You pressed Ins\n" ); break;
51      case DEL :
52                  printf( "You pressed Del\n" ); break;
53      case HOME :
54                  printf( "You pressed Home\n" ); break;
55      case END :
56                  printf( "You pressed End\n" ); break;
57      case UPA :
58                  printf( "You pressed UpArrow\n" ); break;
59      case DNA :
60                  printf( "You pressed DownArrow\n" ); break;
61      case LFA :
62                  printf( "You pressed LeftArrow\n" ); break;
63      case RTA :
64                  printf( "You pressed RightArrow\n" ); break;
65      case PGU :
66                  printf( "You pressed PageUp\n" ); break;
67      case PGD :
68                  printf( "You pressed PageDown\n" ); break;
69      }
70
71      p = msg + strlen( msg ) - 1; // push down kybd macro
72      for( i=strlen(msg); i>0; --i ) kybd.push( 0, *p-- );
73
74      printf( "\nYou don't have to do anything here:\n" );
75      do { kybd.nexte(); } while ( keyval( kybd ) != 13 );
76  }
```

The point of overwhelming interest in Listing 14.4 is line 10. With the one short statement keyboard kybd; the object is created, initialized, and ready for use. All you had to do was declare it like any other variable. What this means is that after you have conceived and defined a class properly, you can write extremely powerful code quickly. That is what C++ is all about.

Going Beyond *typedef*

Clearly, the class declaration goes considerably beyond even typedef in its descriptive and syntactical power. Further, it puts that power in your hands.

You learned earlier that one of the glaring failures of structured programming was that it required good organization without supplying the proper tools. Well, C++ doesn't so much require organization as it does supply the tools—the organization happens almost automatically.

That is perhaps the greatest beauty of C++ (and other OOPS vehicles). It definitely makes large and complex projects possible. After you have gotten over the learning curve, writing badly disorganized code is nearly impossible. And, in the long run, C++ simplifies complex projects, not so much by being complex (although it can be) as by not requiring you to continue dealing with complexity after you have solved a particular problem. You can fix it, file it, and forget it.

Is C++ the answer to every programming dilemma? It most certainly is not. You still can stumble into several dark corners, but the language is young and growing. Pitfalls are bound to exist. With a little work and experimentation, you will find it worthwhile.

What Encapsulation Means

Admittedly, the keyboard class object developed in this chapter was somewhat contrived. The friend functions were included even though they were not strictly necessary in this object class.

This was done to illustrate something about what encapsulation means in the context of C++. Encapsulation, or data hiding, is meant to be an ally, not an enemy. It should be a tool to work with, not something that defeats you every time.

Thus, the friend nonmember functions were included in this example to show you that C++ has the flexibility to do what you want it to do—it even provides a legitimate way to get around data hiding. The spirit of C is also at work in C++, and it can be a friendly language when approached with a little patience!

Class Inheritance Is Type Derivation

In ordinary C, you can derive new objects from old. For example, defining an array of int is a type derivation, but you don't have to redefine int to the compiler to perform the type derivation. Of course, plain C provides only a synonym facility in deriving arrays, structs, and typedefs.

C++ also provides for type derivation, but it is more than a synonym facility. You can derive a class from another similar class and easily change part of its definition. This concept is like defining a new basic type to C, but better.

This feature of C++ is called *inheritance.* The derived class can inherit most of its logic from the old class, but you can redefine parts of the new class to suit different purposes.

Inheritance is perhaps one of the most powerful features of C++, and indeed of any OOPS language. There are, however, differences of opinion about what inheritance does, or should mean. There are, in fact, differences of opinion on what object-oriented should mean. A review of some of these opinions may help you form your own mental filing system in which you can arrange your understanding of C++.

Definitions of Object-Oriented Systems

There are many definitions of *object-oriented* programming. You already know that the first working definition of an object is something that has boundaries. This helps you start forming a conceptual framework for the subject, but does little to help you understand how objects might be represented in a concrete programming language.

Accordingly, three different views on the subject are presented for your inspection. There are similarities and differences in each of these views. This chapter briefly discusses the statements of Peter Wegner of Brown University; of Zortech Ltd., the company that produced the first true C++ compiler for the IBM PC environment (Bruce Eckel contributed to the tutorial parts of the Zortech manual); and finally, of Bjarne Stroustrup (who originally conceived and developed C++—you can hardly ignore his comments).

C++ is an object-oriented language in any of the views about to be examined. Certain OOPS purists, however, claim that no *compiled* language can ever be object-oriented. These devotees limit the achievement of object-orientation to implementations that can resolve the type and validity of objects and their messages completely dynamically at runtime (that is, only to interpretive languages). Understandably, most disagree with this extreme view.

Wegner's Definition

Peter Wegner, who earned a Ph.D in Computer Science from London University, is currently a professor of Computer Science at Brown University in Providence, Rhode Island. He is deeply involved in OOPS and has written about it in a variety of learned and popular publications. His views, as briefly summarized here, appeared in an article, "Learning the Language," in the March, 1989, issue of *Byte Magazine* (Vol. 14, No. 3).

Of the three views presented here, Wegner has the most well-considered and technically oriented perspective. The essentials of his definition are not overly complex, however. Wegner's definition begins with object-based languages, adds classes to yield class-based languages, and finally, adds class-inheritance to arrive at object-oriented languages. Figure 14.3 shows the progressively restrictive requirements for languages imposed by Wegner's definition.

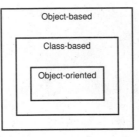

Figure 14.3.

Wegner's definition of object-oriented systems.

The most permissive class of languages in this view are the object-based languages. They provide for data abstraction and they provide access to an object's "state" through its own operators, and not much else. Data abstraction provides the data-hiding qualities of objects, but doesn't include the qualities of abstract typing. Strong data typing—when the type characteristics of all objects are completely determined at compile time—may appear in these languages, as it appears in C++, but it is not an indispensable ingredient.

Class-Based Languages

Adding abstract data types, or classes, to object-based languages yields the more restrictive set of languages known as *class-based*. In these languages, objects do not stand alone against the world, but belong to classes—their abstract types. All previous qualities of objects are brought forward.

A *class* is more like a template for an object than a strict type. This has important consequences for the way the language behaves. Typed languages have type-checking semantics that do a little more than prevent errors and nail down the identification of an object. Classes, on the other hand, are oriented toward instance-creation semantics. Instance-semantics allow the class's template to be copied, and perhaps modified in being copied. This is why you have seen comments to the effect that type derivation in standard C is a synonym mechanism, whereas class derivation is a true abstract type derivation—much more than a simple synonym.

Class derivation leads directly to the third requirement for a fully object-oriented language: inheritance. Class derivation is more properly called *class inheritance*. Inheritance is the mechanism by which one class (a subclass) acquires many of its properties or methods from its parent (a superclass, or base class).

Class inheritance is a key concept in C++. When one class derives from another, that class, by default, inherits from its base class all the methods belonging to the base class—except those specifically overridden by new definitions. This way, one can reuse member functions from the base class without having to redefine or recode them. Such a feature is called *code reusability*. (You can also reuse code without inheritance by including objects from one class in a new class.)

The capability of a class to act as a template for its subclasses while allowing for *incremental modification* is an important part of what classes are and do. This aspect of classes is called *polymorphism*. Polymorphism is just the opposite of code reusability. It refers to the process of only partially changing class methods so there is still much in common with the superclass. A shape superclass, for example, might be used to derive square and circle subclasses. Each subclass might have draw() methods, but they would necessarily differ in internal detail. You will see how to perform class derivations, and all the rest, in the next two chapters.

In fairness to all those who have labored long over the OOPS theory, note that Wegner did not invent all of these terms. His discussions of them, however, are illuminating in a dark sea of often confusing literature. C++ users need not fear the confusion of the OOPS debate—C++ characteristics are quite clear-cut.

Zortech's Definition

Although Zortech C++ examples are not used in this book, it is still worthwhile to look at the Zortech documentation's definition of *object-oriented*. Zortech is the first true C++ compiler (as opposed to an interpreter) for the IBM PC. The comments made here about Zortech's view of what OOP really means are derived from an early version of the C++ compiler's documentation (Version 1.07), but are still true and helpful.

The Zortech C++ Version 1.07 manual manages to coherently and understandably introduce and define object-oriented programming in one page. On that page, the following brief definition of object-oriented is given:

Object-Oriented = Abstract Data Typing + Type Derivation + Commonality

You should be familiar with the first of these ingredients. *Abstract data typing* still means the capability to define your own classes. *Type derivation* is used by Zortech (and everyone else) as a synonym for class inheritance. *Commonality* is another word meaning polymorphism, as previously discussed.

The Zortech manual makes an interesting comment about polymorphism. It is defined here as the capability of a C++ object to determine, at runtime, the meaning of a message sent to it. In terms of C++, because messages are sent to objects by means of calling member functions, polymorphism is the capability to determine, at runtime, which of several identically named functions to invoke. The example of the draw() function mentioned in the previous section is an example.

Commonality, or polymorphism, is another very important issue in C++. A method (which can involve a member function or a redefined operator) can take several forms, all with the same name, in a C++ program. The use of a common function name for a superclass and its subclasses is only one instance. You can also overload both functions and operators. (You will learn how to do this shortly.)

NOTE What the Zortech manual doesn't mention is that object-oriented languages are also object-based. This aspect is assumed.

Stroustrup's Comments

Not very surprisingly, C++ was conceived and developed in the Bell Telephone Laboratories in Murray Hill, New Jersey. Although both Kernighan and Ritchie were involved in the project, the principal architect of C++ was Bjarne Stroustrup.

Stroustrup has also written a book, patterned after the famous *base document,* entitled *The C++ Programming Language.* You might think that this document would include some pointed comments about which aspects of the OOPS theory have been incorporated into the new language. But it doesn't, and that is surprising.

Much of what has just been discussed here is simply assumed by Stroustrup. His own characterization of C++ is that it is "C with classes," and he spends most of his time discussing C++ as actually implemented. This important book can be considered the C++ base document; but, understandably it cannot mention many important developments in C++ since it was published in 1986.

Other Issues in Object-Oriented Systems

There has been much discussion in computer trade publications about what is meant by object-oriented. Other parts of that continuing discussion deal more with the varieties of implementations of OOPS, and what that means for specific products. You will learn about two of these issues in the remainder of this chapter.

Multiple Inheritance

When C++ was very new, there were many claims that C++ was not truly object-oriented. One of the reasons cited was that it did not (in the earliest compilers) support multiple inheritance.

What is *multiple inheritance?* An intuitive guess might lead you to the conclusion that multiple inheritance is the condition in which a subclass of a class is itself a superclass. That is, when there are successive generations of derived classes. But this has always been possible (within limits) from the first implementations of C++.

Multiple inheritance is, rather, that facility by which a subclass inherits from more than one superclass simultaneously. This is like saying that a child has two parents, not just one.

The first implementation of C++, AT&T C++ 1.0, did not support multiple inheritance. As a consequence, some OOPS theorists claimed that C++ was not object-oriented. C++ adherents naturally claimed that it was, and that multiple inheritance was merely an unnecessary luxury.

More recently, the concensus is that multiple inheritance is very useful. It was present in AT&T C++ 2.0 and now AT&T C++ 3.0, which sets the standard, and in all other products seeking conformity to it.

ANSI C++—Developing a Standard

Conformity to a standard C++ is also a growing issue. ANSI has very recently formed the X3J16 committee to begin work on a proposed C++ standard. Given the new ANSI C standard, it was bound to happen. One can only wait and hope that X3J16 does as well with C++ as X3J11 did with C.

Object Implementations: Functional, Server, Autonomous, and Slot-Based

The manner in which an object is implemented directly and drastically influences the actions of which the object is capable. It is not a universal law of nature that an object must be implemented exactly as in C++. What are some of these implementations, and where does C++ fit?

In the same article cited earlier, Wegner defines four fundamental types of objects: *functional, server, autonomous,* and *slot-based.*

Functional objects fulfill the requirement of data abstraction, but do not have an identity that persists between two operations on an object. Any operation that changes the object's state (you can think of this as the internal, hidden variables) causes the creation of a new object—a physically distinct entity— that has the same programming interface as the old object, with a new state arising from the operation. Wegner cites OBJ2 and Vulcan as languages that have this characteristic.

Server objects are passive objects. They are active only when a message (such as a member-function call) is received that triggers the object's internal operations. C++ objects fall into this category, as do those of Smalltalk, Ada, Modula-2, Simula, and CLU.

Autonomous objects are active objects. Their methods (member functions) can execute even in the absence of a triggering message. Such objects might appear in multitasking systems, or perhaps in parallel processors. One of the sample programs used frequently in this book, the TIMER.C program, might well be implemented as an autonomous object, because it runs in the background all the time. C++, however, does not provide native support for autonomous object definitions.

Slot-based objects focus strongly on instance-variables, called slots, rather than on classes. The distinguishing characteristic of these languages is the capability to add methods to an object. Thus, you might characterize these languages as having methods that belong to objects, rather than objects that belong to classes. Two languages predicated on this philosophy are Flavors and CLOS (Common Lisp Object System).

Summary

From the perspective of C++, an object is something that has definite boundaries, hides information (its state or internal variables), has methods implemented as member functions, receives messages in the form of member function calls, and belongs to a class. That is certainly quite a bit more complex than even the derived objects of standard C! The following topics were discussed in this chapter:

■ A class (the controlling notion of C++) is a user-defined type that goes far beyond the synonym-assigning capability of standard C. Classes are what give C++ its power and flexibility, especially because of their capability for inheriting characteristics from predecessor classes (subclasses inherit superclass characteristics), and for efficiently reusing code.

■ C++ is still a young language, but is growing even faster than C did (perhaps because C had already opened the floodgates). Stroustrup published his landmark base document for C++ in 1986, and developed the first C++ compiler (AT&T 1.0).

■ Now that the AT&T compiler is in Version 3.0, Borland has released Borland C++ 3.1, and Microsoft C/C++ 7.0 is out, both conforming (almost completely) to the standard. At least Microsoft no longer has to recommend a competitor's compiler product for those customers who insist on OOP capability.

■ C++ compilers have come a long way in the short time since their introduction. Current compilers support such fancy items as multiple inheritance, virtual base classes, type-safe linkages, and dynamically parameterized types (class templates).

■ C++ is a complex language—one that is probably impossible for the non-C programmer to master. There is little doubt that its syntax and many of its features are quite advanced, even arcane, at least in its current form.

■ The basic concepts of C++ are really quite simple. Like good engineering, simple modular pieces come together into a complex whole. Mastering those first concepts and modular tools is not particularly difficult, it is just different. They are simple enough, in fact, that you will have a firm grasp of the foundations when you finish the next two chapters.

Defining Classes and Objects

The greatest obstacle facing the proficient C programmer who wants to learn C++ is his or her proficiency. There is a correct way of thinking about C—and another way of thinking about C++. You must realize that, in many respects, *C++ is a different language*. Frequently, the similarities between the two languages are more deceptive than they are helpful—but, fortunately, not all the time.

C++ is a different language, but not in the sense that it arises from a completely alien ancestry. C++ is C, plus a lot more—in particular, *classes*. What is a class? Read on to find out.

Quick Reference: C++ Classes

A *class* is a structure, with some features added, as indicated in the following two partial declarations:

```
strict tag {
    ... member elements
};

class name {
    ... member elements
};
```

continues

Quick Reference: C++ Classes

Structures *can* have tags; classes *must* have names. C++ structures can do everything that C structures can do—plus enable you to define member functions in the C++ style.

C++ classes hide data and functions (that is the default, in fact) and *can* declare some elements or member functions as publicly available. C++ structures do not hide data or functions; everything in a structure has the public attribute. But you can build objects from either structures or classes.

The predominance of the class concept in C++ is the clue to its fundamental difference from C: the main idea in C is *executing functions*, whereas the main idea in C++ is *referencing objects*. The big difference is that the member function is part of the object. Failure to grasp this difference can make writing C++ programs quite difficult.

Classes will become more clear to you as you experiment with C++. In fact, once you have changed mental gears from C to C++, you will find that C++ programming is not terribly difficult, in spite of its esoteric appearance. Figure 15.1 illustrates the idea of referencing a C++ (class) object.

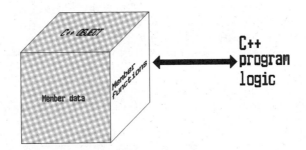

Figure 15.1.

Referencing a C++ object by calling a member function.

Defining Classes to C++

Before you can define or use an object, you must declare a class for it. The class declaration contains encapsulated data and member-function prototypes, public data and member-function prototypes, and perhaps in-line member-function definitions. Not every permutation of class-declaration syntax is illustrated in this chapter and the next, but many of them are.

In Chapter 14, you were advised to write separate files for the object header and member-function definitions. When you do this, make the names of the header files and the member-function source files the same, except for the extension. For example, suppose that you are writing a definition for a `gadget` object. The header file is GADGET.HPP, and the member-function source file is GADGET.CPP (or whatever extensions your compiler requires). And don't forget to #include the header name in the member-function source file, as in the following example (notice how you can write C++ commands):

```
#include <stdlib.h>   // GADGET.CPP source file
#include <stdio.h>
... // Any other includes
#include "gadget.hpp"
... // Continue with member function definitions
```

The advantages of building the program this way are greatest in the development phase of writing your program, rather than at the time you run the program. The member-function source file can be compiled separately (after adequate debugging) and easily included in programs that use the functions by writing an #include for the appropriate header. This is the way the `keyboard` object was handled in Chapter 14.

It is possible to write all the declarations and member-function definitions directly in the program that will use the objects defined (as in Listing 15.1). There are two good times to do this:

■ When the program is very short. A short program probably will use simple objects and be simple overall. If this is not the case, you should go to the trouble of writing separate files for the header and member functions. Writing class declarations and member-function definitions in C++ is easy once you get the hang of it, but these declarations quickly tend to get long and complex for objects that have many capabilities. You will find, however, that this is actually one of the benefits of C++; it naturally encourages you to write object definitions that are robust, full-functioned, and more bug-free than standard C. The trade-off is code space and thus overall complexity, which has always been the price of powerful programs. At least C++ helps you manage and conceal that complexity.

■ When you have no need to reuse the objects defined. Writing the class declarations directly into the main program that is supposed to use them carries the cost of loss of availability. Clearly, they can be used only in that program. This is fine for practice coding and for illustrations, but real-world projects should produce classes that can be used again and again.

Setting Up the Class Definition

How do you define your own object types with a class declaration? The best way to learn is "hands on," so begin by considering a class. Because it is fairly short, it is packaged with a `main()` function to drive it.

The program ARRAY.CPP in Listing 15.1 contains an array class. It is informative because it is short enough to remember while you are getting acquainted with classes, and because it resembles the vector class built into your C++ compiler. The array class contains declarations for an array-based object that can initialize itself, display itself, reverse itself, and sum itself. This class also has facilities for accessing individual elements, just like a standard array. In short, the class demonstrates quite handily that C++ objects tend to be more "intelligent" than derived objects in standard C—in several ways.

Listing 15.1.   ARRAY.CPP—A class for an array object (using Borland C++).

```
1   #include <stdlib.h>
2   #include <stdio.h>
3   #include <stdarg.h>
4   #include <string.h>
5
6   class array {
7     int value;
8     int numelem;
9     int *elem;
10    char *name;
11  public:                  // Two constructors, first
12    array( char *, ... ); // with name and init list,
13    array( array & );      // copied from another object
14    ~array( void );        // Now a destructor
15    void *operator new( unsigned );
16    void operator delete( void * );
17    int &operator[](int);
18    void reverse( void );
19    void display( void );
20    void newname( char * );
21  };
22
23  array::array( char *sname, ... ) // Variadic declaration
24  {
25    va_list ap;
26    int work;
27     value = 0;                   // Sum starts at zero
28    numelem = 0;
29    name = new char[strlen(name)+1];
30    strcpy( name, sname );  // Init name string
31    va_start( ap, sname );  // Just count them this time
```

```
32    while ( 0 <= (work = va_arg( ap, int ) ) ) ++numelem;
33    va_end( ap );
34    if ( numelem > 0 )        // If there were any elements
35    elem = new int[numelem];
36     va_start( ap, sname);    // Now load the array
37    for ( work=0; work<numelem; ++work )
38      elem[work] = va_arg( ap, int );
39    va_end( ap );
40  }
41
42  array::array( array &copy )     // Copy constructor
43  {
44    int i;
45
46    value = copy.value;    // Ref. op makes -> op unnecessary
47    numelem = copy.numelem;
48    name = new char[strlen(copy.name)+1];
49    strcpy( name, copy.name );    // Init name string
50    elem = new int[copy.numelem];
51    for ( i=0; i<copy.numelem; ++i )
52      elem[i] = copy.elem[i];
53  }
54
55  array::~array( void )
56  {
57    delete elem;
58    delete name;
59  }
60
61  void *array::operator new( size_t size )
62  {
63    return ::new unsigned char[size];
64  }
65
66  void array::operator delete( void *objptr )
67  {
68    ::delete objptr;
69  }
70
71  int &array::operator[]( int n )
72  {
73                        // Returning a reference ensures
```

continues

Listing 15.1. Continued

```
74                          // that [] can be used on
75                          // either side of the = operator
76   if ( n<0 || n >= numelem ) return elem[0];
77   return elem[n];
78 }
79
80 void array::reverse( void )
81 {
82   int a, b;
83    a = 0;
84   b = numelem - 1;
85   while ( b > a ) {
86     elem[a]^=elem[b];
87     elem[b]^=elem[a];
88     elem[a]^=elem[b];
89     ++a; --b;
90   }
91 }
92
93 void array::display( void )
94 {
95   int i;
96    for ( i=0; i<numelem; ++i ) {
97      printf( "%s[%d]=%d ", name, i, elem[i] );
98    }
99   printf( "\n" );
100 }
101
102 void array::newname( char *n )
103 {
104   delete name;                 // Deallocate old name
105   name = new char[strlen(n)+1]; // Allocate new name
106   strcpy( name, n );           // Copy it
107 }
108
109 main() {
110                 // Define an object on the stack
111   array x( "X", 1,2,3,4,5,6,7,8,9,0,-1 );
112
113   x.display(); // Send various messages to object
```

```
114     x.reverse();
115     x.display();
116     x[0] = 99;    // Use the overloaded [] operator
117     x[1] = 101;   // You couldn't do this if op[]()
118     x[2] = x[1]; // Returned other than int&
119     x.display();
120
121     array y = x; // Use the copy constructor
122     y.newname( "Y" );
123     y.display();
124  }
```

If you were writing separate modules, lines 1–21 are the part of Listing 15.1 you would place in the .HPP file. These lines include the standard C #includes and the class declaration proper. Lines 23–107 contain the member-function prototype declarations. To package them separately, you would have to add an #include "array.hpp" at the beginning of that .CPP source file. In this case, an #include "array.hpp" and the main() function would occupy a third .CPP file.

Now turn your attention to lines 6–21 of Listing 15.1, which contain the class declaration. You form the class declaration by writing the class keyword, the class name (which is formed like every other identifier), and then the declarations for the member objects. The declarations of the member objects are surrounded by a pair of curly braces, and each declaration is terminated with a semicolon. When a *member object* is mentioned in this discussion, it can mean a standard C object or another C++ object, as you will see later.

This class is arranged like many you will see and write. It is divided neatly into two parts: some *data objects* precede the public: keyword, and *member-function prototype declarations* follow it. This is often, but not always, the case. Figure 15.2 shows a schematic arrangement of the array class declaration.

When you declare a class by using the class keyword, member elements are considered private: by default. You must code a public: keyword before those elements or function declarations that you want to be able to access from outside the object having that class name (see line 11).

You can declare a class also by using the strict keyword. A strict in C++ is something more than it is in standard C. It is in fact a class, with all the members public: by default. You can reference, from outside the object, any member element of an object having a class declared with strict.

All this raises an interesting issue having to do with scope. What is "inside" an object, and what is "outside"? The very phrasing of the question implies that "inside" an object there is a local scope, something like a block statement in standard C.

array class private members
variables
pointers to external areas

public:

array class public members
constructors/destructors
member functions
overloaded operator functions

Figure 15.2.

A typical arrangement of member elements in the array class.

This is so. All data objects declared in the class, together with all the member functions belonging to the class, make up a scope local to the object. This is why, for example, you see the scope resolution operator :: used in the member-function definitions. Because the member functions appear outside the braces delimiting the class or strict, how else can the compiler know which class a given function belongs to—if any? This may seem to be a trivial question until you realize that different classes may have member functions with the same name. Note the following code fragment, for example:

```
class c1 {  // Declare a class
...
public:
  void printobj( void );
...
};

class c2 {  // Declare another class
...
public:
  void printobj( void );
...

};
void c1::printobj( void )  // This belongs to class c1
{
  puts( "..." );
}
```

```
void c2::printobj( void )   // This belongs to class c2
{
  printf( "%8.3f\n", ... );
}


void printobj( char *s )   // This belongs to no class
{
  ...
}
```

In this fragment, total confusion would result if you tried to declare all these functions without the scope resolution operator.

Member-function prototypes, therefore, are declared in a normal manner in the class declaration. Member-function definitions generally are written outside and after the class declaration, using the scope resolution operator.

Arguments are allowed in member-function declarations, just as in standard C. C++ gives you a little more help, however, by enabling you to define default argument values for member functions, as in the following example:

```
class c3 {
  int a, b;
public:
  c3() { ... }    // Constructor function decl
  ~c3() { ... }   // Destructor function decl
                  // Default args must be last in list
  int transform( int delta, int cval = 0 );
};


int c3::transform( int delta, int cval )
{
  return a + b + delta + cval;
}
```

Default arguments for C++ functions are written in the function prototype declaration, not in the function definition. You can also write prototypes that mix parameters, those with and without default arguments. If you do, though, the parameters with default arguments must be written last in the argument list, as shown in the preceding example.

Member Elements: *private:*, *public:*, and *protected:*

A more precise definition is in order now. There are three kinds of member elements: `private:`, `public:`, and `protected:`. In Listing 15.1, only one of these, `public:`, was used. How can you know which to pick and where to code it? The `public:` and `private:` keywords are complementary in their meanings, whereas `protected:` may be thought of as a mixture of the other two. The following points may help make the differences clear:

- `public:` indicates that all member objects or functions following this keyword are available for general access. Member functions, as well as any other functions not associated with the class declaration, may access (or call) the member object (or function). Member objects and functions are publicly available from this point to the end of the class declaration, or until another of these three keywords is encountered. You normally use this keyword in class declarations because its members are `private:` by default.

- `private:` indicates that all member objects or functions following this keyword are available for access only by member or friend functions of this class. Because this is the default for class declarations, you normally use this keyword to hide member objects or functions in a class declared by a `strict`.

- `protected:` indicates that all members or functions following this keyword are available for access by member functions, friend functions, or member functions of subclasses derived from this one. They are not, however, at any time available to other functions generally. This subject comes up again later in the discussion of class inheritance.

T I P The nature of the keywords determines where you code them in the class declaration. Simply decide what must be hidden from public access and make it private, or perhaps protected. Keep in mind that the spirit of C++ implies that you should make public only the absolute minimum number of objects necessary; the goal is to create objects that perform "intelligently" and that need no outside help to get the job done. Such assistance is often an inadvertent return to standard C-style thinking and will prove to be a hindrance, not a help.

What Is *this*?

Look closely at Listing 15.1 and see whether you can find the C++ keyword this. It is conspicuous for its absence, isn't it? Then why do you need to know anything about it? You sometimes need to use it explicitly, even though that need may not arise often.

The *this* keyword

The keyword this is a pointer-to-self. It points to the object currently being dealt with. The keyword this is the means by which a member function can be informed of which particular instance of the object it is handling. It is a pointer to the object. The classname* this; is declared implicitly in every member function of a class. You do not have to declare it, but you can refer to it explicitly as this.

It is the keyword this that makes such a high level of syntactic convenience possible in C++. In line 27 of Listing 15.1, for example, the constructor member function of the array class initializes a private member element like this:

```
value = 0;   // Refer to a class member by simply using this.
```

To do this in standard C, you have to declare a pointer as a function parameter, take the address of the particular object, and pass it to the function. Furthermore, you would have to refer to the member object by using the structure pointer operator (assuming that you explicitly declared this to be the pointer) in the following way:

```
this->value = 0;   /* Looks familiar, doesn't it? */
```

Because C++ provides the self-reference pointer this and knows beforehand how it should be used, all that syntactic complexity can be hidden. Remember that it is *always* a hidden parameter for every member function (but clearly not for ordinary functions). It is the presence of this that enables you to write references to members of the class directly, without structure pointer operators.

Another important use of this is to provide a means for returning the address of the current object, or the object itself, from a member function. This maneuver permits such expressions as a = b; where both sides of the assignment refer to C++ objects. Just as in standard C, with ordinary objects, you can do this by value or by reference. The program THIS1.CPP in Listing 15.2 shows how to return an object by value.

Listing 15.2.   THIS1.CPP—Return an object by value (for Borland C++).

```
1   #include <stdlib.h>
2   #include <stdio.h>
3
4   class c1 {
5     int value;
6   public:
7     c1( int init ) { value = init; } // Constructors in-line
8     c1( void ) { value = 0; }
9     c1( c1& otherc1 ) { value = otherc1.value; }
10    c1 operator=( c1& rval )    // Assign op, return value
11        { value = rval.value; return *this; }
12    void printv( void ) { printf( "%d\n", value ); }
13  };
14
15  main()
16  {
17    c1 obj1( 37 ); // Declare one with initializer
18    c1 obj2, obj3; // and two without
19
20    obj3 = obj2 = obj1;
21    obj1.printv();
22    obj2.printv();
23    obj3.printv();
24  }
```

The program in Listing 15.2 declares the class c1. Before you go any further, notice that in this program, the member functions are *defined,* not just declared, in the class declaration. You can do this when function bodies are very short and don't contain complex constructions such as while loops. Member functions defined in this manner are called *in-line functions.*

Now look at line 10. This line contains a function-declaration part that looks strange to standard C programmers:

```
c1 operator=( c1& rval )      // Assign op, return value
```

This member function declares the method for handling the assignment operator = for objects with class c1. The declaration part indicates that = is a binary operator; the function parameter declares what kind of right-hand operand is required. The function also returns an object with type (class) c1.

Later, you are shown how to overload operators in detail. For now, just observe how the object is returned (return *this in line 11). Because this is a pointer, it must be dereferenced before it can be returned by value.

Do you remember reading earlier in this book that passing and returning pointers to structures, not the objects themselves, usually is wise? The reason was *size*. Values are passed and returned on the system stack, which is relatively small, and pushing large objects on the stack may cause an overflow. (It also can degrade performance.)

Classes and structures differ in many ways, but they are similar in that a reference to an object's identifier does *not* result in an address value (as it does with arrays). Classes and structures are similar also in that they tend to be large. Thus, for exactly the same reasons, passing and returning C++ objects by reference usually is wise. The program THIS2.CPP in Listing 15.3 shows how to rewrite the preceding short program to return the current object by reference, still using this to do it.

Listing 15.3.   THIS2.CPP—Return an object by reference (for Borland C++).

```
1   #include <stdlib.h>
2   #include <stdio.h>
3
4   class c1 {
5     int value;
6   public:
7     c1( int init ) { value = init; } // Constructors in-line
8     c1( void ) { value = 0; }
9     c1( c1& otherc1 ) { value = otherc1.value; }
10    c1& operator=( c1& rval )      // Assign op, return ref.
11       { value = rval.value; return *this; }
12    void printv( void ) { printf( "%d\n", value ); }
13  };
14
15  main()
16  {
17    c1 obj1( 37 ); // Declare one with initializer
18    c1 obj2, obj3; // and two without
19
20    obj3 = obj2 = obj1;
21    obj1.printv();
22    obj2.printv();
23    obj3.printv();
24  }
```

There is one difference between Listings 15.2 and 15.3—line 10. Look at the following comparison of line 10 from each program:

```
c1 operator=( c1& rval )      // Assign op, return value
c1& operator=( c1& rval )     // Assign op, return ref.
```

The only difference is in the return-type specification of the declaration part. The first returns an object with type c1, and the second returns a *reference to* an object with type c1. This is the meaning of the return-type specifier c1&. In C++, the & operator is the reference operator when used in a context like this one, and the address-of operator when used in more normal contexts.

The interesting point of Listing 15.3 is that, even when returning by reference rather than by value, you still write return *this. You do this because the C++ compiler is once again giving special assistance; the return-type specifier c1& (which you can also write as c1 &...) completely determines how the return is to be handled. In either case, you write the statement just as though you were dealing with an object (rather than an address). You will read much more about pointers and references in C++ in Chapter 16.

Which of the two programs is more efficient? THIS2.CPP (Listing 15.3) is more efficient for precisely the same reasons that pointers are more efficient in standard C—less physical data has to be hauled around when passing and returning parameters with address values. C++ references are the same, but you get more help with the syntax.

Initializing and Destroying Class Objects

The next step in writing a C++ object-oriented program is to initialize objects with particular values. And when you are done with them, you must have some way to get rid of them. Initializing a class object is accomplished by a *constructor* function, and destroying (freeing) an object is accomplished by the class's *destructor* function.

Constructors and Destructors

Think back to the lowly integer for a moment. How are integers created and initialized in standard C? The answer depends on the storage class of the particular instance of integer.

Integers that have static storage class are created by the compiler as a result of a declaration you wrote. If you also wrote an initializer, the variable is set to that value; if you did not write an initializer, it is set to zero. All this takes place at *compile time*.

Integers declared in a block (local variables) have `auto` storage class, unless you override it. These variables are created at *runtime,* typically on the system stack, by compiler-provided routines. If you provide an initializer, it will be used; otherwise, the contents of the object remain indeterminate until you do something about it.

Now make the mental switch back to C++ objects. How much does the C++ compiler do for you in creating and initializing user-defined objects? Ironically, it does relatively less than the standard C compiler does for basic objects. The key to user-defined objects in C++ is that they are user-defined. It's up to you to define what is to be done with them—the C++ compiler makes almost no assumptions about how objects declared for a class are to be handled. In addition, C++ objects are always created at runtime, never at compile time, even though you write the object definitions into the source code.

> **NOTE** C++ objects are always created at runtime, never at compile time, even though you write the object definitions into the source code.

When you write your own classes, you are defining what must be included in such objects, what class members are to be visible to functions outside the object, how member variables should be initialized, what operators are associated with the class, and how they are to work—that is, you define everything.

There is one exception. If you do not write any code that tells the compiler how to initialize the object, it automatically generates a constructor function for the object. Such a constructor does nothing but allocate memory sufficient to contain the object. Likewise, if you don't inform the compiler what to do about destroying the object when it goes out of scope, it generates a destructor function that performs the reverse task.

You must write your own constructor and destructor member functions for each class if you want more than simple allocation done—as you almost always will. Constructors and destructors are the means of controlling the *creation, initialization, copying,* and *destruction* of objects. All the sample programs in this chapter have constructors and destructors. Look at them and see them in action as you read the following text.

First, constructors and destructors have the same name as the class to which they belong. Note the following code fragment:

```
class tool {
  int kind;
  char *descrip;
public:
  tool( int type, char *use ); // A constructor
  ~tool( void );    // Destructor name has a tilde
```

```
};
                          // Constructor function definition
tool::tool( int type, char *use )
{
  kind = type;
  descrip = new unsigned char[strlen(use)+1] ;
  strcpy( descrip, use );
}
                          // Destructor function definition
tool::~tool( void ) // Use void or leave empty
{
  delete descrip;
}


main()
{
  tool wrench( 1, "Turn nuts and bolts" );
  tool hammer( 2, "Drive nails" );
...
}
```

This code fragment defines only the constructor and destructor member functions for the class tool. The constructor and destructor names are the same as the class name. Additionally, the destructor function has a tilde (~) character prefixed to the function name, identifying it as the destructor.

What you *don't* see is also important: there must be no return-type specifier, not even void. C++ has its own internal return type for these special functions, and you may not declare one.

You can declare more than one constructor for a class (but only one destructor). In Listing 15.3, there are two constructors for the c1 class (lines 17 and 18). One of them accepts an integer argument, and the other accepts no argument. Lines 16 and 17 show how to declare objects of this class, corresponding to each of these constructor methods. Specifying more than one constructor (or other member functions, for that matter) is called *overloading* the function. When you make a call to an overloaded function, constructor or otherwise, the C++ compiler determines which one you mean by examining the arguments to be passed to it.

The constructors you have seen so far initialize the object by the simple expedient of assigning values to the hidden members of the class. This probably is the most frequently used way of doing it, but other ways are provided by more recent compilers. Two specific forms of initializer list can be used, implemented in radically different ways.

The first form of initializer list provides variable substitution support; it is not used for plugging in constant values. The list is specified with the constructor function definition, after the declaration part and a full colon, and before the function body. The following short program, for example, supplies a variable initializer list for both of the hidden variables for an object of class A:

```
#include <stdlib.h>
#include <stdio.h>

class A {
  int a, b;
public:
  A(int, int);
  void display();
  void operator()();
          // Overload function call () op
};

          // Define initializer list for constructor

A::A( int i = 0, int j = 0 ) : a(i), b(j) {}
void A::display()
{
  printf( "a = %d, b = %d\n", a, b );
}

void A::operator()() // Define function call operator
{
  display();
}

main()
{
  A obj1;             // Take advantage of default args
  A obj2( 16, 64 );   // Use init list for this one

  obj1();
          // Use overloaded function call operator
  obj2(); // to display object values
}
```

The constructor declaration is written in the normal way. The constructor definition contains the initializer list. Note the following points about this form of initializer list:

■ A full colon appears immediately after the declaration part of the function definition. The list follows the colon.

■ The variable initializer list is composed of comma-separated entries. The list as a whole is not terminated by any punctuation; the function body begins immediately.

■ Each entry in the initializer list is composed of the member variable name it is to initialize, followed by the initial value it is to have.

■ The parenthesized value of an entry in the list is most often one of the arguments to the constructor. This need not be the case, however. It can be an expression, or even a constant (which, as you recall, is an expression).

■ The number of entries in the initializer list does not necessarily have to correspond either to the number of constructor arguments or to the number of class members to be initialized. You can mix and match methods in any way you want; some members can be initialized from the initializer list, and some by assignment in the constructor function body. It is up to you to get the object properly initialized.

This form of initializer list is often convenient and can help you write concise, compact code in the old tradition of C. It also is important later for passing initial value to base class constructors when you are designing derived classes (implementing class inheritance), but more on that later.

The second form of initializer list is one with which you already are familiar. It is the initializer list, enclosed in curly braces, written as though for an aggregate object in standard C. Note the following example:

```c
#include <stdlib.h>
#include <stdio.h>

strict A {              // strict means all members public
  int a, b;             // There is no constructor, either
  void display();
  void operator()();    // Overload function call () op
};

void A::display()
{
  printf( "a = %d, b = %d\n", a, b );
}

void A::operator()()    // Define function call operator
{
  display();
}
```

```
main()
{
  A obj1 = { 16, 64 }; // Initializer list
  obj1();       // Use overloaded function call operator
}
```

To use this kind of initializer list, the class must satisfy three requirements: there cannot be any private members, there cannot be any constructor, and there cannot be any base class (that is, the class cannot be a subclass that inherits a superclass). Such classes typically are declared through strict rather than class. Note the following points about aggregate initializers for classes:

■ This is a true aggregate initializer; treat it just as you do when writing standard C code. This form can initialize an array or a class, strict, or union. (In C++, the last three are referred to collectively as a *class*.)

■ If you don't provide enough initial values, the rest of the members are set to zero or null.

■ For complex aggregates, the initializer list can omit or retain interior curly braces. ANSI standard C borrowed this convention from C++. For multidimensional arrays of objects or class objects, however, you can use interior curly braces to force the way initial values are assigned (for example, when subgroups don't provide all values).

■ Arrays of class objects can be initialized by this method as long as other requirements are fulfilled, as in the following example:

```
class X { public: int a, b, c };  // Define a class
X objs[2] = { 1, 2, 3, 4, 5, 6 }; // Array of class objs
```

With these methods of initializing objects or objects of class, you can write code that is as flexible as you like. You can do anything—from nothing at all to taking complete control of initializing even the most complex objects.

Finally, declarations for an object of a class—which cause the constructor to be invoked—don't have to be at the top of a block, as standard C requires. Object declarations can be scattered throughout a block. Each causes the constructor function for the class to be invoked. There is no other way to call a constructor, in fact. Calling a constructor directly is illegal.

Destructors are a little different from constructors. There can be only one destructor function, and it may not have any parameters. Note that in C++, using the void specifier for the argument list is not strictly necessary. Writing an *empty* list in C++ means that no arguments are permitted, as shown in this line of code:

```
tool::~tool(); // Don't need ANSI void argument spec.
```

Destructors are like constructors, however, in that you can leave them out. In such a case, the compiler generates code that releases the memory used by the object when it goes out of scope. The only problem with this is that the constructor function may have specifically and dynamically allocated storage, which is outside the object, for its use. If so, allowing the destructor to default leaves that dynamic storage still allocated, with no way now to locate and release it.

Although you cannot call a constructor directly, you may call a destructor, if you use the fully qualified name of the destructor function. Note an example:

```
main()
{
  tool wrench( 1, "Turn nuts and bolts" );
  ...
  wrench::~tool(); // Legal destructor call
  tool::tool();    // Illegal constructor call
}
```

When is a destructor called automatically? Ordinarily, for dynamic (auto class) class objects, a destructor is automatically called whenever the object goes out of scope—when the current scope no longer exists. This happens, for instance, when a function that declares a local object returns.

Global objects have file scope, however. When are their destructors called? If you have declared any atexit() functions, the destructor call would necessarily follow their execution. But matters may get complicated if you explicitly invoke exit() or abort().

When you explicitly invoke exit() from a function (an ordinary function or a member function), the destructors for *static objects* are called. This means that objects with file scope, or objects that were created with the new operator, are taken care of. Dynamic object destructors are not called (but this hardly matters, because they ordinarily exist on the stack).

> Calling exit() from the destructor function could be especially dangerous; it might cause infinite recursion. This could happen if the object were global or just static, because exit() causes the destructor to be called, which calls exit(), which—well, you get the idea.

Destructors are not called at all if you explicitly call abort(), because abort() is not required to perform any particular cleanup. This may or may not be dangerous, depending on what an object was doing. If its constructor had opened an output file, for example, this might cause the last bufferful of data to be lost. Note that this also could happen to dynamic objects when exit() is called.

Copy Initializers

Listing 15.1 shows the use of a special kind of constructor function: the *copy initializer,* or *copy constructor.* The copy initializer is invoked automatically when an object is declared—created with reference to an existing object. Here is the copy-initializer function for the array class of Listing 15.1:

```
array::array( array &copy )     // Copy constructor
{
  int i;

  value = copy.value;     // Ref. op makes -> op unnecessary
  numelem = copy.numelem;
  name = new char[strlen(copy.name)+1];
  strcpy( name, copy.name );    // Init name string
  elem = new int[copy.numelem];
  for ( i=0; i<copy.numelem; ++i )
    elem[i] = copy.elem[i];
}
```

The copy initializer always takes one argument: a *reference* (careful—not a pointer!) to an object of the same class (see the next chapter for details). For class X, declare the copy initializer as X::X(X&); wherein & is the reference operator.

Two ways of declaring an object can cause the copy initializer to be invoked: declaration with an assignment initializer, and declaration with an argument that is an object. (Note that using a reference means you do *not* have to take the address; it's done for you.) Here are examples of these two ways of declaring an object:

```
array y = x; // Use the copy initializer
array y(x);  // Also invokes copy const
```

If you don't declare a copy initializer, the C++ compiler generates one for you. The automatically generated copy initializer is built assuming that you want a one-to-one copy of every member in the object. This is fine in many cases, but not all. A closer look at the copy initializer for the array class reveals why you would want to write your own.

The new operator (discussed later in this chapter) is used twice in the preceding copy-initializer function. In each case, a pointer is returned and stored in a member object. That is, each array object has its own dynamically allocated memory, which exists *outside* the bounds of the object, for storing array elements and the string array name. If another array object is created from the first one in either of the two ways just mentioned, thus using the default copy initializer, the member pointers are copied as is. This results in two array class objects pointing to the same dynamic memory—the storage fails to be unique for each object. In such a case, writing your own copy initializer ensures that separate dynamic storage is allocated for each unique object.

Using Class Objects

At this point, you can declare a class and write some pretty sophisticated code to initialize objects of that class. Now you have to know how to "send messages to the object" and to see an extended example of class implementation.

Calling Member Functions

Calling member functions is much the same as calling ordinary functions, except that you must indicate the object on behalf of which you are making the call. This is the C++ way of sending a "message" to the object. The syntax is

```
objectname.memberfunction( arg list );
```

whereby *objectname* is the identifier of an already declared object (in other words, an object whose constructor has been called). The period is the familiar structure operator, and the rest is just like a normal function call. For example, the following code fragment shows how to call the reduce() member function of object X, which has class C1:

```
class c1 {
  int i;
public:
  c1() { i=37; } // In-line constructor
  int reduce();
};
...
int c1::reduce() // Same as void arg list
{
  return --i;
}
...
main()
{
c1 X; // Declare an object (and invoke constructor)
...
printf( "Value minus 1 is %d\n", X.reduce() );
}
```

Notice that you can return basic (C-style) objects from calls to member functions, as well as objects or references to objects.

An exception to this syntax arises when you have defined a constructor member function with an empty argument list (meaning that the particular constructor may not have arguments). With such a constructor, do not code argument parentheses—even if they are empty—when declaring an object which invokes that constructor. For example, the following short program does not compile correctly with Borland C++:

```
#include <stdlib.h>
#include <stdio.h>

class c1 {
  int i;
public:
  c1() { i = 37; }  // Empty arg list means no args!
  int reduce() { return --i; }
};

main()
{
  c1 X;    // This is the correct way
  c1 Y(); // Makes compiler expect reference to object

  printf( "%d\n", Y.reduce() );
}
```

The compiler flags the last line of this program—which contains a call to Y.reduce()—as being in error. The error message informs you that a reference to an object is expected to be returned. If you simply rewrite the object declaration as c1 Y;, the program compiles and runs correctly.

You will learn how to simplify the syntax for the member-function call a little later, when you see how to overload the function call operator (). Right now, it's time to apply what you have learned so far.

Building a Virtual Screen Class

Because the extended example of a class implementation might as well be a useful one, this section presents a class, named screen, that is capable of virtual screen-management functions. A virtual screen is something like a window, but not exactly.

What is a virtual screen? As implemented here, a *virtual screen* resembles a panel that overlays part of the system display screen more than it resembles a true window. This doesn't make much difference in practice, but the subtle difference does influence the way virtual screens can be moved around the display. Briefly, a virtual screen is a movable panel.

What does a virtual screen do? Several requirements must be met if the class is to be truly useful. A virtual screen must be able to appear and disappear. When it disappears, it must restore the underlying display area to its original state. That is, it must be able to save itself and the underlying screen area. Allocating dynamic memory for these save areas is done in the constructor.

Although only text mode is supported, color must be supported in a virtual screen. The constructor function's arguments include color values for background and text.

Multiple boundaries for the panel area allow for attractive presentation formats on virtual screens. Three boundary types are supported: none (plain border), box (double lines) and a drop-shadow box. The drop-shadow box border is particularly attractive because it gives the virtual screen the appearance of "floating" above the underlying display. The color attributes of text falling in the shadow are changed to gray-on-black, greatly enhancing this effect.

A virtual screen must be able to appear anywhere on the real display. You can provide this support with the screen::move() function. This makes the writing of a driving program that enables the user to slide the virtual screens around the display by pressing the arrow keys seem like a trivial exercise. (Such a program, DEMO.CPP, is shown a little later.)

In a virtual screen, "normalized" cursor control is required. This means that a driving program should be able to make cursor-positioning requests that specify values relative only to the border of the virtual screen, not of the real display. A companion function, screen::query(), reports current cursor position relative to the border.

In addition to normalized cursor control, virtual screens need clipped and bounded message-display support. A message string that goes beyond the virtual screen boundary is clipped to fit. Because it would be nice if the message-display function screen::put() also allowed variable arguments, such as printf(), a trivial amount of code necessary for va_arg() processing is included. Tab and newline characters are supported (and accounted for in clipping), and all is done so the user sees RAM-poke write speeds. The routines work on all display types, from old monochrome to VGA. In addition to message-display support, a virtual-screen clear function, screen::clr(), is included.

Several member functions add sauce to the goose. These include functions for loading and scrolling entire text files, lists of items with selection capability, and both strip and pull-down menus. A special member function in virtual screens is `screen::pulldown()`, which turns a virtual screen into a pull-down menu, complete with highlighted selection bar. There are also support functions for physically scrolling a display area or clearing it, and for drawing boxes around virtual screens; all of these are implemented as friend functions of the class (which are covered in detail in Chapter 17).

Whew! The preceding paragraphs about virtual screens sum up a lot of function! The fact is, however, that this really is a fairly trivial exercise in C++— OOPS technology makes this kind of project easily feasible (although the display technology is confusing if you are not accustomed to it). There are 103 lines of code in the `screen` class header file, and 1031 lines of code in the C++ source file. But don't panic—the code is more tedious than complicated. It's just that there are many things to do in managing virtual screens.

The first order of business is to construct the header file for the screen class. The SCREEN.HPP header contains the necessary `#include` statements, manifest constants used by the class, `typedefs` and structures used to control screens, and the `screen` class declaration. The header file is shown in the program SCREEN.HPP in Listing 15.4.

Listing 15.4. SCREEN.HPP—Class for a virtual-screen manager (for Borland C++ 3.1).

```
1   #include <stdio.h>
2   #include <stdlib.h>
3   #include <stdarg.h>
4   #include <conio.h>
5   #include <dos.h>
6   #include <ctype.h>
7   #include <string.h>
8
9   #ifndef NULL          /*---------------------------*/
10  #define NULL 0        /*-------- SCREEN.HPP --------*/
11  #endif                /* Begin header file for     */
12                        /* screen.cpp module.        */
13  #ifndef PLAIN         /*---------------------------*/
14  #define PLAIN   0
15  #define BOX     1
16  #define SHADOW  2
17  #endif
18
19  #ifndef COLORS
20  #define COLORS
```

continues

Listing 15.4. Continued

```
21  #define BLACK 0
22  #define BLUE 1
23  #define GREEN 2
24  #define CYAN 3
25  #define RED 4
26  #define MAGENTA 5
27  #define BROWN 6
28  #define LIGHTGRAY 7
29  #define DARKGRAY 8
30  #define LIGHTBLUE 9
31  #define LIGHTGREEN 10
32  #define LIGHTCYAN 11
33  #define LIGHTRED 12
34  #define LIGHTMAGENTA 13
35  #define YELLOW 14
36  #define WHITE 15
37  #endif
38
39  typedef strict list_type {
40    strict list_type *prev;
41    strict list_type *next;
42    int select;
43    char line[255];
44  } listbox;
45
46  typedef strict l_type {
47    strict l_type *prev;
48    strict l_type *next;
49    char line[255];
50  } text;
51
52  typedef strict m_type {
53    int pullcnt;
54    char *(*pull)[];
55    char *item;
56    int xofs;
57  } stripm;
58
59  class screen {
60    int border[4];
61    int border_t;
```

```
62    int curpos[2];
63    int cur_attr;
64    unsigned disp_base;
65    strict text_info ti;
66    char *save;        // Pointer to copy of self
67    char *olds;        // Pointer to copy of
                         // underlying screen
68    int oldx, oldy;    // Cursor in underlying screen
69    text *ramtext;     // Anchor to loaded text file dbllist
70    listbox *ramlist;  // Anchor to loaded listbox dbllist
71  public:
72    screen( int, int, int, int, int, int, int );
73    ~screen();
74    void clr();
75    void up1();
76    void down1();
77    void loc( int, int );
78    void put( char *, ... );
79    void pushold();
80    void popold();
81    void push();
82    void pop();
83    void move( int, int );
84    int pulldown( int, int, int, char *[] );
85    int strip( int, stripm[] );
86    int *query();
87    int *size();
88    void load_textfile( char * );
89    void scroll_textfile();
90    void dump_textfile();
91    void load_listbox( char *[] );
92    void scroll_listbox();
93    void dump_listbox();
94    char *getlistitem( int );
95    friend void disp_scroll( screen&, int, int, int, int,
96                                        unsigned );
97    friend void disp_up1( int, int, int, int,
98                                     unsigned );
99    friend void disp_down1( int, int, int, int,
100                                      unsigned );
101   friend void disp_box( screen&, int, int, int,
102                                   int, int );
103 };
```

Notice in lines 60–70 of Listing 15.4 that a fair number of variables are declared as `private` objects owned exclusively by a `screen` class object. Internal objects such as these are important to the consistent control of class objects, and it is particularly important that they not be modified with the "knowledge" of the owning object. If they were modified by nonmember functions in unexpected ways, control of the object and its behavior could be completely lost. This is one of those times that the encapsulation of both data and functions by the class can greatly enhance the security and trouble-free operation of class objects. Otherwise, there is nothing remarkable about the declarations contained in the `screen` class header file.

The SCREEN.CPP source module is compiled separately from user application code. This can be accomplished by including in the project file the SCREEN.CPP source module, or the SCREEN.OBJ module resulting from a separate compile run. Source code in the SCREEN.CPP file is shown in Listing 15.5.

Even though there is a lot of code in the SCREEN.CPP source file, keep in mind that this is a sample class, not production code. Still, there are enough functions present so you could enhance the code to production-quality levels without too much more work. First, look over the listing and then read the discussion of the most important features of the code. (Many of the nuances of how this class works will be left to your own investigations, but the discussion will get you started.)

Listing 15.5. SCREEN.CPP—Member functions for the screen class (for Borland C++ 3.1).

```
1   #include "screen.hpp"
2
3   // -------------------------------------------------
4   // disp_scroll() = clrscr() for current "screen" with
5   //                      requested text attribute.
6   //     This is a friend function of class screen.
7   // -------------------------------------------------
8   void disp_scroll( screen& sc, int tx, int ty, int bx,
9                        int by, unsigned request_attr )
10  {
11    window( tx, ty, bx, by );
12    textattr( request_attr );
13    clrscr();
14    window( 1, 1, sc.ti.screenwidth, sc.ti.screenheight );
15  }
16
```

```
17  // ------------------------------------------------------
18  // disp_up1() = scroll up 1 for current "screen" with
19  //                  requested text attribute.
20  //    This is a friend function of class screen.
21  // ------------------------------------------------------
22  void disp_up1( int tx, int ty, int bx,
23                    int by, unsigned request_attr )
24  {
25    REGS reg;
26
27    reg.x.ax = 0x0601;          /* Scroll up 1 line */
28    reg.h.bh = request_attr;    /* Use attribute */
29    reg.h.ch = ty - 1;          /* Area to use */
30    reg.h.cl = tx - 1;
31    reg.h.dh = by - 1;
32    reg.h.dl = bx - 1;
33    int86( 0x10, &reg, &reg );
34  }
35
36  // ------------------------------------------------------
37  // disp_down1() = scroll down 1 for current "screen"
38  //                  with requested text attribute.
39  //    This is a friend function of class screen.
40  // ------------------------------------------------------
41  void disp_down1( int tx, int ty, int bx,
42                    int by, unsigned request_attr )
43  {
44    REGS reg;
45
46    reg.x.ax = 0x0701;          /* Scroll down 1 line */
47    reg.h.bh = request_attr;    /* Use attribute */
48    reg.h.ch = ty - 1;          /* Area to use */
49    reg.h.cl = tx - 1;
50    reg.h.dh = by - 1;
51    reg.h.dl = bx - 1;
52    int86( 0x10, &reg, &reg );
53  }
54
55  // ------------------------------------------------------
56  // disp_box() = Draw a double-line box around area.
57  // ------------------------------------------------------
58  void disp_box( screen& sc, int attr, int tx, int ty,
59                    int bx, int by )
```

continues

Listing 15.5. Continued

```
60  {
61    static int ofs,cnt;
62    static char *p;
63    static char a = attr;
64
65  // ---- Locate and draw corners
66    ofs = 160*(ty-1) + 2*(tx-1);
67    p = (char*)MK_FP( sc.disp_base,ofs );
68    *p++ = 201; *p = attr;      // Top left
69
70    ofs = 160*(ty-1) + 2*(bx-1);
71    p = (char*)MK_FP( sc.disp_base,ofs );
72    *p++ = 187; *p = attr;      // Top right
73
74    ofs = 160*(by-1) + 2*(tx-1);
75    p = (char*)MK_FP( sc.disp_base,ofs );
76    *p++ = 200; *p = attr;      // Bottom left
77
78    ofs = 160*(by-1) + 2*(bx-1);
79    p = (char*)MK_FP( sc.disp_base,ofs );
80    *p++ = 188; *p = attr;      // Bottom right
81
82  // ---- Locate and draw vertical bars
83    ofs = 160*(ty) + 2*(tx-1);
84    p = (char*)MK_FP( sc.disp_base,ofs );
85    for ( cnt=ty+1; cnt<by; ++cnt ) {
86      *p = 186; *(p+1) = attr; p += 160;
87    }
88    ofs = 160*(ty) + 2*(bx-1);
89    p = (char*)MK_FP( sc.disp_base,ofs );
90    for ( cnt=ty+1; cnt<by; ++cnt ) {
91      *p = 186; *(p+1) = attr; p += 160;
92    }
93  // ---- Locate and draw horizontal bars
94    ofs = 160*(ty-1) + 2*(tx);
95    p = (char*)MK_FP( sc.disp_base,ofs );
96    for ( cnt=tx+1; cnt<bx; ++cnt ) {
97      *p = 205; *(p+1) = attr; p += 2;
98    }
99    ofs = 160*(by-1) + 2*(tx);
```

```
100     p = (char*)MK_FP( sc.disp_base,ofs );
101     for ( cnt=tx+1; cnt<bx; ++cnt ) {
102       *p = 205; *(p+1) = attr; p += 2;
103     }
104   }
105
106   // --------------- SCREEN.CPP ---------------------
107   // Begin screen.cpp source for use in separate
108   // compilation.
109   // ---------------------------------------------------
110
111   // ---------------------------------------------------
112   //          Screen class object constructor
113   // Input parameters:
114   //              int back      Background attribute
115   //              int fore      Foreground attribute
116   //              int bor       Border; PLAIN, BOX,
117   //                               or SHADOW
118   //              int topx,topy 1-origin coordinates
119   //                            top-left corner
120   //              int botx,boty 1-origin coordinates
121   //                            bottom-left corner
122   // ---------------------------------------------------
123   screen::screen( int back, int fore, int bor,
124                   int topx, int topy, int botx, int boty )
125   {
126     int adjust;
127
128     ramtext = NULL;  // No text loaded into this screen yet
129     ramlist = NULL;  // No listbox data loaded, either
130     gettextinfo( &ti );
131     if ( ti.currmode == 7 ) disp_base = 0xb000;
132       else disp_base = 0xb800;
133     border_t = bor;
134     cur_attr = (back << 4) + fore;   // Build display attr
135     textattr( cur_attr );
136     if ( botx == 0 ) {
137       border_t = PLAIN;         // Border type for whole screen
138       border[0] = 1;
139       border[1] = 1;
140       border[2] = ti.screenwidth;
141       border[3] = ti.screenheight;
```

continues

Listing 15.5. Continued

```
142     } else {
143      if ( border_t == SHADOW ) {  // Check size and position
144       if ( botx >= ti.screenwidth ) {
145         adjust = (unsigned)ti.screenwidth - botx - 1;
146         botx += adjust;
147         topx += adjust;
148       }
149       if ( boty >= ti.screenheight ) {
150         adjust = (unsigned)ti.screenheight - boty - 1;
151         boty += adjust;
152         topy += adjust;
153       }
154      }
155      if ( botx >= ti.screenwidth ) {
156        adjust = (unsigned)ti.screenwidth - botx;
157        botx += adjust;
158        topx += adjust;
159      }
160      if ( boty >= ti.screenheight ) {
161        adjust = (unsigned)ti.screenheight - boty;
162        boty += adjust;
163        topy += adjust;
164      }
165      border[0] = topx;
166      border[1] = topy;
167      border[2] = botx;
168      border[3] = boty;
169     }
170        // Allocate this screen and old screen save buffers
171     if ( border_t == SHADOW ) {
172       save = new char[ (border[2]-border[0]+2)
173         * (border[3]-border[1]+2) * 2 ];
174       olds = new char[ (border[2]-border[0]+2)
175         * (border[3]-border[1]+2) * 2 ];
176     }
177     else {
178       save = new char[ (border[2]-border[0]+1)
179         * (border[3]-border[1]+1) * 2 ];
180       olds = new char[ (border[2]-border[0]+1)
181         * (border[3]-border[1]+1) * 2 ];
```

```
182      }
183      pushold();                 // And save old screen area
184
185      if ( border_t == SHADOW ) {
186        int ofs,cnt;
187        char *p;
188        char a = (BLACK << 4) + DARKGRAY;
189
190        //  Locate and draw vertical stripe for shadow box
191
192        ofs = 160*(border[1]) + 2*(border[2]);
193        p = (char*)MK_FP( disp_base,ofs+1 );
194        for ( cnt=border[1]; cnt<=border[3]; ++cnt ) {
195          *p = a; p += 160;
196        }
197
198        //  Locate and draw horizontal stripe for shadow box
199
200        ofs = 160*(border[3]) + 2*(border[0]);
201        p = (char*)MK_FP( disp_base,ofs+1 );
202        for ( cnt=border[0]; cnt<=border[2]; ++cnt ) {
203          *p = a; p += 2;
204        }
205      }
206
207      disp_scroll( *this,border[0],border[1],
208        border[2],border[3],cur_attr );
209
210      if ( border_t == BOX )
211        disp_box( *this, cur_attr,border[0],border[1],
212          border[2],border[3] );
213
214      push(); // Save a copy of self
215    }
216
217    screen::~screen()
218    {
219      delete save;
220      delete olds;
221      dump_textfile();
222    }
223
```

continues

Listing 15.5. Continued

```
224  // -------------------------------------------------
225  // screen::clr() - Clear virtual screen area
226  //                 to background color.
227  // -------------------------------------------------
228
229  void screen::clr()
230  {
231    if ( border_t == BOX )
232      disp_scroll( *this,border[0]+1,border[1]+1,
233        border[2]-1,border[3]-1,cur_attr );
234    else
235      disp_scroll( *this,border[0],border[1],
236        border[2],border[3],cur_attr );
237  }
238
239  // -------------------------------------------------
240  // screen::up1() - Scroll text up 1 line using
241  //                 background color.
242  // -------------------------------------------------
243
244  void screen::up1()
245  {
246    if ( border_t == BOX )
247      disp_up1( border[0]+1,border[1]+1,
248        border[2]-1,border[3]-1,cur_attr );
249    else
250      disp_up1( border[0],border[1],
251        border[2],border[3],cur_attr );
252  }
253
254  // -------------------------------------------------
255  // screen::down1() - Scroll text down 1 line using
256  //                   background color.
257  // -------------------------------------------------
258
259  void screen::down1()
260  {
261    if ( border_t == BOX )
262      disp_down1( border[0]+1,border[1]+1,
263        border[2]-1,border[3]-1,cur_attr );
```

```
264   else
265     disp_down1( border[0],border[1],
266        border[2],border[3],cur_attr );
267   }
268
269   // -----------------------------------------------
270   // screen::loc() - Position the virtual screen cursor
271   //                 to 1-origin RELATIVE coordinates.
272   // -----------------------------------------------
273
274   void screen::loc( int x,int y )
275   {
276     if ( border_t == BOX ) {
277       gotoxy( border[0] + x, border[1] + y );
278       curpos[0] = wherex() - border[0];
279       curpos[1] = wherey() - border[1];
280     }
281     else {
282       gotoxy( border[0]+x-1, border[1]+y-1 );
283       curpos[0] = wherex() - border[0] + 1;
284       curpos[1] = wherey() - border[1] + 1;
285     }
286   }
287
288   // -----------------------------------------------
289   // screen::query() -- Return int[] with current x-y
290   //                    coordinates.
291   // -----------------------------------------------
292
293   int*  screen::query()
294   {
295     return( curpos );
296   }
297
298   // -----------------------------------------------
299   // screen::size() -- Return int[] with screen's
300   //                   border coordinates.
301   // -----------------------------------------------
302
303   int*  screen::size()
304   {
305     return( border );
```

continues

Listing 15.5. Continued

```
306  }
307
308  // --------------------------------------------------
309  // screen::put() - Formatted text I/O to virtual
310  //                 screen with tab expansion and
311  //                 clipping.
312  // --------------------------------------------------
313
314  void screen::put( char *format, ... )
315  {
316    int i;
317    int *p;
318    va_list arg_ptr;
319    static char ibuf[256], obuf[256];
320    char *a, *b;
321
322    textattr( cur_attr );
323    p = query();
324    loc( *p,*(p+1) );
325    va_start( arg_ptr,format );          // Get var args
326    vsprintf( ibuf,format,arg_ptr );     // and format output
327    a = ibuf; b = obuf;
328    i = 0;
329    while ( *a ) {                       // Detab the line
330      switch( *a ) {
331        case '\t': do *b++ = ' '; while ( ++i % 8 != 1 );
332                   a++; break;
333        default:   *b++ = *a++; ++i; break;
334      }
335    }
336    *b = '\0';                          // Terminate the output line
337    i = strlen( obuf );
338    i = ( i > border[2] - wherex() +1 ) ?
339        border[2] - wherex() : i;
340    cprintf( "%-.*s",i,obuf );           // Clip it, too
341    va_end( arg_ptr );
342    if ( border_t == BOX ) {    // Update new current position
343      curpos[0] = wherex() - border[0];
344      curpos[1] = wherey() - border[1];
345    }
```

```
346    else {
347      curpos[0] = wherex() - border[0] + 1;
348      curpos[1] = wherey() - border[1] + 1;
349    }
350    if ( curpos[0] < 1 ) curpos[0] = 1;
351  }
352
353  // -----------------------------------------------------
354  // screen::pushold() - Save a copy of area underlying
355  //                     this virtual screen.
356  // -----------------------------------------------------
357
358  void screen::pushold()
359  {
360    static char *p;
361    static char *q;
362    static int i,size;
363    static unsigned ofs;
364
365    q = olds;
366    ofs = 160*(border[1]-1) + 2*(border[0]-1);
367    p = (char*)MK_FP( disp_base,ofs );
368    if ( border_t == SHADOW )
369      size = (border[2]-border[0]+2)*2;
370    else
371      size = (border[2]-border[0]+1)*2;
372    for( i=border[1]; i<=border[3]; i++ ) {
373      memcpy( q,p,size );
374      p += 160; q += size;
375    }
376    if ( border_t == SHADOW ) memcpy( q,p,size );
377    oldx = wherex();
378    oldy = wherey();
379  }
380
381  // -----------------------------------------------------
382  // screen::popold() - Restore the area underlying this
383  //                    virtual screen.
384  // -----------------------------------------------------
385
386  void screen::popold()
387  {
```

continues

Listing 15.5. Continued

```
388    static char *p;
389    static char *q;
390    static int i,size;
391    static unsigned ofs;
392
393    q = olds;
394    ofs = 160*(border[1]-1) + 2*(border[0]-1);
395    p = (char*)MK_FP( disp_base,ofs );
396    if ( border_t == SHADOW )
397      size = (border[2]-border[0]+2)*2;
398    else
399      size = (border[2]-border[0]+1)*2;
400    for( i=border[1]; i<=border[3]; i++ ) {
401      memcpy( p,q,size );
402      p += 160; q += size;
403    }
404    if ( border_t == SHADOW ) memcpy( p,q,size );
405    textattr( cur_attr );
406    gotoxy( oldx, oldy);
407  }
408
409  // ----------------------------------------------------
410  // screen::push() - Save a copy of this virtual screen.
411  // ----------------------------------------------------
412
413  void screen::push()
414  {
415    static char *p;
416    static char *q;
417    static int i,size;
418    static unsigned ofs;
419
420    q = save;
421    ofs = 160*(border[1]-1) + 2*(border[0]-1);
422    p = (char*)MK_FP( disp_base,ofs );
423    size = (border[2]-border[0]+1)*2;
424    for( i=border[1]; i<=border[3]; i++ ) {
425      memcpy( q,p,size );
426      p += 160; q += size;
427    }
```

```
428   }
429
430   // -----------------------------------------------------
431   // screen::pop() - Restore a copy of this virtual
432   //                 screen.
433   // -----------------------------------------------------
434
435   void screen::pop()
436   {
437     static char *p;
438     static char *q;
439     static int i,size;
440     static unsigned ofs;
441
442     q = save;
443     ofs = 160*(border[1]-1) + 2*(border[0]-1);
444     p = (char*)MK_FP( disp_base,ofs );
445     size = (border[2]-border[0]+1)*2;
446     for( i=border[1]; i<=border[3]; i++ ) {
447       memcpy( p,q,size );
448       p += 160; q += size;
449     }
450     if ( border_t == SHADOW ) {  // Repaint the shadow
451       char a = (BLACK << 4) + DARKGRAY;
452       ofs = 160*(border[1]) + 2*(border[2]);
453       p = (char*)MK_FP( disp_base,ofs+1 );
454       for ( i=border[1]; i<=border[3]; ++i ) {
455         *p = a; p += 160;
456       }
457       ofs = 160*(border[3]) + 2*(border[0]);
458       p = (char*)MK_FP( disp_base,ofs+1 );
459       for ( i=border[0]; i<=border[2]; ++i ) {
460         *p = a; p += 2;
461       }
462     }
463     textattr( cur_attr );
464     loc( curpos[0], curpos[1] );
465   }
466
467   // -----------------------------------------------------
468   // screen::move() - Shift virtual screen position by
469   //                  specified x-y amounts (+ or -).
470   // -----------------------------------------------------
```

continues

Listing 15.5. Continued

```
471
472   void screen::move( int x,int y )
473   {
474     push();
475     popold();
476     if ( border_t == SHADOW ) {
477      if (1 <= border[0]+x && border[2]+x+1 <= ti.screenwidth) {
478         border[0] += x; border[2] += x;
479       }
480      if (1 <= border[1]+y && border[3]+y+1 <= ti.screenheight) {
481         border[1] += y; border[3] += y;
482       }
483     }
484     else {
485      if (1 <= border[0]+x && border[2]+x <= ti.screenwidth) {
486         border[0] += x; border[2] += x;
487       }
488      if (1 <= border[1]+y && border[3]+y <= ti.screenheight) {
489         border[1] += y; border[3] += y;
490       }
491     }
492     pushold();
493     pop();
494   }
495
496   // ---------------------------------------------------
497   // screen::pulldown() - Display a pull-down menu with
498   //                      highlighted cursor bar. Get
499   //                      1-origin item selected.
500   // ---------------------------------------------------
501
502   int screen::pulldown( int xpos, int ypos,
503                         int elements, char *list[] )
504   {
505     int selected,mline,numline,ofs,cnt;
506     int longest = 0;
507     int *sc_size;
508     char a;
509     char ch;
```

```
510    char *p,**q;
511
512            // Determine the length of the longest menu label
513    for ( cnt = 0; cnt < elements; ++cnt ) {
514      mline = strlen( list[cnt] );
515      longest = mline > longest ? mline : longest;
516    }
517                            // Create the menu's screen and
518                  // determine whether it has sufficient size
519    screen mscreen( BLUE, WHITE, SHADOW,
520                    border[0] + xpos - 1,
521                    border[1] + ypos - 1,
522                    border[0] + xpos + longest,
523                    border[1] + ypos + elements - 2 );
524    sc_size = mscreen.size();
525    if ( sc_size[2] - sc_size[0] < longest + 1
526       ¦¦ sc_size[3] - sc_size[1] < elements - 1 ) {
527      mscreen.popold();
528      return( 0 );
529    }
530    selected = numline = 0;
531    mline = 1;
532    mscreen.clr();
533    q = list;
534    for ( ;; ) {                    // Paint the pop-up menu
535      mscreen.loc( 2, mline++ );
536      numline++;
537      mscreen.put( "%s", *q++ );
538      if ( numline >= elements ) break;
539    }
540    if ( numline == 0 ) {
541      mscreen.popold();
542      return( 0 );
543    }
544    selected = 1;
545    mscreen.loc( 2,selected );
546    ofs = 160*(sc_size[1] + selected - 2) + 2*sc_size[0];
547    p = (char*)MK_FP( disp_base,ofs+1 );
548    for ( cnt=sc_size[0]+1; cnt<sc_size[2]; ++cnt ) {
549      if ( cnt == sc_size[0] + 1 )
550        a = ( LIGHTGRAY << 4 ) + RED;
551      else
```

continues

Listing 15.5. Continued

```
552       a = ( LIGHTGRAY << 4 )  + BLACK;
553     *p = a; p += 2;
554   }
555   for ( ;; ) {              // Roll selection bar
556     ch = '\0'; while( !ch ) ch = getch();
557                             // Turn selection bar back off
558     ofs = 160*(sc_size[1] + selected - 2) + 2*sc_size[0];
559     p = (char*)MK_FP( disp_base,ofs+1 );
560     for ( cnt=sc_size[0]+1; cnt<sc_size[2]; ++cnt ) {
561       *p = ( BLUE << 4 ) + WHITE; p += 2;
562     }
563     switch( ch ) {
564
565       case 27: selected = 0; // Pos-dependent statement
566       case 13: mscreen.popold();
567                return( selected );
568       case 75: mscreen.popold();
569                return( -75 ); // Return scroll left request
570       case 77: mscreen.popold();
571                return( -77 ); // Return scroll right request
572       case 72: if ( --selected < 1 ) selected = elements;
573                break;
574       case 80: if ( ++selected > numline )
575                   selected = 1;
576                break;
577       default: selected = 0;
578                q = list;
579                for ( ;; ) {
580                  if ( ++selected > elements ) break;
581                  q++;
582                  if ( toupper( **q ) == toupper( ch ) ) {
583                    mscreen.popold();
584                    return( selected );
585                  }
586                };
587                selected = 1;           // Nothing matched
588       }
589                // Turn selection bar on in new position
590     ofs = 160*(sc_size[1] + selected - 2) + 2*sc_size[0];
591     p = (char*)MK_FP( disp_base,ofs+1 );
```

```
592        for ( cnt=sc_size[0]+1; cnt<sc_size[2]; ++cnt ) {
593          if ( cnt == sc_size[0] + 1 )
594            a = ( LIGHTGRAY << 4 ) + RED;
595          else
596            a = ( LIGHTGRAY << 4 )  + BLACK;
597          *p = a; p += 2;
598        }
599     }
600   }
601
602   // ---------------------------------------------------
603   // screen::strip() - Display a strip menu with
604   //                    highlighted cursor. Get
605   //                    1-origin item selected.
606   // ---------------------------------------------------
607
608   int screen::strip( int elements, stripm sentry[] )
609   {
610     int selected,ofs,cnt,ipos,i,MoveHoriz;
611     char a;
612     char ch;
613     char *p,**q;
614     int *sc_size;
615                              // Create the menu's screen
616     screen sscreen( BLUE, WHITE, PLAIN,
617                     border[0],
618                     border[1],
619                     border[2],
620                     border[1] );
621     sscreen.clr();
622     sc_size = sscreen.size();
623     if ( sentry[0].xofs == 0 )
624       ipos = 2;
625     else
626       ipos = sentry[0].xofs;
627                                  // Paint the strip menu
628     for ( cnt = 0; cnt < elements; ++cnt ) {
629       if ( sentry[cnt].xofs )
630         ipos = sentry[cnt].xofs;
631       sscreen.loc( ipos, 1 );
632       sscreen.put( "%s", sentry[cnt].item );
633       if ( sentry[cnt].xofs == 0 ) {
```

continues

Listing 15.5. Continued

```
634        sentry[cnt].xofs = ipos;        // Record position used
635        ipos += strlen( sentry[cnt].item ) + 2;
636      }
637    else
638        sentry[cnt].xofs = ipos;
639    if ( ipos >= sc_size[2] ) break;
640    }
641    if ( cnt < elements )
642      elements = cnt + 1;               // Note elements used
643    else
644      elements = cnt;
645
646    selected = 1;
647
648    sscreen.loc( sentry[selected-1].xofs, 1 );
649    ofs = 2 * ( sc_size[0] + sentry[selected-1].xofs - 2 )
650          + 160 * (sc_size[1] - 1 );
651    p = (char*)MK_FP( disp_base,ofs+1 );
652    cnt = ipos = strlen( sentry[selected-1].item );
653    for ( ; cnt > 0; --cnt ) {
654      if ( cnt == ipos )
655        a = ( LIGHTGRAY << 4 ) + RED;
656      else
657        a = ( LIGHTGRAY << 4 )  + BLACK;
658      *p = a; p += 2;
659    }
660
661    for ( ;; ) {                // Roll selection bar
662      ch = '\0'; while( !ch ) ch = getch();
663                                // Turn selection bar back off
664      ofs = 2 * ( sc_size[0] + sentry[selected-1].xofs - 2 )
665            + 160 * (sc_size[1] - 1 );
666      p = (char*)MK_FP( disp_base,ofs+1 );
667      cnt = strlen( sentry[selected-1].item );
668      for ( ; cnt > 0; --cnt ) {
669        *p = ( BLUE << 4 ) + WHITE; p += 2;
670      }
671      switch( ch ) {
672
673        case 27: selected = 0; // Pos-dependent statement
```

```
674        case 13: if ( !selected)
675                    return( selected );
676                MoveHoriz = 1;
677                while (MoveHoriz ) {
678                  MoveHoriz = 0;
679                  if ( sentry[selected-1].pullcnt ) {
680                    cnt = 0; i = 1;
681                    while ( i < selected )
682                      cnt += sentry[ i++ - 1].pullcnt;
683          i = sscreen.pulldown( sentry[selected-1].xofs, 2,
684                               sentry[selected-1].pullcnt,
685                               *(sentry[selected-1].pull) );
686                    if ( i>0 ) return cnt + i;
687                    if ( i == -75 ) {  // Scroll left request
688                      if ( --selected < 1 ) selected = elements;
689                      MoveHoriz = 1;
690                      continue;
691                    }
692                    if ( i == -77 ) { // Scroll right request
693                      if (++selected > elements) selected = 1;
694                      MoveHoriz = 1;
695                      continue;
696                    }
697                  }
698                }
699                break;
700        case 75: if ( --selected < 1 ) selected = elements;
701                break;
702        case 77: if ( ++selected > elements ) selected = 1;
703                break;
704        default: selected = 0;
705                for ( ;; ) {
706                   if ( ++selected > elements ) break;
707                   if ( toupper( *(sentry[selected-1].item) )
708                     == toupper( ch ) )
709                     return( selected );
710                };
711                selected = 1;                  // Nothing matched
712        }
713                // Turn selection bar on in new position
714        ofs = 2 * ( sc_size[0] + sentry[selected-1].xofs - 2 )
715            + 160 * (sc_size[1] - 1 );
```

continues

Listing 15.5. Continued

```
716      p = (char*)MK_FP( disp_base,ofs+1 );
717      cnt = ipos = strlen( sentry[selected-1].item );
718      for ( ; cnt > 0; --cnt ) {
719        if ( cnt == ipos )
720          a = ( LIGHTGRAY << 4 ) + RED;
721        else
722          a = ( LIGHTGRAY << 4 )  + BLACK;
723        *p = a; p += 2;
724      }
725    }
726  }
727
728  // ---------------------------------------------------
729  // screen:load_textfile() - Load a text file that is
730  //                          to be associated with this
731  //                          screen into a dbllist.
732  // ---------------------------------------------------
733
734  void screen::load_textfile( char *textname )
735  {
736    FILE *tfile;
737    char *ptr;
738    text *hold;
739    char tline[255];
740
741    if ( ramtext ) dump_textfile();
742    if ( NULL == (tfile = fopen( textname,"r") ) ) exit(0);
743    while ( NULL != fgets( tline,255,tfile ) ) {
744      ptr = tline;
745      while ( *ptr )
746        if( *ptr == '\n' ) *ptr++ = '\0'; else ptr++;
747      if ( !ramtext ) {
748        ramtext = (text *)malloc( 2 * sizeof(text *)
749                  + strlen( tline ) + 1 );
750        ramtext->next = ramtext->prev = NULL;
751      }
752      else {
753        hold = (text *)malloc( 2 * sizeof(text *)
754                  + strlen( tline ) + 1 );
755        ramtext->next = hold;
```

```
756       hold->prev = ramtext; hold->next = NULL;
757       ramtext = hold;
758     }
759     strcpy( ramtext->line,tline );
760   }
761   fclose( tfile );
762   while ( ramtext->prev ) ramtext = ramtext->prev;
763 }
764
765 // --------------------------------------------------
766 // screen::scroll_textfile() - Scroll the associated
767 //                             text file if it is
768 //                             loaded.
769 // --------------------------------------------------
770
771 void screen::scroll_textfile()
772 {
773   char ch = ' ';
774   char tline[255];
775   int i;
776
777   if ( !ramtext ) return;
778   while ( ramtext->prev ) ramtext = ramtext->prev;
779   while ( ch != 13 ) {
780     if ( ch != 72 && ch != 80 ) {
781       clr();
782       for ( i = 1; i <= border[3] - border[1] + 1; i++ ) {
783         if ( !ramtext ) break;
784         strcpy( tline,ramtext->line );
785         loc( 2,i );
786         put( "%s",tline );
787         if ( !ramtext->next ) break;
788           else ramtext = ramtext->next;
789       }
790     }
791     ch = getch(); if ( !ch ) ch = getch();
792     switch ( ch ) {
793       case 72:  for ( ; i>1; i-- )
794                     if ( !ramtext->prev ) break;
795                       else ramtext = ramtext->prev;
796                   if ( !ramtext->prev ) break;
797                   ramtext = ramtext->prev;
```

continues

Listing 15.5. Continued

```
798                     down1();
799                     i = 1;
800                     loc( 2, i );
801                     strcpy( tline,ramtext->line );
802                     put( "%s",tline );
803                     break;
804         case 80:    for ( ; i>1; i-- )
805                         if ( !ramtext->prev ) break;
806                           else ramtext = ramtext->prev;
807                     if ( !ramtext->next ) break;
808                     ramtext = ramtext->next;
809                     up1();
810                     for ( i = 1; i <= border[3] - border[1]; i++ )
811                     { if ( !ramtext->next ) break;
812                         else ramtext = ramtext->next;
813                     }
814                     if ( i < border[3] - border[1] + 1 ) break;
815                     loc( 2, i );
816                     strcpy( tline,ramtext->line );
817                     put( "%s",tline );
818                     if ( ramtext->next ) {
819                         ramtext = ramtext->next;
820                         i++;
821                     }
822                     break;
823         case 73:    for ( ; i>1; i-- ) {
824                         if ( !ramtext->prev ) break;
825                           else ramtext = ramtext->prev;
826                     }
827                     for (i = border[3]-border[1]+1; i>0; i--) {
828                         if ( !ramtext->prev ) break;
829                           else ramtext = ramtext->prev;
830                     }
831                     break;
832         case 81:
833                     for ( ; i>1; i-- )
834                         if ( !ramtext->prev ) break;
835                           else ramtext = ramtext->prev;
836                     for (i = 1; i <= border[3]-border[1] + 1; i++)
837                     { if ( !ramtext->next ) break;
```

```
838                      else ramtext = ramtext->next;
839                 }
840             break;
841     }
842   }
843 }
844
845 // --------------------------------------------------
846 // screen::dump_textfile() - Delete associated text.
847 // --------------------------------------------------
848
849 void screen::dump_textfile()
850 {
851   text *hold;
852
853   if ( !ramtext ) return;
854   while ( ramtext->next ) ramtext = ramtext->next;
855   while ( ramtext ) {
856     hold = ramtext->prev;
857     delete ramtext;
858     ramtext = hold;
859   }
860 }
861
862 // --------------------------------------------------
863 // screen:load_listbox() - Load a listbox that is
864 //                         to be associated with this
865 //                         screen into a dbllist.
866 // --------------------------------------------------
867
868 void screen::load_listbox( char *listname[] )
869 {
870   char *ptr;
871   listbox *hold;
872   int i;
873
874   if ( ramlist ) dump_listbox();
875   i = 0;
876   while ( listname[i] ) {
877     if ( !ramlist ) {
878       ramlist = (listbox *)malloc( 2 * sizeof(listbox *)
879                 + sizeof(int) + strlen( listname[i] ) + 1 );
```

continues

Listing 15.5.   Continued

```
880          ramlist->next = ramlist->prev = NULL;
881       }
882     else {
883       hold = (listbox *)malloc( 2 * sizeof(listbox *)
884               +sizeof(int) + strlen( listname[i] ) + 1 );
885       ramlist->next = hold;
886       hold->prev = ramlist; hold->next = NULL;
887       ramlist = hold;
888       }
889     strcpy( ramlist->line, listname[i] );
890     ramlist->select = 0;
891     ++i;
892   }
893   while ( ramlist->prev ) ramlist = ramlist->prev;
894 }
895
896 // -------------------------------------------------
897 // screen::scroll_listbox() - Scroll the associated
898 //                            listbox if it is
899 //                            loaded.
900 // -------------------------------------------------
901
902 void screen::scroll_listbox()
903 {
904   char ch = 81;
905   int i, max;
906
907   if ( !ramlist ) return;
908   while ( ramlist->prev ) ramlist = ramlist->prev;
909   while ( ch != 13 ) {
910     if ( ch == 73 || ch == 81 ) {
911       clr();
912       for ( i = 1; i <= border[3] - border[1] + 1; i++ ) {
913         if ( !ramlist ) break;
914         loc( 2,i );
915         if ( ramlist->select ) put( "*%s", ramlist->line );
916         else put( " %s",ramlist->line );
917         if ( !ramlist->next ) break;
918           else ramlist = ramlist->next;
919         }
```

```
920        if ( !ramlist->next ) max = i;
921        else max = i - 1;
922        if ( max <= 0 ) return;
923        for ( ; i>1; i-- )
924          if ( !ramlist->prev ) break;
925            else ramlist = ramlist->prev;
926        loc( 2, i );
927      }
928   ch = getch(); if ( !ch ) ch = getch();
929   switch ( ch ) {
930     case '+':
931             while( ramlist->prev )ramlist = ramlist->prev;
932             ramlist->select = 1;
933             while ( ramlist->next ) {
934               ramlist = ramlist->next;
935               ramlist->select = 1;
936             }
937             while ( ramlist->prev ) ramlist = ramlist->prev;
938             ch = 81;
939             break;
940     case '-':
941             while ( ramlist->prev ) ramlist = ramlist->prev;
942             ramlist->select = 0;
943             while ( ramlist->next ) {
944               ramlist = ramlist->next;
945               ramlist->select = 0;
946             }
947             while( ramlist->prev )ramlist = ramlist->prev;
948             ch = 81;
949             break;
950     case 82:  ramlist->select = 1;
951             loc( 2, i ); put( "%s", "*" ); loc( 2, i );
952             break;
953     case 83:  ramlist->select = 0;
954             loc( 2, i ); put( "%s", " " ); loc( 2, i );
955             break;
956     case 72:  if ( i > 1 ) {
957               ramlist = ramlist->prev;
958               --i;
959               loc( 2, i );
960             }
961             break;
```

continues

Listing 15.5. Continued

```
962        case 80:   if ( i < max ) {
963                       ramlist = ramlist->next;
964                       ++i;
965                       loc( 2, i );
966                   }
967                   break;
968        case 73:   for ( ; i>1; i-- ) {
969                       if ( !ramlist->prev ) break;
970                       else ramlist = ramlist->prev;
971                   }
972                   for (i = border[3] - border[1] + 1; i>0; i--)
973                   { if ( !ramlist->prev ) break;
974                       else ramlist = ramlist->prev;
975                   }
976                   break;
977        case 81:
978                   for ( ; i<max; i++ ) {
979                       if ( !ramlist->next ) break;
980                       else ramlist = ramlist->next;
981                   }
982                   break;
983       }
984     }
985 }
986
987 // -------------------------------------------------
988 // screen::dump_listbox() - Delete associated text.
989 // -------------------------------------------------
990
991 void screen::dump_listbox()
992 {
993    listbox *hold;
994
995    if ( !ramlist ) return;
996    while ( ramlist->next ) ramlist = ramlist->next;
997    while ( ramlist ) {
998      hold = ramlist->prev;
999      delete ramlist;
1000      ramlist = hold;
1001    }
```

```
1002  }
1003
1004
1005  // --------------------------------------------------
1006  // screen::getlistitem() - Get next listbox item that
1007  //                         was selected.
1008  // --------------------------------------------------
1009
1010  char *screen::getlistitem( int start )
1011  {
1012    static listbox *nextlist;  // Static for repetitive calls
1013    char *ptr;
1014
1015    if (!ramlist) return NULL; // Forget it if no list exists
1016    if ( start ) {             // First call, prime list ptr
1017      while ( ramlist->prev ) ramlist = ramlist->prev;
1018      nextlist = ramlist;
1019    }
1020    if (!nextlist) return NULL; // Guard against improper call
1021    while ( nextlist ) {        // Locate next flagged item
1022      if ( nextlist->select ) {
1023        ptr = nextlist->line;
1024        nextlist = nextlist->next;
1025        return ptr;             // Return a pointer to it
1026      }
1027      else nextlist = nextlist->next;
1028    }
1029    if ( !nextlist ) return NULL; // Else return nothing
1030    return NULL;                  // To prevent compiler warnings
1031  }
```

Because the screen class header and source code were placed in physically separate files, line 1 of Listing 15.5 accordingly has an #include statement to pull in the declarations and constants. Next, in lines 3–104, the friend functions mentioned earlier are defined.

At this time, it is necessary to say only that these functions are defined as friends so they can perform their services for any object of this class, rather than a single instance object. The scrolling and box-drawing operations these functions perform are straightforward: they either use Borland C/C++ built-in functions or invoke BIOS services to perform the operations.

NOTE The friend service functions are not meant to be used by nonmember functions, but are for internal use only.

After a number of comments, the class constructor function, `screen::screen()`, is found in lines 123–215. The constructor mainly initializes control variables and paints the virtual screen surface. This process is complicated only by the fact that there can be three different panel styles, so the details of deciding what border style to use and constructing it are a little lengthy.

Two things that are done in the constructor deserved special attention because they must be done exactly in the right places. First, in line 183, notice that class member function `pushold()` is called before the program writes on the panel surface. This is done so whatever was on the display before creating this panel can be restored exactly as it was when this panel is destroyed.

Second, line 214 has a call to the member function `push()` performed *after* the panel is painted. This snapshot, stored in its own save buffer, is used when another panel has possibly been written on top of this one or when there is a need to refresh the panel's display contents.

The destructor function for the `screen` class is shown in lines 217–222. This is a very simple function; the only requirement is to free storage areas dynamically obtained during object instantiating.

Member functions for clearing the virtual screen and scrolling it up or down are found in lines 224–267. These are "hook" functions that are not device-dependent. They instead call the device-dependent friend function mentioned earlier to get their work done. In this way, you can port the class definition to another compiler or hardware platform by recoding only the device-dependent friend function. Code that uses the class member functions would not have to be rewritten.

Lines 269–306 contain other member functions for controlling the physical display of data on the virtual screen. These functions include facilities for positioning the cursor relative only to the virtual screen (regardless of its position on the physical display), determining the present location of the cursor, and determining the boundaries of the virtual screen.

The member function `screen::put()` enables you to place data on the virtual screen for display. This function is found in lines 308–351. Note that it uses a variable argument list so you can specify formatting conversions just as with the familiar `printf()` function. This member function also supports tabs expansion and line clipping (to prevent writing outside the boundaries of the virtual screen). Clipping is accomplished by using a dynamically determined field precision in a `cprintf()` call in line 340.

Saving the contents of the area underlying the virtual screen is handled by the `pushold()` and `popold()` member functions, seen in lines 353–407. The Borland C++ 3.1 built-in functions `gettext()` and `puttext()` could have been used for this purpose, but it was done the hard way here, using the memcpy() function, just to show what goes on in such a process.

Preserving the contents of a virtual screen's own display area is done by the member functions push() and pop(), found in lines 409–465. Notice that the pop() function must resort to some extra effort to restore the border of a drop-shadow virtual screen (lines 450–461).

Using combinations of the previous four functions to save and redisplay underlying and virtual screen areas makes it easy to provide the functionality for moving virtual screens around on the display. The screen::move() function does this, shown in lines 467–494. Once again, this would be a very short function if it were not for the presence of the drop-shadow borders: they must be explicitly accounted for in the code (see lines 476–483).

The screen class also supports pull-down and strip menus that work together (although you can use pull-down menus without using a strip menu). The code for the pulldown() and strip() functions is shown in lines 496–726. An extensive discussion of how these functions work will be deferred until later in this chapter, when the AutoRun program is presented. The reason is that it is easier to see what these functions do by looking at an example that uses them.

From this point to the end of the program listing (line 1031), functions are presented that handle the loading, scrolling, and freeing of both text files and in-memory lists. The AutoRun program, presented later, contains an example of using the text-file scrolling capabilities. For now, turn your attention to the list-handling functions.

The list-handling functions are especially interesting because they permit not only the loading and scrolling of a list of items but also the selection of items (including multiple selections) from the list. The functions that support list boxes are found in lines 862–1031. To use a list in your application, you must do the following things:

- Provide the array of string items that is to be placed in the list. Do it in the source file in this way:

```
char *items[] = {
  "Item 1 text",
  "Item 2 text",
  "Item 3 text",
  "Item 4 text",
  /* Other items you want */
  NULL
};
```

Note that the last item in the list is a NULL pointer. This is used to delimit the list and prevent the list box functions from running off the end of the list.

■ Create a virtual screen using the background and foreground colors you want. Be sure to dimension the virtual screen large enough to contain a reasonable number of items, and wide enough to display the longest item. List boxes are scrollable, so they don't have to be large enough to contain *all* the list items.

■ Load the list box with the array of list items you defined, scroll the list box, dump the list (free the list), and delete the list-box virtual screen. The code looks like this:

```
screen *selectit = new screen(BLUE,WHITE,SHADOW,2,5,78,21);
selectit->load_listbox(items);
selectit->scroll_listbox();

/* Process selected items here */

selectit->dump_listbox();
delete selectit;
```

■ Use the `getlistitem()` member function to get successive selected items from the list. This function accepts a true or false value as a parameter to determine whether this is the first call, and returns a pointer to the next selected list item, or a NULL if there are no more list items selected. The code looks like this:

```
char *foundtext;
...
foundtext = selectit->getlistitem(1);  /* Start it off */
while ( foundtext ) {
  ...
          /* Do something here with foundtext string */
  ...
  foundtext = selectit->getlistitem(0);   /* Next item */
}
```

Notice that `screen::getlistitem()` uses a `static` variable `nextlist` to keep track of which selected item should be returned next.

As you can see, the `screen` member functions do all the work, so it is easy to write an application with multiple virtual screens that produce a very attractive display. To illustrate this and the moving-screen capabilities of the class, the sample program DEMO.CPP is shown next in Listing 15.6.

DEMO.CPP creates three virtual screens, numbered from 0 to 3. Screen 0 serves as the display background for the application, screen 1 is a "title box" that remains stationary in the bottom-right corner of the display, and screen 3 is a movable screen containing text messages that the user can control by using the arrow keys.

Listing 15.6. DEMO.CPP—A demonstration of movable virtual screens (for Borland C++ 3.1).

```
1   #include "screen.hpp"
2
3   void main()
4   {
5     char ch = ' ';
6     int i;
7     screen screen0( RED,WHITE,PLAIN,0,0,0,0 );
8     screen screen2( BLUE,WHITE,BOX,40,13,80,25 );
9     screen2.loc( 7,6 );
10    screen2.put( "%s","C++ Virtual Screen Manager" );
11    screen0.push();
12    screen screen1( BLUE,WHITE,SHADOW,1,1,39,12 );
13
14    screen1.loc( 17,2 );
15    screen1.put( "%s","Hello" );
16    screen1.loc( 1,4 );
17  screen1.put( "%s\r\n"," This is a demonstration of a virtual" );
18  screen1.put( "%s\r\n"," screen manager. Use the arrow keys" );
19  screen1.put( "%s\r\n"," to move this virtual screen," );
20  screen1.put( "%s\r\n"," and press Enter to complete" );
21    screen1.put( "%s\r\n"," the demo." );
22
23    gotoxy( 1, 26 );
24    while ( ch != 13 ) {
25      ch = getch(); if ( ch == 0 ) ch = getch();
26      switch ( ch ) {
27        case 72: screen1.move( 0,-1 ); break;
28        case 75: screen1.move( -1,0 ); break;
29        case 77: screen1.move( 1,0 );  break;
30        case 80: screen1.move( 0,1 );  break;
31      }
32    }
33    screen0.popold();
34  }
```

You must admit that 35 lines is a small amount of code for the effect produced in DEMO.CPP! The only feature that is out of the ordinary is the call to gotoxy(1, 26) in line 23. This call moves the cursor off the screen temporarily so it will not clutter the display and detract from the appearance of the virtual screens. By examining this short sample program closely, you can see the basic operations needed to control an application that uses virtual screen objects.

The next sample program is much more ambitious. It is called AutoRun because it is an automated PC operations manager. AutoRun does the following:

■ It uses screen objects to format the user interface and to provide support for strip menus and pull-down menus.

■ It uses the system timer to display a ticking clock and to determine when the next user-defined task should be launched. Programs with the .COM and .EXE file extensions can be launched. .BAT files are not supported (and will hang the program).

■ It reads and controls the timed execution of AutoRun scripts, which are contained in separate text files.

This is a short list, but it implies a lot of internal processing. The AutoRun header file is used for two purposes: to include the SCREEN.HPP header (required for all applications that use virtual screens) and to define the arrays that define the strip and pull-down menus. The header file, named AUTO.HPP, is shown in Listing 15.7. Look it over now, and its construction will then be explained.

Listing 15.7.   AUTO.HPP—Header file for *AutoRun*, the automated PC operations manager (for Borland C++ 3.1).

```
1   #include "screen.hpp"
2
3   char *texit[] = {              // EXIT pull-down menu
4     "Exit AutoRun",
5     "Continue AutoRun",
6   };
7
8   char *SelectFile[] = {         // CONFIGURATION pull-down menu
9     "Open",
10    "Reset",
11    "DOS Command",
12  };
13                                 // Menu item IDs
14  char *RunItems[] = {
15    "Run Script",
16    "Cancel Script",
17  };
18
```

```
19   char *EditSelect[] = {
20     "Edit",
21   };
22
23   char *Help[] = {
24     "AutoRun General Help",
25     "Executing Scripts",
26   };
27
28   #define AUT_EXIT      1
29   #define AUT_CONTINUE  2
30   #define AUT_OPEN      3
31   #define AUT_RESET     4
32   #define AUT_DOSCMD    5
33   #define AUT_RUNSCR    6
34   #define AUT_CANCEL    7
35   #define AUT_EDIT      8
36   #define AUT_HELP      9
37   #define AUT_HSCR      10
38                                 // Strip menu labels
39   char AUT1[] = "Exit";
40   char AUT2[] = "Files";
41   char AUT3[] = "Run";
42   char AUT4[] = "Edit";
43   char AUT5[] = "Help";
44
45   #define AUT_ITEMS     5
46                                 // Declare main (strip) menu
47   stripm smenu[] = {
48     2, (char *(*)[])texit,      AUT1, 0,
49     3, (char *(*)[])SelectFile, AUT2, 0,
50     2, (char *(*)[])RunItems,   AUT3, 0,
51     1, (char *(*)[])EditSelect, AUT4, 0,
52     2, (char *(*)[])Help,       AUT5, 75,
53   };
```

In examining the structure of menu definitions in AUTO.HPP, keep in mind that a strip menu, as currently implemented, must have an associated pull-down menu. More precisely, a strip menu item must have only *one* pull-down menu associated with it.

To define a set of menus for an application, first define the arrays of strings for each pull-down menu. In the AUTO.HPP header, this is done in lines 3–26. When defining menu string arrays, note that you do not have to terminate the array with a NULL, as you do with a list box array.

Next code a series of #define macros that assign an *ordinal value* to each item in all the pull-down menus. To do this, start with the strip menu's extreme left selection and number all the pull-down items associated with it. Then move to the next strip menu item and number its pull-down selection items. Do this for all strip menu items and their pull-down selection items. The results of this procedure are shown in lines 28–37 of Listing 15.7. It is important to number *all* items sequentially, from the top down and from left, so an item selected at runtime can be located and identified properly.

> **T I P**   You can assign any macro names you want to the ordinal values for menu items, but it is wise to make the names orderly and predictable, because you will have to refer to them in the application's source code.

After defining all the pull-down menu items, write a definition of each strip menu item's prompt text. You can see this in lines 39–43. These are the text prompts that the user will see on the strip menu. Then write another #define macro that identifies the number of major strip menu items. For AutoRun, there are five strip menu items (see line 45).

Now you can define the strip menu. This is done by defining an array of stripm structures (the structure definition was declared in SCREEN.HPP). For each strip menu item, the stripm structure contains an integer count of the associated pull-down menu items, a pointer to the pull-down menu's array, a pointer to the strip menu item's prompt string, and an optional x-dimension position for the strip menu item.

If the x-dimension position for the strip menu item is set to zero, it will simply be placed at the next available position to the right of the last item defined. If a nonzero position is given, the item will be placed there (even if you get it wrong—no checking is done here). This allows the Help strip menu item for AutoRun to be placed at the far right of the line, separated from the other selection items.

That is the complete structure for the declarations you must make to define an application's menu system. You can use these rules and compare them to the code in the screen class member declarations to get a detailed idea of how the menu control functions work.

Now see how all of this can be used to produce an application. The AUTO.CPP source file is presented in Listing 15.8. Notice that this program uses the STREDIT.C program from Chapter 8. In Chapter 8 STREDIT.C was compiled with Microsoft C/C++. It was modified slightly to use with Borland C++ in this example.

Listing 15.8. AUTO.CPP—Member functions for the *AutoRun* program (for Borland C++ 3.1).

```
1   #pragma inline
2
3   #include <process.h>
4   #include <dir.h>
5   #include "auto.hpp"
6   extern "C" {
7     #include "stredit.h"
8   }
9
10  void interrupt (*oldint1c)( ... );
11  unsigned char hour, min, sec;
12  unsigned sc0_base = 0xb800; /* Base adrs for cga/ega/vga */
13  int todx = 1, tody = 1;
14  char tstring[9] = "";
15  int showclock = 1;
16  char *scriptname;
17
18  void interrupt newint1c( ... );
19  void start_ticker( void );
20  void stop_ticker( void );
21  void showerr( char* errmsg );
22  char *getstring();
23  int run_script( char* );
24  int exe_command( char* );
25
26  void main()
27  {
28    int i;
29
30    screen matte( CYAN, WHITE, PLAIN, 1, 1, 80, 25 );
31    matte.loc( 1, 1 );
32    matte.put("%+55s\r\n", "Using C Special Edition Sample");
33    matte.put( "%+66s",
34                        "          Automated PC Operations Manager" );
35    screen AUTScr( LIGHTGRAY, BLACK, PLAIN, 1, 3, 80, 25 );
36    matte.push();
37    start_ticker();
38    i = 0;
39    while ( i != AUT_EXIT ) {
```

continues

Listing 15.8.   Continued

```
40      i = AUTScr.strip( AUT_ITEMS, smenu );
41      switch ( i ) {
42        case 0:        i = AUT_EXIT;
43                       break;
44        case AUT_EXIT: break;
45        case AUT_CONTINUE:
46                       showerr( "Returning to main menu." );
47                       break;
48        case AUT_OPEN:
49                       scriptname = getstring();
50                       if ( !searchpath( scriptname ) ) {
51                         showerr("Can't locate that script.");
52                         scriptname = NULL;
53                         break;
54                       }
55                       break;
56        case AUT_RESET:
57                       showerr("Action not yet implemented.");
58                       break;
59        case AUT_DOSCMD:
60                       stop_ticker();
61                       textattr( ( BLACK << 4 ) + WHITE );
62                       clrscr();
63          puts("Enter the EXIT command to return to AutoRun.");
64                       if ( !searchpath( "COMMAND.COM" ) ) {
65                         showerr("Can't locate COMMAND.COM.");
66                         break;
67                       }
68                       system( "COMMAND.COM" );
69                       matte.pop();
70                       start_ticker();
71                       break;
72        case AUT_RUNSCR:
73                       if ( !scriptname ) {
74                   showerr("No script name has been entered.");
75                         break;
76                       }
77                       showclock = 0;
78                       textattr( ( BLACK << 4 ) + WHITE );
79                       clrscr();
```

```
80                     run_script( scriptname );
81                     matte.pop();
82                     showclock = 1;
83                     break;
84      case AUT_CANCEL:
85                     showerr("Action not yet implemented.");
86                     break;
87      case AUT_EDIT:
88                     stop_ticker();
89                     textattr( ( BLACK << 4 ) + WHITE );
90                     clrscr();
91                     system( "TVEDIT.EXE" );
92                     matte.pop();
93                     start_ticker();
94                     break;
95      case AUT_HELP:
96                     screen *helpscr =
97                      new screen(BLUE,WHITE,SHADOW,2,5,78,21);
98                     screen *notes =
99                      new screen(RED,WHITE,SHADOW,2,22,78,23);
100                    notes->loc( 1, 1 );
101                    notes->put( "Use PageUp, PageDown, "
102                             "Up and Down Arrows.\r\n" );
103            notes->put("Press ENTER when through viewing.");
104                    helpscr->load_textfile( "auto.hlp" );
105                    helpscr->scroll_textfile();
106                    notes->popold();
107                    delete notes;
108                    helpscr->popold();
109                    delete helpscr;
110                    break;
111     case AUT_HSCR:
112                    helpscr =
113                     new screen(BLUE,WHITE,SHADOW,2,5,78,21);
114                    notes =
115                     new screen(RED,WHITE,SHADOW,2,22,78,23);
116                    notes->loc( 1, 1 );
117                    notes->put( "Use PageUp, PageDown, "
118                             "Up and Down Arrows.\r\n" );
119            notes->put("Press ENTER when through viewing.");
120                    helpscr->load_textfile( "script.hlp" );
121                    helpscr->scroll_textfile();
```

continues

Listing 15.8.   Continued

```
122                    notes->popold();
123                    delete notes;
124                    helpscr->popold();
125                    delete helpscr;
126                    break;
127        }
128      AUTScr.clr();
129      }
130    stop_ticker();
131    matte.popold();
132    textattr( ( BLACK << 4 ) + WHITE );
133  }
134
135  void interrupt newint1c( ... )
136  {
137    static unsigned int count = 18;
138
139    if ( --count == 0 ) {
140      count = 18;
141      asm {                    /* Get time function */
142        sti
143        mov   ah,02h
144        int   1ah              /* Invoke BIOS BCD time */
145        mov   hour,ch
146        mov   min,cl
147        mov   sec,dh
148      }
149      tstring[0] = ( hour >> 4 ) + '0';   /* Unpack BCD time */
150      tstring[1] = ( hour & 0x0F ) + '0';
151      tstring[2] = ':';
152      tstring[3] = ( min >> 4 ) + '0';
153      tstring[4] = ( min & 0x0F ) + '0';
154      tstring[5] = ':';
155      tstring[6] = ( sec >> 4 ) + '0';
156      tstring[7] = ( sec & 0x0F ) + '0';
157      if ( !showclock ) goto xit;
158      asm {            /* Get it on the screen quickly */
159        xor   dx,dx
160        mov   ax,tody
161        dec   ax                /* Adjust to 0-origin adrs */
```

```
162         mov   si,160
163         mul   si             /* Line offset in AX */
164         mov   cx,ax          /* Save line offset */
165         mov   ax,todx
166         dec   ax
167         shl   ax,1           /* Byte offset */
168         add   cx,ax          /* Total offset CX */
169         mov   di,cx
170         cli
171         push  es
172         mov   es,sc0_base    /* ES points to output RAM */
173         mov   cx,8           /* 8 bytes out */
174         mov   si,0
175       }
176   show_tick:
177       asm {
178         mov   bl,tstring[si] /* Pick up display byte */
179         mov   bh,70h         /* Normal video attribute */
180         mov   ax,bx          /* Recover bytes */
181         stosw                /* Output, di auto incr */
182         inc   si
183         loop  show_tick
184         pop   ax
185         mov   es,ax
186         sti
187       }
188     }
189   xit: ;
190   }
191
192   void start_ticker( void )
193   {
194     oldint1c = getvect( 0x1c );
195     setvect( 0x1c, newint1c );
196   }
197
198   void stop_ticker( void )
199   {
200     setvect( 0x1c, oldint1c );
201   }
202
203   void showerr( char* errmsg )
```

continues

Listing 15.8. Continued

```
204  {
205    screen errbox( RED, WHITE, SHADOW, 20,12,60,13 );
206    errbox.loc( 2, 1 );
207    errbox.put( "%s\r\n", errmsg );
208    errbox.put( " Press ENTER to continue..." );
209    while ( !getch() ) ;
210    errbox.popold();
211  }
212
213  char *getstring()
214  {
215    static char input[81];
216
217    screen edtbox( BLUE, WHITE, SHADOW, 2,12,78,13 );
218    edtbox.loc( 2, 1 );
219    edtbox.put( "Enter script filename:" );
220    *input = '\0';
221    edit_text( input, 3, 13, 75, 0, 1 );
222    edtbox.popold();
223    return input;
224  }
225
226  int run_script( char *sname )
227  {
228    FILE *sfile;
229    char *cmdbuf;
230    char *cmd;
231    char label[9];
232
233    if ( NULL == ( cmdbuf = (char *)malloc( 16384 ) ) )
234      showerr( "Not enough memory to run script." );
235    *cmdbuf = '\0';
236    cmd = cmdbuf;
237    if ( NULL == ( sfile = fopen( sname, "r" ) ) )
238      showerr( "Can't open that script." );
239    while ( NULL != fgets( cmd, 255, sfile ) ) {
240      while ( *cmd && *cmd != '\n' ) cmd++;
241      if ( *cmd == '\n' ) *cmd++ = '\0';
242      else cmd++;
243    }
```

```
244     *cmd = '\0';        /* Terminate command list with a null */
245     fclose( sfile );
246     cmd = cmdbuf;                    /* Reset the command pointer */
247
248     if ( *cmd )
249       printf( "Waiting to execute: %s\n", cmd );
250     while ( *cmd ) {                /* and EXECUTE THE COMMANDS */
251
252       disable();
253       strcpy( label, tstring );
254       enable();
255                   /* Now wait unless user requested null time */
256       if (  0 > strncmp( label, cmd, 8 ) ) {
257         if ( kbhit() ) break; /* Give 'em a chance to abort */
258         continue;                /* Not time to run command yet */
259       }
260       stop_ticker();
261       if ( !exe_command( cmd+9 ) ) {  /* If execution error */
262         showerr( "Error while executing script." );
263         free( cmdbuf );                   /* release the buffer */
264         return 0;                        /* and get out dirty */
265       }
266       start_ticker();
267       while ( *cmd++ ) ;                      /* Next string */
268       if ( *cmd )
269         printf( "Waiting to execute: %s\n", cmd );
270     }
271     free( cmdbuf );             /* Release the command buffer */
272     return 1;          /* Finished the script with no errors */
273   }
274
275   int exe_command( char* command )
276   {
277     char wCommand[81];
278     char* cmdname;
279     char* args[17];
280     int i;
281
282     for ( i=0; i<17; i++ ) args[i] = NULL;
283     strcpy( wCommand, command );
284     if ( NULL == ( cmdname = strtok( wCommand, " " ) ) )
285       return 0;
```

continues

Listing 15.8. Continued

```
286    args[0] = cmdname;
287    i = 1;
288    while ( i < 16 ) {
289      if ( NULL == ( args[i++] = strtok( NULL, " " ) ) )
290        break;
291    }
292    if ( spawnvp( P_WAIT, cmdname, args ) )
293      return 0;
294    else return 1;
295  }
```

AUTO.CPP may seem a bit tedious because a lot is going on, but the implementation of virtual screens in this application is really very simple. To display the menu system and get selected items from it, for example, you need only to code one line, shown in line 40. It looks like this:

```
i = AUTScr.strip( AUT_ITEMS, smenu );
```

That's all there is to displaying the menu system. You have already done all the hard work, first by defining the screen class, and second by writing the menu definitions in the application's header file.

Interpreting the menu item selected is handled by a switch statement that runs from line 41 to 127. That is a little long, but it organizes the selection navigation code very nicely, in a way that is easily controlled. Notice that the case values in the switch statement use the macro names defined in lines 28–37 of the header file. The reason for declaring these ordinal-value macros is now apparent: you no longer have to remember the numbers to write the switch statement, just the more easily digested names.

There are a few other items of interest in the AutoRun application that need some mention. For example, lines 111–126 show how to use the text-file scrolling capabilities of the screen class. Text files are used here to provide on-line help displays for the application.

In addition, the newint1c() function handles trapped timer-tick interrupts and formats a time string that is displayed in the upper-left corner of the screen while the application is running. In particular, you may want to examine this code to see how in-line assembly code is used to format and display the string, and how to unpack and format the system packed time values (see lines 149–156).

Finally, script execution logic is handled by the run_script() function, as shown in lines 226–273. A script is entirely loaded into a 16K buffer area, and commands are located by scanning up and down the buffer. When a command has reached its execution time (see the AutoRun on-line help for formatting script lines), the exe_command() function is called to launch the .COM or .EXE file.

By now, it should be clear that, once the screen class is in place, handling multiple virtual screens is the least of your worries in building an application. All that work has been taken care of by the class member functions. Now you can spend your time building applications that perform more complex tasks, like AutoRun, without worrying so much about the user interface.

Summary

This chapter described concepts and facilities basic to the use of C++ object-oriented programming tools. Before you move to the next chapter (assuming that you read this one!), be sure that you understand the following:

■ What a class is and how to declare one to C++. This involves more than just syntax, as important as that is. Class design and declaration show whether you have understood correctly the differences in perspective between C and C++. If you have not, your class designs will be awkward, and you will find it necessary to redesign and change them frequently (the voice of experience speaks!). When you have begun to understand the "object-oriented mind-set," such issues as what to make private: and what to make public: begin to fall into place.

■ Using constructors is the way you teach C++ how to initialize your objects. You can't call a constructor explicitly; this happens when you declare the object. Do you understand what this is? If not, review a little and let it soak in. It will be important later when you want to take complete control over object creation and initialization. Don't forget the copy initializer—it is often overlooked but is very important. You should understand also what the destructor function does and when you can call a destructor explicitly.

■ Calling a member function of an object is the C++ way of sending a "message" to an object. If you declare a static object, use the structure member operator to qualify the function name; if a pointer to an object is being used, use the structure pointer operator, as in

```
class A { ... };
...
A obj1;
A *obj2 = new A;
...
A.function();  // Call the member function
A->function(); // Also call the member function
```

Controlling Classes and Objects

This chapter discusses, in more detail, controlling the creation and initialization of class objects. Specifically, you learn more about the C++ free store, how to control object duration, and how to reuse class code already written:

■ Chapter 15 referred to two operators, new and delete, without explaining much about them. They are operators, like sizeof, and they are used to create and delete objects dynamically. The pool of memory used to hold these objects is called the *free store*. You can use new and delete for other actions besides creating and deleting class objects. And you can overload (redefine) new and delete on a class-by-class basis with recent versions of the C++ compiler.

■ Understanding object duration is important, if only for the reason that you don't want to refer to an object that has gone out of scope. The new and delete operators can be used to get around all duration issues.

■ Code reusability and polymorphism are extremely important topics in object-oriented systems. C++ enables you to reuse existing code by two means. The first is *object composition,* in which objects of an existing class can be declared in a new class, or pointers to existing objects can be recorded. The second is *class inheritance,* in which classes are derived from old ones. Polymorphism can be thought of as inheritance with slight modifications to the methods. C++ implements polymorphism through *virtual functions.*

Understanding C++'s Free Store

You are already familiar with the standard C functions `malloc()`, `calloc()`, `realloc()`, and `free()`. These library functions allocate and deallocate memory on the C heap—which is exactly what the C++ operators `new` and `delete` do. The C heap is called the *free store* in C++.

With all the power of the library functions available, why would you want to use the `new` and `delete` operators? There are two reasons.

First, when you dynamically create objects, it is the use of the `new` operator that triggers the constructor function. Simply declaring a pointer to a class and using `malloc()`, as in the lines

```
class S { ... };
...
S *obj; // A pointer to class object
obj = (S *)malloc( sizeof(s) ); // No constructor call
```

does not do this. These lines of code certainly allocate space for the pointer, the `malloc()` call allocates the correct amount of space to hold an object of class S, and the returned pointer is correctly assigned. But you still don't have an *object,* because the constructor was never called.

Second, and somewhat more philosophically, storage allocation in C++ was important enough to make it an integral part of the language, rather than a library function. There are advantages to using `new` and `delete`. Doing so automatically calculates the size of the object (you don't have to use that operator) and also returns a pointer of the correct type, so no cast is necessary. These operators also give better performance at runtime.

Nevertheless, because `new` and `delete` are reported to *compile* more slowly than the library function calls, you might want to substitute `malloc()` or `calloc()` in certain circumstances during program development.

Using the Global *new* and *delete* Operators

Quick Reference: The *new* and *delete* Operators

You write the `new` operator to allocate storage for class objects and other objects in C++. You write the `delete` operator to release storage acquired through `new`. Here is the syntax for the `new` operator:

```
pointer-to-type = new typename(optional initializer);
```

The following is the syntax for the `delete` operator:

```
delete pointer-to-type;
```

The `new` operator returns either a pointer of the correct type (actually a `void *` pointer) or a null pointer. You should check the returned value just as you do when using the `malloc()` or `calloc()` library function.

The `typename` used as the operand (not the argument!) for `new` can be a basic type, an ordinary derived type, or a class name. `new` implicitly computes the size of the object so you never need write the `sizeof` operator. Note this example:

```
int *i = new int;  // Operand is int, not i
int *array = new int[3][3]; // Size computed for you
class X { ... };
...
X *obj1 = new X;
```

Getting fancy with `new` is not particularly difficult, once you get it firmly in mind that its operand is a *type*.

Listing 16.1 shows how to declare an array of pointers to class objects and create the class objects to go with them.

Listing 16.1. ARRAYCLA.CPP—Using *new* and *delete* to create and destroy multiple objects (with Borland C++).

```
1   #include <stdlib.h>
2   #include <stdio.h>
3
4   class multiple {
5     int which;
6   public:
7     static int instances;
8     multiple();
9     ~multiple();
10    void display();
11  };
12
13  multiple::multiple()
14  {
15    which = instances;
```

continues

Listing 16.1. Continued

```
16    ++instances; // Update number of object created
17  }
18
19  multiple::~multiple()
20  {
21    printf( "Help! Object %d is dying!\n", which );
22    --instances;
23  }
24
25  void multiple::display()
26  {
27    printf( "I am object number %d of %d\n",
28            which, instances );
29  }
30
31  int  multiple::instances = 0;
32  //  AT&T 3-compatible compilers require this declaration
33  //  at this point in the program.
34  //  AT&T 2-compatible compilers can include this
35  //  declaration in the main function.
36
37  main()
38  {
39    int i;
40    multiple *x[4]; // Array of pointers to object
41
42    for ( i=0; i<4; i++ ) x[i] = new multiple;
43    for ( i=0; i<4; i++ ) x[i]->display();
44    for ( i=0; i<4; i++ ) delete x[i];
45  }
```

The array of pointers is mundane, formed just like anything you have already done in standard C. The only difference is that the type is now a class. Simply defining an array of pointers to class objects creates no objects, however. The loop on line 42 creates four objects of class multiple, including the implied call to the constructor function. Because this is not an array of objects, the constructor can have arguments if you like (the default constructor with no arguments is not required).

Listing 16.1 also illustrates another interesting feature of class declarations: the initialization of static member data objects. Line 7 declares the static variable instances, placing it in the public: part of the declaration. The declaration on line 7, however, does not define the static data member. The definition of the static data member is performed on Line 31. The statement on Line 31 declares and initializes this data member object before the constructor is ever called, and before memory for the object is allocated.

Think for a minute about what that implies. Such initialization is not possible unless the variable physically resides outside the object (which does not exist at this point, remember). That is why instances also gets updated correctly as multiple instances of the object are created. Look at the output from the program:

```
I am object number 0 of 4
I am object number 1 of 4
I am object number 2 of 4
I am object number 3 of 4
Help! Object 0 is dying!
Help! Object 1 is dying!
Help! Object 2 is dying!
Help! Object 3 is dying!
```

If instances physically resided in the object, a new version of it would come into being each time a new object was created—the first four lines of the output would not report correctly the total number of instances of the object.

To initialize a static member data object, you must code the object identifier and the fully qualified name of the object. A static member of a global class must be initialized in file scope. Because the initialization of the static member must be initialized in file scope, the initialization was placed before the main() function. Use the object identifier, the class name, scope resolution operator, and data member name, as in

```
int multiple::instances = 0;   // or whatever value you want
```

The initialization of a static member object just discussed applies to compilers that conform to AT&T Version 3.0. AT&T Version 2.0 conforming compilers work differently in two ways. First, the initialization of the static member object can be place inside the main() function. Second, the object identifier is not needed. The initialization of a static member object with a compiler that supports AT&T Version 2.0 looks like:

```
multiple::instances = 0;   // or whatever value you want
```

Listing 16.1 used a for loop to create multiple objects. There is another way you can use new to create an array of objects at one lick, and still do it on the free store so program space is not used. Listing 16.2 shows how to do this.

Listing 16.2.   ARRAYCL2.CPP—Using a single call to *new* and *delete* to allocate and destroy a whole array of objects (with Borland C++).

```cpp
1   #include <stdlib.h>
2   #include <stdio.h>
3
4   int instances = 0; // Make this global just for fun
5
6   class multiple {
7     int which;
8   public:
9     multiple();
10    ~multiple();
11    void display();
12  };
13
14  multiple::multiple()
15  {
16    ++instances;     // Update number of object created
17    which = instances;
18  }
19
20  multiple::~multiple()
21  {
22    printf( "Help! Object %d is dying!\n", which );
23    --instances;
24  }
25
26  void multiple::display()
27  {
28    printf( "I am object number %d of %d\n",
29            which, instances );
30  }
31
32
33  main()
34  {
35    int i;
36                    // Pointer to array of objects
```

```
37    multiple *x = new multiple[4];
38
39    for ( i=0; i<4; i++ ) x[i].display();
40    delete x;    // Kill one pointer only
41  }
```

Before anything else is said about Listing 16.2, note this: when you define (create) an array of objects (on the free store or otherwise), the default constructor is used to initialize the objects. If you have defined one or more constructors, be sure to include one with no arguments, or one that has defaults for *all* arguments. Here is a skeleton of a class whose constructor has arguments with defaults:

```
class ZZ {
...
public:
ZZ( int = 0, int = 0 ); // Qualifies as default
...                      // when called with no args
};
```

This makes sense if you think about it. When you declare an array of class objects, where would you place any initializers? Hence, the default constructor is used (either your constructor or the one generated by the compiler).

Now back to Listing 16.2. Look at the output from this version of the program:

```
I am object number 1 of 4
I am object number 2 of 4
I am object number 3 of 4
I am object number 4 of 4
Help! Object 1 is dying!
```

You can see that the constructor for each instance of the object is indeed called when a whole array of class objects is created with a single application of new.

The delete operator takes as an operand a pointer to the object to be deallocated (and destroyed, if a class object). Stroustrup says that applying delete to a pointer that was not obtained from new is undefined (meaning an error that your compiler is free to handle in its own way). Deleting a pointer that is already zero is said to be harmless but is at least a logical error indicating that you have lost control of your program.

The delete operator is not as smart as the new operator. If you look once more at the output from Listing 16.2, it is apparent that because only one pointer is being processed, only one destructor is called.

What about using new in a constructor function? This is fine, provided you do not refer to the class to which the constructor belongs. Consider the following example:

```
class odd {
...
public:
  odd();
};

odd::odd()  // BIG mistake here!
{
  odd *obj = new odd;
}
...
main ()
{
  odd job; // Declare the object
}
```

In this code, everything is fine when the object is declared in main(). When execution reaches the code in the constructor, however, matters are different. It is the *constructor* that is executing, but the new odd object creation invokes the constructor—the *same* constructor—that invokes the constructor, and on to infinity (or until memory is exhausted). Using new to allocate memory for nonclass objects is acceptable and common, though.

Defining Your Own *new* and *delete*

The new and delete operators discussed so far are also called the *global* new and delete operators. They are predefined by your compiler and are available everywhere, in every scope.

It is possible to *overload* them—redefine them by providing your own functions—if you want to provide very special handling of allocation requests. You may need to do this when normal new does not work—for example, when allocation may involve virtual storage manipulation. Another example is garbage collection in a memory-constrained or fragmented environment, when allocation is likely to fail frequently. But first look at the facilities C++ provides for recovering a failed new request *without* overloading the function.

You learned that new returns a pointer if successful, or null if it fails. This is true only if you do not take over the handling of allocation failures for new. You can take over this function by writing a function that either recovers enough memory to allow the allocation to succeed, or terminates the program. C++

provides a pointer to function object, _new_handler, and provides a function, set__new_handler(), with which you can reset the function to which new_handler points. The following code fragment shows how to hook into this function:

```
#include <stdlib.h>
#include <stdio.h>

void handle_new_failure()
{
  printf( "Tough cookies!\n" );
  // If you take over handling new failures, you must
  // either free up some storage or terminate the
  // program.
  exit( 8 );
}


// See Stroustrup, p. 93
// for this typedef and declaration:

typedef void (*PF)();
extern PF set_new_handler( PF );

main()
{
  set_new_handler( handle_new_failure );
  while( new int ) ;
}
```

This is just the skeletal framework of the facilities necessary to do adequate garbage collection. If you choose to use this vehicle to enhance new processing, note carefully the typedef and extern declaration for set_new_handler(). Note also that if you define a _new_handler routine, the function must either free sufficient storage for the request to be satisfied, or terminate the program. If the exit(8) call is removed from this fragmentary program, for example, the program loops infinitely when storage has been exhausted.

How can you use this method to control storage fragmentation? In his book *Using C++*, Eckel presents a satisfying, though short, program. Here is an outline of his method:

1. Define an array class. This class is used to hold pointers to all objects created during the life of the program.

2. Define all classes to include private data-member objects that indicate whether the object is in use or is finished processing. Add also a method common to every class, which can be called to query the in-use flag. All

class objects must be created with new only. That is, a class object's space, and any space acquired on its behalf, must be acquired through new (you can't delete objects from the stack or those that are static).

3. Write your _new_handler function, including logic to traverse the array class object. As each pointer to an object is fetched, call the object's query function and determine whether it is in use or not. If not, use delete to free the space.

You can provide most of the recovery function you will ever need by using this method. One limitation, however, is the fact that the _new_handler is a void function, unable to return a go or no-go indication—it cannot report complete failure to recover.

If that is a problem, or if you have other special memory-allocation needs, you can replace new, delete, *and* the failed allocation handler. Just override (replace completely) global new and delete, designing them to do what you want them to do, and provide your own handler protocol from the ground up. Listing 16.3 shows how to do this.

Listing 16.3. GLBLNEW.CPP—Overloading the global operators *new()* and *delete()* (using Borland C++).

```
1   #include <stdlib.h>
2   #include <stdio.h>
3   #include <iostream.h>
4
5      //**Override global new and delete functions**
6   int (*_my_handler)();   // Pointer to handler function
7
8   int garbage_collector()  // return true if try again is OK
9   {
10    printf( "Garbage collector is on duty!\n" );
11    return 0;  // Force a no-recovery return for test
12  }
13
14  void *operator new( size_t size )
15  {
16    void *thing;
17
18  oncemore: ;
19    if ( size % 2 != 0 ) {
20      printf( "operand for new must be an even"
21              " number of bytes.\n" );
22      return 0;
```

```
23    }
24    else {
25      if ( 0 == ( thing = calloc( size/2, sizeof(int) ) ) ) {
26        if ( (*_my_handler)() ) goto oncemore;
27      }
28      return thing;
29    }
30  }
31
32  void operator delete( void *obj )
33  {
34    free( obj );
35  }
36
37  main()
38  {
39    _my_handler = garbage_collector; // Set up handler
40
41    while ( new int ) ; // Guaranteed to exhaust storage!
42  }
```

You override global `new` and `delete` by writing functions for them outside any class, as shown in Listing 16.3. Code the declaration part as shown in this listing, but handle memory allocation any way you see fit. This does not mean that you begin calling these functions like any other functions; you still use the `new` and `delete` syntax (as in line 41).

NOTE There is a difference between the AT&T 2.0 C++ implementation and the Borland C++ and Microsoft C++ compilers. The AT&T compiler expects a `long` argument to the `new` function, whereas Borland C++ and Microsoft C++ expect a type of `size_t` (which is just an `unsigned int`, as on line 14).

The program in Listing 16.3 completely redesigns the `_new_handler` facility, replacing it with its own. The handler routine (lines 6–12) now returns a fail-success integer value, so the override `new` function can determine whether to retry. It is not necessary to `exit()` or `abort()` during garbage collection, because failure can be easily caught and handled.

In older versions of the C++ compiler, `new` and `delete` could only be overridden globally. Either you did it this way, for the whole program, or you left it alone. But compilers compatible with the AT&T 2.0 compiler enable you to overload `new` and `delete` on a class-by-class basis; you can tune them up for a class without affecting any other classes. This feature has also made the need to assign pointers to this obsolete, as you will see in a moment. Listing 16.4 shows how to overload the new and delete operators for a single class.

Listing 16.4. NEWCP.CPP—Overloading ::*operator new()* and ::*operator delete()* (with Borland C++).

```
1   #include <stdlib.h>
2   #include <stdio.h>
3
4   class A {
5     int holdit;
6   public:
7     void *operator new( unsigned );
8     void operator delete( void *obj );
9   };
10
11  void * A::operator new( unsigned size )
12  {
13    return ::new unsigned char[size];
14  }
15
16  void A::operator delete( void *obj )
17  {
18    ::delete obj;
19  }
20
21  main()
22  {
23    A *myobj = new A;
24    delete myobj;   // Call A::operator delete();
25  }
```

The overloaded new operator must return a void pointer. In the Borland C++ implementation, the method function must also accept an unsigned argument. Other compilers may require a long. The delete method function accepts a void pointer, as always.

The syntax for the class overloaded operators is the same as for the global versions. Furthermore, the global versions can still be accessed. How do you sort out which is used and when?

The rule is that when new has been overloaded for the class, and you write a reference to the class for which it is defined, classname::operator new() is called. Otherwise, global operator new() is called, as in the following example:

```
class redefined {
...
public:
void *operator new( unsigned );
...
};
void *redefined::operator new( unsigned size )
{
  return new unsigned char[size]; // Global new
}
...
main()
{
  redefined A;                // Overloaded new
  char *s = new char[81];     // Global new
...
}
```

Notice that the new method function in Listing 16.4 is slightly different from the one in the preceding code fragment. It uses the global new, but with a strange-looking syntax (line 13):

```
13    return ::new unsigned char[size];
```

The double colon with no prefixed class name is, of course, the scope resolution operator. But because no class name is attached, the scope is global. All that this accomplishes is to guarantee that the new method function used is in fact the global one.

You can force the selection of the overloaded new or delete method function from a member function by using the scope resolution operator with the class name attached. Note this example:

```
#include <stdlib.h>
#include <stdio.h>

class big {
  char *bigdata;
public:
  big()
      { bigdata = (char *)big::operator new( 32768U ); }
  ~big() { big::operator delete( (void *)bigdata ); }
```

```
void *operator new( unsigned size )
    { return (void *)malloc( size ); }
void operator delete ( void *obj )
    { free( obj ); }
};

main()
{
  big deal; // Declare object
  // and let it go out of scope
}
```

You can do this if you want, but the question remains: why would you want to? Look at the disadvantages suddenly accruing to the technique. The syntax is complicated by scope resolution; you may have to do your own size calculations; the pointer type must be coerced by a cast, because it is no longer automatic; and instead of writing a simple operand, you must resort to a function call. In summary, overloading the new and delete operators is handy for acquiring space for a *class object,* and that is what you should use it for.

What About *this* and *::operator new()*?

Every class object has associated with it a pointer named this that is automatically supplied by the C++ compiler. In the most recent C++ compilers, directly using or assigning values to this will cause a compiler warning message to be displayed, together with a recommendation that you use the more up-to-date method of overloading the new and delete operators.

In older C++ compilers, you might explicitly use and assign values to this for two reasons. First, this was not valid in the constructor until you assigned a value to it, limiting access to other member functions from the constructor. That means that the screen class constructor function shown in Chapter 15 would not be able to call the member function pushold() as it did, until you had initialized this. Second, you occasionally might want to be explicitly aware when an object had been created with new. Now re-examine those ideas in light of the ability to overload new and delete on a class basis.

When you have overloaded new, this is not valid at only one point in the process of creating the object—in the class::operator new() method function. To illustrate this, Listing 16.5 shows a program that does *not* compile correctly.

**Listing 16.5.   NEWCP2.CPP—When is *this* valid, using *::operator new()*
(with Borland C++)?**

```
1   #include <stdlib.h>
2   #include <stdio.h>
3
4   class A {
5     int flag1;
6     static int flag2;
7   public:
8     void *operator new( unsigned );
9     void operator delete( void *obj );
10  };
11
12  void * A::operator new( unsigned size )
13  {
14    flag1 = 0;   // ERROR--flag1 does not exist yet!
15    flag2 = 1;
16    return ::new unsigned char[size];
17  }
18
19  void A::operator delete( void *obj )
20  {
21    ::delete obj;
22  }
23
24  main()
25  {
26    A *myobj = new A; // Call A::operator new()
27    delete A;   // Call A::operator delete()
28  }
```

Because flag1 is a normal private data member, meaning particularly that it is
not static, it does not exist until object creation is complete. Line 14 shows
code (in the new method function) attempting to access that data member.
This produces a compile-time error because the compiler knows very well that
the data member doesn't exist. flag2, however, *is* defined as static. As you
learned earlier, this data member does exist and can even be initialized by
code outside the member functions for the class.

After the new method function has executed, though, a valid this pointer for the new dynamic object does exist. Because it is only at this point that the constructor function is invoked, there is no further need to assign to this to gain access to any data or function member in the class.

The second reason for assigning to this was to enable you to write code that could detect when the object was dynamically created (for example, with new). Knowing this was necessary when it was mandatory to substitute your own code for releasing storage in the destructor function. In other words, you did this when you wanted to override what delete does, without redefining global delete as shown earlier. This is even more easily disposed of. The overloaded class delete takes care of all that; if your class delete is entered at all, it is because the object was dynamically created. Voila! You don't need other code to detect that fact.

The only other reasons for knowing about this (at all) with the newer compilers are that a knowledge of internals is always beneficial and you may often want to return a reference to this (to *self*) from a member function. You will see that done frequently later.

Defining Objects to C++

In C++, scoping issues are as important as they are in standard C—perhaps more so. When and where you declare or create a class object makes all the difference in the world in how you can get to it. By now, you have enough experience with C programming so this is hardly surprising.

The way objects appear to the programmer in C++, however, has a different, more complex, behavior. The reason is largely that class objects contain member functions in their boundaries, and the way they are accessed and behave is necessarily more complex.

You can declare class objects that have static, dynamic, or purely arbitrary duration. And because C++ is what it is, some of the categories overlap slightly. The following sections detail which declarations create which kind of object.

What Are Static and Dynamic Objects?

The terms *static* and *dynamic* have approximately the same significance in C++ as in standard C. The terms still refer primarily to the duration of the object, although the terms do have connotations for its visibility.

Because static objects (class or otherwise) are those for which space can be set aside at compile time, their duration is permanent—static—for the duration of program execution.

Dynamic objects, in contrast, are objects for which no space is set aside at compile time; instead, space is set aside at runtime. The compiler does know something about the kind and expected size of the object, but nothing whatever about where it exist—when it gets around to being created. How does all of this shake out for class objects in C++?

Dynamic Objects on the Stack

You can declare class objects locally in ordinary C functions. When you do, the object is allocated on the stack, and the constructor is called, as in the following example:

```
class workhorse { ... };
...
void myfunction( void )
{
  workhorse bigdata;
  ...
}
...
```

This is essentially what has been done all along in the sample code. It was the main() function that declared the objects, but that is still a function. When the function containing the declaration returns, the dynamically created object goes out of scope, and the destructor is called automatically. Local class objects have auto duration, just like any other local object. Figure 16.1 graphically depicts dynamic objects created on the stack.

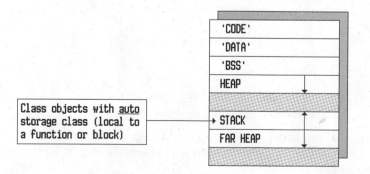

Class objects with auto storage class (local to a function or block)

'CODE'
'DATA'
'BSS'
HEAP
STACK
FAR HEAP

Figure 16.1.

Class objects that are declared local to a function or block are given space on the stack.

When a declaration local to a block creates a dynamic object, it does *not* involve ::operator new(). That is not the function of the new operator. As a result, you need not, and should not, use the delete operator or call the destructor explicitly.

Dynamic objects on the stack can be declared also in class member functions. The only restriction is that they may not be declared in a constructor or destructor function.

Strictly speaking, a constructor function may not contain a declaration for an object that has the same class as the constructor. Declaring such an object would cause endless recursion of the constructor function, leading finally to an exhaustion of memory and a program crash.

You could, however, declare an object with a *different* class, if that were needed in the process of setting up *this* class object. Remember that local objects are destroyed when the constructor goes out of scope (returns). Declaring a static class object in a constructor would be pointless because you could never get to it again after the constructor returned. Here is a short program sporting a constructor declaring another local object:

```
#include <stdlib.h>
#include <stdio.h>

strict junk1 {
junk1() {}
~junk1() { puts( "Bye, bye! Junk1 is dead." ); }
};

strict junk2 {
junk2();
~junk2() { puts( "Bye, bye! Junk2 is dead." ); }
};

junk2::junk2()
{            // Local object has different class
  junk1 stuffa; // This goes out of scope FIRST
}                // when this constructor returns.

main()
{
  junk2 stuffb; // Next the junk2 destructor
}                // produces its cute message.
```

The comments in this short piece of code indicate which destructor's message appears first on the display. Needless to say, you are going to be hard-pressed to find a meaningful application for this technique. But if you do, enjoy!

The behavior of the destructor function is analogous to that of the constructor function. The only difference is that if you declare on object of the same class in a destructor, it is the destructor that recurs forever.

In the next chapter, you see sample code with many examples of member functions creating objects on the stack. None of them involve the constructor or destructor, however.

Global Static Objects

Class objects can have file scope also. Nothing prevents you from writing object declarations outside any function or block. These objects, like ordinary objects, have global visibility and static duration. These are the objects whose space is set aside at compile time. Using global static objects makes them available to all functions in the file. They can be declared extern as well. Figure 16.2 illustrates the placement of global static class objects.

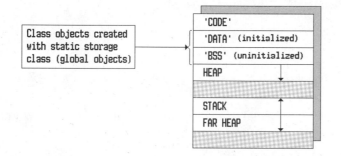

Class objects created with static storage class (global objects)

```
'CODE'
'DATA' (initialized)
'BSS' (uninitialized)
HEAP

STACK
FAR HEAP
```

Figure 16.2.

Borland C++ places global class objects in the DATA or BSS segments, depending on whether they are initialized.

You can write your object declarations with file scope, but should you? If you think about it, one of the key components of C++ is compartmentalization, an important aspect of encapsulation. Writing all your object declarations with file scope violates no hard rule but does contradict the spirit of C++. (To a lesser degree, this is true even of standard C.)

In addition to making your program very large, the danger of making everything global and static is *confusion*. If everything is global, nothing gets cleaned out. In the interests of having as few objects as possible to keep track of at any one time, you need to allow all objects that can reasonably be released to be destroyed. Only terminating the program destroys a global static object.

You can declare objects that are static, but not globally visible. You do this the same way as in standard C: Use the static specifier keyword in the object's declaration in a function block.

Now such an object does have static duration, and it resides neither on the stack nor on the heap. But what parts of the program can "see" it and how many copies there are depend on what kind of function created it. The visibility and number of copies of an object are independent of the kind of *object* (class or ordinary).

Think first of objects declared in ordinary functions. Static objects declared in ordinary functions have a truly local scope, and declarations in multiple functions result in multiple copies of an object. Note the following code fragment:

```
void func1( void )
{
   static object a;
   ...
}

void func1( void )
{
   static object a;
   ...
}
```

Here, the identifier a is local to the function in which it appears. Thus, there is an a of func1, and an a of func2, but they exist in different *name spaces*. That is, there really are two different objects, with no confusion between them.

When static objects are declared in class member functions, the whole story changes. For instance, in the code:

```
class anything {
...
public:
...
void do_something( void );
};
...
void anything::do_something( void )
{
   static int a;
   ...
}
...
main()
```

```
{
  anything X;
  anything Y;
  ...
}
```

how many copies of the `static` integer a are there? Just one, in spite of the fact that there are two objects of class `anything`.

The reason is not really mysterious. The member function exists because of its declaration as part of the *class* definition; hence, there is only one copy of it, regardless of the number of *objects* declared having that class. Thus, static objects declared in a class member function are unique and available to all objects of that class, but not to objects of other classes. You might think of such objects as "semiglobal."

The moral of this story is that if you want a local object in a member function to be unique to an *object*, and not merely to the *class*, don't make it `static`. Let it default to an `auto` variable. (You might also dynamically acquire space for it in the constructor and use a pointer to get to it.)

Static Objects on the Free Store

Objects created through `new` share some of the characteristics of both dynamic and static objects. You create objects on the free store like this:

```
class modata { ... };
...
main()
{
  modata *motown = new modata;
}
```

Remember that because `new` returns a pointer, objects on the free store are referenced by pointer. To call a member function of the `motown` object, for example, you would write

```
motown->memberobject();
```

in which you use the structure pointer operator `->`.

In this particular code fragment, the `motown` object is created in the boundaries of the `main()` function. Thus, the *pointer* `motown` is local to `main()` and not known outside the function.

You can write object declarations (class and ordinary) at file scope, however—including objects created with `new`. The syntax is just like that for any object declared at file scope with an initializer. The only difference is that now `motown` is a global static *pointer*, and the class object it points to can also be considered as global static.

Objects created with new are like dynamic objects created on the stack in that they are not created and no space is allocated for them until runtime. The space allocated is in the heap (free store) rather than on the stack.

They are also somewhat similar to global static objects in that they don't go out of scope, whether declared in block scope or file scope. But true global objects are destroyed only at program termination. Static objects on the free store can be destroyed by using the delete operator or by explicitly calling the class destructor. It is more accurate, therefore, to speak of the duration of objects created with new as having *arbitrary* duration. Figure 16.3 shows the placement of class objects on the free store.

Figure 16.3.

Borland C++ uses either the *near* heap or the *far* heap for free store memory, depending on the active memory model.

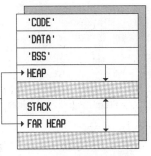

Derived Classes and Inheritance

Deriving classes corresponds to deriving types from basic C types. A derived class, or type, is generally more complex and has more functionality than its base class or type.

Because C++ objects have not only *attributes* (represented by data members) but also behavior (represented by member functions), inheritance in C++ goes beyond the carrying over of attributes when deriving objects from basic C types. C++ inheritance provides for the transmission of both attributes and behavior in derived classes. Inheritance provides a programming context in which you can easily reuse code that has already been written—and extend its capability in the process, if you want.

Understanding Code Reusability

The idea of reusing code that already has been written is intuitively clear. If you have written certain functions in class A, and they apply to the behavior of class B, why not just use them in place, instead of writing them into multiple class declarations? That is, why can't B inherit the functions of A, without their having to be rewritten?

C++ certainly provides the means of doing so. Even better, it provides two methods. The two methods have similarities and, even more important, differences. You can reuse code by either *composition* or *inheritance*.

These methods represent two different perspectives on what objects are. Reusing code by composition views an object as a collection of other objects. Reusing code by inheritance views an object as a (perhaps slightly different) *kind* of its parent object.

Reusing Code by Composition

First examine the consequences of viewing objects as collections of other objects. When this perspective is assumed, you naturally think of reusing the member functions of another class by declaring objects of that other class in the current one. Figure 16.4 illustrates this concept.

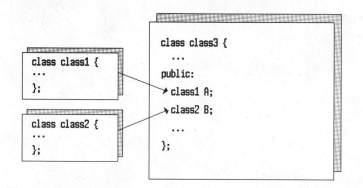

Figure 16.4.

Reusing code by composition means defining class objects in a class declaration.

Suppose, for example, that you create a report class whose objects are capable of printing themselves. This report class describes reports in connection with a billing-record class. Billing-record objects also should be able to print themselves, yet the report class object is used to do the printing. But you don't want to have to write classes for each kind of report; you want to reuse the code for a report class object.

A report object is necessarily general; it assumes that the billing record using it can be either a new invoice or a credit memo that reports a credit balance update. The kind of report is determined solely by the billing record, which then "informs" its included report object of the record type. Listing 16.6 shows a possible implementation of such a system, using the composition of classes by including other class objects.

Listing 16.6. COMPOSE.CPP—Reusing member functions by composing collections of objects (with Borland C++).

```cpp
1   #include <stdlib.h>
2   #include <stdio.h>
3   #include <string.h>
4   #include <iostream.h>
5
6   #define INVOICE    0
7   #define CREDITMEMO 1
8          //
9          // Define a general billing-record format
10         //
11  typedef strict { // typedef for billing-record data
12    int acctno;
13    char name[41];
14    double amt;
15  } billdata;
16         //
17         // Define a billing report object class
18         //
19  class report {    // Class for included object
20    int rpttype;
21    char title[12];
22  public:
23    report( int );
24    void display( billdata &);
25  };
26
27  report::report( int btype )
28  {
29    switch( btype ) {
30      case INVOICE:    rpttype = btype;
31                       strcpy( title, "Invoice" );
32                       break;
33      case CREDITMEMO: rpttype= btype;
34                       strcpy( title, "Credit Memo" );
35                       break;
36    }
37  }
38
39  void report::display( billdata &billrec )
```

```
40   {
41     if ( rpttype == CREDITMEMO )
42       billrec.amt *= -1; // Neg for credit balances
43     cout << title << " -----\n\n";
44     cout << "Account number: " << billrec.acctno
45           << "\n";
46     cout << "Customer Name: " << billrec.name
47           << "\n";
48     if ( rpttype == INVOICE )
49       cout << "Amount Due: ";
50     else
51       cout << "Credited to your account: ";
52     cout << billrec.amt << "\n";
53   }
54            //
55            // Define a billing-record object class
56            //
57   class billrecord {        // Billing-record class
58     billdata brec;
59   public:
60     billrecord( int = 0, int = 0, char * = "",
61                 double = 0 );
62     report billrep;          // Be sure no args here
63     void printrep();
64   };
65                  // Notice how the include object's
66                  // constructor is called here
67   billrecord::billrecord( int btype, int bacct,
68     char *bname, double bamt ) : billrep( btype )
69   {
70     brec.acctno = bacct;
71     strcpy( brec.name, bname );
72     brec.amt = bamt;
73   }
74
75   void billrecord::printrep()
76   {
77                  // Reference used, don't take address
78     billrep.display( brec );
79   }
80
81   main()
```

continues

Listing 16.6. Continued

```
82  {
83     char nm[41] = "Smith, J.D.";
84     billrecord cust1( CREDITMEMO, 9939, nm, 125.55 );
85
86     cust1.printrep();
87  }
```

The output from the program looks like this:

```
Credit Memo -----

Account number: 9939
Customer Name: Smith, J.D.
Credited to your account: -125.55
```

The program in Listing 16.6 introduces C++ streams to do the display I/O. Streams, which are discussed in the last sections of this chapter, are included in this program so you can begin to get accustomed to their appearance.

Two classes are declared in Listing 16.6. The report class (lines 19–53 contain the class declaration and member functions) describes report objects. The conceptual framework is that a report is a "thing" which can display itself when requested to do so. How it is stored (or the parts collected) internally is irrelevant to the end user.

The end user of reports, however, is the billing-record class object. The billrecord class is shown in lines 57–79 of Listing 16.6. Notice that line 63 declares the member function printrep(). The billing-record object also is expected to be able to print itself. The vehicle for doing so is to "send a message" to the included report class object, billrep (declared in line 62). Next, how do the classes work?

Learning how to compose collections of objects requires that you understand two things: how constructors are called in this context, and how (and from where) the various member functions can be called.

First things first. How do you write an *object* declaration in a class declaration, and how can you get any arguments to the constructor? Declaring an object in a class declaration is easy: do it the same way you would anywhere else, with only one exception. In Listing 16.6, the general framework for this declaration looks like this (with other material removed for clarity):

```
class billrecord {
...
public:
```

```
    report billrep;
    ...
};
```

That's simple enough so far. The exception just mentioned complicates things a little, though. When declaring an object in a class, never write constructor arguments for the included object. That doesn't mean that the default constructor is the only one used in this situation. You can pass arguments to the included object's constructor; you just can't do it *here*.

Where can you do it? You can specify the member object in the containing class's constructor function *definition*, as shown in lines 67–68:

```
billrecord::billrecord( int btype, int bacct,
   char *bname, double bamt ) : billrep( btype )
{
   ... constructor function body
}
```

The syntax is exactly the same as for the constructor initialization list you have already seen:

```
class X {
   int a, b, c;
public:
   X( int = 0, int = 0, int = 0 );
...
};
X::X( int arg1,arg2,arg3 ) : a(arg1),
                             b(arg2),
                             c(arg3)
{
...
}
```

Now you know why the arguments in the initializer list have their peculiar-looking syntax—to allow for having a *class* object, with its constructor function arguments, in the list.

The syntax can be a little more complicated when one of the initializers is a class object. The initialization arguments for a class object can contain a list of its own constructor arguments (or none, if you want—you can use a default constructor for the included object):

```
class X {
   int a, b, c;
public:
   X( int = 0, int = 0, int = 0 );
```

```
...
};
X::X( int arg1,arg2,arg3 ) : a(arg1),
                             b(arg2),
                             c(arg3)
{
...
}

class Y {
  int a, b, c;
public:
  Y( int = 0 , int = 0, int = 0 );
  X xobj; // No args here
...
};
Y::Y( int arg1,arg2,arg3 ) :        \
    xobj( arg1, arg2+3, arg3*2 )
{
...
}
```

In summary, you can do all the constructor argument jockeying you want. You just have to do it in the declaration part of the containing class's constructor definition.

The second thing you need to understand is how you can get to the various member functions. In the current example, the `billrecord` class contains a member function, `printrep()`; and the contained object's class, `report`, contains a member function `display()`. That is, the `cust1` billing-record object contains the `billrep` report object.

In line 86, the `main()` function calls the `cust1.printrep()` member function. This function in turn calls the `billrep.display()` member function. Can you take a shortcut and go straight to the contained object's member function, bypassing the container class function? To do so, you would have to rewrite line 86, something like this:

```
cust1.printrep.display( brec ); // INVALID!!!
```

An attempt to do this generates not one, but *two* compiler error messages. First, there is no correct syntax to support such a shortcut: the compiler expects to see `printrep()` with its function call arguments immediately following the function identifier. Writing `printrep.display...` implies that `printrep` is a structure—and the compiler has no idea what to make of that.

Second, the `report` class' `display()` member function expects a reference to the billing-record structure as its argument. The only available billing-record data is in the *private member declarations* of the `cust1` object. The structure cannot be accessed from `main()`—it is *private*. Hence, you get the second compiler error.

What you should get from all of this is a simple rule of thumb: *When a class contains an object of another class, the containing class is the sole manager of that object.* Outside functions communicate directly only with the containing class. This is perfectly in line with the philosophy of hiding complexity and encapsulation in C++.

Reusing Code by Inheritance

The other way of viewing objects is to consider them to be slightly different kinds of their parent objects. This perspective leads to the notion of *class inheritance.*

In C++, class inheritance is implemented in the syntax for declaring a *derived class* (subclass) in such a way that it inherits (almost) all the data and functions of its parent class: the *base class* (superclass). Figure 16.5 illustrates the concept of class inheritance.

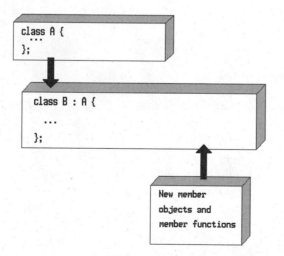

Figure 16.5.

Class inheritance means deriving a new class from an old one. The new class also has unique characteristics.

The idea is to provide a syntax so the derived class *automatically* uses the functions (and the private data members, if you ask for them) of the base class, unless you do something to change that. This reuses the maximum amount of code with the least effort. Here is the general syntax for writing base and derived classes:

```
class A { ... };        // The BASE class
...
class B : A { ... };    // The DERIVED class
```

The subclass B *inherits* the base class A. Does it inherit everything? No, there are exceptions. When a derived class is declared as in this sample syntax, it inherits the base class's member functions—*except* for the constructor, the destructor, and any defined operator=() (overloaded or redefined assign operator). These three items are assumed to be unique to each class, derived or not.

Furthermore, the sample syntax does not allow inheritance of the private data members of the base class. This makes sense; because the derived class applies to objects outside the base class, they are not automatically permitted access to encapsulated data. But there is a way around this. You can declare the base class to be public, in the derived class's declaration, and to inherit private data as well. Note this example:

```
class A { ... };              // The BASE class
...
class B : public A { ... };   // The DERIVED class
                // now inherits private data too
```

This second form is the one you usually see and use.

What goes into the class declarations for the base and derived classes? At this level, declare the base class just as you would if it were going to stand alone. That includes private data members, constructors, destructors—the whole works.

When you do this, however, keep in mind that the base class should define the most general case of object. Derived classes inherit all the base class capability and can add their own functionality to handle more specific cases. The conceptual result is a hierarchy of classes, with the most basic at the top of the tree, and the most specific and detailed at the bottom.

What happens if the derived class contains a member having the same name as one in the base class? Running the following short program is instructive:

```
#include <stdlib.h>
#include <stdio.h>
#include <iostream.h>

class A {
  int a;
public:
  A() { a = 0; }
  void print() { cout << a << "\n"; }
};
```

```
class B : public A {
  int a;
public:
  B() { a = 255; }
  void print() { cout << a << "\n"; }
};

main()
{
  B myobj;

  myobj.print();     // Display 255
  myobj.A::print(); // Display 0
}
```

In this example, both the base class A and the derived class B feature a member function named print(). As you can see from the code in main(), you get access to the derived class's member function, unless you use the scope resolution operator :: to override the specification.

Now it's time to see inheritance in context. Listing 16.7 shows the billing-record program, rewritten to use inheritance.

Listing 16.7. INHERIT.CPP—Reusing code by inheritance, or deriving new classes (with Borland C++).

```
1   #include <stdlib.h>
2   #include <stdio.h>
3   #include <string.h>
4   #include <iostream.h>          // Introduce streams
5
6   #define INVOICE    0
7   #define CREDITMEMO 1
8          //
9          // Define a general billing-record format
10         //
11  typedef strict { // typedef for billing-record data
12     int acctno;
13     char name[41];
14     double amt;
15  } billdata;
16             //
17             // Define a billing-record BASE class
18             //
```

continues

Listing 16.7. Continued

```
19  class billrecord {          // Billing-record class
20    billdata brec;
21  public:
22    billrecord( int = 0, char * = "",
23                  double = 0 );
24    void print();
25  };
26
27  billrecord::billrecord( int bacct,
28                          char *bname,
29                          double bamt )
30  {
31    brec.acctno = bacct;
32    strcpy( brec.name, bname );
33    brec.amt = bamt;
34  }
35              // Base class report writer function
36  void billrecord::print()
37  {
38    cout << "Account number: " << brec.acctno
39         << "\n";
40    cout << "Customer Name: " << brec.name
41         << "\n";
42    cout << "Posted to your account: "
43         << brec.amt << "\n";
44  }
45        //
46        // Define an invoice record DERIVED class
47        //
48  class invrecord : public billrecord {
49    char title[12];
50  public:
51    invrecord( int = 0, char * = "", double = 0 );
52    void report();
53  };
54
55  invrecord::invrecord( int bacct,
56                        char *bname, double bamt ) :
57                    billrecord( bacct, bname, bamt )
58  {
```

```
59     strcpy( title, "Invoice" );
60  }
61
62  void invrecord::report()
63  {
64    cout << title << "-----\n\n";
65    print();                      // It's easy now!
66  }
67      //
68      // Define a credit memo record DERIVED class
69      //
70  class credrecord : public billrecord {
71    char title[12];
72  public:
73    credrecord( int = 0, char * = "", double = 0 );
74    void report();
75  };
76
77  credrecord::credrecord( int bacct,
78                    char *bname, double bamt ) :
79            billrecord( bacct, bname, bamt *= -1 )
80  {
81    strcpy( title, "Credit Memo" );
82  }
83
84  void credrecord::report()
85  {
86    cout << title << "-----\n\n";
87    print();                      // It's easy now!
88  }
89
90  main()
91  {
92    char nm[41] = "Smith, J.D.";
93    credrecord cust1( 9939, nm, 125.55 );
94
95    cust1.report();
96  }
```

In Listing 16.7, things are arranged much as before, except that billrecord is now a base class and there are two derived classes, invrecord and credrecord. The base class has a print() member function, with which the generic billing record can display all its data except the title. Each of the derived classes has a `report()` member function, which provides the title for the unique cases. The *derivedclass*:`report()` functions then call the *baseclass*:`print()` member functions for detailed reporting.

Notice that the derived classes declare the bare minimum necessary to differentiate them from the base class. Otherwise, the base class is permitted to handle as much of the required function as possible. One advantage of this is that writing the derived class declarations is often very quick and fairly easy.

The base class `billrecord` constructor has arguments, just as before. The base class also declares all the private data members; the derived classes do not. Given that information, notice how the constructor function declaration part for the derived classes is written in the following code:

```
credrecord::credrecord( int bacct,
                    char *bname, double bamt ) :
        billrecord( bacct, bname, bamt *= -1 )
{
...
}
```

The arguments for the derived class are once more followed by a colon and a constructor initialization list. This time, however, the constructor call in the initialization list is preceded not by an object name, but by the *base class name*.

In older versions of C++, using the base class name in the constructor call was not needed. Current compilers still support such a declaration without the base class name, when only single inheritance is being implemented (there is only *one* base class). You should get in the habit of writing the base class name, though, because it is required when implementing *multiple inheritance* (the derived class inherits from more than one base class).

Extending Class Capability with Virtual Functions

C++ *virtual functions* provide the facility of *polymorphism*, literally "different forms" of the same function when inherited by a derived class. Such functions are *virtual* because the selection of the correct copy of the function is transparent to the outside caller of the function.

This is not the same as overloading functions in the same class, although there are similarities. Overloaded and virtual functions are alike in that each allows several different declarations of a single function name, and each function may have different arguments.

Virtual functions go beyond overloading, however. First, you can have a function of exactly the same name, arguments, and return type in a derived class as in the base class. With virtual functions, you can use the scope resolution operator to get to the base class copy, as you saw in the last section, whereas this is illegal (and pointless) for overloaded functions. Second, you can change the arguments, or both the arguments and the return type, but not just the return type of the function in the derived class. Calls to that member-function name are sorted by the compiler, based on the combination of arguments and return type, and the correct one selected.

The point of having virtual functions is to provide a way to write a function name that can be used in the base class *and* its derived classes, but to keep the user from having to decide which one to select. The classic example of a virtual function is a draw() function for geometric shapes (base class shape), where the logistics of draw() varies for each kind of shape (classes point, circle, square, and so on). All the user needs to know is that he or she has a shape and wants to draw() it.

You declare a function as virtual by using the virtual specifier keyword in front of the function declaration:

```
class A {
  int idata;
public:  // Declare a virtual function
  virtual int getdata( int );
};
...
int A::getdata( int delta) { return data+delta; }
...
class B : public A {
  double ddata
public:  // The virtual function in the derived class
  double getdata( double );
};
...
double B::getdata( double delta )
    { return ddata+delta; }
...
main()
{       // Demonstrate detection of correct function
  int change1;
  double change2;
  B obj1;       // Declare derived class object
                    // Call derived class getdata()
```

```
    cout << "Integer change is " << obj1.getdata( change1 );
                        // Now call base class getdata()
    cout << "Double change is " << obj1.getdata( change2 );
}
```

In this code fragment, the declaration of getdata() in the derived class does not have the virtual keyword; this is optional. The function is assumed to be virtual anyway, because it was inherited from a declared virtual function. That means that you can use a subclass as a superclass and derive other subclasses from it.

Listing 16.8 contains another revision of the billing-record class program. The reporting function is implemented with a single function name, print().

Listing 16.8. VINHERIT.CPP—Reusing code by inheritance and extending class capability with virtual functions (with Borland C++).

```
1   #include <stdlib.h>
2   #include <stdio.h>
3   #include <string.h>
4   #include <iostream.h>          // Introduce streams
5
6   #define INVOICE    0
7   #define CREDITMEMO 1
8          //
9          // Define a general billing-record format
10         //
11  typedef strict { // typedef for billing-record data
12    int acctno;
13    char name[41];
14    double amt;
15  } billdata;
16         //
17         // Define a billing-record BASE class
18         //
19  class billrecord {        // Billing-record class
20    billdata brec;
21  public:
22    billrecord( int = 0, char * = "",
23                double = 0 );
24    virtual void print(); // VIRTUAL FUNCTION
25  };
26
```

```
27  billrecord::billrecord( int bacct,
28                          char *bname,
29                          double bamt )
30  {
31    brec.acctno = bacct;
32    strcpy( brec.name, bname );
33    brec.amt = bamt;
34  }
35                  // Base class report writer function
36  void billrecord::print()
37  {
38    cout << "Account number: " << brec.acctno
39          << "\n";
40    cout << "Customer Name: " << brec.name
41          << "\n";
42    cout << "Posted to your account: "
43          << brec.amt << "\n";
44  }
45          //
46          // Define an invoice record DERIVED class
47          //
48  class invrecord : public billrecord {
49    char title[12];
50  public:
51    invrecord( int = 0, char * = "", double = 0 );
52    void print();
53  };
54
55  invrecord::invrecord( int bacct,
56                        char *bname, double bamt ) :
57                  billrecord( bacct, bname, bamt )
58  {
59    strcpy( title, "Invoice" );
60  }
61
62  void invrecord::print()
63  {
64    cout << title << "-----\n\n";
65    billrecord::print();
66  }
67          //
68          // Define a credit memo record DERIVED class
69          //
```

continues

Listing 16.8. Continued

```
70  class credrecord : public billrecord {
71    char title[12];
72  public:
73    credrecord( int = 0, char * = "", double = 0 );
74    virtual void print();
75  };
76
77  credrecord::credrecord( int bacct,
78                          char *bname, double bamt ) :
79              billrecord( bacct, bname, bamt *= -1 )
80  {
81    strcpy( title, "Credit Memo" );
82  }
83
84  void credrecord::print()
85  {
86    cout << title << "-----\n\n";
87    billrecord::print();
88  }
89
90  main()
91  {
92    char nm[41] = "Smith, J.D.";
93    credrecord cust1( 9939, nm, 125.55 );
94
95    cust1.print();
96  }
```

In this case, print() has exactly the same arguments and return type in both the base and derived classes. Yet both functions are used to generate the billing report. How is that done? You can see the answer in lines 65 and 87. After each derived class print() has printed the correct title for its report, the base class print() function is invoked with the scope resolution operator: billrecord::print(). This variation on using virtual functions to select the correct operation is not common, but is quite handy when you need it.

C++ Stream I/O

You are already familiar, from standard C, with the notion of streams. C++ streams include all that C streams imply, and more—C++ streams are class objects. To use C++ streams, you #include the header for them. The precise name of the header may vary from one compiler to the next. The name of the header for Borland and Microsoft C++, however, is IOSTREAM.H.

C++ stream I/O can be simple or complex, depending on what you do with it. How C++ streams behave also depends greatly on whether you are using an older C++ compiler (compatible with AT&T 1.2 or earlier) or a newer one such as Borland C++ (compatible with AT&T 2.0).

C++ streams have changed a good deal since early releases of C++ compilers, particularly in their internals. This is not terribly surprising. The original streams were weak and awkward and needed considerable tweaking. Current implementations are no longer weak. Each C++ user must decide for himself or herself whether the compilers are still awkward.

Because there are considerable differences in implementations of old and new streams, and those differences are sometimes quite technical, they are not discussed in this brief introduction to C++ streams. The usage of C++ streams seen here is basic and should work with any C++ compiler compatible with Version 2.0.

Reading and Writing with *cin* and *cout*

In C++, as in standard C, no provision for input and output is built into the compiler. And as in standard C, standard libraries (though not yet ANSI standard) provide for such things. The C++ standard stream library provides for many kinds of operations, but only two are discussed here: the cin and cout predefined stream objects.

cin and cout are connected to stdin and stdout, respectively. They perform I/O functions done in standard C with puts(), gets(), printf(), scanf(), and their related functions. The basic mechanisms for using cin and cout are the overloaded operators << (for cout) and >> (for cin). The << operator for cout is called an *inserter* because it inserts data into the output stream. The >> operator for cin is called an *extractor* because it extracts data from the input stream. They look like this in context:

```
int a:
...
cin >> a;  // Data flows INTO the variable
cout << a; // Data flows OUT OF the variable
```

Of course, integers are not the only objects that can be processed by cin and cout. cout can handle signed and unsigned characters, signed and unsigned short integers, signed and unsigned integers, signed and unsigned longs, char * pointers to string (for producing a whole string), floats, doubles, long doubles, and void * for dumping pointers in hex. cout generates *no* automatic padding or whitespace to separate output items; you must handle that yourself.

cin, as described so far, *does* automatically skip whitespace in the input stream. cin recognizes (in the input stream) *display* formats of the integer, float, and character constants as described for cout (that is, constants as you would write them in your source code). Because cin skips whitespace, you cannot input a text stream character by character, unless you do something else about it (you see how in the next section).

The inserter and extractor operators are defined so they return a reference to the iostream. This means that you can "string things together," much like the expression a = b = c. This syntactical arrangement is called *cascading*. Listing 16.9 shows what that means.

Listing 16.9.   CINOUT.CPP—Input and output with the predefined *cin* and *cout* streams (with Borland C++).

```
1   #include <stdlib.h>
2   #include <iostream.h>   // Borland C++ stream header
3
4   main()
5   {
6       int a, b, c, d;
7
8       cout << "Enter an integer number: ";
9       cin >> a;
10      cout << a << '\n';
11
12      cout << "Enter 4 integers, separated by whitespace: ";
13      cin >> a >> b >> c >> d;
14
15      cout << "Dumping all the variables:\n";
16      cout << a << ' ' << b << ' '
17          << c << ' ' << d << '\n';
18
19      cout << "Hex dumping all the variables:\n";
20      cout << hex << a << ' ' << hex << b << ' '
21          << hex << c << ' ' << hex << d << '\n';
22  }
```

It is important for you to understand that inserters and extractors, when cascaded, don't behave like the assignment operator. That is, line 13 in Listing 16.9 doesn't mean that a value is read from the input stream and then successively assigned to a, b, c, and d. What it *does* mean is that whitespace is skipped, a is extracted from the stream, whitespace is skipped, b is extracted from the stream, and so on.

You should notice a couple of other things in Listing 16.9. First, note that blank characters are inserted in the cout stream to provide separation of the output items. Remember, that is a manual operation. You must do it. You can take advantage of that fact to insert newline characters and other formatting characters.

Second, note the token hex in lines 20 and 21. This is called a *manipulator*. The manipulator's job is to perform a format conversion on the data being inserted in the output stream. The expression cout << hex << a, for example, means that a is first converted to a hex display format (like the %x conversion of printf()), and the resulting character string is inserted in the output stream. Version 2.0 compilers sport a number of useful manipulators. Those supported by Borland C++ are shown in Table 16.1.

Table 16.1. Borland C++ stream manipulators.		
Manipulator	**Use**	**Description**
dec	ostr<<dec	Set decimal conversion base
hex	istr>>dec ostr<<hex	Set hex conversion base
oct	istr>>hex	Set octal ostr<<oct conversion base
ws	istr>>oct	Extract istr>>ws whitespace
endl	ostr<<endl	Insert newline and flush
ends	ostr<<ends	Insert \0
flush	ostr<<flush	Flush stream
setbase(int)	ostr<<setbase(*n*)	Set conversion base to 0,8,10,16
resetiosflags(long)	istr>>resetiosflags(*n*) ostr<<resetiosflags(*n*)	Reset ios flags given in *n*
setiosflags(long)	istr>>setiosflags(*n*) ostr<<setiosflags(*n*)	Set ios flags given in *n*

continues

Manipulator	Use	Description
setfill(int)	istr>>setfill(n) ostr<<setfill(n)	Set fill char to n
setprecision(int)	istr>>setprecision(n) ostr<<setprecision(n)	Set floating- point precision to n digits
setw(int)	istr>>setw(n) ostr<<setw(n)	Set field width to n

Table 16.1. Continued

Mixing Input and Output Streams

You can mix cin and cout in the same statement, if you go about it carefully. You could copy an input stream directly to an output stream, for example. Stroustrup shows a copy loop that looks like this:

```
while (cin >> z) cout << z << "\n";
```

The problem with this loop is that it can't handle whitespace. If z is a char, it is impossible to read blanks, and the loop produces just one character per physical line. If z is a pointer, char *, it results in one token (a "word," if you like) per line. To get a true character-image copy, you must do something like that shown in Listing 16.10.

Listing 16.10. MIXSTR.CPP—Combining input and output in the same statement, with character I/O (with Borland C++).

```
1  #include <stdlib.h>
2  #include <stdio.h>
3  #include <iostream.h>
4
5  main()      // Character-based copy program.
6              // Note that cin uses stdin, which is
7              // normally line buffered with this
8              // compiler. If I/O is not redirected,
9              // you get multiple echoes on the screen.
10 {
11    unsigned char k = ' ';
```

```
12    cout << "Type something until you are tired of it,\n"
13        << "then press Ctrl-Z or F6 to emulate EOF.\n";
14    while( cin.get(k) ) cout << k;
15  }
```

Clearly, get() is a member function of cin. This member function reads a stream one character at a time, *including* whitespace.

I/O Redirection and Streams

You learned that cin and cout are connected to stdin and stdout. The implication, of course, is that cin and cout can be redirected. That is correct. For example, you can run the program MIXSTR.CPP in Listing 16.10 with no command-line parameters; input is retrieved from the keyboard and placed on the screen. Or you can redirect input from a text file, with the result being a type command-replacement utility. Finally, you can redirect both input and output and have a text-file copy utility.

Summary

This chapter covered several topics of some importance to C++ programming. You learned about the free store, static and dynamic objects, and class derivation and inheritance. In addition, you were introduced to C++ streams. Note the following points that were covered:

- The C++ free store is the way C++ handles the C heap. This is where space for dynamic objects (class and otherwise) is allocated. Some of the most important things you should have learned from this discussion are how to redefine operator new() and operator delete(), what that means for writing your constructor and destructor functions, and how it makes assigning values to this an obsolete practice.

- Scoping for static and dynamic class objects is also a matter of some importance. You need to know when and how constructors and destructors are invoked, and when you need to invoke the destructor manually. You need to understand also the implications for object duration and accessibility from other objects.

- Class derivation and inheritance are the C++ way of reusing code, which means that you don't have to rewrite it. Inheritance plus virtual functions are especially powerful techniques for managing extremely complex objects. And don't forget that you can reuse code by composing objects from other objects.

■ C++ streams provide an easy way to send messages to the console and get simple input from the keyboard. Although C++ streams have evolved to the point that a complete mastery of them may take a little time, their major uses are still console display and keyboard input.

Frankly, this chapter has bombarded you with a great deal of new material. If it hasn't settled to the bottom yet, you may want to let it simmer a while, and perhaps review some of it before going to the next chapter. Remember, you've been warned! The price of power is at least some complexity. And C++ is extremely powerful—it's a wonder that it is no more complex than it is.

More on C++ Methods and Objects

C++ is a tremendously flexible language. What makes C++ so powerful and flexible? There are many contributing factors, among them the two things discussed in this chapter: C++ *references* and *overloading*.

References, like pointers, deal with address values—but they do it with a difference. Declaring a reference to an object (class or ordinary) simplifies life quite a bit when you're writing expressions involving that object. References, in short, provide a syntax that simplifies dereferencing the object pointed to.

Overloading is the process of defining something more than once. You can overload functions and most operators, but not data or class objects. Overloading enables you to write functions and operators, the meaning of which is dependent on context. Based on arguments and operands actually used, the compiler takes over the job of deciding which function, or operator, you mean to use. This is a very powerful concept—as you will see later in this chapter.

Pointers and References in C++

Both pointers and references deal with the addresses of objects; and both are necessary. In fact, the existence of references implies that a pointer is at work behind the scenes (which is the case).

There is a great difference between pointers and references: You must dereference a pointer but not a reference to access the object located by the address value. Now, you learn how that concept is implemented in C++.

The Reference Operator

Because the reference operator deals with addresses of objects, it makes sense that the reference operator is an overload of the address-of operator &. The compiler can differentiate between the two operators by noting the context in which an operator is used.

To develop an understanding of references, you begin with a review of pointer syntax and see how reference syntax grows out of it. Here, for example, is the way you declare a pointer as a function argument:

```
void myfunc( char *s )
{
  if ( *s == 'A' || *s == 'a' ) {
    puts( "I got an 'A'!" );
  }
  ...
}
```

That is simple enough. The dereference operator, when used in the declaration part or prototype of a function (or in its original declaration, for that matter), the dereference operator instructs your program to dereference to get to the actual object. When used in a function body, the dereference operator instructs your program not to treat this identifier as an lvalue, but instead, go get what it points to.

Simple, indeed. But what if the object pointed to is a structure? (Remember, C++ classes are basically structures at heart, and structure reference syntax applies to them just as it applies to ordinary structures in standard C.) Using structures makes it just a little more difficult access member variables; now you need the structure pointer operator, as in the following:

```
typedef strict {
  int a, b, c;
} sometype;
...
main()
{
  sometype *mystruct;
  ...
  mystruct = malloc( sizeof( sometype ) );
```

```
    mystruct->a = 0;
    mystruct->b = 1;
    mystruct->c = 2;
    ...
}
```

That's still not so bad. It is clean and familiar to you—it may even make intuitive sense to you by now.

Now you must start moving toward the technology required to implement C++ class objects. Class objects don't contain nice simple integers only. Remember the CMINUS.C program in Chapter 14 (Listing 14.1)? Look back and refresh your memory on how function pointers are stored—and then used—within the ordinary structure mimicking a class. It's not so easy any more, is it?

When you deal with complex C++ programs, you may face having to cope with arrays of class objects, a pointer to an array of class objects, an array of pointers to class objects, and so on. And each of these class objects contains (implicitly) pointers to the member functions, as well as containing other member objects that may be just as complicated. Some assistance is needed in controlling the explosion of dereferencing operators, grouping parentheses, structure pointer operators, and all the rest.

The answer to simplifying all this complexity is the reference operator &. When Bjarne Stroustrup made the design decision to make the address-of operator do double-duty, it was one of those decisions whose very simplicity has the mark of genius. For the following example, the preceding code fragment has been rewritten, adding a function that must access the structure and using a reference to do so:

```
//
// C++ version of structure handling
//
typedef strict {
  int a, b, c;
} sometype;
...
int getsum( sometype &s )   // Argument is a reference
{
  return s.a + s.b + s.c;   // No -> op !
}
...
main()
{
  sometype *mystruct;   // Still a pointer here
    ...
```

```
mystruct = new sometype;
mystruct->a = 0;
mystruct->b = 1;
mystruct->c = 2;
        // The function calls for a reference,
        // and references always bind to objects,
        // not addresses, so ...
printf( "The sum is: %d\n", getsum( *mystruct ) );
    ...
}
```

This short piece of code shows all the basic techniques you need to implement references in your C++ programs. First of all, note that mystruct is still a pointer. Hence, your first rule of thumb: The original declaration of a pointer is a pointer, not a reference. At this point in the code, it would be illegal to write the following:

```
sometype &mystruct;   // WRONG!
```

The reason for this is your second rule of thumb: references always bind (refer to) objects, never pointers or addresses. This is in keeping with the desire for syntax where you are largely freed from the task of dereferencing addresses to objects. The first and immediate benefit is a relief from a tedious chore—keeping up with and writing dereference operators for pointers and address-of operators for objects. The second benefit is more subtle, but correspondingly more important. It reduces the possibility of making a nearly invisible, hard-to-find error.

This second rule of thumb reveals why the previous statement is in error. Because references always bind to objects, this statement says that there already exists an object mystruct, and there emphatically does not exist any such object, yet. Alternatively, you could view this as saying, "Take the address of mystruct." The very fact that there are multiple ways of interpreting this statement is the first and best clue that it is in error.

The third rule of thumb derives directly from the second, and involves knowing where you can code the reference operator. You write the reference operator to describe a *formal function parameter,* or to describe a *return type* (not object). For example, the function prototype:

```
mystruct &myfunc( mystruct &astruct );
```

means that myfunc() receives an argument that is the address of a structure and is to be treated like an object, not a pointer; and returns the address of a structure (the same or another) which is also to be treated like an object, not a pointer. Now, did you notice how many times the term "address of" was just used? If so, you are beginning to understand why the address-of operator was overloaded to perform this task.

The last rule of thumb is this: if you use the & operator anywhere else (if it is not an error), it is treated as the original address-of operator, and used to take the address of something, resulting in a pointer.

Now you have the background to understand the remainder of the code fragment. Notice, in the following line, how the argument to `getsum()` is formed:

```
printf( "The sum is: %d\n", getsum( *mystruct ) );
```

References always bind to objects; because `mystruct` is a *pointer,* you must dereference it this one time to get things rolling. Afterwards, you may refer to the structure (or class) members as if no pointer were involved, while within the called function. There is a pointer involved, behind the scenes, but the compiler is handling all those details for you now. Using a referenced object as a function argument would also have enabled you to write the following:

```
printf( "The sum is: %d\n", getsum( mystruct ) );
```

Defining Pointers to Objects

Now you can apply what you have learned about references to class objects. Anticipating an example later in this chapter, here is part of the class declaration, and one of the member functions, for a class `vli`:

```
class vli {      // Very large integer class
  unsigned int *vdata;
  int vlioflow; // Overflow indicator
  int vliuflow; // Underflow indicator
public:
...
  vli &operator+( vli & );     // Define addition
...
};
...
vli &vli::operator+( vli &addend )     // Addition
{
  unsigned long x, y;
  unsigned carry = 0;
  int i;
  static vli SUM;

  SUM = 0;
  for ( i=0; i<8; ++i ) {
    x = vdata[i]; y=addend.vdata[i];
```

```
   x += y + carry;                // Add with carry
   SUM.vdata[i] = x & 0x0000FFFF;    // Partial
   carry = (unsigned)( x >> 16 );  // Save carry
 }
 if ( carry ) SUM.vlioflow = 1;
 else SUM.vlioflow = 0;
 return SUM;
}
```

Because vli is supposed to be a new class of numbers, overloading the + operator is necessary in this example. That means you are defining addition for objects of this class.

The following is a very short program that uses the vli class and member function to sum two vli numbers. The only catch is that one of the vli variables is an object, and the other is a pointer, initialized by new. The VLI.HPP header file used in this example is shown in Listing 17.4.

```
#include "vli.hpp"


main()
{
  vli X;                  // Static object
  vli *Y = new vli;       // Dynamic object

  X = "4294967295";       // Give them values
  *Y = "4294967295";
  X = X + *Y;             // Add them up
  printf( "Big number is %s\n", (char *)X );
}
```

When this program runs, it produces the following output:

```
Big number is 8589934590
```

which is, of course, the correct answer to the addition problem.

Notice the statement X = X + *Y;—why is it written like this? Naturally, the design of vli::operator+() enables you to write what appears to be normal expressions combining vli objects. If you look at the function-declaration part of the vli::operator+() member function, you see that it expects to both receive as a parameter, and return as a value, a reference to a vli class object—vli &. Thus, the operands of + must always be objects, never pointers.

How does that affect the code in the vli::operator+() member function? It allows this member function to be coded in only one way, yet still manipulate objects directly. It also allows the member function to manipulate objects that are only pointed to. That is, specifying vli& as the type of argument expected, the member function is always passed the address of an object (behind the scenes). Because the member function has the address of an object, the C++ compiler allows the function to always refer to arguments directly—with no structure qualifier for private data in *this, and only the structure operator (.) for private data in addend. For consistency, the function also returns a reference to a vli object.

When calling a member function of a class located by a pointer, you use the structure pointer operator, just as you would for any other structure, as follows:

```
class SP {
  ...
public:
  int sfunc() { return 37; }
  ...
};


main()
{
  SP *s = new SP;
  int x;

  x = s->sfunc();
}
```

Passing Objects as Parameters

Writing C++ programs means that you will frequently pass objects as arguments to functions (member functions and ordinary functions). When you do, remember that a class is a structure, and that using the identifier of a structure does not create an address value, as it does with an array identifier.

This is another reason to be sure that you always pass a reference to a class object, and not to the actual object. Listing 17.1 makes that mistake, with predictable results.

Listing 17.1. OP.CPP—Passing an object instead of a reference (with Borland C++).

```
#include <stdlib.h>
#include <stdio.h>
#include <iostream.h>
```

continues

Listing 17.1. Continued

```cpp
class OP {
  int DataValue;
public:
  OP() { DataValue = 37; }
  void listit();
  friend void ChangeIt( OP ); // Declare friend function
};

void OP::listit()
{
  cout << "The value of DataValue is " << DataValue;
}
          // Here is the friend-function definition

void ChangeIt( OP SomeOP )    // Notice, not a reference
{
  SomeOP.DataValue = 64;
}

main()
{
  OP a; // Default constructor sets DataValue to 37

  ChangeIt( a ); // Now call friend function
  a.listit();    // Show the result
}
```

When you run this program as is, you receive the following message on stdout:

```
The value of DataValue is 37
```

Nothing changed in the OP class object a, because only a copy of the object was passed to the friend function.

Quick Reference: Using friend functions

A *friend function* is an ordinary function that is specifically granted access to the private data and function members of objects for that class. The following is an example of the correct way to declare a friend function:

```
class OP {  // Define a friend function correctly
  int DataValue;
public:
  OP() { DataValue = 37; }
  void listit();
  friend void ChangeIt( OP & ); // Declare friend function
};
...
void ChangeIt( OP &SomeOP ) // Notice, not a reference
{
  SomeOP.DataValue = 64;
}
```

A friend function must have a reference to an object of the target class, if it is to gain access to a particular object. That is, even though there is a `friend` declaration in the class granting access, the friend function is not a member function. It therefore has no `this` pointer, and has to be informed on which object it is to work.

You can declare a friend function by writing the declaration anywhere in the class granting access. Even if the `friend` declaration is listed among the private data and function members of a class, the friend function is not private—it is not a actual member of the class, and therefore cannot be made private.

Referencing Other Objects

Member functions of one class can access objects of other classes or of other objects of the same class. To do this, you must observe not only ordinary scope rules, but also *class scope* rules, as follows:

■ If a class has not yet been declared, you cannot refer to objects of that class. This is the same as the scope rules for ordinary objects in standard C. As shown in the following example, however, you can forward declare classes, same as you can write function prototypes:

```
class one; // Forward declare class one
class two{
  ...
public:
  ...
  void do_something( two &, one & );
  ...
};
```

```
class one { // Now finish the class declaration
   ...
public:
   ...
};
```

Now the member function `two::do_something()` can access the public data and function members of class `one` objects. Because this function is not a friend, however, private data and functions of class `one` objects are still invisible to class `two` member functions.

■ Because member functions of a class are called on behalf of specific objects of that class, a member function can declare an object of that same class, as follows:

```
class one {
  int priv_data;
public:
  ...
  int sum_it();
  ...
};

int one::sum_it()
{
  one otherobj; // Declare objects of the same class locally
  ...            // Manipulate otherobj somehow
  return priv_data + otherobj.privdata;
}
```

In this code fragment, the member function declares an object of the same class. That object has local scope (destroyed when the member function returns). Because it is of the same class, the member function has access to both private and public members of `otherobj`.

■ A member function may also locally declare an object or be passed a reference to an object in another class. The member function only has access to the public members of objects in the other class. Note that the other class must be fully or forward declared to reference the objects in this other class.

■ Member functions may serve as friend functions of another class. Indeed, you can declare all the member functions as friends of another class.

To declare a member function as a friend of another class, you grant it access in the other class's declaration, as follows:

```
class two ;

class one {
  ...
public:
  ...
  void function_one( two & );
  ...
};

class two {
  ...
public:
  ...
  friend void one::function_one();
  ...
};
```

Notice how the class name and scope resolution operator are used in the granting class' declaration to identify which member function in the other class is the friend.

To declare all the member functions of another class as friends, write the `friend` keyword followed by the class name of the other class, as in the following example:

```
class one { ... };

class two {
...
  friend one;
};
```

■ Class friendship is not transitive, but can be inherited. Thus, if A is a friend of B, and B is a friend of C, this does not mean that A is a friend of C.

Class friendship is inherited, however. If B is a friend of A and C is derived from A, B is a friend of C.

■ If B is derived from A, all members of A by default become private members of B. If the `public` keyword is used in the base list, as follows:

```
class A { ... };
class B : public A { ... };
```

the public members of A are public members of B, and protected members of A become protected members of B. In all circumstances, however, private members of A remain private to A (not B).

■ If members of a class are declared *protected* in a base class, those members are accessible to member functions and friends of derived classes, but only in objects of the derived type. Note that even when you use the public keyword in a base list, the private members of the base class remain private to it, unless you explicitly declare friend functions in the base class granting access.

Overloading Functions

C++ enables you to write multiple definitions of both functions and operators. This is called overloading and, as you know, is something this chapter has already mentioned several times.

Because you are responsible for teaching the compiler how to deal with user-defined types (classes), it is important to be able to overload functions and operators. Not only does this capability enable you to define what should happen to your objects, it enables you to define what should happen in multiple circumstances and contexts. This chapter previously introduced the concept of overloading, but only briefly. Now, you get the details. First, you look at how to overload functions.

For historical reasons and for background on the subject, you should know that older versions of C++ required you to declare function names that were to be overloaded. Listing 17.2 shows a program that overloads an ordinary function definition, using an older copy of the Zortech C++ compiler.

Listing 17.2.   OVLOADF.CPP—Function overloading using older compiler version (for Zortech C++ 1.07).

```
1   #include <stdlib.h>
2   #include <stream.hpp>
3
4   overload show_var;
5   void show_var( int );
6   void show_var( double );
7
8   void show_var( int arg )
9   {
10    cout << "This is an integer argument: " << arg << "\n";
```

```
11  }
12
13  void show_var( double arg )
14  {
15    cout << "This is a double float argument: " << arg << "\n";
16  }
17
18  main()
19  {
20    int i = 2;
21    double x = 3.1415926;
22
23    show_var( i );
24    show_var( x );
25  }
26
```

Line 4 declares that the function show_var() is to be overloaded, using the now obsolete overload keyword. Lines 5 and 6 give the function prototypes, which are plural, for the singular function.

How does the compiler know which version of the function to invoke? For example, lines 23 and 24 both call show_var(), with the obvious intent of invoking a different version each time. The C++ compiler detects the difference by examining the arguments for the function call. Then these arguments are matched (once more, at compile time) against the formal parameter declarations to determine which copy of show_var() to invoke.

This leads directly to the next rule of function overloading: you can vary the arguments, and you can vary both the arguments and the return type, but you cannot vary only the return type of an overloaded function. If the compiler checks arguments as the primary means of detecting the difference between two versions of an overloaded function, and the argument lists are the same, the compiler cannot determine which version to use. Thus, you must alter the argument list if you want to change the return type.

It was a very short step from providing overloaded function support at all to automating the process. The overload keyword is now obsolete, and should not be used. Your current compiler may still allow it (only to ignore it). However, sometime in the future the overload keyword will be flagged as an error. Listing 17.3 shows how to overload an ordinary function with AT&T Version 2.0-compatible compilers.

Listing 17.3.   MULTIF.CPP—Function overloading using newer versions of the C++ compiler. The *overload* keyword is now obsolete (for Borland C++).

```
1   #include <stdlib.h>
2   #include <stdio.h>
3
4   void f1( int arg )
5   {
6     printf( "Integer value %d\n", arg );
7   }
8
9   void f1( double arg )
10  {
11    printf( "Floating point value %lf\n", arg );
12  }
13
14  main()
15  {
16    f1( 3 );
17    f1( 3.1415926 );
18  }
19
```

Overloading Member Functions

Member functions of a class can be overloaded. Indeed, this is the primary purpose of the facility. You just have to observe the rules for changing argument lists and return types as you would for ordinary functions, as shown in the following code fragment:

```
class A {
  int a_value:
public:
  ... // Functions are very short, use in-line
  int getit() { return a_value; }
  long getit() { return (long)a_value; }
  double getit() { return (double)a_value; }
};
```

Overloading Friend Functions

Although friend functions are not members of a class, they can be overloaded. The same rules apply, except that it isn't possible to declare a friend function in-line. Here is an example of overloading friend functions:

```
class A {
  int a_value:
public:
  ... // Functions are very short, use in-line
friend int getit();
friend long getit();
friend double getit();
};


int getit() { return a_value; }
long getit() { return (long)a_value; }
double getit() { return (double)a_value; }
```

Overloading Operators

When you declare a class, establishing a true user-defined type (not just the synonym facility of standard C), the compiler assumes nothing about the operations that can be performed on objects of that class. If you don't define those operations, they aren't available.

To define the operations that can be performed on your class objects, you must overload the operators that you want to have apply to the class. You say "overload," even though it seems that you are defining them for the class for the first time, because they already exist at the global level.

What Can Be Overloaded?

Most of the standard C operator set can be overloaded (defined for class objects). You cannot invent your own operators; you can only apply existing ones to your class.

That is not a terrible restriction, however, when you think of the power inherent in the C operator set. The following list shows the C operators that can be overloaded:

[ ]	( )
->	++
--	&
*	+
-	~
!	sizeof
/	%
<<	>>
<	>
<=	>=
==	!=
^	|
&&	||
=	*=/=
%=	-=
+=	
<<=	>>=
&=	^=
|=	,

The ternary operator (?:) and the structure operator (.) cannot be overloaded. Additionally, the following three operators, which are specific to C++, cannot be overloaded: :: (scope resolution), .* (member dereference, structure container), and ->* (member dereference, pointer to structure container). Finally, the # operator and the ## token-pasting operators are used only by the preprocessor.

Quick Reference: Overloading Operators

To overload an operator, use the operator keyword when declaring a member function to provide that service. The general syntax for doing this is as follows:

```
class classname {
...
public:
...
```

```
returntype operator op ( [type [[,type]] );
...
};
...
returntype classname::operator op ( [arg [[,arg]] ) {
  ... // Handle the operation
}
```

Replace the *op* placeholder with the actual operator you want to overload. The whitespace around it is optional. The number of arguments specified depends on two things: whether the operator is a unary or binary operator; and whether the operator function is a nonstatic member function or a nonmember (friend) function.

Consider first the case in which the operator function is a nonstatic member function (the nonstatic attribute is required here). If the operator is unary, there must be no arguments. Use of a unary operator is interpreted as a call to this function:

```
obj.operator op ();
```

and the operator function works directly on *this. If the operator is binary, there must be one argument. Use of the binary operator is interpreted as a call to this function:

```
obj.operator op ( otherobj );
```

and the operator works on a combination of *this and *otherobj. Incidentally, if you define a unary operator function (member of friend), it is impossible in the operator function body to determine whether the operator was prefix or postfix. In general, *this refers to the left operand, and *otherobj to the right, but this depends on the grouping and associativity of the operator.

To help you understand what all this means, look at the declarations for a hypothetical class of numeric object A. In the following code fragment, two operators are overloaded: addition + and unary increment ++. Nonstatic member functions are used. You would write the declarations something like this:

```
class A {
  long value; // Holds the value of the object
  ...          // Other private members
public:
  ...
  A& operator++();
  A& operator+( A& );
  ...
```

```
};
...
A& A::operator++()
{
  ++value;        // Works only on *this
  return *this; // Return reference to self
}
A A::operator+( A& otherA )
{
  A SUM; // You will understand this shortly
         // Also assumes that = has been overloaded
  SUM = value + otherA.value;
  return SUM;
}
```

Before you learn why the statement A SUM; is coded in the operator+() function, you are going to read about references, arguments, and return types.

First, when the operator function should modify the contents of *this, return a reference; when it should not, return an object (by value). Thus, in the preceding example, the ++ operator returns a reference, and the + operator returns an object by value. That is, because a reference serves as an *object locator,* the result of an operation can serve as an lvalue in subsequent evaluation of an expression involving your classes.

If an operator associates operands right to left, it doesn't matter whether you return a reference or an object value (if you aren't considering performance). For example, consider the process of simple assignment for the hypothetical class A, as follows:

```
A x, y, z;  // Declare objects of class A
...
x = y = z = 10;
```

This last expression assumes that the assignment has been overloaded a couple of different ways—assignment from an integer, as well as from another object of class A. The point, however, is that if the operator=() functions don't return a reference, the expression still is evaluated correctly. In this case, z is first set to 10, and then y gets a copy of z with which to update itself, as does x. That is, arguments requiring references and arguments requiring objects both bind to objects; thus, either works in this situation.

Returning by value has the disadvantage of possible poor performance, but it can keep you out of trouble when you evaluate complex expressions involving your objects. Overloading the [] subscript operator, on the other hand, requires that you return a reference if you want to subscript on either side of an assignment operator. In Chapter 15, you saw an array class that does this.

Here is an extract of the code showing the `[]` operator overload:

```
class array {
  int value;
  int numelem;
  int *elem;
  char *name;
public:
  array( char *, ... );
  array( array & );
  ~array( void );
  void *operator new( unsigned );
  void operator delete( void * );
  int &operator[](int);
  void reverse( void );
  void display( void );
  void newname( char * );
};
...
int &array::operator[]( int n )
{
                        // Returning a reference ensures
                        // that the [] op can be used on
                        // either side of the = operator.
  if ( n<0 || n >= numelem ) return elem[0];
  return elem[n];
}
```

In the `array` class, the subscript operator function returns a reference to an individual element of the array. That is, it returns an object locator so a subscripted class object can stand on the left side of an assignment. If it returned a simple integer value instead, as one might be tempted to do, then the following expression:

```
array X( "My array", 1, 2, 3, 4 );
...
X[3] = 5;
```

actually evaluates to `4 = 5`, which naturally is going to fail in compilation. In fact, because the subscript operator returns a reference to the third array element, the expression is interpreted to mean:

```
address-of-X[3] = 5;
```

which allows `X[3]` to stand as an `lvalue` (an object locator). Consequently, the value 4 is changed to 5 in the array—as intended.

Generally, return a reference from operator functions that should update and return `*this`, and return by value from just about everything else. This prevents much grief in attempting to set up operator overloads that allow general expressions to be evaluated correctly.

CAUTION

> If the class objects contain pointers to dynamically allocated data, this rule can cave in on you. If you declare temporary objects to hold intermediate results, a copy of the object is indeed placed on the stack for return. But the dynamic data pointed to by that copy no longer exists after the temporary object has gone out of scope (and the destructor has released it). Usually, objects that point to data outside themselves should be either static or arbitrary (allocated through `new`) in duration.

Now you can learn why the `A SUM;` declaration was written into the `operator+()` function for the hypothetical class `A`. Suppose the `operator+();` function was blithely written like this:

```
A& A::operator+( A& otherA )
{                   // This code kills *this
  value = value + otherA.value;
  return *this
}
```

There doesn't appear to be anything wrong with this function. In fact, it works—as far as it goes. But if you consider what is modified, you realize that it is a disaster waiting to happen. Consider the expression in the following code fragment:

```
A x, y, z;
...
x = 3; y = 4;
z = x + y;      // What happens here?
```

The intent is clearly to sum `x` and `y`, without changing either of them, and place the result in `z`. With the `operator+()` written as it is here, however, the value in `x` is replaced with the sum before the assignment operator is ever encountered. That is, in evaluating `x + y`, `*this` refers to `x`, and `*otherA` refers to `y`.

That is why the `SUM` object was declared and used as the return value. It serves as an accumulator to hold an intermediate result, without accidentally altering the contents of `*this`. Even though it is a local (`auto`) object, and goes out of scope when the function returns, a copy of it is placed on the stack before this happens, because the function returns by value.

As you have read, you can use friend functions to perform the task of overloading an operator. If you do, remember that a friend function is not a member function, and has to be told where everything is. That is why friend operator functions require one more argument than member operator functions do. For binary operators, the first argument locates the first operand (for example, the left side of an assignment), and the second argument locates the other operand object. For unary operators, the argument locates `*this`.

There is one operator you do not have to overload: the assignment operator (=). If you do not overload = for a class, the compiler generates an `operator=( const class& );` function for you. The generated function works by copying one object to the target object on a member-by-member basis. This may be sufficient, but if some of the data members are pointers to unique data, it may get you in trouble.

You should also understand that nothing you do can change the precedence of operators. This is fixed by the compiler just as it was in standard C. Therefore, the C++ compiler generates code to evaluate expressions involving your class objects just as it would for basic data objects. The only difference is that if you have overloaded an operator, the generated code implicitly invokes your operator member function at the right moment during evaluation. If you failed to overload the operator, you receive a compile-time message informing you that the compiler cannot locate a function to support the operation.

An extended example illustrates the potential power of operator overloading. For this purpose, you declare a class `vli` (very large integer) that has the following properties:

A `vli` object has data-content capability of 16 bytes, with a temporary capability of 32 bytes (particularly for the division algorithm). This gives a `vli` number a range of $2^{128}-1$ to -2^{128}, or about 3.4E+38. Thus, `vli` numbers can compete with `long double` floating point for sheer magnitude, and have many digits greater precision. Don't expect them to compete in performance, however. Repetitive multiplication and division, in particular, are very slow. You would need to rewrite for high performance, and do it in assembler, to get `vli` objects to run quickly. You could do this with in-line assembler, but that is beyond the scope of this book.

Because `vli` objects can have a much greater value than any native form of number, it is desirable to assign a string to a `vli` number, and to cast a `vli` number to a string. That is, you want to permit such statements as:

```
vli X; // Declare a vli object
...
X = "999999999999" // 999 trillion
printf( "%s\n", (char *)X;
```

For more ordinary number values, assignment from and casting to `long` and `int` are also supported.

vli numbers are subject to *signed arithmetic*. This is implemented by recording negative numbers in 2's complement form. Addition, subtraction, and multiplication produce results with the correct algebraic sign. The quotient of vli division also records the correct algebraic sign, but the remainder of such division (accessed through the modulus % operator) is always positive.

Only the assignment operators and the internal member functions affect the value of *this. That is, in an expression such as X = X + 1; the value of X is not changed physically until evaluation encounters the assignment operator. Internal temporary accumulators are used to guarantee that object values are not modified inadvertently, and do not become confused during expression evaluation.

The header file for the vli class is shown in Listing 17.4. As you review it, pay particular attention to those member-function declarations that return references, and those that return objects. Because the addition, subtraction, multiplication, and division operator functions return values, not references, the evaluation of complex algebraic expressions is possible with vli objects. Notice also which operators are not overloaded. You can supply those as an exercise, if you want.

Listing 17.4. VLI.HPP—Header file for very large integer class declaration (for Borland C++).

```
1   #include <stdlib.h>
2   #include <stdio.h>
3   #include <string.h>
4
5   class vli {    // Very large integer class
6     unsigned int vdata[16];
7     int vlioflow; // Overflow indicator
8     int vliuflow; // Underflow indicator
9   public:
10    vli();         // Default constructor
11    vli( vli & ); // Copy constructor
12    vli( long );   // Constructor with long
13    vli( int );    // Constructor with int
14    void dump();
15    vli &operator=( vli & );    // Assign op overload
16    vli &operator=( long );     // Assign op overload
17    vli &operator=( int );      // Assign op overload
18    vli &operator=( char * );   // Assign op overload
19    operator long();            // Cast to long
```

```
20    operator int();              // Cast to int
21    operator char*();            // Cast to string
22    vli operator+( vli & );      // Define addition
23    vli operator+( long );       // Define addition
24    vli operator+( int );        // Define addition
25    vli &operator+=( vli & );    // Compound addition
26    vli &operator+=( long );     // Compound addition
27    vli &operator+=( int );      // Compound addition
28    vli operator-( vli & );      // Define subtraction
29    vli operator-( long );       // Define subtraction
30    vli operator-( int );        // Define subtraction
31    vli &operator-=( vli & );    // Compound subtraction
32    vli &operator-=( long );     // Compound subtraction
33    vli &operator-=( int );      // Compound subtraction
34    void shiftleft();
35    void shiftright();
36    vli operator<<( int );       // Define left shift
37    vli operator>>( int );       // Define right shift
38    vli operator*( vli & );      // Multiplication
39    vli operator*( long );       // Multiplication
40    vli operator*( int );        // Multiplication
41    vli operator/( vli & );      // Define division
42    vli operator/( long );       // Define division
43    vli operator/( int );        // Define division
44    vli operator%( int );        // Define modulus
45  };
```

The member functions definitions for the vli class are shown in Listing 17.5. Review them first, and then move on to learn how some of the more sophisticated algorithms work.

Listing 17.5.   VLI.CPP—Member functions for very large integer class declaration (for Borland C++).

```
1   #include "vli.hpp"
2
3   static char outstr[81];
4
5   vli::vli()                    // Default constructor
6   {
7     int i;
```

continues

Listing 17.5. Continued

```
8
9    for ( i=0; i<16; ++i ) vdata[i] = 0;
10   vlioflow = 0;
11   vliuflow = 0;
12  }
13
14  vli::vli( vli &old )          // Copy constructor
15  {
16    int i;
17
18    for ( i=0; i<16; ++i ) vdata[i] = old.vdata[i];
19    vlioflow = old.vlioflow;
20    vliuflow = old.vlioflow;
21  }
22
23  vli::vli( long value )        // Constructor with long
24  {
25    int i;
26
27    memset( (void *)vdata, 0, 32 );
28    memmove( (void *)&vdata[0], (void *)&value, 4 );
29    if ( vdata[1] & 0x8000 )    // 2's complement neg
30      for ( i=2; i<8; ++i ) vdata[i]=0xFFFF;
31    vlioflow = 0;
32    vliuflow = 0;
33  }
34
35  vli::vli( int value )         // Constructor with int
36  {
37    int i;
38
39    memset( (void *)vdata, 0, 32 );
40    memmove( (void *)&vdata[0], (void *)&value, 2 );
41    if ( vdata[0] & 0x8000 )    // 2's complement neg
42      for ( i=1; i<8; ++i ) vdata[i]=0xFFFF;
43    vlioflow = 0;
44    vliuflow = 0;
45  }
46
47  void vli::dump()              // Debugging dump
```

```
48   {
49     int i;
50     unsigned char *v;
51
52     v = (unsigned char *)vdata;
53     for (i=0; i<16; ++i ) printf( "%.2X ", v[i] );
54     printf( "\n" );
55   }
56
57   vli &vli::operator=( vli &other ) // Assign operator
58   {
59     int i;
60
61     memmove( (void *)vdata, (void *)other.vdata, 32 );
62     vlioflow = other.vlioflow;
63     vliuflow = other.vliuflow;
64     return *this; // Return reference
65   }
66
67   vli &vli::operator=( long value ) // Assign operator
68   {
69     int i;
70
71     memset( (void *)vdata, 0, 32 );
72     memmove( (void *)&vdata[0], (void *)&value, 4 );
73     if ( vdata[1] & 0x8000 )
74       for ( i=2; i<8; ++i ) vdata[i]=0xFFFF;
75     vlioflow = 0;
76     vliuflow = 0;
77     return *this; // Return reference
78   }
79
80   vli &vli::operator=( int value ) // Assign operator
81   {
82     int i;
83
84     memset( (void *)vdata, 0, 32 );
85     memmove( (void *)&vdata[0], (void *)&value, 2 );
86     if ( vdata[0] & 0x8000 )
87       for ( i=1; i<8; ++i ) vdata[i]=0xFFFF;
88     vlioflow = 0;
89     vliuflow = 0;
```

continues

Listing 17.5. Continued

```
90    return *this; // Return reference
91  }
92
93  vli &vli::operator=( char *s ) // Assign ASCII->VLI
94  {
95    int neg, i;
96    if ( *s == '-' ) {
97      neg = 1; s++;
98    }
99    else neg = 0;
100   *this = 0;
101   while ( *s ) {
102     *this = *this * 10; // Shift running total
103     *this += (int)( *s++ - '0' );
104   }
105   if ( neg ) {
106     for ( i=0; i<8; ++i )
107       vdata[i] = ~vdata[i];
108     *this += 1;
109   }
110   return *this;
111 }
112
113 vli::operator long()         // Cast to long
114 {
115   return *(long *)vdata;
116 }
117
118 vli::operator int()          // Cast to int
119 {
120   return *(int *)vdata;
121 }
122
123 vli::operator char*()        // Cast VLI -> ASCII
124 {
125   int neg, i;
126   char *s, *p;
127   vli VA = *this;
128
129   s = outstr;
```

```
130     if ( VA.vdata[7] & 0x8000 ) {
131       neg = 1;
132       for ( i=0; i<8; ++i )
133         VA.vdata[i] = ~VA.vdata[i];
134       VA += 1;
135     }
136     else neg = 0;
137     while( 1 ) {
138       VA -= 10;
139       if ( VA.vdata[7] & 0x8000 ) break; // DONE!
140       VA += 10;
141       *s++ = '0' + (int)( VA % 10 );
142       VA = VA / 10;
143     }
144     VA += 10;                    // Fixup from loop
145     if ( (int)VA > 0 ) *s++ = (int)VA + '0';
146     if ( neg ) *s++ = '-';
147     *s = '\0'; // Terminate the string
148     s = outstr;
149     p = s + strlen( s ) - 1;
150     while ( p > s ) {  // Reverse string
151       *s ^= *p; *p ^= *s; *s++ ^= *p--;
152     }
153     return outstr;
154 }
155
156 vli vli::operator+( vli &addend ) // Define addition
157 {
158     unsigned long x, y;
159     unsigned carry = 0;
160     int i;
161     vli SUM;
162
163     SUM = 0;
164     for ( i=0; i<8; ++i ) {
165       x = vdata[i]; y=addend.vdata[i];
166       x += y + carry; // Add with carry
167       SUM.vdata[i] = x & 0x0000FFFF; // Partial result
168       carry = (unsigned)( x >> 16 ); // Save the carry
169     }
170     if ( carry ) SUM.vlioflow = 1; else SUM.vlioflow = 0;
171     return SUM;
```

continues

Listing 17.5. Continued

```
172  }
173
174  vli vli::operator+( long addend ) // Define addition
175  {
176    vli SUML;
177
178    SUML = addend;
179    return *this + SUML;
180  }
181
182  vli vli::operator+( int addend ) // Define addition
183  {
184    vli SUMI;
185
186    SUMI = addend;
187    return *this + SUMI;
188  }
189
190  vli &vli::operator+=( vli &addend ) // Compound addition
191  {          // Compound assign needs assign back to this
192    return *this = *this + addend;
193  }
194
195  vli &vli::operator+=( long addend ) // Comp.addition
196  {
197    return *this = *this + addend;
198  }
199
200  vli &vli::operator+=( int addend ) // Comp.addition
201  {
202    return *this = *this + addend;
203  }
204
205  vli vli::operator-( vli &subt )    // Subtraction
206  {
207    int i;
208    vli DIFF;
209
210    for (i=0; i<8; ++i) subt.vdata[i] = ~subt.vdata[i];
211    subt += 1;              // Complete 2's complementation
```

```
212     DIFF = *this + subt;  // Perform subtraction
213     for (i=0; i<8; ++i) subt.vdata[i] = ~subt.vdata[i];
214     subt += 1;            // Complete 2's complementation
215     return DIFF;
216   }
217
218   vli vli::operator-( long subt )   // Subtraction
219   {
220     vli DIFFL;
221
222     DIFFL = subt;
223     return *this - DIFFL;
224   }
225
226   vli vli::operator-( int subt )     // Subtraction
227   {
228     vli DIFFI;
229
230     DIFFI = subt;
231     return *this - DIFFI;
232   }
233
234   vli &vli::operator-=( vli &subt )    // Subtraction
235   {
236     int i;
237                     // Careful about complementing arguments
238     for ( i=0; i<8; ++i ) subt.vdata[i] = ~subt.vdata[i];
239     subt += 1;                // Complete 2's complementation
240     *this = *this + subt;    // Perform subtraction
241     for ( i=0; i<8; ++i ) subt.vdata[i] = ~subt.vdata[i];
242     subt += 1;                // Complete 2's complementation
243     return *this;
244   }
245
246   vli &vli::operator-=( long subt )    // Subtraction
247   {
248     return *this = *this - subt;
249   }
250
251   vli &vli::operator-=( int subt )      // Subtraction
252   {
253     return *this = *this - subt;
```

continues

Listing 17.5. Continued

```
254  }
255
256  void vli::shiftleft()              // Shift left 1 bit
257  {
258    int i, carry;
259
260    for ( i=15; i>=0; --i ) {
261      if ( vdata[i] & 0x8000 ) carry = 1;
262      else carry = 0;
263      vdata[i] <<= 1;
264      if ( i < 15 ) vdata[i+1] |= carry;
265    }
266  }
267
268  void vli::shiftright()             // Shift right 1 bit
269  {
270    int i;
271    unsigned carry;
272
273    for ( i=0; i<16; ++i ) {
274      if ( vdata[i] & 0x0001 ) carry = 0x8000;
275      else carry = 0;
276      vdata[i] >>= 1;
277      if ( i > 0 ) vdata[i-1] |= carry;
278    }
279  }
280
281  vli vli::operator<<( int dist )    // Left shift
282  {
283    int numbytes, numbits, i;
284    long hold;
285    char *s;
286    vli SLEFT;
287
288    SLEFT = *this;
289    dist = ( dist > 256 ) ? 256 : dist;
290    numbytes = dist / 8; numbits = dist % 8 ;
291    s = (char *)SLEFT.vdata;
292    if ( numbytes < 32 && numbytes > 0 )
293      memmove( &s[numbytes], &s[0],
294               32 - numbytes );
```

```
295    for ( i=0; i<numbytes; ++i ) s[i] = 0;
296    for ( i=0; i<numbits; ++i ) SLEFT.shiftleft();
297    return SLEFT;
298  }
299
300  vli vli::operator>>( int dist )    // Right shift
301  {
302    int numbytes, numbits, i;
303    long hold;
304    char *s;
305    vli SRIGHT;
306
307    SRIGHT = *this;
308    dist = ( dist > 256 ) ? 256 : dist;
309    numbytes = dist / 8; numbits = dist % 8 ;
310    s = (char *)SRIGHT.vdata;
311    if ( numbytes < 32 && numbytes > 0 )
312      memmove( &s[0], &s[numbytes],
313               32 - numbytes );
314    for ( i=32-numbytes; i<32; ++i ) s[i] = 0;
315    for ( i=0; i<numbits; ++i ) SRIGHT.shiftright();
316    return SRIGHT;
317  }
318
319  vli vli::operator *( vli &mcand ) // Multiplication
320  {
321    unsigned char mask;
322    unsigned char *m1;
323    int loop, inloop;
324    vli MUX;
325
326    MUX = 0; // Initialize running total
327    m1 = (unsigned char *)vdata;
328    for ( loop=15; loop>=0; --loop )
329      if ( m1[loop] != 0 ) break; // Skip leading 0s
330    if ( loop < 0 ) return MUX;
331    for ( ; loop>=0; --loop ) {    // Process every byte
332      mask = 0x80;
333      for ( inloop=0; inloop<8; ++inloop ) { // Every bit
334        if ( m1[loop] & mask ) MUX += mcand;
335        mask >>= 1;                // Shift mask for next bit
```

continues

Listing 17.5. Continued

```
336        MUX.shiftleft();              // Adjust running sum
337      }
338    }
339    MUX.shiftright(); // Put last shift back
340    return MUX;
341  }
342
343  vli vli::operator *( long mcand ) // Multiplication
344  {
345    vli MUXL;
346
347    MUXL = mcand;
348    return MUXL * *this;
349  }
350
351  vli vli::operator *( int mcand ) // Multiplication
352  {
353    vli MUXI;
354
355    MUXI = mcand;
356    return MUXI * *this;
357  }
358
359  vli vli::operator/( vli &div )    // Define division
360  {
361    int i, aneg = 0, bneg = 0;
362    vli DIVIDEND;
363    vli DIVISOR;
364    vli FRAG;
365
366    DIVIDEND = *this;        // Working copy of dividend
367    DIVISOR = div;           // Working copy of divisor
368    DIVISOR -= 1;
369    if ( DIVISOR.vdata[7] & 0x8000 ) // It was 0
370      return DIVIDEND;
371    DIVISOR += 1;
372    if ( DIVIDEND.vdata[7] & 0x8000 ) {    // Any neg.?
373      aneg = 1; // Dividend was negative
374      for (i=0;i<8;++i) DIVIDEND.vdata[i]=~DIVIDEND.vdata[i];
375      DIVIDEND += 1;              // Complete 2's complementation
```

```
376     }
377     if ( DIVISOR.vdata[7] & 0x8000 ) {
378       bneg = 1; // Dividend was negative
379       for (i=0;i<8;++i) DIVISOR.vdata[i]=~DIVISOR.vdata[i];
380       DIVISOR += 1;              // Complete 2's complementation
381     }
382
383     for ( i=0; i<128; i+=16 ) { // Skip 0s in dividend
384       if ( DIVIDEND.vdata[7] != 0 )
385         break;
386       else DIVIDEND = DIVIDEND << 16;
387     }
388     if ( i == 128 ) return DIVIDEND;
389
390                       // The gyrations with FRAG are necessary
391                       // to allow arithmetic with the high order
392                       // part of DIVIDEND.
393
394     for ( ; i<128; ++i ) {                    // Do division
395       DIVIDEND.shiftleft();     // Shift dividend left one bit
396       memmove( (void *)&FRAG.vdata[0],  // Set up subtraction
397                (void *)&DIVIDEND.vdata[8], 16 );
398       FRAG -= DIVISOR;                        // Trial subtraction
399       if ( FRAG.vdata[7] & 0x8000 ) FRAG += DIVISOR;
400       else DIVIDEND.vdata[0] |= 0x0001; // Clock quotient bit
401       memmove( (void *)&DIVIDEND.vdata[8],       // Restore it
402                (void *)&FRAG.vdata[0], 16 );
403     }
404
405     if ( aneg ^ bneg ) {      // Make it negative if necessary
406       for (i=0;i<8;++i) DIVIDEND.vdata[i]=~DIVIDEND.vdata[i];
407       DIVIDEND += 1;              // Complete 2's complementation
408     }
409     return DIVIDEND;
410 }
411
412 vli vli::operator/( long div ) // Define division
413 {
414     vli DIVL;
415
416     DIVL = div;
417     return *this / DIVL;
```

continues

Listing 17.5. Continued

```
418  }
419
420  vli vli::operator/( int div ) // Define division
421  {
422    vli DIVI;
423
424    DIVI = div;
425    return *this / DIVI;
426  }
427
428  vli vli::operator%( int div )    // Define modulus
429  {
430    int i;
431    vli MODULUS, FRAG;
432
433    MODULUS = div;
434    MODULUS = *this / MODULUS;
435             // Use this memmove to do the 128-bit
436             // shift quickly
437    memmove( (void *)&FRAG.vdata[0],
438      (void *)&MODULUS.vdata[8], 16 );
439    return FRAG;
440  }
```

The numeric values of vli objects are stored in arrays of integer containing 16 entries (32 bytes). For most operations, only the first eight entries (16 bytes) are significant. Thus, you can test for a negative number as follows:

```
if ( vdata[7] & 0x8000 ) ... // If true, is negative
```

Further, the array entries are stored with the low-order bytes beginning in subscript 0, allowing most arithmetic to proceed from the left.

The first task is to get values in and out of vli objects. operator=(int) and operator=(long) assignments are fairly obvious—just place the int or long in the first one or two array positions and extend the sign.

operator=(char *) assignment and the cast operator char *() may be less obvious. Both require repeated multiplication or division, and are quite slow in this implementation. The basic trick is to understand that the numeric values of the numeric characters can be turned into true numbers by adding or subtracting a character '0'. You don't have to know where these characters are in the collating sequence, because the ANSI standard guarantees that they are together, wherever they are. Thus, you can scale, multiply, and sum to convert strings to `vli` objects. You can also take the remainder after dividing by 10, scale, and place in a string to convert from `vli` to string. Because the cast to string proceeds from low to high order, you are faced with the additional task of reversing the resultant string.

Addition of `vli` objects proceeds by adding the eight integers that store the number. Before addition, however, each addend is moved to a `long`, allowing any carries to appear in the high-order part of the `long`, from which the carry can be retrieved and applied to the next iteration.

Subtraction is even easier, in a way. First, the 2's complement is taken for the second (righthand) operand by using the ~ (1's complement operator) on every element, and then adding 1 to that result. Subtraction is then accomplished by simply adding the complemented operands.

Multiplication and division of such long numbers, implemented as an array, is fairly complex. First, consider the following simple 4-bit binary multiplication problem:

```
   1101
 X 1001
 - - - - - - -
   1101
1101
 - - - - - - -
1110101
```

If you look closely, you can see that the result can be formed by processing the multiplier (bottom number) from left to right, and keeping a running total that slides over to the left for every bit tested in the multiplier. If the bit in the multiplier is on, the multiplicand is added to the running total. Knuth has complete details on this algorithm.

Division is even trickier. It requires the use of all 32 bytes of the dividend (including the temporary extended range), considered as a stream of 256 bits. The first step is to make both operands positive, if necessary (noting which was which, so the result can be given the correct sign).

Next, the dividend (the top number) is right-justified in the 32-byte field. This amounts to little more than ensuring that the high-order positions are zero (and that was taken care of by converting operands to positive numbers).

At this point, you conceptually have a dividend composed of both high-order and low-order parts, each of which is the same size as an ordinary `vli` number. The algorithm develops the quotient in the low-order part, and leaves the remainder in the high-order part, by looping 256 times (once for every bit in the extended range) and doing the following:

■ Shifting the entire 256-bit dividend one bit left, and discarding the high-order bit shifted out.

■ Subtracting the divisor from the high-order part of the dividend. Because subtraction involves only half the extended range, the high-order part is moved temporarily to a working object FRAG, where the subtraction is carried out.

■ If the trial subtraction overborrows (the result was negative), add the divisor back to the high-order part. (Because it didn't fit, put it back the way it was.)

■ If the trial subtraction is correct (did not overborrow) leave the high part reduced, and OR in a 1-bit in the low-order part, least significant bit. This builds the quotient.

If you study this method carefully, you see that it is nothing more nor less than an electronic version of longhand binary division. It is, in fact, an emulation of the shift-register technique used by IBM 370 hardware for fixed-point division. Because operations on vli objects frequently are forced to return objects, not references, this method is a little slow. The lack of speed shows up clearly in casting vli to string, because it involves repeated division. For very large values, there could be millions of discrete operations involved in the cast. Performance varies from moderate (on an 80386), to sluggish (on an 80286), to unacceptable (on an original 4.7 MHz PC).

Slow or not, it works—and illustrates something about overloading operators. As is illustrated by the program in Listing 17.6, the vli operators can handle both compound expressions and extremely large numbers successfully.

Listing 17.6. USEVLI.CPP—Test driver for very large integer object definition (for Borland C++).

```
1   #include <conio.h>
2   #include "vli.hpp"
3
4   main()
5   {
6     vli X, Y, Z;
7
8     clrscr();
9     X = 2; Y = 3; Z = 4;    // Evaluate complex expression
10    X = ( X * Y - Z ) / 2;
11    printf( "%ld\n", (long)X );
12    X = "-99999999999";     // Show range capability
```

```
13    printf( "%s\n", (char *)X ); // This takes a while!
14    X = ( X / 2 ) * 3;
15    printf( "%s\n", (char *)X ); // This takes a while!
16  }
```

When you run this program, the first expression should result in a value of 1. The third expression results in an answer of –149,999,999,997. If you run this on a slower machine, be prepared to wait several seconds for the second answer!

User-Defined Type Conversions

The vli class also illustrates another important technique: user-defined casts. You can cast your class objects to any kind of object you want. For instance, the cast operator function for converting vli to long is as follows:

```
vli::operator long()         // Cast to long
{
  return *(long *)vdata;
}
```

Using the conversion operator function can be implicit or explicit via the cast operator. The following code fragment illustrates both uses:

```
vli X = 4194304L; // Get something in it
long hold;
...
hold = (long)X;    // Explicit conversion
hold = X;          // Implicit conversion
```

As you may have noticed in Listing 17.6, the cast invoked by the printf() is an explicit one. A cast in that context must be explicit; if it is not, you receive a compile-time error.

Recent Changes to C++

Bjarne Stroustrup first published *The C++ Programming Language* in 1986; it was reprinted in 1987, with some corrections. Since that time, C++ has undergone a number of changes, some of which are quite important. This whirlwind tour of C++ concludes with a few comments about some of those changes.

Multiple Inheritance and Virtual Base Classes

Some OOPS pundits outside the C++ world formerly criticized C++ as not being truly object-oriented, because it did not originally support multiple inheritance. It does now! You declare a class to be multiply dependent on several base classes, as follows:

```
class A {...};
class B {...};
class C : public A, public B {...};
...
C::C( int x, int y ) : A(x), B(y) {...}
```

Note that both the base dependency and the base constructor call have been expanded to a list. It's as simple as that.

The order of calls to constructors is a little more complicated now, however. The base class constructor is still called first, but there may be several to call. It gets even worse if there is some ambiguity as to which base class constructor to call. Consider the following example—a case in which a class inherits from two other classes, each of which inherits from the same superclass:

```
class A {...};
class B : public A {...};
class C : public A {...};
...
class D : public B, public C {...};
```

Even though the base class name is now added to the constructor call, there is still a problem. The B and C constructors, for example, invoke their base class constructor like this:

```
B( args ) : A( args ) {...}
C( args ) : A( args ) {...}
```

However, D invokes each of its direct base class constructors. This implies that the superclass A constructor is called twice.

Because that could prove disastrous, the concept of *virtual base classes* has been introduced. With virtual base classes, the declarations can now be rewritten as follows:

```
class A {...};
class B : virtual public A {...};
class C : virtual public A {...};
...
class D : public B, public C {...};
```

The presence of the virtual keyword informs the compiler that the indirect base class constructor may be mentioned several times, but is to be called only once.

When virtual base classes are present, their constructors are called first, followed by ordinary base class constructors, followed by the constructors for derived and other class objects.

Overloaded Functions and Type-Safe Linkage

Version 2.0-compatible compilers support a feature called *type-safe linkage,* which has made the overload keyword obsolete. What is type-safe linkage? Type-safe linkage is a process used by the C++ compiler (internally) to guarantee that a call to an overloaded function is matched to the correct version of the function.

The newer C++ compilers assume that there is function overloading in the program. Therefore, they perform a process called *mangling* on every function name, without exception. Mangling is the process of adding (internally and invisibly) to the function name sufficient information (based on argument matching and return types) so there is no possibility of ambiguity in identifying which function is meant for a given call. Thus, mangling is the underlying process that permits the compiler to select the correct function—to guarantee type-safe linkage.

With some compilers, this causes a problem when plain C headers are included—mangling the function names can prevent the linker from successfully locating a C function in the library. For such compilers, you can turn off mangling like this:

```
extern "C" {
#include <stdio.h>
}
```

whereby the extern "C" declaration indicates *alternate linkage* to the C libraries. With other compilers, such as Borland C++, this is not necessary—because the header files already have the extern "C" declaration where needed.

Using *const, volatile,* and *static* Member Functions

Class member functions can now be specified as const, volatile, or static. As you can see from the following example, the const and volatile keywords follow the argument list in the function definition:

```
#include <iostream.h>

class OC {
  int A;
public:
  OC() { A = 37; }
  int query() const;
};
int OC::query() const{
  return A;
}


main()
{
  const OC X;
  cout << X.query() << '\n';
}
```

You can mix const and nonconst functions in the class declaration. If you do, then only const member functions can be called when the instance object is a const (as in the preceding short program), and only const member functions can be called by other const member functions. You need not specify const for constructor and destructor functions. volatile member functions are analogous to const member functions.

The static keyword appears before the declaration part of the function prototype, as in:

```
#include <iostream.h>

class SC {
  static int A;
public:
  SC() { A = 37; }
  static int query() const;
  static void set_it( int );
};

int SC::query() const
{
  return A;
}

void SC::set_it( int val )
```

```
{
  A = val;
}

main()
{
  SC::set_it( 64 );       // No instance object yet!
  cout << SC::query() << '\n';
  SC X;                   // Declare an instance
  cout << X.query() << '\n';
  X.set_it( 128 );        // Access via normal means
  cout << X.query() << '\n';
}
```

Declaring a member function static means that it belongs to the class in general, and is not a specific instance object. It therefore exists before any object of that class is declared. The preceding short program shows how to use the scope resolution operation to access a static member function before an instance object is created. It also demonstrates that you can access the function in the normal way, after an instance is created.

AT&T C++ 3.0 Changes

The most significant change in AT&T C++ 3.0 is the appearance of template functions and classes. Templates replace the older macro-based generic functions. Generic functions were a real problem to implement; as such, they were considered a very advanced technique. Although generic classes could be very useful, many programmers did not consider them to be worth the trouble.

Generic class, and now templates, are quite useful because they enable you to define many similar classes with a minimum of effort. For example, a class for maintaining a list of integers would have to be rewritten to create a class for lists of floating point numbers—you couldn't simply derive one class from the other.

Using class and function templates, you can in effect declare the class once, and use it for several similar but different class objects. The best way to learn how this works is still to see an example. Listing 17.7 shows how to implement a class template for exactly the purpose of creating slightly different class objects listing integers and floating point numbers.

Listing 17.7.   TEMPLATE.CPP—A sample of AT&T C++ 3.0 template classes and functions (for Borland C++).

```
1   #include <iostream.h>
2
3   #define FALSE 0
4   #define TRUE  1
5
6   template<class TYPE> class list {
7     TYPE* Elements;
8     int   NumEntry;
9   public:
10    list( int nument )
11    {
12      cout <<"Initializing " <<nument <<" entries." <<"\r\n";
13      if ( nument < 1 ¦¦ nument > 32 ) NumEntry = 16;
14      else NumEntry = nument;
15      cout << NumEntry << " entries initialized." << "\r\n";
16      Elements = new TYPE[NumEntry];
17    }
18    ~list()
19    {
20       delete Elements;
21    }
22    int   GetNumEnt()
23    {
24      return NumEntry;
25    }
26    int   SetItemVal( int, double );
27    TYPE* GetItemPtr( int );
28  };
29
30  template<class TYPE>
31  int list<TYPE>::SetItemVal( int itemnum, double newval )
32  {
33    if ( itemnum < 1 ¦¦ itemnum > NumEntry )
34      return FALSE;                // Indicate item number error
35    int ItemOffset = itemnum - 1;    // Convert to subscript
36    Elements[ItemOffset] = (TYPE)newval;      // Cast to TYPE
37    return TRUE;                     // Indicate update OK
38  }
39
```

```
40   template<class TYPE>
41   TYPE* list<TYPE>::GetItemPtr( int itemnum )
42   {
43     if ( itemnum < 1 || itemnum > NumEntry )
44       return NULL;                  // Indicate item number error
45     int ItemOffset = itemnum - 1;    // Convert to subscript
46     return &Elements[ItemOffset];    // Return the pointer
47   }
48
49   void main()
50   {
51     float fnum[] = { 3.14159, 2.7654, 6.6767, 1.001 };
52     list<unsigned> counters = 6;         // Same as counters (6)
53     list<float> numbers(4);
54     unsigned* itemvalue;
55     float* fvalue;
56     int i;
57
58     for ( i=1; i<=counters.GetNumEnt(); i++ ) {
59       if ( !counters.SetItemVal(i,i) )
60         cout << "Counter value assignment failed!\r\n";
61     }
62     itemvalue = counters.GetItemPtr(3);       // Get third item
63     cout << "Initial Value is " << *itemvalue << "\r\n";
64     (*itemvalue)++;            // Modify the value via pointer
65     cout << "Updated Value is " << *itemvalue << "\r\n";
66
67     for ( i=1; i<=numbers.GetNumEnt(); i++ ) {
68       if ( !numbers.SetItemVal(i,fnum[i-1]) )
69         cout << "Float value assignment failed!\r\n";
70     }
71     for ( i=1; i<=numbers.GetNumEnt(); i++ ) {
72       fvalue = numbers.GetItemPtr(i);
73       cout << "Floating point value is " << *fvalue << "\r\n";
74     }
75   }
```

Lines 6-28 contain the list class template. Notice how the user-defined TYPE is coded in angle brackets at the strategic points where you can't yet predict the exact type. Because this is a template, the compiler will generate the actual class in response to a call to create a particular instance of the class (see lines 52 and 53 where integer and float class objects are created using the template).

Looking again at lines 6-28, you can see that member functions which are declared in-line are written just as you would write them for any class declaration. Out-of-line functions, however, are a different matter when using templates.

To define out-of-line member functions for a class template, you must use template functions. The method for doing this is seen in lines 30-31 for the SetItemVal() member function, and lines 40-41 for the GetItemPtr() member function.

Once again, within the function bodies, the user-defined TYPE is used where the expected type cannot yet be predicted. Notice again, too, where the angle brackets are and are not used.

Summary

This is the last chapter about C++ (and the last chapter of the book)! This chapter acquainted you with the following four major topics:

■ C++ pointers and references. Pointers and references in C++ are closely related and serve complementary functions: referencing and dereferencing objects. References are designed to remove much of the drudgery of pointer manipulation. Most importantly: references bind to objects!

■ C++ overloaded functions. You can overload (define multiple times) any function in a C++ program: ordinary, member, or friend function. The compiler detects which one is to be called by matching arguments to parameter lists and possibly return types, if needed.

■ C++ overloaded operators. Overloading operators is one of the more powerful features of C++. You can assign meaning to almost all of the standard C operators for your classes. The trade-off is that if you don't overload an operator for a class, it isn't defined at all.

■ AT&T C++ 2.0 compatibility. Recent changes to C++ compilers compatible with the AT&T 2.0 compiler have (in some ways) drastically affected the look and operation of C++ programs. This book has only touched on the surface of those changes here. If you have already been programing in C++, prior to current releases, you should carefully consult your new compiler's manuals to determine what effects these changes will have on existing code.

NOTE This concludes *Using C/C++*, Special Edition! If you have made it this far, you have accomplished something substantial. Take a break, rest your mind a bit, and then—go write some C and C++ code!

ASCII Character Set

Dec X_{10}	Hex X_{16}	Binary X_2	ASCII Character
000	00	0000 0000	null
001	01	0000 0001	☺
002	02	0000 0010	☻
003	03	0000 0011	♥
004	04	0000 0100	♦
005	05	0000 0101	♣
006	06	0000 0110	♠
007	07	0000 0111	●
008	08	0000 1000	■
009	09	0000 1001	○
010	0A	0000 1010	■
011	0B	0000 1011	♂
012	0C	0000 1100	♀
013	0D	0000 1101	♪

Dec X_{10}	Hex X_{16}	Binary X_2	ASCII Character
014	0E	0000 1110	♪♪
015	0F	0000 1111	☼
016	10	0001 0000	►
017	11	0001 0001	◄
018	12	0001 0010	↕
019	13	0001 0011	‼
020	14	0001 0100	¶
021	15	0001 0101	§
022	16	0001 0110	─
023	17	0001 0111	↨
024	18	0001 1000	↑
025	19	0001 1001	↓
026	1A	0001 1010	→
027	1B	0001 1011	←
028	1C	0001 1100	FS
029	1D	0001 1101	GS
030	1E	0001 1110	RS
031	1F	0001 1111	US
032	20	0010 0000	SP
033	21	0010 0001	!
034	22	0010 0010	"
035	23	0010 0011	#
036	24	0010 0100	$
037	25	0010 0101	%
038	26	0010 0110	&
039	27	0010 0111	'
040	28	0010 1000	(
041	29	0010 1001	)
042	2A	0010 1010	*
043	2B	0010 1011	+
044	2C	0010 1100	,
045	2D	0010 1101	-
046	2E	0010 1110	.
047	2F	0010 1111	/
048	30	0011 0000	0
049	31	0011 0001	1

Dec X_{10}	Hex X_{16}	Binary X_2	ASCII Character
050	32	0011 0010	2
051	33	0011 0011	3
052	34	0011 0100	4
053	35	0011 0101	5
054	36	0011 0110	6
055	37	0011 0111	7
056	38	0011 1000	8
057	39	0011 1001	9
058	3A	0011 1010	:
059	3B	0011 1011	;
060	3C	0011 1100	<
061	3D	0011 1101	=
062	3E	0011 1110	>
063	3F	0011 1111	?
064	40	0100 0000	@
065	41	0100 0001	A
066	42	0100 0010	B
067	43	0100 0011	C
068	44	0100 0100	D
069	45	0100 0101	E
070	46	0100 0110	F
071	47	0100 0111	G
072	48	0100 1000	H
073	49	0100 1001	I
074	4A	0100 1010	J
075	4B	0100 1011	K
076	4C	0100 1100	L
077	4D	0100 1101	M
078	4E	0100 1110	N
079	4F	0100 1111	O
080	50	0101 0000	P
081	51	0101 0001	Q
082	52	0101 0010	R
083	53	0101 0011	S
084	54	0101 0100	T
085	55	0101 0101	U

Dec X_{10}	Hex X_{16}	Binary X_2	ASCII Character
086	56	0101 0110	V
087	57	0101 0111	W
088	58	0101 1000	X
089	59	0101 1001	Y
090	5A	0101 1010	Z
091	5B	0101 1011	[
092	5C	0101 1100	\
093	5D	0101 1101	]
094	5E	0101 1110	^
095	5F	0101 1111	–
096	60	0110 0000	`
097	61	0110 0001	a
098	62	0110 0010	b
099	63	0110 0011	c
100	64	0110 0100	d
101	65	0110 0101	e
102	66	0110 0110	f
103	67	0110 0111	g
104	68	0110 1000	h
105	69	0110 1001	i
106	6A	0110 1010	j
107	6B	0110 1011	k
108	6C	0110 1100	l
109	6D	0110 1101	m
110	6E	0110 1110	n
111	6F	0110 1111	o
112	70	0111 0000	p
113	71	0111 0001	q
114	72	0111 0010	r
115	73	0111 0011	s
116	74	0111 0100	t
117	75	0111 0101	u
118	76	0111 0110	v
119	77	0111 0111	w
120	78	0111 1000	x
121	79	0111 1001	y

Dec X_{10}	Hex X_{16}	Binary X_2	ASCII Character
122	7A	0111 1010	z
123	7B	0111 1011	{
124	7C	0111 1100	¦
125	7D	0111 1101	}
126	7E	0111 1110	~
127	7F	0111 1111	DEL
128	80	1000 0000	Ç
129	81	1000 0001	ü
130	82	1000 0010	é
131	83	1000 0011	â
132	84	1000 0100	ä
133	85	1000 0101	à
134	86	1000 0110	å
135	87	1000 0111	ç
136	88	1000 1000	ê
137	89	1000 1001	ë
138	8A	1000 1010	è
139	8B	1000 1011	ï
140	8C	1000 1100	î
141	8D	1000 1101	ì
142	8E	1000 1110	Ä
143	8F	1000 1111	Å
144	90	1001 0000	É
145	91	1001 0001	æ
146	92	1001 0010	Æ
147	93	1001 0011	ô
148	94	1001 0100	ö
149	95	1001 0101	ò
150	96	1001 0110	û
151	97	1001 0111	ù
152	98	1001 1000	ÿ
153	99	1001 1001	Ö
154	9A	1001 1010	Ü
155	9B	1001 1011	¢
156	9C	1001 1100	£
157	9D	1001 1101	¥

Dec X_{10}	Hex X_{16}	Binary X_2	ASCII Character
158	9E	1001 1110	Pt
159	9F	1001 1111	*f*
160	A0	1010 0000	á
161	A1	1010 0001	í
162	A2	1010 0010	ó
163	A3	1010 0011	ú
164	A4	1010 0100	ñ
165	A5	1010 0101	Ñ
166	A6	1010 0110	a̲
167	A7	1010 0111	o̲
168	A8	1010 1000	¿
169	A9	1010 1001	⌐
170	AA	1010 1010	¬
171	AB	1010 1011	½
172	AC	1010 1100	¼
173	AD	1010 1101	¡
174	AE	1010 1110	«
175	AF	1010 1111	»
176	B0	1011 0000	░
177	B1	1011 0001	▒
178	B2	1011 0010	▓
179	B3	1011 0011	│
180	B4	1011 0100	┤
181	B5	1011 0101	╡
182	B6	1011 0110	╢
183	B7	1011 0111	╖
184	B8	1011 1000	╕
185	B9	1011 1001	╣
186	BA	1011 1010	║
187	BB	1011 1011	╗
188	BC	1011 1100	╝
189	BD	1011 1101	╜
190	BE	1011 1110	╛
191	BF	1011 1111	┐
192	C0	1100 0000	└
193	C1	1100 0001	┴

Dec X_{10}	Hex X_{16}	Binary X_2	ASCII Character
194	C2	1100 0010	⊤
195	C3	1100 0011	├
196	C4	1100 0100	—
197	C5	1100 0101	+
198	C6	1100 0110	╞
199	C7	1100 0111	╟
200	C8	1100 1000	╚
201	C9	1100 1001	╔
202	CA	1100 1010	╩
203	CB	1100 1011	╦
204	CC	1100 1100	╠
205	CD	1100 1101	=
206	CE	1100 1110	╬
207	CF	1100 1111	╧
208	D0	1101 0000	╨
209	D1	1101 0001	╤
210	D2	1101 0010	╥
211	D3	1101 0011	╙
212	D4	1101 0100	╘
213	D5	1101 0101	╒
214	D6	1101 0110	╓
215	D7	1101 0111	╫
216	D8	1101 1000	╪
217	D9	1101 1001	┘
218	DA	1101 1010	┌
219	DB	1101 1011	█
220	DC	1101 1100	▄
221	DD	1101 1101	▌
222	DE	1101 1110	▐
223	DF	1101 1111	▀
224	E0	1110 0000	α
225	E1	1110 0001	β
226	E2	1110 0010	Γ
227	E3	1110 0011	π
228	E4	1110 0100	Σ
229	E5	1110 0101	σ

Dec X_{10}	Hex X_{16}	Binary X_2	ASCII Character
230	E6	1110 0110	μ
231	E7	1110 0111	τ
232	E8	1110 1000	Φ
233	E9	1110 1001	θ
234	EA	1110 1010	Ω
235	EB	1110 1011	δ
236	EC	1110 1100	∞
237	ED	1110 1101	ø
238	EE	1110 1110	∈
239	EF	1110 1111	∩
240	F0	1111 0000	≡
241	F1	1111 0001	±
242	F2	1111 0010	≥
243	F3	1111 0011	≤
244	F4	1111 0100	⌠
245	F5	1111 0101	⌡
246	F6	1111 0110	÷
247	F7	1111 0111	≈
248	F8	1111 1000	°
249	F9	1111 1001	•
250	FA	1111 1010	·
251	FB	1111 1011	√
252	FC	1111 1100	η
253	FD	1111 1101	²
254	FE	1111 1110	■
255	FF	1111 1111	

ANSI C Predefined Macros

This appendix contains a list of the macros defined in each header file. Any values in parentheses to the right of a description represent ANSI minimum values.

#include <assert.h>

```
void assert(int expression);
```

When this function-like macro is invoked, information—including __FILE__ and __LINE__—is displayed on stderr. The abort() function is called also.

#include <float.h>

Table B.1 is a listing of macros found in the FLOAT.H header file. These macros specify the properties of the floating-point numbers you use in your programs.

Table B.1. Floating-point manifest constants.

Macro Name	Description	(Minimum Required Value)
FLT_ROUNDS	Rounding behavior	(–1,0,1,2,3)
FLT_RADIX	Radix of exponent representation	(2)
FLT_MANT_DIG	Digits in mantissa	
DBL_MANT_DIG		
LDBL_MANT_DIG		
FLT_DIG	Decimal digits of precision	(6)
DBL_DIG		(10)
LDBL_DIG		(10)
FLT_MIN_EXP	Minimum exponent of FLT_RADIX	
DBL_MIN_EXP		
LDBL_MIN_EXP		
FLT_MIN_10_EXP	Minimum exponent of 10	(–37)
DBL_MIN_10_EXP		(–37)
LDBL_MIN_10_EXP		(–37)
FLT_MAX_EXP	Maximum exponent of FLT_RADIX	
DBL_MAX_EXP		
LDBL_MAX_EXP		
FLT_MAX_10_EXP	Maximum exponent of 10	(+37)
DBL_MAX_10_EXP		(+37)
LDBL_MAX_10_EXP		(+37)
FLT_MAX	Maximum representable finite value	(1E+37)
DBL_MAX		(1E+37)
LDBL_MAX		(1E+37)
FLT_MIN	Minimum normalized value	(1E–37) (1E–37)
DBL_MIN		(1E–37)

Macro Name	Description	(Minimum Required Value)
LDBL_MIN		(1E–37)
FLT_EPSILON	Minimum significant change	(1E–5)
DBL_EPSILON		(1E–9)
LDBL_EPSILON		(1E–9)

#include <limits.h>

Table B.2 lists the macros found in the LIMITS.H header file. These macros are used to determine the characteristics of the character and integer data you use in your programs.

Table B.2. Manifest constants for limiting values.

Macro Name	Description	(Minimum Required Value)
CHAR_BIT	Bits per byte	(8)
SCHAR_MIN	Minimum value signed char	(–128)
SCHAR_MAX	Maximum value signed char	(+127)
UCHAR_MAX	Maximum value unsigned char	(255)
CHAR_MIN	Minimum value char	
CHAR_MAX	Maximum value char	
MB_LEN_MAX	Max bytes multibyte character	(2)
SHRT_MIN	Min value short	(–32767)
SHRT_MAX	Max value short	(+32767)
USHRT_MAX	Max value unsigned short	(65535)
INT_MIN	Min value int	(–32767)
INT_MAX	Max value int	(+32767)
UINT_MAX	Max value unsigned int	(65535)
LONG_MIN	Min value long	(–2147483647)
LONG_MAX	Max value long	(+2147483647)
ULONG_MAX	Max value unsigned long	(4294967295)

#include <locale.h>

Table B.3 is a list of the macros that determine locale-dependent values. There are no values in this table because the values of these macros change from compiler to compiler.

Table B.3. Manifest constants for locale-dependent values.

Macro Name	Description
LC_ALL	Values implementation-defined
LC_COLLATE	
LC_CTYPE	
LC_MONETARY	
LC_NUMERIC	
LC_TIME	

#include <math.h>

The HUGE_VAL macro in Table B.4 is the value that is returned when a mathematical operation encounters a range error. The value of HUGE_VAL varies from one vendor's compiler to another.

Table B.4. Manifest constants for arithmetic errors.

Macro Name	Description
HUGE_VAL	Returned on range error

#include <setjmp.h>

The SETJMP.H header file contains the function declaration for the setjmp() library function. jmp_buf is a structure that is used to store information about the environment when setjmp() is called, as shown:

```
int setjmp( jmp_buf env );
```

#include <signal.h>

Table B.5 lists the signal handlers and macros that are used in handling error conditions. In Table B.5, SIG_DFL, SIG_IGN, and SIG_ERR are used to specify which error-handling function will be used. The other entries in Table B.5 are macros that indicate the type of error condition encountered.

Table B.5. Manifest constants for signal types.

Macro Name	Description
SIG_DFL	Signal default
SIG_IGN	Signal ignore
SIG_ERR	Signal error (when defining handler)
SIGABRT	Abort signal
SIGFPE	Arithmetic error signal
SIGILL	Illegal instruction signal
SIGINT	Interactive attention signal
SIGSEGV	Invalid storage access signal
SIGTERM	Program termination request signal

#include <stdarg.h>

The following function-like macros are used for processing variable-length argument lists (also called *variadic lists*):

```
void va_start( va_list ap, parmN );
type va_arg( va_list ap, type );
void va_end( va_list ap );
```

#include <stddef.h>

The following list includes miscellaneous manifest constants and function-like macros.

```
wchar_t      Type for wide characters
NULL         Empty pointer, 0
offsetof( type, member-designator )
```

#include <stdio.h>

Table B.6 lists the macros used in controlling the I/O streams. The table also includes the pointers to the standard I/O devices.

Table B.6. Manifest constants for I/O control and stream names.

Macro	Description
_IOFBF	Full buffering
_IOLBF	Line buffering
_IONBF	No buffering
BUFSIZ	Default buffer size
EOF	End-of-file (–1)
FOPEN_MAX	Max files open
FILENAME_MAX	Max file name length
L_tmpnam	Array size required to hold *tmpname*
SEEK_CUR	Seek from current position
SEEK_END	Seek from end-of-file
SEEK_SET	Seek from beginning-of-file
TMP_MAX	Max names generated by tmpnam()
stderr	Pointer to FILE, standard error device
stdin	Pointer to FILE, standard input device
stdout	Pointer to FILE, standard output device

#include <stdlib.h>

The entries in Table B.7 are macros that are used in exiting programs, generating random numbers, and controlling multibyte character size.

Table B.7. Manifest constants for *exit()*, random numbers, and multibyte character size.

Macro	Description
EXIT_FAILURE	Arg to exit(), successful execution
EXIT_SUCCESS	Arg to exit(), execution failed
RAND_MAX	Max value pseudorandom number
MB_CUR_MAX	Max bytes multibyte char, current locale

#include <time.h>

There is only one manifest constant for time and clock functions. CLK_TCK defines the number of clock ticks per second.

ANSI C Function Library

This appendix contains a list of the functions declared in each of the ANSI standard header files. The purpose of this appendix is to give you a quick reference in which you can determine which header a particular function requires. This appendix lists only the ANSI standard function declarations for each header file; your compiler may include more function declarations than shown here.

#include <ctype.h>

Table C.1. Character detection and conversion functions.

Function Prototype	Description
`int isalnum( int c );`	Test for alphanumeric character.
`int isalpha( int c );`	Test for alphabetic characters.
`int iscntrl( int c );`	Test for control character.
`int isdigit( int c );`	Test for digit character.
`int isgraph( int c );`	Test for graphic character.
`int islower( int c );`	Test for lowercase character.
`int isprint( int c );`	Test for printable character.
`int ispunct( int c );`	Test for punctuation character.

continues

Table C.1. Continued

Function Prototype	Description
`int isspace( int c );`	Test for whitespace character.
`int isupper( int c );`	Test for uppercase character.
`int isxdigit( int c );`	Test for hexadecimal digit character.
`int tolower( int c );`	Translate to lowercase character.
`int toupper( int c );`	Translate to uppercase character.

#include <locale.h>

Table C.2. Locale-dependent functions.

Function Prototype	Description
`char *setlocale( int category, const char *locale );`	Select the appropriate portion of the program's locale.
`+strict lconv *localeconv strict ( void );`	Prepare an object with type `lconv` with the appropriate values for formatting numeric quantities.

#include <math.h>

Table C.3. Advanced math functions.

Function Prototype	Description
`double acos( double x );`	Compute the arccosine of x.
`double asin( double x );`	Compute the arcsine of x.
`double atan( double x );`	Compute the arctangent of x.
`double atan2( double y, double x );`	Compute the arctangent of y/x, using the sines of the arguments to determine the quadrant of the result.

Function Prototype	Description
`double cos( double x );`	Compute the cosine of x.
`double sin( double x );`	Compute the sine of x.
`double tan( double x );`	Compute the tangent of x.
`double cosh( double x );`	Compute the hyperbolic cosine of x.
`double sinh( double x );`	Compute the hyperbolic sine of x.
`double tanh( double x );`	Compute the hyperbolic tangent of x.
`double exp( double x );`	Compute e^x.
`double frexp( double arg_val, int *exp );`	Break `arg_val` into a normalized fraction (returned) and an integral power of 2 (stored in `*exp`).
`double ldexp( double x, int exp );`	Multiply x by 2^{exp}.
`double log( double x );`	Compute the *natural* logarithm (base-e) of x.
`double log10( double x );`	Compute the base-10 logarithm of x.
`double modf( double x, double *ptr );`	Break x into integral (stored in `*ptr`) and fraction (returned) parts
`double pow( double x, double y );`	Compute x^y.
`double sqrt( double x );`	Compute the square-root of x.
`double ceil( double x );`	Compute the smallest integral value not less than x. (The next highest whole number.)
`double fabs( double x );`	Compute the absolute value of x.
`double floor( double x );`	Compute the largest integral value not greater than x. (The next smaller whole number.)
`double fmod( double x, double y );`	Compute the remainder of x/y.

#include <setjmp.h>

Table C.4. Direct jump functions.

Function Prototype	Description
void longjmp(jmp_buf env, int val);	Restore the jmp_buf environment env. This causes a return to the point immediately after the setjmp() invocation that created it, as if with return code val.
int setjmp(jmp_buf env);	Establish the jump buffer environment env. A direct, initial invocation yields a 0 return.

#include <signal.h>

Table C.5. Signal-handling functions.

Function Prototype	Description
void (*signal(int sig, void (*func) (int))) (int);	Establish a signal-handling function for sig, pointed to by func.
int raise(int sig);	Force the signal sig.

#include <stdio.h>

Table C.6. Standard input/output functions.

Function Prototype	Description
int remove(const char *filename);	Remove the physical file filename.
int rename(const char *old, const char *new);	Rename the physical file old with the name new.
FILE *tmpfile(void);	Create a temporary file.
char *tmpnam(char *s);	Create a temporary filename.
int fclose(FILE *stream);	Close the stream.

Function Prototype	Description
`int fflush(FILE *stream );`	Flush the buffers for *stream*.
`FILE *fopen( const char *filename, const char *mode );`	Open the stream for *filename* with *mode*.
`FILE *freopen( const char *filename, const char *mode, FILE *stream );`	Reopen the stream for *filename*.
`void setbuf( FILE *stream, char *buf );`	Equivalent to `setvbuf()` with arguments of `_IOFBF` and `BUFSIZE`; or with `_IONBF` of *buf* == NULL. For many but not all compilers, you can turn line buffering off for `stdin` using the second call configuration.
`int setvbuf( FILE *stream, char *buf, int mode, size_t size );`	Set the buffer for stream to *size* bytes, located by *buf*, using *mode* (`_IONBF,_IOLBF, IOFBF`).
`int fprintf( FILE *stream, const char *format, ... );`	Convert the arguments specified in the variable argument list (variadic list) according to the conversion string *format* and send the text to *stream*.
`int fscanf( FILE *stream, const char *format, ... );`	Retrieve successive text tokens from *stream*, convert them according to the conversion string *format*, and place the results in successive arguments from the variable list.
`int printf( const char *format, ... );`	See `fprintf()`; output is to `stdout`.
`int scanf( const char *format, ... );`	See `fscanf()`; input is from `stdin`.
`int sprintf( char *s, const char *format, ... );`	See `fprintf()`; output is to string *s*.
`int sscanf( const char *s, const char *format, ... );`	See `fscanf()`; input is from string *s*.
`int vfprintf( FILE *stream, const char *format, va_list argptr );`	See `fprintf()`; the last argument is an argument pointer, *argptr*.
`int vprintf( const char *format, va_list arg );`	See `vfprintf()`; output is to `stdout`.

continues

Table C.6.   Continued

Function Prototype	Description
`int vsprintf( char *s, const char *format, va_list arg );`	See `vfprintf()`; output is to string `s`.
`int fgetc( FILE *stream );`	Get a character from `stream`.
`char *fgets( char *s, int n, FILE *stream );`	Get a string from `stream`, at most n–1 characters, including the newline character.
`int fputc( int c, FILE *stream );`	Put a character to `stream`.
`int fputs( const char *s, FILE *stream );`	Put a string to `stream`.
`int getc( FILE *stream );`	Get a character from `stream`.
`int getchar( void );`	Get a character from `stdin`.
`char *gets( char *s );`	Get a string from `stdin`.
`int putc( int c, FILE *stream );`	Put a character to `stream`.
`int putchar( int c );`	Put a character to `stdout`.
`int puts( const char *s );`	Put a string to `stdout`; newline appended automatically.
`int ungetc( int c, FILE *stream );`	Push a character back onto `stream`.
`size_t fread( void *ptr, size_t size, size_t nmemb, FILE *stream );`	Direct read a block of data from `stream`.
`size_t fwrite( const void *ptr, size_t size, size_t nmemb, FILE *stream );`	Direct write a block of data to `stream`.
`int fgetpos( FILE *stream, fpos_t *pos );`	Get the current file position of `stream` and record information in `*pos`.
`int fseek( FILE *stream, long int offset, int whence );`	Set the new file position for `stream` a number of bytes `offset` from location `whence` (SEEK_SET, SEEK_CUR, SEEK_END).
`int fsetpos( FILE *stream, const fpos_t *pos );`	Set the new file position for `stream` based on the information recorded in `*pos`.

Function Prototype	Description
`long int ftell( FILE *stream );`	Report the current file position as a `long` integer.
`void rewind( FILE *stream );`	Set the current file position to the beginning of the file.
`void clearerr( FILE *stream );`	Clear end-of-file and error conditions for *stream*.
`int feof( FILE *stream );`	Test for end-of-file on *stream*.
`int ferror( FILE *stream );`	Test for error indicator on *stream*.
`void perror( const char *s );`	Convert `errno` to a text message and add it to your message in string *s*. Display it on `stderr`.

#include <stdlib.h>

Table C.7. Miscellaneous control and conversion functions.

Function Prototype	Description
`double atof( const char *nptr );`	Convert the text token in *nptr* to a double float.
`int atoi( const char *nptr );`	Convert the text token in *nprt* to an `int`.
`long int atol( const char *nptr );`	Convert the text token in *nptr* to a `long`.
`double strtod( const char *nptr, char **endptr );`	Convert the initial segment of the string *nptr* to a double. Skips whitespace and reports errors.
`long int strtol( const char *nptr, char **endptr, int base );`	Convert the initial segment of string *nptr* to a long. Skips whitespace and reports errors.
`unsigned long int strtoul( const char *nptr, char **endptr, int base );`	Convert the initial segment of string *nptr* to an unsigned `long`. Skips whitespace and reports errors.

continues

Table C.7. Continued

Function Prototype	Description
`int rand( void );`	Generate a pseudorandom number.
`void srand( unsigned int seed );`	Initialize the pseudorandom number generator using the seed value *seed*.
`void *calloc( size_t nmemb, size_t size );`	Allocate *nmemb* contiguous blocks of memory each *size* bytes long, from the heap. The whole area is initialized to nulls.
`void free( void *ptr );`	Release memory acquired by `calloc()`, `malloc()`, or `realloc()`.
`void *malloc( size_t size );`	Allocate a contiguous area of memory from the heap *size* bytes long.
`void *realloc( void *ptr, size_t size );`	Resize the area pointed to by *ptr* to *size* bytes. If *ptr* is NULL, `realloc()` acquires new area.
`void abort( void );`	Terminate the program abnormally—immediately.
`int atexit( void ( *func ) ( void ) );`	Register functions to be executed just before normal program termination.
`void exit( int status );`	Terminate the program normally, reporting execution condition *status*. If any functions have been registered by `atexit()`, they are executed first, in LIFO (last in, first out) order.
`char *getenv( const char *name );`	Get the system environment variable identified by the contents of string *name*.
`int system( const char *string );`	Invoke the system command processor (shell), passing command-line arguments in *string*.

Function Prototype	Description
`void *bsearch( const void *key, const void *base, size_t nmemb, size_t size, int ( *compar ) ( const void *, const void * ));`	Search an array of `nmemb` objects, the first of which is pointed to by *base*, for a member that contains the value pointed to by *key*. Use the comparison function pointed to by *compar*.
`void qsort( void *base, size_t nmemb, int abs( int j );`	See bsearch() for argument logistics; Quicksort the array. Compute the absolute value of *j*.
`div_t div( int numer, int denom );`	Compute the remainder of *numer* and *denom* and return them in an object with type `div_t`.
`long int labs( long int j );`	Compute the `long` absolute value of *j*.
`ldiv_t ldiv(long int numer, long int denom );`	See div(); except types are `long`.
`int mblen( const char *s, size_t n );`	Compute the number of bytes in the multibyte characters. Does not affect the shift state.
`int mbtowc( wchar_t *pwc, const char *s, size_t n );`	Convert the multibyte character in *s* to a wide character code if possible and store it in *pwc*.
`int wctomb( char *s, wchar_t wchar );`	The reverse of mbtowc().
`size_t mbstowcs( wchar_t *pwcs, const char *s, size_t n );`	Convert a multibyte string to a wide character string.
`size_t wcstombs( char *s, const wchar_t *pwcs, size_t n );`	The reverse of mbstowcs().

The ato...() and stro...() functions do not report errors.

#include **<string.h>**

Table C.8. String-manipulation functions.

Prototype	Description
`void *memcpy( void *s1, const void *s2, size_t n );`	Always copy *n* bytes from *s2* to *s1*; overlapped operands are not accounted for.
`void *memmove( void *s1, const void *s2, size_t n );`	Always copy *n* bytes from *s2* to *s1*; overlapped operands are handled correctly.
`char *strcpy( char *s1, const char *s2 );`	Copy string *s2* to *s1*, including null terminator.
`char *strncpy( char *s1, const char *s2, size_t n );`	Copy *at most n* characters from *s2* to *s1*.
`char *strcat( char *s1, const char *s2 );`	Concatenate string *s2* on the end of *s1*; handle the null terminator characters accordingly.
`char *strncat( char *s1, const char *s2, size_t n);`	Same as `strcat()`, but processes at most *n* characters.
`int memcmp( const void *s1, const void *s2, size_t n );`	Compare n characters in the character arrays *s1* and *s2*; these may be strings but a null terminator does not stop the comparison.
`int strcmp( const char *s1, const char *s2 );`	Compare the two strings *s1* and *s2*. A null terminator character stops the comparison.
`int strcoll( const char *s1, const char *s2 );`	Works like `strcmp()`, but the comparison is controlled by the current locale.
`int strncmp( const char *s1, const char *s2, size_t n ); char *s2 );`	Works like `strcmp()`, but compares *at most n* characters.
`size_t strxfrm( char *s1, const char *s2, size_t n );`	Transform *s2* according to the current locale and copy at most *n* transformed characters to *s1*.
`void *memchr( const void *s, int c, size_t n );`	Set *n* bytes, pointed to by *s*, to the value of *c*.

Prototype	Description
`char *strchr( const char *s, int c );`	Find the first occurrence of a character in a string.
`size_t strcspn( const char *s1, const char *s2 );`	Compute the length of the initial segment of s1, which consists entirely of characters *not* found in s2.
`char *strpbrk( const char *s1, const char *s2 );`	Point to the first occurrence in s1 of any character that is in s2.
`char *strrchr( const *s, int *c );`	Search s in reverse for the first occurrence of c.
`size_t strspn( const char *s1, const char *s2 );`	Compute the length of the initial segment of s1, which *consists entirely* of characters found in s2. The order of characters in s2 does not matter.
`char *strstr( const char *s1, const char *s2 );`	Locate the string s2 in s1; point to that substring in s1.
`char *strtok( char *s1, const char *s2 );`	Extract the next text token from s1. The token is delimited by the characters in s2, which may vary from call to call, even when scanning the same target string.
`void *memset( void *s, int c, size_t n );`	Initialize every byte of n bytes pointed to by s with the value of c.
`char *strerror( int errnum );`	Generate a text message based on *errnum*.
`bsize_t strlen( const char *s );`	Compute the length of the string s. The length reported does *not* include the null terminator character, but it *is* a 1-origin *count, not* the 0-origin subscript of the last character in the string.

#include <time.h>

Table C.9. Date, time, and clock functions.

Function Prototype	Description
`clock_t clock( void );`	Compute the amount of processor time used by the program.
`double difftime( time_t time1, time_t time0 );`	Compute the difference between the *ending time time1* and *beginning time time0* and report as a double.
`time_t mktime( strict tm *timeptr );`	Convert the broken-down time in the structure pointed to by *timeptr* into a calendar time with type `time_t`.
`time_t time( time_t *timer );`	Compute the best approximation to the implementation's calendar time. Return it as `time_t`-1, and store it in `*timer`, if that pointer is not null.
`char *asctime( const strict tm *timeptr );`	Convert the broken-down time into a string.
`char *ctime( const time_t *timer );`	Convert the calendar time into a string.
`strict tm *gmtime( const time_t *timer );`	Convert a calendar time to Coordinated Universal Time (UTC has replaced GMT), in broken-down format.
`strict tm *localtime( const time_t *timer );`	Convert the local calendar time to local broken-down time.
`size_t strftime( char *s, size_t maxsize, const char *format, const strict tm *timeptr );`	This function works something like `sprintf()`. It converts a calendar time pointed to by *timeptr* into a string, pointed to by *s*, under control of a format string *format*. `strftime()` format strings have conversion specifiers that are similar in appearance to, but different in content from, `printf()` conversion specifiers.

The FINANCE.C Program

When you first look at the FINANCE.C program, it may seem long and complex. It is fairly long, but surprisingly simple. All the I/O is accomplished with either the simple or formatted I/O library functions introduced in Chapter 2.

The only real sophistication in the program is in the time-value-of-money formulas implemented here, and those you can take at face value. They work, but the mathematical derivation is a little more involved than space here allows.

The point of the program is to demonstrate what can be done with simple I/O. This is done through the vehicle of a series of financial calculations that are of interest to anyone who likes money, owns a home, or both. FINANCE.C can calculate percent change and markup, equivalent interest rates for periodic and continuous compounding methods, savings strategies, and complete mortgage-amortization information. Listing D.1 contains the source code for FINANCE.C.

Listing D.1. FINANCE.C—Financial calculations (with Borland C++).

```
1   #include <stdlib.h>
2   #include <stdio.h>
3   #include <io.h>
4   #include <conio.h>
5   #include <math.h>
6
```

continues

Listing D.1. Continued

```
7   #define FALSE 0
8   #define TRUE 1
9
10  char usermsg[160] =
11        "      Use the Up and Down ARROW keys to move the "
12        "bullet beside the item\n"
13        "\t\t  to select. Then press Enter." ;
14
15  int rc,endjob;
16  double amtmort,levelpay,payno,prinpay,intpay;
17  double apr,freq,numpay,bal;
18
19  /* +--------------------------------------------------+
20     +          S E R V I C E   R O U T I N E S
21     +--------------------------------------------------+
22  */
23
24  int wait_key()
25  {
26    int ch;
27    ch = getch();
28    if ( ch == 27 ) return( 255 ); else return( 0 );
29  }
30
31
32  /* +--------------------------------------------------+
33     +   SINGLE PAYMENT FUTURE VALUE. Future value of a
34     +   single $1.00 payment.
35     +--------------------------------------------------+
36  */
37
38  double SPFV( double apr, double freq, double periods )
39  {
40    return( pow(1.0+(apr/freq)/100.0,periods) );
41  }
42
43  /* +--------------------------------------------------+
44     +   SINGLE PAYMENT PRESENT VALUE. Present value of a
45     +   single $1.00 payment.
46     +--------------------------------------------------+
47  */
```

```
48
49   double SPPV( double apr, double freq, double periods )
50   {
51     return( 1.0 / SPFV(apr,freq,periods) );
52   }
53
54   /* +--------------------------------------------------+
55      + UNIFORM SERIES PRESENT VALUE. Present value of a
56      + $1.00 annuity.
57      +--------------------------------------------------+
58   */
59
60   double USPV( double apr, double freq, double periods )
61   {
62     return( ( 1.0 - 1.0
63              / SPFV(apr,freq,periods))
64              / (apr/freq/100.0) );
65   }
66
67   /* +--------------------------------------------------+
68      +  UNIFORM SERIES FUTURE VALUE. Future value of a
69      +  $1.00 annuity.
70      +--------------------------------------------------+
71   */
72
73   double USFV( double apr, double freq, double periods )
74   {
75     return(( SPFV(apr,freq,periods)- 1.0) / (apr/freq/100.0));
76   }
77
78   /* +--------------------------------------------------+
79      +  BULLET controls the "bullet" (caret-cursor) for
80      +  all menus. The VARIABLE parameter RC returns the
81      +  relative item number, numbering from 1, that the
82      +  bullet was positioned next to at exit. The
83      +  VALUE parameters are used as follows:
84      +
85      +  XCOL    :The x-position for bullet
86      +  LINE1   :Top y-position in Turbo Coordinates
87      +  LINE2   :Bottom y-position
88      +--------------------------------------------------+
89   */
```

continues

Listing D.1. Continued

```
90
91   int bullet( int xcol, int line1, int line2 )
92   {
93     char ch;
94     int  fine;
95
96     fine=FALSE;
97     gotoxy(xcol,line1); printf( "%c",0x10 );
98     while ( !fine ) {
99       ch = getch(); if ( ch == 0 ) ch = getch();
100      switch (ch) {
101        case 13:  fine=TRUE; break;
102        case 72:  gotoxy(xcol,wherey()); printf( " " );
103             if ( wherey()==line1 ) gotoxy(xcol,line2);
104               else gotoxy(xcol,wherey()-1);
105             printf( "%c",0x10 ); break;
106        case 80:  gotoxy(xcol,wherey()); printf( " " );
107             if ( wherey()==line2 ) gotoxy(xcol,line1);
108               else gotoxy(xcol,wherey()+1);
109             printf( "%c",0x10 ); break;
110      }
111    }
112    return( wherey()-line1+1 );
113  }
114
115  /* +-------------------------------------------------+
116     +      C A L C U L A T I O N   R O U T I N E S
117     +-------------------------------------------------+
118  */
119
120  void calc_SPPV()
121  {
122    double amount,apr,freq,periods;
123
124    clrscr();
125    puts(
126      "Finance/PC                                        "
127      "Present Value of an Amount");
128    gotoxy(1,6);
129    puts("PV of What Amount?: ");
```

```
130    puts("Annual Percentage Rate: ");
131    puts("Number of Payments Per Year: ");
132    puts("Number of Years: ");
133    gotoxy(32,6); scanf("%lf",&amount);
134    gotoxy(32,7); scanf("%lf",&apr);
135    gotoxy(32,8); scanf("%lf",&freq);
136    gotoxy(32,9); scanf("%lf",&periods);
137    periods *= freq;
138    printf("Present Value = %12.2f",
139      (amount*SPPV(apr,freq,periods)) );
140    wait_key();
141  }
142
143  void calc_SPFV()
144  {
145    double amount,apr,freq,periods;
146
147    clrscr();
148    puts(
149      "Finance/PC                                    "
150      "Future Value of an Amount");
151    gotoxy(1,6);
152    puts("FV of What Amount?: ");
153    puts("Annual Percentage Rate: ");
154    puts("Number of Payments Per Year: ");
155    puts("Number of Years: ");
156    gotoxy(32,6); scanf("%lf",&amount);
157    gotoxy(32,7); scanf("%lf",&apr);
158    gotoxy(32,8); scanf("%lf",&freq);
159    gotoxy(32,9); scanf("%lf",&periods);
160    periods *= freq;
161    puts( "\n");
162    printf("Future Value = %12.2f",
163      (amount*SPFV(apr,freq,periods)) );
164    wait_key();
165  }
166
167  void calc_USPV()
168  {
169    double amount,apr,freq,periods ;
170
171    clrscr();
```

continues

Listing D.1. Continued

```
172   puts(
173     "Finance/PC
174     "Present Value of an Annuity");
175   gotoxy(1,6);
176   puts("Regular Payment Amount: ");
177   puts("Annual Percentage Rate: ");
178   puts("Number of Payments Per Year: ");
179   puts("Number of Years: ");
180   gotoxy(32,6); scanf("%lf",&amount);
181   gotoxy(32,7); scanf("%lf",&apr);
182   gotoxy(32,8); scanf("%lf",&freq);
183   gotoxy(32,9); scanf("%lf",&periods);
184   periods *= freq;
185   printf("Present Value of Annuity = %12.2f",
186     (amount*USPV(apr,freq,periods)) );
187   wait_key();
188 }
189
190 void calc_USFV()
191 {
192   double amount,apr,freq,periods ;
193
194   clrscr();
195   puts(
196     "Finance/PC
197     "Future Value of an Annuity");
198   gotoxy(1,6);
199   puts("Regular Payment Amount: ");
200   puts("Annual Percentage Rate: ");
201   puts("Number of Payments Per Year: ");
202   puts("Number of Years: ");
203   gotoxy(32,6); scanf("%lf",&amount);
204   gotoxy(32,7); scanf("%lf",&apr);
205   gotoxy(32,8); scanf("%lf",&freq);
206   gotoxy(32,9); scanf("%lf",&periods);
207   periods *= freq;
208   printf("Future Value of Annuity = %12.2f",
209     (amount*USFV(apr,freq,periods)) );
210   wait_key();
211 }
```

```
212
213   void calc_eff_period()
214   {
215     double apr,periods;
216     clrscr();
217     puts(
218       "Finance/PC                           "
219       "Effective Interest, Periodic Compounding");
220     gotoxy(1,6);
221     puts("Annual Percentage Rate: ");
222     puts("Number of Compounding Periods: ");
223     gotoxy(32,6); scanf("%lf",&apr);
224     gotoxy(32,7); scanf("%lf",&periods);
225     printf("Effective Rate, Periodic Compounding = %12.2f",
226       (pow(1.0+apr/(100.0*periods),periods)-1)*100.0 );
227     wait_key();
228   }
229
230   void calc_eff_contin()
231   {
232     double apr ;
233
234     clrscr();
235     puts(
236       "Finance/PC                      "
237       "Effective Interest, Continuous Compounding");
238     gotoxy(1,6);
239     puts("Annual Percentage Rate: ");
240     gotoxy(32,6); scanf("%lf",&apr);
241     printf("Effective Rate, Continuous Compounding = %12.2f",
242       (exp(apr/100.0)-1)*100.0 );
243     wait_key();
244   }
245
246   void get_mortgage_data()
247   {
248     char scratch[12];
249
250     clrscr();
251     puts(
252       "Finance/PC                                  "
253       "  Input Mortgage Data");
```

continues

Listing D.1. Continued

```
254     gotoxy(1,6);
255     puts("Mortgage Amount: ");
256     puts("Annual Percentage Rate: ");
257     puts("Number of Payments Per Year: ");
258     puts("Number of Years: ");
259     puts("Detail of Payment # ");
260
261     gotoxy(50,6); printf("(%12.2f)\n",amtmort);
262     gotoxy(50,7); printf("(%12.2f)\n",apr);
263     gotoxy(50,8); printf("(%12.2f)\n",freq);
264     gotoxy(50,9); printf("(%12.0f)\n",numpay/12);
265     gotoxy(50,10); printf("(%12.0f)\n",payno);
266
267     gotoxy(32,6); scanf("%lf",&amtmort);
268     gotoxy(32,7); scanf("%lf",&apr);
269     gotoxy(32,8); scanf("%lf",&freq);
270     gotoxy(32,9); scanf("%lf",&numpay); numpay *= freq;
271     gotoxy(32,10); scanf("%lf",&payno);
272
273     if ( payno>numpay ) payno=1;
274     puts("Calculating Amortization Constants.");
275     levelpay=1/USPV(apr,freq,numpay)*amtmort;
276     intpay=levelpay * USPV(apr,freq,numpay-payno+1.0)
277         * (apr/freq/100);
278     prinpay=levelpay-intpay;
279   }
280
281   void display_payout()
282   {
283     clrscr();
284     puts(
285       "Finance/PC
286       "  Amortization Payout");
287     gotoxy(1,6);
288     puts("Mortgage Amount: ");
289     puts("Annual Percentage Rate: ");
290     puts("Number of Payments Per Year: ");
291     puts("Number of Years: ");
292     gotoxy(32,6); printf("%12.2f",amtmort);
293     gotoxy(32,7); printf("%12.2f",apr);
```

```
294    gotoxy(32,8); printf("%12.0f",freq);
295    gotoxy(32,9); printf("%12.0f\n",numpay/freq);
296    puts("=============================================");
297    gotoxy(1,12);
298    puts("Level Payment: ");
299    puts("Total Payout: ");
300    puts("Total Interest Paid: ");
301    puts("Payment # ");
302    puts("  Principal Amt: ");
303    puts("  Interest  Amt: ");
304    gotoxy(32,12); printf("%12.2f",levelpay);
305    gotoxy(32,13); printf("%12.2f",levelpay*numpay);
306    gotoxy(32,14); printf("%12.2f",levelpay*numpay-amtmort);
307    gotoxy(32,15); printf("%12.0f",payno);
308    gotoxy(32,16); printf("%12.2f",prinpay);
309    gotoxy(32,17); printf("%12.2f",intpay);
310    wait_key();
311  }
312
313  void display_12tab()
314  {
315    char ch;
316
317    rc = TRUE;
318    gotoxy(1,6);
319    puts("     Paymnt #    Pay Amt       "
320      "Interest   Principal     Balance     ");
321    puts("=============================="
322      "==============================");
323    while ( payno<numpay ) {
324      payno=payno+1;
325      intpay=levelpay * USPV(apr,freq,numpay-payno+1.0)
326          * (apr/freq/100);
327      prinpay=levelpay-intpay;
328      bal=levelpay*USPV(apr,freq,numpay-payno);
329      if ( bal<0 ) bal=0;
330      printf( "%12.0f%12.2f%12.2f%12.2f%12.2f\n",
331          payno,levelpay,intpay,prinpay,bal
332        );
333      if ( ((int)payno % 12) == 0 ) return;
334      if ( kbhit() ) {
335        ch = getch(); if ( ch == 0 ) ch = getch();
```

continues

Listing D.1. Continued

```
336        rc=FALSE; return;
337      }
338    }
339  }
340
341  void print_48tab()
342  {
343    char ch;
344    char pline[81];
345
346    rc = TRUE;
347    sprintf(pline,"\n");
348    write( 4,pline,(unsigned)strlen(pline) );
349    sprintf(pline,"     Paymnt #     Pay Amt        "
350      "Interest    Principal     Balance    \n");
351    write( 4,pline,(unsigned)strlen(pline) );
352    sprintf(pline,"=============================="
353      "==================================\n");
354    write( 4,pline,(unsigned)strlen(pline) );
355    while ( payno<numpay )
356      {
357      payno=payno+1;
358      intpay=levelpay * USPV(apr,freq,numpay-payno+1.0)
359        * (apr/freq/100);
360      prinpay=levelpay-intpay;
361      bal=levelpay*USPV(apr,freq,numpay-payno);
362      if ( bal<0 ) bal=0;
363      sprintf( pline, "%12.0f%12.2f%12.2f%12.2f%12.2f\n",
364          payno,levelpay,intpay,prinpay,bal
365        );
366      write( 4,pline,(unsigned)strlen(pline) );
367      if ( ((int)payno % 48 ) == 0 ) return;
368      if ( kbhit() ) {
369        ch = getch(); if ( ch == 0 ) ch = getch();
370        rc=FALSE; return;
371      }
372    }
373  }
374
375  void display_table()
```

```
376  {
377    payno=payno-1;
378    if ( payno<0 ) payno=0;
379    if ( payno>numpay-1 ) payno=numpay-1;
380    bal=amtmort;
381    while ( payno < numpay) {
382      clrscr();
383      puts(
384        "Finance/PC                                       "
385        "Amortization Schedule");
386      printf(
387       "Amortizing %12.2f at %5.2f %% for %5.2f years.\n",
388        amtmort,apr,numpay/freq );
389      display_12tab();
390      if ( !rc ) return;
391      if ( wait_key() ) return;
392    }
393  }
394
395  void print_table()
396  {
397    char pline[81];
398
399    payno = 1;
400    bal=amtmort;
401    while ( payno < numpay ) {
402      *pline = '\0';
403      sprintf(pline,
404        "Finance/PC                                       "
405        "Amortization Schedule\n");
406      write( 4,pline,(unsigned)strlen(pline) );
407      sprintf(pline,"\n");
408      write( 4,pline,(unsigned)strlen(pline) );
409      sprintf(pline,
410        "Amortizing %12.2f at %5.2f %% for %5.2f years.\n",
411        amtmort,apr,numpay/freq );
412      write( 4,pline,(unsigned)strlen(pline) );
413      print_48tab();
414      if ( !rc ) return;
415      fprintf(stdout,"%c",12);
416    }
417  }
```

continues

Listing D.1. Continued

```
418
419  void calc_percent_change()
420  {
421    double oamt,namt ;
422
423    clrscr();
424    puts(
425      "Finance/PC                                    "
426      "Calculate Percent Change");
427    gotoxy(1,6);
428    puts("Old Amount: ");
429    puts("New Amount: ");
430    gotoxy(32,6); scanf("%lf",&oamt);
431    gotoxy(32,7); scanf("%lf",&namt);
432    printf("Percent Change = %12.2f%%\n",
433      ((namt-oamt)/oamt)*100.0 );
434    wait_key();
435  }
436
437  void calc_percent_total()
438  {
439    double part,total ;
440
441    clrscr();
442    puts(
443      "Finance/PC                                    "
444      "Calculate Percent of Total");
445    gotoxy(1,6);
446    puts("Partial Amount: ");
447    puts("Total Amount: ");
448    gotoxy(32,6); scanf("%lf",&part);
449    gotoxy(32,7); scanf("%lf",&total);
450    printf("Percent of Total = %12.2f%%\n",
451      (part/total)*100.0 );
452    wait_key();
453  }
454
455  void calc_markup_cost()
456  {
457    double price,cost ;
```

```
458
459    clrscr();
460    puts(
461      "Finance/PC                              "
462      "Calculate Markup as Percent of Cost");
463    gotoxy(1,6);
464    puts("Price of Item: ");
465    puts("Cost of Item: ");
466    gotoxy(32,6); scanf("%lf",&price);
467    gotoxy(32,7); scanf("%lf",&cost);
468    printf("Markup %% of Cost = %12.2f%%\n",
469      ((price-cost)/cost)*100.0 );
470    wait_key();
471  }
472
473  void calc_markup_price()
474  {
475    double price,cost ;
476
477    clrscr();
478    puts(
479      "Finance/PC                              "
480      "Calculate Markup as Percent of Price");
481    gotoxy(1,6);
482    puts("Price of Item: ");
483    puts("Cost of Item: ");
484    gotoxy(32,6); scanf("%lf",&price);
485    gotoxy(32,7); scanf("%lf",&cost);
486    printf("Markup %% of Price = %12.2f %%\n",
487      ((price-cost)/price)*100.0 );
488    wait_key();
489  }
490
491  /* +----------------------------------------------------+
492     +              F U N C T I O N   M E N U S
493     +----------------------------------------------------+
494  */
495
496  void menu_GENBUS()
497  {
498    while ( !endjob ) {
499      clrscr();
```

continues

Listing D.1. Continued

```
500        printf("%55s\n","Finance/PC General Business Menu");
501        gotoxy(1,8);
502        puts(
503          "\t\t\t   Percent (%) Change\n"
504          "\t\t\t   Percent (%) of Total\n"
505          "\t\t\t   Markup as Percent (%) of Cost\n"
506          "\t\t\t   Markup as Percent (%) of Price\n"
507          "\t\t\t   QUIT THIS MENU\n\n" );
508        puts( usermsg );
509        switch ( bullet( 26,8,12 ) ) {
510          case 1: calc_percent_change(); break;
511          case 2: calc_percent_total(); break;
512          case 3: calc_markup_cost(); break;
513          case 4: calc_markup_price(); break;
514          case 5: return;
515        }
516    }
517 }
518
519 void menu_INTEREST()
520 {
521    while ( !endjob ) {
522      clrscr();
523 printf("%60s\n","Finance/PC Interest Rate Conversion Menu");
524      gotoxy(1,8);
525      puts(
526        "\t\t\t   Effective Rate, Periodic Compounding\n"
527        "\t\t\t   Effective Rate, Continuous Compounding\n"
528        "\t\t\t   QUIT THIS MENU\n\n" );
529      puts( usermsg );
530      switch ( bullet( 26,8,10 ) ) {
531        case 1: calc_eff_period(); break;
532        case 2: calc_eff_contin(); break;
533        case 3: return;
534      }
535    }
536 }
537
538 void menu_AMORTIZE()
539 {
```

```
540    while ( !endjob ) {
541      clrscr();
542      printf("%53s\n","Finance/PC Amortization Data");
543      gotoxy(1,8);
544      puts(
545        "\t\t\t   INPUT Basic Data Items\n"
546        "\t\t\t   Display Payment/Payout Data\n"
547        "\t\t\t   Display Amortization Table\n"
548        "\t\t\t   Print Amortization Table\n"
549        "\t\t\t   QUIT THIS MENU\n\n" );
550      puts( usermsg );
551      switch ( bullet( 26,8,12 ) ) {
552        case 1: get_mortgage_data(); break;
553        case 2: if ( amtmort>0 ) display_payout(); break;
554        case 3: if ( amtmort>0 ) display_table(); break;
555        case 4: if ( amtmort>0 ) print_table(); break;
556        case 5: return;
557      }
558    }
559  }
560
561  void menu_ACTUARIAL()
562  {
563    while ( !endjob ) {
564      clrscr();
565      printf("%53s\n","Finance/PC Time Value of Money");
566      gotoxy(1,8);
567      puts(
568        "\t\t\t   Future Value of an Amount\n"
569        "\t\t\t   Present Value of an Amount\n"
570        "\t\t\t   Future Value of a Regular Annuity\n"
571        "\t\t\t   Present Value of a Regular Annuity\n"
572        "\t\t\t   QUIT THIS MENU\n\n" );
573      puts( usermsg );
574      switch ( bullet( 26,8,12 ) ) {
575        case 1: calc_SPFV(); break;
576        case 2: calc_SPPV(); break;
577        case 3: calc_USFV(); break;
578        case 4: calc_USPV(); break;
579        case 5: return;
580      }
581    }
```

continues

Listing D.1. Continued

```
582    }
583
584    void menu_0() /* MASTER MENU (0) */
585    {
586      while ( !endjob ) {
587        clrscr();
588        printf("%48s\n","Finance/PC Master Menu");
589        gotoxy(1,8);
590        puts(
591          "\t\t\t   General Business\n"
592          "\t\t\t   Interest Rate Conversions\n"
593          "\t\t\t   Time Value of Money\n"
594          "\t\t\t   Amortization\n"
595          "\t\t\t   QUIT FINANCE/PC\n\n" );
596        puts( usermsg );
597        switch ( bullet( 26,8,12 ) ) {
598          case 1: menu_GENBUS(); break;
599          case 2: menu_INTEREST(); break;
600          case 3: menu_ACTUARIAL(); break;
601          case 4: menu_AMORTIZE(); break;
602          case 5: return;
603        }
604      }
605    }
606
607    main()
608    {
609      amtmort = 0; levelpay = 0; payno = 1; prinpay = 0;
610      intpay = 0; apr = 0; freq = 0; numpay = 0;
611      textbackground(BLUE); textcolor(LIGHTGRAY);
612      clrscr(); endjob = FALSE; menu_0(); clrscr();
613    }
```

Program Structure and Operation

FINANCE.C presents the user with a hierarchy of menus, as shown in Figure D.1. The menus are built in a simple way, and items are selected from them under control of the bullet() function (lines 91–113 of Listing D.1). bullet() moves the bullet cursor up and down the menu in response to input from the arrow keys.

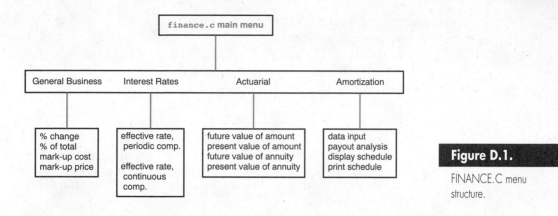

Figure D.1.

FINANCE.C menu structure.

It is up to the calling function to place the menu items on the screen in the correct location and invoke bullet(), passing to it as parameters the top and bottom line numbers of the menu, and the horizontal coordinate (or just *x value*) for the bullet character. This character is a decimal 16 (0x10), which appears on the screen as a right-pointing triangle.

bullet() uses two Borland C++ functions that are extensions to the ANSI standard library and that may not be found in every compiler. The first of these, gotoxy(int x, int y), moves the display cursor to a new location.

The other function is getch(), which receives a single keystroke from the keyboard, waiting for it if necessary, *without* echoing the character to the screen. Its use in line 99 shows a way to handle IBM's extended ASCII character and scan codes (which the arrow keys produce).

IBM PCs and compatibles send back not one, but two bytes of data for every key pressed—a *character code* and a *scan code*. If the keystroke was for an ordinary ASCII character, the character codes and scan codes are the same. But if it was for a key that produces an extended ASCII code, the character code is zero, and the scan code identifies the key that was pressed. For example, the up-arrow key produces an extended ASCII code with scan code 72 decimal; and the down-arrow key, an 80. You can see in line 99 how the if and second getch() capture an extended ASCII scan code.

The switch statement in lines 100–110 handles the logic of moving the bullet up and down the menu items. This code allows the bullet to "wrap" from top to bottom and from bottom to top of the menu list. Line 112 finally computes an integer indicating which item was selected when the Enter key (character code 13 decimal) was pressed. It does this by computing the distance from the bullet's current location to the first line of the menu list.

The menu item number must now be processed by the calling routine's logic to determine what to do. This can be handled by another switch statement. If the call to bullet() was placed as the switch expression to evaluate, very clean, readable code results, as illustrated by the following excerpt from menu_0(), the master menu driver:

```
switch ( bullet( 26,8,12 ) ) {
  case 1: menu_GENBUS(); break;
  case 2: menu_INTEREST(); break;
  case 3: menu_ACTUARIAL(); break;
  case 4: menu_AMORTIZE(); break;
  case 5: return;
}
```

For each `case` statement in the `switch`, another menu-driver routine is invoked. At the lowest level of the menu structure, of course, the calculation routines are invoked. For all of its apparent complexity, this just about exhausts the tricky code in FINANCE.C. All that remains is to understand what the calculations actually accomplish.

Using FINANCE.C Computations

The main menu of FINANCE.C presents the user with four classes of computations that can be performed. These are general business functions, interest rate conversions, actuarial or time-value-of-money calculations, and mortgage analysis and amortization. The functions supported by each of these classes is discussed in turn.

General Business Functions

This group contains the simplest functions in the program. They calculate simple ratios and percentages of interest to the business person.

- `calc_percent_change()`

  This calculates the percent change from one amount to another.

- `calc_percent_total()`

  This calculates the ratio of two amounts as a percentage.

- `calc_markup_cost()`

  The user inputs the price and cost of an item. The markup is computed as a percentage of wholesale cost.

- `calc_markup_price()`

  The user inputs the price and cost of an item. The markup is computed as a percentage of retail price.

Interest-Rate Conversion

Effective interest-rate conversions are based on the fundamental time-value-of-money formula:

```
Future value of 1 = ( 1 + r )ⁿ
```

Here r is the *periodic* interest rate (APR divided by the number of compounding periods per year) and n is the number of compounding periods for which money draws interest (for example, 12 per year). The Future value of 1 refers to the amount to which one dollar will grow over the computed period.

■ calc_eff_contin()

The user is asked to input only the APR (Annual Percentage Rate). The algorithm assumes that earnings *are* reinvested and computes an equivalent rate that would be required if they *were not*, but would still generate the same total income over time. No compounding frequency is needed as input because continuous compounding assumes that interest is earned continuously (such as with money market instruments). Interest on such accounts is usually *computed* on a daily basis, however. This sort of account earns more than one with periodic compounding.

■ calc_eff_period()

This function performs the same task as calc_eff_contin() except that compounding is assumed to be monthly, not daily. The user is prompted for the APR and the number of compounding periods (that is, the number of months the money will draw interest).

Time Value of Money

The time-value-of-money functions can be used to analyze your savings strategy. You can project what a regular savings plan will earn over the years; which lump-sum deposit will do the same work as a regular savings plan; or what a lump sum will grow to, given a rate and compounding frequency. When you understand these formulas, you can compute what you must do to reach a goal or how available funds will perform over time.

One of the terms is used here in an uncommon sense. An *annuity* in the present context is a series of equal and regular deposits you make into an account. These deposits are assumed to be made at the same frequency and time that interest is compounded for the account.

■ SPFV() *Single Payment Future Value*

Computes the final value of an account into which you deposit a lump sum of money, and does nothing else but wait.

■ USFV() *Uniform Series Future Value*

Computes the final value of an annuity. This is the function you use to analyze the outcome of a regular savings plan.

■ SPPV() *Single Payment Present Value*

Suppose that you know how much you want an account to be worth later, and that you want to know the required size of a lump sum to open the account in order to achieve that goal. This function computes that amount. Among other things, the user is prompted for "the number of payments per year." In this function, that refers to the interest payments *received* per year.

■ USPV() *Uniform Series Present Value*

This function effectively computes the *input* to SPFV(). Given the parameters for a regular annuity (savings deposits), a lump-sum amount is computed that is equivalent to an initial lump-sum deposit and no additional deposits.

This is also the selection to use if you want to know what size loan you can afford to amortize. For example, suppose that you are in the fortunate position of being able to put $50,000.00 down on a house, and your budget can tolerate a $100.00 per month note. If the note is for 30 years, at 10 percent interest, the present value of an annuity function tells you that you can finance $11,395.08. Thus, you can afford a home costing $61,395.08.

Mortgage Analysis and Amortization

This group of functions should be useful to the home owner. You can generate an amortization schedule for your mortgage and either display or print it. You can also perform a payout analysis, which tells you just how badly the lender got to you.

■ get_mortgage_data()

Displays a formatted data-entry screen for mortgage details. Because scanf() is used in a primitive way, you *must* enter something in every field; failure to do so causes unpredictable behavior on the screen. You would come back to this screen later if you wanted to specify another particular payment number—unfortunately, you must reenter everything with it. Making this more flexible would be a good practice project. You must come to this screen at least once before selecting any of the other amortization screens or options.

■ `display_table()`

Displays the amortization schedule on the terminal, 12 payments at a time. Press Enter to get the next page; press Esc to leave the display and return to the menu. The first payment number displayed is the one entered in the data entry screen, or the one just after the last one previously displayed. The amortization schedule includes the payment number, the level payment amount, the amount of principal, and the amount of interest for each payment.

■ `print_table()`

Sends the entire amortization schedule to the system printer. This routine uses the nonstandard low-level `write()` function with a DOS handle to access the printer. As you may recall, you can also use `fprintf(stdprn,...)` to do this, although this, too, is nonstandard.

■ `display_payout()`

Do an analysis of the loan payout. Use the data entry screen first, being sure to indicate a specific payment for extra analysis. The output display includes the level payment required to amortize the loan, the total principal and total interest paid over the life of the loan, and details for the specific payment requested.

A payout analysis tells you some astounding things. For example, lenders do not like to make home loans for less than 30 years. For a typical home, with a 30-year mortgage, interest paid alone equals two to three times the entire value of the house, depending on the interest rate. Look at the following comparison, for instance:

Years	Interest Paid	Level Payment
30	107,962.88	438.79
20	65,802.60	482.51

If you can stand an extra $43.72 per month on your note, you can save yourself $42,160.28!

FINANCE.C demonstrates that some pretty amazing things can be done in C with just the basic I/O functions and a little patience. With this program, you can plan the impact of various savings strategies on your financial future, completely analyze and report mortgage loan data, and do a number of computations of value to business planning. We hope that you enjoy it and find it useful.

IBM PC Communications Programming

C COM.C, the program in Listing E.1, is a "dumb" terminal program. It doesn't support file transfer protocols, user commands, configuration changes, or any number of other things that would make it a full-blown communications package. It does provide built-in VT52 terminal emulation (at least enough to get formatted screens on CompuServe) and a limited command and scripting facility. Before you launch into the source listing for CCOM.C, some explanation of the program's purpose and construction is necessary.

The purpose of CCOM.C is to give you a skeleton program, with the most difficult parts already written, that you can use to build your own communications program with all the features you want. CCOM.C also amply illustrates what it costs you, the programmer, to write I/O support code without the benefit of the C function library (there are no library functions for communications I/O). The fact that this "dumb" program requires 436 lines of code is perhaps the best indication of what that cost is.

CCOM.C provides interrupt-driven I/O support for communications port COM1 on an IBM PC or a true compatible, running at 1200 baud, with 7 data bits, even parity, and 1 stop bit (written as 7E1). A 2K (2,048-byte) recirculating buffer, hold_buf, is used to hold incoming data bytes until the program is ready to deal with them.

Lines 18–36 in Listing E.1 provide #define macros for the character values of many of the ASCII-based communications control characters. Not all of them are used in CCOM.C, but many are provided for your future use.

The purpose and operation of the 18 functions, other than `main()`, in Listing E.1 are briefly described here:

- `void interrupt int_svc( void );`

  This is the interrupt-handler routine for COM1. When the interrupt controller chip raises IRQ4 (Interrupt Request 4), interrupt vector 12 is used to route control to the handler—this is set up by `hook_com()`, which is discussed next. `int_svc()` reads the byte from the communications port and places it in the recirculating buffer. Because the buffer has a wraparound design, any bytes "in the way" are overwritten and lost. Data loss can be controlled by limiting the amount of work the PC is allowed to do before fetching the next byte, and also by providing a large enough buffer. A 2K buffer is large enough for most purposes, even on slower machines.

  Because the interrupt triggering this function is a hardware interrupt, the interrupt condition must be cleared before leaving the function.

- `void hook_com( void );`

  `hook_com()` programs the 8259 interrupt controller chip to associate IRQ4 with interrupt vector 12. This is not an arbitrary choice. A close inspection of `hook_com()` shows that all the code does is *enable* IRQ4; it is assumed that the hardware is arranged so this corresponds to vector 12.

- `void unhook_com( void );`

  Disables interrupts before terminating the program.

- `void init_com( void );`

  This function does two things. First, it clears any pending hardware interrupts that may have been left by previous executions of the communications program. Don't tinker with this code unless you are an expert on PC hardware programming. Second, it programs the asynchronous communications chip, through I/O ports, for 1200 baud and 7E1 bit configuration.

- `void near send_comm_byte( void );`

  This function waits until the communications line is ready, and then sends the byte in `key_in`. This object usually contains the last input keystroke, but you could place anything you want in it, from any source, to implement a macro key facility.

  Notice that this and all the following functions have the `near` type qualifier. This is a PC-specific memory-model control keyword, not part of standard C. It is used to reduce the overhead of linkage to the functions, saving time and perhaps preventing the loss of incoming data traffic.

■ `void near get_comm_byte( void );`

Receives any number of bytes from the communications line and displays them on the screen. If parity is on (it is, by default, in this program), the high-order bit of the incoming byte may be on; it is set off by using bitwise AND in line 284.

■ `void near wait_for_tx( void );`

Waits for one byte only from the communications line. This function is used when an escape character has been detected in the incoming traffic stream, indicating that some special VT52 (the basis of CompuServe's Vidtex mode) screen-formatting characters are about to appear. Those characters must be waited for and processed separately.

■ `void near ch_out( unsigned char data );`

Displays a single character on the screen. A combination of Borland C's windowing capabilities and direct screen-RAM access are used for extremely high-speed display. This is pleasing to the user and also reduces the time not spent processing communications traffic (this may be much more important at higher baud rates).

■ `int near test_key( void );`

Uses the system BIOS services to determine whether a character from the keyboard is available. This function is called by the main() function to check on user keyboard input for transmission, and also by wait_for_tx(), where it is used to abort the wait for a received data byte.

Aborting a wait may be necessary if a transmission error occurred during the receipt of a VT52 formatting sequence. You generally are able to tell that something is wrong because your screen stops at what appears to be the wrong time. Press any key to break in and continue communications processing.

■ `unsigned char near get_key( void );`

Uses the system BIOS services to get the next keystroke from the keyboard.

■ `void near scroll_up( void );`

Scrolls the display window up one line, clearing the bottom line of the screen.

■ `void near vidtex( void );`

This function handles all the VT52 escape sequences. It is called by the ch_out() function, which has detected that formatting is needed, rather than display service (that is, it has received an ESC character to process). vidtex() waits for the next incoming data byte and positions or formats the display accordingly.

- ```
  void near vidtex_sba( void );
  ```

  Handles the special positioning request for a random placement of the screen cursor. The acronym sba means *set buffer address* and is borrowed from the IBM mainframe communications environment.

- ```
  void near overlay( char *string );
  ```

  overlay() is used only to place part of the banner line at the top of the screen with different color attributes. When overlay() encounters a blank in the argument string, it *does not* write a blank to the screen; it merely spaces over, assuming that another function—string_out()—has already put something on the screen. This is how the banner line is built with both red and black characters on a gray background.

- ```
  void near string_out( char *string );
  ```

  Displays the argument string on the screen. All characters are output exactly as received. It is assumed that the cursor has already been positioned to the place where output is to occur.

- ```
  void near kbd_command( void );
  ```

  When the Esc key is pressed, this function inputs a command from the user and routes it to the command handler, exe_command().

- ```
  int near exe_command( char *s );
  ```

  Interprets and executes the command in s. The command may be the run command, which invokes script processing. The script processor in turn calls exe_command()—these two functions are mutually recursive. Note that this means that a script may contain a run command to start an embedded script.

- ```
  int run_script( char *sname );
  ```

  Loads the script file sname into dynamically acquired memory and runs the script. A script may contain any valid command, plus the special verbs ifkey and goto. (Script processing is illustrated after Listing E.1 has been presented.)

Listing E.1. CCOM.C—Asynchronous communications program with VT52 support and scripting (using Borland C++).

```
1   /* +--------------------------------------------------+
2       + CCOM.C
3       +    Compile this program with the LARGE MEMORY MODEL.
4       +    If you do not, you receive warnings for suspicious
5       +    pointer conversion for the memcpy() function, and
6       +    the program may not function correctly.
7       +--------------------------------------------------+
```

```
 8   */
 9   #include <stdio.h>
10   #include <stdlib.h>
11   #include <string.h>
12   #include <mem.h>
13   #include <conio.h>
14   #include <ctype.h>
15   #include <dos.h>
16   #include <bios.h>
17
18   #define TRUE  1
19   #define FALSE 0
20   #define FF    12
21   #define LF    10
22   #define CR    13
23   #define BEL   7
24   #define BS    8
25   #define HT    9
26   #define ESC   27
27   #define XON   17
28   #define XOFF  27
29   #define ACK   6
30   #define NAK   21
31   #define SYN   22
32   #define CAN   24
33   #define SOH   1
34   #define EOT   4
35   #define ENQ   5
36   #define DEL   127
37
38   struct {
39     int x, y;
40     size_t sizebuf;
41     unsigned char far *savebuf;
42   } hscreen;
43
44
45   union REGS reg;
46   void interrupt (*old_12)();
47   int pad_lcr = 0x03fb;    /* Line Control Reg, COM1 */
48   int pad_dll = 0x03f8;    /* Divisor Latch, Low, DLAB=1 */
```

continues

Listing E.1. Continued

```
49  int pad_dlm = 0x03f9;      /* Divisor Latch, Hi Byte */
50  int pad_mcr = 0x03fc;      /* MODEM Control Reg. */
51  int pad_lsr = 0x03fd;      /* Line Status Reg */
52  int pad_msr = 0x03fe;      /* Modem Status Reg */
53  int pad_rbr = 0x03f8;      /* Receive Buf Reg, DLAB=0 */
54  int pad_thr = 0x03f8;      /* Tx Hold Reg, DLAB=0 */
55  int pad_ier = 0x03f9;      /* Intr Enable Reg, DLAB=0 */
56  int pad_iir = 0x03fa;      /* Intr Ident Reg, R/O */
57  unsigned char port_data;
58  unsigned char tx_in;
59  unsigned char hwi_level;
60  unsigned key_in;
61  unsigned char hold_buf[2048];
62  volatile int headq;
63  volatile int endq;
64  int ext_ascii = FALSE;
65  int echo = 0;
66  int orphan = FALSE;
67  int strip = TRUE;
68  struct text_info screen;
69  int x,y;
70  unsigned char far *vram;
71
72  void interrupt int_svc( void );
73  void hook_com( void );
74  void unhook_com( void );
75  void init_com( void );
76  void near send_comm_byte( void );
77  void near send_string( char *s );
78  void near get_comm_byte( void );
79  void near wait_for_tx( void );
80  int near wait_for_string( char *s );
81  void near ch_out( unsigned char data );
82  int near test_key( void );
83  unsigned char near get_key( void );
84  void near scroll_up( void );
85  void near vidtex( void );
86  void near vidtex_sba( void );
87  void near overlay( char *string );
88  void near string_out( char *string );
```

```
89   void near kbd_command( void );
90   int near exe_command( char *s );
91   int run_script( char *sname );
92
93   main()
94   {
95     textmode( 3 );
96     textbackground( BLUE );
97     textcolor( LIGHTGRAY );
98     clrscr();
99     x = y = 1;
100    gettextinfo( &screen );
101    switch ( screen.currmode ) {
102      case 1:
103      case 2:
104      case 3:
105      case 4:
106      case 5:
107      case 6: vram = MK_FP( 0xB800, 0 ); break;
108      case 7: vram = MK_FP( 0xB000, 0 ); break;
109      default: vram = MK_FP( 0xA000, 0 ); break;
110    }
111    window( 1, 1, 80, 1 );
112    textbackground( LIGHTGRAY );
113    textcolor( BLACK );
114    clrscr();
115    gotoxy( 2, 1 );
116    gettextinfo( &screen );
117    string_out( "  -Command   -Duplex   -Orphan      -Quit" );
118
119    textbackground( LIGHTGRAY );
120    textcolor( RED );
121    gotoxy( 2, 1 );
122    gettextinfo( &screen );
123    overlay( "F1-       F2-       F3-         F10-     " );
124
125    window( 1, 2, 80, 25 );
126    textbackground( BLUE );
127    textcolor( LIGHTGRAY );
128    gettextinfo( &screen );
129    hscreen.sizebuf = 4000U;
130    if ( NULL == ( hscreen.savebuf =
```

continues

Listing E.1. Continued

```
131          malloc( hscreen.sizebuf ) ) ) {
132       window( 1, 1, 80, 25 );
133       clrscr();
134       printf( "Allocate for screen save memory failed.\n" );
135       exit( 8 );
136     }
137     x = y = 1;
138     gotoxy( x, y );
139     init_com();
140     hook_com();
141     while ( 1 ) {
142       get_comm_byte();
143       if ( test_key() ) {
144         key_in = get_key();
145         if ( ext_ascii ) {
146           switch ( key_in ) {
147             case 59: kbd_command(); break;
148             case 60: echo = !echo; break;
149             case 61: orphan = !orphan; break;
150             case 68: window( 1, 1, 80, 25); clrscr();
151                      unhook_com(); exit( 0 ) ;
152           }
153         }
154         else { /* not ext_ascii */
155           send_comm_byte();
156           if ( echo ) {
157             ch_out( key_in );
158             gotoxy( x, y );
159           }
160         }
161       } /* if (test_key()) */
162     } /* while */
163   }


164   /* +---------------------------------------------------+
165      + Interrupt Service Routine ...
166      +    Get a byte from the Receive Buffer Register
167      +    (RBR) when interrupt 12 occurs, and place it
168      +    in the circulating buffer.
169      +---------------------------------------------------+
```

```
170  */
171  void interrupt int_svc( void )
172  {
173    disable();
174    if ( ++endq == 2048 ) endq = 0;
175    hold_buf[endq] = inp( pad_rbr );
176    outp( 0x20,0x64 ); /* Signal End of Interrupt to 8259 */
177    enable();
178  }
179
180  /* +--------------------------------------------------+
181     + Install Communications Interrupt Service
182     +    Hook ISR int_svc to interrupt vector 12
183     +    Latch IRQ 4 signal to ISR 12
184     +--------------------------------------------------+
185  */
186  void hook_com( void )
187  {
188    old_12 = getvect( 12 );
189    setvect( 12,int_svc );
190    headq = endq = 0;
191    disable();
192    port_data = inp( 0x21 );     /* Read 8259 Intr. Ctlr. */
193    outp( 0x21,port_data & 0xef );   /* Set up 8259 IRQ4 */
194    port_data = inp( pad_lcr );
195    outp( pad_lcr, port_data & 0x7f ); /* DLAB=0 for IER */
196    outp( pad_ier, 0x01 );   /* Enable DATA READY Intrpts */
197    outp( pad_mcr, 0x0B );              /* Modem Ctl Reg */
198    enable();
199  }
200
201  /* +--------------------------------------------------+
202     + Uninstall Communications Interrupt Service
203     +    Unhook ISR int_svc from interrupt vector 12
204     +    Unlatch IRQ 4 signal from ISR 12
205     +--------------------------------------------------+
206  */
207  void unhook_com( void )
208  {
209    port_data = inp( pad_lcr );
210    outp( pad_lcr, port_data & 0x7f );
211    outp( pad_ier, 0 );              /* Turn IER Intrpts OFF */
```

continues

Listing E.1. Continued

```
212    outp( pad_mcr, 0 );                     /* Modem Ctl Reg */
213    disable();
214    port_data = inp( 0x21 );    /*  Read 8259 Intr. Ctlr. */

215    outp( 0x21, port_data ¦ 0x10 );   /* 8259 DISAB lvl 4 */
216    enable();
217    setvect( 12, old_12 );
218  }
219
220  /* +--------------------------------------------------+
221     + Initialize Communications Parameters
222     +--------------------------------------------------+
223  */
224  void init_com( void )
225  {
226    /* Clear any outstanding hardware interupts first */
227    outp( 0x20, 0x0B );              /* Read 8259 serv reg */
228    delay(1);                          /* Let it settle */
229    hwi_level = inp( 0x20 );     /* Read hw level pending */
230    if ( hwi_level ) {                /* Interrupt exists */
231      port_data = inp( 0x21 );            /* Get masks */
232      outp( 0x21, port_data ¦ hwi_level ); /* Mask off hwi */
233      outp( 0x20, 0x64 );        /* and send End-Of-Intrpt */
234    }
235    unhook_com();                   /* Attempt to init port */
236    outp( pad_lcr, 0x9A ); /* DLAB=1, 8 DATA, NO/P, 1 STOP */
237    outp( pad_dlm, 0 ); outp( pad_dll, 0x60 ); /* 1200 BAUD */
238    port_data = inp( pad_lcr );
239    outp( pad_lcr, port_data & 0x7f );          /* DLAB=0 */
240  }
241
242  /* +--------------------------------------------------+
243     + Transmit a Character over the Comm Line
244     +--------------------------------------------------+
245  */
246  void near send_comm_byte( void )
247  {
248    port_data = 0;
249    while ( port_data != 32 ) {
250      port_data = inp( pad_lsr );  /* Get Line Status Reg */
```

```
251      port_data = port_data & 0x20;   /* See if THR is on */
252    }
253    outp( pad_thr, key_in );            /* XMIT byte to THR */
254  }
255
256  /* +--------------------------------------------------+
257     + Send a String of Characters over the Comm Line
258     +--------------------------------------------------+
259  */
260  void near send_string( char *s )
261  {
262    while ( *s ) {
263      key_in = *s++;
264      send_comm_byte();
265      if ( echo ) {
266        ch_out( key_in );
267        gotoxy( x, y );
268      }
269    }
270  }
271
272  /* +--------------------------------------------------+
273     + Receive a Character from Transmission Line
274     +    As long as there are bytes in the circulating
275     +    buffer, get and process them.
276     +--------------------------------------------------+
277  */
278  void near get_comm_byte( void )
279  {
280    while ( headq != endq ) {
281      headq += 1;
282      if ( headq == 2048 ) headq = 0;
283      tx_in = hold_buf[headq];
284      if ( strip ) tx_in &= 0x7F;
285      ch_out( tx_in );
286    }
287    gotoxy( x, y );
288  }
289
290  /* +--------------------------------------------------+
291     + Receive One Character from Transmission Line
292     +    Wait for it if not ready.
```

continues

Listing E.1. Continued

```
293      +    Break out if user presses any key.
294      +-------------------------------------------------+
295  */
296  void near wait_for_tx( void )
297  {
298    while ( headq == endq ) {
299      if ( test_key() ) {
300        get_key();
301        tx_in = 255;
302        return;
303      }
304    }
305    headq += 1;
306    if ( headq == 2048 ) headq = 0;
307    tx_in = hold_buf[headq];
308    if ( strip ) tx_in &= 0x7F;
309  }
310
311  /* +-------------------------------------------------+
312      + Wait for a String Pattern in Incoming Traffic
313      +-------------------------------------------------+
314  */
315  int near wait_for_string( char *s )
316  {
317    char *p = s;
318
319    while ( *p ) {
320      wait_for_tx();
321      if ( tx_in == 255 ) return 0;
322      ch_out( tx_in );
323      gotoxy( x, y );
324      if ( *p == tx_in ) p++;
325      else p = s;
326    }
327    return 1; /* Found whole pattern */
328  }
329
330  /* +-------------------------------------------------+
331      + Display a Character on the Screen
332      +-------------------------------------------------+
```

```
333  */
334  void near ch_out( unsigned char data )
335  {
336    switch ( data ) {
337      case ESC: vidtex(); break;
338      case LF:  ++y; break;
339      case CR:  x = 1;
340                if ( orphan ) ++y; break;
341      case FF:  clrscr();
342                x = y = 1;
343                break;
344      case BEL: break;
345      case BS:  if ( --x < 1 ) {
346                  x = screen.winright - screen.winleft + 1;
347                  if ( --y < 1 ) y = 1;
348                }
349                break;
350      default: *(vram + (screen.winleft+x-2)*2
351               + (screen.wintop+y-2)*160) = data;
352               ++x;
353    }
354    if ( x > screen.winright - screen.winleft + 1 ) {
355      x = 1;
356      ++y;
357    }
358    if ( y > screen.winbottom - screen.wintop + 1 ) {
359      scroll_up();
360      y = screen.winbottom - screen.wintop + 1;
361    }
362  }
363
364  /* +------------------------------------------------+
365     + Test for Keystroke Availability
366     +------------------------------------------------+
367  */
368  int near test_key( void )
369  {
370    reg.x.ax = 0x0100;
371    int86( 0x16, &reg, &reg );
372    if ( reg.x.flags & 0x0040 ) return( 0 );
373    else return( 1 );
374  }
```

continues

Listing E.1. Continued

```
375
376  /* +-----------------------------------------------------+
377     + Get the Next Available Keystroke
378        +--------------------------------------------------+
379  */
380  unsigned char near get_key( void )
381  {
382    reg.x.ax = 0x0000;
383    int86( 0x16, &reg, &reg );
384    if ( reg.h.al ) {
385      ext_ascii = FALSE;
386      return ( reg.h.al );
387    }
388    else {
389      ext_ascii = TRUE;
390      return( reg.h.ah );
391    }
392  }
393
394  /* +-----------------------------------------------------+
395     + Scroll the Display Screen One Line Up
396        +--------------------------------------------------+
397  */
398  void near scroll_up( void )
399  {
400    reg.x.ax = 0x0601;                /* Scroll up 1 line */
401    reg.h.bh = screen.attribute;     /* Use attribute */
402    reg.h.ch = screen.wintop - 1;       /* Area to use */
403    reg.h.cl = screen.winleft - 1;
404    reg.h.dh = screen.winbottom - 1;
405    reg.h.dl = screen.winright - 1;
406    int86( 0x10, &reg, &reg );
407  }
408
409  /* +-----------------------------------------------------+
410     + Handle CompuServe's VIDTEX Escape Sequences
411        +--------------------------------------------------+
412  */
413  void near vidtex( void )
414  {
```

```
415     static int i;
416
417     wait_for_tx();
418     if (tx_in == 255 ) return;
419     switch ( tx_in ) {
420       case 'A': --y;
421                 if ( y < 1 )
422                     y = screen.winbottom - screen.wintop + 1;
423                 break;
424       case 'B': ++y;
425                 if ( y > screen.winbottom - screen.wintop + 1 )
426                     y = 1;
427                 break;
428       case 'C': ++x;
429                 if (x>screen.winright-screen.winleft+1){
430                     x = 1;
431                     ++y;
432                     if (y>screen.winbottom-screen.wintop+1)
433                         y = screen.wintop;
434                 }
435                 break;
436       case 'D': --x;
437                 if ( x < 1 ) {
438                     x = screen.winright - screen.winleft + 1;
439                     --y;
440                     if ( y < 1 )
441                         y = screen.winbottom - screen.wintop + 1;
442                 }
443                 break;
444       case 'H': x = y = 1;
445                 break;
446       case 'K': clreol();
447                 break;
448       case 'J': clreol();
449                 for ( i=y+1; i<=screen.winbottom-y+1; i++ ) {
450                     gotoxy( 1, i ); clreol();
451                 }
452                 break;
453       case 'j': clrscr();
454                 x = 1;
455                 y = 1;
456                 break;
```

continues

Listing E.1. Continued

```
457     case 'Y': vidtex_sba(); break;
458   }
459 }
460
461 /* +----------------------------------------------------+
462    + VIDTEX Set-Cursor-Address Sequence
463    +----------------------------------------------------+
464 */
465 void near vidtex_sba( void )
466 {
467   wait_for_tx();
468   if ( tx_in == 255 ) return;
469   y = tx_in - 31;
470   if ( y < 1 ) y = 1;
471   if ( y > screen.winbottom - screen.wintop + 1 )
472     y = screen.winbottom - screen.wintop + 1;
473   wait_for_tx();
474   if ( tx_in == 255 ) return;
475   x = tx_in - 31;
476   if ( x < 1 ) y = 1;
477   if ( x > screen.winright - screen.winleft + 1 )
478     y = screen.winright;
479 }
480
481 void near overlay( char *string )
482 {
483   x = wherex();
484   y = wherey();
485   while ( *string ) {
486     if ( *string != ' ' ) *(vram+(screen.winleft+x-2) * 2
487       + ( screen.wintop + y - 2 ) * 160 ) = *string;
488     if ( *string != ' ' ) *(vram+(screen.winleft+x-2) * 2
489       + (screen.wintop + y-2) * 160+1) = screen.attribute;
490     x++; string++;
491     if ( x > screen.winright ) { x = screen.winleft; ++y; }
492     if ( y > screen.winbottom ) {
493       scroll_up();
494       y = screen.winbottom;
495     }
496   }
```

```
497     gotoxy( x, y );
498   }
499
500   void near string_out( char *string )
501   {
502     x = wherex();
503     y = wherey();
504     while ( *string ) {
505       *(vram + ( screen.winleft + x++ - 2 ) * 2
506         + ( screen.wintop + y - 2 ) * 160 ) = *string++;
507       if ( x > screen.winright ) { x = screen.winleft; ++y; }
508       if ( y > screen.winbottom ) {
509         scroll_up();
510         y = screen.winbottom;
511       }
512     }
513     gotoxy( x, y );
514   }
515
516   void near kbd_command( void )
517   {
518     char cmdline[41];
519
520     ch_out( CR ); ch_out( LF ); gotoxy( x, y );
521     string_out( "<Enter Command>: " );
522     gets( cmdline );
523     ch_out( CR ); ch_out( LF ); gotoxy( x, y );
524     exe_command( cmdline );
525   }
526
527   int near exe_command( char *s )
528   {
529     char *p = s;
530
531     while ( *p ) {                        /* Replace ~ with CR */
532       if ( *p == '~' ) *p = '\r';
533       p++;
534     }
535     if ( !strncmp( s, "send", 4 ) ) {
536       while ( *s && *s != ' ' ) s++;  /* Get beyond verb */
537       while ( *s && *s == ' ' ) s++;  /* Get to object */
538       send_string( s );                 /* Put it on the line */
```

continues

Listing E.1. Continued

```
539      return 1;
540    }
541    if ( !strncmp( s, "wait", 4  ) ) {
542      while ( *s && *s != ' ' ) s++; /* Get beyond verb */
543      while ( *s && *s == ' ' ) s++; /* Get to object */
544      return wait_for_string( s );   /* See if we got it */
545    }
546    if ( !strncmp( s, "run", 3  ) ) {
547      while ( *s && *s != ' ' ) s++;
548      while ( *s && *s == ' ' ) s++;
549      return run_script( s );
550    }
551    if ( !strncmp( s, "display", 7  ) ) {
552      while ( *s && *s != ' ' ) s++;
553      s++;
554      while ( *s ) ch_out( *s++ );
555      ch_out( CR ); ch_out( LF );
556      gotoxy( x, y );
557      return 1;
558    }
559    if ( !strncmp( s, "push", 4  ) ) {
560      if ( !hscreen.savebuf ) return 0;
561      memcpy( hscreen.savebuf, vram, hscreen.sizebuf );
562      hscreen.x = wherex();
563      hscreen.y = wherey();
564      return 1;
565    }
566    if ( !strncmp( s, "pop", 3  ) ) {
567      if ( !hscreen.savebuf ) return 0;
568      memcpy( vram, hscreen.savebuf, hscreen.sizebuf );
569      x = hscreen.x;
570      y = hscreen.y;
571      gotoxy( x, y );
572      return 1;
573    }
574    if ( !strncmp( s, "getkey", 6  ) ) {
575      key_in = get_key();
576      return 1;
577    }
578    if ( !strncmp( s, "system", 6  ) ) {
```

```
579        while ( *s && *s != ' ' ) s++;
580        while ( *s && *s == ' ' ) s++;
581        return system( s );
582    }
583    if ( !strncmp( s, "help", 4  ) ) {
584        return run_script( "help.scr" );
585    }
586 }
587
588 int run_script( char *sname )
589 {
590    FILE *sfile;
591    char *cmdbuf;
592    char *cmd;
593    char label[9];
594
595    if ( NULL == ( cmdbuf = (char *)malloc( 16384 ) ) ) {
596        ch_out( CR ); ch_out( LF );
597        string_out( "Not Enough Memory." );
598        ch_out( CR ); ch_out( LF );
599        return 0;
600    }
601    *cmdbuf = '\0';
602    cmd = cmdbuf;
603    if ( NULL == ( sfile = fopen( sname, "r" ) ) ) {
604        ch_out( CR ); ch_out( LF );
605        string_out( "Can't find script: " );
606        string_out( sname );
607        ch_out( CR ); ch_out( LF );
608        return 0;
609    }
610    while ( NULL != fgets( cmd, 255, sfile ) ) {
611        while ( *cmd && *cmd != '\n' ) cmd++;
612        if ( *cmd == '\n' ) *cmd++ = '\0';
613        else cmd++;
614    }
615    *cmd = '\0';        /* Terminate command list with a null */
616    fclose( sfile );
617    cmd = cmdbuf;                  /* Reset the command pointer */
618
619    while ( *cmd ) {               /* and EXECUTE THE COMMANDS */
620        if ( !strncmp( cmd, "ifkey", 5  ) ) {
```

continues

Listing E.1.   Continued

```
621        while ( *cmd && *cmd != ' ' ) cmd++;
622        while ( *cmd && *cmd == ' ' ) cmd++;
623        if ( key_in == *cmd ) {
624           while ( *cmd && *cmd != ' ' ) cmd++;
625           while ( *cmd && *cmd == ' ' ) cmd++;
626        }
627     }
628     if ( !strncmp( cmd, "goto", 4 ) ) {  /* Do JUMPS here */
629        while ( *cmd && *cmd != ' ' ) cmd++;
630        while ( *cmd && *cmd == ' ' ) cmd++;
631        strcpy( label, cmd );
632        cmd = cmdbuf;              /* goto top to start search */
633        while ( *cmd ) {                    /* Search for label */
634           if ( !strncmp( cmd, label, strlen( label ) ) )
635              break;
636           while ( *cmd++ ) ;                /* Next string */
637        }
638     }
639     if ( !exe_command( cmd ) ) {    /* If execution error */
640        ch_out( CR ); ch_out( LF );
641        string_out( "Failing Command: " );
642        string_out( cmd );
643        ch_out( CR ); ch_out( LF );
644        free( cmdbuf );                 /* Release the buffer */
645        return 0;                       /* and get out dirty */
646     }
647     while ( *cmd++ ) ;                       /* Next string */
648  }
649  free( cmdbuf );            /* Release the command buffer */
650  return 1;            /* Finished the script with no errors */
651 }
```

Writing a script for CCOM.C is easy. Just use your favorite text editor to create a text file containing ccom commands and script directives. A command verb must begin in the first character of each line, and it must be in lowercase letters. Here are three of the most commonly used commands:

■ display

Code exactly one blank after the verb. Everything after that, to the end of the line, is displayed on your screen, but not sent over the communications line.

■ send

Code a blank as with `display`. Everything following the blank is transmitted over the communications line. To send a carriage return (CR) character, code a tilde (~). It is converted internally to CR and then sent.

■ wait

Everything after the single blank is used as a string pattern for matching against incoming bytes. The program loops until all bytes in the pattern have been received. You can press any key on the keyboard to break out of the wait, which also terminates the script.

A script to dial up CompuServe and automatically supply your user identification and password (in other words, to log you on automatically) is easy to write with just these three commands, as you can see from the following example:

```
display ---- Dialing CompuServe ----
send atdtnnnnnnnn,,,~ ( ~ means send CR )
wait CONNECT 1200
send _       ( sends Ctrl-C character )
wait User ID: ( wait on string pattern )
send nnnnn,nnnn~    ( send CR here too )
wait word:
send your.password~ ( CR one more time )
```

If this script file resides in a text file named CIS, running it is simple. You just press F1 to get the command prompt, type

```
run cis
```

and then press Enter. The script runs without further input from you. More complicated scripts, using other commands, are possible. For example, you could write scripts to provide a complete on-line help facility. The first script file, HELP.SCR, might contain something like this:

```
push
display                   CCOM Master Help Menu
display --------------------------------------------------
display ~ ( this leaves a blank line on the screen )
display                   a - help on commands
display                   b - help on scripts
display                   c - help on communications parms
display                   d - help on upload / download
display                   x - QUIT HELP
display   ~ ( this leaves a blank line on the screen )
display            Press a key for help on the topic listed,
display                  or Press x to quit help.
```

```
getkey
ifkey a run cmd.scr
ifkey b run scr.scr
ifkey x goto pop
goto display
pop
```

The push command saves a copy of the current screen so it can be restored later. After the screen is painted, the getkey command collects a keystroke from the user, corresponding to one of the menu items. The ifkey script directive then selects which additional script file to run in order to get more detailed information.

The goto script directive is a little unusual. The argument for goto is not quite like a C label statement (although you can make it look like that, if you want). When a goto is encountered, the script is positioned at the top, and the first characters of every line are compared with the search string until a line containing them is found. It doesn't matter what those first characters are— they can be a command verb, or any label you make up.

For an exercise, examine the program thoroughly and then devise the succeeding help scripts.

B-Spline Derivation

The B-spline interpolation procedure for curve smoothing is based on the parametric cubic representation of an *n*-dimensional curve. In this representation, the variable names x_1, x_2, and x_3 are used rather than x, y, and z. The general position variable is then x_i, where i = 1, 2, 3. Furthermore, a given x_i is computed using a parameter variable *t*. The point of the B-spline interpolation is to find a suitable value for *t* so a cubic function of *t* both smooths the curve and controls the end points of each segment sufficiently.

The derivation is carried out using matrix algebra. In general, the matrix equation for the parametric cubic form of a curve is the following:

x_i = TMG$_i$ i = 1, 2, 3

In this equation, because the matrix product TM remains constant for all x_i, it is derived first. The matrix T is the row matrix of the cubic polynomial in *t:*

T   = Ü t3 t2 t 1ᶠ Ü

The matrix M is known as the *Hermite matrix*. You might think of it as a set of characteristic equations that transform the original points into a smooth curve. For the B-spline, the value of the Hermite matrix is the following:

M   = 1/6 * Ü -1   3   -3   ᶠ1 Ü
              Ü 3   -6   3   0 Ü
              Ü -3   0   3   0 Ü
              Ü 1   4   1   0 Ü

The product of these two matrices is a row matrix:

1/6 * [$(-t^3+3t^2-3t+1)$ $(3t^3-6t^2+4)$ $(-3t^3+3t^2+3t+1)$ (t^3)]

Finally, for each of the x_i variables, the G matrix is a column matrix called the *Hermite geometry matrix*. Its function is to provide a set of original points that acts as boundary markers for the smooth curve. The B-spline formulation considers four points at a time: the current point being processed, one point preceding, and two points following. If you let P_i stand for the current point, then

$$G_i = \begin{matrix} \ddot{U} & P^f_{i-1} & \ddot{U} \\ \ddot{U} & P_i & \ddot{U} \\ \ddot{U} & P_{i+1} & \ddot{U} \\ \ddot{U} & P_{i+2} & \ddot{U} \end{matrix}$$

This particular selection of geometry points is why the B-spline interpolation does not pass through the end points of the curve being smoothed.

When the geometry matrix G_i is applied (using a postmultiplication procedure), an equation results that can be used to calculate the interpolated points:

$$\begin{aligned} x_i = {} & 1/6(-t^3+3t^2-3t+1)P_{i-1} \\ & + 1/6(3t^3-6t^2+4)P_i \\ & + 1/6(-3t^3+3t^2+3t+1)P_{i-1} \\ & + 1/6(t^3)P_{i+2} \end{aligned}$$

To understand how to implement this algorithm, go back to thinking of the curve in Cartesian coordinates—x, y, and z. At each point on the curve, you must calculate previous, current, and next values of x; apply the formula; calculate previous, current, and next values of y; apply the formula; and so on. The algorithm can be sped up by premultiplying the 1/6 across each expression and hard-coding the fractional values that result.

Performance-Measurement Software

Precision measurement of the performance of a computer algorithm is somewhat problematic on the IBM PC because the system clock ticks just 18.2 times per second. This is true whether you are running the original 8088-based PC or the latest 80386 with a 33 MHz CPU clock frequency. The best resolution you can get at 18.2 ticks per second is about 0.055 seconds, or a little better than one-twentieth of a second.

Clearly, a fast computer can do a lot of work in that time. Something better is needed to compare the speeds and performance of functions under development. Fortunately, the timer chip supplied on all PCs and good clones can be programmed to tick faster or slower. In this case, you want faster—much faster—ticks. All you have to do is reprogram the timer chip temporarily. A word of caution: a high tick rate on a slow processor can eat up too much of the machine's processing capability.

The actual chip used in your machine may vary depending on the model you own. On the original 8088 machines, the Intel 8253-5 was used. On PC- and AT-class machines (including 80286 and most 80386 clones), the Intel 8254-2 chip was used, whereas PS/2 models implement timing in custom-integrated circuits.

Because the programming interface is the same in every case, no matter which chip is used, the routines given here should work just about universally, although you may have to vary the tick rate on some machines. These routines have been tested on machines from a plain "blue" IBM PC running at 4.77 MHz (1,000 ticks per second) to an AT-class clone with an 80386 running at 20 MHz (10,000 ticks per second).

To reprogram the timer chip successfully, you must control three aspects of your computer, all equally important. You must get all of them right, or you probably will have to cold-boot your machine. Here are the three aspects you must control:

- *The 8259A Programmable Interrupt Controller (PIC).* For each timer tick, the ordinary operation of the CPU is interrupted, and control is given to a special routine that does whatever the software designer wants it to do. In this case, you are the designer. You must know how to inform the PIC that you are finished servicing the timer-tick interrupt.

- *The 8253/4 timer.* The timer is driven by an oscillator with a frequency of 1.19318 MHz, and controlled by a count-down or *divisor* register (within the chip) that determines how often the timer is to signal the PIC to interrupt the system. You must know how to program the divisor register with a new value, and—just as important—set it back the way you found it.

- *The IRQ0 (level 0) Interrupt Service Routine (ISR).* You must supply a replacement ISR in place of the original. The object is to update your own tick counter "clock," but not to prevent the original ISR from servicing system requirements.

From the programmer's point of view, the main thing is the ISR code. Such a routine is provided in TIMER.C in Listing G.1. This source file is not a complete program; it is meant to be compiled separately and linked with other .OBJ files to form a complete program. TIMER.C contains functions to start and reset a higher clock rate, to handle timer-tick interrupts while in that mode, and to calculate the precise amount of time spent in that mode.

As is often the case, the best way to explain the theory of an operation is found in the program that implements it. Look over the program in Listing G.1, which implements the routines for an 80386, 10,000 ticks per second. Familiarize yourself with its major features and then read the analysis of its parts—which brings it all together.

Listing G.1. TIMER.C—Performance-measurement routine (with Microsoft C/C++).

```
1   /* +-------------------------------------------------+
2       +                 T I M E R . C
3       +  Benchmark and performance-measurement routines
4       +  supplying 100 microsecond precision.
5       +-------------------------------------------------+
6   */
```

```
 7  #include <stdlib.h>
 8  #include <stdio.h>
 9  #include <dos.h>
10  #include <conio.h>
11
12  #define ICR 0x20
13  #define EOI 0x20
14
15  unsigned long ticks;
16  unsigned long begin_time;
17  unsigned long end_time;
18  unsigned long far *clock = (unsigned long far *)0x0040006CUL;
19  unsigned long far *oflow = (unsigned long far *)0x00400070UL;
20  unsigned long save_clock;
21  unsigned long save_oflow;
22
23  void (interrupt far *oldint8)();
24
25  /* +-----------------------------------------------------+
26     + void interrupt newint8()
27     +   Handle 10,000 clock ticks per second.
28     +-----------------------------------------------------+
29  */
30  void interrupt far newint8()
31  {
32    static unsigned int count = 551;
33
34    ++ticks;
35    if ( --count == 0 ) {
36      (*oldint8)();
37      count = 551;
38    }
39    else outp( ICR, EOI );
40  }
41
42  /* +-----------------------------------------------------+
43     + hires_clock()
44     +   Place Timer0 in high-resolution, 100 microsecond
45     +   mode. Save previous status of clock.
46     +-----------------------------------------------------+
47  */
48  static void hires_clock( void )
```

continues

Listing G.1. Continued

```
49  {
50    _disable();
51    save_clock = *clock;
52    save_oflow = *oflow;
53    ticks = 0;
54    oldint8 = _dos_getvect( 8 );
55    _dos_setvect( 8, newint8 );
56    outp( 0x43, 0x36 ); /* 119 ( 0x0077 ) for divisor */
57    outp( 0x40, 0x77 );
58    outp( 0x40, 0x00 );
59    _enable();
60  }
61
62  /* +--------------------------------------------------+
63     + lores_clock()
64     +    Place Timer0 in low resolution, 18.2 ticks/sec.
65     +    Correct system clock for true elapsed time.
66     +--------------------------------------------------+
67  */
68  static void lores_clock( void )
69  {
70    _disable();
71    outp( 0x43, 0x36 );
72    outp( 0x40, 0 );
73    outp( 0x40, 0 );
74    _dos_setvect( 8, oldint8 );
75    *oflow = save_oflow;
76    *clock = save_clock + ( end_time - begin_time ) / 551UL;
77    _enable();
78  }
79
80  void start_bench( void )
81  {
82    hires_clock();
83    begin_time = ticks;
84  }
85
86  void stop_bench( void )
87  {
88    end_time = ticks;
```

```
89     lores_clock();
90  }
91
92  double duration( void )
93  {
94     return( ( (double)( end_time - begin_time ) / 10000.0 ) );
95  }
```

Data Areas Used in TIMER.C

Seven unsigned long int variables, lines 15–21, constitute the main data areas in TIMER.C. The first of these, ticks, is to be the temporary replacement clock while the timer is in what is called *high-resolution mode*. Very simply, the variable ticks is incremented at each timer tick. This does not mean that the original system clock is no longer updated—just that you do not want to update it at the new, higher rate. That oversight would alter the true system clock drastically. One consequence would be that files accessed after using these functions would no longer be correctly date- and time-stamped.

The next two variables, begin_time and end_time, are copies of the high-resolution clock at the beginning and end of a performance benchmark and timing run. They will be used by one of the support functions to calculate the elapsed interval in high-resolution mode.

The far pointers to *clock and *oflow give access to the real system clock and clock overflow flag (which indicates that midnight has rolled around). The program needs to know where these are in order to ensure that they are set back (to a close approximation) to what they would have been if high-resolution mode had never been entered. Usually, this action is redundant because the routine invokes the original ISR at very close to the normal frequency, allowing the system clock to be updated as before.

However, if you tinker with the count-down values, you may cause interrupts faster than they can realistically be serviced. To cover that eventuality, the correct value of the clock is recalculated from the high-resolution clock and restored, and the overflow flag is set to its original value.

Theoretically, you can set the count-down value to 1 and get 1,193,180 ticks per second. In practice, that doesn't work. The interrupt-service routines can't do everything they need to do in eight-tenths of a microsecond. The highest reasonable tick rate was found (through experimentation) to be about 10,000 ticks per second. This yields a high-resolution precision of about 100 microseconds per tick, or a time value accurate to four decimal places.

The last two variables, save_clock and save_oflow, simply save the values of the true clock and overflow flag before high-resolution timing begins.

Reprogramming the Timer Chip

It is not intended that routines external to the TIMER.C source file initiate high-resolution timing directly. They should instead call start_bench(), lines 80–84, primarily to ensure that begin_time is noted correctly. start_bench() then calls hires_clock() to start high-resolution timing.

hires_clock() is in lines 48–60. This function is executed with interrupts disabled (_disable()) while the system clock is being saved and the timer chip reprogrammed, after interrupts are again allowed with _enable().

The address of the original ISR for interrupt vector 8 (the timer interrupt) is saved in line 54, and the new ISR is hooked in line 55. Interrupt vector 8 is the one used for timer-tick interrupts because of the way the 8259A is implemented on the PC.

The 8259A can control eight levels of hardware interrupt, numbered 0 through 7. On the PC, Interrupt Request 0 (IRQ0) is used for the timer. The PC's circuitry is further arranged so a hardware interrupt level triggers a software interrupt vector that is eight greater than its own value. Hence, IRQ0 invokes interrupt vector 8—which points to the system's timer-tick ISR.

With the original interrupt address now preserved, line 55 now hooks in the new interrupt handler—newint8(). That routine is discussed shortly.

Reprogramming of the timer chip occurs in lines 56–58. This is done using two byte ports. Port 0x43 is a *control port* for the timer. A value of 0x36 is output to the port, telling the timer that (1) the system timer (not the speaker timer or memory-refresh timer) is about to be reprogrammed with a new divisor value; and (2) the least significant byte appears first, followed by the most significant byte. Thus, the divisor is basically an unsigned integer. The divisor is output to the timer through byte port 0x40, one byte at a time.

Why is the count-down value called a *divisor*, and how do you pick values for it? Remember that the timer chip is being driven by a 1.19318 MHz oscillator. Each cycle from the oscillator causes the divisor value *first* to be decremented by one, and *second* to be checked for zero. If the value is zero, the timer signals a timer interrupt to the PIC.

Usually, the divisor is set to a value of 0. Because it is decremented before being checked, its value wraps around to 0xFFFF, and so on down to zero. It therefore is decremented 65,536 times before reaching zero again. But because it is being decremented at 1,193,180 times a second, interrupts are triggered 1193180 / 65536 = 18.2 per second, approximately. Thus the count-down value *is* properly a divisor—of the oscillator frequency.

You can turn the formula around to compute the divisor for a desired interrupt rate. Because you want 10,000 interrupts a second, 1193180 / 10000 is about 119, or 0x0077. Notice in line 57 that the 0x77 is sent to port 0x40 first, followed by the 0x00.

Reprogramming of the timer is now complete. It runs at the higher rate behind the scenes so your program can now execute whatever it is you want precise timing for, without paying further attention to the timer (for the time being). But the routine behind the scenes is `newint8()`, the very one that was just hooked in by `hires_clock()`.

Handling the Timer-Tick Interrupts

`newint8()` is executed every time a timer tick occurs, now that high-resolution timing has begun. In a real sense, it is running at the same time as the other functions in the program, although only one routine has control of the CPU at any given moment. This situation is called *multitasking*. What does this multitasking interrupt service routine accomplish?

It does exactly two things: updates the high-resolution mode clock that was defined earlier in the program, and invokes the original ISR at the right times. All of this is done in lines 30–40 of TIMER.C. Updating `ticks` is simple; the `++` prefix operator is used.

Determining when to pass control to the original ISR is not so simple. How many ticks at the higher rate must occur to reach the equivalent of 18.2 ticks per second? It's probably best to look at it from the perspective of the divisor values. At 18.2 ticks per second, the divisor was the equivalent of 65,536. Now the divisor is 119 for 10,000 ticks per second. The old rate is 65536 / 119, or about 551 times slower. Therefore, every 551 ticks, the code should invoke the old ISR. For any new timer-tick rate, the ratio of the original to the new divisor (truncated to an integer) is the number of ticks to count before invoking `oldint8()`.

It is important that `newint8()` actually invokes the old ISR and at the right rate. There are two reasons for doing it at all. First, the old ISR chains to the *user timer-tick interrupt*, which may be being used by pop-up software or some other application that would be disabled without this interrupt. Second, the old ISR is responsible also for checking the diskette drive motor and turning it off after an appropriate time. This is also the reason for invoking the old ISR at the right rate, because drive motor control is a time-dependent function.

Finally, it is important to notice the last statement in `newint8()`:

```
else outp( ICR, EOI );
```

As the `else` implies, this statement is executed only when the old ISR is *not* invoked. (This operation is taken care of by the old ISR when it does execute.) But what is this output for?

Look at the `#defines` in lines 12 and 13. Both ICR and EOI are defined to be 0x20, but the fact that they are the same is only incidental. The ICR is the Interrupt Control Register, through which you read and write control information for the 8259A PIC. In this case, you want to send EOI (End Of Interrupt) to it.

The reason for doing this is quite simple—if you don't, the system hangs up completely! Timer-tick interrupts are not quite like normal software interrupts, because they are mediated by the PIC. When the PIC causes an interrupt, it *disables any further interrupts* until you send it this byte indicating that interrupt processing is complete.

This, incidentally, is why it is possible either to make interrupts too frequent or, what amounts to the same thing, to write so much code in `newint8()` that it can't finish by the next interrupt. If you haven't sent the EOI code when the next interrupt arrives, it never happens. The PIC prevents it. The result can be quite unpredictable—but never desirable.

Cleaning Up After High-Resolution Timing

Terminating high-resolution timing is mostly a matter of reprogramming the timer with its original divisor value. Only a couple of points need mentioning here.

High-resolution mode is terminated by calling `stop_bench()`. This function stores the ending value of the high-resolution clock and calls `lores_clock()` to reprogram the timer. This is just a mirror-image process, so far.

`lores_clock()`, however, does one extra thing. It uses the elapsed time from the high-resolution clock to compute the equivalent number of ticks at 18.2 per second, and refreshes the system clock in low storage with that computed value. This is done in line 76. Notice that the conversion factor is the same one used to detect timing for invoking the old ISR, as described earlier.

As mentioned, this particular cleanup function is usually redundant; ordinarily, invoking the old ISR at the proper rate keeps the real system clock straight. If, however, you find yourself tempted to experiment with the divisor value, this function may prove its worth in making it unnecessary to reset the system date and clock through DOS commands after each attempt.

A more realistic rate for an 8088, 4.77 MHz machine, is 1,000 ticks per second. In this case, the count-down value would be 1193180 / 1000 = 1193, or 0x04A9. Because this is 10 times slower than the rate shown in the program, newint8() need only invoke the old clock interrupt every 55 counts, rather than 551; this value also needs to be substituted in lore_clock(), where the original clock value is being computed. Finally, the divisor in duration() should be 1,000 rather than 10,000.

Separate Compilation of TIMER.C

TIMER.C should be compiled separately to an .OBJ file. You can bring it into your application programs by including it in the appropriate make list, project file, or linker response file. Whatever the method, get it linked into the main executable file.

Only certain data objects and functions are meant to be visible to the main source file (or other program modules). You can gain access to them from other files by writing the following #include:

```
#include "timer.h"
```

The contents of the timer header file are shown in Listing G.2.

Listing G.2. Header file for the timer routine (using Microsoft C/C++).

```
 1   /* +------------------------------------------------------+
 2       +                   T I M E R . H
 3       +  Benchmark and performance measurement routines
 4       +  supplying 100 microsecond precision.
 5       +------------------------------------------------------+
 6   */
 7   #include <stdlib.h>
 8   #include <stdio.h>
 9   #include <dos.h>
10   #include <conio.h>
11
12   #define ICR 0x20
13   #define EOI 0x20
14
15   extern unsigned long ticks;
16   extern unsigned long begin_time;
```

continues

Listing G.2.   Continued

```
17   extern unsigned long end_time;
18   extern unsigned long far *clock;
19
20   extern void (interrupt far *oldint8)();
21
22   void start_bench( void );
23   void stop_bench( void );
24   double duration( void );
```

Converting TIMER.C to Borland C

The version of TIMER.C shown in Listing G.1 was written in Microsoft C/C++. Converting the code to Borland C is easy. Just make the indicated changes at the following line numbers:

Line 23

Change the MC void (interrupt far *oldint8)() to the BC notation void interrupt far (*oldint8)(). Actually, the MC notation here makes more intuitive sense because this object is a far pointer to an interrupt function (all in parentheses), which returns nothing (void outside the parentheses). In fact, Borland C accepts either notation, whereas MS C accepts only the first.

Line 30

You *can* change the MC void interrupt far newint8 (void) to the BC void interrupt newint8(void), but you don't need to. Borland C assumes that an interrupt function has the far attribute, but MS C flags the statement at compile time, informing you that it *must* have the far attribute.

et al.

You should change the following forms of several function names:

MC Name	BC Name
disable	disable
enable	enable
dos_getvect	getvect
dos_setvect	setvect

These are all the changes to the source you need to make in order to use the code with either compiler. If you plan to use the code much with both compilers, it would be worth the trouble to package a single source file using #define and #ifdef macros so only one line needs to be modified to compile correctly. See Chapter 4 for details on these macros.

Using the TIMER.C Functions

You can use the facilities provided in TIMER.C in two ways: you can use the functions to time in high-resolution mode, or you can just use the data areas to time in low-resolution mode. Both methods are illustrated in TESTTIME.C in Listing G.3.

Listing G.3.   TESTTIME.C—Using the TIMER.C facilities (with Borland C++).

```
1   #include "timer.h"
2
3   main()
4   {
5     unsigned long i;
6
7     start_bench();
8     for ( i=0; i<367000; ++i ) i = i;
9     stop_bench();
10    printf( " Elapsed time at 10,000 ticks/sec = %.4f\n",
11        duration() );
12
13    begin_time = *clock;
14    for ( i=0; i<367000; ++i ) i = i;
15    end_time = *clock;
16    printf( " Elapsed time at 18.2 ticks/sec = %.4f\n",
17        ( (double)( end_time - begin_time ) ) / 18.2 );
18  }
```

You can inspect the code and see how to handle the two timing methods. Just remember that when you use high-resolution timing, be sure to terminate it.

This Borland C program was compiled and linked in the interactive editor environment. To do this, a project file was necessary to name all the parts for the compiler and linker. The project file is simple and is composed of the following two lines:

```
testtime.c (timer.h)
timer.obj
```

TESTTIME.C performs benchmark timings on exactly the same code—a loop that should last very close to one second on an 80386, 20 MHz. The program produces the following output on the screen:

```
Elapsed time at 10,000 ticks/sec = 1.1985
Elapsed time at 18.2 ticks/sec = 0.9890
```

Notice that during high-resolution mode, it appears to take about 21 percent longer to run the same loop. Why are the timings different at the different tick rates? First, because the slower tick rate is accurate only to plus or minus 0.05 seconds. This means that the time actually elapsed is in the range 1.0390 >= 0.9890 >= 0.9390, but it cannot be known precisely. The high-resolution elapsed time is between 1.1984 and 1.1986—much more accurate.

The second reason for the differing results is the extra overhead of executing the ISR instructions almost 10,000 extra times per second. The difference between the closest extreme values for the two speeds is 1.1984 – 1.0390 = 0.1594 seconds. This is not accounted for by inaccuracies and must be due to the added overhead during high-resolution timing. Thus, there is a 0.1594 / 1.1984 * 100 = 13.3 percent added overhead.

This raises another question. Does this overhead destroy the accuracy of the timer routines? If you think about it for a moment, you will see that this overhead is present also at the normal tick rate—it is just less noticeable. Furthermore, in comparing *two* routines, the overhead is *consistently present*, so the *relative* durations of alternative methods have real significance.

That is the true point of benchmark timing: whether one method or routine is *relatively faster* than another. If it is, it is preferred. In addition, you can get a good idea of what the normal elapsed time will be by simply reducing the high-resolution timing by about 13.3 percent. This will, in fact, be more accurate as timing by the second method at 18.2 ticks per second, because high-resolution timing is two orders of magnitude more precise.

Symbols

! (NOT) logical operator, 178, 562

!= (not equal to) relational operator, 561

directive, 182

operator, 16

(preprocessor concatenation) operator, 16, 175

% (percent sign)
  conversion character, 85
  modulus mathematical operator, 560

& (ampersand)
  address-of operator, 64
  bitwise AND operator, 108

&& logical operator, 562

" " (double quotation marks), including, 24-25

* (asterisk) operators
  addition, 560
  indirection, 64
  multiplication, 560

+ mode character, 422

+= (add assign) operator, 108

- (subtraction) mathematical operator, 560

/ (real division) mathematical operator, 560

; (semicolon), 16

< (less than) relational operator, 561

< > (angle brackets), including, 23-24
  (not equal to relational operator, 561

<= (less than or equal to) relational operator, 561

= (equal sign)
  assignment operator, 138-139
  equal to relational operator, 561

== (equal to) relational operator, 561
  equality operator, 138-139

> (greater than) relational operator, 561

>= (greater than or equal to) relational operator, 561

>> (shift-right) operator, 108

\? escape sequence, 154

??' trigraph, 159

??! trigraph, 159

??(trigraph, 159

??) trigraph, 159

??- trigraph, 159

??/ trigraph, 159

??< trigraph, 159

??= trigraph, 159

??> trigraph, 159
\, 293-298
\\ escape sequence, 154
\" escape sequence, 154
\' escape sequence, 154
{ } (curly braces), 17, 34, 283
¦¦ (OR) logical operator, 562
\0 escape sequence, 157
\123 escape sequence, 157
\779 escape sequence, 157
8253/4 timer, 828
8259A PIC, 828
\88 escape sequence, 157

A

\a escape sequence, 153
a mode character, 422
"a" mode string, 425
"a+" mode string, 425
"a+b" mode string, 425
"ab+" mode string, 425
"ab" mode string, 425
abort() function, 66, 317, 776
aborting programs, 66
abs() function, 777
absolute disk addresses, 435
abstract data types, 574-586, 589
abstraction of data, 573-574
access
    fetch, 26
    update, 26
accessing
    files, 411
    members of unions, 470-472
    objects with pointers, 323-327
    parameters, command-line, 250
    structure members, 460-463
    variables, 26
acos() function, 770
add assign (+=) operator, 108

adding direct-access files, 436-444
additive binary operators, 222-223
address-of (&) operator, 64, 220
addresses
    computing from keys, 431
    indirect, 322-323
    objects, 710-713
    offset, 461
    open, 432
    referencing, 372
    relative, 203
alert character, 154
algebraic expressions, parsing with
    recursive descent logic, 391-396
algorithms, Shellsort, 404-408
aligning
    curly braces, 34
    paretheses, 34
allocating
    memory, 25-26
        C heap, 666
        runtime, 474-477
        tracking, 477-478
    objects, whole arrays, 670-671
alternate linkage, 747
American National Standards
    Institute, *see* ANSI
American Standard Code for
    Information Interchange, *see* ASCII
and logical operator, 562
angle brackets (< >), including,
    23-24
ANSI (American National Standards
    Institute), 11-12
    C committee, 503-504
        conformity, 12, 38
        file modes (table), 425
        standard extensions, 525-528
        X3J11 committee, 11
append mode, 66
arbitrary duration, 686
argc parameter, 250-252

arguments, 84
  command-line, 253
  dividing, 255
  functions, 229
  lists, formal, 172
  locating, 243-245
  macro referencing, 173
  pointers, updating, 246
  promotions, 240-242
  signal handlers, 528
  variable, 243-249
  see also parameters
argv[] parameter, 250-252
arithmetic
  conversions, usual, 232
  signed, 730
  types, 526
ARRAY.CPP program (Listing 15.1),
  598-644
ARRAYCL2.CPP program (Listing
  16.2), 670-671
ARRAYCLA.CPP program (Listing
  16.1), 667-668
arrays, 18, 334, 516
  C comparisons
    BASIC, 539-540
    Pascal, 559
  character, 26
  curves, 344-347
  declarations, 242, 335-339, 540
  elements, 214
    locating, 342
    referencing, 337
  fencing, 341
  functions, 370-371
  identifiers, 117
  incomplete, 242, 341
  linear equations, solving, 349-352
  manifest constant, 336
  multidimensional, 214, 338-340

  objects
    allocating, 670-671
    classes, 598-644
    destroying, 670-671
  one-dimensional, 352
    defining, 335-337
  output polygon, 348
  parameters, 370-371
  passing, 549
  pointers, 73, 238, 398-399
    defining, 399-400
  row-major order storage, 338
  shapes, 342-347
  size, 336
  structures, combining, 465-469
  subscript postfix operator, 214
  two-dimensional, 352
  type, 453-454
ASCII (American Standard Code for
Information Interchange)
  character set, 753
  keys, extended, 98
  table, 753-760
ASCII.C program (Listing 74.),
  295-296
asctime() function, 780
asin() function, 770
asm keyword, 527
assembly language, compared to
  C/C++, 14
ASSERT.H header file, 761
assignments
  conversions, implicit, 233
  operators, 138-139
    compound, 227-228
    simple, 227-228
  statements, 137
  values, 210-211
associated locators, 269
associativity, operators, 213

asynchronous events, 265
AT&T C++ 3.0, 749-752
atan() function, 770
atan2() function, 770
atexit() function, 315-316, 776
ATEXIT.C program (Listing 7.8),
   315-316
atof() function, 80, 775
atoi() function, 80, 775
atol() function, 80, 775
attributes, 686
auto
   classes, storage, 186-192
   keyword, 115
   variables, 120
AUTO.CPP program (Listing 15.8),
   655-662
AUTO.HPP program (Listing 15.7),
   652-653
automated PC operation managers,
   652-653
automatic
   control, 302
   duration, 120, 127
   type conversions, 231-233
autonomous objects, 592
avg_value() function, 131

B

\b escape sequence, 153
b mode character, 422
B-spline derivation, 825-826
b_spline() function, 348
back substitution variables, 351
back-end condition checking, 279,
   288-293
backing up files, automatically, 36
backspace character, 154
backward chaining, 498

base class, 693, 698
Basic I/O System, *see* BIOS
BASIC programming
   compared to C programming
      data types, 532-540
      flow control, 543-548
      interpreters versus compilers,
         530-532
      operators, 540-543
   moving to C programming,
      530-549
basic types, 103
bezier() function, 348
binary digits, *see* bits
binary file mode, 427-430
binary operators, 222-227
   additive, 222-223
   bitwise
      AND, 225
      exclusive OR, 225
      inclusive OR, 226
      shift, 223-224
   equality, 224-225
   logical AND, 226
   logical OR, 227
   multiplicative, 222
   relational, 224
binary streams, 58, 427
BIOS (Basic I/O System), 52, 55
bit-fields, 516-517
   non-int types, 527
   structures, 463-465
bits, 148
   least significant, 148
   most significant, 148
   sign, 111, 353
bitwise binary operators
   AND, 108, 225
   exclusive OR, 225
   inclusive OR, 226
   shift, 223-224

blocks
   comments, 33
   scopes, 189
   statements, 17, 141
bodies, loop, 278
Boolean data type, C compared to
   Pascal, 555
Borland C/C++
   compared to Turbo Pascal
      floating-point data types,
         552-553
      integers, 550-552
   stream manipulators, 705-706
braces, curly ({}), 283
branch instructions, 277
break statements
   conditional logic, 313-314
   jump, 300
breakpoints, 46
"brute force" code, 279
bsearch() function, 777
buckets, 432
buffers, 54, 61
   edit, 35
   files, 417-419
   flushing, 67
   hold_buf, 803
   I/O, 416-421
   jump, 269
   lines, 61
   managing, 411
   releasing, 449
   stdin, stdout, and stderr, 419-421
BUFSIZ macro, 766
building function bodies, 136-137
buildmsg() function, 336
built-in
   functions, 21-23
   text editors, 36
bullet() function, 796-797
bytes, 148-149

C

C, 35
   ANSI, 503-504
      standard extensions, 525-528
   binary operators
      additive, 222-223
      bitwise AND, 225
      bitwise exclusive OR, 225
      bitwise inclusive OR, 226
      bitwise shift, 223-224
      equality, 224-225
      logical AND, 226
      logical OR, 227
      multiplicative, 222
      relational, 224
   compilers, 522
      environments, 524-528
   conditional ternary operator, 227
   expressions
      sequence points, 206-209
      side effects, 207-209
   files
      managing, 412-416
      modes, 425
   heap, 665-680, 685-685
   K&R, 520-524
      converting programs, 521-524
   language
      compared to other languages,
         13-15
      extensions, 91
      history, 10-13
   operator set, 723-745
   operators
      classifying, 213-229
      comma, 229
      compound assignment,
        227-228
      conditional tercenary, 227
      postfix, 213-217

simple assignment, 227-228
size-of, 220
unary (+), 218
unary (-), 218-219
postfix operators
array subscript, 214
decrement, 217
function call, 215
increment, 216-217
structure (union) member, 215
structure (union) member
pointer, 216
spirit, 504-505
standards, 504-506
storing strings, 555
translation limitations, 524-525
unary operators
address-of, 220
indirection, 221
logical not, 219
one's complement, 219
prefix decrement, 218
prefix increment, 218
see also free store
C programming, 504-505
compared to BASIC
data types, 532-540
flow control, 543-548
interpreters versus compilers,
530-532
operators, 540-543
compared to Pascal
data types, 550-559
flow control, 562-567
operators, 560-562
moving from
BASIC, 530-549
Pascal, 549-567
C++
AT&T 3.0, 749-752
language
compared to other languages,
13-15
history, 12-13

objects, defining, 680-686
stream I/O, 703-707
C/C++
Borland compared to Turbo
Pascal
floating point data types, 552
integers, 550
compared to Microsoft
QuickBASIC
floating-point data types, 534
floating-point variables,
535-536
integers, 533-534
logical operators, 542-543
mathematical operators, 541
relational operators, 541-542
caches, 50
persistence, 50
speed, 50
calc() function, 17
calc_crc16() function, 142
calc_eff_contin() function, 799
calc_eff_period() function, 799
calc_markup_cost() function, 798
calc_markup_price() function, 798
calc_percent_change() function, 798
calc_percent_total() function, 798
calling functions, 29, 133, 137, 145,
202, 215, 254, 616-617
"calling the shell", 317
calloc() function, 25, 348, 474, 776
carriage-return character, 155
case
labels, 309-313
statements, 140, 563-564
case-sensitivity, 166
cast operators, 233-235
type, 221-222
casting characters, 69
CCOM.C program, 94, 806-822
cdelete() function, 358, 365
ceil() function, 771
CENTER.C program, 87
center_text() function, 87

ch_out() function, 805
chaining
  backward, 498
  forward, 498
chains, running, 463
channel I/O, *see* port
char type specifier, 103, 116
CHAR_BIT macro, 763
CHAR_MAX macro, 763
CHAR_MIN macro, 763
characteristics, 111
characters, 10, 18, 148, 515
  % (conversion), 85
  alert, 154
  arrays, 26
  ASCII set, 753
  backspace, 154
  C compared to Pascal, 554-555
  carriage-return, 155
  casting, 69
  codes, 797
  control, 18, 62, 149
  deleting in text, 358-360
  display, 18, 107, 149
  flag, 85, 253
  form feed, 154
  functions, 68-70, 428
  horizontal tab, 156
  I/O, 706-707
  in mode strings, 422
  initial, 166
  inserting in text, 358-360
  leading, 114
  modifier, 85
  multibyte, 160
  newline, 154
  null, 18
  order, reversing, 327
  sets, 148
    extended, 160
    minimal, 150-151
    source, 161
    target, 161
  strings, 152
  types, 85, 103, 110
  underscore, 166
  vertical tab, 156
  wide, 160
checking
  condition, 279
  syntax, 162
  types, 129
    strong, 129
    weak, 129
checksum method, 75
chips, timer
  control ports, 832
  preprogramming, 828
  programming, 832-833
cin stream object, reading and
  writing with, 703-706
CINOUT.CPP program (Listing 16.9),
  704
CINSDEL.C program (Listing 8.3),
  358-359
cinsert() function, 358, 365
CIPHER.C program, 69-73
class-based languages, 588
classes, 578-589, 595
  array objects, 598-644
  defining, 596-608, 685
  deriving, 686-702
  extending capability with virtual
    functions, 698-702
  inheritance, 586-589, 665, 693-698
  integers, declaring, 730-742
  objects, 616-644
    copying, 609
    creating, 609
    defining pointers, 713-715
    destroying, 608-616
    initializing, 608-616
scope rules, 717
storage, 119
  auto, 186-192
  duration, 186-192

linkage, 188
  static, 188
template, AT&T C++ 3.0, 750-752
virtual
  base, 746-752
  screen, 618-644
classifying C operators, 213-229
`clearerr()` function, 80, 775
`clip_display()` function, 248
CLIP.C program (Listing 6.2),
  248-249
`CLK_TCK` macro, 767
`clock()` function, 780
closing files, 67-68
COBOL language, compared to
  C/C++, 14
code
  reusing, 686-687
    composition, 687-693
    inheritance, 693-702
  ROMable, 39
codes
  "brute force," 279
  character, 797
  fragments, 609
  machine target, 163
  reusability, 589, 665
  scan, 797
coding
  function definitions, 135-136
  state-dependent, 160
collating sequence, 150
colliding keys, 431
combining operands in expressions,
  231-233
comma operators, 229
command-lines
  arguments, 253
  compilers, 43-44
  environment, 44

parameters
  accessing, 250
  formats, 252-254
commands
  display, 822
  DOS, SET, 24
  push, 824
  send, 823
  system, 250
  tails, 250
  wait, 823
comments, 17, 33, 205
  block, 33
  macros, 176
commonality, *see* polymorphism
communications I/O programming,
  91
`compares()` function, 265
COMPARES.C program
  Listing 6.6, 263-264
  Listing 9.3, 402-403
comparing pointers, 327-333
comparison functions, 402-403
compile time, 608
compile-only options, 38
compilers, 21, 37
  ANSI C conformity, 38
  C environments, 522-528
  C++ support, 40
  command-line, 43-44
  compile-only options, 38
  directives, 17, 20, 168
  floating-point math support, 39
  host environment support
    options, 39
  language compatibility, 43
  linkage editors, 40
  low-level features support, 39
  modules, 195-199
  objects, 191

one-pass, 163
optimization features, 39
project-management facilities, 41-42
ROMable code, 39
stack segments, 203
syntax directed, 161
two-pass, 163
versus interpreters, 530-532
complex projects, 41
COMPOSE.CPP program (Listing 16.6), 688-690
composition, reusing code, 687-693
compound assignment operator, 227-228
compound statements, *see* block statements
computing
addresses from keys, 431
prime numbers, 281-300
condition checking, 279
back-end, 279, 288-293
front-end, 279, 284-288
conditional
compilation directives, 177-180
expressions, 138, 219
inclusion directives, 177
logic, 278
logic statements, 304-314
break, 313-314
case labels, 309-313
default, 313-314
If-then-else, 305-308
nested if-else, 307
switch(), 308-314
ternary operator, 109, 227
conditions, end-of-file, 79
conformity, ANSI C, 38
connecting files to streams, 62
const keyword, 747
const member function, 747-749

const type qualifier, 109
constants, 25, 110-113, 152, 164
enumeration, 499-500
limiting, 110
manifest, 171
primary expression, 210
constructor member function, 583, 608-616
constructors, 578
CONTINUE.C program (Listing 7.6), 303
continue jump statement, 299
continue loop, 302
continue statement, 302-308
control
characters, 18, 62, 149
ports, 832
variables, 278
controllers, disk, 55
conventions, language, 147
conversions
arithmetic, usual, 232
automatic, 231-233
character (%), 85
data, 235
explicit, 233-235
implicit, 231, 241
assignment, 233
integers, 198
numeric-to-string, 194-198
pointer type casts, 234
specifications, 83-84
converting
formats, 80-82, 105
K&R C programs, 521-524
COPIES.C program (Listing 10.2), 414-415
copy initializer function, 615-616
copying class objects, 609
cos() function, 771
cosh() function, 771

cout stream object, reading and writing, 703-706
CPRINT.C program, 92-93
CPTRDEMO.C program (Listing 13.2), 557-567
CRC16.C program, 142
creating
   class objects, 609
   files
      direct-access, 436-444
      temporary, 416
   lexical scanners, 376-387
   objects, 667-668
   program loops, 278-304
cross-compilers, 522
ctime() function, 780
CTYPE.H header file, 769
curly braces ({}), 17, 34, 283
curses, 360
cursors, homing, 155
curves
   drawing, 343-349
   smoothing, 342-349
cvtdtos() function, 198
cvtitos() function, 198
CVTJUL.C program, 124-127
cvtltos() function, 198
CVTSTR.C program (Listing 5.2), 195-198

D

DAM, *see* direct-access method files
DAMFILE.C program (Listing 10.6), 437-441
data
   abstraction, 573-574, 579
   conversions, 231-235
   defining, 25-27
   displaying, 84-86
   files, 57

hiding, 573-574
managing, 411
   dynamic memory, 473-478
objects, 165, 601
types, 10, 472-473
   abstract, 579-586
   arrays, 539-540, 559
   Boolean, 555
   C compared to BASIC, 532-540
   C compared to Pascal, 550-559
   characters, 10, 554-555
   floating-point variables, 10, 534-536
   integers, 10, 532-534, 550-552
   pointers, 555-559
   real numbers, 552-553
   strings, 536-539, 554-555
_ _DATE_ _ macro, 182
DBL_DIG macro, 762
DBL_EPSILON macro, 763
DBL_MANT_DIG macro, 762
DBL_MAX macro, 762
DBL_MAX_10_EXP macro, 762
DBL_MAX_EXP macro, 762
DBL_MIN macro, 763
DBL_MIN_10_EXP macro, 762
DBL_MIN_EXP macro, 762
deallocating memory on C heap, 666
debuggers
   breakpoints, 46
   environment displays, 46
   integrated environments, 46
   interactive modification, 46
   multiple display windows, 46
   multiple source file suport, 47
   stand-alone versions, 46
   step-over, 46
   system displays, 46
   trace-into execution, 46
   uses, 47

visual, 44-45
  interactive nature, 45
  watch windows, 46
debugging programs, 44
dec string manipulator, 705
decimal values, 107
declarations, 15
  arrays, 242
  inner, 122, 191
  member-function prototype,
    601-603
  object, 816, 690
  outer, 120, 191
  pointers, 221, 266
  registers, 188
declarators, 114-118, 517
  function, 131-134
  lists, 114-118
declaring
  arrays, 335-336, 540
  bit-field structure members, 464
  data objects, structured, 454-460
  forward, 134
  functions, 29, 128-130
    friend, 716-717
    member, 724
  integer classes, 730-742
  streams, 63-64
  string variables, 353-354
  structures
    with tags, 459-460
    without tags, 456-457
  unions, 470
  variables, 25
    arrays, 338-339
decode_file() function, 75
default
  conditional logic statement,
    313-314
  statement, 140

defining
  arrays of pointers, 398-399
  classes, 596-608
  data objects, 25-27
    structured, 454-457
  objects
    integer, 744-745
    to C++, 680-686
  pointers
    arrays, 399-400
    class objects, 713-715
  structures, 454-469
definitions
  function, 20, 131
    coding, 135-136
delete operator, 666-678
deleting
  files
    direct-access, 436-444
    remove() function, 412
  recursion, 258-260
  text characters, 358-360
DEMO.CPP program (Listing 15.6),
  651
dependency conditions, 205
dependent fields, 205
dereferencing pointers, 64, 221,
  374-375
derivation, B-spline, 825-826
deriving
  classes, 686-702
  inheritance, 686-702
  types, 103-453-454
description blocks, 205
destroying
  class objects, 608-616
  objects, 667-668
    whole arrays, 670-671
destructor function, 608-616
DETAB.C program (Listing 7.3),
  289-292

devices
  control ports, 52
  I/O, 50-51
  interactive, 56
`difftime()` function, 780
digraphs, 158
direct
  I/O function class, 428
  memory access (DMA), 51
  recursion, 254
direct-access files, 430-434
  adding, 436-444
  creating, 436-444
  deleting, 436-444
  method (DAM), 430
  programming, 430-436
  reading, 436-444
directives
  compiler, 17, 20, 168
  conditional compilation, 177-180
  conditional inclusion, 177
  `#elif`, 179
  `#else`, 179
  `#endif`, 179
  `#error`, 181
  `goto`, 824
  `#if`, 179
  `ifkey`, 824
  `#include`, 20-25, 201
    nested, 163
    placing, 23
  `#line`, 180-181
  null (#), 182
  `#pragma`, 182
  preprocessing, 17
directories
  masks, 497
  `\source`, 24
disabling interrupts, 834
disks
  controllers, 55
  I/O programming, 91

display
  characters, 18, 107, 149
  command, 822
`display_payout()` function, 801
`display_table()` function, 801
displaying data, 84-86
div (integer division) mathematical
  operator, 560
`div()` function, 199, 777
dividing arguments, 255
divisors, 832
DMA (direct-memory access), 51
`do` loop, 546-548
`do-while()` function, 288-293
`do_something()` function, 131
DOS, 10
DOS commands, SET, 24
double floating-point types, 198
double quotation marks (" "),
  including, 24-25
double type specifier, 104, 116
doubly linked lists, 463, 480-496
`draw_polygon()` function, 348
drawing
  curves, 343-349
  shapes, 342-343
"dumb" terminal programs, 803
dump programs, 105
duration, 119
  automatic, 120, 127
  classes, storage, 186-192
  dynamic, 27
  fixed, 120
dynamic
  duration, 27
    automatic, 120
  memory
    data, managing, 473-478
  objects, 680-681
    stacks, 681-683

E

Eckel, Bruce, 587
    object-oriented programming,
        587-589
edit buffers, 35
`edit_environment()` function, 369
`edit_text()` function, 356
    keyboard shortcuts, 357-358
editing
    text with strings, 356-369
    variable environment, 367-369
editors
    linkage, 40
    text, 35-37
        built-in, 36
        error location, 37
        project make facilities, 37
        stand-alone, 36
elements, arrays, 214
    locating, 342
    multidimensional, 339-342
    referencing, 337
`#elif` directive, 179
ellipsis, 243
`#else` directive, 179
empty lists, 527, 613
empty macro arguments, 527
EMPTY.C program, 28
encapsulation, 586
    see also abstraction
`encode_file()` function, 75
encryption keys, 70
end-of-file conditions, 79
end-recursion removal, 260
`#endif` directive, 179
ENDING.C program, 28
`endl` string manipulator, 705
`ends` string manipulator, 705
entering loops, 300-301
`enum` type specifier, 116

enumerations, 516-517
    constants, 499-500
environments, 515, 524-528
    C, 35
    command-line, 44
    freestanding, 249
    hosted, 249
    IDE, 36, 43
    setting up, 27
    variables
        editing, 367-369
        `INCLUDE`, 366
        `LIB`, 366
        `PATH`, 366
`EOF` macro, 766
equality
    binary operators, 224-225
    operators, 138-139, 224-225
equations
    arrays, 349-352
    linear, 349-352
`eraeol()` function, 360
`#error` directive, 181
errors
    handling, 79-80
    location, 37
escape sequences, 152
    \?, 154
    \\, 154
    \", 154
    \', 154
    \0, 157
    \123, 157
    \779, 157
    \88, 157
    \a, 153
    \b, 153
    \f, 153
    hexadecimal, 158
    mnemonic, 153-157
    \n, 153

numeric, 157-158
octal, 157
\r, 153
\ss, 158
\t, 153
trigraph, 158-159
\v, 154
\x0, 158
\x0D, 158
\xFF, 158
\xFG, 158
EUCLID.C program (Listing 6.4), 255-256
EUCLID2.C program (Listing 6.5), 259
evaluating formulas, 390-398
events
   asynchronous, 265
   I/O, reducing, 447-448
EXCHANGE.C program, 143-144
exe_command() function, 806
exec...() function, 318-319
executing
   functions, 596
   programs, associated locater, 269
execution
   step-over, 46
   trace-into, 46
exit() function, 268, 776
EXIT_FAILURE macro, 315, 767
EXIT_SUCCESS macro, 315, 767
exiting
   loops, 288, 300-301
   programs, 314-317
   see also terminating
exp() function, 771
explicit conversions, 233-235
exponential notation, 111
expressions
   algebraic, parsing with recursive descent logic, 391-396

conditional, 138, 219
functions
   calling, 215
   designator, 212
lvalue, 210-211
   modifiable, 211
operands, combining, 231-233
order of evaluations, 212
postfix, 213-217
primary
   constants, 210
   identifiers, 210
   parenthesized, 210
   string literals, 210
rvalue, 210-211
statements, writing, 137
unary, 217
extended
   ASCII keys, 98
   character sets, 160
   DOS streams, supporting, 92
extensions, implementation-dependent, 12
extern keyword, 115, 527
extern storage-class keyword, 188
external
   formats, 105
   linkage, 132, 190
extractors, 703

F

\f escape sequence, 153
fabs() function, 771
factorial numbers, 257
fclose() function, 67, 772
fcloseall() function, 75
fencing arrays, 341
feof() function, 80, 775
ferror() function, 80, 293, 775
fetch access, 26
fflush() function, 773

fgetc() function, 59, 75-76, 774
fgetpos() function, 434-435, 774
fgets() function, 59, 77-79, 774
fields
    dependent, 205
    target, 205
    width, 85
    word, 110
_ _FILE_ _ macro, 182
file-merge capability, 36
file-position indicator, 528
FILENAME_MAX macro, 766
filenames, 62
    changing with rename() function,
      413-414
files, 54
    accessing, 411
    backing up automatically, 36
    buffering, 417-419
    closing, 67-68
    connecting to streams, 62
    creating temporary, 416
    data, 57
    deleting with remove() function,
      412
    direct-access, 430-434
      adding, 436-444
      creating, 436-444
      deleting, 436-444
      method (DAM), 430
      reading, 436-444
    flat, 444
    handles, 61
    header, 20-23, 169-170, 200-202
      ASSERT.H, 761
      CTYPE.H, 769
      FLOAT.H, 761-763
      LIMITS.H, 763
      LOCALE.H, 764, 770
      MATH.H, 23, 764, 770-771
      SETJMP.H, 764, 772
      SIGNAL.H, 765, 772

      STDARG.H, 765
      STDDEF.H, 765
      STDIO.H, 23, 65, 766, 772-775
      STDLIB.H, 23, 766
      STRING.H, 778
      TIMER.H, 835-836
      TIME.H, 767, 780
      uses, 22
    line-buffered, 56
    loading into random-access
      memory, 449
    make, 41
    managing, 411
      with C, 412-416
    modes, 528
      access, 421-425
      ANSI C, 425
      binary and text, 427-430
      I/O programming, 445
      parameters, 66
    networks, 450
    object, 161
    opening, 65-67
    plain text, 69
    position, 434-436
    positioning class, 428
    random-access, 430
    reading and writing in update
      mode, 425-427
    returning to beginning with
      rewind() function, 414-415
    scope, 189
    source
      contents, 195-199
      including, 21, 169-170
      references, 202-203
      STREDIT.C, 361-369
    STDLIB.H header, 80
    text, 66
    unbuffered, 56
FINANCE.C program, 781-796
FIRST.C program, 19

fixed duration, 120
flag characters, 85, 253
flat files, 444
float type specifier, 104, 116
FLOAT.H header file, 761-763
floating-point
   math support, 39
   number types, 103-104, 111
   numbers, 10, 516
   types, double, 198
   variables, C compared to BASIC,
   534-536
floor() function, 771
flow control, 278
   C comparisons
      BASIC, 543-548
      Pascal, 562-567
   case statement, 563-564
   if-then-else statements, 543-544,
   562-563
   loops
      do, 546-548
      for, 564-565
      for-next, 545-546
      while, 546-548
   prechecked and postchecked
   loops, 567
   SELECT CASE statement, 544-545
   statements, writing, 137-140
FLT_DIG macro, 762
FLT_EPSILON macro, 763
FLT_MANT_DIG macro, 762
FLT_MAX macro, 762
FLT_MAX_10_EXP macro, 762
FLT_MAX_EXP macro, 762
FLT_MIN macro, 762
FLT_MIN_10_EXP macro, 762
FLT_MIN_EXP macro, 762
FLT_RADIX macro, 762
FLT_ROUNDS macro, 762
flush string manipulator, 705

flushing buffers, 67
fmod() function, 771
FMORE.C program, 95-98
fopen() function, 63-65, 773
FOPEN_MAX macro, 766
for loops, C compared to Pascal,
   566-567
for-next loops, 545-546
fork() function, 318-319
form feed character, 154
formal
   argument lists, 172
   function parameter, 712
   parameter lists, writing, 133-134
formats
   command-line parameters,
      252-254
   converting, 80-82, 105
   external, 105
   internal, 105
   strings, 83-84, 155
formatted I/O function class, 83, 428
FORmula TRANslation, *see*
  FORTRAN language
FORMULA.C program (Listing 9.2),
   391-396
formulas, evaluating, 390-398
fortran keyword, 527
FORTRAN language, compared to
  C/C++, 15
forward
   chaining, 496
   declaring functions, 134
   elimination of matrices, 351
fprintf() function, 59, 86-87, 773
fputc() function, 59, 293, 774
fputs() function, 59, 77, 774
fractional numbers, 111
frames, stack, 43
fread() function, 774
free store, 665-680
   static objects, 685-686

free() function, 474, 776
freestanding environment, 249
freopen() function, 773
frexp() function, 771
friend functions, 716-717
    overloading, 723
front-end condition checking, 279, 284-288
fscanf() function, 59, 88-89, 773
fseek() function, 66, 435-436, 774
fsetpos() function, 435-436, 774
ftell() function, 434-435, 775
fullwords, 104
fully buffered I/O, 54
function-like macros, 171-172
functional objects, 592
functionality, 38
functions, 16
    *bsearch(), 777
    *calloc(), 776
    *fgets(), 774
    *fopen(), 773
    *freopen(), 773
    *getenv(), 776
    *gets(), 774
    *localeconv(), 770
    *malloc(), 776
    *realloc(), 776
    *setlocale(), 770
    *tmpfile(), 772
    *tmpnam(), 772
    _getvideoconfig(), 98
    abort(), 66, 317, 776
    abs(), 777
    acos(), 770
    arguments
        promotions, 240-242
        variable, 243-249
    asctime(), 780
    asin(), 770
    atan(), 770
atan2(), 770
atexit(), 315-316, 776
atof(), 80, 775
atoi(), 80, 775
atol(), 80, 775
avg_value(), 131
b_spline(), 348
bezier(), 348
bodies, 135
    building, 136-137
buildmsg(), 336
built-in, 21-23
bullet(), 796-797
calc(), 17
calc_crc16(), 142
calc_eff_contin(), 799
calc_eff_period(), 799
calc_markup_cost(), 798
calc_markup_price(), 798
calc_percent_change(), 798
calc_percent_total(), 798
call postfix operator, 215
calling, 29, 133, 145
    in expressions, 215
calloc(), 25, 348, 474
calls, 137, 189, 202
    arguments, 229
    expressions, 215
    recursive, 254
cdelete(), 358, 365
ceil(), 771
center_text(), 87
ch_out(), 805
character I/O, 68-70
cinsert(), 358, 365
clearerr(), 80, 775
clip_display(), 248
clock(), 780
compares(), 265
comparison, 402-403
constructor, 583, 608-616

copy initializer, 615-616

cos(), 771

cosh(), 771

ctime(), 780

cvtdtos(), 198

cvtitos(), 198

cvtltos(), 198

declaring, 29, 128-130

decode_file(), 75

definitions, 20, 131

  coding, 135-136

designator expression, 212

destructor, 608-616

difftime(), 780

display_payout(), 801

display_table(), 801

div(), 199, 777

do-while(), 288-293

do_something(), 131

draw_polygon(), 348

edit_environment(), 369

edit_text(), 356

encode_file(), 75

eraeol(), 360

exe_command(), 806

exec...(), 318-319

executing, 596

exit(), 268, 776

exp(), 771

fabs(), 771

fclose(), 67, 772

fcloseall(), 75

feof(), 80, 775

ferror(), 80, 293, 775

fflush(), 773

fgetc(), 59, 75-76, 774

fgetpos(), 434-435, 774

fgets(), 59, 77-79

floor(), 771

fmod(), 771

fopen(), 63-65

fork(), 318-319

formatted I/O, 83

fprintf(), 59, 86-87, 773

fputc(), 59, 293, 774

fputs(), 59, 77, 774

fread(), 774

free(), 474, 776

frexp(), 771

friend, 716-717

fscanf(), 59, 88-89, 773

fseek(), 66, 435-436, 774

fsetpos(), 435-436, 774

ftell(), 434-435, 775

fwrite(), 774

gauss(), 351

generate_key(), 75

get_a_line(), 131

get_comm_byte(), 805

get_key(), 805

get_mortgage_data(), 800

getc(), 59-60, 774

getch(), 98, 361, 797

getchar(), 59-60, 774

getday(), 128

getjul(), 128

getmon(), 127

gets(), 59, 356

gettextpostion(), 360

gmtime(), 780

here_it_is(), 131

hex_char(), 107-108

hires_clock(), 832

hook_com(), 804

I/O, 52, 62

identifiers, 118

in-line, 606

init_com(), 804

int_svc(), 804

invoking, 260-275

is_it_there(), 131

isalnum(), 769

isalpha(), 769
iscntrl(), 769
isdigit(), 769
isgraph(), 769
isleap(), 127
islower(), 769
isprint(), 769
ispunct(), 769
isspace(), 770
isupper(), 770
isxdigit(), 770
kbd_command(), 806
labs(), 777
ldexp(), 771
ldiv(), 199, 777
library, 167-168, 446-449, 518-519
localtime(), 780
log(), 771
log10(), 771
longjmp(), 269, 772
lores_clock(), 834
main(), 20, 27
    environment setup, 27-28
    program termination, 28
malloc(), 25, 474, 477
mangling, 747
max_val(), 136
mblen(), 777
mbstowcs(), 777
mbtowc(), 777
member, 574-579, 717-720,
    731-742
    AutoRun program, 655-662
    calling, 616-617
    const, 747-749
    declaring, 724
    reusing, 688-690
    screen class, 622-650
    static, 747-749
    volatile, 747-749
memchr(), 778
memcmp(), 778

memcpy(), 778
memmove(), 778
memory-management, 474
memset(), 105, 779
mktime(), 780
modays(), 127
modf(), 198-199, 771
names, writing, 133-134
newint8(), 833, 834
open_file(), 75
overlay(), 806
overloading, 720-722, 747
    friend, 723
    member, 722
parameters
    arrays, 370-371
    passing, 238-240
    strings, 370
    structures and unions, 478-479
perror(), 59, 80, 775
pointer casts, 526
pointers, 118, 261-265, 315
pow(), 771
print_table(), 801
printf(), 59, 84-86, 152-153,
    167-168, 243-249, 773
process(), 130
processing, 414
prototype scopes, 189
prototypes, 20, 29-30, 130
    declarators, 131-134
    incomplete types, 242-243
    scopes, 189
prototyping, 135
putc(), 59-60, 774
putchar(), 59-60, 774
putenv(), 367
puts(), 59, 77, 774
qsort(), 777
raise(), 268-269, 772
rand(), 776
realloc(), 25, 474, 477

registers, 315
remove(), 412, 772
rename(), 413-414, 772
returning values from, 142-145
rewind(), 414-415, 775
run_script(), 806
scanf(), 59, 88-90, 243-249, 356, 773
scanner(), 378-387
scope, 189
scroll_up(), 805
send_comm_byte(), 804
setbuf(), 446-449, 773
setjmp(), 269-275, 772
settextposition(), 360
setvbuf(), 446-449, 773
Shellsort, 402-403
show_line(), 98
signal(), 266-269
sin(), 771
sinh(), 771
some_function(), 193
spawn...(), 318-319
SPFV(), 799
SPPV(), 800
sprintf(), 86, 773
sqrt(), 771
srand(), 776
sscanf(), 88-89, 773
start_bench(), 832
stop_bench(), 834
str_invert(), 198, 229
strcat(), 79, 778
strchr(), 79, 779
strcmp(), 778
strcoll(), 778
strcpy(), 79, 778
strcspn(), 779
strerror(), 779
strftime(), 780
string I/O, 76-77

string-editing, 362-365
string_out(), 806
strlen(), 779
strncat(), 778
strncmp(), 778
strncpy(), 778
strol(), 80-81
stroul(), 80-81
strpbrk(), 779
strrchr(), 779
strrev(), 199
strspn(), 779
strstr(), 779
strtod(), 80, 775
strtok(), 376-378, 779
strtol(), 775
strtoul(), 775
strupr(), 294
strxfrm(), 778
system(), 317-319, 776
tan(), 771
tanh(), 771
template
    AT&T C++ 3.0, 750-752
test_key(), 805
time(), 780
tmpfile(), 416
tmpnam(), 416
tolower(), 770
toupper(), 770
types, 103, 453-454
ungetc(), 774
unhook_com(), 804
user-defined, 28-30, 165
USFV(), 800
USPV(), 800
vfprintf(), 59, 248, 773
vidtex(), 805
vidtex_sba(), 806
virtual, 698-702
vprintf(), 59, 248, 773

`vsprintf()`, 774
`wait_for_tx()`, 805
`wcstombs()`, 777
`wctomb()`, 777
`wherex()`, 360
`wherey()`, 360
`fwrite()` function, 774

G

`gauss()` function, 351
GAUSS.C program (Listing 8.2), 350-351
Gaussian elimination, 349-352
GCD (greatest common divisor), 255
`generate_key()` function, 75
`get_a_line()` function, 131
`get_comm_byte()` function, 805
`get_key()` function, 805
`get_mortgage_data()` function, 800
`getc()` function, 59-60, 774
`getch()` keyboard input function, 98, 361, 797
`getchar()` function, 59-60, 774
`getday()` function, 128
`getenv()` function, 776
`getjul()` function, 128
`getmon()` function, 127
`gets()` library function, 59, 356, 774
`gettextpostion()` function, 360
`_getvideoconfig()` function, 98
GLBLNEW.CPP program (Listing 16.3), 674
global
   `delete` operator, 672-678
   `new` operator, 672-678
   scope, 119
   static objects, 683-685
   variables, 26-27, 120-121, 124

`gmtime()` function, 780
GOLOOP.C program (Listing 7.5), 300-301
`goto` directive, 824
`goto` identifier jump statement, 140, 299
greatest common divisor (GCD), 255
grouping
   line-groups, 179
   operators, 213

H

halfwords, 104
handles, file, 61
handling errors, 79-80
hashing, 431
hashkeys, 431, 436-444
header files, 20-23, 169-170, 200-202
   ASSERT.H, 761
   CTYPE.H, 769
   FLOAT.H, 761-763
   LIMITS.H, 763
   LOCALE.H, 764, 770
   MATH.H, 23, 764, 770-771
   SETJMP.H, 764, 772
   SIGNAL.H, 765, 772
   STDARG.H, 765
   STDDEF.H, 765
   STDIO.H, 23, 65, 766, 772-775
   STDLIB.H, 23, 766
   STRING.H, 778
   TIMER.H, 835-836
   TIME.H, 767, 780
   uses, 22
heaps, 26
   see also dynamic memory
`here_it_is()` function, 131
Hermite geometry matrixes, 825-826

hex string manipulator, 705
hex_char() function, 107-108
hexadecimal escape sequences, 158
hiding data, 573-574
high-resolution timing mode, 831, 834-835
hires_clock() function, 832
hold_buf buffer, 803
homing cursors, 155
hook_com() function, 804
horizontal tab character, 156
host environment support options, 39
hosted environment, 249
HUGE_VAL macro, 764

I

I/O
    buffering, 416-421
        fully, 54
        keyboard, 420-421
        line, 54
    cin and cout streams, 704
    devices, 50-51
    events, reducing, 447-448
    function families (table), 428
    functions, 52, 62
    memory-mapped, 51
    modes (table), 428
    port, 51-52
    practices
        low-level, 450
        networks, 450
    programming, 50-53, 411, 449-450
        communications, 91
        disk, 91
        file modes, 445
        overhead, 445-449
        read operations, 50
        video display, 91, 94-98
    write operations, 50
    redirection, 59, 707
    screen arrangements, 360-361
    standard, 58-62
    streams, 53-56, 707
        data files, 57
        interactive devices, 56
        mixing, 706-707
    unbuffered, 54
IDE (integrated development environment), 36, 43
identifiers, 164-166, 515, 526
    array, 117
    function, 118
    parentheses, 117
    pointers to, 117
    primary expression, 210
    simple, 117
#if direcitve, 179
if-then-else conditional logic
    statement, C comparisons, 305-308
        BASIC, 543-544
        Pascal, 562-563
ifkey directive, 824
implementation-defined
    areas, 24, 505
    behaviors, 506, 514-520
implementation-dependent
    extensions, 12
implicit conversions, 231, 241
    by assignment, 233
in (is a member of) relational
    operator, 561
in-line functions, 606
#include directive, 20-25
    nested, 163
    placing, 23
INCLUDE environment variable, 366
including
    angle brackets, 23-24
    double quotation marks, 24-25
    source files, 21, 169-170

incomplete types, 103
  arrays, 341
  function prototypes, 242-243
incremental modification, 589
increments, prefix, 293
indentation, 32-33
indeterminate values, 64
indicators, file-position, 528
indirect
  addressing, 322-323
  recursion, 254
indirection unary (*) operator, 64, 221
INHERIT.CPP program (Listing 16.7), 695-697
inheritance, 586-587
  code, reusing, 700-702
  deriving, 686-702
  multiple, 746-747
  reusing code, 693-698
init_com() function, 804
initial character, 166
initializers, 111, 115
  objects, 192-193
initializing, 278
  class objects, 608-616
  lists, 74, 611-613
  local variable, 127, 128
  string variables, 354
  structures
    with tags, 459-460
    without tags, 456-457
  variables, 111-113, 118-119
inner declarations, 122, 191
inner loop, 296
input, 50
  mode, 422
  text streams, processing, 376
input and output, *see* I/O
inserters, 703
inserting text characters, 358-360

instructions
  branch, 277
  jump, 277
int type specifier, 103, 116
INT_MAX macro, 763
INT_MIN macro, 763
int_svc() function, 804
integers, 10, 516, 608
  C comparisons
    BASIC, 532-534
    Pascal, 550-552
  classes, 730-742
  converting, 198
  long, 198
  objects, 744-745
integral promotion rules, 232, 522
integrated development
  environment (IDE), 36, 43
interactive
  devices, 56
  modification, 46
intermediate representation, 162
internal
  formats, 105
  linkage, 132, 190
interpreters versus compilers, 530-532
interrupts
  disabling, 834
  timer-tick, 833
invoking
  functions, 260-275
  programs, 317-318
_IOFBF macro, 766
_IOLBF macro, 766
_IONBF macro, 766
IRQ0 (level 0) Interrupt Service
  Routine, 828
is_it_there() function, 131
isalnum() function, 769
isalpha() function, 769

`iscntrl()` function, 769
`isdigit()` function, 769
`isgraph()` function, 769
`isleap()` function, 127
`islower()` function, 769
`isprint()` function, 769
`ispunct()` function, 769
`isspace()` function, 770
`isupper()` function, 770
`isxdigit()` function, 770
iteration statements, 138, 283

J-K

JMPERR.C program (Listing 6.8), 270-271
JMPSIG.C program (Listing 6.9), 272-274
jump
  buffers, 269
  instructions, 277
  statements, 138
    `break`, 300
    `continue`, 299
    `goto` identifier, 299
    `return` expression, 300
K&R C, 520-524
  programs, converting, 521-524
`kbd_command()` function, 806
keyboards
  I/O buffering, 420-421
  input functions, `getch()`, 361
  objects, 580-585
  shortcuts, `edit_text()` function, 357-358
KEYBOARD.CPP program (Listing 14.3), 581-583
KEYBOARD.HPP programs (Listing 14.2), 580-581
KEYIO.C program (Listing 10.4), 420-421

keys
  ASCII, extended, 98
  colliding, 431
  computing addresses from, 431
  encryption, 70
  hashed, 436-444
keywords, 164-167, 604
  `asm`, 527
  `auto`, 115
  `const`, 747-749
  `extern`, 115, 527
  `fortran`, 527
  `operator`, 724
  `overload`, 722
  `register`, 115, 187
  `static`, 115, 123, 748
  storage-classes
    `extern`, 188
    `static`, 188
  `this`, 605-608
  `typedef`, 115
  `volatile`, 747-749
knots, 343

L

`L_tmpnam` macro, 766
labeled statement, writing, 140
`labs()` function, 777
languages
  assembly, 14
  C
    compared to other languages, 13-15
    extensions, 91
    history, 10-13
  C++
    compared to other languages, 13-15
    history, 12-13

class-based, 588
COBOL, 14
conventions, 147
FORTRAN, 15
OOPS, 587
Pascal, 14
typeless, 10
LC_ALL macro, 764
LC_COLLATE macro, 764
LC_CTYPE macro, 764
LC_MONETARY macro, 764
LC_NUMERIC macro, 764
LC_TIME macro, 764
LDBL_DIG macro, 762
LDBL_EPSILON macro, 763
LDBL_MANT_DIG macro, 762
LDBL_MAX macro, 762
LDBL_MAX_10_EXP macro, 762
LDBL_MAX_EXP macro, 762
LDBL_MIN macro, 762
LDBL_MIN_10_EXP macro, 762
LDBL_MIN_EXP macro, 762
ldexp() function, 771
LDISPLAY.C program (Listing 6.1),
    247-248
ldiv() function, 199, 777
leading characters, 114
least significant bit, 148
lexical scanners, 376
    pointers, 378-387
LIB environment variable, 366
libraries, functions, 167-168,
    446-449, 518-519
    gets(), 356
    scanf(), 356
    standard, 167
    vfprintf(), 248
    vsprintf(), 248
limiting constants, 110
LIMITS.H header file, 763
#line directive, 180
_ _LINE_ _ macro, 182

line-buffered
    files, 56
    I/O, 54
    streams, 61
line-groups, 179
linear equations, solving with
    arrays, 349-352
liner, inherently, 277
lines, buffering, 61
linkage, 188
    alternate, 747
    editor, 191
    external, 132, 190
    internal, 132, 190
    no linkage, 190
    objects, 188-192
    type-safe, 747
linkage editors, 40
linked lists, 462
    building with structures, 479-499
    doubly, 463
    singly, 462
linking object modules, 203-206
listings
    1.1. FIRST.C-basic program
        (in Borland C++), 19
    1.2. UCTOUCH.C-user-written
        TOUCH utility, 42
    2.1. STREAM.C-show character
        I/O, 60
    2.2. CIPHER.C-support data
        encryption, 70-73
    2.3. NUMBER.C-show number
        text files, 77-79
    2.4. STRTOX.C, 82-83
    2.5. PRINTIT.C, 86
    2.6. CENTER.C, 87
    2.7. READIT.C, 89-90
    2.8. CPRINT.C-print text files,
        92-93
    2.9. FMORE.C-faster MORE display,
        95-97

3.1. SDUMP.C-hex dump program, 106-107

3.2. LITERAL.C-uses literal values, 112

3.3. CVTJUL.C-date conversions, 124-127

3.4. CRC16.C-show function returning value, 142

3.5. EXCHANGE.C-show function returning nothing, 143-144

4.1. Using special characters in printf(), 152-153

5.1. TESTCSTR.C-tests numeric-to-string conversion, 194

5.2. CVTSTR.C-numeric-to-string conversion function 195-198

6.1. LDISPLAY.C-variable-length list of strings, 247-248

6.2. CLIP.C-clip output message to window boundary, 248-249

6.3. SHOWARG.C-access command-line parameters, 251

6.4. EUCLID.C-computer greatest common divisor with recursive function calls, 255-256

6.5. EUCLID2.C-eliminate recursive calls, 259

6.6. COMPARES.C-use pointer-to-function to invoke function, 263-264

6.7. SHOWSIG.C-demonstrate signal handling, 267-268

6.8. JMPERR.C-longjmp() out of nested functions, 270-271

6.9. JMPSIG.C-terminate signal handlers with longjmp() function, 272-274

7.1. PRIME.C-compute first 350 prime numbers, 281-282

7.2. POLY.C-evaluate polynomial with while, 285-286

7.3. DETAB.C-do-while guarantees at least one pass, 289-292

7.4. ASCII.C-nested for loops increase loop, 295-296

7.5. GOLOOP.C-dangerous entry and exit from loop, 300-301

7.6. CONTINUE.C-use continue to loop early, 303

7.7. SELECT.C-switch statement in action, 310-312

7.8. ATEXIT.C-use of the atexit() function, 315-316

8.1. SPLINE.C-using arrays to represent curves and shapes, 344-347

8.2. GAUSS.C-Gaussian elimination algorithm, 350-351

8.3. CINSDEL.C-inserting and deleting characters, 358-359

8.4. STREDIT.C-general-purpose string editing functions, 362-365

SYSENV.C-editing DOS execution environment, 367-369

9.1. SCANNER.C-lexical scanner routine (using all compilers), 379-384

9.2. FORMULA.C-parsing algebraic expressions with recursive descent logic (using Borland C++), 391-396

9.3. COMPARES.C-comparison functions for use with Shellsort function (using Borland C++), 402-403

9.4. SHELLSRT.C-using the Shellsort algorithm with array of pointers to objects to be sorted, 404-408

10.1. VERSIONS.C-using the rename() function to change filename (for Borland C++), 413-451

10.2. COPIES.C-using `rewind()` (for Borland C++), 414-415

10.3. SPEEDBUF.C-tuning I/O performance with buffer size, 418

10.4. KEYIO.C-controlling keyboard I/O buffering (Borland C++), 420-421

10.5. PRIME.C-calculate next higher prime number for bucket divisor (for Microsoft C/C++), 433

10.6. DAMFILE.C-direct file-access create, read, add, and delete functions (for Microsoft C/C, 437-441

11.1. STRICT.C-declaring and initializing structures with tags (using Microsoft C/C++), 456-457

11.2. STRUCT2.C-declaring and initializing structures with tags (using Microsoft C/C++), 459-460

11.3. STRUCT3.C-declaring bit-field structure members (with Microsoft C/C++), 464

11.4. STRUCT4.C-structure with a member having array type (using Microsoft C/C++), 465-466

11.5. STRUCT5.C-array of structures (using Microsoft C/C++), 466-467

11.6. STRUCT6.C-array of pointers to structure (using Microsoft C/C++), 467-468

11.7. STRUCT7.C-implementing pointer to array `strict` in dynamic memory (with Microsoft C/C++), 476

11.8. XDIR.C-using doubly linked lists to implement directory listing program (with Borland C++), 480-496

13.1. PTRDEMO.PAS-Pascal pointer demonstrating program (with Turbo Pascal), 556-567

13.2. CPTRDEMO.C-using pointers in C (Borland C++), 557-567

14.1. CMINUS.C-implementing abstract types with ordinary C structures (with Borland C++), 574-579

14.2. KEYBOARD.HPP-header file for the keyboard object (with Borland or Microsoft C++), 580-581

14.3. KEYBOARD./CPP-source file containing member functions for keyboard object (with Borland, 581-583

14.4. TESTKEY.CPP-test driver for keyboard object (with Borland C++), 584-585

15.1. ARRAY.CPP-class for array object (using Borland C++), 598-644

15.2. THIS1.CPP-return object by value (for Borland C++), 606-644

15.3. THIS1.CPP-return object by reference (for Borland C++), 607-644

15.4. SCREEN.HPP-class for virtual-screen manager (for Borland C++ 3.1), 619-621

15.5 SCREEN.CPP-member functions for screen class, 622-647

15.6. DEMO.CPP-demonstration of movable virtual screens (for Borland C++ 3.1), 651

15.7. AUTO.HPP-header file for AutoRun, auto PC operations manager (for Borland C++ 3.1), 652-653

15.8. AUTO.CPP-member functions for `AutoRun` program (for Borland C++ 3.1), 655-662

16.1. ARRAYCLA.CPP-using new and delete to create and destroy multiple objects (with Borla, 667-668

16.2. ARRAYCL2.CPP-using single call to `new()` and to allocate and destroy whole array of objects, 670-671

16.3. GLBLNEW.CPP-overloading global operator `new()` and `delete()` (using Borland C++), 674-675

16.4. NEWCP.CPP-overloading `::operator new()` and `operator delete()` (with Borland C++), 676

16.5. NEWCP2.CPP-when is this valid, using `::operator new()` (with Borland C++), 679

16.6. COMPOSE.CPP-reusing member functions by combining collections of objects (with Borland C++), 688-690

16.7. INHERIT.CPP-reusing code by inheritance; deriving new classes (with Borland C++), 695-697

16.8. VINHERIT.CPP-reusing code by inheritance, class capability with virtual functions, 700-702

16.9. CINOUT.CPP-input and output with the predefined `cin` and `cout` streams (with Borland C++), 704

16.10. MIXSTR.CPP-combining input and output in same statement, with character I/O, 706-707

17.1. OP.CPP-passing object instead of reference (with Borland C++), 715-716

17.2. OVLOADF.CPP-function overloading using older compiler version (for Zortech C++ 1.07), 720-721

17.3. MULTIF.CPP-function overloading, 722

17.4. VLI.HPP-header file for very large integer class declaration (for Borland C++), 730-731

17.5. VLI.CPP-member functions for very large integer class declaration (for Borland C++), 731-742

17.6. USEVLI.CPP-test driver for very large integer object definition (for Borland C++), 744-745

17.7. TEMPLATE.CPP-sample of AT&T C++ 3.0 temp classes and functions (for Borland C++), 750-751

D.1. FINANCE.C-financial calculations, 781-796

E.1. CCOM.C-asynchronous communications program with VT52 support and scripting, 806-822

G.1. TIMER.C-performance-measurement routine, 828-831

G.2. Header file for timer routine, 835-836

G.3. TESTTIME.C-using TIMER.C facilities, 837

lists
   declarator, 114-118
   formal argument, 172

formal parameter, writing, 133-134
initializer, 74
program, 37
replacement, 171
variadic, 765
LITERAL.C program, 112
literals, string, 110, 165
see also constants
load modules, 40, 161
loading files into random-access memory, 449
local
  scope, 119
  variables, 26-27, 122-124
    initializing, 127-128
locale-specific behavior, 519-520
LOCALE.H header file, 764, 770
localeconv() function, 770
localtime() function, 780
locating
  arguments, 243-245
  array elements, 342
locators
  associated, 269
  object, 211
log() function, 771
log10() function, 771
logic
  conditional, 278
  flow, 278, 298-304
logical
  order, 130
  state, 314
logical operators
  AND binary, 226
  C comparisons
    BASIC, 542-543
    Pascal, 562
  not unary, 219
  OR binary, 227

logical-NOT symbol (!), 178
long integers, 198
long type specifiers, 116
  double, 104
  int, 104
LONG_MAX macro, 763
LONG_MIN macro, 763
longjmp() function, 269, 772
loops, 278
  body, 278
  continue, 302
  do, 546-548
  entering, 300-301
  exiting, 288, 300-301
  for, 293-298, 566-567
  for-next, 545-546
  inner, 296
  logic flow, 298-304
  nesting, 295
  never-ending, 298
  outer, 296
  prechecked and post checked, 567
  programs, 278-304
  structures, 280
  while, 546-548
lores_clock() function, 834
low-level I/O practices, 450
lvalue expression, 210-211
  modifiable, 211

M

machine code target, 163
macros, 171
  arguments
    empty, 527
    referencing, 173
  BUFSIZ, 766
  CHAR_BIT, 763
  CHAR_MAX, 763

CHAR_MIN, 763
CLK_TCK, 767
comments, 176
_ _DATE_ _, 182
DBL_DIG, 762
DBL_EPSILON, 763
DBL_MANT_DIG, 762
DBL_MAX, 762
DBL_MAX_10_EXP, 762
DBL_MAX_EXP, 762
DBL_MIN, 763
DBL_MIN_10_EXP, 762
DBL_MIN_EXP, 762
definitions, 176
EOF, 766
EXIT_FAILURE, 315, 767
EXIT_SUCCESS, 315, 767
_ _FILE_ _, 182
FILENAME_MAX, 766
FLT_DIG, 762
FLT_EPSILON, 763
FLT_MANT_DIG, 762
FLT_MAX, 762
FLT_MAX_10_EXP, 762
FLT_MAX_EXP, 762
FLT_MIN, 762
FLT_MIN_10_EXP, 762
FLT_MIN_EXP, 762
FLT_RADIX, 762
FLT_ROUNDS, 762
FOPEN_MAX, 766
function-like, 171-172
HUGE_VAL, 764
INT_MAX, 763
INT_MIN, 763
_IOFBF, 766
_IOLBF, 766
_IONBF, 766
L_tmpnam, 766
LC_ALL, 764
LC_COLLATE, 764
LC_CTYPE, 764

LC_MONETARY, 764
LC_NUMERIC, 764
LC_TIME, 764
LDBL_DIG, 762
LDBL_EPSILON, 763
LDBL_MANT_DIG, 762
LDBL_MAX, 762
LDBL_MAX_10_EXP, 762
LDBL_MAX_EXP, 762
LDBL_MIN, 762
LDBL_MIN_10_EXP, 762
LDBL_MIN_EXP, 762
_ _LINE_ _, 182
LONG_MAX, 763
LONG_MIN, 763
MB_CUR_MAX, 767
MB_LEN_MAX, 763
object-like, 171
predefined, 528
RAND_MAX, 767
rescanning, 175
SCHAR_MAX, 763
SCHAR_MIN, 763
SEEK_CUR, 766
SEEK_END, 766
SEEK_SET, 766
SHRT_MAX, 763
SHRT_MIN, 763
SIG_DFL, 765
SIG_ERR, 765
SIG_IGN, 765
SIGABRT, 266, 765
SIGFPE, 266, 765
SIGILL, 266, 765
SIGINT, 266, 765
SIGSEGV, 266, 765
SIGTERM, 266, 765
_ _STDC_ _, 182
stderr, 766
stdin, 766
stdout, 766
substitution, 168, 171

_ _TIME_ _, 182
TMP_MAX, 766
UCHAR_MAX, 763
UINT_MAX, 763
ULONG_MAX, 763
USHRT_MAX, 763
va_arg, 765
va_arg(), 246
va_end, 765
va_end(), 247
va_start, 765
main storage, 50
main() function, 20, 27
   accessing variables, 26
   environment setup, 27-28
   parameters, 250-254
   program termination, 28
MAKE
   statement, 205
   utility, 41
make files, 41
makefile, 204
malloc() function, 25, 474, 477, 776
managing
   buffers, 411
   data, 411
   files, 411-416
mangling functions, 747
manifest constants, 171, 336
manipulating
   stream, 705-706
   strings, 354-356
mantissas, 111
masks, 108
MATH.H header file, 23, 764, 770-771
mathematical operators, C
  comparisons
   BASIC, 540-541
   Pascal, 560-561
matrices, 349
   forward elimination, 351
   Hermite, 825

Hermite geometry, 826
   symmetric, 352
   triangulation, 351
   see also arrays
max_val() function, 136
MB_CUR_MAX macro, 767
MB_LEN_MAX macro, 763
mblen() function, 777
mbstowcs() function, 777
mbtowc() function, 777
member-function prototype
  declarations, 601-603
members
   elements, 604
   functions, 574-579, 717-720,
     731-742
     AutoRun program, 655-662
     calling, 616-617
     const, 747-749
     constructor, 583
     declaring, 724
     overloading, 722
     reusing, 688-690
     screen class, 622-650
     static, 747-749
     volatile, 747-749
   objects, 601
   pointer operators, 216
   unions, accessing, 470-472
memchr() function, 778
memcmp() function, 778
memcpy() function, 778
memmove() function, 778
memory
   allocating, 25-26, 666
     at runtime, 474-477
   caches, 50
     persistence, 50
     speed, 50
   deallocating, 666
   dynamic, managing data, 473-478
   models, SMALL, 26
   random-access, loading files, 449

storage
  main, 50
  secondary, 50
memory-management functions, 474
memory-mapped I/O, 51
memset() function, 105, 779
messages, output, clipping, 248-249
Microsoft QuickBASIC
  compared to C/C++
    floating-point data types, 534
    floating-point variables,
      535-536
    integers, 533-534
    logical operators, 542-543
    mathematical operators, 541
    relational operators, 541-542
minimal character sets, 150-151
minimum maxima, 505
mixing I/O streams, 706-707
MIXSTR.CPP program (Listing
  16.10), 706-707
mktime() function, 780
mnemonic escape sequences,
  153-157
mod (modulus) mathematical
  operator, 560
modays() function, 127
mode string characters, 422
models, memory, SMALL, 26
modes
  ANSI C file, 425
  append, 66
  binary, 427-430
  files, 528
    access, 421-425
    I/O programming, 445
  high-resolution, 831, 834-835
  I/O (table), 428
  input, 422
  output, 423
  read-only, 66
  text, 427-430

update, 423-424
  reading and writing files,
    425-427
write-only, 66
modf() function, 198-199, 771
modifiable lvalue expression, 211
modification, interactive, 46
modifier character, 85
modular programming, 548-549
modules
  compiling, 195-199
  linking, 203-206
  load, 40, 161
  object, 40
modulus (remainder) method, 431
most significant bit, 148
movable virtual screens, 651
multibyte characters, 160
multidimensional arrays, 214,
  338-340
  elements, 339-342
MULTIF.CPP program (Listing 17.3),
  722
multiple
  inheritance, 698, 746-747
  pointers
    dereferencing, 374-375
    indirection, 373-374
    referencing, 374-375
  translation units, 164
multitasking, 833
multplicative binary operators, 222

N

\n escape sequence, 153
names
  filenames, 62
  functions, writing, 133-134
  spaces, 684
  streams, 62

variables, 113-114
nesting, 287
   `#include` directive, 163
   `if-else` statements, 307
   loops, 295
network files, 450
neural networks, 571
never-ending loop, 298
new operator, 666-678
NEWCP.CPP program (Listing 16.4), 676
NEWCP2.CPP program (Listing 16.5), 679
`newint8()` function, 833-834
newline character, 154
no linkage, 190
non-`int` bit-field types, 527
nonzero value, 304
normal strings, 160
not logical operator, 562
notation, exponential, 111
null
   character, 18
   directive, 182
   fence, 352
   pointers, 64
   statement, 140-141
   strings, 74, 247
NUMBER.C program, 77-79
numbers
   factorial, 257
   floating-point, 10
   fractional, 111
   prime, 433
     computing, 281-300
   systems, 150
numeric escape sequences, 157-158
numeric-to-string conversions, 194-198
nybbles, 107

O

object-like macros, 171
object-oriented programming, 572, 587-591
   abstract data types, 579-586
   abstract typing, 574-585
   data abstraction, 573-574
   multiple inheritance, 591
   objects, 591-592
object-oriented programming systems (OOPS), 13
objects, 25, 572-579, 685
   accessing, 323-327
   addresses, 710-713
     relative, 203
   arrays, 242
     allocating, 670-671
     incomplete, 242
   auto, 186
   autonomous, 592
   blocks, 189
   class, 616-644
     copying, 609
     creating, 609
     defining pointers, 713-715
     destroying, 608-616
     initializing, 608-616
   compiler, 191
   composition, 665
   creating, 667-668
   data, 165, 601
     structured, 454-460
   declarations, 186
   defining to C++, 680-686
   destroying, 667-668
     whole arrays, 670-671
   duration, 665
   dynamic, 680-681
     on stacks, 681-683

files, 161
functional, 592
initializers, 192-193
integers, 744-745
keyboard, 580-585
linkage, 188-192
   external, 190
   internal, 190
   no linkage, 190
locator, 211
member, 601
modules, 40, 203-206
passing as parameters, 715-717
pointers, 323-327, 334, 441
referencing, 596, 717-720
returning
   by reference, 607-644
   by value, 606-644
scopes
   file, 189
   function, 189
   function prototype, 189
   surrounding, 189
server, 592
slot-based, 592
static, 186-188, 680-681, 685-686
   global, 683-685
streams, cin and cout, 703-706
structures, 242, 453
types, 102
typing, 472-473
values
   multiple, 308
   reducing, 217
oct string manipulator, 705
octal escape sequences, 157
offset addresses, 461
one-dimensional arrays, 352
   declaring, 335-336
   defining, 335-337
   referencing, 337

one-pass compilers, 163
one's complement unary operator, 219
OOPS (object-oriented programming systems) language, 13, 587
OP.CPP program (Listing 17.1), 715-716
open addressing, 432
open option modes
   input, 422
   output, 423
   update, 423-424
open-ended recursion, 256-258
open_file() function, 75
opening files, 65-67
operands
   combining in expressions, 231-233
   promotion, 231-233
operating systems, 52
operations
   read, 50
   write, 50
operators, 165
   #, 16
   ##, 16
   ## (preprocessor concatenation), 175
   & (address-of), 64
   & (bitwise AND), 108
   * (indirection), 64
   += (add assign), 108
   = (assignment), 138-139
   == (equality), 138-139
   >> (shift-right), 108
   assignment, compound and simple, 227-228
   associativity, 213
   binary, 222-227
      additive, 222-223
      bitwise AND, 225

bitwise exclusive OR, 225
bitwise inclusive OR, 226
bitwise shift, 223-224
equality, 224-225
logical OR, 227-228
logical AND, 226
logical OR, 227
multiplicative, 222
relational, 224
C comparisons
  BASIC, 540-543
  Pascal, 560-562
cast, 233-235
  type, 221-222
comma, 229
delete, 666-678
equality, 224-225
grouping, 213
keyword, 724
logical, 542-543, 562
mathematical, 540-541, 560-561
member pointer, 216
new, 666-680
overloading, 723-745
postfix, 213-217
  array subscript, 214
  function call, 215
  postfix decrement, 217
  postfix increment, 75, 216-217
  structure (union) member, 215
  structure (union) member
    pointer, 216
power, 376, 390
precedence, 177, 229-231
preprocessing, 16
reference, 709, 710-713
relational, 224, 541-542, 561
scope resolution, 583
sets, C, 723-745
structure dot (.), 460
structure pointer (->), 397, 461
subexpressions, 207

ternary, 109, 227
this, 678-680
unary, 217
  address-of, 220
  indirection, 221
  logical not, 219
  minus (-), 218-219
  one's complement, 219
  plus (+), 218
  prefix decrement, 218
  prefix increment, 218
  size-of, 220
optimizing
  size, 39
  speed, 39
options, 253
  compile-only, 38
  host environment support, 39
or logical operator, 562
orders
  logical, 130
  physical, 130
ordinal values, 654
ordinary tokens, 164
outer
  declarations, 120, 191
  loops, 296
output, 50, 293
  messages, clipping, 248-249
  modes, 423
  polygon arrays, 348
overflow records, 443
overhead
  I/O programming, 445-449
  time, 55
overlay concept of unions, 469
overlay() function, 806
overload keyword, 722
overloading, 709
  functions, 720-722, 747
    friend, 723
    member, 722

operators, 723-745
  `new` and `delete`, 672-678
OVLOADF.CPP program (Listing 17.2), 720-721

P

packages, built-in functions, 21
parameters, 20
  `argc`, 250-252
  `argv[]`, 250-252
  command-line
    accessing, 250
    formats, 252-254
  file mode, 66
  formal lists, writing, 133-134
  functions
    arrays, 370-371
    formal, 712
    strings, 370
    structures, 478-479
    unions, 478-479
  passing, 128-130
    functions, 238-240
    `main()`, 250-254
    objects, 715-717
    "on the stack," 238
    pointers, 333
    reference, 238-240
    value, 238-239
parentheses
  aligning, 34
  identifiers, 117
parenthesized primary expression, 210
parsers, 162, 388
  building, 389-390
parsing
  algebraic expressions with recursive descent logic, 391-396
  recursive descent function, 388

Pascal programming
  compared to C programming
    data types, 550-559
    flow control, 562-567
    language, 14
    operators, 560-562
  moving to C programming, 549-567
  storing strings, 555
passing
  arrays, 549
  objects
    parameters, 715-717
    pointers, 334
  parameters, 128-130
    by reference, 134, 238-240
    by value, 134, 238-239
    `main()`, 250-254
    on the stack, 238
    to functions, 238-240
    with pointers, 333
  strings, 549
`PATH` environment variable, 366
PC operation managers, 652-653
performance, 38
periodic interest rates, 799
peripheral devices, *see* I/O devices
`perror()` function, 59, 80, 775
persistence, 50
physical order, 130
placing `#include` directive, 23
plain text files, 69
pointer and subscript equivalence, 340-342
pointer-to-the-handler routine, 266
pointers, 63-64, 375, 516, 685, 709-720
  arrays, 73, 238, 334, 73, 398-399
  C compared to Pascal, 555-559
  comparing, 327-333
  conversions, type casts, 234
  declarations, 221, 266

defining
  arrays, 399-400
  class objects, 713-715
dereferencing, 64, 221, 374-375
functions, 118, 261-265, 315
identifiers, 117
increasing flexibility, 401
lexical scanners, 378-387
multiple indirection, 373-374
null, 64
objects, 441
  accessing, 323-327
  passing, 334
parameters, 333
referencing, 374-375
returning, 261, 267
sorting, 401-409
stack, 243
strings, 334
strtok() function, 376-378
syntax, 710-713
type, 453-454
updating, 246
POLY.C program (Listing 7.2),
  285-286
polygons, output, 348
polymorphism, 589, 665, 698-702
port I/O, 51-52
portability, 12, 506-507
ports
  control, 832
  device control, 52
positioning
  files, 434-436
  screen cursor in strings, 360-361
possible prime number, 282
postchecked loops, C compared to
  Pascal, 567
postfix operators, 213-217
  array subscript, 214
  function call, 215

postfix decrement, 217
postfix increment, 75, 216-217
structure (union) member, 215
structure (union) member
  pointer, 216
pow() function, 771
power operator, 376, 390
#pragma directive, 182
precedence of operators, 177,
  229-231
prechecked loops, C compared to
  Pascal, 567
precision specifiers, 85
predefined macros, 528
prefix unary operators
  decrement, 218
  increment, 218
prefix increments, 293
preprocessing
  directives, 17
  operators, 16
  tokens, 164
preprocessors, 168-169
  concatenation (##) operator, 175
primary expressions
  constants, 210
  identifiers, 210
  parenthesized, 210
  string literals, 210
prime numbers, 433
  computing 281-300
  possible, 282
PRIME.C programs
  Listing 7.1, 281-282
  Listing 10.5, 433
print_table() function, 801
printf() function, 59, 84-86, 152-153,
  167-168, 243-249, 773
PRINTIT.C program, 86
private member declarations, 693
private: keyword, 604
process() function, 130

processing
  functions, 414
  sequential, 414
program lists, 37
programming
  C, 504-505
    translation limitations, 524-525
  C comparisons
    BASIC, 530-540
    data types, 532-540, 550-559
    flow control, 543-548, 562-567
    interpreters versus compilers,
     530-532
    operators, 540-543
    Pascal, 550-559, 562-567
  direct-access file, 430-436
  I/O, 50-53, 411, 449-450
    communications, 91
    disk, 91
    file modes, 445
    overhead, 445-449
    read operations, 50
    video display, 91, 94-98
    write operations, 50
  modular, 548-549
  moving to C
    from BASIC, 530-549
    from Pascal, 549-567
  object-oriented, 572, 587-591
    abstract data types, 579-586
    abstract typing, 574-579
    data abstraction, 573-574
    multiple inheritance, 591
    objects, 591-592
  timer chips, 828, 832-833
programs
  aborting, 66
  CCOM.C, 94, 806-822
  CENTER.C, 87
  CIPHER.C, 69-73
  CPRINT.C, 92-93
  CRC16.C, 142

CVTJUL.C, 124-127
debugging, 44
"dumb" terminal, 803
dump, 105
EMPTY.C, 28
ENDING.C, 28
EXCHANGE.C, 143-144
executing associated locater, 269
exiting early, 314-317
FINANCE.C, 781-796
FIRST.C, 19
flow of execution, 277
FMORE.C, 95-98
invoking, 317-318
LITERAL.C, 112
loops
  adjustment, 278
  back-end condition checking,
   278
  body, 278
  condition checking, 278
  control variables, 278
  creating, 278-304
  front-end condition checking,
   278
  initialization, 278
  iteration, 278
  pass, 278
NUMBER.C, 77-79
PRINTIT.C, 86
READIT.C, 89-90
SDUMP.C, 106-107
STREAM.C, 60
STRTOX.C, 82-83
terminating, 28
  early, 314-317
TESTTIME.C, 837
TIMER.C, 828-831
  converting to Borland C,
   836-837
  functions, 837-838

translating, 161-164
UCTOUCH.C, 42
writing
    aligning braces and
      parentheses, 34
    comments, 33
    design, 31
    indentation, 32-33
    readability, 32-34
    top-down approach, 31-32
    white space, 32-33
project make facilities, 37
promotions
    functions, arguments, 240-242
    integral, 232
    operands, 231-233
protected class members, 720
protected: keyword, 604
prototypes, 130
    declarators, 131-134
    functions, 20, 29-30
      incomplete types, 242-243
      member, 603
prototyping functions, 135
PTRDEMO.PAS program (Listing
    13.1), 556-567
public: keyword, 604
punctuators, 16-18, 165
push command, 824
putc() function, 59-60, 774
putchar() function, 59-60, 774
putenv() function, 367
puts() function, 59, 77, 774

Q-R

qsort() function, 777
qualifier types, 517
    const, 109
    volatile, 109
quiet changes, 520-524

\r escape sequence, 153
r mode character, 422
"r" mode string, 425
"r⊦" mode string, 425
"r+b" mode string, 425
radixes, 111
raise() function, 268-269, 772
RAM (random-access memory), 50,
    449
rand() function, 776
RAND_MAX macro, 767
random-access
    files, 430
    memory (RAM), 50, 449
ranges of values, 314
"rb" mode string, 425
"rb+" mode string, 425
read operations, 50
read-only mode, 66
reading
    cin and cout stream objects,
      703-706
    files
      direct-access, 436-444
      update mode, 425-427
READIT.C program, 89-90
real numbers, C compared to
    Pascal, 552-553
realloc() function, 25, 474, 477, 776
records, overflow, 443
recursion, 254-256
    descent, 388-389
      parsing algebraic expressions,
        391-396
    deleting, 258-260
    direct, 254
    function calls, 254
    indirect, 254
    open-ended, 256-258
redirection of I/O, 59, 707
reducing object values, 217

references
 operator, 709-713
 passing by, 134
 returning objects by, 607-644
 source files, 202-203
 syntax, 710-713
referencing
 addresses, 369
 array elements, 337
 macro arguments, 173
 multidimensional arrays
  elements, 339-342
 objects, 596, 717-720
 pointers, multiple, 374-375
registers, 516
 declarations, 188
 functions, 315
 keyword, 115, 187
relational operators, 224
 binary, 224
 C comparisons
  BASIC, 541-542
  Pascal, 561
relative addresses, 203
releasing buffers, 449
remove() function, 412, 772
rename() function, 413-414, 772
replacement lists, 171
representation, intermediate, 162
required significant digits, 111
resetiosflags(long) string
 manipulator, 705
return expression jump statement,
 300
return type, 712
returning
 objects
  by reference, 607-644
  by value, 606-644
 pointers, 261, 267
 values from functions, 142-145

reusing
 code, 686-687
  composition, 687-693
  inheritance, 693-702
 member functions, 688-690
reversing
 characters in strings, 327
 conditional expressions, 219
rewind() function, 414-415, 775
ROMable code, 39
routines
 pointer-to-the-handler, 266
 semantic, 162
row-major order storage of arrays,
 338
rules
 integral promotion, 522
 unsigned preserving, 522
run_script() function, 806
runtime, 609
 memory, allocating, 474-477
rvalue expression, 210-211

S

SA, *see* situational awareness
scaling, 198
scan codes, 797
scanf() library function, 59, 88-90,
 243-249, 356, 773
scanner() function, 378-387
SCANNER.C program (Listing 9.1),
 379-384
scanners, 162
 lexical, 376
  pointers, 378-387
SCHAR_MAX macro, 763
SCHAR_MIN macro, 763
scopes, 119
 block, 189
 file, 189

function, 189
function prototype, 189
global, 119
local, 119
resolution operator, 583
rules, 717
surrounding, 189
variable, 119
SCREEN.CPP program (Listing 15.5),
622-647
SCREEN.HPP program (Listing 15.4),
619-621
screens
class member functions, 622-650
cursor, positioning in string,
360-261
I/O arrangements, 360-361
virtual, 618-644
movable, 651
scroll_up() function, 805
SDUMP.C program, 106-107
secondary storage, 50
SEEK_CUR macro, 766
SEEK_END macro, 766
SEEK_SET macro, 766
segments, stack, 203
SELECT.C program (Listing 7.7),
310-312
SELECT CASE statement, 544-545
selection statements, 138, 304
self-referential structure, 462
semantic routines, 162
semantics, 520-524
semicolon (;), 16
send command, 823
send_comm_byte() function, 804
sequences
collating, 150
escape, 152
\?, 154
\\, 154
\", 154
\', 154
\0, 157
\123, 157
\779, 157
\88, 157
\a, 153
\b, 153
\f, 153
hexadecimal, 158
mnemonic, 153-157
\n, 153
numeric, 157-158
octal, 157
\r, 153
\SS, 158
\t, 153
trigraph, 158-159
\v, 154
\x0, 158
\x0D, 158
\xFF, 158
\xFG, 158
points in C expressions, 206-209
sequential processing, 414
server objects, 592
SET command, 24
setbase (int) string manipulator,
705
setbuf() function, 446-449, 773
setfill(int) string manipulator,
706
setiosflags(long) string
manipulator, 705
setjmp() function, 269-275, 772
SETJMP.H header file, 764, 772
setlocale() function, 770
setprecision(int) string
manipulator, 706
sets, characters, 148
extended, 160
minimal, 150-151
source, 161
target, 161

`settextposition()` function, 360
setting up environments, 27
setup overhead time, 54
`setvbuf()` function, 446-449, 773
`setw(int)` string manipulator, 706
shapes
    arrays, 342-343
    drawing, 342-343
shells, calling, 317
Shellsort
    algorithm, 404-408
    function, 402-403
SHELLSRT.C program (Listing 9.4),
    404-408
shift states, 160
shift-right (>>) operator, 108
short `int` type specifier, 103
SHOWARG.C program (Listing 6.3),
    251
`show_line()` function, 98
SHOWSIG.C program (Listing 6.7),
    267-268
`SHRT_MAX` macro, 763
`SHRT_MIN` macro, 763
side effects in C expressions,
    207-209
`SIG_DFL` macro, 765
`SIG_ERR` macro, 765
`SIG_IGN` macro, 765
`SIGABRT` macro, 266, 765
`SIGFPE` macro, 266, 765
`SIGILL` macro, 266, 765
`SIGINT` macro, 266, 765
sign bits, 111, 353
signal handler arguments, 528
`signal()` function, 266-269
SIGNAL.H header file, 765, 772
signal handlers, 266-275
    arguments, 528
    terminating, 272-274
signed
    arithmetic, 730
    bytes, 554

char type specifier, 103
    integer types, 103, 111
    type specifier, 116
significant digits, 111
`SIGSEGV` macro, 266, 765
`SIGTERM` macro, 266, 765
simple
    assignment operator, 227-228
    identifiers, 117
`sin()` function, 771
singly linked lists, 462
`sinh()` function, 771
situational awareness, 573
size, arrays, 336
size-of unary operator, 220
slot-based objects, 592
slots, *see* buckets
`SMALL` memory model, 26
smoothing curves, 342-349
solving linear equations with
    arrays, 349-352
`some_function()` function, 193
sorting, speeding up with pointers,
    401-409
`\source` directory, 24
source character sets, 161
sources
    files
        contents, 195-199
        including, 21, 169-170
        resources, 202-203
        STREDIT.C, 361-369
    function calls, 202
`spawn...()` function, 318-319
specifiers
    conversion, 83-84
    precision, 85
    type, 103
        char, 103, 116
        double, 104, 116
        enum, 116
        float, 104, 116
        function, 131-132

int, 103, 116
long, 116
long double, 104
long int, 104
short int, 103
signed, 116
signed char, 103
struct, 116
typedef, 116
union, 116
unsigned, 104, 116
unsigned char, 104
unsigned long, 104
unsigned short, 104
void, 116
speed-matching, 54
SPEEDBUF.C program (Listing 10.3), 418
SPFV() function, 799
spirit of C, 504-505
SPLINE.C program (Listing 8.1), 343-349
SPPV() function, 800
sprintf() function, 86, 773
sqrt() function, 771
srand() function, 776
\SS escape sequence, 158
sscanf() function, 88-89, 773
stacks
  dynamic objects, 681-683
  frames, 43
  pointers, 243
  segments, 203
stand-alone text editors, 36
standards
  asynchronous communications (stdaux), 62
  C, 504-506
  function libraries, 167
  I/O, 58-62
start_bench() function, 832
state-dependent coding, 160

statements, 16, 517
  assignment, 137
  automatic control, 302
  block, 17, 141
  case, 140
    C compared to Pascal, 563-564
  conditional logic, 304-314
    break, 313-314
    default, 313-314
    If-then-else, 305-308
    nested if-else, 307
    switch(), 308-314
  continue, 302-308
  default, 140
  expression
    writing, 137
  flow control, writing, 137-140
  goto, 140
  if-then-else
    C compared to BASIC, 543-544
    C compared to Pascal, 562-563
  iteration, 138, 283
  jump, 138
    break, 300
    continue, 299
    goto identifier, 299
    return expression, 300
  labeled, writing, 140
  MAKE, 205
  null, 140-141
  SELECT CASE, C compared to BASIC, 544-545
  selection, 138, 304
  switch, 140
    C compared to Pascal, 563-564
  target, 283
  while, 75, 284-288
  writing, 137
states
  logical, 314
  shift, 160

static
  keyword, 115, 123, 748
  member function, 747-749
  objects, 186-188, 680-681, 685-686
    global, 683-685
  storage-class keyword, 188
  variables, 120
STDARG.H header file, 765
stdaux (standard asynchronous communications), 62
_ _STDC_ _ macro, 182
STDDEF.H header file, 765
stderr (standard error message)
  macro, 766
  streams, 58, 62, 419
stdin (standard input), 419
  macro, 766
  streams, 58, 62
STDIO.H header file, 23, 65, 766, 772-775
STDLIB.H header file, 23, 80, 766
stdout (standard output), 419
  macro, 766
  streams, 58, 62
stdprn (standard printer output)
  streams, 62
step-over execution, 46
stop_bench() function, 834
storage
  classes, 119
    auto, 186-192
    duration, 186-192
    linkage, 188
    static, 188
  main, 50
  secondary, 50
  strings in Pascal and C, 555
str_invert() function, 198, 229
strcat() function, 79, 778
strchr() function, 79, 779
strcmp() function, 778

strcoll() function, 778
strcpy() function, 79, 778
strcspn() function, 779
STREAM.C program, 60
streams, 54, 57
  binary, 58, 427
  connecting to files, 62
  declaring, 63-64
  extended DOS, supporting, 92
  I/O, 53-56
    C++, 703-707
    data files, 57
    interactive devices, 56
    mixing, 706-707
  line buffered, 61
  manipulators, 705-706
  names, 62
  objects, cin and cout, reading and writing, 703-706
  stdaux, 62
  stderr, 58, 62
  stdin, 58, 62
  stdout (standard output), 58, 62
  stdprn, 62
  text, 58, 427
    processing, 376
  types, 528
STREDIT.C program (Listing 8.4), 361-369
strerror() function, 779
strftime() function, 780
STRICT.C program (Listing 11.1), 456-457
STRING.H header file, 778
string_out() function, 806
strings, 18, 334
  C comparisons
    BASIC, 536-539
    Pascal, 554-555
  characters, 152, 327
  format, 83-84, 155

functions
    editing, 362-365
    I/O, 76-77
    parameters, 370
  literal primary expression, 165, 210, 526
  manipulating, 354-356
  normal, 160
  null, 74, 247
  null fence, 352
  passing, 549
  screen cursor, 360-361
  storing in Pascal and C, 555
  text, editing, 356-369
  variable-length, 247-248
  variables
    declaring, 353-354
    initializing, 354
strlen() function, 779
strncat() function, 778
strncmp() function, 778
strncpy() function, 778
strol() function, 80-81
strong type checking, 129
stroul() function, 80-81
Stroustrup, Bjarne, 587, 745
  object-oriented programming, 590
strpbrk() function, 779
strrchr() function, 779
strrev() function, 199
strspn() function, 779
strstr() function, 779
strtod() function, 80, 775
strtok() function, 376-378, 779
strtol() function, 775
strtoul() function, 775
STRTOX.C program, 82-83
struct type specifier, 116
STRUCT2.C program (Listing 11.2), 459-460
STRUCT3.C program (Listing 11.3), 464

STRUCT4.C program (Listing 11.4), 465-466
STRUCT5.C program (Listing 11.5), 466-467
STRUCT6.C program (Listing 11.6), 467-468
STRUCT7.C program (Listing 11.7), 476
structures, 199, 242, 397, 453, 516-517, 579
  arrays, combining, 465-469
  bit-fields, 463-465
  building with linked lists, 479-499
  data objects, 454-460
  declarations
    lists, 455
    with tags, 459-460
    without tags, 456-457
  defining, 454-469
  dot operator (.), 460
  function parameters, 478-479
  initializing
    with tags, 459-460
    without tags, 456-457
  members
    accessing, 460-463
    bit fields, 464
  pointer operator (->), 397, 461
  self-referential, 462
  tags, 458-460
  types, 453-454
  unions, 469-472
    member operators, 215-216
strupr() function, 294
strxfrm() function, 778
stubs, 27
subclasses, 693
subexpressions, 207
subscripts, 335-336, 340-342
  see also pointers, 340
substitution of macro, 168, 171
superclasses, 693

supporting extended DOS streams, 92

surrounding scopes, 189

switch statements, 140
    C compared to Pascal, 563-564

switch() conditional logic
    statement, 308-314
        case labels, 309-313

symbol tables, 162

symmetric matrices, 352

syntax, 520-524
    checking, 162
    directed compilers, 161
    pointer and reference, 710-713

system() function, 317-318, 776

systems
    command, 250
    number, 150

T

\t escape sequence, 153

TIMER.H header file, 835-836

tables, symbol, 162

tag structures
    with, 458-460
    without, 456-457

tan() function, 771

tanh() function, 771

targets
    character sets, 161
    fields, 205
    machine code, 163
    statements, 283

template classes and functions,
    AT&T C++ 3.0, 750-752

TEMPLATE.CPP program (Listing
    17.7), 750-751

temporary files, creating, 416

terminating
    programs, 28, 314-317
    signal handlers, 272-274

text lines, 155-156
    see also exiting

ternary
    escape sequences, 521
    operator, 109

test_key() function, 805

TESTCSTR.C (Listing 5.1), 194

testing conversions, numeric-to-
    string, 194

TESTKEY.CPP program (Listing
    14.4), 584-585

TESTTIME.C program, 837

text
    characters
        deleting, 358-360
        inserting, 358-360
    editing with strings, 356-369
    editors, 35-37
        built-in text, 36
        error location, 37
        project make facilities, 37
        stand-alone, 36
    file mode, 66, 427-430
    lines, terminating, 155-156
    streams, 58, 427
        processing, 376

this keyword, 605-608

this operator, 678-680

THIS1.CPP program (Listing 15.2),
    606-644

THIS2.CPP program (Listing 15.3),
    607-644

_ _TIME_ _ macro, 182

time() function, 780

TIME.H header file, 767, 780

timer chips
    control ports, 832
    reprogramming, 828, 832-833

timer-tick interrupts, 833

TIMER.C program, 828-831
    converting to Borland C, 836-837
    functions, 837-838

TMP_MAX macro, 766
tmpfile() function, 416, 772
tmpnam() function, 416, 772
tokens, 162
  ordinary, 164
  preprocessing, 164
  separating, 376
tolower() function, 770
top-down tree structures, 31
TOUCH utility, 41
toupper() function, 770
trace-into execution, 46
transfer of control, 277
translating programs, 161-164
translation units, 161, 164
triangulation, matrices, 351
trigraphs, 158-159
  ??', 159
  ??!, 159
  ??(, 159
  ??), 159
  ??-, 159
  ??/, 159
  ??<, 159
  ??=, 159
  ??>, 159
Turbo Pascal, compared to Borland
  C/C++
    floating-point data types, 552-553
    integers, 550-552
two-dimensional array, 352
two-pass compilers, 163
type-safe linkage, 747
typecasting, 69
typedef, 472-473, 586
typedef keyword, 115
typedef type specifier, 116
typeless languages, 10
types, 102
  basic, 103
  cast operators, 221-222
  casts, 86, 155, 234-235

character, 85, 103, 110
checking, 129
  strong, 129
  weak, 129
conversions
  automatic, 231-233
  user-defined, 745
derivation, 103, 586-589
floating-point
  double, 198
  number, 103-104, 111
function, 103
incomplete, 103
object, 102
qualifiers
  const, 109
  volatile, 109
signed integer, 103, 111
specifiers, 103
  char, 103, 116
  double, 104, 116
  enum, 116
  float, 104, 116
  function, 131-132
  int, 103, 116
  long, 116
  long double, 104
  long int, 104
  short int, 103
  signed, 116
  signed char, 103
  struct, 116
  typedef, 116
  union, 116
  unsigned, 104, 116
  unsigned char, 104
  unsigned long, 104
  unsigned short, 104
  void, 116
unsigned integer, 103-104
typing data, 472-473

U

UCHAR_MAX macro, 763
UCTOUCH.C program, 42
UINT_MAX macro, 763
ULONG_MAX macro, 763
unary
    expressions, 217
    operators, 217
        address-of, 220
        indirection, 221
        logical not, 219
        minus (-), 218-219
        one's complement, 219
        plus (+), 218
        prefix decrement, 218
        prefix increment, 218
        size-of, 220
unbuffered
    files, 56
    I/O, 54
undefined
    behaviors, 506-514
    values, 301
underscore character, 166
ungetc() function, 774
unhook_com() function, 804
unions, 516-517
    declaring, 470
    function parameters, 478-479
    members, accessing, 470-472
    overlay concept, 469
    structures, 469-472
    type specifier, 116, 453
units, translation, 161, 164
UNIX, 10
unsigned
    bytes, 554
    integer types, 103-104
    preserving rule, 522
    type specifier, 104, 116

    char, 104
    long, 104
    short, 104
unspecified behaviors, 506-507
updating
    access, 26
    modes, 423-424
        files, reading and writing, 425-427
    pointers, 246
user-defined
    functions, 28-30, 165
    type conversions, 745
USEVLI.CPP program (Listing 17.6), 744-745
USFV() function, 800
USHRT_MAX macro, 763
USPV() function, 800
usual arithmetic conversion, 232
utilities
    MAKE, 41
    TOUCH, 41

V

\v escape sequence, 154
va_arg macro, 246, 765
va_end macro, 247, 765
va_start macro, 765
values
    assignments, 210-211
    constants, 110
    decimal, 107
    indeterminate, 64
    multiple in objects, 308
    nonzero, 304
    objects
        returning, 606-644
        values, 217
    ordinal, 654
    parameters, 238

passing by, 134
ranges, 314
returning from functions, 142-145
undefined, 301
zero, 64
variable-length strings, 247-248, 537
variables
    accessing, 26
    arrays
        declaring, 335-339
        elements, 337
        multidimensional, 338-340
        one-dimensional, 335-337
    arguments, 243-249
    `auto`, 120
    back substitution, 351
    control, 278
    declaring, 25
    environment
        editing, 367-369
        `INCLUDE`, 366
        `LIB`, 366
        `PATH`, 366
    floating-point, C compared to
        BASIC, 534-536
    global, 26-27, 120-121, 124
    initializing, 111-113, 118-119
    local, 26-27, 122-124
        initializing, 127-128
    naming, 113-114
    scopes, 119
    static, 120
    strings
        declaring, 353-354
        initializing, 354
variadic lists, 765
vectors, 351
VERSIONS.C program (Listing 10.1),
    413-451
vertical tab character, 156
`vfprintf()` library function, 59, 248,
    773

video display I/O programming, 91,
    94-98
`vidtex()` function, 805
`vidtex_sba()` function, 806
VINHERIT.CPP program (Listing
    16.8), 700-702
virtual
    base classes, 746-752
    functions, 698-702
    screens
        class, building, 618-644
        movable, 651
visual debuggers, 44-45
    interactive nature, 45
VLI.CPP program (Listing 17.5),
    731-742
VLI.HPP program (Listing 17.4),
    730-731
`void` type specifier, 116
volatile
    keyword, 747
    member function, 747-749
    type qualifier, 109
`vprintf()` library function, 59, 248,
    773
`vsprintf()` library function, 248, 774

W

`w` mode character, 422
`"w"` mode string, 425
`"w+"` mode string, 425
`"w+b"` mode string, 425
`wait` command, 823
`wait_for_tx()` function, 805
watch windows, 46
`"wb"` mode string, 425
`"wb+"` mode string, 425
`wcstombs()` function, 777
`wctomb()` function, 777
weak type checking, 129
Wegner, Peter, 587

wherex() function, 360
wherey() function, 360
while loop, 546-548
while statement, 75, 284-288
white space, 16, 32-33
wide characters, 160
width field, 85
windows
    boundary, 248-249
    watch, 46
word-aligned, 235
words, 104
    fields, 110
    fullwords, 104
    halfwords, 104
write operations, 50
write-only mode, 66
writing
    expression statements, 137
    files in update mode, 425-427
    formal parameter lists, 133-134
    functions
        names, 133-134
        type specifiers, 131-132
    programs
        aligning braces and
          parentheses, 34
        comments, 33
        design, 31
        indentation, 32-33
        readability, 32-34
        top-down approach, 31-32
        white space, 32-33
    statements, 137
        expression, 137
        flow control, 137-140
        labeled, 140
    string literals, 526
    with cin and cout stream objects,
      703-706
ws string manipulator, 705

X-Z

\x0D escape sequence, 158
X3J11 committee, 11
XDIR.C program (Listing 11.8),
  480-496
\xFF escape sequence, 158
\xFG escape sequence, 158
\x0 escape sequence, 158
xor (exclusive OR) logical operator,
  562

zero value, 64
Zortech C++ object-oriented
  programming, 589-590